EDITION

3

Principles of Everyday Behavior Analysis

EDITION
3

Principles of Everyday Behavior Analysis

L. Keith Miller

University of Kansas

Brooks/Cole Publishing Company

I(T)P® ***An International Thomson Publishing Company***

Pacific Grove • Albany • Bonn • Boston • Cincinnati • Detroit • London • Madrid • Melbourne
Mexico City • New York • Paris • San Francisco • Singapore • Tokyo • Toronto • Washington

Editor: *Marianne Taflinger*
Representative: *Carolyn Crockett*
Assistant: *Laura Donahue*
on Editor: *Tessa A. McGlasson*
ript Editor: *David Hoyt*
ssions Editor: *May Clark*
ior and Cover Design: *Katherine Minerva*

oto Credits are on page 602

Art Editor/Interior Illustration: *Kathy Joneson*
Photo Editor: *Kathleen Olson*
Marketing Team: *Gay Meixel / Romy Fineroff*
Indexer: *James Minkin*
Typesetting: *CompuKing Typesetting*
Cover Printing: Phoenix Color Corp
Printing and Binding: Phoenix Color Corp

For more information, contact:

BROOKS/COLE PUBLISHING COMPANY
511 Forest Lodge Road
Pacific Grove, CA 93950
USA

International Thomson Publishing Europe
Berkshire House 168-173
High Holborn
London WC1V 7AA
England

Thomas Nelson Australia
102 Dodds Street
South Melbourne, 3205
Victoria, Australia

Nelson Canada
1120 Birchmount Road
Scarborough, Ontario
Canada M1K 5G4

International Thomson Editores
Campos Eliseos 385, Piso 7
Col. Polanco
11560 México D. F. México

International Thomson Publishing GmbH
Königswinterer Strasse 418
53227 Bonn
Germany

International Thomson Publishing Asia
221 Henderson Road
#05-10 Henderson Building
Singapore 0315

International Thomson Publishing Japan
Hirakawacho Kyowa Building, 3F
2-2-1 Hirakawacho
Chiyoda-ku, Tokyo 102
Japan

Printed in the United States of America

10 9 8 7

Library of Congress Cataloging-in-Publication Data
Miller, L. Keith.
Principles of everyday behavior analysis / L. Keith Miller. — 3rd ed.
p. cm.
Includes bibliographical references and index.
ISBM 0-534-16146-4
1. Behavior modification—Programmed instruction. I. Title.
BF637.B4M53 1996
153.8'3—dc20 96-2625
CIP

To my father, C. Dana Miller, and my wife, Ocoee Lynn Miller, and Reiko Mizutani

Contents

Preface

I am happy to offer the Third Edition of *Principles of Everyday Behavior Analysis*. This book retains its original features. Students read short lessons focused on one set of closely related concepts. After finishing the reading they may answer questions that review the reading. If they wish to, they may also practice applying the concepts to everyday examples. Finally, they take one form of a short quiz that tests their mastery of the lesson. If they pass, they know that they can go on to the next lesson. If they fail, they know they should study the lesson again. Thus the book continues to have a self-instructional form.

The Third Edition is thoroughly revised and updated. I have added hundreds of examples illustrating the application of behavioral principles to everyday problems. I have added dozens of stories showing how behavioral concepts can help us understand the behavior of everyday people. I have highlighted these stories by placing them within boxes. I have revised the first unit to help students understand the unique approach to science on which behavior analysis is based. Thus this edition of the book includes the latest examples of applying behavioral principles of everyday behavior.

The Third Edition, like its predecessors, has been thoroughly tested and revised. I used a computer version of the book to test different revisions of the book with over 100 University of Kansas students. The result is that most questions have an error rate of less than 15%. Students should find the writing clear and to the point. They should find the questions easy to answer correctly and helpful in learning the material thoroughly. Thus the book is student friendly.

I began revision of this book in 1985. I did not complete it until the summer of 1995. This lengthy birthing reflects my attempts to retain the features that made the book so successful in prior editions, while making it as current and accessible as possible.

I would like to thank the many people who made this book possible. I owe a boundless debt to my wife, Ocoee. She supported my efforts over these many years to revise the book. She probably discussed with me every important change once, if not many times. She helped me more than I can ever repay.

I owe an enormous debt to my daughter-in-law, Mary Miller, for her countless hours of work on the database that contained the book. She entered student error rates, made suggestions for changes, implemented changes, and generally produced the final product.

I owe a great debt to the many students who helped in a variety of ways: Deborah Altus, for her background research and resulting revisions; Charlie Cleanthous, for helping me keep alive the spirit of Socrates; Bryan Midgley, for his thorough reading and rereading, his research on Skinner, his interesting examples of research, and his ongoing help throughout; and Paul Crosby, for a critical but supportive reading of the book.

I would like to thank the many people at Brooks/Cole who have made it possible for this book to become a bestseller. In particular I am grateful that Jack Thornton took the initial gamble on the unusual format of the book. More recently, Marianne Taflinger and the rest of the Brooks/Cole staff provided encouragement, resources, and talent in nurturing this edition to its birth.

I am grateful to the reviewers: William M. Beneke, Lincoln University; John C. Birkimer, University of Louisville; Paul K. Brandon, Mankato State University; Gerald D. Guthrie, Portland State University; James Kopp, University of Texas at Arlington; Robert Madigan, University of Alaska, Anchorage; and David Schmitt, University of Washington. They helped me avoid many problems, particularly in my initial attempts to explain what is unique and powerful about the scientific approach of behavior analysis.

I am also grateful to the many behavior analysts who have shared with me insights into how to improve the book. Richard O'Connell has shared data, problems, class notes, and a rich variety of insights over many years. Bob Peterson encouraged me at a critical moment in the revision process. Lanny Fields freely suggested several ways that the stimulus control unit might be improved. Dave Schmidt has been supportive in a critical but helpful way.

I am grateful for the help provided by these many people over the last 20-plus years. The book owes many of its best features to our collaborative efforts. Since I made the final decisions, I bear the responsibility for its hopefully few defects.

I hope that students and instructors will find this book of personal value and easy to use. I trust that readers finding errors will inform me of them. I invite readers to tell me about their favorite examples of both research and anecdotal applications of behavior analysis to everyday life.

L. Keith Miller

Introduction: The Science of Learning and the Technology of Education

(Note to the student: The book uses **boldface** to emphasize basic concepts and underlining to highlight key words. I will ask you questions about these terms on the Reading Quiz later. Please pay careful attention to those terms that are boldfaced or underlined.)

This book introduces you to the science of behavior analysis. Behavior analysis studies how the events in your daily life affect your behavior. This science has three branches: experimental, applied, and conceptual. The experimental analysis of behavior studies the basic principles that determine people's behavior. It conducts "basic research." Applied behavior analysis studies the application of those principles to behavioral problems. It conducts "applied research." Conceptual behavior analysis discusses theoretical issues. It conducts "theoretical research." The name given to the basic, applied, and conceptual branches together is behavior analysis. This book focuses on applied behavior analysis while drawing on elements of the other two branches. (Notice that I underlined the important words *behavior analysis*.)

1. This book introduces you to the science of behavior ________________. (Note: Answers are found at the end of the book.)

Behavior Analysis and Learning

Behavior analysis studies how people learn the rich variety of behaviors that mark their lives. It examines how children learn new skills as they grow up, how adults learn to work and love, and how older people learn to adjust to retirement. It studies how people learn both rational and emotional behavior. It investigates how we can help people with retardation learn to run their own lives. It studies how normal people can learn to live cooperatively. These studies enable behavior analysts to help people learn new behaviors that enrich their lives. (I have emphasized the word *learn* because behavior analysis is the science of learning.)

2. Behavior analysis studies how people ________ the rich variety of behaviors that mark their lives.

Behavior analysis helps people with many kinds of problems improve their lives. In particular, it has developed numerous ways to help people overcome disabilities. It has helped college students to overcome learning problems. It has assisted all kinds of people in dealing with problems in social relationships. It has helped parents handle problems in raising their children. (Notice what behavior analysis helps people with.)

3. Behavior analysis helps people with many kinds of ___________ improve their lives.

This book is not only about behavior analysis; it is also an example of behavior analysis. In writing it, I have used many of the discoveries behavior analysis has made about learning. You will probably find that you are learning more material with less effort. Because the book is an example of behavior analysis, you will be learning about behavior analysis simply by using it. If you like using it, then you like at least one example of behavior analysis. (Notice the words emphasized in this paragraph.)

4. This book is not only about behavior analysis; it is also a(n) _________ of behavior analysis.

The book differs from most other introductory textbooks by inviting you to actively respond to it throughout. It invites you to respond by answering questions about what you have just read, by extending that understanding to everyday situations, and by applying your understanding to examples. By answering, extending, and applying your understanding, you will be actively responding to the book. You will thereby participate in the process that is at the very heart of behavior analysis: modifying behavior! (Did you notice the important word in this paragraph?)

5. The book differs from most other introductory textbooks by inviting you to actively ________ to it throughout.

The Sections of a Lesson

The book divides each of the 25 lessons into four sections. Each section prompts your active responses to its ideas. The sections of each lesson appear in the following order: the Reading section, the Reading Quiz section (or Practice Review in review lessons), the Examples section (in all except review lessons), and the Class Quiz section. I will explain what you can expect to learn from each of these sections in the following paragraphs.

6. The book divides each of the 25 lessons into four ______________.

Reading Section

You begin each lesson by reading about one or more behavioral concepts in the Reading section. The Reading section defines each concept, gives examples of research that uses it, and illustrates how it can help you understand everyday situations. (Note: What section of the Introduction are this and the previous paragraphs a part of?)

7. You begin each lesson by reading about one or more behavioral concepts in the ________ section.

Reading Quiz Section

The book then invites you to answer questions about your reading in the Reading Quiz section. The quiz questions help you identify and remember the most important points from the Reading section. I have added extra questions to help you remember and learn the correct answers. These extra questions make this section into a program on the ideas in the lesson. The answers to the quiz questions appear at the end of the book.

8. The book then invites you to answer questions about your reading in the Reading ______ section.

After you answer the questions in the Reading Quiz section, you should check your answers! This is very important. If you make a mistake and don't check your answer, you will end up practicing that mistake! If you find a mistake, you should also consider rereading the corresponding part of the Reading section.

9. After you answer the questions in the Reading Quiz section, you should ________ your answers!

Examples Section

The book next invites you to apply your new skills to short stories about everyday events in the Examples section. I call it the *Examples section* because each story gives you an example to analyze using the concepts you have learned in the Reading section. Your analysis of the examples is guided by a series of questions. The questions help you decide whether you can use one of the concepts from the lesson to analyze the situation. If not, the questions lead you to a concept from an earlier lesson that can help you analyze the example.

10. The book next invites you to apply your new skills to short stories about everyday events in the ______________________________ section.

To help you answer the questions in the first few examples, the Examples section gives hints. These hints draw your attention to the most important parts of the examples. The book provides many hints to help you learn to use the basic ideas. After the first few examples, the number of hints decreases until you get no hints at all for the last ten examples. By slowly reducing the number of hints, the book gradually puts you on your own. The answers to all questions appear at the end of the book.

11. To help you answer the questions in the first few examples, the Examples section gives ____________.

After you answer the questions in the Examples section, you should check your answers to see if they are correct!

12. After you answer the questions in the Examples section, you should ____________ your answers to see if they are correct!

Class Quiz

The last section of each lesson is the Class Quiz. For most lessons, there are three class quizzes bound in the back of the book. Normally your teacher will use one of these quizzes in class. You can prepare for these quizzes by trying to answer the Class Quiz questions without writing on them.

13. The last section of each lesson is the Class ____________.

You now know that each lesson consists of four parts. The first part is the Reading section, in which you read about different aspects of behavior analysis. The second part is the Reading Quiz section, where you answer questions about what you just read. The third part is the Examples section, in which you analyze stories in terms of behavior analysis concepts. The fourth and last part of each lesson is the Class Quiz, based on the ideas in the lesson.

14. The four sections of a lesson are the part you read, called the ____________ section; the part that tests you on the reading, called the Reading ____________ section; the part with short fictional stories, called the ____________ section; and the part that tests you on the whole lesson, called the Class ____________ section.

Practice Review Section

In addition to the regular lessons, the book contains four review lessons. Each review lesson includes a Practice Review section. The questions in this section are drawn from everything that you have learned up to that point, to help you study for your review exam. If you can answer these question correctly, you will be able to answer the similar questions on your review exam correctly.

15. In addition to the regular lessons, the book contains four ____________ lessons.

How to Study for Review Exams

After you study a review lesson, your instructor will probably give you a Review Exam. This 25-item exam will contain questions from every lesson that you have already studied. Your instructor will probably base your course grade primarily on your scores on the four Review Exams.

16. After you study a review lesson, your instructor will probably give you a major exam called a Review ____________.

Don't confuse the Class Quiz and the Review Exam. The Class Quiz is a minor test that appears as a section of each lesson. You can look at it ahead of time and make sure you know the answers. The Review Exam is a major test that is not a section of the book. You will not be able to look at it ahead of time.

17. Don't confuse the Class Quiz and the Review Exam. A minor test included in the book is a ____________ Quiz. A major test not included in the book is a ____________ Exam.

If you can answer 90% or more of the questions in a Class Quiz, you should have little trouble scoring well on the Review Exam covering all material previously presented. If you answer fewer correctly, then consider changing the way you prepare for the quizzes. I recommend three practices that I will call the read-write-check method.

18. If you do not score 90% on the Class Quizzes I recommend the read-write-check method: First, you ____________ every section of the lesson; second, you ____________ answers to every question; and third, you ____________ every one of your answers.

First, read every section of the lesson. Read every sentence of the Reading section—the text, the boxes, the examples, the notes, and the Helpful Hints. Read all of the Reading Quiz. It will help you determine whether you have read the Reading section carefully enough to remember the major ideas. Read the Examples section. It will help you learn how to apply the behavioral concepts you have read about to real-life situations. You cannot learn everything you need to know just by reading the Reading section.

19. First, you ____________ every section of the lesson.

Second, <u>write</u> your answers to the Reading Quiz and to the Examples in the book. Many students just *think* their answers without writing them. Others simply look up the answers, perhaps without even reading the Reading section. Educational research has demonstrated that writing your answers is likely to improve your learning (e.g., Holland, 1965; Tudor & Bostow, 1991).

20. Second, you __________ your answers to the Reading Quiz and to the Examples in the book.

Third, <u>check</u> to see if all of your responses are correct by looking them up. If you make an incorrect response and don't check it, you will be practicing making the wrong response. Checking your responses can help you correct misunderstandings that may have developed. This will prepare you for tests given by your teacher.

21. Third, you ____________ to see if all of your responses are correct by looking them up.

Summary

This book introduces you to the science of behavior analysis. I designed it using the behavior analysis of learning. It differs from most other introductory textbooks by inviting you to actively respond to it throughout. Each lesson is divided into a Reading section, Reading Quiz section, Examples section, and Class Quiz section. In addition, the four review lessons have a Practice Review section. If you have trouble scoring 90% on the class quizzes, consider using the read-write-check method. First, read every section of the lesson. Second, write your answers to every question. Third, check all of your answers.

Helpful Hints

I have put a section entitled Helpful Hints in each lesson. You will find it at the end of the Reading section, just before the Reading Quiz. These hints will help you prepare for quizzes and exams on your readings. I have included questions based on the hints in the Reading Quiz section. I have also included questions in the Class Quizzes and Review Exams to test you on some of the <u>Helpful Hints</u>.

Helpful Hint #1

Words referring to basic concepts initially appear in **boldface** type. You will encounter them throughout the book. Key words crucial to understanding a concept are <u>underlined</u>. These key words often answer questions posed by the book.

22. Basic concepts appear in __________ type. Key words are __________.

Helpful Hint #2

Some of the questions on the Class Quiz will come from the <u>Reading Quiz</u> you completed after the Reading section. This means that one way to study for the Class Quiz is to make sure you can correctly answer every question in the Reading Quiz.

23. One way to study for the Class Quiz is to make sure you can correctly answer every question in the __________ Quiz.

Helpful Hint #3

I include references to behavior analysis books and articles. You can look up more details by going to the source for my statements. I put these references in the standard form for behavior analysis. They appear in parentheses, with the names of the authors first, followed by the year of publication. For example, a reference to this book would look like this: (Miller, 1996). You could then go to the <u>References</u> section of the book to find the title, where it was published, and what pages I refer to. When you do not wish further details, you will be safe ignoring these references.

24. If you wish further details, look up the reference in the __________ section.

Helpful Hint #4

Some of the questions on the Class Quiz will be shortened forms of examples from the Examples section. Being familiar with the original version is helpful. This means that a second way to study for the Class Quiz is to make sure you can correctly answer questions about the examples.

25. A second way to study for the Class Quiz is to make sure you can correctly answer questions about the __________.

Helpful Hint #5

I have adopted an unusual way of numbering quiz questions. For example, I might label the first question 14, the second 5, and so on. I have scrambled them so you won't accidentally see the answer to the second question while checking the first one to see if your response is correct. Seeing the second answer would prevent you from recalling that answer on your own. You may check the answer to the first question labeled 14, by looking at the answer section at the end of the book and finding 14.

26. Scrambling the answers in this way prevents you from seeing the answer to other questions while __________ to see if your response is correct.

Helpful Hint #6

I have changed some of the Class Quiz questions that are based on the Reading Quiz and the Examples enough to make a different answer correct. Be sure to read the Class Quiz questions closely even if they look familiar. I have made these changes so that you must read each question carefully to determine your answer. By doing so, I have ensured that students can't simply memorize answers.

27. You can't memorize answers, because I have sometimes changed Class Quiz questions that are based on the Reading Quiz and Examples enough to make a(n) __________ answer correct.

Helpful Hint #7

Pay special attention to sentences with underlined words, but read every sentence in the Reading section. In this lesson, I have made the questions by simply copying those sentences with an underlined word and leaving out the underlined word. This makes your reading quiz simple; in future lessons, I will gradually make things harder. I will often reword the question so that it is no longer identical to the Reading section. I will also ask questions based on sentences without underlined words.

28. Pay special attention to sentences with underlined words, but still read __________ sentence.

Helpful Hint #8

One final hint: Make sure you have a calculator for two lessons that require computations. The lesson on reliability and the lesson on visual analysis both require computations. Many students make errors because they can't divide 3 by 8 without a calculator.

Additional Readings

Holland, J. G. (1965). Research on programming variables. In R. Glaser (Ed.), *Teaching machines and programming learning II: Data and directions*. Washington, DC: National Education Association.

Tudor, R. M., & Bostow, D. E. (1991). Computer-programmed instruction: The relation of required interaction to practical application. *Journal of Applied Behavior Analysis*, 24, 361–368. This article describes recent research on the importance of actively responding to questions.

Reading Quiz

I have provided a set of questions about the ideas that you have just read. They may help you learn those ideas. Some of the questions are designed to teach you. They may have obvious clues, be extremely easy to answer, or have several possible answers listed. These questions lead up to harder questions that I have labeled Review questions. Pay particular attention to the Review questions. I urge you to write out and check your answers to these questions. If you don't always get them right, then you should write out and check your answers to the more obvious teaching questions as well.

33. This book introduces you to the science of behavior __________.
29. Students sometimes decide that the name of the field is *behavioral analysis*. It is not! It is incorrect to add an "al" onto *behavior*. The correct term is *behavior analysis*. Your answer is wrong unless you call it __________ analysis.
25. Review: The name of the field applies to all three of its branches taken together. Thus the name for the basic, applied, and conceptual branches together is __________ analysis.
5. Behavior analysis studies how people ______ the rich variety of behaviors that mark their lives.
4. Behavior analysis helps people with many kinds of __________ improve their lives.
34. This book is not only *about* behavior analysis, it is also a(n) __________ of behavior analysis.
30. The book differs from most other introductory textbooks by inviting you to actively ______ to it.
31. The book divides each of the 25 lessons into four __________.
27. Review: You begin each lesson by reading about one or more behavioral concepts in the __________ section.
23. Review: The book then invites you to answer questions about the reading in the Reading ________ section.
1. After you answer the questions in the Reading Quiz, you should __________ your answers!
22. Review: The book next invites you to apply your behavior analysis skills to stories about everyday events in the __________ section.
35. To help you answer the questions in the first few examples, the Examples section gives you __________.
2. After you answer the questions in the Examples section, you should __________ your answers to see if they are correct!
24. Review: The last section of each lesson is the __________ Quiz.
28. Review: You review groups of regular lessons with four special lessons. I call these special lessons __________ lessons.
3. After you study a review lesson, your instructor will probably give you an exam called a Review __________, containing questions from every lesson you have already studied.
13. If you can answer 90% or more of the questions in a Class Quiz, you should have little trouble scoring well on the __________ Exam that reviews all the material previously presented.
17. Review: If you are not able to answer 90% of the questions correctly on the Class Quiz, first be sure that you __________ every section of each lesson from then on.
18. Review: If you are not able to answer 90% of the questions correctly on the Class Quiz, second, you should ________ down your answers to the Reading Quiz and to the Examples.
19. Review: If you are not able to answer 90% of the questions correctly on the Class Quiz, third, you should __________ to see if all of your responses are correct by looking them up.
32. The Class Quizzes and Review Exams test you on the Helpful __________.
14. Remember to read the Helpful Hints section. From Hint #1: Words referring to basic concepts initially appear in __________ type.
6. From Hint #1: Key words crucial to understanding a concept are __________.
7. From Hint #2: Some of the questions on the Class Quiz will come from the section that asks you questions about the reading: the __________ Quiz section.
8. From Hint #4: Some of the questions on the Class Quiz will be shortened forms of stories from the section called the __________ section.
9. From Hint #5: I have scrambled question numbers so you won't accidentally see the answer to the second question when you __________ the first one to see if your response is correct.
10. From Hint #6: I have changed some of the Class Quiz questions that are based on the Reading Quiz and the Examples enough to make a/the __________ (different, same) answer correct.

11. From Hint #7: Pay special attention to sentences with underlined words in this book, but read ____________ sentence in the Reading section.
12. From Hint #8: If you can't divide 3 by 8 without a calculator, then you should be ready on two lessons to use a ____________ (calculator, friend).
26. Review: When you have finished answering the questions in the Reading Quiz, you should ____________ your answers!
20. Review: If you have trouble scoring 90% on the Class Quizzes, consider three practices. First, ____________ every section of the lessons. Second, ____________ down your answers to every question. Third, ____________ all of your answers.
21. Review: Some of the questions on the Class Quiz will come from the ____________ Quiz you have already completed; others will be shortened forms of ____________ from the Examples section.
16. Review: I have changed some of the Class Quiz questions that are based on the Reading Quiz and the Examples enough to make a(n) ____________ answer correct.
15. Review: Carefully note sentences in the Reading section with underlined words, but be sure to ____________ every sentence, whether or not it contains an underlined word.

UNIT
1

The Behavioral Strategy

LESSON

1 Introduction to Everyday Behavior Analysis

Introduction to Unit One

The purpose of this book is to teach you how to apply behavior analysis to solve human problems. You will learn four broad strategies for doing so. In this unit, you will learn about the behavioral strategy for solving human problems. You will learn that simply gathering information about the role of behavior in a human problem will often lead to its solution. You will learn five specific tactics for using this strategy. In future units, you will learn additional strategies, but first I will introduce you to the historical roots of behavior analysis.

Behavior analysis is the modern form of the philosophy of behaviorism. Behavior analysis began in the 1930s and started to grow rapidly in 1970, helping people solve many behavioral problems and leading to the development of new fields such as behavioral medicine. Using the methods of natural science, behavior analysis has become the most successful approach to understanding human behavior. Behavior analysis has succeeded in solving many problems that plagued the study of human behavior. One such problem is understanding the role of private events in causing behavior. I will start with a short history of behavior analysis.

1. Behavior analysis is the modern form of the philosophy of behaviorism.

Modern Behaviorism

The historical roots of behavior analysis lie in the philosophy of behaviorism, which first appeared on the American scene around 1900. It took an approach to human conduct that looked for facts. It tried to find out what people do and why they do it. Behaviorism favored using the methods of natural science to discover the causes of human behavior. It aimed to use this information to solve the many social problems of that time. Behaviorist philosophy influenced economics, political science, and sociology even before psychology (Samelson, 1985).

2. The philosophy of behaviorism took an approach to human conduct that looked for facts.

Most people interested in the study of human behavior in 1900 resisted the philosophy of behaviorism. They preferred the time-honored approach to human conduct, engaging in theories, guesses, and learned debate, and spending many hours in the library reading what other "experts" had to say. They remained philosophers, not scientists. Rather than facts, they used logic to explain human behavior. They gathered data through people's reports of their own thoughts, assuming that thoughts cause behavior.

John B. Watson (Figure 1-1) argued passionately that psychology should adopt the philosophy of behaviorism (Watson, 1914). He was the first widely known psychologist to do so. Watson based his approach on the laws of reflex behavior (Pavlov, 1927). Reflex behavior is responding caused by a stimulus. It is responding that you cannot avoid; it is involuntary. For example, the eye blink is an involuntary reflex caused by an object moving toward the eye. Watson argued that simple reflexes combine to form complex behavior. He proposed the first stimulus-response behaviorism. Watson's behaviorism accounts for much behavior in primitive organisms, but only a small amount of human behavior. Its most important weakness is that it cannot explain voluntary behavior. Behavior analysts argue that this kind of behaviorism cannot explain complex human behavior.

Figure 1-1. John B. Watson urged psychology to adopt a form of stimulus-response behaviorism in 1914.

Figure 1-2. B. F. Skinner founded modern behaviorism in the 1930s. The scientific field is called *behavior analysis.* Photograph courtesy of B. F. Skinner.

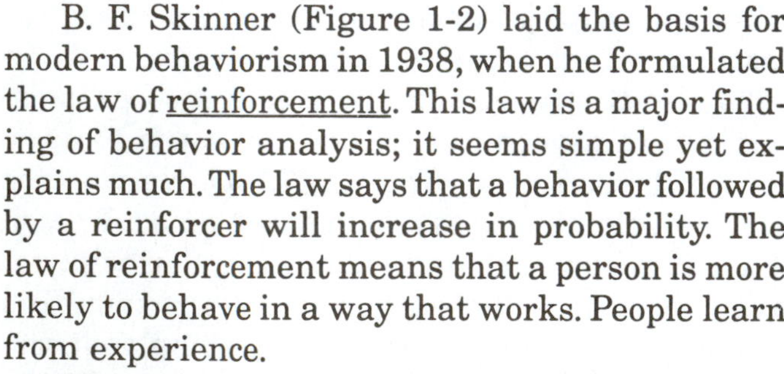

B. F. Skinner (Figure 1-2) laid the basis for modern behaviorism in 1938, when he formulated the law of reinforcement. This law is a major finding of behavior analysis; it seems simple yet explains much. The law says that a behavior followed by a reinforcer will increase in probability. The law of reinforcement means that a person is more likely to behave in a way that works. People learn from experience.

Skinner gave the name *operant* to behavior affected by reinforcement. He thereby set it apart from reflex behavior. Reflex behavior is involuntary behavior, but operant behavior is voluntary behavior. Skinner argued that "operant behavior is the field of intention, purpose and expectation" (Skinner, 1986: p. 716). He contended that the laws of operant behavior can explain complex human behavior.

Skinner founded modern behaviorism. He added operant behavior to Watson's and Pavlov's reflex behavior to get a rounded picture of the causes of behavior. In doing so, he went beyond the stimulus-response behaviorism advocated by Watson. His approach has been much more successful with human behavior, so much of which is voluntary. Skinner called his brand of behaviorism behavior analysis.

Many people have ranked Skinner's work next to other major advances in science. According to Vaughan (1984), it is one of three major advances: The first major advance was to stop seeing Earth as the center of the universe; the second was to stop seeing humans as totally different from animals; and the third was to give up the idea that private events cause behavior.

Many people view Skinner as the world's greatest psychologist. The American Psychological Association cited his work as "unparalleled among contemporary psychologists" (Graham, 1990). The APA gave him an award for his lifetime contribution to psychology—an honor no other psychologist has received.

The Growth of Behavior Analysis

Skinner did not gain instant recognition for his formulation of the law of reinforcement. But his work caused a few others to study reinforcement, and they made additional discoveries. The number of behavior analysts grew slowly from this start in the 1930s. By 1958, they founded their first journal. They studied basic laws of reinforcement during those early years but did not try to apply the laws to practical problems.

Behavior analysts found variables that strongly affect behavior. These variables were the basis for the first laws of voluntary behavior, which allowed this new field to begin solving practical behavioral problems. Behavior analysts called this practical application of behavioral laws to solve behavioral problems applied behavior analysis. The first examples of applying behavioral laws to real problems occurred in the early 1960s. They created a sensation among students of human behavior.

3. When behavior analysts first applied behavioral laws to solve behavioral problems, they called it applied behavior analysis.

Applied behavior analysts first used these laws to help people with only the most severe problems. Often the problems were so bad that all other approaches had failed. They taught long-term mental patients to take care of themselves (Ayllon & Azrin, 1968). They helped people with severe retardation learn how to talk (Guess, 1969). They got children with devastating autism to stop hurting themselves (Lovaas, Schaeffer, & Simmons, 1965). Such successes with severe problems convinced many students of human behavior that behavior analysis was a major breakthrough. You will have the chance to judge for yourself as you read this book.

Figure 1-3. Charles Ferster was the first editor of the first journal devoted to behavior analysis. It publishes basic research.

Figure 1-4. Montrose Wolf was the first editor of the first journal devoted to applied behavior analysis. It publishes applied research.

Drawing strength from these triumphs, behavior analysts used behavioral laws to help people with moderate problems. They helped adults change their stuttering (James, Ricciardelli, Hunter, & Rogers, 1989). People with mild retardation learned to prepare their own meals (Sanders & Parr, 1989). Troubled teens improved their social and academic skills (Phillips, Phillips, Fixsen, & Wolf, 1971). Behavior analysts had thousands of similar successes. Their methods worked not only with severe problems, but also with a wide range of moderate problems.

Behavior analysts use these laws to improve the lives of everyday people. Children are helped to form healthy sleep habits (Durand & Minell, 1990). College students learn better how to learn (Kulik, Kulik, & Cohen, 1979). Low-income children learn more in school (Bereiter & Midian, 1978; Bushell, 1978). Behavior analysts even help groups learn to cooperate more fully (Comunidad-Los-Horcones, 1986; Miller, 1976). You will find many other everyday examples in this book.

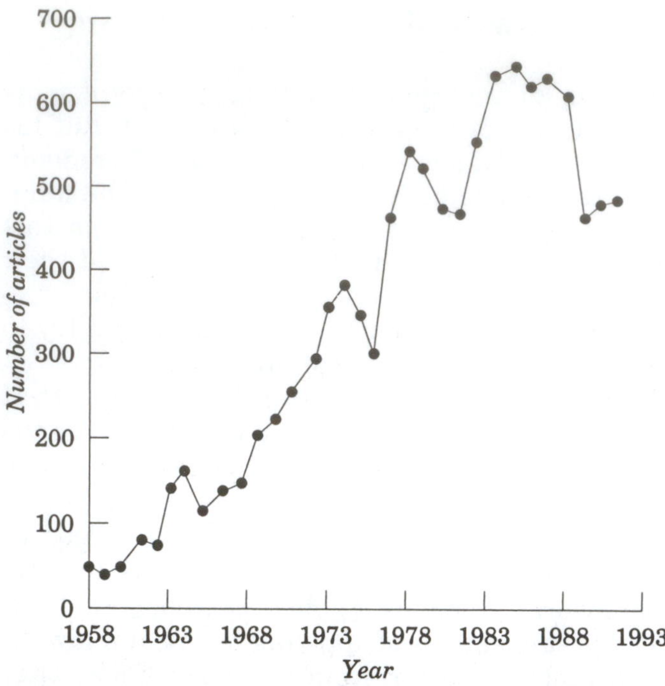

Figure 1-5. Number of behavior analysis papers published each year.

4. Applied behavior analysts started helping people with severe or moderate problems that one doesn't run into every day. They have finally begun improving the lives of people with ___moderate___ problems.

Behavior analysts are opening up whole new fields of study with the power of these laws. Behavioral medicine has replaced psychosomatic medicine (Pattishall, 1989). This new field of behavioral medicine is important because people's behavior causes as much as half of all disease (Dush & Spoth, 1988). Behaviors that cause disease include overeating, careless sex, smoking, lack of exercise, drinking alcohol, using drugs, poor driving, and fighting. There are other new fields. Behavioral pediatrics improves the care of infants (Gross & Drabman, 1990). Behavioral gerontology helps keep old people active and healthy (Carstensen, 1988). Behavioral dentistry improves self-care through better brushing and flossing (Melamed & Bennett, 1985).

Behavior analysts believe that behavioral laws provide a foundation for all behavioral sciences. They are the basis of behavioral sociology (Burgess & Bushell, 1969; Kunkel, 1975), behavioral economics (Hursh, 1984; Kagel & Winkler, 1972), behavioral social work (Thyer, 1988), and behavioral anthropology (Lloyd, 1985). Glenn (1986) has suggested that the operant is the "gene" for all of the social sciences. Thus, behavior analysis may be more than just another approach to human behavior (Kazdin, 1975).

Behavior analysis burst on the American scientific scene about 1970. Figure 1-5 shows the growth in number of scientific papers, starting in 1958 with the first journal devoted exclusively to behavior analysis. Behavior analysts were publishing many more by 1970, and since 1977 more than 500 papers a year have been published. Behavior analysis grew explosively during the 1970s because of its success with a wide range of human problems.

5. Behavior analysis burst on the American scientific scene about ___1970___.

As you might expect, behavior analysts view B. F. Skinner as the founder of their field. Skinner discovered many of the basic laws of behavior

Note: Graph shows papers published in behavioral journals, cited in Wyatt, Hawkins, & Davis, 1986. Articles published after 1973 were counted from the PsychLit database.

analysis and foresaw the possibility of applying these laws to solving practical problems. He also laid out the basis for the methods and philosophy of behavior analysis (e.g., Skinner, 1945, 1950).

What Is Behavior Analysis?

Just what is behavior analysis? Here is your first definition. **Behavior analysis** is the science that studies environmental events that change behavior (Baer, Wolf, & Risley, 1968).

6. Behavior analysis is the science that studies environmental events that do what to behavior? They ________ it.

Behavior analysis studies environmental events that change behavior. Environmental events are any events outside the person. The physical world provides many such events: Rain is an environmental event that changes the way you dress and what you do; the presence of a cliff is an environmental event that changes the direction of your walking. The social world of other people also provides innumerable environmental events. When your mother tells you to stop teasing your brother, she creates an event that may change how you play. When your boss gives you a raise, she may influence how well you do your job. Environmental events are all of those events in your world that may influence your behavior.

Here is an example of behavior analysis. Suppose Tom is having trouble in fifth-grade spelling. We might guess that studying does not lead to any environmental events that have an obvious benefit for Tom. His parents may not praise him, the teacher may not notice his effort, and his friends may like other things about him. We could help Tom change by arranging for some benefits. The easiest place to start might be with the teacher. We could induce the teacher to pay attention to Tom when he studies. His teacher might praise him whenever he is studying. Studying is an observable behavior; praise is an environmental event. If Tom's studying increases, then we have found an environmental event that seems to change behavior. If Tom's studying does not increase, we could look at other events. Behavior analysis is the science that studies environmental events like praise, to determine whether such events can change behaviors like studying.

Notice that praise is an environmental event. Also notice that we can observe studying. We can experiment with praise to see if it changes Tom's studying. The defining feature of behavior analysis is this focus on environmental events that change behavior.

The Problem with Using Private Events to Explain Behavior

Skinner invented a natural science method for the study of behavior. His method was to focus on environmental events rather than private events as causes of behavior.

People often explain behavior with private events. Private events include thoughts, feelings, emotions, attitudes, and the like. They are private because only the person who has them can observe them. Here are some examples of explanations based on private events. "I ate vegetables because I decided I needed more vitamins." You are explaining the behavior of eating vegetables by the thought that you need more vitamins. Your decision is private because you are the only person who can observe your thoughts. "I went to a movie because I felt like laughing." You are explaining the behavior of going to the movie with the feeling of wanting to laugh. "I voted for Dole because I like his sense of humor." You are explaining the behavior of voting for Dole by your attitude toward his sense of humor. "I hit him because I was angry." You are explaining your behavior of hitting the person by your emotion of anger.

There is a problem with these explanations. The problem is that we need to explain the private events just as much as we need to explain the public behavior. For example, we might say, "Joe decided to do his homework." This invites the next question, "Why did Joe decide to do his homework?" If we cannot answer that question, we cannot increase the chances that Joe will do his homework. Common sense suggests that Joe decided to do his homework for a reason. Perhaps he has a test coming up. Perhaps his allowance depends on doing his homework. Perhaps he has some free time. Notice that these causes are environmental events, not private events. If we can find an environmental event that explains Joe's decision, then we can use it to increase the chance that he will do his homework. As long as we find only private events, we can't do anything that will help Joe. When we use private behavior like Joe's decision to explain not doing his homework, we still need to explain his decision.

7. The problem with using private events to explain behavior is that we still must explain the private events!

The Principle of Public Events

Skinner advocated the principle of public events. **The principle of public events** seeks the causes of behavior in environmental events, not in private events such as thinking or feeling. This approach required Skinner to establish two facts. The first fact was the observed behavior, and the second was the state of the environment. If Skinner observed Ann swearing and yelling, he would look for an environmental event that causes the behavior. Maybe Ann's Dad is often helping her when she swears and yells. Getting Dad's help could be an explanation for Ann's swearing and yelling. It is an event in Ann's environment that could be observed. Skinner did not have to use unexplained causes to explain Ann's behavior; he sought the explanation in environmental events.

Notice that Skinner did *not* deny the existence of private events. He did not deny that Ann had feelings of anger. But in Skinner's view, the study of public events, like Dad's offer to help, permits a natural-science approach to behavior. You will learn in the next chapter that behavior analysts regard private events as behavior. Ann's feelings of anger are complex and subtle behaviors that only Ann can observe. They are private. Skinner argued that Ann's feelings are caused by the same kind of public events that caused her yelling and cursing.

Many people still explain behavior by private events. However, Skinner's arguments convinced many researchers to reject the use of private events as causes. Skinner and his colleagues call this approach *behavior analysis*. It seeks causes of behavior in the environment rather than private events.

Skinner on Feelings

According to critics, "Behaviorists are not supposed to have feelings, or at least to admit that they have them. Of the many ways in which behaviorism has been misunderstood for so many years, this is perhaps the commonest" (Skinner, 1989: p. 3).

8. Skinner calls this a "misunderstanding"; he has never denied that people do have Feelings. In fact, he calls them private events.

A Leading Anthroplogist's View of Private Events

"The human intuition concerning the priority of thought over behavior is worth just about as much as our human intuition that the earth is flat" (Harris, 1979). In other words, Marvin Harris thinks that thought does not have priority over behavior; he does not think that thought causes behavior. Remember, behavior analysts do not deny the existence of thoughts. In fact, they claim that thoughts are a form of behavior. They seek environmental causes of our thoughts, just as they seek environmental causes of all behavior.

9. Do you think behavior analysts agree with Marvin Harris that thoughts do not cause other behavior? yes (no, yes)

The Behavioral Strategy

This book is about applied behavior analysis. Applied behavior analysis seeks to help people solve their problems by changing their behavior. Therefore, the focus of the book will be on ways to change behavior. The book will present four strategies for changing behavior. I have divided the book into four units, each devoted to one of the four strategies. I introduce each strategy in the order that you would usually try them. If the first doesn't work, then you would try the second. If the second doesn't work, you would try the third.

I call the first strategy for changing behavior the behavioral strategy. The behavioral strategy is the simplest strategy. Its core idea is that people will often be able to solve their problems if they clearly define them as behavioral problems. People often require nothing more. The **behavioral strategy** is to define human problems as behavioral problems. This is the easiest strategy to use.

10. The first strategy for solving human problems is to define them as behavioral problems. I will call this strategy the behavioral strategy.

I will teach you five tactics in applying the behavioral strategy. One lesson will be devoted to each of these tactics.

If the behavioral strategy doesn't work, then you can try the reinforcement strategy that you will learn in Unit Two. If that doesn't work, then you can try the stimulus control strategy that you will learn in Unit Three. Finally, if all else fails, you can try the aversive control strategy that you will learn in Unit Four.

Why the First Part of This Book Is About Scientific Methods

Astrophysicist Carl Sagan asserts that we live in a society deeply influenced by science, but most of us know little about it. "Virtually every newspaper in America has a daily astrology column. How many have a daily science column? Science is much more than a body of knowledge. It is a way of thinking. This is central to its success. Science invites us to let the facts in, even when they don't conform to our preconceptions. It counsels us to carry alternative hypotheses in our heads and see which ones best match the facts. It urges on us a fine balance between no-holds-barred openness to new ideas and established wisdom. We need wide appreciation of this kind of thinking. It works" (Sagan, 1989). In other words, science is a method for understanding. Therefore, I have placed first in this book the scientific methods used by behavior analysis.

11. I have placed first in this book the scientific methods used by behavior analysis.

Summary

Behavior analysis is modern behaviorism. It differs from stimulus-response behaviorism because it studies "voluntary" behavior. It started in the 1930s. It built a foundation of basic knowledge until its explosive growth in the 1970s. Behavior analysis is the science that studies environmental events that change behavior. Its most important contribution may be that it seeks the causes of behavior in environmental events rather than in private events. The behavioral strategy for solving human problems is to define them as behavioral problems. You will learn about that strategy in Unit One.

Notes

I have put a section entitled Notes in most lessons. You will find it at the end of the reading, and just before the Helpful Hints and the Reading Quiz. These notes expand on some of the ideas presented in the lesson. They may help you prepare for quizzes and exams on your readings. I have included questions based on the notes in the Reading Quiz Section. I have also included questions in the Class Quizzes and Review Exams to test you on some of the notes.

Note #1

Place (1993) asserts that advances in behavior analysis may lead to methods for measuring private events. He contends that we may learn when self-reports are accurate and when they are not. Some studies have begun exploring the conditions under which people make accurate reports (e.g., Critchfield & Perone, 1990). Other studies have shown ways to teach children to report public events accurately (e.g., Baer & Detrich, 1990). Perhaps people can be taught to report private events accurately; we may then discover how to predict when people will do so.

12. Such advances may lead to methods for accurately measuring private events.

Helpful Hints

Helpful Hint #1

When asked for a person's name, give only the last name. Do not include the first name or initials.

13. For example, when asked who is the founder of the science of behavior analysis, give only the single name skinner.

Helpful Hint #2

The first time that I present a question in this lesson, I often use exactly the same wording as in the text. Each time I repeat that question, I will change some of the words, to encourage you to learn the idea rather than some mechanical formula. Notice, however, that I insist that you use the exact term or the exact underlined key words as your answers. I do this so that you will learn technical terms.

For example, here is the initial definition of behavior analysis: "Behavior analysis is the science that studies environmental events that change behavior."

I use the exact same wording the first time I ask you about behavior analysis: "Behavior analysis is the science that studies environmental events that (blank) behavior." To make the question a little easier, I omit only one key term.

When I ask you about behavior analysis a second time, I change "the science that studies" to "the science of" and leave out two key terms: "Behavior analysis is the science of (blank) events that (blank) behavior." Notice that this time I left out two key terms.

When I ask you about behavior analysis for the third time, I change a few words and I change the order. This time I ask for the term being defined. "What science looks at environmental events to find ways to help people change their behavior? (blank)"

When I ask you about behavior analysis a fourth time, I reword further. "The name of the science that studies external events that change people's behavior is (blank)."

Much later I change the wording still further: "If you wanted to develop techniques that used external events to change behaviors, what behavioral science would you use? (blank)"

14. To recap: the first time I ask about a concept, I often use the exact same words as appear in the readings. The next time I ask about that concept, I use somewhat different words.

Helpful Hint #3

When asking the first question about an idea, I will sometimes give you a multiple-choice instead of a fill-in question. When I give you multiple choices, I will always list the choices alphabetically.

15. If the choices are "same" and "different," which word would I list second? same

Helpful Hint #4

I will ask you to define the major concepts in the book in many different places and in many different ways. You can help yourself by memorizing each definition. The simplest way to do that is to memorize the key terms in the definition. For example, I have defined behavior analysis as the science that studies environmental events that change behavior. I have underlined the key terms in the definition. If you learn only these, you will probably be able to recite the whole definition. So, to memorize the definition of behavior analysis, you need to remember that the two key terms are *environmental* and *change*. You will help yourself further if you repeat the full definition of the concept without looking at it several times during each lesson. Thus, after you read the definition of behavior analysis, try closing your eyes and reciting the definition. Try it now!

16. I have defined behavior analysis as the science that studies environmental events that change behavior. To memorize the definition of behavior analysis you need to remember that the two key terms are environoental and change.

Additional Readings

Bandura, A. (1969). *Principles of behavior modification*. New York: Holt, Rinehart, & Winston. This book gives an overview of behavior modification. It shows the broader meaning of the term *behavior modification* in psychology.

Goodall, K. (1972, November). Shapers at work. *Psychology Today*, p. 6. This is an extremely well-written introduction to the founders of behavior analysis.

Moore, J. (1980). On behaviorism and private events. *Psychological Record, 30*, 459–475. This paper presents an extensive discussion of the behavior analysis of private events, using many examples. It is a classic.

Pryor, K. (1984). *Don't shoot the dog*. New York: Bantam Books. One of the original porpoise trainers, the author used behavioral procedures. These worked so well that she became an advocate of behavior analysis. This wonderfully readable book will help you to a better understanding of behavior analysis.

Skinner, B. F. (1989). *Recent issues in the analysis of behavior*. Columbus, OH: Merrill. In the most recent collection of Skinner's papers, he discusses a variety of misunderstandings about behavior analysis. He includes an analysis of feeling, cognitive thought, the role of genes in behavior, and behavior therapy.

Ullman, L. P., & Krasner, L. (1965). *Case studies in behavior modification*. New York: Holt, Rinehart, & Winston. This book gives a sample of early research on specific behavioral problems.

Willis, J., & Giles, D. (1976). *Great experiments in behavior modification*. Indianapolis, IN: Hackett. This book provides brief accounts of 100 great experiments in behavior analysis. It is a good book from which to get an overview of behavior analysis research.

Reading Quiz

16. I will ask you many questions about behavior analysis in this Reading Quiz. Remember that the science is not named behavior<u>al</u> analysis. It is called ________ analysis!
15. I invite you to learn about the science of behavior ________ from this book.
54. The modern form of the philosophy known as <u>behaviorism</u> is called ________ analysis.
11. Behaviorism favored natural-science methods to discover <u>facts</u> about the causes of human behavior. It took a new approach to human conduct — it looked for the ________.
19. Most students of human behavior in 1900 ________ (accepted, resisted) the philosophy known as behaviorism.
58. Watson argued that simple reflexes combine to form complex behavior. Because a reflex involves a stimulus that causes a response, psychology calls Watson's approach *stimulus-* ________ behaviorism.
34. Review: Reflex behavior is <u>involuntary</u> behavior. Skinner argued that operant behavior is unlike reflex behavior, because it is ________.
47. Skinner called his approach to behaviorism behavior ________.
57. Vaughan ranks Skinner's work next to other ________ (major, minor) advances in science.
18. Many people consider Skinner the world's ________ psychologist.
48. Skinner did not gain instant ________ for his formulation of the law of reinforcement.
10. Behavior analysts started <u>applying</u> the laws of behavior in the 1960s to solve behavioral problems. They called this new field *applied behavior* ________.
8. Behavior analysts call the practical <u>application</u> of laws of behavior to solve behavioral problems ________ *behavior analysis*.
62. You might describe the kinds of problems that applied behavior analysts have dealt with in the following way: They started by helping the few people with severe or moderate problems that don't happen every day. Now they are also improving the lives of people with ________ problems.
3. Applied behavior analysts first used behavioral laws to help people with only the most ________ problems.
2. After behavior analysts learned how to help people with severe problems, they then tried to help people with ________ problems.
9. Behavior analysts have begun to use these laws to improve the lives of those people with ________ problems.
20. One of the new fields behavior analysts have opened with the power of their laws has replaced psychosomatic medicine. Because it focuses on behavior and uses <u>behavioral</u> laws, they call it ________ *medicine*.
7. Behavior analysts believe that behavioral laws give a foundation for such fields as <u>behavioral</u> sociology, <u>behavioral</u> economics, and <u>behavioral</u> anthropology. They believe that these laws provide a natural science foundation for all ________ sciences.
27. Review: Behaviorism appeared about 1900 in America. Skinner's discoveries started about 1930. However, applied behavior analysis didn't

burst on the American scientific scene until about ________.

23. Review: As you might expect, behavior analysts view ____________ as the founder of their field.
59. What is the correct name for the science that studies <u>environmental</u> events that <u>change</u> behavior: behavior analysis or behavioral analysis? ____________
1. *Environmental* is a word that many students rarely use. Behavior analysts use it to refer to events in the world outside of a person, as opposed to the world within his or her own body. Copy *environmental* to become familiar with its spelling: ____________.
6. Behavior analysis is the science that studies environmental events that ____________ behavior.
56. The science of behavior analysis is the study of ____________ events that change behavior.
44. Review: What science studies environmental events that change behavior? ____________
52. The defining feature of the science of behavior analysis is its focus on ____________ events that change behavior.
49. Skinner's method required a new approach to private events. Thoughts, feelings, emotions, and attitudes are all examples of what behavior analysts call ________ (private, public) events.
21. People often try to explain <u>behavior</u> by pointing to such inner causes as thoughts, feelings, and emotions that behavior analysts call ____________ events.
22. People often try to use private events to explain ________________.
55. The problem with explaining behavior using private events is that we need to <u>explain</u> these ____________ events just as much as we need to explain public behavior.
29. Review: For example, someone might try to explain that Mary hit Ted because she was mad at him. They are explaining the behavior of hitting by the private event of feeling mad. The problem with this explanation is that we still need to ____________ why Mary feels mad!
4. As another example, someone might try to explain why Mozart composed such beautiful music. They might assert that Mozart was creative. The problem is that we don't understand Mozart's composing behavior any better as a result. In order to understand Mozart's composing behavior, we still need to ____________ the private event of creativity.
17. In general, when someone states that a private event causes a behavior, we are still left with the need to explain the ____________ event.
5. Because the person who experiences thoughts, feelings, emotions, and attitudes is the only person who can observe them, behavior analysts call them ____________ events.
35. Review: Remember, the problem with private events is that we still need to ____________ them.
61. When people try to explain behavior by pointing to private events, you might say that they are using the principle of private events. When behavior analysts try to explain behavior by pointing to environmental events that are public, you might say that they are using the principle of ____________ events.
60. When I ask you for the name of the approach that looks for causes of behavior in public, environmental events, do not call it the principle of environmental events. Rather, call it the principle of ____________ events.
46. Skinner advocated the principle of public events. Students are often tempted to say that this approach seeks the causes of behavior in public events. A better answer is that this approach seeks the causes of behavior in environmental ____________.
37. Review: So when you are asked to explain the principle of public events, the best answer is that this approach seeks the causes of behavior in ____________ events.
31. Review: Looking for the causes of behavior in environmental events is called the *principle of* ____________ *events*.
45. Skinner (1989) asserted that the most prevalent misunderstanding of behaviorism is that "behaviorists are not supposed to have ____________."
28. Review: Did Skinner deny the existence of private events? ____________
51. The book teaches strategies for changing behavior. How many does it teach? ________
53. The first <u>strategy</u> for solving human problems is to define them as behavioral problems. Note that I do not call this the *behavior strategy* but rather the behavior<u>al</u> ____________.
32. Review: Notice that the correct name for the

science is *behavior analysis,* but the correct name for the strategy of defining human problems as behavioral problems is the behavioral *strategy*.

50. The behavioral strategy is to define human problems as behavioral problems.
12. From Helpful Hint #1: When asked for a person's name, give only the last name. Do not include the first name or initials. For example, when asked who is the founder of the science of behavior analysis, give only the single name Skinner.
13. From Helpful Hint #2: The first time I ask about a concept, I often use the exact same words as appear in the readings. The next time I ask about a concept, I will usually use a/the different (different, same) words.
14. From Helpful Hint #3: When asking the first question about an idea, I will sometimes give you a multiple-choice instead of a fill-in question. If two choices of a multiple-choice question are: "multiple-choice" and "fill-in," which choice would I list last? multiple-choice
24. Review: Behavior analysis is the science that studies environmental events that change behavior.
33. Review: Publication of articles about applied behavior analysis became widespread about 1970.
43. Review: What science looks at environmental events to find ways to help people change their behavior? behavior analysis
41. Review: The problem with private events is that we must still explain the private events.
25. Review: Behavior analysts view Skinner as the founder of their field.
30. Review: I call defining human problems as behavioral problems the behavioral *strategy*.
36. Review: Skinner argued that operant behavior is different from reflex behavior because it is voluntary behavior.
42. Review: This book shows how behavior analysis can help you understand and deal with not only severe and moderate problems but also problems from everyday life.
40. Review: The principle of public events is to look for the causes of behavior in environmental events.
39. Review: The name of the science that studies external events that change people's behavior is behavior analysis.
26. Review: Behavior analysis is the science that studies events outside of a person that can change the person's behavior.
38. Review: The behavioral strategy is to define human problems as behavior problems.

LESSON

2 Definitions of Everyday Behaviors

You will learn in this lesson the first tactic in solving human problems by using the behavioral strategy. The first tactic in using the behavioral strategy is to develop a behavioral definition of the problem. You may help people solve a problem with this tactic alone. It will focus their attention on their behavior rather than on inner causes. But that doesn't mean that you will be restricted to superficial or trivial problems. Indeed, behavior is not a trivial or superficial aspect of human conduct; it is all of human conduct. You can apply the idea of behavior to everything that people do. You can define everything that people do and every problem that people have in terms of behavior.

When you learn how to define problems in terms of behavior, you will realize that many vague terms, such as *bad attitude,* ultimately refer to behaviors. You will see that self-reports such as questionnaires and interviews usually do not let you get accurate information about behaviors. The alternative is to use the principle of direct observation. The great value of studying behavior is that it permits direct observation, which is the most important tool in changing behavior.

What Is Behavior?

Behavior analysts study behavior. However, many students of human behavior believe that studying only behavior leaves out the most interesting human phenomena. They believe that behavior analysis deals with only trivial and mechanical aspects of human activity. So that you won't think that focusing on behavior is limiting, I will start by showing you what behavior analysts mean by *behavior*.

Behavior is anything that a person does (cf. Catania, 1984). Behavior is physical, and it functions to do something. The best test of whether it is physical is whether you can observe it. You might use your unaided senses, or you might use electronic instruments. Running is an obvious example of behavior: You can observe the action of the legs as they move the body somewhere. I will describe four broad categories of human activity that behavior analysts consider behavior, starting with examples that are clear to most people. I will progress to examples that confuse most people, such as many activities that people usually call *mental.* I hope to change your understanding of the unclear and murky examples so that they are clear to you.

1. Behavior is anything that a person ______.

Clear examples of behavior for most people involve obvious body actions. You would probably label biting into an apple as behavior. You might also call hitting a ball, walking a mile, and jumping over a ditch behavior. You would probably label shouting as behavior. Behavior analysts consider such actions behavior because they are physical

A Leading Philosopher's View on Mental Events

"Mental events are identical with physical events" (Davidson, 1980: p. 209). Behavior analysts view anything that people do, including mental and physical activities, as forms of behavior.

2. Behavior analysts view anything that people do, including mental and physical activities, as forms of ______.

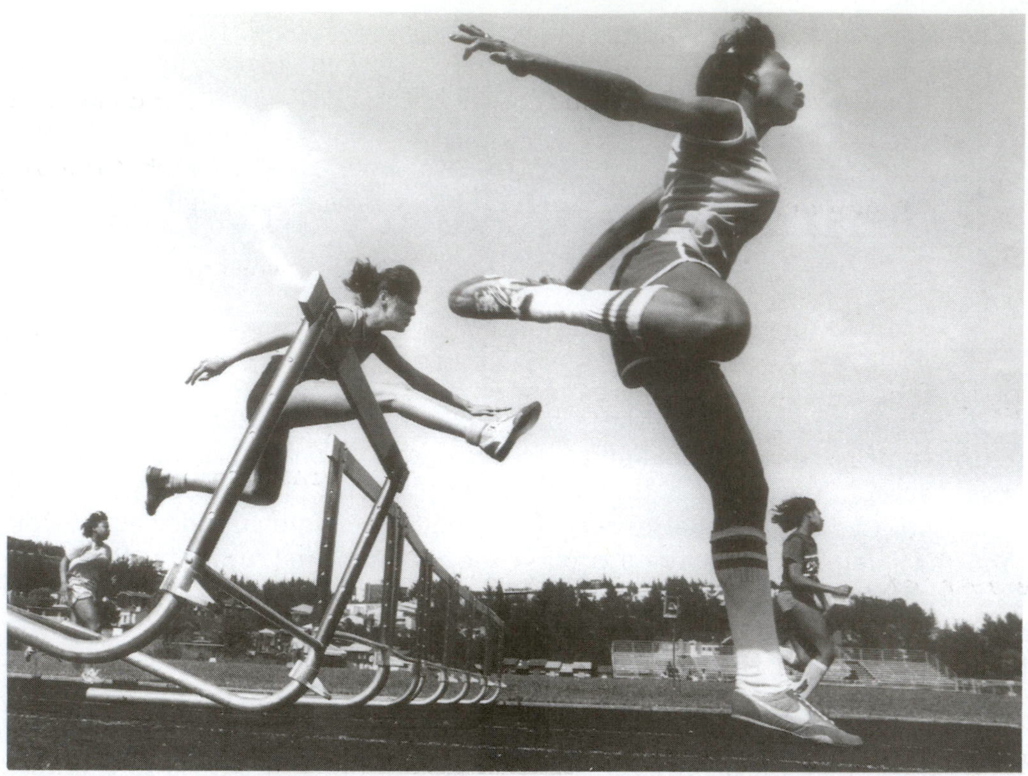

Figure 2-1. Most people would call what this person is doing a form of behavior. This is obvious behavior.

and they function to do something. Everyone agrees that the obvious movements of major muscles are behavior. (See Figure 2-1.)

Less clear examples of behavior for most people involve subtle body actions. You might waver before calling talking, looking, and reading *behaviors*. Behavior analysts argue that affecting someone's behavior by talking to them is behavior. Talking involves small physical movements of vocal, mouth, and tongue muscles to produce sounds. Moving these small muscles to say something is as much behavior as moving the bigger muscles. These movements don't require a different label just because the muscles are small and hard to observe. Behavior analysts also consider reading, which teaches you facts and skills, to be behavior. Reading involves small physical movements of head, eye, and neck muscles to face the book and to focus on the page. Reading functions to change what you can say or do after reading. Behavior analysts regard the subtle movement of small visible muscles, as in talking and reading, as behavior because they are physical and they function to do something.

Unclear examples of behavior for most people involve internal body actions. You might not label secreting stomach acids to digest a steak as a behavior, but behavior analysts argue that it is. They point out that valves must open in tiny stomach glands to release the acid into the stomach. Electronic equipment can detect the stomach acids coming from these glands (Whitehead, Renault, & Goldiamond, 1975). Again, these movements don't require a different label just because they are tiny and hard to see. They are physical because we can observe their movement with proper equipment. They function to digest food. We cannot now measure all, or even most, internal body actions. However, we will be able to measure more and more of them as our instruments improve. Behavior analysts consider internal movements as behavior because they are physical and produce results.

Murky examples of behavior for most people involve private events. Behavior analysts use the term *private events* to refer to complex actions that people often consider to be mental. People usually regard thinking as mental activity and assert that it is not physical (e.g., Chaplin, 1985). They assert that mental activity occurs in a world separate from the physical world of the brain. Their approach reflects the old idea that the world is divided into two realms: physical and mental.

As you already know, behavior analysts do not deny that thinking exists. They argue that it exists in the physical world; we do not need to call upon a hypothetical mental world that we can never observe directly. They propose that thinking is a form of behavior that is very private. You will see in this lesson that such "cognitive" activities as learning and creativity can be observed. There will be additional examples throughout the book. Interpreting private events as complex, hard-to-observe behavior has led to a great deal of misunderstanding. Insisting that private events must themselves be explained may have led to even more. Because behavior analysts deny that private events cause behavior, many people believe that they deny the existence of thinking. This is wrong! Behavior analysts simply claim that private events are a type of behavior.

You might resist labeling silent reading as behavior. Many people experience reading as saying the words in a book to themselves. One idea is that those words occur in their minds; but another idea is that the words may occur in their speech muscles. People appear to use the same muscles when saying words to themselves as when saying them aloud (Hardycke, Petrinovich, & Ellsworth, 1966). They may be silent only because the silent reader does not expel the *air* required to sound the word out loud. Of course, silent reading may involve other parts of the body as well. By viewing silent reading as an activity of the body, behavior analysts do not have to consider it a mental activity located in the mind. Instead they regard it as behavior that isn't obvious to others. Silent reading may involve behavior in another way as well. It may change some of the reader's observable behavior such as repeating facts or demonstrating skills. For behavior analysts, silent reading is an example of private behavior.

Problem solving as a form of thinking may also be private behavior. Most people consider "saying things in your head" to be what happens when you problem solve. They regard it as mental activity occurring in the mind. Yet "saying things in your head" may simply be silent talk and therefore similar to silent reading. Suppose you say to yourself, "I could improve my grade by studying more for tests." That seems to involve doing everything you do when you say it out loud, except that you don't expel air to make an audible sound. Try saying "ouch" to yourself. Notice the slight tension in your throat as you say it. If you don't notice anything, try humming "The Star Spangled Banner" and saying "ouch" to yourself at the same time. Chances are that using the vocal cords to hum will interfere with the tiny movements of "thinking" the word *ouch*. Similar tiny movements may account for other forms of thinking. They may also account for "seeing images in your imagination" in the same way (Skinner, 1953).

Behavior analysts regard thinking, imagining, and feeling as things that people do. They call human conduct of this kind *private events* and consider it behavior. Most private events involve complex activities that we don't know how to observe yet. Often they also involve complex functions such as those involved in conveying meaning to other people.

You may have read about behavior analysis in another course. You may have learned that behavior analysts deny that thinking and visualizing exist. That is not the case! Behavior analysts argue that thinking is private behavior. In their view, private behavior does not cause public behavior, although it often precedes it. They argue that behavioral scientists must analyze the causes of private behavior just as they must analyze the causes of public behavior. They assume that people's experience with past environments determines what they think as well as what they do. Behavior analysts see private events simply as additional behavior for them to explain.

Behavior analysis has been very successful in

Skinner on Awareness

"Instead of taking awareness as a given, Skinner views the act of becoming aware... as another learned behavior" (Bry, 1991: p. 9). Awareness involves looking and listening. It involves noticing the differences between things. It involves acting differently under different conditions. In short, awareness is something that people do. We learn to look, listen, notice, and act differently.

3. Because it involves people doing things, behavior analysts like Skinner view awareness as a form of ____________.

helping people change their irrational self-talk. Behavior analysis has helped people change many behaviors. Some of those behaviors have been very complex, very subtle, and even very private. I hope you will notice from the examples you have just read how broadly the concept of behavior applies. I hope you will conclude that *behavior* refers to more than the trivial or mechanical doings of human beings.

In summary, behavior analysts study everything that people do. They study actions that are physical and produce a result. They study obvious, subtle, internal, and private behaviors. They focus on behavior. Studying behavior does not limit their study of human activity.

Behavioral Definitions

Remember that I defined behavior analysis in the first lesson. Behavior analysis is the study of environmental events that change behavior. Applied behavior analysts apply the principles of behavior to solve human problems. Their goal is to modify human behavior that causes difficulties. A lonely teenager may wish to increase her social skills to get more dates. A harassed parent may wish to decrease a child's crying or nagging. A concerned teacher may wish to increase the amount of time that a student spends studying. An annoyed university student may want to improve his roommate's neatness. An overweight person may wish to alter his eating patterns to lose weight.

Behavior analysts often help solve problems like these. They first try to specify the exact behavior causing the problem. The goal would be to specify it in a way that allows clear and precise observation. Behavior analysts call such a specification a *behavioral definition.* A **behavioral definition** is a statement that specifies exactly what behavior to observe.

4. A behavioral definition is a statement that specifies exactly what behavior to observe.

A behavioral definition specifies the included behavior. It also specifies the excluded behavior. For example, suppose that Fred's father complains to Dr. Lopez that Fred punches other children. Dr. Lopez would first need to define punching. Her first attempt might be "A punch is any blow that Fred gives to another child with his hand." That leaves open the question of how hard the contact must be. A better definition might be "A punch is any blow by Fred hard enough to move any part of the other child's body." This helps Fred's father, Dr. Lopez, and even Fred to know what counts as a punch. Punching is not hard to define because it is an obvious behavior.

For a slightly harder example, suppose that his mother complains that Fred cries when put to bed at night. Dr. Lopez would interview Fred's mother to find exactly what she means by *crying*. Her definition might include obnoxious and loud crying. It might exclude talking and other soft noises. Dr. Lopez might define crying as "any vocal noise made by the child that the parents can hear outside the child's room and that does not involve recognizable words." The definition specifies exactly what behavior everyone has agreed to call crying. Therefore, it is a behavioral definition.

Crying is not hard to define, because it refers to an easily heard behavior. However, many terms refer to behavior that is much more subtle. For example, suppose that Mr. Teller, Fred's fourth-grade teacher, complains of his "bad attitude." Most of us would guess that Fred must be doing something that annoys Mr. Teller, but we don't have a clue what it is. In fact, Fred may be doing more than one thing. To avoid punishment, Fred is probably being pretty subtle. The term *bad attitude* doesn't begin to specify this complex, subtle behavior.

Dr. Lopez must interview Mr. Teller to find out what he means by *bad attitude*. She might find that Mr. Teller doesn't like Fred whispering to friends, talking back to him, or rattling papers at his desk. She now knows that Mr. Teller uses the vague term *bad attitude* to mean these three behaviors. She would probably use a more descriptive term like *disruptive behavior*. Dr. Lopez's task of defining disruptive behavior requires defining these three behaviors.

You benefit in two ways by talking about specifically defined behaviors. You have clearer communication with others, and you have consistent observations.

First, behavioral definitions produce clearer communication with others about the behavioral problem. You could badly misunderstand the complaints of Fred's father, mother, and teacher. If you do not specify the behaviors, you might not be talking about the same behavioral problem as they are. You may even find that many nonbehavioral

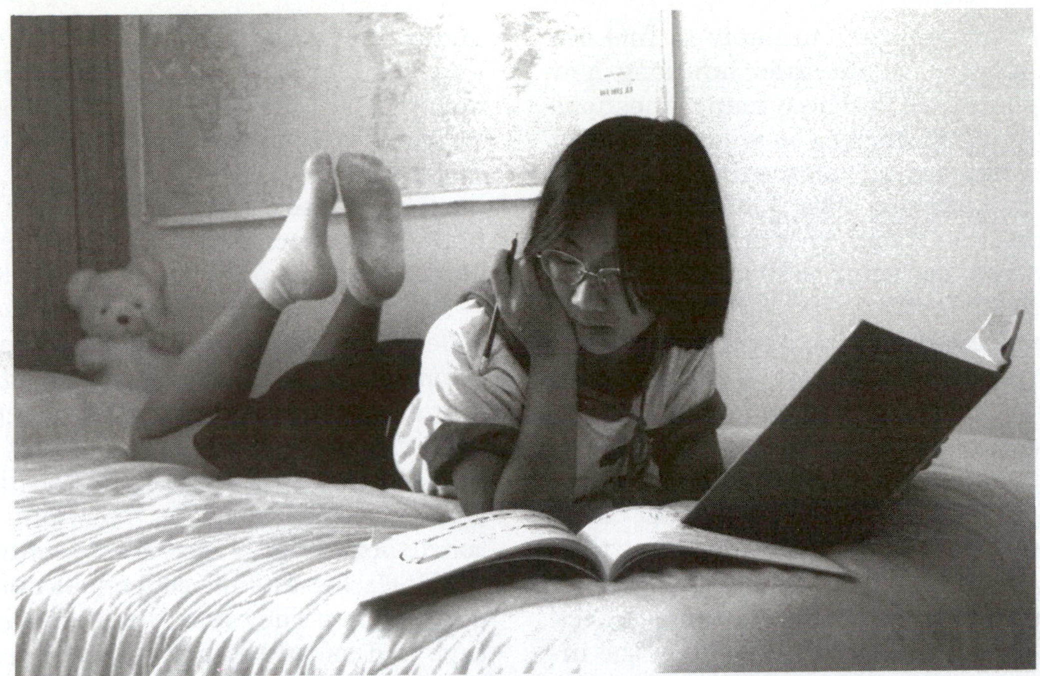

Figure 2-2. Many people would pause before calling what this person is doing a form of behavior. This is subtle behavior.

terms that they use, such as *bad attitude*, refer to subtle behavior once you have discovered what they mean by these terms.

Second, behavioral definitions produce more consistent observations. People often let their hopes influence their observations when they are unsure of what they are observing. Suppose Mr. Teller tries to change Fred's "bad attitude" by being more loving and accepting. Fred's whispering, backtalk, and paper-rustling might originally have upset Mr. Teller. However, his hopes of changing Fred's bad attitude might change his definition. He might ignore whispering and paper-rustling because they are minor problems. He would end up observing fewer instances of "bad attitude" even if Fred's behavior did not change. Mr. Teller's observations would show that Fred's attitude had changed for the better even if it had remained exactly the same. Only Mr. Teller's definition of what constituted a bad attitude would have changed. Maintaining consistency of observations is an important benefit of using specific behavioral definitions.

The Problem with Self-Reports

Once you decide exactly what behavior you want to observe, you have to decide what approach you will take to observe it. The most common approach used by those who are not behavior analysts is called *self-report observations*. I will first describe this approach. I will explain why it usually does not produce data that help behavior analysts discover laws. In the following section, I will describe the approach used by behavior analysts.

Many people interested in human behavior rely heavily on self-report observations made by *informants*. Informants are simply people who report from memory their own behavior or someone else's. You might call them *untrained observers*. I am sure you frequently read or hear findings based on the most common forms of self-reports: questionnaires and interviews.

Behavior analysts usually avoid questionnaires and interviews because of the problem with self-reports. The problem is that they are usually inaccurate or of unknown accuracy. They are inaccurate in three ways.

5. The problem with self-reports is that they are usually ________ or of unknown accuracy.

First, self-reports usually lack detail. From asking people, you may find out that they often study. However, you usually will not find out the details of their studying. You are not likely to find out exactly when they start, how long they study, or when they stop. You are unlikely to find out exactly when they space out or for how long, how many pages they read, or how many questions they answer. In other words, you will not find out precisely what happened. Given such vague data, the behavior analyst can learn little about what causes studying. It's like physicists trying to learn about gravity from someone telling them that an object falls "pretty fast."

Second, self-reports often cannot be checked. When people report on internal events, we usually cannot check their accuracy. When they report events with no one else present, we usually cannot check their accuracy. When they report events that happen rarely, we often cannot check on them. When they report on events that they hide from others, such as crime, deviant acts, or behavior they feel guilty about, we cannot check on them. We probably should not rely on the information contained in self-reports that cannot be checked.

Third, self-reports are often wrong. Even when self-reports provide sufficient detail, we may find that they are simply not accurate. When we can check up on them, we often find that they are not correct reports of what happened. The errors sometimes arise because memory is imperfect, but there is also the fact that people want to present a particular image to others. We should never assume that self-reports are correct unless we have verified that they are likely to be accurate.

Over the years I have collected a number of examples of problems with self-reports. These examples do not prove that all self-reports lack detail, are wrong, or cannot be checked, but they can give you a feeling for some of the problems that arise.

For example, Mertz and his colleagues asked 266 people how many calories they usually eat (Mertz, Tsui, Judd, Reiser, Hallfrisch, Morris, Steele, & Lashley, 1991). He then fed them only the amount of calories they claimed to be eating. They lost weight! He concluded that most of his informants had been eating 25% more than they reported. This study clearly shows the dangers of relying on the self-report observations of informants.

Mertz's findings are not unusual. La Pierre wrote a letter in 1934 to 128 owners of restaurants and motels, asking whether they would accept Chinese guests. Over 90% of them said "no." Yet every single one of them had served La Pierre and his Chinese friend on a recent cross-country trip (La Pierre, 1934). La Pierre did this study before most Americans felt ashamed of discriminating. The owners probably feared that La Pierre didn't like Chinese and that they would lose his business if they admitted serving Chinese. If he had drawn conclusions from these self-report observations, he would have been seriously wrong!

When Brickman asked students walking on a college campus if they would pick up litter, 94% of them said "yes." Yet 20 feet from where they answered the question, the researcher planted some litter near a trash can. Only 1% of the students picked it up (Brickman, 1972). Based on the self-report observations, he would have drawn conclusions exactly opposite to reality.

Hoelscher and his colleagues studied 21 anxiety patients. They lent the patients a relaxation tape and asked them to practice using it. Later the researchers asked how much time each patient practiced (Hoelscher, Lichstein, & Rosenthal, 1984). They also secretly observed how much time each patient practiced, using a hidden timer that recorded how long the patients turned the tape recorder on. The patients reported that they practiced 26% longer than the time shown by the hidden timer. This is another example of the inaccuracy of self-report observations, but the researchers made an even more important discovery. When the researchers used the patients' self-report observations, they found no correlation with anxiety. However, when they used the time from the hidden timer, the researchers found an inverse correlation with anxiety. The more the patients practiced, the less anxiety they had. Thus, if the researchers had relied on self-report observations, they would have drawn the wrong conclusion. They would have concluded that relaxation practice had no effect, when it actually did.

Many similar studies exist. Wicker reviewed 31 studies showing that what people say and do differ (Wicker, 1969). Lloyd reviewed additional studies concluding that self-report observations are not accurate (Lloyd, 1980).

Much research shows just how inaccurate untrained observers are. For example, studies of rumor illustrate how inaccurately people report events (Allport & Postman, 1945). For another example, studies of eyewitness testimony show how inaccurately untrained observers report events. Read the box on nearly 2000 eyewitnesses who were wrong!

Nearly 2000 Witnesses Can Be Wrong

Robert Buckhout (1980) staged a mock crime, consisting of a mugging and a purse snatching, which he videotaped and showed to 2145 people. Afterwards, he asked each viewer to pick the "criminal," whom they just saw, out of a lineup from memory. Only 301 identified the correct person; 1844 were unable to do so. This experiment shows the problem of remembering even the most important aspects of situations. It may also illustrate the importance of training. A trained police officer would probably have little difficulty identifying the "criminal." Police officers are trained to write down a criminal's outstanding features immediately. They would note such details as hair color and style, face, scars, and clothing. Similar training might have helped the eyewitnesses pick the "criminal" out of the lineup. Only a few viewers were able to identify the "criminal" correctly.

6. The problem with such self-reports is that they are usually inaccurate or of unknown accuracy.

Self-report observations, such as answers given to questionnaires and interviews, are based on memory. People giving self-report observations may report inaccurately for many reasons. They may not want to admit how much they eat. In the 1930s, they might not have wanted to admit serving minorities. In modern times, they may not want to admit *not* serving minorities. They may want to claim concern about litter without having to pick it up. They may not remember what really happened. They may be using a different behavioral definition than you use. They can seldom provide detailed descriptions of the behavior. The problem with self-reports is that they are usually inaccurate or of unknown accuracy. Behavior analysts usually do not trust informants as a primary source of data.

Having argued that behavior analysts usually do not rely on self-report observations, I hasten to add that self-reports can sometimes be useful. People often answer questions from a census taker accurately. They often answer questions about political preferences accurately. Businesses often gain useful consumer information. All of us learn a great deal about other people from their reports. Self-reports, then, can be useful under some conditions.

Because self-reports are something that people do, behavior analysts sometimes study them as a form of behavior. Behavior analysts might study people's statements about a situation. When studying self-reports, behavior analysts would describe their results very carefully. For example, suppose we ask Mrs. Patel how many calories she usually eats. She might admit to eating 1300 calories per day. Behavior analysts would describe this finding as "Mrs. Patel reported eating 1300 calories a day." They would not say, "Mrs. Patel eats 1300 calories a day." Rather, they would state only that she *reported* eating 1300 calories a day. This permits them to remain neutral about whether she really did eat only 1300 calories!

While behavior analysts sometimes study self-reports as a form of behavior, they do not rely on them as basic data. They do not rely on them because of the fact that self-reports are usually inaccurate or of unknown accuracy. Behavior analysts rely on a different approach to observing behavior, which I will describe in the next section.

The Principle of Direct Observation

The second approach to observing behavior is to directly observe the behavior of interest. This permits behavior analysts to avoid depending on untrained observers relying on memory. They may be interested in obvious behaviors like punching or crying, subtle behaviors like whispering or talking back to a teacher, internal behavior like a stomachache, or private events like thoughts and feelings. Whatever behavior they are interested in, behavior analysts solve the problem with self-reports by directly observing these behaviors.

Behavior analysts arrange to be present so that they can directly observe obvious behaviors like punching, crying, and dancing. They arrange to be present for direct observation of more subtle behaviors like listening to music and whispering. They use biofeedback instruments to observe stomach acidity and other internal events. Sometimes they even find ways to directly observe such private events as self-talk and pain. Behavior analysts usually directly observe whatever behavior they are interested in.

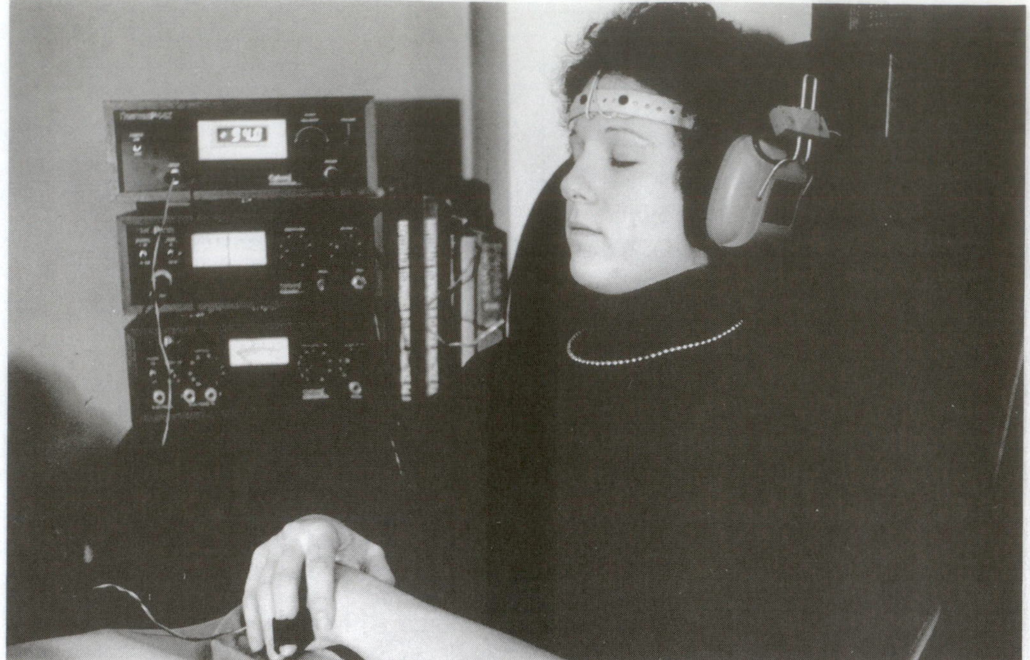

Figure 2-3. Many people would not call what this person is doing a form of behavior. Biofeedback amplifies tiny responses by using electronic equipment. It measures internal behavior.

The principle of direct observation involves the use of trained observers to personally see and immediately record behavior. Behavior analysts require the observers to immediately record what they see. In this way, they avoid the factor of memory. They carefully formulate and test behavioral definitions for these observers to use. They then train the observers to use the definitions correctly. Further, they spot-check the observers to ensure correct use of the definitions. These steps ensure accurate behavioral observations. Observations based on the principle of direct observation are called *direct observations*. They provide an improved approach to observing behavior that reduces the problem with self-reports.

7. The principle of direct observation involves the use of trained observers to personally observe and immediately record behavior.

Notice the differences between the approach used to make self-report observations and that used for direct observations. Self-report observations are made from memory by observers untrained in the use of a consistent definition. Direct observations are made by observers who personally see (or hear) the behavior and immediately record it. The observers are trained to use an explicit behavioral definition.

There are two exceptions to the requirement that the observer see the behavior. One exception is that the observer may listen for a sound such as talking or shouting. In that case, the requirement is that the observer personally hear the behavior and immediately record it.

The other exception to seeing the behavior is that sometimes the observer looks for a physical result to determine whether the behavior occurred. For example, he or she might look for a clean floor to decide whether someone swept the floor. I will describe this method, called *outcome recording*, in a future lesson. Notice that even here, the observer must be personally present to see or hear the result of the behavior.

Behavior analysts sometimes ask people to observe their own behavior if they have taken steps to ensure that the data are accurate. Behavior analysts can increase accuracy by insisting that people use a behavioral definition and write their observations immediately. This eliminates the failings of memory. If Mrs. Patel kept a diary of meals and snacks, writing as she was eating them, her accuracy would be greater. Behav-

Figure 2-4. Behavior analysts consider thinking to be a form of behavior, though it is a behavior that others cannot see. Thinkers may not call what they are doing *behavior*, but they are doing something. Behavior analysts call this *private* behavior.

ior analysts can increase accuracy further by having someone else make an independent report. Accuracy would be greater if Mr. Patel openly checked up on one of his wife's meals each week. Accuracy would be greater if the behavior analyst told Mrs. Patel about any disagreements in the reports. These and other steps can improve the accuracy of such observations. Observing your own behavior is a form of direct observation when these safeguards are followed.

When people use a behavioral definition and write their observations immediately, and someone else makes an independent report, behavior analysts call this a direct observation. When people do not use a behavioral definition, when they report from memory, or when no one makes an independent report, behavior analysts call this a self-report.

Is Attention a Behavior? Part 1

Do you think of attention as something that goes on in the hidden recesses of the mind? One dictionary defines it as "applying the mind to an object of sense or thought... a selective narrowing or focussing of consciousness and receptivity" (Webster's New Collegiate Dictionary, 1977, p. 72). Behavior analysts view it as something that people do. They view it as behavior! Jim Holland found one way to observe it. He placed a U.S. Navy recruit in a dark room with a button. When the recruit pressed the button, a light came on showing the pointer on a dial for a moment. The recruit's task was to report whenever the pointer was deflected. Holland could tell when the recruit looked by observing when he pressed the button. He could tell whether the recruit was paying attention by whether or not he correctly reported deflections of the pointer (Holland, 1958).

8. Holland turned the concept of attention from a private event into one that can be directly ______________.

Summary

This lesson teaches you the first tactic in using the behavioral strategy to solve human problems: to develop a behavioral definition that specifies exactly how to observe the behavior. Observing behavior is not a limitation, because behavior is anything that people do. You can observe obvious, subtle, internal, or private behavior. One approach to observing behavior is through self-reports. Unfortunately, that leads to problems: self-reports are usually inaccurate or of unknown accuracy. You can solve this problem by using the principle of direct observation to observe behavior. Using direct observations is usually a more accurate approach to observing behavior.

Behavior Analysis Examples

Some examples of behavioral definitions are given in the paragraphs that follow. They show how behavior analysts define behaviors that are subtle, internal, or private. These are only a few of the many creative behavioral definitions devised by behavior analysts.

Tension

I am sure you have been in situations where you felt "tense." You may have thought of your tension as a mental problem, but you might look at it as a behavioral problem instead. Your tension may have consisted entirely of muscles in your body becoming tight. In particular, your forehead muscles may have become so tight that they hurt. Tension is usually associated with tight forehead muscles, but this often cannot be observed by others. Luckily, these muscles produce electrical activity when they are tightened. Researchers use this fact to define tension as "a high level of electrical activity in the forehead muscles." They measure it with a sensitive electronic device.

Many researchers have used this behavioral definition to treat tension as an internal behavior needing change, rather than as a mental event. They provide people with immediate electronic feedback to help them learn how to relax their forehead muscles. Note that if people can reduce the electrical activity, they are no longer "tense." The electrical activity is the same thing as tension. This approach is called *biofeedback*. It is widely used as an alternative to medication.

Biofeedback provides a strategy for observing human activity that is otherwise difficult to observe. Clearly, tension does not involve obvious movements of major muscles that are easily visible, but rather subtle movements of muscles. Nor is it so private that it cannot be directly observed. The strategy for observing tension is based on the fact that it consists of tiny changes in electrical activity within the muscles. This same approach can be applied to any internal activity that involves tiny changes in muscles or glands that can be detected with specialized equipment. Such behavior can be observed as directly as obvious or subtle behavior. (Based on Budzynski & Stoyva, 1969.)

9. The statement "Tension is a high level of electrical activity in the forehead muscles" specifies exactly what internal behavior you should observe if you are interested in tension. Behavior analysts call such a statement a *behavioral* __definition__.

Creativity

Creativity is mysterious; we know little about what it is. We know even less about how to encourage it in ourselves and others. Some people seem wildly creative, while others seem to have no creativity at all. Most people regard creativity as the result of some mental process deep inside a person.

Goetz and Baer (1973) studied the creativity with which 4-year-old preschool children use building blocks. They defined creative block building as "building a form that the child hadn't used before." They found that complex structures were made up of 20 basic forms. For example, one basic form is a "story." A story is "any two or more blocks placed one atop another, the upper block(s) resting solely upon the lower." Another form is a "balance." A balance is "any story in which the upper block is at least four times as wide as the lower." They found that the children built almost no new forms until reinforced by the teacher for doing so. When reinforced, the children produced many novel forms. The children built structures that were far more creative than they had built before. Goetz and Baer helped these children become more creative by treating creativity as an observable behavior instead of an unobservable mental activity.

Notice that the researchers are interested in the behavior itself. They want the children to use new forms. They are not inferring some internal creativity from the children's use of novel forms. Rather, the creativity lies directly and completely in using the new forms.

When a child, let's call her Keesha, builds two different forms, she uses similar motions. She usually does not use obvious movements of major muscles. Clearly, Keesha's creative behaviors are not so tiny or internal that they require electronic instruments to measure. Nor are her creative behaviors so private that we need to infer them from other behaviors. Rather, Keesha's creative behaviors involve the smallest muscles of her fingers and hands as she stacks, turns, or rotates the blocks. Only if you watch very closely would you notice a difference between novel and repetitive forms. (Based on Goetz & Baer, 1973.)

10. Because building creative forms is something that Keesha does, it can be called a subtle form of __behavior__.

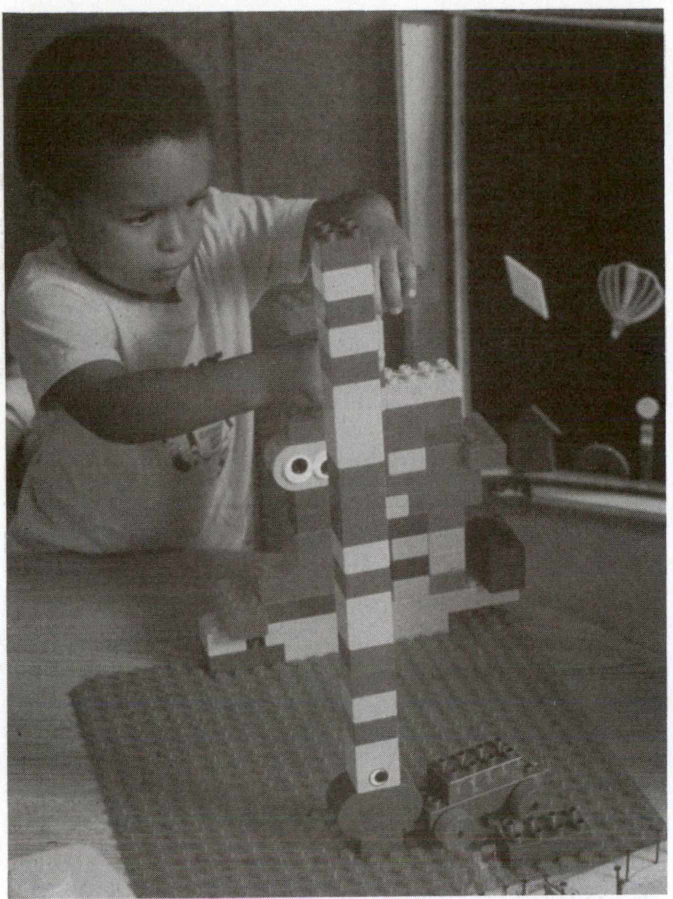

Figure 2-5. This is a picture of a fanciful Lego structure. Goetz and Baer (1973) studied ways to increase the creativity of such structures built by children.

Learning

Learning is often regarded as a magical process occurring deep within the mind. But if you think about it, you only know if someone has learned a fact if they state the fact. You only know if they have learned to identify a species of tree if they point to the tree. All learning eventually must be displayed at an appropriate time and place. While learning may be displayed privately so that only the learner can observe it, learning in the classroom must be displayed publicly. No teacher will credit a student with having learned the answer to a question if they cannot produce that answer. So learning cannot be separated from behavior.

Skinner (1954) went a step further. He argued that learning is the development of new behaviors. He defined learning in the classroom as "giving correct answers to increasingly difficult questions."

The behavioral definition of learning eventually led to a new approach to teaching. Skinner developed written programs that presented small units of information. He posed frequent questions to determine student mastery over the small units. He then revised the programs until most students answered the questions correctly. His behavioral definition led to a new approach to learning. He did not use tests to find out which students learned and which did not. Rather, he sought to ensure that all students could learn. He changed the emphasis from dumb students to dumb teaching. This book uses Skinner's definition of learning.

Notice that Skinner was interested in the behavior of giving correct answers itself. He was not interested in inferring that something was going on inside of the person that he might call learning. The learning consists completely of acquiring correct answers to the questions. You learn American history by acquiring answers to questions about dates, persons, and events. You learn even more by acquiring answers to questions about trends, epochs, and related world conditions. You learn still more by acquiring answers to questions that compare different eras. Learning does not exist somewhere apart from the answering behavior; learning is acquiring the behavior of answering questions.

Skinner's definition of learning did not focus on movements of major muscle groups or use electronics to detect tiny internal events. It did not involve behavior so private that you can't observe it. Writing a correct answer involves only slightly different movements of the fingers and hand from writing a wrong answer. Skinner specified that if you wanted to observe the subtle behavior of learning, you must observe "writing correct answers." (Based on Skinner's writings on programmed instruction, particularly Skinner, 1954.)

11. Because it specifies exactly what to observe if you're interested in learning, the statement "Learning is writing correct answers" is called a behavioral __________

Pain

You might imagine that the pain of cancer is far from being a behavior of any kind. It may seem like something that the cancer patient must endure alone. It may seem that no one else could know anything about it; it seems to be totally private. The doctor can see the tumor, but only the patient can experience the pain.

Behavior analysts maintain that anything that a person does is behavior. Therefore, the action of a person feeling pain must be behavior. Ahles and his colleagues (1990) found a way to measure some parts of this behavior. They found that cancer patients emit subtle pain behaviors that most of us could easily overlook. These pain behaviors correlate with the patient's experience of pain. The patients "guard" painful parts of their bodies when moving. They brace themselves to reduce pain. They express pain through sighing, sobbing, and cursing. They rub or hold sore areas. They grimace and make terrible faces when in pain. Ahles and his associates defined pain behavior as "guarding, bracing, expressing, rubbing, or grimacing." The researchers inferred the private experience of pain from these behaviors and justified this inference by showing that the total number of these pain behaviors that they observed correlates with the patient's own rating of his or her pain.

This example is interesting because it illustrates a method for observing private behavior. Pain is largely private behavior, but it is accompanied by subtle but observable behaviors such as guarding, bracing, expressing, rubbing, or grimacing. By observing these subtle behaviors, we can infer when the more private aspects of pain are also likely to be occurring. We are not interested in the observable pain behaviors so much as the private experience of pain. To put it another way, eliminating the pain behaviors would not necessarily eliminate the pain. This approach to pain is quite different from the earlier examples of tension, creativity, and learning, in which the researchers were interested in the observed behavior alone. The approach to pain that Ahles and his colleagues developed can be used to observe any private events that are accompanied by observable behaviors.

The researchers' method provided an objective measure for when to give terminal cancer patients narcotic drugs to ease their pain. Similar studies of pain have sought to find other ways that don't involve drugs, such as meditation, relaxation, and "cognitive restructuring."

Ahles and his colleagues observed cancer patients guarding, bracing, rubbing, expressing, and grimacing so that they could infer their pain. Clearly, such behaviors as bracing and grimacing do not involve obvious movements of major muscles. Nor are they internal actions detectable only with electronic devices. The researchers were interested in a cluster of behaviors that included those they could observe plus the feeling of pain itself. (Based on Ahles, Coombs, Jensen, Stukel, Maurer, & Keefe, 1990.)

12. Because the private behavior of feeling pain is something that a person does, feeling pain is a form of behavior.

Notes

Note #1

Psychologists use the term *operational definition*. They define it as the operations used to measure the concept being defined. They often use it to refer to a concept involving a private event. This term differs from *behavioral definition*. Behavioral definitions always refer to some aspect of behavior. For this reason, the two terms are not synonymous (Moore, 1975; Skinner, 1945).

13. Remember that an operational definition isn't (is, isn't) the same as a behavioral definition.

Note #2

Behavior analysts emphasize that all behavior involves the whole body. The most obvious aspect of running is movement of the legs. However, running also involves moving the arms and upper body. Other aspects of it are breathing, pumping blood, and looking. It also involves the coordination of looking and moving. Thus, running involves legs, arms, lungs, heart, and brain. The behavior analysis of thinking points to saying words to yourself "under your breath." However, thinking also involves breathing, sitting, and looking. Thus, thinking involves the vocal cords, lungs, spine, eyes, and brain. We may readily label running as behavior, because of the obvious movement. We may incorrectly label thinking as mental, because of the lack of obvious movement.

14. Whether a behavior is obvious, subtle, internal, or private, it involves the whole body.

Helpful Hints

Helpful Hint #1

People can make direct observations of their own behavior. If they use a behavioral definition and record their behavior as soon as it occurs, they are using direct observation. Be careful not to confuse direct observations, where people record their own behavior immediately, with self-reports, where people rely on memory!

15. Behavior analysts call the use of a behavioral definition by someone to immediately record observations of their own behavior direct observation.

Helpful Hint #2

I will always refer to a statement that specifies exactly what to observe as a *behavioral definition*. By using the term *behavioral definition,* I will distinguish a definition that refers to behavior from one that does not. I will consider your answer wrong if you call a statement that specifies exactly what to observe simply a *definition*.

16. When you are answering questions, you should always refer to a statement that specifies exactly what to observe as a(n) behavioral definition.

Helpful Hint #3

I will always refer to personally seeing and immediately recording an observation as *direct observation*. By doing so, I will distinguish direct observation from self-report observations. I will consider your answer wrong if you call personally seeing and immediately recording simply an *observation*. You must take a stand on whether it is a self-report observation or a direct observation.

17. When you are answering questions, always refer to personally seeing and immediately recording an observation as direct observation.

Helpful Hint #4

Students sometimes conclude that both approaches to studying behavior involve reports to someone else. If a researcher asks informants about their behavior, the informants clearly "report" their memories to the researcher. But a researcher who directly observes a person's behavior records what he or she just saw. The researcher need never report the observation to anyone else. A report may eventually be made to other behavior analysts, but not immediately. I have used the word *record* to stress that researchers write their observations as soon as they make them.

18. Define direct observation as "the use of a trained observer who personally sees and immediately records his or her observations."

Helpful Hint #5

Here is a hint that will help you understand some of the questions I will ask you later. If you understand the questions, you are more likely to answer them correctly! When I want to ask you about self-report observations or direct observations, I will ask you what approach the observers took to observing behavior.

19. You can be sure that I am asking you about self-report observations or direct observations if my question concerns observations and uses the specific word approach.

Additional Readings

Danskin, D. G., & Crow, M. A. (1981). *Biofeedback: An introduction and guide*. Palo Alto, CA: Mayfield. These authors give a very brief rationale for biofeedback. There is also an interesting chapter on the use of biofeedback in education.

Hatch, J. P. (1990). Growth and development of biofeedback: A bibliographic update. *Biofeedback and Self-Regulation, 15*(1), 37–46. Hatch charts the recent growth of biofeedback research, finding that research began in the early 1970s and averaged over 200 articles per year since 1976.

Hatch, J. P., Fisher, J. G., & Rugh, J. D. (1987). *Biofeedback: Studies in clinical efficacy*. New York: Plenum.

Irwin, D. M., & Bushnell, M. M. (1980). *Observational strategies for child study*. New York: Holt, Rinehart, and Winston.

Mager, R. F. (1962). *Preparing instructional objectives*. Belmont, CA: Fearon. This book explains how to prepare sound behavioral definitions, particularly in educational settings.

Sackett, G. P., Rupenthal, G. C., & Gluck, J. (1978). *Observing behavior: Data collection and analysis methods* (Vol. II). Baltimore: University Park Press.

Skinner, B. F. (1945). The operational analysis of psychological terms. *Psychological Review, 52*, 270–277. Skinner gives his rationale for behavioral definitions. He also argues that behavior analysis can study both overt and covert activities.

Von Bozzay, G. D. F. (1984). *Projects in biofeedback: A text/workbook.* Dubuque, IA: Kendall/Hunt. This is an elementary introduction to biofeedback. It covers instruments, relaxation, and how to conduct a biofeedback project.

Reading Quiz

21. Developing a behavioral definition is the first tactic in using the ______________ (behavior, behavioral) strategy.
46. Review: Behavior is anything that a person ______________.
86. The philosopher Davidson (1980) states, "Mental events are identical with physical events." Likewise, because mental and physical activities are things that people do, behavior analysts view both of them as forms of ______________.
85. The obvious movement of big muscles used in hitting or running are activities that people do. They are clear examples of ______________ for most people.
92. The subtle movements of smaller muscles used in reading or looking are also examples of behavior. They are examples of behaviors because they are things that people ______________. Many people would be less clear about calling them behavior.
84. The internal actions of secreting stomach acids or tensing muscles are something that people do. Because they are something that people do, behavior analysts regard them as examples of ______________. The reasons for labeling them as behavior may be unclear to many people.
89. The private events of thinking or feeling are examples of behavior. Behavior analysts regard them as behavior because they are something that people ______________. Most people, even psychologists, might find the reasons for calling them behavior to be murky at best.
35. Most people might find the reasons for labeling silent reading as a behavior murky. Yet silent reading involves moving the head, focusing the eyes, turning pages, saying the words to oneself, taking notes, and ultimately describing what one reads. It differs from reading out loud only in not expelling the air required to say the words. Because it is something that people do, behavior analysts regard silent reading as a form of ______________.
18. Bry writes, "Instead of taking awareness as a given, Skinner views the act of becoming aware ...as another learned behavior." Because it involves activities that people do, Skinner views awareness as a form of learned ______________.
49. Review: Here is a fact that you should be absolutely clear about: Behavior analysts ______________ (do, don't) deny that such private events as thinking, feeling, visualizing, and even self-awareness exist.
1. The term *behavior* ______________ (does, doesn't) refer only to the trivial or mechanical activities of human beings.
17. Behavior analysts view private behavior such as thinking and feeling simply as additional ______________ for them to explain.
34. In summary, behavior analysts study everything that people ______________.
91. The science that studies environmental events that change behavior is called ______________.
12. Behavior analysis is the behavioral science that studies ______________ events that ______________ behavior.
94. When students first learn the definition of *behavioral definition*, they sometimes start adding an "al" to the name of the field, making it *behavioral analysis*. That is wrong! The name of the field is ______________ analysis.
14. Behavior analysts label a statement that defines exactly what behavior to observe a *behavioral* ______________.
24. For example, behavior analysts label the statement "Eye contact occurs whenever Tommy looks directly in your eyes" as a(n) ______________ *definition*.
10. Because the statement "Eye contact occurs whenever Tommy looks directly in your eyes" tells you exactly what behavior to observe when looking for eye contact, behavior analysts call it a(n) ______________ *definition*.
39. Review: A behavioral definition tells you exactly what behavior to ______________.
58. Review: The name of the science that studies environmental events that change behavior is ______________ *analysis*; the name for statements that specify exactly what to observe is ______________ *definition*.
2. A behavioral definition specifies both the behavior to include and the behavior to ______________.

23. Dr. Lopez might define crying as any vocal noise made by the child that the parents can hear outside the child's room and that does not involve recognizable words. Because this statement specifies what behavior everyone has agreed to call *crying*, it is a(n) ________ *definition*.

22. Dr. Lopez found out what Mr. Teller called Fred's "bad attitude." It was Fred's whispering to friends, talking back, and rattling papers. If Dr. Lopez uses this information to state exactly how to observe Fred's "bad attitude," he creates a(n) ________

40. Review: A statement that describes exactly what behavior one should observe is called a(n) ________.

9. Because it helps you consistently look for the same behavior, one advantage of a behavioral definition is that you have ________ observations.

11. Because you are more likely to talk clearly about the same behavior, a second advantage of using a behavioral definition is ________ communication.

7. Because an observer is guided by an unchanging definition of the behavior to observe, behavioral definitions produce more consistent ________.

8. Because both people are talking about the same behavior, using a behavioral definition may lead to clearer ________

47. Review: Behavioral definitions have two advantages. First, when people are talking about a behavioral problem, using a behavioral definition leads to clearer ________. Second, when an observer is observing a behavior over a long period of time, using a behavioral definition leads to more consistent ________

3. A statement that describes the exact behavior to look for is called a(n) ________

37. Review: "Disruptive behavior includes whispering in class, leaving your desk, or hitting other children" tells you what behavior to look for if you are looking for "disruptive behavior." Behavior analysts call a sentence of this kind a(n) ________.

78. Students of human behavior who are not behavior analysts often observe behavior by asking people questions. Behavior analysts call a person's answers about their own behavior or someone else's behavior *self-reports* if they are based on memory and don't use a behavioral definition. Questionnaires and interviews are examples of the approach called *self-* ________ *observations.*

77. Some students of human behavior rely heavily on questionnaires and interviews, which are examples of the approach called ________ *-report observations*.

62. Review: The problem with self-reports is that they are usually ________ or of unknown accuracy.

83. The inaccuracy of reports that people make about their own behavior without a behavioral definition and based on memory is the problem with ________

75. Self-reports usually lack detail, can be wrong, and often can't be checked. I've summarized these three problems by saying that the problem with self-reports is that they are usually ________ or of unknown accuracy.

32. I described several studies showing that people's reports of what they do are inaccurate. People's reports of how much they eat are inaccurate. Reports of whether hotel owners served Chinese were inaccurate. Patients' reports of how much they practiced relaxation were inaccurate. Brickman (1972) found that 94% of students reported that they picked up litter, but when they encountered litter a few feet from where they were interviewed, only ________ (0, 1, 5, 10) percent picked it up.

96. Wicker reviewed 31 studies showing that people's reports of what they or others do are often ________.

19. Buckhout found that 1844 out of 2145 people identified the wrong person from a videotaped mugging. These inaccurate reports about the behavior of other people are another example of the problem with ________

90. The problem with self-reports is that they are usually ________ or of unknown accuracy.

15. Behavior analysts solve the problem with self-reports by using the approach called *direct* ________ with all behaviors.

13. Behavior analysts almost always use the approach called ________ *observation* with the behaviors of interest.

70. Review: When behavior analysts use trained observers who personally see and immediately record behavior, they are using the principle of ________

87. The principle of direct observation is to use

trained observers to personally see and immediately record behavior.

95. When the observer sees the behavior and records it immediately, we call this approach __________ *observation.*
36. Observations based on the principle of direct observation are called __________ *observations.*
88. The principle of direct observation is to use trained observers to personally __________ (or hear) and immediately record behavior.
53. Review: The direct observation approach is being used when the observer personally __________ the behavior and immediately __________ it.
79. Sweeping the floor produces the result of a clean floor. If a trained observer cannot see the act of sweeping but can see the physical result of the clean floor, it is still an example of the approach called direct __________.
74. Seeing a cleanly swept floor is an example of direct observation where the observer does not personally see the behavior itself but does personally see the physical __________ of the behavior.
81. The direct observation approach requires that the observer either personally see the behavior or personally see the physical __________ of the behavior.
51. Review: Students sometimes confuse direct observation and behavioral definition. A statement specifying what to observe is called a(n) __________; personally seeing and immediately recording observations is called a(n) __________.
52. Review: Suppose a behavior analyst wants Nguyen to observe how often Don hits other children. The behavior analyst would train Nguyen to use a specific behavioral definition of hitting. If Nguyen then personally sees and immediately records the hitting, he is using the following approach to observation: __________.
16. Behavior analysts sometimes ask a person to observe his or her own behavior. They teach the person a behavioral definition and then get someone else to check on the person's accuracy. Because the person personally sees the behavior and immediately records it, he or she is using the direct __________ approach.
93. When behavior analysts ask a person to directly observe his or her own behavior by personally seeing and immediately recording it, they call this approach *direct observation* instead of the __________ observation approach.
80. The approach to observation in which a person observes his or her own behavior and immediately records it __________ (is, isn't) called *self-report observation.*
71. Review: When people use a behavioral definition and write their observations immediately, and someone else makes an independent report, behavior analysts call this approach a(n) __________ *observation.* When people do not use a behavioral definition, when they report from memory, or when no one makes an independent report, behavior analysts call this approach a(n) __________ *observation.*
69. Review: When an untrained observer reports a behavior from memory alone, we call this approach a(n) __________ *observation.*
65. Review: When a person observes his or her own behavior with a behavioral definition and immediately records it, and another person checks the accuracy, behavior analysts regard this approach as __________ observation.
31. Holland (1958) let Navy recruits flash a light to observe the pointer on a dial. Holland defined the private event of attention as flashing the light and reporting when the pointer deflected. By doing so, he turned the concept of attention from a private event into one that can be directly __________.
82. The first tactic in using the behavioral strategy is to specify the problem in terms of what behavior to observe. To use the term you learned in this lesson, the first tactic is to develop a(n) __________ definition of the problem.
33. If a parent says the problem is that Jerry is lazy, then the behavior analyst tries to get the parent to specify exactly what behavior Jerry is not doing. Thus, the behavior analyst tries to develop a behavioral __________ of Jerry's laziness.
55. Review: The first tactic in using the behavioral strategy is to develop a(n) __________.
20. According to Budzynski and Stoyva (1969), what we call *tension* can be observed as a "high level of electrical activity in the fore-

head muscles." Behavior analysts call their statement a(n) ____________.

30. Goetz and Baer (1973) behaviorally defined creativity as "building a form that Mary hadn't used before." Two advantages to using this behavioral definition are that when they talk with parents about creativity, they will have clearer ____________; and when observers record Mary's creativity, they will have more consistent ____________.
76. Skinner (1954) defined learning as "a student giving correct answers to more and more difficult questions." Behavior analysts call the approach of asking a student to remember how much he learned yesterday a(n) ____________ *observation*; they call the approach of asking a student to use this definition, and immediately record every instance of giving a correct answer, then having someone check on accuracy, a(n) ____________ *observation*.
4. Ahles and colleagues (1990) defined feeling pain. Because the activities of guarding, bracing, expressing, rubbing, or grimacing are things that people do, feeling pain is a form of ________.
5. Be sure to read the section titled Notes. Here's a question from Note #1: Because it refers to a private event, the term *operational definition* ____________ (does, doesn't) mean the same as *behavioral definition*.
29. From Note #2: Because running involves not only the legs but also the heart, lungs, and even arms, behavior analysts emphasize that all behavior involves the ____________ body.
6. Be sure to read the Helpful Hints section. From Hint #1: People can directly observe their own behavior if they have a behavioral definition and immediately ____________ their behavior.
25. From Hint #2: You should always refer to a statement that specifies exactly what to observe as a(n) ____________ *definition*.
26. From Hint #3: You should always refer to personally seeing and immediately recording an observation as ____________ *observation*.
27. From Hint #4: Many students confuse *record* and *report*. Be sure to define *direct observation* as the use of a trained observer who personally sees and immediately ____________ the observation.
28. From Hint #5: You can be sure that the question is asking you about either self-report observation or direct observation if it uses the word ____________ in connection with observing.
63. Review: The science that studies environmental events that modify what people do is called ____________.
41. Review: Behavior analysts ____________ (do, don't) deny that thinking and feeling exist.
73. Review: You benefit in two ways by talking about specifically defined behaviors. You ____________ more clearly with others, and your observations remain ____________.
61. Review: The problem with self-reports is that they are usually ____________.
59. Review: The principle of direct observation is to use observers to personally ____________ and immediately ____________ behavior.
38. Review: A behavioral definition clearly states what behavior to ____________.
42. Review: Behavior analysts call everything that a person does ____________.
67. Review: When an observer personally sees and immediately records a behavior, analysts call the approach ____________ *observation*. This usually involves an observer trained to use a behavioral definition. When an observer relies on memory without such a definition, behavior analysts call the approach ____________ *observation*.
43. Review: Behavior analysts call a statement about exactly what behavior to observe a(n) ____________; they call personally seeing and immediately recording their observations ____________.
48. Review: By describing exactly what everyone has agreed to call *crying*, Dr. Lopez has created a(n) ____________.
57. Review: The most accurate approach to observing behavior is usually ____________.
60. Review: The principle of direct observation is to use observers to personally ____________ a behavior and immediately ____________ it.
44. Review: Behavior analysts solve the problem with self-reports by using the principle of ____________.
72. Review: When observers immediately record observations that they personally see (or hear), behavior analysts call the approach ____________.
54. Review: The first tactic in using the behav-

ioral strategy for solving human problems is to develop a(n) ____________.

68. Review: When an untrained observer reports observations from memory, we call the approach ________________ *observation.*

56. Review: The name for statements that specify exactly what to observe is ________________ *definition*; the name of the science that studies environmental events that change behavior is ________________ *analysis.*

66. Review: When people observe their own behavior using a behavioral definition and record instances of the behavior at the time they occur, they are using the following approach: ________________ *observation.*

64. Review: There are two exceptions to the requirement of direct observation that the observer personally see the behavior. One exception is that the person can personally hear it if it is a sound. A second exception is that the observer can personally see a physical ________________ of the behavior.

45. Review: Behavior analysts view private events like thinking simply as additional __________ for them to explain.

50. Review: In summary, behavior analysts study everything that people ________________.

Examples

I have developed a set of examples illustrating the ideas in this lesson. The first few examples may teach you how to analyze everyday situations in terms of behavior, direct observations, and other behavior analysis concepts. These examples include clues and show you how to analyze situations in a step-by-step manner. I then present some examples that don't include such clues. These are labeled *Review,* similar to questions in the Reading Quiz section. You will find that Review examples may include concepts from prior lessons. Be sure to focus on these Review examples carefully. Write out and check your answers. If you have trouble with Review examples or Review questions from the Reading Quiz, or if you have trouble with Class Quizzes, you should also write out and check your answers to the easier examples.

1. Ms. James observed the amount of time that Fred spent studying. She recorded that Fred was studying when "He had a book in front of him and was looking at it." Her statement of when to record studying is a(n) ________________ definition of studying. By using that definition to personally look for studying and then immediately record it, Ms. James was using the principle of __________ observation.

2. Dorm members complained that Sarah cleaned the lounge poorly. Ali disagreed. He made a checklist of tasks: (a) floor clean, (b) furniture returned, (c) surfaces dusted, (d) rugs vacuumed, (e) ashtrays emptied, (f) picked up, and (g) trash emptied. Ali inspected for two weeks. He found that Sarah was a good cleaner who completed 85% of the tasks. Ali used direct observation because, even though he didn't see Sarah actually cleaning, he personally saw the physical ____________ of Sarah's cleaning behavior. Further, because the checklist of tasks is a kind of statement that specified the exact results to observe, it is a(n) ________________ of cleaning behavior.

3. Ms. Caltado read a book on acting assertively. The book stated that it is assertive to openly accept praise. She decided to count each time that she looked directly at anyone who praised her and said, "Thank you." She used a wrist counter to immediately record her successes. Ms. Cataldo's use of the wrist counter to record her own behavior is an example of the approach called __________ *observation.* If Ms. Cataldo waited till the end of the day to record the number of times she had accepted praise that day, she would have been using the approach called ________________ observation.

4. Bill's son, Don, was in fifth grade. Don had often been "aggressive" in the past and had gotten into a lot of trouble. Bill decided to visit Don's class to see if he was being aggressive. However, Bill knew that the word *aggressive* is vague and could actually refer to many different behaviors. He decided to limit the term to times when Don hit or pushed another child. He specifically ruled out yelling or talking in an angry way at another child. The statement "Aggression refers only to hitting or pushing another child" describes what Bill should observe to measure Don's aggression. Therefore, it is called a(n) ________________.

5. Frank thought he was selfish. He said "no" to any request by his son for a favor, such as letting him have extra ice cream, giving him a ride to the movies, and playing games with him. Then Frank read a book by Skinner. He decided that

"selfish" was something that he did, not something that he was. Every time he said "no" he pushed a button on a wrist counter, and every time he said "yes" he pushed a button on another counter. By using the counters, Frank recorded his observations when they occurred. He said "no" 17 times and "yes" 3 times the first day. By the tenth day his behavior had changed to the extent that he said "no" only 4 times and "yes" 12 times. Frank recorded what he heard himself saying when he heard it. Therefore, he was using the approach called ________________ *observation*. Because the counts of "yes" and "no" are environmental events that changed his behavior, Frank's use of the counters to change his selfish behavior is a good example of what science? ______________ ____________________________

6. Review: Because Andy felt depressed, he went to see Dr. Shaw. After Dr. Shaw talked with Andy, he guessed that Andy's depression involved a cluster of related behaviors. First, it involved the obvious behavior of poor social skills that resulted in people ignoring him. Second, there were the subtle behaviors of speaking in a whisper, slumping, and looking down. Third, the depression involved internal behaviors such as shallow breathing. Fourth, Andy had the private behavior of telling himself that he wasn't likable. Dr. Shaw kept track of Andy's progress by observing the postural behaviors and what Andy said about himself. Because Dr. Shaw saw and heard these behaviors himself and promptly noted them, he used the principle of ________________. Dr. Shaw helped Andy to learn more positive ways to talk about himself. Dr. Shaw also taught him the skills to participate in social activities. The doctor's help is an environmental event that could change Andy's behavior. Dr. Shaw's treatment is therefore an example of the science of ______________ ______________.

7. Review: Darrell decided that Vince was "mad at him" because someone told him that Vince thought he was a mean guy. Is Darrell's conclusion based on direct observation of Vince's behavior? ____________

8. Review: Ann decided that Vince was mad at her. By "mad" she meant that Vince made negative comments about her. Vince told her that she must be eating too much because she had gotten fat. She immediately wrote the comment down in her notebook. Is Ann's conclusion based on direct observation of Vince's behavior? ____________

9. Review: Rob set his watch alarm to go off every 15 minutes. When it did, he noted what he was saying to himself. At the end of the day, he found that he was thinking about sex 93% of the time. Because Rob immediately recorded instances of his self-talk when he noticed them, he was using the approach called ____________ *observation*.

10. Review: Juan measured the littering behavior of his family on a picnic. He observed this behavior by measuring its result—namely, the amount of litter left behind. Juan carefully picked up all litter as his family was leaving the area, weighed it, and wrote the weight down. He also was careful to clean the area completely before the picnic started. He defined litter as human-made objects bigger than a quarter-inch across that were not permanent parts of the picnic area. The principle that Juan followed to measure litter is called ______________________.

LESSON

3 Methods for the Observation of Everyday Behaviors

You have learned that the first tactic in using the behavioral strategy to solve human problems is to develop a behavioral definition. When the resultant focus on a behavior does not solve the problem, you can use a second tactic. You can gather information about when and how often the behavior occurs. This information will sometimes motivate people to change the behavior. At other times, it will provide enough information to let others help them make the change. With this tactic, you will build on your behavioral definition, which gives you the basis for observing the problem behavior. This lesson teaches you how to get accurate data by using the approach of direct observation.

The second tactic in using the behavioral strategy is to use the approach of direct observation to gather information about the problem behavior. This lesson teaches the four most common methods you can use to observe behavior directly. These methods are also the most commonly cited methods in leading behavior analysis journals. Each of these methods is useful for different situations: outcome recording when the behavior leaves a unique result; event recording when instances of the behavior are uniform; interval recording when the behavior is nonuniform; and time sample recording when you wish to sample the behavior. You will learn how and when to use each of these methods.

Outcome Recording for Behaviors That Leave Unique Results

Here is the first idea you will need to help you analyze examples of different methods of observation. Some behaviors are uniform in length, while others are nonuniform. For example, consider saying a syllable. Every syllable takes about the same length of time to say—the sounds are relatively uniform in length. Compare saying a syllable with speaking. You may speak only long enough to say "hello," you may speak long enough to ask a friend how she is feeling, or you may speak long enough to tell a story. You might even make a speech taking one hour. Clearly, you may speak for vastly different lengths of time; the occurrences of speaking are nonuniform in length.

Behavior analysts use two methods to observe behaviors that are uniform. If a uniform behavior produces a unique result, they use outcome recording. If a uniform behavior does not produce a unique result, they use event recording.

You can use outcome recording with behaviors that leave unique results. Many behaviors produce unique results. Writing with a pencil leaves marks on the paper. Washing a window leaves the window clean. Cooking food produces a meal. Filling out a form leaves a form with writing on it. Driving a car leaves the odometer (mileage meter) with a new number on it. (It may also leave the car in a new spot.) All of these behaviors leave some unique result that proves the behavior took place. Notice that the durability of the result may vary from one behavior to the next. The form may stay filled out for years. Meals that I cook stay around for only a few minutes.

Observing a behavior that leaves a unique result is easy. Observers can look for the result at their convenience. They can even look for it long after the behavior occurred. Further, it may take them only a moment to see the result, but it may have taken hours to create it. Thus, looking at the result is much quicker. Observing the result of a behavior is the easiest method of observation when feasible. It is the simplest instance-type method. Behavior analysts call this method *outcome recording*.

Outcome Recording

You record a response when you see the result of the behavior. You use a behavioral definition to

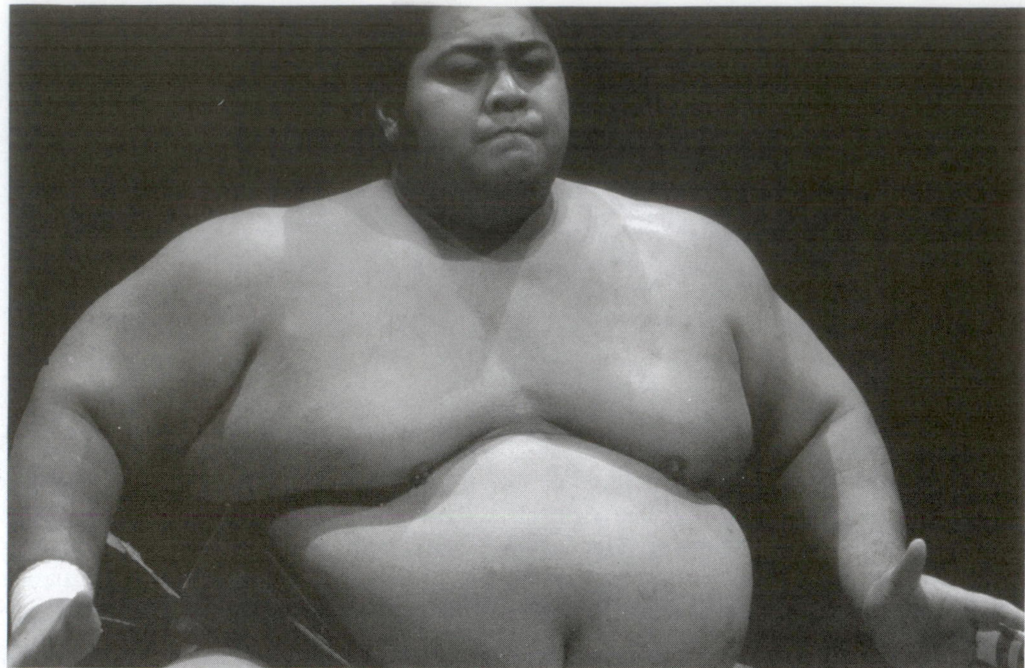

Figure 3-1. You might measure how much someone eats by weighing them. Because you are measuring the result of eating rather than the act of eating, you would be using outcome recording.

state the result to look for. You select a result that is a good indicator of that behavior. Behavior analysts use this method with behaviors that leave a unique change in the environment. Because they look for the result, they do not have to watch the behavior itself.

1. For outcome recording, you record a response when you see the outcome of the behavior.

A mark of outcome recording is that the observation takes place after the response—possibly long after. This is because the result occurs after the response and continues to exist after the response has ended. Sometimes you may have trouble deciding whether an observer looked at a response or a result. If observers look after a response ends, you can conclude that they looked at its result. You can always be sure that observers are using outcome recording if they observe after the response has ended.

An example of outcome recording might involve Ann's dishwashing behavior. Washing dishes leaves the unique result that dirty dishes are now clean. They can't get clean in any way other than by someone washing them. Therefore, you can define dishwashing in terms of whether the dishes are clean. You needn't watch Ann's dishwashing behavior. Rather, you can check to see if the dishes are clean. If they are clean, then you can conclude that she washed them. Notice that you check for the result of washing dishes—clean dishes—rather than the actual dipping of a dish in soapy water and scrubbing. How do you know that checking dishes is outcome recording? Because you can check for clean dishes only after the dishwashing has been done.

You must be able to see the results of a behavior for them to be useful. For example, suppose you wanted to observe whether Tom was making nasty comments to Maria. One result of Tom's nasty comments might be Maria's hurt feelings. But you can't observe hurt feelings, so you can't use that result to observe whether Tom makes nasty comments.

Likewise, you must be sure that the result is unique to the behavior for it to be useful. Suppose you wanted to observe how often Karim does favors for other people. One result of Karim's doing favors might be that he will tell you how often he does them. But his report is based on memory, and it does not use a behavioral definition. Further, he might lie to make himself look good. So his reports do not have a known relation to actually doing favors. You could not use them with any confidence to observe Karim's favors.

Observers can use outcome recording to observe a variety of behaviors. You can observe plaque deposits on the teeth of children to determine the frequency of their flossing (Dahlquist & Gil, 1986). You can count workbook pages completed by pupils to observe their productivity (Jones, Fremouw, & Carples, 1977). You can weigh litter deposited in a trash bin to observe cleanup behavior (O'Neill, Blanck, & Joyner, 1980). You can build a special cassette recorder that plays only a relaxation tape and that has a built-in time meter, so that you can observe the duration that someone listens to the tape at home (Hoelscher, Lichstein, & Rosenthal, 1984). You can ask students diagnosed with sexually transmitted diseases to tell their partner to seek treatment; then you can observe whether they do by whether the partner shows up at the clinic (Montesinos, Frisch, Greene, & Hamilton, 1990). These observations focus on the result of a behavior rather than on the behavior itself.

You may use outcome recording to observe a complex behavior. One way is to use a checklist to observe a series of behavioral results. You might use a checklist to determine whether the teaching staff of a large introductory course was helping students. One researcher checked quizzes scored, worksheets scored, computer printouts posted, student records updated, and daily instructions checked to see whether the staff was helping (Bacon, Fulton, & Malott, 1982). You might observe whether a person washed all the tableware dirtied at dinner by making up a list of all types of utensils used. These might include plates, glasses, silverware, pots, and serving spoons. If you found all the plates clean you would check them off; if you found the glasses clean you would check them off; and you would continue with each type of utensil. This approach permits very detailed observation of dishwashing behavior. It would, of course, still be an example of outcome recording, even though a list of behavioral results is being observed.

Classify a method as outcome recording only if it looks for a result of the behavior. Do not consider it outcome recording if it looks at the behavior itself. The result must occur after the behavior. If you are observing a result of behavior rather than the behavior itself, then always label the method as *outcome recording.*

To decide whether a method of observation is outcome recording, start by asking the question: Does the behavior occur as uniform instances? If the answer is "yes," then ask: Does the behavior leave a result? If the answer is "yes," then the method is outcome recording.

Learning Simple Arithmetic Takes 50,000 Responses!

People often explain the differences between how easily children learn math by saying that some children are "smart" and others are "dumb." Skinner (1954) explains it differently. He guesses that children make about 50,000 responses to learn arithmetic. Teachers, parents, and books help children with some of these responses, but they don't help all children equally. Skinner explains differences between children in terms of the amount of help they get. He invented a "teaching machine" that provides help on every single response! He showed that almost all children learned well with the machine. The children wrote their answers directly on paper in the machine. Skinner used outcome recording because he looked at the result of their writing behavior: their written answers on the paper (Skinner, 1954).

2. Because Skinner looked at the result of their writing, he was using what method of observing? outcome recording

Event Recording for Uniform Behaviors

If a behavior does not leave a unique result, you must observe during the occurrence of the response. Many behaviors do not leave unique results. Waving your hand at someone, saying "thank you," and reading a book do not leave a result. They occur and then they are gone. Your hand is back in your pocket, your voice has died away, and the book is back in its place. You must observe these behaviors when they are performed.

Some behaviors that do not leave unique results are uniform, while others are nonuniform. A behavior is uniform if each instance of the behavior takes about the same length of time as every other instance. For example, stuttering is uniform because each stutter involves only the brief moment. Solving math problems is uniform if students take about the same time for each problem. Even long sequences of behaviors like swimming laps can be uniform. A swimmer usually takes about the same time to complete each lap. For uniform behaviors that do not leave a result, you can use a second instance-type method of observation. This method is called *event recording*.

Event Recording

You record a response when you see an instance of the behavior. Behavior analysts use this method when they observe behavior that is relatively uniform in length. You observe the behavior during the response.

3. For event recording, you record a response when you see an __________ of the behavior.

An example of event recording might involve counting each time that a student raises his or her hand in class. You would record hand-raising when you see someone raise a hand. You can use event recording because each hand-raising response takes about the same amount of time. Usually the whole episode takes only a few moments to complete.

You can use event recording to record many simple behaviors. You might observe the number of times third-grade peer tutors praised the spelling efforts of the pupils they were tutoring (Kohler & Greenwood, 1990). You can observe the number of children engaging in disruptive behavior on a playground (White & Bailey, 1990). You might even count the number of curveballs hit well by players trying out for the college team (Osborne, Rudrud, & Zezoney, 1990). Behavior analysts usually use event recording to find out how many times the behavior occurs. The observer counts praises, disruptive acts, or well-hit balls. (See Figure 3-2.)

You can also use event recording to observe the performance of complex behaviors. You would break the complex behavior down into its parts, then use event recording to fill out a checklist of the parts. For example, you might wish to observe a public speech that a friend makes, to see if it is complete. You might list the major parts of a speech—for example, opening comments, main body of the speech, closing comments, and inviting questions (Fawcett & Miller, 1975). As your friend spoke, you would record the occurrence of each category.

Figure 3-2. Umpires call balls and strikes. Because they are observing instances of uniform behaviors, you would call this event recording.

Classify a method as *event recording* only if it involves observing uniform instances of a behavior. The observer must watch the behavior during its occurrence. Be very careful when trying to decide between event recording and outcome recording! Suppose you are observing the result of an instance of behavior after the behavior occurs. You are not using event recording. Behavior analysts always call the observation of results by the name *outcome recording*. They call the observation of instances of a behavior *event recording* only if those instances are behaviors, not results. Be careful not to look only for the word *results* or the word *instances*.

To decide whether a method of observation is outcome recording, start by asking the question: Does the behavior occur as uniform instances? If the answer is "yes," then ask: Does the behavior

The Making of an Observation System

David Lombard studied whether people protect themselves against skin cancer from the sun. His behavioral definition of "safe sunning" included wearing a shirt, being in the shade, wearing a hat, wearing sunglasses, wearing zinc oxide, and using sunscreen lotion. He went to a private pool every day at 2:00 P.M., walking the same path around the pool each day, and counted the number of people using each of those steps. He found that the lifeguards used about 25% of the steps and patrons 19%. He then asked lifeguards to model safe sunning. They increased their use to 65%, and the patrons increased their use to about 25% as a result. The observation system made it possible to see the effect of using lifeguards as models (Lombard, Neubauer, Canfield, & Winett, 1991).

4. Because Lombard recorded each instance of safe sunning behavior that he observed, he was using what method of observation? __event__ (event, outcome) recording

Delinquent Children Learn through Thousands of Parental Conflicts

Some people explain gang violence by an inner mechanism such as a violent personality or identity crisis. But Gerry Patterson wouldn't. He spent a lifetime studying the causes of delinquent behavior. He gathered data on families in their own homes, observing instances of children's conflicts with their parents. Children who become delinquent have twice as many conflicts as do normal children. Delinquents have up to ten times as many conflicts! Children have the opportunity to conflict with their parents as many as one million times before they leave home. The parents have that many chances to teach their children kindness or violence. Patterson has developed classes to teach parents of potential delinquents how to reduce conflict. (Based on Patterson, 1993.)

5. By observing instances of conflict, Patterson uses what method of observation? __event__ (event, outcome) recording

leave a result? If the answer is "no," then the method is event recording.

Interval Recording for Nonuniform Behaviors

This section introduces you to the first of the interval-type methods of observation. If you decide that you cannot use an instance-type method of observation, you will probably need to use an interval-type method.

Many behaviors are nonuniform in length. For example, study behavior is nonuniform. Often you may study for a few minutes and then look out the window, get a drink, or think about something else. Studying for an hour may mean studying on and off like that for an hour. It might mean studying for an hour straight. Other similar behaviors might be reading, talking, listening to music, or even walking. Behavior analysts use different methods to observe nonuniform behaviors than they do to observe uniform behaviors.

For example, you might think of using event recording with a nonuniform behavior to count how often it occurs. However, if you count nonuniform behaviors, you will probably produce meaningless results. Suppose Deb starts watching TV football at 3:00. If Deb watches straight through to a commercial at 3:15, you might call her viewing one TV-watching response. Suppose you also observe Andre. He takes his first commercial break at 3:12, returns at 3:13, and watches until the next commercial at 3:15. Should you count his viewing as two TV-watching responses? The trouble is that Andre watches less of the program than Deb, but you count him as having twice as many responses. Doesn't make much sense, does it?

I can imagine an even worse case. Suppose that Ann starts watching the same program at 3:00. She may have told her 5-year-old son, Dan, to stay in the yard. She might stop watching the program after every play to see if Dan is still in the yard. Should you count each time she checks on Dan as the end of a watching response? If the teams made 15 plays, then you would count Ann with 15 TV-watching responses. However, she might spend more time checking on Dan than she spent watching the plays. So you would count Ann as having more responses than Deb or Andre, even though she spent the least time watching. This makes even less sense.

The problem with nonuniform behavior is that each response can take very different amounts of time. In the TV-watching example, we found that people may look at the screen for different lengths of time. Deb looked once, for 15 minutes. Andre looked twice, for 12 and 2 minutes. Ann looked 15 times, for less than a minute each time. The different people watch for widely varying times. Even one person can watch for times that vary widely.

Behavior analysts observe nonuniform behaviors by dividing the overall observation time into short intervals. For example, you might divide the football game into intervals one minute long. You would divide the time from 3:00 to 3:15 into 15 intervals. You would then look to see if Deb appears to be watching TV at any time during each one-minute interval. If so, you would record a response. You would end up with a count of how many intervals contained some watching; you would have a crude measure of the amount of time spent watching TV during the 15 minutes. This method would probably show that Deb, Andre and Ann each watched for 14 or 15 intervals. You could get an even more accurate measure by dividing the time between 3:00 and 3:15 into smaller intervals. For example, if you are concerned about the frequent glances out the window by Ann, you could use 30-second intervals. That might show Deb with 30 intervals, Andre with 28 intervals, and Ann with 15.

Using a series of continuous intervals gives a rough estimate of the amount of time for that behavior. You observe during each interval and count the number of intervals during which you saw the behavior. This number gives you an idea of what percent of the time the behavior occurs.

Interval Recording

You record a response if the behavior occurs in one of a series of continuous intervals. The term *continuous* just means that each additional interval starts right after the end of the prior interval. The observer divides the entire observation period into intervals that follow one another. Note that the behavior doesn't have to occur in each interval. However, the observer has to look for it throughout each interval. You can also say that the observer looks continuously.

6. For interval recording, you record a response only if the behavior occurs in one of a series of ____________ intervals.

Behavior analysts use this method to observe instances of a nonuniform behavior that vary greatly in length. Because such behavior is unstructured, you must use a structured observational method. You create the structure by dividing the observation period into a series of short intervals. Sometimes the response will fit into one interval because it is short. At other times, it will cover more than one interval because it is longer. Sometimes there will be no response during an interval in which you have observed. Your job is to decide whether any part of these nonuniform responses occurs within each of the intervals.

For example, all of the following behavioral events would be considered an occurrence of a behavior in interval recording: (1) The behavior starts within the interval; (2) The behavior ends within the interval; (3) The behavior starts before the interval and continues past the end of the interval; (4) The behavior starts and ends during the interval; (5) The behavior starts and stops more than once during the interval. In this last case, you would not record that the response occurred more than once. You are interested only in whether any part of a response occurs within the interval. To summarize, a behavior is scored as occurring in interval recording if any part of the behavior takes place within the interval. Figure 3-3 illustrates these different cases.

Interval recording is used to observe instances of behaviors that are nonuniform in length. The overall observation period is then divided into a series of intervals of a convenient length. The intervals are continuous because each interval immediately follows the prior interval.

For example, you might use interval recording to determine whether Jay's TV show spends more time telling funny stories in the monologue than David's. You would first divide each show's monologue into a series of short intervals. If you picked 15-second intervals, and if each monologue is 30 minutes long, then you would have a series of 120 continuous intervals. You can then observe during each interval and record whether the host was telling any part of a funny story during the interval. A long joke might cover six intervals. A very short joke might take just one interval. At the conclusion of Jay's and David's shows, you could easily determine which show spent more

Cases of Recording Nonuniform Behaviors During Intervals

Time line:	Int. 1:	Int. 2:	Int. 3:	Record:	1	2	3
Case A:	----------	-sxxxxxxxx	xxxxe-----		N	Y	Y
Case B:	------sxxx	xxxxxxe---	----------		Y	Y	N
Case C:	----------	--sxxxxe--	----------		N	Y	N
Case D:	----sxxxxx	xxxxxxxxxx	xxxxxxxe--		?	Y	?
Case E:	----------	sxe--sxe-s	xxxxxxe---		N	Y	Y

Figure 3-3. The time line shows each second of three ten-second intervals for five cases. The "- " shows where no behavior occurred. The "s" shows where the behavior starts, the "x" where it continues, and the "e" where it ends. Case A: Behavior analysts record the behavior as No in interval 1, Yes in 2 and 3. Case B: record as Yes in interval 1 and 2. Case C: record as Yes only in interval 2.

7. Case D: Record interval 1 as _______, interval 2 as Yes, and interval 3 as _______. Case E: You record interval 2 as Yes (but only one Yes!) and interval 3 as Yes.

time with funny stories in its monologue by comparing the number of intervals containing funny stories. You would not know which show told the most funny stories.

Notice three aspects of interval recording. First, you use interval recording to observe nonuniform behavioral episodes. Funny stories can last a few seconds or a few minutes. Five of Jay's stories might take a couple of minutes to tell, while five of David's might take ten minutes to tell. If you counted stories, you would score them both as five stories. Second, you divide the overall observational period into continuous intervals that follow right after one another. You then observe during each interval to determine whether or not the behavior occurs during some portion of the interval. A long story might occur in many intervals; two short ones might occur in one interval. Remember, recording that a response occurred during an interval does not indicate whether the response covered the entire interval or only a moment of it. Nor does it indicate the number of occurrences. Third, note that the overall record indicates the amount of time the behavior occurred.

Consider another example. Interval recording would be an ideal method for observing the study behavior of a child. Suppose you want to watch the child from 4:00 to 5:00 in the afternoon. You divide the hour into a series of continuous time intervals of a convenient length—perhaps 30 seconds. You then record, for each of those 30-second intervals, whether or not the child studies during any part of that interval. You do not record whether the behavior occurs for all or part of the interval. Your objective is to discover what percentage of intervals contain some studying.

You might also observe the behavior of a group of children using interval recording. For example, you might be interested in how much of the time the children are playing quietly. You might observe them during 20-second intervals. If all of them are playing quietly, then you would score them as quiet; if any of them are screaming or yelling, you would not score them as quiet. In this example, you are not observing each child but the group as a whole.

You might also use interval recording to find out how much of the time an infant emits positive behavior such as smiling or looking at toys in the crib (Derrickson, Neef, & Cataldo, 1993). You might use it to find out how high the activity of preschool children is after consuming cola drinks (Baer, 1987). You might use it to measure the amount of time that junior high students study or socialize appropriately (Ninness, Fuerst, Rutherford, & Glenn, 1991).

Be very careful when trying to distinguish between interval recording and outcome recording. Suppose you look every 30 minutes for the result of some behavior. Behavior analysts would call this outcome recording, because you are looking for a result after the behavior occurs. Looking for a result is always considered outcome recording. Looking every 30 minutes is simply a systematic way to look for the result.

Also be very careful when trying to distinguish between event recording and interval recording. Looking for instances of a nonuniform behavior during a series of continuous 30-second intervals is not event recording. You may record a particular instance in more than one interval. You find out about how much of the time this nonuniform behavior occurs. You do not find out how many times the behavior occurs. Therefore, this would be interval recording.

Classify a method as interval recording only if the intervals are continuous. Remember, the response does not have to fill the interval; and it may extend over more than one interval. Many of the intervals will contain no response. Also, you record only one response per interval.

Time Sample Recording for Sampling a Behavior

Time sample recording is a variation of interval recording. Behavior analysts use it when they can't continuously record one behavior. Instead, they sample a behavior—that is, observe it only part of the time. You may wish to observe Andre's peculiar habit of reading while watching TV. You might have trouble accurately recording both behaviors at the same time. Behavior analysts handle this by sampling one behavior and then sampling the other. In other words, you would switch back and forth between the two behaviors. First you look for reading, then you look for TV watching. This same approach can be used with more than two behaviors.

Interestingly enough, you can use the same approach to observe a single behavior when it is not convenient to observe it continuously. For example, you may wish to observe Andre's study behavior over an eight-hour day, but you may not be able to observe every moment of the eight hours. You can estimate the amount of his study behavior throughout the day by sampling a 15-second interval once every half-hour.

Time Sample Recording

You record a response if one behavior occurs within one of a series of discontinuous intervals. Behavior analysts use time sample recording to sample one or more behaviors during an observation period. The name comes from observing the behavior during a sample of the total time period rather than during all of it.

8. For time sample recording, you record a response if one behavior occurs within one of a series of ______ intervals.

Time sample recording differs from interval recording in that discontinuous intervals are used. The word *discontinuous* means that the beginning of each time interval does not start at the end of the prior time interval. Rather, there is an interruption between intervals. If the intervals used to observe one behavior are discontinuous, the method is time sample recording. If the intervals used to observe one behavior are continuous, then the method is interval recording.

For example, you might use time sample recording to observe Andre watching TV and reading. Suppose you use 30-second intervals. You might observe TV watching during the first interval and reading during the second interval. You would continue switching from one behavior to the other. You would observe Andre's TV watching during the odd-numbered intervals: 1,3,5, etc. You would observe Andre's reading during the even-numbered intervals: 2,4,6, etc. Notice that you would observe TV watching during discontinuous intervals. The beginning of a TV-watching interval does not immediately follow the end of the previous TV-watching interval. Rather, a reading interval intervenes. Figure 3-4 illustrates the way an observer switches back and forth between these two behaviors.

One variation of time sample recording involves observing multiple people one after the other. For example, suppose that a teacher checks for 30 seconds to see if Willie is studying, then shifts to observe Diane for 30 seconds, and then

Observing Two Behaviors with Time Sampling

15-second intervals:	1	2	3	4	5	6	7	8	9	10
Is Andre watching TV?	Y	-	N	-	Y	-	N	-	Y	-
Is Andre reading a book?	-	N	-	Y	-	N	-	N	-	N

Figure 3-4. During odd-numbered intervals, the observer records a "Y" for "yes" when Andre is watching TV and an "N" for "no" when he is not watching TV. The observer records a "-" for "no observation" during the even-numbered intervals. During the even-numbered intervals, the observer used the same code to record when Andre is reading a book. Notice that the observer looked for TV watching during the first but not the second interval and then looked for TV watching again during the third interval.

9. Note that a new interval devoted to looking for TV watching does not follow immediately after the last interval devoted to looking for TV watching. Therefore, the intervals devoted to looking for TV watching ______ (are, aren't) continuous.

returns to observe Willie again. Notice that she checks on Willie's behavior for 30 seconds and then doesn't check on his behavior again for another 30 seconds. She observes his behavior every other interval. Thus, she would be using time sample recording, because she is observing Willie's behavior during discontinuous 30-second intervals. Likewise, she is observing Diane's behavior during discontinuous intervals. Figure 3-5 illustrates the switching back and forth between two people.

Notice that you might observe a group of individuals as a group and not be using time sample recording. Remember the example of interval recording involving children playing quietly. In that example, you observed to see if all the children were quiet during each 20-second interval. You were observing for quiet during continuous intervals. You didn't switch from child to child, thus creating discontinuous intervals. You didn't switch from behavior to behavior. You observed only one behavior, even though it was the behavior of a group. You observed it for continuous intervals. Therefore, it was interval recording, not time sample recording.

Another variation on time sample recording is to observe only <u>one</u> behavior during discontinuous intervals. This variation is often used to sample the behavior over a long period of time. For example, you might want to see if Dan is really studying during most of his "all-nighter." To find out, you might look into his room for 5 seconds every 30 minutes all night. Each 5-second interval is discontinuous, because there is a gap of almost 30 minutes before the next 5-second interval of observation. Therefore, you would be using time sample recording. Similarly, you might want to find out how much of the time elderly patients in a nursing home were moving instead of sitting. You could observe for a brief interval every 40 minutes during the day (Burgio, Burgio, Engel, & Tice, 1986). This is time sample recording, because each brief interval is separated by almost 40 minutes. The arrangement of observational intervals is illustrated by Figure 3-6.

Observing Two People with Time Sampling

15-second intervals:	1	2	3	4	5	6	7	8	9	10
Is Willie studying?	Y	-	Y	-	Y	-	N	-	Y	-
Is Diane studying?	-	N	-	Y	-	Y	-	Y	-	N

Figure 3-5. During odd-numbered intervals, the observer records whether or not Willie is studying. The observer records a "-" for "no observation" during the even-numbered intervals. During the even-numbered intervals, the observer uses the same code to record whether Diane is studying. Notice that the observer looked at Willie during the first but not the second interval and then looked at Willie again during the third interval. Notice that a new interval devoted to looking at Willie does not follow immediately after the last interval devoted to looking at Willie.

10. The intervals devoted to looking at Willie are __________ (continuous, discontinuous).

Time Sample Recording of One Behavior

Time line: | ------- | ------- | ------- | ------- | ------- | ------- |
Observer: [--- don't look ---][look][--- don't look ---][look]

Figure 3-6. When observers use time sample recording for just one behavior, they don't look for long periods of time and then they look for a brief period of time.

11. Each interval during which the observer is supposed to look in this figure is discontinuous from the others because it __________ (does, doesn't) follow right after the prior look.

Time sample recording is also used by applied behavior analysts when they simply need more time to record their observations. Researchers observed a child for a one-second interval every ten seconds to see how he was playing (Esposito & Koorland, 1989). This approach gave them nine seconds to write down the result and prepare for the next observation.

Another variation of time sample recording is to observe one behavior during <u>randomly</u> selected observational periods. For example, suppose that a professor checked for 5 seconds to see whether a particular student was awake. The professor might check after 5 minutes, 9 minutes, 17 minutes, and 25 minutes. The 5-second intervals are discontinuous, because the next interval is not observed immediately after the prior interval. Therefore, the professor would be using time sample recording. Likewise, researchers sampled staff performance in a hospital for a brief interval on the average of every 12 minutes to find out how much of the time they were doing their job (Burgio, Whitman, & Reid, 1983). The researchers used time sample recording because the brief intervals of observation were separated by an average of 12 minutes.

Classify an observational method as time sample recording only if the intervals for one behavior are <u>discontinuous</u>. Be very careful when trying to distinguish between time sample recording and outcome recording. If you observe every hour whether the behavior has produced a result, then you are not using time sample recording, but rather outcome recording.

Summary

This lesson showed you the second tactic in using the behavioral strategy for solving human problems. The second tactic is to use the approach of <u>direct observation</u> to gather information about the problem behavior. The lesson showed you the four most commonly used and cited methods of direct observation. You can use outcome recording to observe the <u>result</u> of a behavior. You can use event recording to observe <u>instances</u> of a uniform behavior. You can use interval recording to observe nonuniform behavior during <u>continuous</u> intervals. You can use time sample recording to observe a sample of a behavior during <u>discontinuous</u> intervals.

Behavior Analysis Examples

This section gives you some examples of how behavior analysts actually use the four methods of direct observation. (Hint: The examples of the methods do not necessarily appear in the same order that you learned them.)

Study Behavior

Studying is mental activity, right? Behavior analysts couldn't possibly study it, right? Walker and Buckley were among the first to find a way. They analyzed the study behavior of Phillip, a bright fourth-grader. Phillip did very little work in school, so he was not getting good grades. They defined study behavior as "looking at the assigned page, working problems, and recording responses." They divided their ten-minute observation period into ten-second intervals. Figure 3-7 shows a sample of their observation form. The authors found that Phillip studied during about 40% of the intervals. They then let him work toward a model airplane by studying. They found that his study behavior increased to over 90% of the intervals. (Based on Walker & Buckley, 1968.)

12. Because they observed study behavior during <u>continuous intervals</u>, Walker and Buckley used what observational method? ______________ (event, interval, outcome, time sample) recording

Self-Recording

You might think that behavior analysts can't study the behavior of an isolated individual, since there is no one else around to observe the behavior. Lindsley suggested using people to observe their own behavior directly. Direct observation requires that they use a behavioral definition and that they immediately record the behavior. Lindsley suggested that people use golf wrist counters to record their own behavior. These counters can be operated by pressing a button, which doesn't interfere with other activities. Figure 3-8 shows a wrist counter. People use wrist counters to record a variety of discrete behaviors, including smoking, smiling, making positive comments to others, and even anxious thoughts. Note that self-recording is not another method of recording behavior. Note also that it is not self-report if people use a behavioral definition and record their observations immediately. (Based on Lindsley, 1968.)

14. Because Lindsley suggests using a wrist counter to count <u>instances</u> of uniform behaviors, he is suggesting what method of observation? ______________ (event, interval, outcome, time sample) recording

Interval:	1	2	3	4	5	6	7	8	9	10	11	12	13	14	15	16	17	18	19	20
Studying:		x	x	x	x	x										x	x	x		

Figure 3-7. This is the recording sheet for observing Phillip's study behavior. The sheet permits recording whether Phillip was studying during each of 20 intervals, each ten seconds long. The observer placed an "x" in boxes corresponding to intervals where Phillip studied. You can see that he did not study during the first interval, but he did during the second, third, fourth, fifth, and sixth. (Based on Walker & Buckley, 1968.)

(13) Write the number of the next interval that he studied. __________

Figure 3-8. People can use a wrist counter to record such behaviors as smoking, smiling, and complaining.

Cooperative Dormitory

One approach to helping people be more cooperative may be to define cooperation behaviorally. Then we could observe it and make sure everyone acts fairly. Feallock and Miller developed the checklist of behaviors shown in Figure 3-9. The members of a cooperative dorm used it to observe their own lounge-cleaning. The behavior analysts gave each of the entries, such as "pick up trash," a careful behavioral definition so that the members knew exactly what results to record. Members appointed one of the group as inspector, who then used the checklist after another member cleaned the lounge. The inspector used similar checklists for the results of all basic housework. The data clearly revealed that members did very little cleaning. However, by giving a rent reduction to members who did their share of the cleaning, they were able to get everyone to clean. (Based on Feallock & Miller, 1976.)

15. Because the inspector observed the results of lounge cleaning, they used what method of observation? ____________ (event, outcome, interval, time sample) recording

Positive Interactions

Could we observe whether interacting with normal children improves the behavior of children with retardation? If it does, maybe we could find ways to increase their interactions. Beckman and Kohl studied positive interactions by children with mild retardation. They compared the amount of positive interactions when only children with retardation were in the group with the amount of positive interactions when normal children were also in the group. Examples of positive interaction are saying something nice, hugging, waving, sharing toys, and smiling. They observed each of six children every ten seconds. During the first ten seconds, they recorded whether the first child was engaging in positive interaction. Then a timer went off, and they observed the second child for ten seconds; the timer went off again, and the process was repeated for the remaining children. After the six children had been observed once, they again observed the first child, repeating the process with all six children. They observed 30 intervals per day.

Beckman and Kohl found that children with retardation engaged in positive interactions about 6 times out of 30 when in segregated groups consisting only of children with retardation. They found that children with retardation engaged in positive interactions in integrated groups about 9 times out of 30. Thus, the children with retardation engaged in about 50% more positive interactions when normal children were around. (Based on Beckman & Kohl, 1987.)

[x] Pick up trash in lounge
[x] Sweep up dirt in lounge
[x] Vacuum and shake out rugs
[x] Empty and clean ashtrays
[ ] Empty trash basket, replace liner
[x] Mop tile floor
[x] Return items to proper place
[x] Pick up trash in phone room
[x] Sweep up dirt in phone room
[x] Mop floor in phone room
[x] Provide clean paper and pen
[x] Return items for phone room
[ ] Replace burned-out bulbs

Figure 3-9. This is the inspection checklist for lounge cleaning in a cooperative dorm. The observer writes an "x" for each task completed. (Based on Feallock & Miller, 1976.)

16. In this example, the lounge cleaner did not empty the trash basket and replace the liner. Nor did he or she ____________ burned-out bulbs.

17. Because they observed the children in <u>discontinuous</u> intervals, what method of observation did Beckman and Kohl use? ___time sample___ (event, interval, outcome, time sample) recording

Notes

Note #1

In the remainder of the book, I will make a distinction between behavior and response. When referring to a <u>type</u> of activity, I will use the word *behavior*. When referring to a single <u>occurrence</u> of a behavior, I will use the word *response*.

18. When referring to a single <u>occurrence</u> of a behavior, I will use the word ___response___.

Note #2

This lesson provides an introduction to the four most commonly used methods of observation. Kelly (1977) reported that these four methods accounted for about 90% of the cases reported in the *Journal of Applied Behavior Analysis*. More precisely, 8% used outcome recording, 50% used event recording, 15% used interval recording, and 15% used time sample recording. For information on additional methods of observation, consult the additional readings section at the end of this lesson.

19. The most widely used method was ___Event___ recording. These four methods accounted for ___90___ percent of the cases.

Note #3

Behavior analysts have found that when the frequency of behaviors is high, interval recording and time sample recording underestimate them (Repp, Roberts, Slack, Repp, & Berkler, 1976). Event recording, on the other hand, does not produce either an overestimate or an underestimate.

20. When the frequency of a behavior is high, which method will produce the most accurate estimate of the frequency of the behavior? ___Event___ (event, interval, time sample)

Note #4

Behavior analysts have found that interval recording and time sample recording are inaccurate when intervals are long compared to the duration of responses (Mann, Ten Have, Plunkett, & Meisels, 1991). Event recording, on the other hand, does not produce either an overestimate or an underestimate.

21. Therefore, when the intervals are longer than the behavior, which method will produce the most accurate estimate of the frequency of the behavior? ___event___ (event, interval, time sample)

Helpful Hints

Helpful Hint #1

To figure out what method of observation is being used, you need ask only two questions. First, you need to establish whether or not the presence of a behavior during an interval is observed. If so, then the method has to be either interval or time sample recording. If the presence of a behavior during an interval is not observed, then the method has to be either outcome or event recording. So by establishing whether the presence of a behavior during an interval is observed, you eliminate two of the four methods. One follow-up question will then determine the method. The second question depends on the answer to the first question. If the presence of a behavior during an interval is observed, then you need only find out whether the intervals are continuous or not. If the presence of a behavior during an interval is not observed, then you need only find out whether a result is being observed.

So here are the two questions to ask. You always start by asking question #1. You then follow up by asking a different second question, depending upon the answer to question #1.

Question #1: "Is the presence of a behavior observed during <u>intervals</u>?"

If "yes," ask "Does this method use <u>continuous</u> intervals?"

"Yes" means it is interval recording.

"No" means it is time sample recording.

If "no," ask "Does this method involve a <u>result</u>?"

"Yes" means it is outcome recording.

"No" means it is event recording.

Asking these two questions gives you an easy way

Question #1:	Answer #1:	Question #2:	Answer #2:	Recording method:
Intervals?	no	Result?	yes	Outcome
Intervals?	no	Result?	no	Event
Intervals?	yes	Continuous?	yes	Interval
Intervals?	yes	Continuous?	no	Time sample

Figure 3-10. Use these questions to figure out what observational method is being used. First, ask if the method uses intervals. If the answer is "No, it does not use intervals," then ask if it observes results. If it does, it is outcome; if it doesn't, it is event. If the answer is "yes, it does use intervals," then ask if the intervals are continuous.

23. If they are not, then you know that the recording method is ____time sample____ (event, interval, outcome, time sample) recording.

to figure out what method of observation someone is using.

I want you to remember these questions, because I will use them as a prompt many times in this lesson. First, you ask about intervals. Then, depending on the answer, you ask about either continuous or results. So remember: intervals? Then continuous? Or results? In fact, make it even shorter: intervals: continuous/results (where the "/" means "or"). Can you remember those three words? Figure 3-10 shows a flow diagram of these questions.

22. Suppose you ask "intervals?" and answer "no." You would then ask whether the method involves ____results____. If so, the method is outcome recording. You can easily figure out the method if you remember to ask first "intervals?" and then, depending on the answer, either "____continous____" or "results."

Helpful Hint #2

The behavior does not have to occur during each consecutive interval in interval recording. The only requirement is that the observer look for it during each interval. You will encounter examples where an observer uses 15-second intervals. The behavior will usually not occur during every single interval. Some students have reasoned that because the behavior did not occur during continuous intervals, the observer did not look for it during continuous intervals. Therefore, he or she must have looked for it during discontinuous intervals. The students conclude that the observational method was time sample recording. This is incorrect. The definition requires only that you observe the person during continuous intervals. It does not require that the behavior occurs during each of those intervals.

24. For example, suppose you observe Franz during 100 intervals, each 15 seconds long. Suppose that each new interval starts when the previous interval ends. If you find that Franz listens to music during some but not all intervals, would you be using interval recording or time sample recording? ____interval____ recording

Helpful Hint #3

Normally, when I am asking you to distinguish between self-report and direct observation, I will ask you what approach to observation is used. This is the same term I used in the prior lesson. When I am asking you to distinguish between the four methods of observation, I will ask you what method of observation is used. I will also place the word *recording* after the blank, so that you don't have the busywork of writing that out.

25. When I want you to distinguish between the different methods of observation, I will ask you what ____method____ of observation was used.

Helpful Hint #4

I have underlined the key words in the definition of each method of observation in order to call your attention to a major idea. Be careful not to look only for those words, however, as they may appear in an example of another method. To answer a question, you must understand the concept rather than just memorize a key word. For example, suppose that you count the number of words that someone says in one minute to measure their speed of talking. Clearly that is event recording. It is not interval recording, because you are not looking for the presence or absence of talking in that interval. It is not interval recording just because you are counting for one minute. It would not be interval recording even if you were to start a new count for each new minute. You would still be counting instances of saying a word rather than whether or not talking occurs in the interval. So focusing on the presence or absence of an interval is a very helpful clue, but you need to look at every aspect of the method.

26. Counting the number of words spoken in consecutive one-minute intervals is an example of what method of observation? Event ___________ recording

Helpful Hint #5
You should have access to a calculator for the next lesson unless you are very good at math.

Additional Readings

Bass, R. F., & Aserlind, R. (1984). Interval and time-sample data collection procedures: Methodological issues. In K. V. Gadow (Ed.), *Advances in learning and behavioral disabilities* (Vol. 3, pp. 1–39). Greenwich, CT: JAI Press. A brief discussion of the history and prevalence of direct measures is presented, as well as a critique of the comparability of interval and time sample. There is also a discussion of the variables affecting observer records. Finally, a case is put forth for the development of an observer technology that emphasizes the strength of observational procedures.

Bijou, S. W., Peterson, R. F., & Ault, M. H. (1968). A method to integrate descriptive and experimental field studies at the level of data and empirical concepts. *Journal of Applied Behavior Analysis, 1*, 175–191. This article discusses the use of objective direct observation procedures in the description and analysis of everyday behavior.

Brandt, R. (1972). *Studying behavior in natural settings*. New York: Holt, Rinehart & Winston. This book describes a variety of observational procedures that can be used in the study of everyday behavior: narrative data, ratings, and data from simulated situations are described.

Hartmann, D. P., & Peterson, L. (1975). A neglected literature and an aphorism. *Journal of Applied Behavior Analysis, 8*, 231–232. This article cites 12 references to discussions of observational technology in social psychology, education, and child psychology.

O'Leary, K. D. (Ed.). (1979). Behavioral assessment [special issue]. *Journal of Applied Behavior Analysis, 12*(4), 489. A special issue of *JABA* devoted to behavioral assessment, including articles on behavioral assessment, the functions of assessment, graphic aids, and various commentaries related to these issues.

Rosenthal, R., & Rosnow, R. L. (1969). *Artifact in behavioral research*. New York: Academic Press. This book discusses the effect that being observed has on people's behavior. Because people may act differently when they know they are being observed, the resulting data can be misleading. This phenomenon, known as *reactivity*, is an important issue in behavior analysis.

Wright, H. (1960). Observational child study. In P. Mussen (Ed.), *Handbook of research methods in child development* (pp. 71–139). New York: Wiley. The application of "ecological" psychology to direct observation is described. The article contains explanations of methods that have been adopted by behavior analysts. Many are documented in this reading as early as the 1920s.

Reading Quiz

97. To use the behavioral strategy: (1) create a behavioral definition, (2) use the approach of ___________ (direct observation, self-report observation) to gather information about the problem behavior.

91. The second tactic in employing the behavioral strategy is to use the approach of direct ___________ to gather information.

92. The second tactic in using the behavioral strategy is to use the approach of ___________ observation to gather information.

89. The four most common methods of observing behavior are event recording, interval recording, outcome recording, and ___________ sample recording.

39. Remember, I will ask you to distinguish between self-report and direct observation by asking you which <u>approach</u> to observation was used. I will ask you to distinguish between event, interval, outcome, and time sample recording by asking you which ___________ to observation was used.

79. Review: You use outcome recording with behaviors that leave unique ___________.

35. Observing a behavior that leaves unique re-

sults is easy. At their convenience, even long after the behavior occurs, observers can look for that unique ________________ of the behavior.

1. A mark of outcome recording is that the observation of the result takes place ________ (before, during, after) the response.

53. Review: If you record a response when you see the unique result of a behavior after the response takes place, you are using what method of observation? ______________ recording

36. Observing Ann's dishwashing behavior by checking to see if the dishes are clean is an example of outcome recording because you are checking the ______________ of her dishwashing.

59. Review: Observing Mary's paper grading by seeing whether a stack of graded papers exists is an example of ________________ recording.

107. You cannot use every kind of result to make an outcome observation. For example, if you can't observe the result because it is a feeling inside of someone, is in a different location, can be caused by other behaviors, or just doesn't last long enough, you ________ (can, can't) use it to prove that the behavior occurred.

70. Review: Tom had a date with beautiful Barb. The result of the date is that afterwards he bragged to his friends about the date. Of course, Tom could have lied about his date. Could an observer use the result that his friends "knew" he had a date to prove that Tom had a date with Barb? ____________

19. Fran might yell at Jane. The result might be that Jane felt bad. However, an observer could not directly observe whether Jane feels bad. Therefore, the observer ____________ (could, couldn't) use that result to observe Fran yelling at Jane.

30. Juan got a haircut. The result of the haircut is that Juan's long locks were reduced to a short crewcut. Could an observer use the short crewcut to directly observe whether Juan had a haircut? ______________

100. When Mom bakes chocolate chip cookies, they disappear in a few hours. Could an observer look for chocolate chip cookies this evening to see if Mom had baked any at noon? ______________

14. Do not count on seeing the word *result* in the description of an example of outcome recording. For example, Skinner's teaching machine recorded every answer that a student wrote. Afterwards, Skinner looked at their written answers on paper. Clearly Skinner was not watching the students write their answers. Rather, he was looking afterwards at the answers they had written. This is an example of outcome recording because the written answer ______________ (is, isn't) the result of their writing behavior.

28. In analyzing descriptions of observing methods, you must ask if the method involves observing a result of the behavior rather than the behavior itself. For example, Dad observed Ken's car-washing behavior by looking to see if all the dust had been removed after Ken supposedly washed the car. You must notice that Dad didn't observe Ken while he was washing the car. Rather he observed what Ken had changed by washing the car. What method of observation did Dad use to observe Ken's car washing behavior? ______________ recording

10. Classify a method as outcome recording only if the method looks for a unique and observable ______________ of the behavior.

82. Some students get confused and think that when an observer records the occurrence of a behavior, their record is a result of the behavior. They then label the method as outcome recording. Since every method of observation requires an observer to record the occurrence of the behavior, these students usually get the ____________ (right, wrong) answer.

26. If a behavior does <u>not</u> leave a unique result, then you must observe it ______________ (before, during, after) its occurrence.

81. Some behaviors that do not leave unique results are nonuniform, while others are ____________________.

17. Event recording: You record a response when you see a(n) ____________ (result, instance) of the behavior.

16. Each time that Maria raises her hand would be called an <u>instance</u> of that behavior. Counting how many times Maria raises her hand in class would be observing how many instances of that behavior occurred. Therefore, counting how many times Maria raises her

hand is what method of observing? _______ recording

110. You might count how often Barry interrupts Charlie. You would be using event recording, because each time that Barry interrupts Charlie is a(n) _______________ of that behavior (Note: do not answer with "example." Use the exact term used to define event recording).

71. Review: Using a checklist to observe instances of a complex behavior, such as whether Jose remembered every part of his speech, would be an example of what method of observation? _______________ recording

88. Suppose you use a checklist of the different kinds of tableware to observe whether Darnell washed all the tableware dirtied at dinner. If you check the results after Darnell was supposed to wash them to see if every item of each kind is clean, you would be using what method of observation? _______________ recording

83. Suppose I ask you what method of observation is involved if you observe someone saying "ain't." First ask yourself whether "ain't" is an instance of the behavior or a result of the behavior. You would no doubt conclude that it is a(n) _______________ of the behavior.

12. David Lombard counted the instances of swimmers who wore a shirt; got in the shade; wore a hat, sunglasses, and zinc oxide; and put on sunscreen lotion. What method of observation did he use? _______________ recording

42. Review: Classify a method as event recording only if it involves observing _______________ of a behavior during their occurrence.

112. You should classify a method as outcome recording only if it looks for a(n) _______________ of the behavior.

62. Review: Remember, if you are looking for an instance of the behavior, you are using _______________ recording. If you are looking for a result of the behavior, you are using _______________ recording.

4. Be very careful when trying to decide between event recording and outcome recording. If a method involves observing a result, always call the method outcome recording. For example, when observers look for the result of an instance of behavior after the behavior occurs, they are using the following method of observation: _______________ recording.

2. Also do not look only for the key word *instance*. Make sure you read to understand what is being observed. Suppose that Mom is observing Darius while he tugs on weeds to produce the result of pulling the roots out. In this case, Mom observes the weed pulling while it is happening. She sees the result, but she watches and records the weed pulling. The best label for Mom's method of observing weed pulling is _______________ recording. If Mom did not watch weed pulling but came back later to count weeds pulled, then the best label would be _______________ recording.

13. Do not count on always finding the word *instance* in the description of event recording. Instead, decide whether the observer is looking for a relatively uniform response. Suppose you count how often Lew says "Thank you" when his parents pass him some food. You should label the method of observation as event recording, because each "Thank you" that Lew says takes about the same amount of time. Therefore, you are observing a(n) _______________ (instance, result) of behavior.

111. You observe each time Ted hits another child in preschool. Because each hit takes about the same amount of time, you are observing instances of the behavior. You are using what method of observation? _______________ recording

93. Time for a review: Louise immediately recorded every time that Pablo said a new word. She learned that Pablo was saying new words at the rate of two a week. She was using what method of observation? _______________ recording

34. More review: Dad saw that the gas gauge was now half empty rather than full. He knew that his son had driven the car while he was away on vacation. Dad was using what method of observation? _______________ recording

37. People normally don't engage in studying, reading, or watching TV steadily. They look away, go get a snack, or talk to someone at random times. Therefore, studying, reading,

and watching TV are examples of behaviors that occur for ________________ (uniform, nonuniform) periods of time.

90. The problem with nonuniform behavior is that each response can take ________________ (different, identical) amounts of time.

106. You can produce meaningless data if you use event recording to observe nonuniform behavior. A better approach is to observe nonuniform behavior by dividing the observation period into intervals and using what method of observation? ________________ recording

8. Behavior analysts use <u>interval</u> recording to observe nonuniform behaviors by dividing the overall observation time into a series of <u>continuous</u> ________________ of time.

103. When you observe using interval recording, you divide the observation period into a series of continuous intervals. Students often make errors when answering questions about interval recording because they misspell the word *continuous*. Spell it here: ________________.

56. Review: Interval recording: You record a response if the behavior occurs in one of a series of ________________ intervals.

96. To use interval recording, divide the overall observation period into a series of <u>continuous intervals</u>. Continuous intervals follow one another immediately. For instance, you divide an hour into 15-second intervals. When interval #1 stops, interval #2 immediately begins, and so on for the entire hour. If the intervals in an observation period follow one another immediately, they are ________________ intervals.

78. Review: You record an occurrence of a behavior in interval recording in four situations. (1) When the person starts the behavior within the interval, you record an occurrence. (2) When the person doesn't start the behavior within the interval, but does finish it within the interval, you record an occurrence. (3) When the person starts the behavior prior to the interval and continues it past the end of the interval, you record an occurrence. (4) When the person makes the complete response during the interval, you record an occurrence. A behavior is scored as an occurrence of a behavior in interval recording if any part of the behavior takes place within the ________________.

113. You use interval recording to observe behaviors that are nonuniform in length. The overall observation period is then divided into a series of ________________ (continuous, discontinuous) intervals of a convenient length.

86. Suppose you divide Jay's TV show into 15-second intervals to see how much time he spends telling funny stories in the monologue. Because the intervals are continuous, you would be using what method of observation? ________________ recording

29. Jay spends 10 of the 15-second intervals telling funny stories during his TV show. Notice that you can find out the amount of time taken telling funny stories. All you have to do is multiply the number of observations (in this case, 10) by the length of the intervals (in this case, 15). Therefore, the total amount of time taken by telling funny stories is about 10 times 15 or ________________ seconds.

98. Using a series of continuous intervals to observe a behavior gives you a rough estimate of the amount of ________________ that someone performs that behavior.

63. Review: Suppose you are observing the study behavior of a child by watching the child from 4:00 to 5:00 in the afternoon. You divide the hour into a series of time intervals of a convenient length, perhaps 30 seconds. The 30-second intervals follow one another immediately. For each of those 30-second intervals, you then record whether or not the child studies during any part of that interval. You are using interval recording, because the intervals are ________________.

77. Review: You observe Larry in preschool to see how much time he spends playing with other children. To do so, you break a 30-minute play period into 60 half-minute periods. You record during each interval whether Larry is playing with another child. You are using ________________ recording.

38. Remember three aspects of interval recording. First, you use interval recording to observe <u>nonuniform</u> behavioral episodes. Second, you divide the overall observational period into <u>continuous intervals</u> of a convenient length. Third, note that you can multiply the number of observations by the length of the interval to find out the amount of ________________ taken by the behavior.

11. Classify a method as interval recording only if the intervals are ________________.
5. Be very careful when trying to distinguish between interval recording and outcome recording. Suppose an observer looks for the results of a behavior every 30 minutes. Because the observation takes place after the behavior occurs, the observer is using what method of observation?________________ recording
9. Call the method of observation that looks for instances of a behavior ________________ recording. The method that looks for behavior during continuous intervals is called ________________ recording. The method that looks for the results of a behavior is called ________________ recording.
109. You may observe several behaviors during discontinuous intervals by using the method called time ________________ recording.
61. Review: Recording behavior during <u>discontinuous</u> intervals is called ________________ recording.
68. Review: Time sample recording: You record a response if the behavior occurs within one of a series of ________________ intervals.
101. When one time interval does not begin at the end of the prior time interval, we call the intervals ________________.
47. Review: If the intervals used to observe one behavior are <u>discontinuous</u>, then the method is ________________ recording. If the intervals used to observe one behavior are <u>continuous</u>, then the method is ________________ recording.
87. Suppose you observe Andre watching TV and snacking, with 30-second intervals. You observe TV watching during the first interval and snacking during the second interval. You return to observe TV watching during the third interval and then snacking during the fourth interval. You continue switching from one behavior to the other. During intervals 1, 3, 5, and 7, you observe TV watching. Thus, the intervals for observing TV watching ________________ (are, aren't) continuous.
32. Let's talk more about observing two behaviors during ten-second intervals. You observe behavior A during the odd intervals such as 1, 3, 5, etc. You observe behavior B during the even intervals such as 2, 4, 6, etc. Notice that overall, you are observing continuously. The end of interval 1 is the beginning of interval 2, and so on. Because the intervals are continuous overall, you might be tempted to label this method interval recording. You would be wrong. Because the intervals for each behavior are discontinuous, the method of observing each behavior is called ________________ recording.
102. When the method involves observing two behaviors (or two people) by switching back and forth between them, I will usually ask a very specific question. I will not ask "What is the method of observation?" but rather "What is the method of observation for behavior A?" I will do that to call attention to the fact that the intervals for behavior A in this situation are ________________ (continuous, discontinuous).
85. Suppose you are answering a question about observing two or more behaviors. Suppose the intervals for behavior A are discontinuous, while the intervals overall are continuous. What method of observation is used to observe behavior A? ________________ recording
58. Review: Mrs. Hobbs checks for 30 seconds to see if Willie is studying, then shifts to observe Diane for 30 seconds, and then returns to observe Willie again. Because she observes each of them for discontinuous 30-second intervals, she is using ________________ recording to observe multiple people at the same time.
3. At another time, Mrs. Hobbs observes during each 30-second interval to see if Willie and Diane are both studying. So she observes one behavior, "group study behavior," for continuous 30-second intervals. Therefore, she is using ________________ recording to observe a group during the same interval.
84. Suppose we observe Julio's lawn-mowing for one interval, then do not observe him for four intervals while we observe other individuals. Suppose we observe him again. This is an example of time sample recording, because the intervals of observing Julio are ________________.
49. Review: If we observe Julio's lawn-mowing during a series of randomly selected intervals, the method of observation is ________________ recording.
15. Do not count on the word *interval* appearing

in the description of time sample recording. Suppose a question reads as follows. You look for a few seconds every hour to see if Mary is partying. A few seconds makes up an interval even though the description may not say that. You look only during those few seconds every hour, so the periods of looking are ________________ (continuous, discontinuous). Because you are looking for the partying behavior during intervals that are discontinuous, this is an example of time sample recording.

108. You look at Van's playing for a period of 20 seconds, then at Ann's playing, and finally at Jan's playing. What method are you using to observe Van's playing? ____________ recording

31. Let's do some review. Suppose we observe Julio's lawn-mowing for one minute and then immediately observe his lawn-mowing during the next minute. Suppose we observe his lawn-mowing for 30 one-minute intervals. What method of observation are we using? ________________ recording

25. Gerry Patterson observed interactions beween parents and children in the home. He recorded each parent–child conflict. What method of observation did Patterson use to observe conflict? ________________ recording

104. You are curious how often Verna eats. You briefly check on her eating every 30 minutes during the day. She's eating 76% of the times you check. What method of observation are you using? ________________ recording

105. You are curious how much Verna eats. You give her a total of exactly six pounds of food each day. You weigh how much is left over three times a day (after each meal). You subtract to find out how much she eats. You find that she eats an average of 5.8 pounds of food each day! What method of observation are you using? ________________ recording

6. Be very careful when trying to distinguish between time sample recording and outcome recording. Suppose an observer records every hour whether the behavior produced a result. Because the observation takes place after the behavior occurs, the method of observation being used is ________________ recording.

75. Review: You can use the behavioral strategy to help change a problem behavior (1) by developing a behavioral definition and (2) by using the approach to observing called ________________ to gather information about the behavior.

55. Review: In summary, behavior analysts use four methods of observation. When they record nonuniform behaviors during continuous intervals, we call it ______________ recording. When they record results after the behavior, we call it ______________ recording. When they record nonuniform behavior during discontinuous intervals, we call it ______________ recording. When they record instances of uniform behavior, we call it ______________ recording.

99. Walker and Buckley (1968) analyzed the study behavior of Phillip, a bright fourth-grader. They divided their ten-minute observation period into ten-second intervals. They made a check mark in each interval that they observed Phillip studying. The name of the observational method is ______________ recording.

33. Lindsley (1968) suggested that people use golf wrist counters for recording their own behavior. Lindsley suggested using a wrist counter to count instances of uniform behaviors. He suggested people use what method of observation? ______________ recording

18. Feallock and Miller (1976) developed a checklist for dorm members to observe the results of their own lounge-cleaning. What method of observation did the dorm members use? ______________ recording

7. Beckman and Kohl (1987) studied positive interactions by six children with mild retardation. They observed the first child for ten seconds, and the second child for the next ten seconds. They observed each child during his or her own ten-second period. That meant that they observed each child for a period of 10 seconds and then did not observe that child again for the next 50 seconds (while they were observing the other five children). What method of observation did they use to observe the first child? ______________ recording

46. Review: From Note #1: In the remainder of the book, I make a distinction between *behavior* and *response*. When referring to a

type of activity, I will use the word *behavior*. When referring to a single occurrence of a behavior, I will use the word ______________.

80. So remember to distinguish between behavior and response. When you want to refer to a single occurrence of a behavior, use the word *response*. When you want to refer to a type of activity, use the word ______________.

57. Review: John sees a beer. John chugalugs the beer. You should call that particular chugalugging a(n) ________________. You should call the type of activity known as chugalugging a(n) ______________.

24. From Note #2: This lesson provides an introduction to the most commonly used methods of observation. Kelly (1977) reported that these methods accounted for about ________ (10, 50, 90) percent of the cases reported in the *Journal of Applied Behavior Analysis.*

20. From Helpful Hint #1: To figure out what method of observation someone is using, you need to remember three words formed into two questions. First, ask about intervals. If intervals were used, then ask whether they are ________________. If intervals were not used, then ask about results.

94. To figure out what method of observation someone is using, you need to remember three words with which you can ask two questions. First ask about intervals. If intervals were used, ask whether the intervals are ________________. If no intervals were used, then ask about ________________.

95. To figure out what method of observation someone is using, you need to remember three words with which you can ask two questions. First ask about ______________. If intervals, ask whether they are ________ ________________. If not intervals, then ask about ________________.

21. From Helpful Hint #2: The definition of interval recording requires only that you look for the behavior during continuous intervals. Does it also require that the behavior occur during each of those intervals? ___________

27. If an observer checks for a behavior during a series of 15-second intervals, but the behavior does not occur during every interval, what method of observation is the observer using? ____________________ recording. The reason this is interval recording is that the observer looks for the behavior during each 15-second interval. The behavior does not have to occur during each interval.

22. From Helpful Hint #3: Use the terms for specific methods of direct observation where possible. A question may ask you to name the method of observation where the observer immediately records all behavioral instances. Which is the better answer: direct observation or event recording? ______________ recording. If I had asked you the name of the approach to observation, which would be the better answer? ________________

23. From Helpful Hint #4: Counting the number of words that someone speaks in consecutive one-minute intervals is an example that contains two clues. You might notice first that the observation is during consecutive one-minute intervals and jump to the conclusion that the method of observation is interval recording. You would be wrong, because there is a second clue. The observer is also counting each instance of a word spoken. The observer is not looking for the presence or absence of speaking during the interval. Rather, the observer is looking for each instance of a word being spoken. Therefore, this is an example of what method of observation? ________________ recording

73. Review: When one time interval does not begin at the end of the prior time interval, we call the intervals ________________.

43. Review: Classify a method as event recording only if it involves observing ____________ of a behavior while the person is making them.

44. Review: Classify a method as interval recording only if the intervals are ____________.

65. Review: The behavior is observed while it happens for the following three methods of observation: ________________ recording, ____________ recording, and ____________ recording.

67. Review: The second tactic in using the behavioral strategy is to use one of the four methods based on the approach of ________ ________________.

45. Review: Classify a method as outcome recording only if it looks for a ______________ of the behavior.

41. Review: Behavior analysts observe nonuniform behaviors by dividing the overall observation time into short ______________.

60. Review: One form of time sampling involves the observation of behavior during a series of ________________ time intervals.

52. Review: If you observe a behavior during a 30-minute observation period, divided into 60 30-second intervals, and the behavior occurs only during some of those intervals, what method of observation are you using? ______ ________________ recording

74. Review: Which of the following behavioral events would be scored as an occurrence in interval recording? (a) The person starts the behavior within the interval. (b) The person doesn't start the behavior within the interval but does finish it within the interval. (c) The person starts the behavior prior to the interval and continues it past the end of the interval. (d) The person makes the complete response during the interval. (e) All of the above ______________

72. Review: When referring to a <u>type</u> of activity, I will use the word ________________. When referring to a single <u>occurrence</u> of an activity I will use the word ________________.

48. Review: If the observer records a response only when she sees the result of an instance of some behavior, what method is she using? ________________ recording

66. Review: The first tactic in using the behavioral strategy to solve human problems is to create a(n) ________________ of the problem behavior.

64. Review: Suppose you observe once an hour whether the behavior produced the result. You are using what method of observation? ________________ recording

54. Review: If you score a response occurrence each time an instance of behavior is observed, what method are you using? ______________ recording

50. Review: If we observe John for 10 minutes in 40 intervals, each 15 seconds long, what method are we using? ________________ recording

51. Review: If we observe one individual for brief intervals separated by a considerable amount of time, what method is being used? ________ __________ recording

69. Review: To find out what method of observation is being used, you need to remember three words. First, you ask: "Does this method involve time ________________?" If it does involve intervals, ask: "Does this method involve ________________ time intervals?" If it doesn't involve intervals, ask: "Does this method involve the ________________ of a behavior?"

76. Review: You can use the behavioral strategy to help change a problem behavior (1) by developing a(n) ________________ and (2) by using the approach to observing called ________________ to gather information about the behavior.

40. Review: A statement that specifies exactly what to observe is called a(n) ____________ definition. The science that studies environmental events that change behavior is called ________________ analysis.

Examples

1. David took English 159 from Professor McNault. He wanted a discussion course. David divided the class into 100 30-second intervals. He observed all intervals and noted those in which the professor talked. The professor talked during 65% of the intervals. You can analyze David's method of observation by asking two questions. Remember the first question by the key word *interval*. That word reminds you to answer the question: Does David's method involve looking for the behavior during <u>intervals</u>? ___________ (yes, no). Once you've answered the first question, then remember "continuous/result." If your first answer was "yes," then your key word is *continuous*. That reminds you to answer the question: Does the method use <u>continuous</u> intervals? _________ (yes, no). Since your answer was "yes," you can conclude that he used ________________ recording.

2. John was terrible in spelling. Mr. Fernandez counted the number of correct answers in John's book. You can analyze Mr. Fernandez's method of observation by asking two questions. Remember the first question by the key word *interval*. That word reminds you to answer the question: Does Mr. Fernandez's method involve looking for the behavior during <u>intervals</u>? ________________. Once you've answered the first question, then remember "continuous/result." If your first answer was "no," then your key word is *results*. That reminds you to answer the question: Does the method observe the <u>result</u> of behavior? ________

Since your answer was "yes," you can conclude that he used ____________________ recording.

3. Tyrell felt that the cooperative dorm should not buy a new couch, because nobody ever used the living room. To prove this, Tyrell visited the living room for a brief time every 15 minutes to observe whether anyone was sitting there. You can analyze Tyrell's method of observation by asking two questions. Answer the first question that the key word *interval* reminds you of: ____________. Once you have answered the first question, then remember "continuous/result." Pick the correct key word based on your answer. Answer the second question that the key word reminds you of: ________________. You can conclude that Tyrell used ________________ recording.

4. John got a "B" on his essay paper because he had used one split infinitive. The professor told him that the essay was excellent but that his incorrect English had cost him an A. John counted the number of times that he heard the professor use a split infinitive during his lectures. He found that the professor had split infinitives seven times during five class periods. John gave him a C. You can analyze John's method of observation by asking two questions. Answer the first question that the key word *interval* reminds you of: __________. Once you've answered the first question, then remember "continuous/result." Pick the correct key word based on your answer. Answer the second question that the key word reminds you of: ______________. You can conclude that John used ________________ recording.

5. The Bales wanted to teach their 5-year-old daughter to make her bed and clean her room every day. She was supposed to do this right after school. To find out if she cleaned her room, the Bales checked every day to see whether the bed was made, the floor swept, the trash taken out, and all toys put away. You can analyze the Bales' method of observation by asking two questions. Remember "interval: continuous/result." Answer the first question that the key word reminds you of: ________________. Once you've answered the first question, pick the correct key word for the second and answer it: ______________. You can conclude that the Bales used ________________ recording.

6. Heddy observed littering in a local park. She began by watching four families at the same time. She observed family #1 for 15 seconds. Then she switched to family #2 for 15 seconds. Then she observed family #3. Finally she observed family #4. After she had watched each family once, she started over again. You can analyze Heddy's method of observation by asking two questions. Remember "interval: continuous/result." Answer the first question that the key word reminds you of: ________________________. Once you've answered the first question, pick the correct key word for the second and answer it: ______________. You can conclude that Heddy observed family #1 by what method of observation? ________________ recording

7. Maria and Rex believed that Ronny dominated the meetings of their committee. They decided to measure his domination and report their results at a future meeting of the committee. They recorded each time Ronny talked during a 15-second interval of the meeting. They found that he spoke during 76% of the intervals. You can analyze Maria and Rex's method of observation by asking two questions. Remember "interval: continuous/result." Answer the first question that the key word reminds you of: ________________. Once you've answered the first question, pick the correct key word for the second and answer it: ________________________. You can conclude that Maria and Rex used ____________________ recording.

8. Dee worried that Alice was bullying her son at school. She recorded whether Alice bullied her son in the classroom during a series of 15-second intervals while they were on the playground. She found that Alice bullied her son about 23% of the time. You can analyze Dee's method of observation by asking two questions. Remember the clue. Answer the first question that the key word reminds you of: ________________. Once you've answered the first question, pick the correct key word for the second and answer it: ________________. You can conclude that Dee used ________________ recording.

9. The cooperative dorm had successfully set up programs for keeping the dorm clean, but they hadn't been very successful in keeping the house repaired. They decided to pay cash for each repair job completed. They decided on the amount of pay for each job by inspecting to see how well the damaged area had been repaired. Analyze their method of observation by remembering the clue and then asking the questions. What method of observation did they use to decide on payments? ________________ recording

10. Review: It's time to mix in some review questions from earlier lessons. Fernanda observed Professor Young to see how arrogant he was. She decided that she would record every time that the professor said to a student, "No, you're wrong." The statement "arrogant behavior is saying 'No, you're wrong'" is a(n) ______________.

11. Review: Mary was concerned about the rampant sexism appearing in TV shows. She wanted to write a paper about it, containing specific numbers as to how much sexism was occurring. Since she did not have time to watch every show all the way through, she arranged to observe for ten randomly scheduled intervals of ten seconds each during each program. She was using what method of observation? ______________ recording

12. Review: Al wanted to find out how much of the class period his child spent studying in math class. He went to school and observed whether his child was studying during each 20-second period of the math class. He used what method of observation? ______________ recording

13. Review: Donnell went to counseling because he constantly got his feelings hurt by others. Dr. Barton decided that Donnell was an expert at seeing any indication in a situation that the other person might not like him. But he was poor at seeing other aspects of the situation. Dr. Barton taught Donnell how to seek out other aspects of situations in which his feelings got hurt. He then suggested that he count each time that he could describe other aspects of a situation that caused him to have hurt feelings. What method of observation was Donnell using? ______________ recording

14. Review: Fred was interested in the extent to which people were positive and supportive of one another in casual interactions. His sociology professor suggested that he use a questionnaire approach and ask people how often they were positive toward other people. Fred wanted better information than that, however, so he recorded only what he personally heard and saw at the time of the observation. Because Fred immediately recorded what he personally heard and saw, he was using what approach to observation? ______________

15. Review: Being a bit of a gossip, you want to know how often Ali has his girlfriend in his room, so you make a note every time that you see her visit. You would be using what method of observation? ______________ recording

16. Review: To decide whether the public areas of a dorm have been cleaned well enough, you might make a checklist of things that should be clean (such as floors, ashtrays, trash baskets, and so on) and check once a day to see whether they are clean. You would be using what method of observing? ______________ recording

17. Review: Your living group is having trouble with Selma griping during the dinner hour. You sit at the dinner table and note whether she is griping during each 30-second interval. You would be using what method of observing? ______________ recording

18. Review: Martha wants to determine the actual amount of violence on prime-time TV. She decides to record as violent every scene in which there is a weapon present, every scene that involves physical assault on a person, and all scenes in which one person is yelling in anger at another. By describing exactly what she is going to observe, Martha is stating a(n) ______________.

19. Review: Barb was a new student senator. She was very concerned that parliamentary procedure was not being followed when the chairperson's friends wanted to get something done. She counted the number of times that a motion was passed without correct procedure being fully observed. She noted an average of about three per meeting. What method of observation was Barb using? ______________ recording

20. Review: Maria got reports each Friday from Mrs. Green about how sociable her daughter Lucia was at school. Maria did not tell Mrs. Green exactly what she meant by sociability. She simply asked Mrs. Green to describe Lucia's sociability for the whole week as well as she could remember. What approach to observation did Maria use to observe Lucia's sociability? ______________ observations

LESSON

4

Reliability and Validity of Everyday Observations

You've learned the first two tactics in using the behavioral strategy to help solve human problems. First, you create a behavioral definition of what you want to study. Second, you use a method of direct observation to study it. When those tactics don't solve the problem, you may need to use the third tactic: to check the reliability and social validity of your observations. Reliability is a measure of the accuracy of your observations. Social validity is a measure of whether you are observing what you are really interested in. If your observations are not reliable and socially valid, you may be getting inaccurate or useless information. Improving your information may lead to a solution for the problem.

1. The third tactic when using the behavioral strategy is to check the reliability and social ________ of your observations.

(Note: If you have trouble dividing 3 by 8 or 91 by 20, you should borrow a calculator for this lesson.)

Repeated Observations

The most basic question about an observation is whether you can repeat it. By "repeat it," I mean get the same value. Suppose you measure the length of a table and find it is 36 inches. You would have little trust in that length if you measured twice more and got 35 and then 38 inches. Suppose you measure the amount that a child studies during one hour and find 90%. You would have little trust in that amount if you measured two more days and found 25% and 99%. While a certain amount of change is OK, large variations undermine your trust.

Behavior analysts measure people's behavior for many days until it reaches a stable level. When people learn a new task, their skill may improve for days before it becomes stable. For example, Kate, a 12-year-old girl with retardation, almost never responded to questions. Behavior analysts gave her special training. She learned very slowly to respond to more questions. She took over 35 days to reach her maximum level (Krantz & McClannahan, 1993). Normal adults may also take time to learn new behaviors. Teachers were still improving their performance ten days after learning an innovative teaching method (Ingham & Greer, 1992). Police were instructed to ticket parents who failed to put their infants in car safety seats (Lavelle, Hovel, West, & Wahlgren, 1992). They were still increasing the rate of ticketing six months after adoption of the new procedure.

These examples suggest that many factors may influence behavior in a complex situation. It may take days and weeks for a clear picture of the total effect of these factors to emerge. Thus, behavior analysts often observe behavior for long periods of time. Behavior analysts get data they can trust by repeating their observations many times.

This practice contrasts with the methods often used by other approaches to human behavior. They often interview a person for an hour to learn about that person's behavior. They often ask a person to take a few minutes answering a questionnaire. People are far too complex for this approach to work very well. Measurements taken for a few minutes don't deal with this complexity. Researchers may find it easier to make only one observation or to observe people for a short period of time. However, the result will be that they won't get data that they can trust.

Reliability and Accuracy

Applied behavior analysts use direct observations made by human observers to learn about behavior.

Can observations made by human observers be trusted? Are they accurate? Behavior analysts have found no way to measure the accuracy of their data directly. To understand why, suppose that you want to observe how often Don says "ain't" in a conversation. You might observe Don for an hour and count 27 "ain'ts," but how can you be sure that Don said "ain't" 27 times? You might tape-record what Don says and then count the "ain'ts" from the tape. Surely, you think, that would be exact. But suppose that you count 23 "ain'ts" on the tape. Which count is correct? Don might have said four "ain'ts" too softly for the tape to pick up. You could ignore soft responses and have another observer count from the tape recording. If she counts 25 "ain'ts," which of you is right? She might hear Don say, "She ain't it," where you heard "She ate it." There is no way to find out exactly how many times Don said "ain't." You can never compare your count with the "real" count to find your accuracy.

Behavior analysts have solved this problem by measuring accuracy indirectly. They compare observations of the same responses made by two independent observers using the same behavioral definition. They assume that the more the observers agree, the more accurate the observations. In other words, agreement between two observers is evidence of accuracy. Behavior analysts call this agreement *reliability*. **Reliability** is the agreement between two independent observers.

2. Reliability is the ________________ between two independent observers.
3. The agreement between two independent observers is called ________________.

Measuring reliability requires two conditions. The two observers must use the same behavioral definition. They must observe the same responses.

First, both observers must use the same behavioral definition of the behavior. Suppose that Carlos and Jane agree on a behavioral definition of reading: "John looks at the book and makes eye sweeps from one side of the page to the other." Perhaps they both note that John reads during the first interval. Their agreement suggests that John was really reading. On the other hand, suppose that Carlos used his behavioral definition and Frank used a different behavioral definition. Frank's definition might be "John sits in front of an open book." Agreement between Carlos and Frank doesn't suggest that John was making eye sweeps during the first interval. Maybe Carlos made a mistake while Frank noted that John was sitting in front of the book. Their agreement would no longer be evidence that they were both carefully observing.

Second, both observers must observe the same responses. Suppose Carlos and Jane use the same behavioral definition. Perhaps Carlos finds John reading at 9:00. Perhaps Jane finds John reading the next day at 9:00. Perhaps not. Either way, Jane's finding doesn't help us guess whether Carlos's finding is accurate. Their agreement does not tell us anything about what John was really doing.

4. Measuring reliability requires that the observers use the same ________________ and that they observe the same ________________.

Reliability comes in two forms (Martin & Pear, 1988). I will call one form trial reliability and the other frequency reliability. Behavior analysts use trial reliability when they can compare each observation of two observers. They use frequency reliability when they can only compare the total observations.

Computing Trial Reliability

Trial reliability compares each observation of the two observers. The name arises because we call every chance to observe the behavior a *trial*. One example of a trial is every time a pitcher throws a ball to a batter. We have the chance to observe whether the batter hits it well (e.g., Osborne & Himadi, 1990). Another example is every question directed at a student. We can then see whether the student can answer the question (e.g., Secan, Egel, & Tilley, 1989). The pitch and the question create a trial of the person's behavior. Each trial permits two observers to use the same behavioral definition on the same responses. They can then compare their observations to find out whether they agreed. Trial reliability is the most rigorous form of reliability.

5. Trial reliability compares ________ observation of the two observers.

You find trial reliability by counting the number of agreements and disagreements between the two observers. Reliability is the percentage of agreements out of all observations. Here is the formula. Use A to stand for the number of agreements. Use D to stand for the number of disagreements. The formula for reliability is 100%xA/(A+D) (Araujo & Born, 1985). In other words, you multiply 100% times the agreements. You divide by the sum of the agreements and disagreements. Note that agreements plus disagreements equals the total number of trials. Note also that the parentheses require that you add agreements and disagreements before dividing.

6. Reliability is the percentage of all observations that are ________________ between the two observers.

You cannot use trial reliability with outcome or event recording of simple behaviors. These

Figure 4-1. Even skilled craftsmen have to measure and remeasure their work to get it right. Hence the old saying, "Measure twice, cut once." Accurate, repeatable measurement is important in all fields.

Figure 4-2. Referees huddle to discuss a call. Believe it or not, players and coaches sometimes disagree with their observations! Huddling with other referees provides a check on reliability.

methods lead to a total count, but they don't produce a trial-by-trial record. You can use trial reliability with these methods only when observing complex behaviors with a checklist. You can then compare each item on the checklist as though it were one trial.

You can always use trial reliability with interval and time sample recording. That is because each interval defines a trial. You can compare the records of two observers interval by interval. The only complication is that the two observers must start each interval at the same time. Researchers do this with a signal that both observers can hear.

Johnathon and MaryEllen observe how much Juan reads his history book while the TV is on. They define reading as "Juan looks at the book and makes eye sweeps from one side of the page to the other." Here are their first five observations (R equals reading; N equals nonreading):

Observation:	1	2	3	4	5
Johnathon	R	R	R	R	N
MaryEllen	R	N	R	R	N

Both observers agree that Juan read in the first, third, and fourth intervals. They agree that he did not read in the fifth interval. Their observations agree for these four intervals. However, they disagree on whether Juan read during the second interval. Johnathon marked that Juan was reading while MaryEllen marked that he was not. (You will find it helpful to circle disagreements when asked to compute reliability.)

7. Reliability equals 100% times the number of agreements (4) divided by agreements and disagreements (4+1). In algebraic form, 100% x A/(A+D) = 100% x 4/(4+1). That formula gives 100% times 4 divided by the sum ____. Finally, 4/5 equals 80% reliability.

Here's an example of using trial reliability with an outcome recording checklist. Suppose that the members of a cooperative dorm observe how well the table setter does his job. They might observe whether the table setter places a knife, two forks, a spoon, a plate, and a glass at each position. Two observers might produce the record below. "Yes" indicates that the table setter placed the item. "Not" indicates that the table setter did not place the item.

Items:	Knife	Forks	Spoon	Plate	Glass
Ann	yes	yes	not	yes	not
Bob	not	yes	not	yes	yes

8. To compute trial reliability, circle the pairs of observations that do not agree. Then use the formula for reliability, 100% x A/(A+D) to get 100% x 3/(3+2). That formula equals 100% times _____ divided by the sum _____. Thus, the reliability is 60%.

Here's an example of trial reliability for an event recording checklist. Suppose two observers record whether a tutor did each task on a checklist. Professor Hsieh may have told the tutor to greet students, smile, probe them with questions, praise their correct answers, record their score, and then tell them their grade. This simple list of chores may yield better tutoring than leaving tutors on their own (Weaver & Miller, 1975). The record for the two observers might look like this:

Chores:	Greet	Smile	Probe	Praise	Record	Grade
Mark	not	yes	yes	not	yes	not
Jan	not	not	yes	yes	yes	yes

Analyze this case yourself by circling and then counting disagreements.

9. Use the formula 100% x A/(A+D) to compute reliability. The formula for these observations equals 100% times _______ (enter number of agreements) divided by ______ (enter number of agreements plus disagreements). Thus, reliability is 50%.

Computing Frequency Reliability

You cannot use trial reliability when using outcome or event recording with simple behavior. Both methods yield a count of frequency of the behavior. For example, you might find that Ruth Ellen left 753 candy-bar wrappers in her dressing room on Wednesday morning. Even if Tom also reports exactly 753 wrappers, we have no way of knowing whether he counted the same wrappers. We do not know if you and he agree on each wrapper.

In the same way, you might observe that Hakim smiled 50 times on Monday. Suppose Ann reports 40 smiles. You both might have observed the same 40 smiles, with Ann missing 10 smiles. On the other hand, Ann might have observed 40 smiles that you did not observe. Since this is extremely unlikely, we usually assume that she simply missed some of the ones that you saw.

Frequency reliability compares the total count between two observers. It is used when each observation cannot be compared, such as with simple outcome or simple event recording. You can't find the exact agreement between the observers when you work only with the total count. Therefore, we assume that the overlap in the two counts represents agreement and that nonoverlap represents disagreement. In the case of the candy wrapper observations, reliability would be 100% x 753/(753+0) or 100%. In the case of Hakim and Ann, reliability would be 100% x 40/(40+10) or 80%. Behavior analysts assume that the 40 observations that you and Ann report are agreements. They assume that the ten smiles that you reported and Ann didn't are disagreements.

10. Frequency reliability compares the total ____ ________ between two observers.

The formula for frequency reliability is the same as for trial reliability: 100%xA/(A+D). Notice that this amounts to dividing the larger number into the smaller number. This form of reliability is less rigorous; you do not compare the observers as closely.

Goal for Reliability

Most researchers aim for a reliability of 90% or more. However, they may accept less with a new behavioral definition for subtle or complex behavior. This book accepts a figure of 80% or more for such "new" behavioral definitions. Be sure to read each example to find out if the behavioral definition is new or old. You may assume that an example involves an old behavioral definition unless otherwise specified.

11. Most researchers aim for a reliability of _____ percent, except for new behavioral definitions, for which they usually accept 80%.

Suppose you observe whether 4-year-old Dave engages in anxious behavior when the dentist works on his teeth. You might define *anxious* as "moving his head or body more than a half inch, or crying or complaining." If you made this behavioral definition yourself, it would be a new one. This behavioral definition is fairly complicated. It requires the observer to notice three different aspects of Dave's behavior: movements of Dave's head, his crying, and his complaining. Therefore, you can be satisfied with 80% or greater reliability. However, suppose you got this behavioral definition from the work of Stark, Allen, Hurst, Nash, Rigney, and Stokes (1989). Then it would be an old behavioral definition. You would have the benefit of their experience in developing a workable behavioral definition. If you used their behavioral definition, you should seek reliability of 90% or greater. Remember, if you're inventing it, seek 80%; if you're adapting from someone else, seek 90%. If it's old, seek 90%; if it's new, seek 80%.

Behavior analysts often do not attain the goal on their first try. Often they must refine their behavioral definition before observers can reliably agree. Sometimes they must train their observers longer or give more examples. If you don't attain the goal, you must revise your observational system until you do.

Social Validity of Behavioral Definitions

Applied behavior analysts often observe complex and subtle aspects of human behavior. The resulting behavioral definitions are not always obvious to the average person. Kazdin (1977a) and Wolf (1978) suggested that behavior analysts measure the social validity of such behavioral definitions. **Social validity** is the rating of a behavioral definition by outside judges. These judges tell us if the behavioral definition matches their meaning. We call them outside judges because they are outside behavior analysis. They help us understand what normal adults mean by a word.

12. Social validity is the rating of a behavioral definition by __________ judges.
13. The rating of a behavioral definition by outside judges is called its social ______________.

Imagine that an observer trained to use a particular behavioral definition observes a trial. She records either a response or a nonresponse, according to the behavioral definition. Meanwhile, an outside judge observes the same trial. He reports whether he saw an example of that behavior. Since he is not using the behavioral definition, his report would reflect the common understanding of what is an example of that behavior. If the observer and the outside judge observed many trials together, we could find out whether or not their observations correlated. If they did so, then the behavioral definition would have social validity. If they did not, the behavioral definition would lack social validity.

For example, suppose that you defined smiling as "lips parted with teeth showing and the edges of the mouth upturned." You might train an observer to look at a photo of Mary and use the behavioral definition to decide whether she was smiling. You might have an outside judge do the same, without the behavioral definition. You could repeat this with many photos of Mary. I am sure you can imagine many facial expressions that meet the behavioral definition but which someone not using it would not judge to be smiles. Certainly the lips can be parted, the teeth showing, and the edges of the mouth upturned while showing disdain, superiority, or perhaps even hatred. The trained observer and the outside judge might well disagree on photos of such expressions. We might expect the trained observer and the outside judge to agree on some smiles and agree on some nonsmiles but to disagree on at least some photos. If their observations mostly did correlate, we would conclude that the behavioral definition has pretty good social validity. If their observations mostly did not correlate, we would conclude that the behavioral definition has poor social validity.

Researchers usually use a modification of this procedure to measure social validity. They try to create a "low behavior situation" and a "high behavior situation." They train their observer to observe the behavior in both situations according to the behavioral definition. However, they do not ask the outside observer to report on each instance of the behavior. Rather, they ask the outside judge to give an overall rating of the behavior in both situations. They then correlate the detailed count by the observer with the overall rating by the outside judge.

For example, the researchers might find someone who didn't smile very often because he was depressed. They would have their trained observer look for smiles from him during an observation period. They would have the outside judge rate how often he smiled during that same period of time. Then they would help the person solve his depression, perhaps over many days, weeks, or even months. They would then again have the trained observer look for smiles while the outside judge rated how often the person smiled.

The researchers might find that the observer saw three smiles during an hour of observation before helping with the depression. The outside judge might give a rating of "few smiles" during the same period. After treating the person for depression, the observer might see 29 smiles during an hour of observation. The outside judge might give a rating of "many smiles" during the same period. While this approach does not show a smile-by-smile correlation, it does show a correlation between the trained observer's observations and the outside judge's ratings. It provides evidence that the behavioral definition captures much of the meaning of *smile* held by everyday people. It provides evidence of social validity.

Fawcett and Miller (1975) provide a real example of this approach. They developed a behav-

Figure 4-3. A wine taster judges the characteristics and acceptability of a batch of wine. He is judging its social validity.

ioral definition of good public speaking, having several parts. They guessed that good public speaking takes a high rate of eye contact with the audience, animated gestures, a central position on stage, and greeting the audience. The researchers specified these and a number of other behaviors. As you can see, their behavioral definition is debatable. Maybe it misses some very important but subtle parts of being a good public speaker. This raises the question of social validity. The researchers answered the question by measuring the social validity of their behavioral definition.

The researchers used two steps to validate their behavioral definition. First, they had someone who they thought was low in good public speaking behaviors talk to an audience. Their trained observer found that the speaker performed few of the good public speaking behaviors. The researchers then asked the members of the audience to serve as outside judges. These outside judges rated the person as a "poor" speaker. Second, they trained the speaker to engage in the good public speaking behaviors. They had the person speak to another audience, during which time the observer found that the person engaged in more of the required behaviors. They found that the audience now rated the speaker as "good." Thus, they found a correlation between the amount of the speaking behaviors found by the observers and the ratings given by the audience. This correlation suggests that the behavioral definition caught the audiences' more subjective and unspecified meaning. Note that the members of each audience were outside judges—they were not behavior analysts.

You know that behavior analysts rely on direct observation and rarely use questionnaires. One of the few times when they use questionnaires is to measure social validity. They use questionnaires to find out how outside judges rate their behavioral definition. They regard the ratings as a sample of what the outside judges say about the behavior. If the ratings agree with the observations, then the behavioral definition is socially valid. The behavior analyst does not study the rating to infer an inner cause.

Social validity has found a permanent place in behavior analysis (Fuqua & Schwade, 1986). It provides evidence that the behavioral definition is or is not reasonable.

Thinking May Involve Tiny Muscular Movements

Delprato (1977) had people hold a pendulum above three words and think about one of them. They usually swung the pendulum toward that word without being aware of it! "Thinking" involved "making tiny movements toward the selected word." It may also involve tiny movements of the speech apparatus, looking toward the word and focusing on it, and activation of brain responses. All of these responses, and more, are involved in thinking about the selected word. No single one of them, such as the brain response, is by itself "thinking" about the selected word. Behavior analysts label thinking as a behavior because it involves these active and potentially observable responses. Is this a reasonable label?

14. Suppose you found that when these responses are present, people report thinking about the word. You would be using these people as outside judges to measure the social ________________ of calling these responses *thinking*.

Summary

This lesson taught you the third tactic in using the behavioral strategy to help solve human problems: to check for reliability and social validity. You learned how to check for accuracy by measuring reliability. Reliability assumes that two observers use the same behavioral definition to observe the same responses. You can use trial reliability to compare two observers' reactions to the same trial. You can use frequency reliability when each observer produces only a total count. Both forms multiply 100% times agreements over agreements plus disagreements. You can write the formula as 100%xA/(A+D). You should seek 90% agreement with old behavioral definitions and 80% with new ones. This lesson taught you how to check the social validity of your observations. Social validity is the extent to which outside judges agree with your behavioral definition.

Behavior Analysis Examples

Social Skills

Some people seem born with smooth social skills. We often wish our own skills were better. Too often, we assume that our present level is "just the way we are." Behavior analysts have tried to define many of these skills behaviorally. If they can define them behaviorally, then they can help people learn them. For example, Quinn and his colleagues defined the parts of "accepting criticism." Nonverbal parts include facing the critic; not moving away; and keeping eye contact, a neutral expression, and straight posture. Verbal parts include paraphrasing the criticism, apologizing when appropriate, asking for sugggestions, and accepting feedback. Other parts include using a normal voice, not making angry statements, and not interrupting.

Most people are tempted to ask, "Can you define a subtle skill like accepting criticism with such simple behaviors?" Quinn and colleagues decided to find out. They videotaped scenes in which one roommate criticized the other. Sixty-one adult judges rated "how well the person handled the situation." When the roommates performed all the behaviors well, the outside judges rated them as quite acceptable (6 on a 7-point scale). When the roommates performed all the behaviors poorly, the outside judges rated them as unacceptable (1.5 out of 7). When the roommates performed only one area badly, such as the nonverbal parts, the outside judges gave a moderate rating (about 4 out of 7). Thus, the outside judge's ratings correlated with the performance of these behaviors. This means that these behaviors do indeed define the subtle skill of accepting criticism. (Based on Quinn, Sherman, Sheldon, Quinn, & Harchik, 1992.)

15. The correlation between the performance of the behaviors and the ratings by outside judges shows that Quinn's behavioral definition of skilled acceptance of criticism has __________ validity.

Cooperation with Dentists

Children seldom want to visit the dentist. During visits, they may be very uncooperative. In 1983, Williams and his colleagues set up a way to observe this behavior. They observed uncooperative behavior during 15-second intervals. They defined four types of uncooperative behavior: head movements, body movements, complaining, or any behavior that led the dental assistant to restrain the child. They found that two observers agreed 84% of the time. This was good for a new behavioral definition. Researchers refined the behavioral definition in 1987 and found 85% agreement. Other researchers revised it again in 1992 and found 93% agreement. This was good for an old behavioral definition. Many behavioral definitions are revised many times before observers reach high reliability. (Based on articles by Williams, Hurst, & Stokes, 1983; Allen & Stokes, 1987; and Allen, Loiben, Allen, & Stanley, 1992.)

16. When Williams and colleagues compared the agreement between two observers on noncooperative behavior, they were measuring the __________________________ (reliability, social validity) of the observations.

Conversational Skills

Conversing in a skillful way might seem even more difficult to define behaviorally than accepting criticism. Minkin and his colleagues studied a group of 12- to 14-year-old girls with poor conversational skills. They defined three parts of skilled conversational behavior: asking many conversational questions, providing positive conversational feedback, and talking a reasonable amount. They defined each component carefully. For example, they defined providing positive conversational feedback as "three or fewer words that approve, concur with, or understand what the other conversant is saying." They tested whether this behavioral definition captured what most people regard as skilled conversation. They videotaped conversations showing high or low rates of the three behaviors. They showed these videotapes to a cross section of adults and asked them to rate the conversational skills of the girls. When the three behaviors were high, the ratings were high. When the behaviors were low, the ratings were low. (Based on Minkin et al., 1976.)

17. The correlation between the amount of three conversational behaviors and the ratings of conversational skill by outside judges shows that the Minkin behavioral definition has ____________________ (reliability, social validity).

Notes

Note #1

This lesson provides only a brief introduction to reliability, but it is a critical issue in behavior analysis. Kelly (1977) found that 94% of all articles published in one journal report reliability. Most behavior analysts see it as a major aspect defining behavior analysis (e.g., Kazdin, 1975). Part of the spring 1977 issue of the *Journal of Applied Behavior Analysis* discusses additional aspects of reliability.

18. Kelly found that 94% of all articles published in one journal report ________________ among observers.

Note #2

Sometimes you must provide added information about reliability—for example, by comparing the obtained reliability with chance reliability (Harrop, Foulkes, & Daniels, 1989). Sometimes you must compute the reliability of the intervals in which at least one observer records the behavior (e.g., Hopkins & Hermann, 1977).

19. Sometimes you must provide added information about ________________.

Note #3

Behavior analysts may use social validity to validate more than the behavioral definition. They may use it to evaluate the social appropriateness of intervention procedures. They may also use it to evaluate the social importance of the effects of behavioral procedures. Schwartz and Baer (1991) argue that the most important use of social validity is to ensure the survival of behavioral programs.

20. Behavior analysts may evaluate the social appropriateness of intervention procedures by asking outside judges to rate the intervention. They would be evaluating the ________________ ________________ of the intervention.

Note #4

Social validity is becoming a routine part of behavior analysis. Schwartz and Baer (1991) report that 29% of behavior analysis articles surveyed used some measure of social validity.

Social Validity of Different Treatments

Alan Kazdin invented a clever way to find the social validity of different treatments. He described a normal 5-year-old who didn't follow Mom's instructions. He described a 10-year-old child with mental retardation who was disruptive in class. He asked students to read his descriptions and then to act as outside judges of the acceptability of four treatments. The order of acceptability was reinforcement, isolation, drugs, and shock. This suggests that the behavioral procedures are more acceptable than psychiatric drug treatments (Kazdin, 1980).

21. The ratings of the outside judges are a measure of the ________________ (reliability, social validity) of the treatment.

22. Reliability is reported by more than 90% of research articles, but social validity is reported by only ______ percent.

Helpful Hints

Helpful Hint #1

Remember, when answering questions, you must assume that the behavioral definition is old, with two exceptions. One exception is when the question tells you that the behavioral definition is new. Another is when the question tells you that the observers developed it. Never assume that the observers developed it unless the book tells you. I will give many examples where the reliability is 80% or 85%. The correct answer to questions about these examples will depend on whether the behavioral definition is old or new, so be ready.

23. Remember, when analyzing examples and quizzes, always assume that the behavioral definition is ______. You must assume that the behavioral definition is old unless the question or example clearly states that it is ________________.

Helpful Hint #2

Here's a hint about how to tell reliability from social validity. If an example involves agreement between two observers, that agreement is called *reliability*. The goal is to find out whether the observers can use the same behavioral definition to score the same responses in the same way. On the other hand, if the example involves the correlation between one observer and one or more outside judges, the correlation is called *social validity*. The goal is to find out whether the observer's behavioral definition points to the same responses as does the outside judge's common-sense definition.

24. If an example involves the agreement between one observer and one or more outside judges, that agreement is called ________________.
If an example involves correlation between two observers, that correlation is called ____________________.

Remember, agreement between two observers is reliability. Correlation between outside judges and an observer is social validity.

Helpful Hint #3

The formula for reliability is 100%xA/(A+D). The formula has only two parts. First, the 100% means simply that you are converting the fraction that follows to a percent. The uncapitalized letter x stands for multiplication. It means that you are multiplying the fraction times the 100% to make it into a percent. Second, the fraction A/(A+D) means that you are dividing the number of agreements by the sum of the agreements plus the disagreements. If you have one agreement and one disagreement, then you multiply 100% times the fraction "1 divided by (1 plus 1)." Of course, you can simplify that by adding (1 plus 1) to get 2. Then you have 100% times 1 divided by 2, or one-half. 100% times one-half is 50%. You may need a calculator for bigger numbers, but the idea is simple.

You might easily make five mistakes in writing or using this formula. First, you might omit the percent sign after 100. Be sure to write "100%." Second, you might not use the small x for the multiplication sign. Some students insist that the "*" is the multiplication sign on their computer. Do not use it! Use the uncapitalized letter "x." Third, you might omit the parentheses. If you omit them, then you incorrectly make the formula 100%xA/A+D. This means that you divide A by A and later add D instead of dividing by A+D. So be sure to include the parentheses. Fourth, you might type the backward slash (\ ) instead of the forward slash (/). The backward slash does not stand for division; be sure to use the forward slash. Fifth, you might put spaces between the characters. Do not add any spaces when writing the formula!

25. Write the whole formula for reliability (without looking if possible). ____________________

Helpful Hint #4

Unless you are told otherwise, assume that two observers use the same definition and observe the same responses. If you are told, even indirectly, that the observers do not use the same definition on the same responses, you cannot compute reliability. For example, suppose an example states that you observe Beth on Wednesday and find that she hits Paul five times. The example might go on to say that your friend observes Beth on Thursday and finds that Beth hit Paul ten times.

26. If you observe Beth on Wednesday and your friend observes Beth on Thursday, 50% agreement is not an example of reliability, because you and your friend __________ (did, didn't) observe the same responses.

Helpful Hint #5

If you are not good at arithmetic and percentages, borrow a calculator before you go any further. Otherwise you may get wrong answers to many of the questions requiring computation of reliability. Why be frustrated? Also note that in this book, percentages and decimals are only carried to two digits.

Additional Readings

Baer, D. M. (1977). Reviewer's comments: Just because it's reliable doesn't mean that you can use it. *Journal of Applied Behavior Analysis, 10*, 117–119. This article argues that statistical estimates of reliability are not functional for behavior analysis.

Bass, R. F. (1987). Computer-assisted observer training. *Journal of Applied Behavior Analysis, 20*, 83–88. Although direct observation techniques continue to be the most used data collection procedures reported in *JABA*, they also involve a number of problems. Bass found that training observers on a computer resulted in accurate observational repertoires, which met or exceeded current standards for interobserver accuracy.

Fuqua, R. W., & Schwade, J. (1986). Social validation of applied behavioral research: A selective review and critique. In A. Poling & R. W. Fuqua (Eds.), *Research methods in applied behavior analysis: Issues and advances* (pp. 265–292). New York: Plenum. A review of the role of social validation in the selection of target behaviors, intervention procedures, and judgment of effects.

Reading Quiz

97. You can use the behavioral strategy to help solve a human problem. First, you create a behavioral definition of what you want to study. Second, you use a method of direct observation to study it. Third, you check the reliability and _______________ (behavioral definition, social validity) of your observations.
84. This lesson teaches you about reliability and _______________ validity.
94. You call an indirect measure of the accuracy of your observations their *reliability*. You call the degree to which your observations measure what you are interested in their *social* _______________.
81. The most basic question about an observation is whether you can repeat it—that is, whether you can get the/a _______________ (same, different) value a second time.
5. Behavior analysts repeatedly observe a person's behavior for many days until the rate of the behavior is _______________ (changing, stable).
30. Researchers get data that they trust by making _______________ (few, many) observations.
3. Behavior analysts indirectly measure the accuracy of their data by computing reliability. They compute reliability because they cannot directly measure the accuracy of their data. _______________ (true, false)
4. Behavior analysts indirectly measure the accuracy of their data by computing _______________ (reliability, social validity).
32. Review: Agreement between two observers is called _______________.
42. Review: Reliability is the _______________ between two independent observers.
77. The formula for reliability is 100%xA/(A+D). This means that you multiply 100% times the agreements between two observers and divide by the total number of observations. The total number of observations is represented in the formula by _______________. (Be sure to include the parentheses.)
78. The formula for reliability is 100%xA/(A+D). This gives you the percentage (100%) of all observations (A+D) on which two observers _______________ (A).
24. Measuring reliability requires two conditions. The first requirement is that the two observers must use (a/the) _______________ (different, same) behavioral definition of the behavior. The second requirement is that they must observe (the) _______________ (different, same) responses.
76. The first requirement for reliability is that both observers must observe the same behavior while using the same _______________.
83. The second requirement for measuring reliability is that the observers must use the same behavioral definition while observing the same _______________.
68. Suppose one observer defines play as "all activity outside the classroom," and the other observer defines play as "all fun activity." They would not be able to measure the reliability of their observations, because they were using different _______________.
69. Suppose one observer observes Freddy's play in the morning and the other observer observes his play in the afternoon. They would not be able to measure the reliability of their observations, because they are observing different _______________.
66. Suppose Betty observes Kim's cooperative play on Friday and Ted observes it on Monday. Did the observers meet the requirement that they observe the same responses? _______________ (no, yes)
88. Vern was trained to use the behavioral definition of depressed behavior. Ben was not. They observe Marie's depressed behavior during the afternoon. Do their observations meet the requirement of using the same behavioral definition? _______________ (no, yes)
71. Suppose Jim observes that Patty smiles 25 times in the morning, while Kim observes

that Patty smiles 25 times in the afternoon. You might say that they agreed on 25 smiles. However, because they observe the 25 smiles at different times, they have not agreed on particular responses. Measuring reliability requires agreeing on particular smiles. Therefore, you ____________ (can, can't) measure reliability in this case.

31. Review: A measure of reliability makes sense only when two requirements are met. Both observers must must use the same ________ ________, and they must observe the same ____________________.

6. Behavior analysts use two forms of reliability: trial reliability and frequency reliability. I will start by describing trial ____________.

64. Sometimes two observers can look for a behavior during defined periods called trials. For example, suppose two observers are looking for a batter to swing at a pitch. The batter may swing when a pitch is thrown but will not swing when a pitch has not been thrown. Each pitch defines a trial. When behavior analysts compare how each observer scores a trial, they are using ____________________ reliability.

7. Behavior analysts use trial reliability with the two methods of observation that use intervals. Because each interval defines a trial, you can always use trial reliability with interval recording and with ____________ recording.

13. Here's an example of trial reliability with time sample recording. Dave and Ann observed Gloria's studying during discontinuous 15-second intervals. The table below gives their first five pairs of observations. S stands for studying, N for nonstudying.

Dave:	S	N	S	S	N
Ann:	S	N	N	S	S

Because the example does not tell you otherwise, you can assume that the observers used the same behavioral definition on the same responses. Because you can compare each interval, you can use trial reliability. They agreed on observations 1, 2, and 4. Thus, A= ____. They disagreed on observations 3 and 5. Thus, D= ____. (A+D)= ____. Reliability equals 100% times A/(A+D). Therefore, reliability equals 100% times ____ divided by ____. When you divide 3 by 5, you get the decimal _____. Finally, multiply the decimal by 100% to find out the percent agreement. The result equals _____ percent. If you got the wrong number, use a calculator next time.

14. Here's an example of trial reliability with interval recording. Carl and Jane observed Ken's reading during continuous 15-second intervals. The table below gives their first five pairs of observations. R stands for Ken reading. N stands for nonreading.

Carl:	R	R	R	R	N
Jane:	R	N	R	R	N

Because the example does not tell you otherwise, you can assume that the observers used the same behavioral definition and that they observed the same responses. Because you can compare each observation, you can use trial reliability. Reliability equals 100% x A/(A+D). Count agreements to get the value of A and disagreements to get the value of D. Then add to get (A+D). Then divide A by (A+D) to get the decimal _____. Multiply the decimal by 100% to find out the percent agreement. The result equals _____ percent. If you got the wrong number, use a calculator.

95. You can also use trial reliability when observing a complex behavior using a checklist. For example, a salesperson should perform four steps when customers enter his or her sales area. They should promptly approach the customers, greet them, ask if they need help finding anything, and accompany them to the item they seek. Because each step in a complex behavior defines a trial, you can compute ____________________ (frequency, trial) reliability.

15. Here's an example of computing trial reliability with a complex behavior. Ann and Bob observed table setting. Compute the reliability of these observations made by Ann and Bob:

Items:	Knife	Fork	Spoon	Plate	Glass
Ann	yes	yes	not	yes	not
Bob	not	yes	not	yes	yes

Can you assume that Ann and Bob observed the same responses with the same behavioral definition? ________ Again, you can use trial reliability because you can compare each observation. Reliability equals 100% times A/(A+D). A= _____. (A+D)= _____. A/(A+D)= _____

(Note: give fraction). Then multiply the decimal by 100% to get _____ percent.

16. Here's another example of computing trial reliability with observations of complex behavior. Tom and Ken observed teaching chores. Compute the reliability of their observations:

Chores:	Greet	Smile	Probe	Praise	Record	Grade
Tom	not	yes	yes	not	yes	not
Ken	not	not	yes	yes	yes	yes

Computing reliability is meaningful in this case, because you can assume that the observations were made using the same behavioral definition with the same ______________________. Computed trial reliability equals 100% times A divided by (A+D). In this case A= ____ and (A+D)= _____. A/(A+D)= _____. Convert to a decimal and multiply by 100% to get the trial reliability of ____ percent.

23. Juanita and Carlos were trained to use a complex behavioral definition to observe gracefulness of ballet dancing. Juanita observed Doris on Tuesday and found that she danced gracefully during all 50 of the intervals. Carlos observed Doris on Friday and also found that she danced gracefully during all 50 of the intervals. Since the example states that the observers observed on different days, should you assume that Juanita and Carlos observed the same dancing responses of Doris? ____ (no, yes). Therefore, you cannot measure their reliability.

27. Outcome and event recording with simple behaviors do not produce a trial-by-trial record. Rather, they produce a total count of the behavior. Therefore, when observing a simple behavior, you cannot use trial reliability with either _______________ or _______________ recording.

43. Review: Remember, when observing a simple behavior, you cannot use trial reliability with either _______________ or _______________ recording.

90. When each observer produces only a total count, as with event or outcome recording, you must use _______________ (frequency, trial) reliability.

9. Frequency reliability assumes that two observers agree on all overlapping observations. For example, you might observe that Meg smiled 3 times. However, Lettie might observe that Meg smiled 4 times. Frequency reliability assumes that Lettie agrees with all of the smiles that you counted. It assumes that you disagree on the one extra smile that Lettie observed. Therefore, in this case, A= ___. Also, D= ____ and (A+D)= ____.

17. Here's another example of frequency reliability. You might observe that Hakim smiled 50 times on Monday. Ann might observe 40 smiles. Frequency reliability assumes that you agree with Ann on each of the smiles that she observed. In this case, A= ___, D= ___, and (A+D)= ___.

85. Time to compute a frequency reliability. You and Ken observe Ted littering with candy wrappers. Suppose you observe ten candy wrappers, but Ken sees only eight. In this case, A= ___, and (A+D)= ___. "A" divided by (A+D) equals the decimal ____. Multiply that by 100% to find that frequency reliability is _____ percent.

72. Suppose that Ted observed that the Millers recycled ten pieces of plastic on Monday, and May observed only three pieces on Tuesday. You might jump to the conclusion that their reliability is 30% and that it is not acceptable. You would be wrong, however. Ted and May observed on different days; they did not observe the same responses. Therefore, you ________ (can, can't) measure reliability.

12. Here's a simplification of the formula for reliability. Remember that in another example, you observed ten wrappers and Ken observed eight. Agreement was 8 and (agreement plus disagreement) was 10. Notice that the smaller number equaled the agreements, and the larger number equaled the agreements plus the disagreements. Therefore, the formula for frequency reliability amounts to dividing the larger number into the __________ number and then multiplying by 100%.

91. When you can compare only the total count found by two observers, you use frequency reliability. When you can compare all the observations as they appear in trials, you use ________________ reliability.

59. Review: When you can compare each observation for two observers, you use ___________ reliability. When you can compare only the total count found by two observers, you use _______________ reliability.

79. The formula for reliability is simple. You multiply 100% times the agreements divided by

the sum of agreements plus disagreements, which is the total observations. You can symbolize the formula as 100% x A/______. (Be sure to include the parentheses.)

80. The formula for reliability is 100% times agreements divided by total observations. Symbolize it as 100%x ______________. (Be sure to include the division sign and the parentheses.)

96. You can symbolize the formula for reliability as ______ x A/(A+D).

98. You should now be able to write out the formula for reliability. It is ________________. (Be sure to include the percentage sign, the uncapitalized letter x as the symbol of multiplication, the division sign, and the parentheses.)

18. How large should reliability be? Most researchers aim for a reliability of 90% or more with old, well-established definitions. However, most researchers accept a figure of 80% or more for __________ (new, old) behavioral definitions.

28. Remember, if you're inventing a new behavioral definition, seek 80%; if you're using an established, old behavioral definition invented by someone else, seek the higher figure of ______ percent.

93. You and Bob use a new behavioral definition to observe relaxation. You use a checklist and get 85% reliability. Since your reliability is greater than the 80% required for new behavioral definitions, you ____________ (can, can't) conclude that your behavioral definition is acceptable.

22. Jan and Ted use an old behavioral definition to observe how often Flora greets customers. They find that the reliability of their observations is 86%. Since their reliability is less than the 90% required for old behavioral definitions, they _________ (can, can't) conclude that their behavioral definition is acceptable.

2. Barb and Fred use a new behavioral definition to observe how often Nicole glances in her rear-view mirror. They find that the reliability of their observations is 73%. Since they used a new behavioral definition, they ______ (can, can't) conclude that their behavioral definition is acceptable.

89. Wendy and Mel use an old behavioral definition to observe how often Sam tells Bobby he loves her. They find that the reliability of their observations is 88%. Since they used an old behavioral definition, they ______ (can, can't) conclude that their behavioral definition is acceptable.

58. Review: When using a new behavioral definition, reliability is acceptable if it reaches ______ percent. When using an old behavioral definition, reliability is acceptable if it reaches ______ percent.

73. Suppose you develop a new behavioral definition that produces only 73% reliability. That is not acceptable, so you must improve the behavioral definition until it produces a reliability acceptable for new behavioral definitions of at least ________ percent.

20. If I tell you that two observers agreed on 92% of their observations, you should assume that the acceptable level of agreement is that needed for a(n) ______________ (new, old) behavioral definition. That level is ________ percent.

67. Suppose I tell you that two observers developed a behavioral definition for thoughtfulness and that they agreed on 92% of their observations. You should assume that the acceptable level of agreement is that needed for a(n) __________ (new, old) behavioral definition. That level is _____ percent. (If they developed it, it has to be new.)

62. So if you find out that two observers used someone else's behavioral definition, the level for acceptable reliability is ______ percent. If you find out that they developed the behavioral definition, then the level for acceptable reliability is ____ percent.

74. The agreement between two observers is called reliability. The rating of a behavioral definition by outside judges is called ______________ ______________ (reliability, social validity).

63. Social validity is the rating of a behavioral definition by outside ______________ (judges, observers).

70. Suppose an observer uses a behavioral definition to observe whether or not a person is smiling. Suppose an outside judge looks at the same facial gestures. If their reports about which ones are smiles correlate, can you conclude that the behavioral definition has social validity? _______

65. Suppose an observer using a behavioral definition sees a depressed person smile three times in an hour. Suppose an outside judge rates smiling as "very rare." Now suppose that the person becomes less depressed. Suppose

the observer sees 29 smiles, and the outside judge rates smiling as "frequent." The correlation between observations and ratings provides evidence that the behavioral definition has ______________ (reliability, social validity).

82. The question of whether Fawcett and Miller had a reasonable behavioral definition of public speaking is the question of __________ validity.
75. The audience members who rated the speaker for Fawcett and Miller are called __________ (inside, outside) judges.
50. Review: The rating of a behavioral definition by outside judges is called ______________.
44. Review: Social validity is the rating of a behavioral definition by ______________.
53. Review: To summarize, the agreement between two observers is called ______________. The correlation between ratings by outside judges and observations based on a behavioral definition is called ______________.
86. To use the behavioral strategy, (1) create a behavioral definition of the problem behavior, (2) use a method of direct observation to gather information, and (3) check the <u>reliability</u> and ______________ of your observations.
87. To use the behavioral strategy, (1) create a behavioral definition of the problem behavior, (2) use a method of direct observation to gather information, and (3) check the ______________ and social validity of your observations.
54. Review: To use the behavioral strategy, (1) create a behavioral definition of the problem behavior, (2) use a method of direct observation to gather information, and (3) check the __________ and ______________ of your observations.
8. Delprato (1977) found that people swung a pendulum toward the word they were thinking about. Thinking about a word may involve many tiny behaviors, including swinging the pendulum toward a word, tiny movements of the speech apparatus, looking toward the word, and focusing on the word. You might ask these people to serve as outside judges by reporting when they were thinking about the word. You would be measuring the social ______________ of calling these responses *thinking*.
38. Review: Quinn et al. (1992) found that outside judges rated accepting criticism as very high when observers reported that roommates kept calm and repeated the criticism, but rated accepting criticism low otherwise. This finding shows that the behavioral definition of accepting criticism based on these behaviors has ______________.
92. Williams et al. (1983) compared the agreement between two observers on the amount of noncooperative behavior that occurs. They were measuring the ______________ of the observations.
25. Minkin defined skilled conversational behavior by three behaviors. He showed videotapes of conversations with much or little of these behaviors and asked a cross section of adults to rate how skilled the conversations were. The adults are called ______________ of social validity.
26. Minkin et al. (1976) asked adults to serve as outside judges, rating videotapes of teenage conversations. The researchers trained an observer to use a behavioral definition of skillful conversation behavior, viewing the same videotapes. They then compared the observations with the ratings. They were assessing the ______________ of their behavioral definition.
10. From Helpful Hint #1: Remember, when analyzing examples and quizzes, always assume that the behavioral definition is old. You must assume that the behavioral definition is old unless the question or example clearly states that it is ______________.
21. If the researchers or observers developed a behavioral definition, then obviously it is new. If the question does <u>not</u> tell you that the observers developed a behavioral definition, you should assume that the behavioral definition is ______________.
11. From Helpful Hint #2: If an example involves agreement between two observers, that agreement is called *reliability*. If an example involves the correlation between one observer and one or more outside judges, that correlation is called ______________.
19. If an example involves the correlation between one observer and one or more outside judges, that correlation is called *social validity*. If an example involves agreement between two observers, that agreement is called __________.
1. Agreement between two observers is ________.

Correlation between outside judges and an observer is ________________.

29. Remember, reliability is ________________ between two observers. Social validity is correlation between an observer and one or more ________________.

37. Review: From Helpful Hint #3: The exact formula for reliability is: ________________.

35. Review: Comparing two observers' observations about the same trial is called ________________ reliability.

60. Review: You can use the behavioral strategy to solve a human problem. First, create a behavioral definition. Second, use a method of direct observation to observe. Third, check the ________________ and ________________ of your observations.

45. Review: Social validity is the extent to which ________________ agree with your behavioral definition.

40. Review: Reliability requires two conditions. The two observers must use the same ________________. They must observe the same ________________.

51. Review: The second tactic in using the behavioral strategy to solve a human problem is to use the approach of ________________ to observe the problem behavior.

57. Review: When each observer produces only a total count, you must compute what is called ________________ reliability.

34. Review: Both forms of reliability multiply 100% times ________________ divided by agreements plus disagreements.

46. Review: The extent to which outside judges agree with your behavioral definition is called ________________.

33. Review: Behavior analysts compare the observations of two observers to get an indirect measure of their accuracy. Sometimes they base the measure on frequency and sometimes on trials. In either case, they call this measure ________________.

39. Review: Recording a behavior during a series of discontinuous intervals is called ________________ recording; recording a behavior during a series of continuous intervals is called ________________ recording.

47. Review: The formula for checking reliability is ________________.

61. Review: You should seek ________________ percent agreement with old behavioral definitions and ________________ percent with new ones.

56. Review: Two forms of reliability are ________________ reliability and ________________ reliability.

55. Review: To use the behavioral strategy, first create a behavioral definition of the problem behavior. Second, use the approach of ________________ to gather information about it. Third, check the ________________ and ________________ of your observations.

49. Review: The name of the science that studies environmental events that change behavior is ________________.

36. Review: Frequency reliability is used when observers produce only a total count, such as with ________________ and ________________ recording of simple behaviors.

41. Review: Reliability assumes that two observers use the same ________________ to observe the same ________________.

52. Review: Time sample recording involves the observing of a behavior during a series of ________________ intervals.

48. Review: the formula for reliability is: ________________.

Examples

1. Sammy and Marge used a new and complicated behavioral definition of sleep to see if their new baby was sleeping. They observed every half hour. Their first ten observations were (S=sleep; A=awake):

Sammy:	S	S	A	S	A	S	S	A	S	A
Marge:	S	A	A	S	A	S	A	A	S	A

First, does the example let you assume that the observers used the same behavioral definition and observed the same responses? ________. Then, A= ____. D= ____. (A+D)= ____. A/(A+D) equals the decimal ____. Multiply the decimal by 100% to find that their reliability is ____ percent.

2. Fred and Charlie counted the number of beers that Murray drank on Saturday. Fred counted 10, while Charlie counted only 9. Decide whether their observations are reliable. First, does the information given in the example let you assume that the observers used the same behavioral definition on the same responses? ____. Second, compute reliability using 100%xA/(A+D). In this

case, you should assume that Fred agrees with all of Charlie's observations. Thus, the number of agreements is A= ____. Likewise, you should assume that Charlie disagrees with the extra beer that Fred counted. Thus, the number of disagreements is D= ____. (A+D)= ____. Thus, A/(A+D) equals the decimal ____. Multiply that decimal by 100% to find that reliability equals ____ percent.

3. On Saturday, Roger counted the number of times that Terry threw his clothes down rather than putting them away. He counted eight times. Bunny, his friend, counted ten times on Sunday. First, does the example let you assume that Roger and Bunny used the same behavioral definition and observed the same responses? ____. Please notice that if one observer counts on Saturday and the other counts on Sunday, they are not observing the same responses.

4. Tam and Fay developed a behavioral definition. They made their observations at 8:00 at their coop dorm (yes=pass; not=fail).

Chore:	Floor	Walls	Table	Trash	Chair
Tam	yes	not	yes	not	yes
Fay	yes	not	not	not	not

First, does the example let you assume that they observe using the same behavioral definition with the same responses? ____. Second, count how many observations agree and how many disagree. Then use the formula 100% x A/(A+D) to find that their computed reliability is ____ percent. Third, notice that they developed their own behavioral definition, which means that it is new. To be acceptable, their reliability must be at least ____ percent. Is their reliability high enough for a new behavioral definition? ____. Enter the letter of the correct conclusion. (a) No conclusion is possible because the same responses were not observed; (b) the observations are reliable; (c) the observations are not reliable. ____

5. Owen was appointed to obtain an objective measure of the number of gripes made during dinner at the dorm. Mary was appointed to record the gripes once a week to measure Owen's reliability. On Thursday, when they were both observing, Owen counted nine gripes and Mary counted ten. First, can you assume that they used the same behavioral definition on the same responses? ____. Second, their reliability is ____ percent. Third, decide what level of reliability they must meet to be acceptable. Are their observations reliable enough to be acceptable? ____ (no, yes)

6. Joan and Al feel that Professor Brainbuster says "uh" too often during lectures. Joan counted 48 "uh's" during Monday's lecture. To make sure Joan was accurate in her counting, Al counted "uh's" during Tuesday's lecture and found 50. They decided that their counts were so close that Joan's count must have been correct. Should you assume in this case that the observers used the same behavioral definition and observed the same responses? ____. Is their high agreement evidence of acceptable reliability? ____

7. You and a friend observe the amount of time that a TV show's host talks in a sexist way to his women guests. You develop a behavioral definition of sexist talk. You find that 67% of the intervals on Monday's show contain sexist talk. On Tuesday, a well-known feminist guest tells the host to stop being a sexist. You find that only 5% of the intervals in Wednesday's show contain sexist talk. Suppose you ask a local women's group to rate videotapes of Monday's and Wednesday's shows. The group rates Monday's show as "highly sexist" and Wednesday's as "slightly sexist." The correlation between your observations and the group's ratings suggests that your behavioral definition has ____.

8. The church members were considering whether to continue using some of their space for private worship. There were differing opinions on how often the private worship room was used, so the members appointed Sue to measure its use. She asked Tom to help test the reliability of her observations. She noted that the room was used during only one of those times, but Tom noted two uses of the room. Their records were as follows (U=used; N=not used):

Sue:	N	N	N	U	N	N	N	N	N	N
Tom:	N	N	N	U	U	N	N	N	N	N

Is reliability meaningful (same time and behavioral definition)? ____. Their reliability equals ____ percent. Does the reliability meet the goal? ____

9. Review: The dorm members wanted to know how much their sauna was used before agreeing to buy a second one. Fran and Will agreed to observe its use once an hour. Their data for the first ten hours were as follows (U=use; N=nonuse):

Fran: U U U U N U N U U U
Will: U U U U U U N N U U

What is the reliability of these observations? __________ percent. Is it acceptable?__________

10. Review: Marie was using behavioral methods to teach a group of women how to be more assertive. She had a behavioral definition of assertiveness. Some of her students questioned her behavioral definition, so she took videotapes of her students' performance before and after training and showed them to a cross section of adults, asking them to rate how assertively the taped individuals were acting. They rated the students as more assertive after training than before, just as the behavioral definition did. Marie was attempting to establish the __________ of her behavioral definition.

11. Review: Rob and Jan observed Professor Brainbuster to find out whether he was looking at students when he lectured. They did this in 15-second intervals. The first ten observations were:

Rob: O O O O X O O X O O
Jan: O X O O O O O X O O

Compute the reliability: ________ percent. Is this an acceptable level? ______

12. Review: Time to include some review questions from prior lessons. Marc sometimes thought of himself as the sultan. He made up a checklist of 15 services that he expected of Anna every day. He watched to see if she served him breakfast in bed, brought him his clothes, poured his bath, and so on. His plan was to record immediately when she performed each service. During the first day of his system, he asked Anna to bring him breakfast in bed. She looked at him kind of funny but did it. He then marked it down on his checklist. Next he asked her to pour his bath and to be sure to put cologne in it. She looked real funny this time, went into the kitchen, and then threw a pot of water on the sultan. What method of observation was the sultan hoping to use? ________________ recording

13. Review: Dave observed the study behavior of each of 16 pupils in the fifth grade for ten seconds before moving on to the next pupil. Every four minutes, he started over again with the first pupil. What method of observation was he using with the first pupil? ________________ recording

14. Review: Dom observed each story on the evening news for a week. He found that 50 of the news items were biased toward the status quo. John wanted to see if Dom was correct, so he watched the evening news the next week and applied the same behavioral definition. He found that 46 of the items were biased toward the status quo. Enter the letter of your conclusion: (a) No conclusion is possible, because the same responses were not observed; (b) the observations are reliable; (c) the observations are not reliable. ______

15. Review: The coach diagrammed a football play that showed exactly what the fullback should do. The coach assigned an assistant to observe whether the fullback made the right play according to the diagram. Behavior analysts would call the diagram a(n) ________________ of "made the right play."

16. Review: Barb inspected the cleaning jobs according to a 50-item checklist at 8:00 P.M. Thursday. She found that 30 items had been completed. Jan inspected them at 8:00 P.M. Friday, using the same behavioral definition. She found only 20 done. Is this evidence that their observations were <u>not</u> reliable? ________

17. Review: Two members of NOW counted the number of shoppers going into Nick's store before NOW started its boycott over the wages of Nick's women employees. One member counted 18 shoppers, and the other member counted 20 shoppers. They used the same behavioral definition. Compute the reliability: __________ percent. Is it acceptable? ________

18. Review: Alice was chairperson of the local Wilderness Society. She worried that she dominated monthly meetings. She asked two other members to observe the number of ten-second intervals during which she talked. The first ten observations were (A=Alice talked; O=others talked):

Observer 1: A A A O A O A O A A
Observer 2: A A A A A O A O A A

Does this evidence permit you to conclude that the observations are reliable? ____________

19. Review: Alice and Janet watched ten commercials shown on late-night TV to determine how many of them were advertising products that were ecologically harmful. Their results were (H=harmful; N=not harmful):

Alice: H H N H N H H H N H
Janet: H H H H N H H H H H

Compute the reliability: _______ percent. Is it acceptable? _________

20. Review: Barb and Gary wanted to find out how much time the children at the Yellow Brick Road Alternative School were spending learning to read, write, and do arithmetic. They observed in 30-second blocks of time using a new behavioral definition. Their first ten observations were (S=studying basics; N=not):

Barb:	S	S	N	N	N	N	N	N	N	N
Gary:	S	S	S	N	N	N	N	S	N	N

Compute the reliability: _________ percent. Is it acceptable? _______ (Check)

LESSON

5 Experimental Designs for Studying Everyday Behavior

You have learned the first three tactics in using the behavioral strategy to solve a problem. You develop a behavioral definition, use a method of direct observation, and check the reliability and social validity of your observations. When those tactics don't solve the problem, you can use a fourth tactic. The fourth tactic is to design a single-subject experiment. You can use single-subject experiments to find out if a particular "treatment" for the problem behavior works. Treatments involve environmental events like praising or giving tangible items.

1. The fourth tactic in using the behavioral strategy to solve a problem is to design a single-subject ______________.

Behavior analysts speak of "designing" these experiments. The design is a plan for presenting and withholding the treatment. The simplest design compares the rate of the behavioral variable before and after treatment; if the rate is higher after treatment, this suggests that the treatment caused the change. As you will see, there are several more complex designs.

The most important aspect of an experimental design is whether it can rule out alternative explanations of the results. You might use any one of three widely used designs. Behavior analysts use these three designs so that they can discover laws of behavior. These designs use the principle of single-subject experiments. You will learn about the three single-subject designs commonly used by behavior analysts.

Alternative Explanations

You can use behavioral experiments to find out whether a particular treatment works. For example, you might wish to increase the amount of chores done by children. Most parents give their children an allowance regardless of whether or not they do chores. I will call this *free allowance*. You might guess that an earned allowance would produce more chores than free allowance, but there is only one way to find out whether that is true. You must design an experiment that compares the effects of giving earned allowance with the effects of giving free allowance.

You might find that children do more chores with earned allowance. However, your results might be subject to alternative explanations, of two particular types: individual differences and time coincidences.

Consider two examples of time coincidences. Suppose you decide to compare chore behavior using free allowance during November with chore behavior using earned allowance during December. You might find that the children did more chores during December. Maybe this means that earned allowance works better than free allowance, but maybe it doesn't. Can you think of an alternative explanation? Of course: Most children are on their best behavior just before Christmas. They might increase their chore behavior to get more presents. Another alternative explanation is that their mother might have given them a lecture about neatness in the beginning of December. Both these alternatives involve a coincidence between when you switch from free allowance to earned allowance and some other factor such as Christmas or Mom's lecture. The number of possible coincidences is endless. Because of them, you can't be sure your results mean that an earned allowance works better.

Consider two examples of individual differences. Suppose you observe the amount of chores done by Tom and Tracey, two children getting earned allowances. Suppose you also observe the amount done by Bob and Becky, two children getting free allowances. You might find that Tom and

Tracey do more chores than Bob and Becky. Can you conclude that earned allowance works better? Can you think of alternative explanations? For example, Tom and Tracey may have held real jobs prior to the experiment and learned to do what is asked of them. Bob and Becky may never have held real jobs. The result might appear to favor earned allowances, but the real cause of Tom and Tracey doing more chores may be their job experience. Other individual differences, such as age, IQ, or cooperativeness, might also explain any differences. In fact, the possible alternative explanations based on individual differences are endless. So you can't be sure your results mean that earned allowance works better.

Until you can rule out all alternative explanations, you can't be sure that the increased chores are the result of earned allowance. You must rule out time coincidences, and you must also rule out individual differences. The more alternative explanations that an experiment rules out, the more sure you can be about what caused any change in a behavioral variable.

Experimental Conditions

In this lesson, I will describe three experimental designs and discuss the ability of each one to rule out alternative explanations. First, I need a few terms to help talk about experimental designs.

Behavior analysts seek methods of changing behavior to help solve problems. They call these methods *treatments*. The **treatment** is the method introduced to modify the rate of a behavior. The treatment may be designed either to increase or to decrease the behavior. Thus, giving an earned allowance for chores is the treatment. Behavior analysts call the period of time during an experiment when they are delivering the treatment the *treatment condition*. Thus, the period of time when the children receive an earned allowance is the treatment condition.

2. The treatment is the method introduced to ________ the rate of a behavior.
3. The method introduced to modify the rate of a behavior is called the ___________.

Behavior analysts usually compare the effect of using a treatment with the effect of not using it. They call absence of the treatment the *baseline*. The **baseline** is the period of an experiment without the treatment. In your experiment with chores, the period of time when you observe chores with free allowance would be called the baseline or the baseline condition.

4. The period of an experiment without the treatment is called the ___________.

Behavior analysts run experiments to find out whether a treatment modifies a behavioral variable. Their experiments have at least a baseline condition and a treatment condition. They compare the rate of the behavior in each condition. The rate during treatment might be similar to baseline, or it might be different from baseline. Finding a similar rate suggests that the treatment did not modify the behavior; finding a different rate suggests the obvious explanation that the treatment modified behavior. However, the obvious explanation may not be correct. There may be an alternative explanation for the change.

Ruling Out Alternative Explanations

Ruling out alternative explanations means showing that events other than the treatment did not cause an observed difference. For example, you might be able to show that Christmas didn't cause the children to do their chores. You might be able to show that Mom didn't just have a talk with them. If so, you have ruled out those alternative explanations.

5. Ruling out alternative explanations means showing that events other than the treatment did not ________ an observed difference.
6. Showing that events other than the treatment did not cause an observed difference is called ruling out ___________ explanations.

Suppose you find a difference in behavior with and without treatment and rule out all alternative explanations. You are left with the treatment as the only explanation of the difference. You have designed an experiment that proves the treatment causes the difference! The remainder of this lesson will introduce you to designing such experiments.

The Principle of Single-Subject Experiments

Single-subject experiments provide a powerful way to establish causality. These designs experiment with one person at a time. You observe the behavior of one person before treatment, then observe the same person during treatment. This simple step immediately rules out individual differences between baseline and treatment. Since you use only one individual, there can be no individual differences. As you will see, behavior analysts have additional ways to rule out time coincidences as alternative explanations. When you have ruled out alternative explanations, you are left with the treatment as the only remaining explanation for changes in that single person's behavior. If you find the same result with additional individuals, you have evidence that it is true in general. The **principle of single-subject experiments** is to expose one person to the baseline and treatment.

7. The principle of single-subject experiments is to expose ________ person to the baseline and treatment.

An experiment is single-subject if it exposes one subject to both the baseline condition and the treatment condition. However, the term *single-subject* does not refer to how many subjects there are in the experiment, but rather to the minimum number of subjects—one—needed to compare baseline and treatment. Most single-subject experiments use more than one subject, but each subject is exposed to both the baseline and the treatment condition. The individuals in the baseline condition are the same individuals as those in the treatment condition. Single-subject experiments use more than one subject to see if their findings apply to just that one person or to many. They use more than one subject to assess the generality of their findings.

For example, suppose you want to find out if teaching relaxation can help people reduce their tension headaches. You might start by teaching Kendall a simple method of relaxation. Perhaps you find that pain behaviors linked to headaches decrease by half. By comparing Kendall's pain before relaxation with his pain after relaxation, you have ruled out individual differences. If you rule out other alternative explanations, then you can conclude that relaxation caused the reduction of Kendall's pain. If you want to see whether this finding applies to many people, you could repeat your comparison of baseline and treatment with other people suffering from tension headaches. Suppose you repeat the experiment with eight people. If you find that they all improve, you can conclude that relaxation causes a reduction in headache pain. Your results would be similar to those obtained in a recent study (Applebaum et al., 1990). Notice that the design is single-subject even though it involves more than one person, because you expose each subject to baseline and treatment.

Behavior analysts argue that single-subject experiments are powerful designs (e.g., Barlow & Hersen, 1984). They have used single-subject experiments to discover many laws of behavior; Skinner's discovery of the law of reinforcement was only the first. You will read about additional laws throughout this book. Single-subject experiments let behavior analysis discover many causes of behavior.

Behavior analysts most often use three experimental designs suitable for single subjects. I will describe and illustrate the comparison design first; then I will introduce you to the reversal design and the multiple-baseline design.

Comparison Design

Behavior analysts call the simplest design a *comparison design*. A **comparison** design involves comparing the baseline condition with the treatment condition. It observes the behavior for the same person (or persons) in both conditions. You use this design by first observing a behavior prior to the start of treatment, while the "normal" conditions are still in effect. You call this your baseline. You then observe the behavior during the treatment. Figure 5-1 shows the baseline condition of Sarge's "rational leadership" behavior. Suppose you wished to study the effects of leadership training as a treatment to improve his leadership behavior. You would train Sarge and then observe his rational leadership behavior with training.

8. A comparison design involves comparing the baseline condition with the ____________ condition.

Figure 5-1. Observing Sarge "before" and "after" leadership training would be a comparison design. Cartoon copyright 1973 King Features Syndicate. Reproduced by permission.

9. The design that involves comparing the baseline condition with the treatment condition is called the ___________ design.

As a more serious example, let's return to the chore behavior of children. You wish to compare free allowance with earned allowance. You would select a specific child for your experiment—let's say, Terry. You would start by observing Terry's chore behavior during a baseline period, when you used free allowance rather than earned allowance. Let's say you find that he did about 25% of his chores for the 15 days of baseline. Then you would observe his chore behavior during the following 15 days. During that period, you would give Terry the treatment of earned allowance. Let's say you find that Terry's chore behavior improved; he did about 75% of his chores for those 15 days. Figure 5-2 shows a graph of this result.

Can you rule out alternative explanations of this finding? You can rule out individual difference because you have studied only Terry, but you cannot rule out time coincidences (Parsonson & Baer, 1978a). For example, Terry may have started inviting a playmate home at the same time that you started earned allowance. If so, Terry may have improved his chore behavior to impress the friend, not because of your earned allowance. Or there may have been a decrease in schoolwork, job, or other duties that had interfered with Terry's chore behaviors during baseline. Or perhaps he simply wanted to please you. You can imagine many events that might have coincided with the start of your treatment. Since this design does not rule any of them out, you can't have complete confidence in the effect of the treatment. The change simply may have been a coincidence.

```
                      Free        Earned
            100 |
Chore        75 |            x ------------ x
behavior     50 |            x              x
             25 | ---------- x              x
              0 | ---------- x ------------ x
Day number:   0             15             30
```

Figure 5-2. Comparison design: A hypothetical experiment to increase Terry's chore behavior by using earned allowance. This is a comparison design because it studies one behavior with just baseline and treatment conditions. The first condition is free allowance, and the second condition is earned allowance. (Note that this graph shows only the average chore behavior, not the data points for each of the 15 days.)

Sometimes you might use a *backward* comparison design: introducing the treatment rather than the baseline first. Your experiment would have the same two conditions as with any comparison design, but the first condition would be treatment and the second would be baseline. The logic of the design is identical to the standard comparison design.

You can always tell whether a single-subject experiment uses a comparison design by asking one question. Does the experiment compare the treatment with only one baseline? If so, it uses a comparison design.

Comparison designs do not rule out alternative explanations based on time. However, behavior analysts have developed two experimental designs that do rule out alternative explanations based on time coincidences. These designs provide strong evidence about whether or not a treatment works. They are called the *reversal design* and the *multiple-baseline design*. Because they rule out alternative explanations, I will call these *strong* designs.

Reversal Designs

The reversal design is similar to the comparison design. You start with a comparison of behavior during the baseline and treatment conditions. In other words, you start with a comparison design. You then go one step further and "reverse" from treatment to baseline. This creates a third condition called the *reversal to baseline* or simply the *reversal* condition. The **reversal design** looks at a behavior during baseline, treatment, and reversal.

10. The reversal design looks at a behavior during baseline, treatment, and ____________.
11. The design that looks at a behavior during baseline, treatment, and reversal is called the ______________ design.

You could use this design to determine the effect of earned allowance on the chore behavior of Terry. You would start the same way you did with the comparison design. Let's say the results are the same: You find that Terry did 25% of his chores during an initial 30 days of baseline (with free allowance) but 75% during the following 30 days of treatment (with earned allowance). You create the reversal design by adding a third condition.

```
                          Free        Earned          Free
                 100 |
Chore             75 |               x ------------ x
behavior          50 |               x              x
                  25 | ---------- x              x ------------ x
                   0 | ---------- x ------------ x ------------ x
Day number:  0                30             60             90
```

Figure 5-3. Reversal design: A hypothetical experiment to increase Terry's chore behavior by using earned allowance. This is a reversal design because it studies one behavior with three conditions. The first condition is the baseline of free allowance; the second condition is the treatment of earned allowance; and the third condition is the reversal to free allowance again. (Note that this graph shows only the average chore behavior, not the data for each of the 30 days.)

You would observe Terry's rate of chores when you once again gave him free allowance. Behavior analysts call this the *reversal to baseline condition*, or simply the *reversal condition*. Let's say you find that Terry's chores decreased to 25% during the 30 days of this condition. You would have conducted a reversal design on earned allowance for chores. Figure 5-3 shows a graph of this experiment.

Can you rule out alternative explanations for your finding? Your results make alternative explanations for Terry's changed behavior very unlikely. First, you have ruled out individual differences, because you are comparing Terry to himself. Second, you have made a time coincidence with some other event very unlikely. The other event would have to begin when you started using earned allowance and cease when you stopped using it. The coincidence is too great, so you can conclude that the earned allowance caused the change.

Suppose the experiment had come out differently. If Terry had persisted in his chore behavior during the reversal, then you could not have ruled out alternative explanations. Suppose Terry's chores stayed at 75% during the reversal. You should suspect that some unknown event began when you started to use earned allowance and was still working when you were no longer using earned allowance. In other words, you should suspect that some unknown event, rather than earned allowance, explains Terry's improved chore behavior. The failure of Terry's chore behavior to decrease during the reversal would mean that you could no longer rule this possibility out.

You can use more than one reversal if the results are ambiguous. For example, suppose Terry's chores didn't reverse back to baseline levels. Maybe chores decreased to only 55% when you stopped giving Terry an earned allowance. In other words, you saw a decrease of 20% (75% to 55%) when you stopped earned allowance. That compares to an increase of 50% (25% to 75%) when you started earned allowance. The difference sugGests that another factor coincided with earned allowance to cause the initial increase. To clarify this alternative explanation, you could try the treatment a second time. You might find that Terry once again did 75% of his chores. This suggests that some coinciding factor helped produce the first increase and is still operating. However, with this additional reversal, you would be much more confident that earned allowance produced part of the difference.

Sometimes you might use a backward reversal design. The first two conditions would be identical to a backward comparison design. You would start with the treatment rather than baseline first. You would have three conditions: start with treatment, change to baseline, and then reverse to treatment. For example, one researcher started by helping older people with a memory aid (Bourgeois, 1993). She then took away the aid. Finally, she returned the memory aid. The logic of the design is identical to the forward reversal design.

The reversal design permits you to rule out alternative explanations of any change in behavior associated with the treatment. It is a very convincing and powerful design.

You can always tell whether a single-subject experiment uses a reversal design by asking one question. Does the experiment have a third condition that is the same as the initial condition? If so, it uses a reversal design.

Multiple-Baseline Design

Behavior analysts call a second strong design the *multiple-baseline* design. A **multiple-baseline** design introduces the treatment at different times for two or more behaviors. The multiple-baseline design is two (or more) comparison designs. The only difference is that you start the treatment at different times for the behaviors (or persons or situations).

> ***Data from Well-Designed Experiments Outlive Theories***
>
> "The investigator is... faced with a dilemma. Shall he follow the lead of sophisticated theoreticians and design experiments whose data may be of interest only in reference to the theory in question? Or shall he perform experiments that he believes will yield data of general interest, irrespective of whether current theories have been designed to handle them?... Good data are notoriously fickle. They change their allegiance from theory to theory, and even maintain their importance in the presence of no theory at all" (Sidman, 1960: pp. 6–7).
>
> 12. Data from single-subject experiments are likely to be of lasting interest because they rule out ________________ explanations.

13. A multiple-baseline design introduces the treatment at different times for ________ or more behaviors.
14. The design that introduces the treatment at different times for two or more behaviors, persons, or situations is known as the multiple ________________ design.

For example, suppose Terry not only doesn't do his share of chores but also doesn't answer the phone very often. Suppose you obtain a baseline for both of these behaviors. Maybe Terry does 25% of his chores and 50% of the phone answering. After the second week, you might give him earned allowance based only on doing his chores, whether or not he answers the phone. In other words, you introduce the treatment for chores but not for phone answering. You might find that Terry's chores increase to 75% while his phone answering stays at 50%. After the third week, you might give him earned allowance based on both chores and phone answering. In other words, you introduce the treatment for the phone answering as well as for the chores. You might find that chores stay at 75% and that phone answering goes up to 100%. Figure 5-4 shows a graph of these results. What is unique about this design is that you in-

```
                      Free        Earned        Earned
              100 |
Chore          75 |             | ------------x------------ |
behavior       50 |             |             x             |
               25 | ----------  |             x             |
                0 | ----------  | ------------x------------ |

                      Free         Free         Earned
              100 |                           x------------ |
Phone          75 |             |             x             |
behavior       50 | ----------  | ------------x             |
               25 |             |             x             |
                0 | ----------  | ------------x------------ |
```

Figure 5-4. Multiple-baseline design: A hypothetical experiment to increase Terry's chore and phone behavior by using earned allowance. (Note that this graph shows only the average chore behavior.)

troduced the treatment at different times for the two behaviors.

You now want to know if you can rule out alternative explanations of the difference. Restricting your study to Terry rules out individual differences. Starting earned allowance at a different time for each behavior makes a coinciding event very unlikely. Such an event would have to occur by coincidence after one week for chores and also after two weeks for phone answering. Two such coincidences are very unlikely. You can be pretty sure that a time coincidence does not give an alternative explanation for the difference in chores and phone answering.

If you had found that chores increased but phone answering did not, you could not conclude that the change in chores was a result of the earned allowance. In this case, a coincidence with the introduction of the treatment for chores is possible.

One variation on the multiple-baseline design uses the same behavior with two or more people. For example, suppose that you have two lazy children, Bob and Sue, instead of only one. You might start by measuring Bob and Sue's chore behavior during a baseline. Next, you might begin treatment for Bob's chores but not for Sue's on the tenth day. Third, you might begin treatment for Sue's chores while continuing the treatment for Bob's on the twentieth day. If the treatment is effective for both Bob and Sue, the chances are slim that some unknown alternative explanation was responsible for the change. Notice that you have used two persons instead of two behaviors. What is unique here is that you introduce the treatment at different times for the two persons.

Be careful not to confuse a multiple-baseline design that uses two persons with a simple comparison design using two persons. For example, you might measure a baseline for Ted and Ann. Next, you might introduce earned allowance for both of them on the tenth day. This is a comparison design, because you are introducing the treatment at the same time for both persons. The example with Bob and Sue differs because you introduced the treatment at different times for each person.

Sometimes you might use a backward multiple-baseline design. You would start with the treatment first and then introduce the baseline. You would have two conditions for each person, starting with treatment and then changing to baseline.

Multiple-baseline designs are used when a behavior change will not reverse. For example, if your treatment teaches a child that 2 and 2 equals 4, you can't unteach him. By using a multiple baseline, you simply use the same treatment on a different behavior. You can still rule out time coincidences. Perhaps the earliest use of a multiple-baseline design was in 1967 (Marks & Gelder, 1967).

You can always tell whether a single-subject experiment uses a multiple-baseline design by asking one question. Does the experiment introduce the treatment condition at different times for two (or more) behaviors (or persons)? The key fact to look for is starting the treatment at different times. If the treatment starts at different times, you can be sure the experiment uses a multiple-baseline design.

One-Time Treatments

Most treatments continue until stopped. For example, if you give your children earned allowance, that remains the treatment only until you stop it; we know when treatment started and when treatment ended. Other treatments occur only once. Once you teach Barb how to do long division, you have delivered the treatment. Now she knows how to do it. I will consider one-time treatments as though they are ongoing. Thus, the treatment period starts when you teach Barb long division. It never ends. The treatment may be over, but its effects continue, so the treatment period continues.

You can't use a reversal design with a one-time treatment. You can't undo your treatment. You can't eliminate your friend's knowledge of how to do long division. You can use a comparison design or a multiple-baseline design, but you must be looking for this kind of situation to identify it. The experiment might involve comparing your friend's accuracy after teaching her the skill. The baseline would be the period before you teach her, and the treatment would be the period after you teach her. That period would have no ending.

Summary

The fourth tactic in using the behavioral strategy is to design a single-subject experiment. The principle of single-subject experiments is to expose one person to all conditions in the experiment. The comparison design involves a comparison between baseline and treatment. This design rules out individual differences but does not rule out time coincidences. Reversal and multiple-baseline designs rule out both individual differences and time coincidences. A reversal design uses the sequence of baseline, treatment, and reversal to baseline. A multiple-baseline design compares the baseline and treatment conditions where the treatment condition is introduced at different times for each behavioral variable. Single-subject experiments expose at least one person to all the conditions.

Behavior Analysis Examples

This section presents several examples taken directly from the research literature. The examples show actual uses of all three experimental designs. (Hint: They are not in the same order as you learned them.)

Coaching Football

Behavior analysis doesn't always deal with earth-shaking problems. One study reported a method for coaching football with 9- and 10-year-old boys in a Pop Warner League. Komaki and Barnett (1977) applied their method to three plays: quarterback option, power sweep, and counter. Their method involved four steps. First, the coaches told each boy his assignment on each play. Second, they rehearsed each play. Third, they recorded the boys' performance during practice scrimmages and games, using a checklist to record the plays as they occurred. Fourth, they told the boys how they did; they praised those who carried out their assignments. They hoped to improve the performance of each boy by using these four steps. Thus, these four steps are the treatment they used. I will call their treatment *praise*.

The baseline condition for all three types of plays was the old coaching method before the coaches started using the praise treatment. The researchers introduced the treatment condition for each play at different times. They introduced it for the quarterback option play first, leaving the power sweep and counter plays in the baseline condition of no praise. They then introduced the treatment for the power sweep, leaving the counter play in baseline. This condition lasted four games. They then introduced the treatment condition for the counter play for eight games. At that point, they had all three plays in the treatment condition. Figure 5-5 shows this design. Correct performance was about 60% for all plays before praise and over 80% during praise.

15. Because they introduced the treatment at different times for two or more behaviors, what design did they use? ________________ (comparison, multiple-baseline, reversal)

Energy Conservation

Here's another example of a behavioral approach to conservation. Palmer and his associates studied a treatment to reduce the use of electricity. First, they observed the Smiths' daily usage of electricity for 16 days during baseline. Second, they observed the Smiths' usage during treatment for 10 days. The treatment was to tell the Smiths the cost of the electricity they used each day. Third, they observed usage for 30 days during a reversal to baseline. During the reversal, they stopped telling the Smiths how much their electricity cost. Figure 5-6 shows this design. The researchers found that providing cost information reduced usage more than 10%. They studied three other families and found similar results. Because the researchers studied each family during baseline and treatment conditions, they used a single-subject experiment. (Based on Palmer, Lloyd, & Lloyd, 1977.)

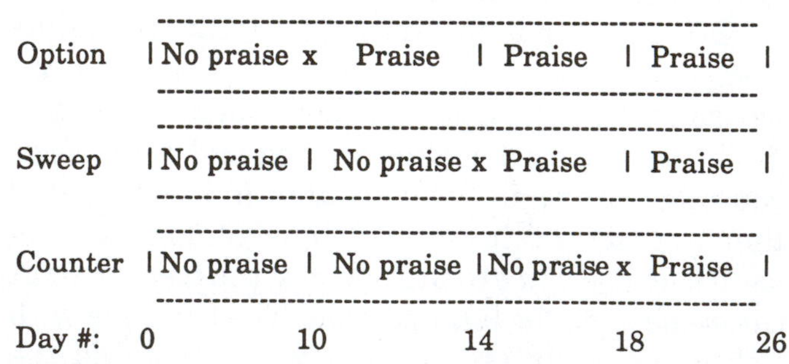

Option | No praise x Praise | Praise | Praise |
Sweep | No praise | No praise x Praise | Praise |
Counter | No praise | No praise | No praise x Praise |
Day #: 0 10 14 18 26

Figure 5-5. Design of an experiment to see the effect of praising the player's execution of three football plays. This is a multiple-baseline design, because praise was started at different times for three different plays.

16. Praise started after day 10 for option, after day 14 for sweep, and after day ____ for the counter play.

```
                      No cost info  x  Cost info  x  No cost info
                  37 I              x             x---------------- x
Kilowatt          36 I ------------ x             x                 x
hours of          35 I              x             x                 x
electricity       34 I              x             x                 x
used              33 I              x             x                 x
                  32 I              x------------ x                 x
                  31 I ------------ x------------ x---------------- x
Day #:               0             16            26                58
```

Figure 5-6. Results of an experiment to reduce the use of electricity.

17. This is a reversal design because the families were initially given no cost information, then cost information, and finally (starting on day _____) they were again given no cost information.

18. Because they returned to the baseline condition after treatment, they used what type of design? _______________ (comparison, multiple-baseline, reversal)

Recycling

Conservation of global resources is critical to our world. Jacob Keller (1991) invented a simple way to increase recycling. What is unique about this example is that he was only 10 years old when he did the study. Jacob wrote notes to the 44 families on his street. He told them how many families on their street had put out material to recycle the previous week. Keller found that the notes increased the number of families recycling. (See Figure 5-7.) He studied each family during baseline and treatment, so he used a single-subject experiment.

19. Because Keller observed recycling only during baseline and treatment, what design did he use? _______________ (comparison, multiple-baseline, reversal)

```
                      No notes                Notes
Percent        50 I            x                              I
of             45 I            x------------------------------ I
homes          40 I            x                              I
recycling      35 I ---------- x                              I
               30 I ---------- x------------------------------ I
          Week #: 0            1                              4
```

Figure 5-7. Results of an experiment to increase the percent of families recycling. This is a comparison design, because the treatment was compared to the baseline condition.

20. Keller's baseline condition was no notes, and the treatment condition was _______________.

Notes

Note #1

Behavior analysts use the single-subject designs outlined in this lesson to find the effect of a particular treatment on the behavior of one individual. The generality of the treatment is tested by repeating the experiment. If it works with a second individual, you have proven some generality. You can try it on more or different types of individuals. If it works, you've shown more generality. Sidman discusses the issue of generality extensively (Sidman, 1960).

21. Behavior analysts test the generality of the treatment by repeating the _______________.

Note #2

Behavior analysts sometimes use group designs instead of single-subject designs. They often use them when they are interested in statistical information. For example, they might want to know how a behavioral treatment compares with a standard treatment. Does it increase studying and lead to higher achievement than standard classroom approaches? They would then try the behavioral treatment with one group and the standard treatment with another. They might find that the behavioral treatment produced an advance of 1.2 grade levels a year. If the standard treatment produced .7, they would conclude that the behavioral treatment worked better (Bushell, 1978). This is not a question of what causes the improvement, but of how much improvement the treatment produces compared to other treatments.

22. I don't want you to conclude that behavior analysts always use single-subject designs. Sometimes they use _________ designs.

Note #3

Behavior analysts call another experimental design the *multi-element* design. It involves alternating the experimental conditions frequently, often every day. Treatment effect shows up as different rates of behavior under the two conditions. This design also rules out alternative explanations. Behavior analysts compared third-grade studying with and without a teacher's aide in the room (Loos, Williams, & Bailey, 1977). To determine if an aide was helpful, they alternated randomly between having an aide and not having one. When the aide was present, the students completed 28% more units.

23. The multi-element design involves ________ the experimental conditions many times, often every day.

Helpful Hints

Helpful Hint #1

As you have seen, the single-subject experiment is designed around the presentation and withdrawal of the treatment condition. When you are asked questions about what modifies a behavior, you may be tempted to answer "experiment." However, the experiment only studies the causes that may change behavior. The correct answer would be "treatment," since that is the part of the experiment that has modified or changed the behavior.

24. Therefore, when asked a question about what has modified a behavior, you should answer ________________ (experiment, treatment).

Helpful Hint #2

You can identify each experimental design by asking key questions. First, ask if the treatment condition is introduced at different times for two or more behaviors. If so, it is a multiple-baseline design. Second, ask if the third condition returns to the initial condition. If so, it is a reversal design. Third, ask if the design involves only a baseline and a treatment condition. If so, it is a comparison design.

25. Remember, the very first question to ask is whether the treatment condition is introduced at ________________ times for two or more behaviors.

Helpful Hint #3

If you have trouble with simple division, such as dividing 3 by 8 or 19 by 20, then you should use a calculator for the next lesson.

Additional Readings

Baer, D. M., Wolf, M., & Risley, T. R. (1968). Some current dimensions of applied behavior analysis. *Journal of Applied Behavior Analysis, 1,* 91–97. This is a classic statement of the methods and goals of applied behavior analysis.

Barlow, D. H., Hayes, S. C., & Nelson, R. O. (1984). *The scientist practitioner: Research accountability in clinical and educational settings.* New York: Pergamon. This book discusses various experimental designs that can be used in clinical and educational settings. It also discusses the ethics of using these designs.

Barlow, D. H., & Hersen, M. (1984). *Single case experimental designs: Strategies for studying behavior change* (2nd. ed.). New York: Pergamon. A text on the history, issues, and use of single-case designs, including statistics and replication procedures. A good text for determining the pros and cons of these designs.

Campbell, D. T., & Stanley, J. C. (1963). *Experimental and quasi-experimental designs for research.* Chicago: Rand McNally. This book is the best exposition of complex comparison designs available. It outlines methods by which many alternative explanations of differences can be eliminated.

Johnston, J. M., & Pennypacker, H. S. (1981). *Strategies and tactics of human behavioral research.* Hillsdale, NJ: Laurence Erlbaum. Introduction to research methods for the advanced student.

Kazdin, A. E. (1977a). Assessing the clinical or applied importance of behavior change through social validation. *Behavior Modification, 1,* 427–452. Kazdin provides a thorough overview of social validation techniques for assessing the importance of behavior change.

Risley, T. R., & Wolf, M. M. (1972). Strategies for analyzing behavioral change over time. In J. Nesselroade & H. Reese (Eds.), *Life-span developmental psychology: Methodological issues.* New York: Academic Press. This is an advanced statement of the methodological ideas underlying the two complex designs taught in this chapter.

Sidman, M. (1960). *Tactics of scientific research.* New York: Basic Books. This is a classic statement of the logic underlying single-subject research designs. It was written before such designs were commonly used with applied human research, so it focuses on basic research.

Reading Quiz

80. To use the behavioral strategy: (1) create a behavioral definition of the problem behavior, (2) use a method of direct observation to observe it, (3) check the reliability and social validity of your observations, (4) design a ________________ (group, single-subject) experiment.
90. You may use environmental events like praising, ignoring, or explaining to modify behavior. In an experiment, you call those events ________________.
71. The design of an experiment is a plan for comparing the rate of a behavior during baseline with the rate during ________________.
38. Review: The most important aspect of an experimental design is whether it can rule out ________________ explanations of the results.
79. To find out whether a treatment works, you must compare the rate of the behavior during baseline with the rate of the behavior during treatment. The word *experiment* refers to this comparison of baseline and ____________.
81. Two types of alternative explanations are time coincidences and individual differences. Some alternative event may occur at the same time as the experimenter introduces the treatment; such an event may explain the modification of behavior. Such a happening is called a *time coincidence*. Some alternative event may occur for one individual, but different events occuring for another individual may explain why the behavior of only one individual changes. Such a difference is called a(n) ____________ difference.
64. Suppose you compare the effect of free allowance versus earned allowance on chore behavior. Suppose you use free allowance during November and earned allowance during December. You might find more chore behavior during earned allowance. A friend might argue that this increase was caused by the coincidence of Christmas rather than earned allowance. Behavior analysts regard such a time coincidence as one type of ____________ (alternative, causal) explanation.
66. Suppose you observe the amount of chores done by Tom and Tracey, two children getting earned allowances. Suppose you also observe the amount of chores done by Bob and Becky, two children getting free allowances. You might find that Tom and Tracey do more chores. A friend might argue that the difference was caused by Tom and Tracey having previously held jobs. Behavior analysts call this a(n) ________________ explanation.
75. The treatment can either increase or decrease the rate of the behavior. To include both possibilities, we define it as the method introduced to ____________ (increase, decrease, modify) the behavior.
82. When called upon to define *treatment*, remember to choose the key word that includes both increasing and decreasing the behavior. Define it as the method introduced to ________ the rate of a behavior.
73. The period of time when the treatment is in effect is called the ____________ (baseline, treatment) condition.
36. Review: The baseline is the period of an experiment without the ____________.
43. Review: The treatment is the method introduced to __________ the rate of a behavior.
39. Review: The period of time without a method to modify the behavior is called the ________ condition; the period of time with a method to modify the behavior is called the ________ condition.
91. You might show that events other than the treatment did not cause an observed difference between baseline and treatment. This is known as ruling out ________________ explanations.
1. Ruling out alternative explanations means showing that events other than the treatment ________ (did, didn't) cause an observed change in behavior.
13. Poorly designed experiments permit alternative explanations of the cause of any change in the rate of behavior. Well-designed experiments rule out alternatives. Ruling out alternatives means showing that events other than the treatment did not ________ any change in the rate of behavior.
17. Review: Ruling out alternatives means showing that events other than the treatment did not ____________ any change in the rate of behavior.
56. Showing that events other than the treatment did not cause any change in the rate of behavior is called ruling out ____________ explanations.
47. Review: Two types of alternative explanations

are ________________ coincidences and ____________ differences.

10. If you can't rule out alternative explanations of behavior, you can never prove that your __________ caused any observed difference.

65. Suppose you find that when you praise your child for eating vegetables, she eats more vegetables. If you can't rule out alternative explanations for her increase, then you _______ (can, can't) be sure that praise caused the increase.

94. You use the principle of single-subject experiments by exposing the same person to both the baseline condition and the __________ condition.

6. Exposing one person to both the baseline and the treatment is the principle of single-_______ experiments.

24. Review: Exposing many people to both the baseline condition and the treatment condition also follows the principle of single-subject experiments. The term s*ingle-subject* doesn't refer to how many people are in the experiment. It refers to whether each person is exposed to both the baseline condition and the __________ condition.

83. When using the principle of single-subject experiments, are the individuals in the baseline condition the same individuals as those in the treatment condition? _____ (yes, no)

23. Review: By comparing Ken's pain before he knew how to relax with his pain when he knew how to relax, you have ruled out __________ differences between Ken and someone else. There is no one else.

34. Review: Some experiments compare the baseline condition used with one person with the treatment condition used with the same person. Such an experiment is the simplest form of single-subject design that involves only two conditions. Behavior analysts call such a design a(n) __________ design.

57. Suppose Terry does 25% of his chores with free allowance and 75% with earned allowance. You can rule out individual difference, because you have studied only Terry. However, you can not rule out __________ coincidences.

2. A design that rules out individual differences (but not time coincidences) is the _________ design.

85. When you start by introducing the treatment rather than the baseline first, you are using a __________ (backward, forward) comparison design.

87. When you use a backward comparison design, you start by introducing the ____________ condition rather than the baseline condition first.

51. Review: You can always tell whether a single-subject experiment uses a comparison design by asking one question. Does the experiment involve only baseline and __________?

76. There are three single-subject experimental designs that rule out alternative explanations based on individual differences: the reversal design, the multiple-baseline design, and the ________________ design.

5. Behavior analysts have invented two strong experimental designs, called the *reversal design* and the *multiple-baseline design*, that not only rule out individual differences but also alternative explanations based on __________ coincidences.

72. The first strong design is the reversal design. A reversal design is an experiment that looks at one behavior during baseline, during treatment, and during ____________ to baseline.

22. Review: A single-subject experiment that looks at one behavior during baseline, treatment, and reversal to baseline is called a ________ design.

58. Suppose Terry does 25% of his chores with free allowance, 75% with earned allowance, and 25% when returned to free allowance. The name for this experimental design is the ________________ design.

59. Suppose Terry's chores increase from 25% to 75% when you introduce earned allowance. Suppose that they decrease from 75% to 25% when you return him to free allowance. You have ruled out individual differences by studying only Terry. Notice that Terry's rate of chores changes every time you change the method of allowance. This correlation rules out ____________ coincidences.

60. Suppose Terry's chores increased from 25% to 75% when you introduce earned allowance but then stayed at 75% when you went back to free allowance. You should suspect that some unknown event caused Terry to increase his chore behavior at the same time that you started earned allowance. You should suspect that this unknown event continues to keep Terry doing his chores even after you stopped

earned allowance. The failure of Terry's chore behavior to decrease during the reversal means that you __________ (can, can't) rule out this possibility.

62. Suppose that the behavior increased from 25% to 75% when you changed from baseline to treatment. Suppose it decreased from 75% to 25% when you reversed from treatment to baseline. If you are still not sure that the treatment caused the change, rather than some unknown event, you can reverse once more from baseline to ____________________.

84. When you cannot rule out an alternative explanation for a change in behavior, then you __________ (can, can't) conclude that the treatment caused the change.

86. When you start with treatment (rather than baseline), change to baseline, and then reverse to treatment, you have a __________ (backward, forward) reversal design.

49. Review: When you use a backward reversal design, you start with the ______________ condition.

16. Remember, to confirm a comparison design, you asked if the experiment involved only baseline and treatment. To confirm a reversal design, ask: Does the experiment involve a third condition that is the same as the condition number ____ (1, 2)?

55. Review: You will more accurately identify experimental designs if you ask the right questions. The design that studies only baseline and treatment is the _________ design; the design that has a third condition that is the same as the first condition is the __________ design.

74. The second strong experimental design is the multiple-baseline design. The key feature of the multiple-baseline design is that it begins treatment at ____________ (different, identical) times for two or more behaviors.

3. Behavior analysts call the experimental design that introduces treatment at <u>different times</u> for <u>two or more</u> behaviors the multiple-________________ design.

4. Behavior analysts call the experimental design that begins treatment at <u>different times</u> for <u>two or more</u> behaviors the ______________ ______________ baseline design.

70. The word *multiple* in "multiple-baseline" refers to at least two behaviors. A design is called multiple-baseline if it begins treatment at different times with at least _______ behaviors. The design could have three, four, or even more behaviors.

15. Remember what <u>multiple</u> means. A multiple-baseline design involves introducing the treatment at different times for ___ or more behaviors.

35. Review: Suppose Terry does 25% of his chores and 50% of the phone answering when both are on free allowance. Suppose he does 75% of his chores and 50% of the phone answering when you treat chores (but not phone) with earned allowance. Suppose finally that he does 75% of chores and 100% of the phone answering when you treat both behaviors with earned allowance. Notice that you started treatment at different times for the two behaviors. Therefore, you are using a(n) __________________ design.

61. Suppose Terry's chore behavior increases when you treat it with earned allowance. Suppose his phone answering increases when you later treat it with earned allowance. Each behavior increased only when you introduced earned allowance. This rules out __________ coincidences. Also, by studying only Terry, you have ruled out _______________ differences. This lets you conclude that earned allowance caused the change in chore behavior.

69. Suppose you study Terry using a multiple-baseline design. First you require Terry to do his chores to get his allowance. Later you also require him to answer the phone to get his allowance. If you find that chores increase but phone answering does not, you ____________ (can, can't) rule out alternative explanations. Therefore, you can't conclude that the change in chores was a result of the earned allowance.

67. Suppose you observe Tom's studying for math and spelling. After a month, you introduce treatment for studying math but not spelling. After another month, you introduce treatment also for studying spelling. Have you introduced treatment at different times for math and for spelling? ________. Therefore, this is what type of single-subject design? __________ ________________ design

68. Suppose you observe Tom's studying of math with no treatment. After a month, you introduce treatment for studying math. After another month, you withdraw treatment for studying math. Have you introduced the treat-

ment at two different times? ______. Because the third condition returns to the no treatment of the first condition, this is what single-subject experimental design? ____________ design

33. Review: Researchers may introduce treatment at different times for two people instead of two behaviors. This is a variation of which single-subject design? ____________ design
63. Suppose this week you observe Tom's and Ann's studying for math. Next week you introduce treatment for Tom's studying math. The third week, you introduce treatment for Ann's studying math. Have you introduced treatment at different times? ______. Therefore, this is what single-subject design? ____________ design
28. Review: If you introduce treatment for one behavior and then, later, for another behavior, you are using what single-subject design? ____________ design. If you introduce treatment after baseline and then return to baseline after treatment, you are using what single-subject design? ____________ design
88. When you use a backward multiple-baseline design, you start with the ____________ condition.
89. You can always tell whether a single-subject experiment uses a multiple-baseline design by asking one question. Does the experiment introduce the treatment condition for each behavior at ____________ (different, identical) times?
78. There are two single-subject experimental designs that rule out alternative explanations based on time coincidences: the reversal design and the ____________ design.
77. There are three single-subject experimental designs that rule out alternative explanations based on individual differences: the comparison design, the multiple-baseline design, and the ____________ design.
93. You should call a single-subject design that compares one person's behavior during baseline and treatment a(n) ____________ design.
53. Review: A design that introduces the treatment at different times for two or more behaviors should be called a(n) ____________ design.
92. You should call a design that compares one person's behavior during baseline, treatment, and reversal to baseline a(n) ____________ design.
21. Review: A multiple-baseline design introduces the treatment to two behaviors at ____________ times.
14. Remember the rule for one-time treatments like teaching someone long division. The rule is that the treatment period ____________ (does, doesn't) end.
44. Review: To use the behavioral strategy: (1) create a behavioral definition, (2) use a method of direct observation, (3) check the reliability and social validity of your observations, and (4) design a(n) ____________ experiment.
11. Komaki and Barnett (1977) provided praise for performance of three football plays. They introduced praise after 10 sessions on the option play, after 14 sessions for the power sweep, and after 18 sessions for the counterplay. What experimental design were they using? ____________ design
12. Palmer and associates (1977) measured electricity usage by a middle-class household during three periods of time: (1) when not giving them cost information, (2) for a period of time while giving them cost information, and (3) again after no longer giving them cost information. They used a(n) ____________ design.
9. Here's a review from an earlier lesson. Palmer and associates (1977) determined the electricity usage of a middle-class family by reading an electric meter rather than by directly observing the people using electrical equipment. What method of observation did they use? ____________ recording
30. Review: Keller (1991) compared the amounts recycled by families before he wrote them notes and while he wrote them notes. What single-subject design did he use? ____________ design
7. From Helpful Hint #1: An experiment involves comparing baseline and treatment conditions. The treatment condition uses a method to try to modify someone's behavior. Therefore, when asked a question about what has modified a behavior, you should answer ____________ (experiment, treatment).
8. Helpful Hint #2: You can identify each experimental design by asking key questions. The best question to start with is whether the treatment condition is introduced at ______ times. If so, it is a multiple-baseline design.
48. Review: Two types of alternative explanations

are __________ differences and __________ coincidences.

45. Review: To use the behavioral strategy: (1) create a behavioral definition, (2) use a method of direct observation, (3) check the reliability and social validity of your observations, and (4) design a(n) ______________ experiment.
54. Review: You use the principle of single-subject experiments by exposing one person to the baseline and ______________ conditions.
32. Review: List three single-subject designs that can rule out individual differences: __________ design, ________ design, and __________ design.
42. Review: The third tactic in using the behavioral strategy is to check the __________ and ______________ of your observations.
37. Review: The formula for reliability is _______ __________.
20. Review: A method designed to modify the rate of a behavior is called a(n) _________.
27. Review: If experimenters compare a baseline condition with the treatment condition using the same person, they are using which single-subject design? ______________ design
18. Review: A design in which two or more behaviors are subjected to the same treatment at different times is called a(n) ______________ design.
26. Review: If an experimenter starts the treatment of two of Terry's behaviors at the <u>same</u> time, be sure to recognize that this is not a multiple-baseline design. It is not a reversal design, because there is no reversal to baseline. Because it studies each behavior during baseline and treatment, it is which single-subject design? __________________ design
29. Review: In an experiment, a baseline is the record of a behavior prior to the use of a(n) ____________________ designed to modify that behavior.
50. Review: With time sample recording, the observer records during a series of __________ intervals.
25. Review: Exposing the same person to both the baseline and the treatment is the principle of ______________________ experiments.
40. Review: The period of time before starting the treatment is called the ______________ condition. The period of time when the treatment is in effect is called the ______________ condition.
31. Review: List two single-subject designs that can rule out time coincidences: the __________ ______________________ design and the ______________________ design
46. Review: To use the behavioral strategy to solve human problems: (3) check the reliability and ______________ of your observations and (4) design a(n) ______________________ experiment.
19. Review: A design in which a behavior is measured before treatment, during treatment, and during a return to baseline is called a(n) ____________ design.
41. Review: The period of an experiment prior to introducing the treatment is the __________.
52. Review: You might show that events other than the treatment did not cause an observed difference between baseline and treatment. Behavior analysts call this ruling out ________ explanations.

Examples

1. Regan wanted to be a more effective teacher. She decided to investigate the effect of praising her second-grade students when they were working hard. She measured Tony's study time before using praise and during praise. Behavior analysts call the period before using praise the __________ condition. They call the period of using praise the ______________ condition. To find out what experimental design she was using, ask questions. Did she start treatment at different times? ____. Did she use a third condition that returned to the first condition? ____. Did she study only baseline and treatment? _____. Therefore, she was using what single-subject design? A(n) ________________ design

2. From January to June, Ms. Mendez politely listened to everything that Mr. James said when he interrupted her work. He interrupted her about 17 times a week. In July, she started to ignore him. His interruptions decreased to less than twice a week. In September, Ms. Mendez began to feel sorry for him. She began listening to him again. His rate of interruptions increased to more than 16 a week. Behavior analysts call the initial period of listening the __________ condition. They call the period of ignoring him the ____________ condition. They call the period of once again lis-

tening to him the reversal to ________________.
To find out what experimental design Ms. Mendez was using, ask questions. Did she start the treatment of ignoring him at different times? ______. Did she use a third condition that returned to the first condition? ______. Did she study only baseline and treatment? ______. Therefore she was using what single-subject design? A(n) ______________ design.

3. Roger was not a socially skilled person. He never greeted friends or even smiled at them. Carol observed greeting and smiling for two weeks before trying to change his behavior. After two weeks, she started praising him when he greeted her. Two weeks later, she started praising him when he smiled at her. Roger became a new and friendlier man. Notice that after two weeks she started praising greeting. Then, after another two weeks, she began praising smiling. So when you ask if she started treatment at different times, the answer is: ____________. Therefore, she was using what single-subject design? A(n) ____________ design

4. Mrs. Green usually fixed a meat-and-potatoes kind of meal. Mr. Green kept track for six months and found that she prepared a vegetarian meal an average of once a week. Then he started telling her how much better he felt every time she fixed a vegetarian meal. She slowly increased the number of such meals, and after six months she was preparing an average of five a week. To find out what design Mr. Green was using, ask: Did he introduce the treatment at different times? ______. Did he use a third condition identical to the first? ______. Did he use only baseline and treatment? ______. You can conclude that he used what single-subject design? ____________ design

5. Sonny had asked Ann and Patsy out for a date each week for two months, with no success. Then Sonny put on some RutAftershave and asked Patsy out for a date each week for a month, with more success. He still asked Ann, but he never remembered to wear Rut. Finally he started wearing Rut when asking both Ann and Patsy out. You want to figure out what design Sonny was using to find out how effective Rut was at changing both women's behavior. Ask: treatment at different times, a third condition same as first, or only baseline and treatment? The answers show that Sonny was using what single-subject design? A(n) ________________ design

6. Mary seems to start talking most often in the middle of Franco's studying. Franco decided to record the interruptions for several days before discussing the situation with Mary. Notice that a discussion is a one-time treatment. That means that the treatment never ends. The period of time starting with the discussion is called the ______________ condition. Ask: treatment at different times, a third condition, or only baseline and treatment? The answers show that Franco was using what single-subject design to find out if discussion changed Mary's interrupting? A(n) ________________ design

7. Freda wore a wrist counter and found that she was critical of other people's ideas an average of 89 times per day for a two-week period. Then she started meditating on being more accepting at the start of every day. Her rate of critical reactions dropped to less than eight per day for two weeks. Then she forgot to meditate for the next two weeks and found that the rate of critical reactions increased to an average of 56 per day. You can ask three questions to figure out what design Freda used (by accident) to find out whether meditating reduced her critical reactions. Ask: treatment at different times, a third condition, or only baseline and treatment? The answers show that Freda was using what single-subject design to find out if meditating changed her critical reactions? A(n) ________________ design

8. Review: Let's see if you still remember ideas from prior lessons. Marie and Harry observed the frequency with which Steve played his new record. The agreement between their observations would be called ____________.

9. Review: Darnell had two friends, each of whom complained a lot about life. Darnell listened to them for years, but he finally decided that, by listening, he was only encouraging their complaints rather than helping them. So he decided to do an experiment to see whether ignoring them would be a help to them. He first recorded the number of complaints each one made for a month. Then he ignored his first friend while continuing to listen to his second friend's complaints. After another month, he ignored the plaints of both. He found that ignoring their complaints did reduce the amount of complaining without any other evidence of problems. Ask yourself the three questions. What single-subject experimental design did Darnell use? ______________ design

10. Review: Forgetful Fred always brought his books back to the library late. The library committee had charged only $.05 a day for overdue books. When they realized they had many patrons like Fred, they increased the fine to $.25 a day. Forgetful Fred became Fast Fred, always returning his books promptly. What single-subject experimental design did the library committee use to see if the increased fine would work? (Remember to ask your questions.) ______________ ______________ design

11. Review: Vern and his friend counted the number of times that Dee hit the tennis ball with a good level swing, and they immediately told her the results. Vern counted 100 level hits, while his friend counted only 87. What is the reliability of their observations? ______________ percent. Is this acceptable? ______________

12. Review: Jaime counted the number of headaches he got before enrolling in a transcendental meditation class. He got an average of five per week. His record of headaches before enrolling in the class would be called a(n) ______________.

13. Review: Bob was excited about the new audiovisual material he had for teaching his junior high social studies class. He found that the students' grades averaged 85% compared with only 78% last year. The problem with Bob's experimental design is that it cannot rule out ______________ explanations for the observed increase (such as better students this year).

14. Review: Mom observed Sally's little-league batting average by recording each hit and at-bat immediately. After five weeks, she was delighted to find that Sally usually got at least one hit per game. What method of observation did Mom use? ______________ recording

15. Review: Marvin gradually became aware that he talked about the circumstances of his life in a negative and self-defeating manner. He decided to go to a class in self-actualization. The class would be called a(n) ______________ that might change his way of talking.

16. Review: Professor Brainbuster was actually a very kindly old guy. He did everything he could to help any student who was really trying in his courses. He considered students to be trying if "they came to class regularly, asked questions, did their assignments, and asked for help when they needed it." The words in quotes would be called a(n) ______________ of *trying*.

17. Review: Sarah normally weighed 130. She tried a new quick diet to find out how well it worked, and she lost 13 pounds. She then stopped using the diet, and her weight returned to 130. What experimental design was she using to determine the effectiveness of her new diet? ______________ ______________ design

18. Review: When Billy nagged her for cookies just before dinner, Mom usually ended up giving him one. Billy nagged her every day as a result. Finally one day, she got tired of this routine and vowed to resist giving Billy any cookies before dinner. She found that he eventually stopped asking. After this had been going along well for six months, Billy asked for a cookie again one day, quite by surprise. Without thinking, Mom gave him a cookie. Now Billy nags her for a cookie every day. Mom ended up using a strong experimental design to discover the effect of giving Billy a cookie before dinner. This design effectively rules out ______________ explanations of Billy's nagging.

19. Review: Hal and Fay had been appointed umpires for the annual softball game. They decided to keep track of how they called action plays. Here is a record of their first five calls.

Calls	Hal	Fay
throw	out	out
steal	out	safe
slide	safe	safe
catch	out	out
homer	safe	safe

What is their reliability? ______________ percent. Would a behavior analyst consider it acceptable? ______________.

20. Review: Dad defined *friendly* as "smiles, offers to do favors, and always stops to talk." He observed his daughter Sally's behavior and found that she rarely engaged in those behaviors. He discussed his ideas with her, and she decided to work hard to increase those behaviors. Dad found that she now engaged in them frequently. He was not sure other people would agree that these behaviors made Sally friendly. He asked five family friends to rate Sally's friendliness before and after his talk with her. By comparing how the friends rated her friendliness with his observations, he was trying to determine the ______________ of his behavioral definition of *friendly*.

LESSON

6 Visual Analysis of Behavioral Experiments

You have learned four tactics in using the behavioral strategy: how to develop a behavioral definition; how to use methods of direct observation; how to check for reliability and validity; and how to design a single-subject experiment. The fifth tactic in using the behavioral strategy is to do a visual analysis of the data. Your analysis must answer a simple question: Did the treatment cause the behavior to change? The answer requires two steps. First, you must decide whether the data show a convincing difference between baseline and treatment; second, you must rule out alternative explanations for the difference. You learned how to rule out alternatives in the last lesson. This lesson shows you how to decide whether there is a convincing difference between baseline and treatment.

Behavior analysts usually use visual analysis to decide if their treatment makes a difference. They usually use it in preference to statistical analysis, the most common alternative method of analysis. I will show you how behavior analysts use visual analysis. I will describe the principle of visual analysis. I will show you how to use it with each single-subject design to decide whether the treatment caused a difference.

(Note: This lesson involves many simple calculations. If you are not good at dividing 3 by 8 or 19 by 20, be sure you have a calculator handy. You should get one right now before proceeding further.)

> ***Who Needs Statistics?***
>
> "It is not the obligation of the research worker to bow to the dictates of statistical theory until he or she has conclusively established its relevance to the technique of inquiry. On the contrary, the onus lies on the exponent of statistical theory to furnish irresistible reasons for adopting procedures which still have to prove their worth against a background of three centuries of progress in scientific discovery accomplished without their aid" (Hogben, 1957: p. 344, cited in Parsonson & Baer, 1978a).
>
> 1. In other words, scientific progress ______ (did, didn't) need statistics.

The Principle of Visual Analysis

The principle of visual analysis is to find differences between baseline and treatment that look convincing. You want confidence that the differences are not accidental and that additional data would still show a difference. Behavior analysts usually consider a difference to be important only if it is obvious. Visual analysis discovers powerful causes of behavior change.

2. The principle of visual analysis is to find differences between baseline and treatment that look ______________.

You can ask a question with two parts to decide whether data show a convincing difference between conditions. You can ask if the observations in different conditions overlap, and you can ask if they show a trend toward each other. To the extent that they do not overlap or show a trend, you can predict that added observations would continue to show a difference. I will teach you first how to decide whether the conditions overlap.

3. To decide whether data show a convincing difference between conditions, you can ask if the observations in different conditions ______ or if they show a ____________ toward each other.

Computing Overlap

To decide if the data show a convincing difference, first ask if the observations in each condition overlap. To the extent that the observations do not overlap, a convincing difference exists. The term *overlap* simply refers to the extent to which the range of numerical values in both sets of observations are equal. For example, if you find that Tom gets a 75% on his spelling and so does David, then both of their scores have the same value. We say that they overlap completely. As a more complex example, if Mary's first two scores are 80% and 90% and Alice's first two scores are 70% and 80%, then each has one score that is identical. Half their scores overlap.

Observations do not have to be identical to overlap. For example, suppose Barb has scores of 75% and 95%. If Tyrell has scores of 65% and 80%, his highest score is higher than her lowest score. Thus, each person has one score that overlaps. Half of their scores overlap. However, if Barb has scores of 80% and 95% and Tyrell has scores of 65% and 75%, they have no overlap. So *overlap* refers to whether the ranges of both people's scores are totally separated, or whether the ranges share values.

Here is how you count overlap between two sets of numbers. Suppose you are counting the overlap between Barb's test scores of 75% and 95% and Tyrell's scores of 65% and 80%. First you decide which set of numbers generally has the larger numbers. Call this the larger set, and call the other set the smaller set. Clearly Barb's scores are the larger set, and Tyrell's scores are the smaller set.

Smaller set:

11 12 (13 13 15) Overlap = 3

Larger set:

(13 14) 16 17 18 Overlap = ?

Total overlap = ?

Figure 6-1. Computing overlap. Find the smallest number in the larger set, which is 13. Then count the number of numbers in the smaller set that are equal to or larger than 13. (I have put them in parentheses to emphasize them.) There are three numbers equal to or larger than 13.

4. In Figure 6-1, find the largest number in the smaller set, which in this case is 15. Count the number of numbers in the larger set that are equal to or smaller than 15. There are how many? ______. What is the total overlap? _____. The percent of numbers overlapping is 5 out of 10, or 50%.

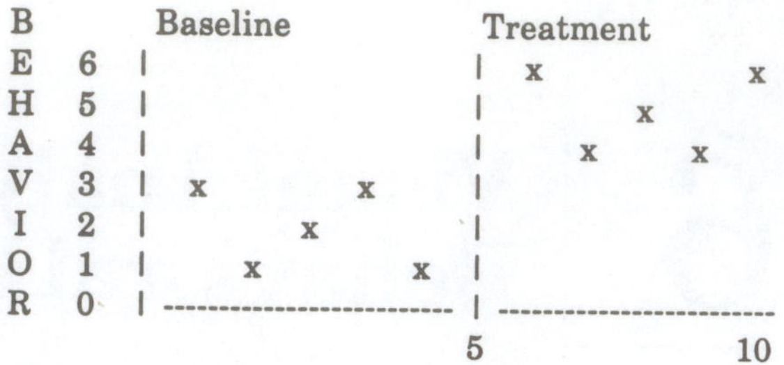

Figure 6-2. Total overlap. This graph shows no overlap in the amount of behavior in baseline and treatment. The highest value of baseline, 3, is less than the lowest value of treatment, 4.

5. In Figure 6-2, zero out of ten points overlap. Thus, there is ________ percent overlap. You can be quite sure that you would still find a difference with added observations.

Second, count how many numbers in the smaller set are larger than the smallest number in the other set. The smallest of Barb's is 75%. Only one of Tyrell's scores is larger—the 80%. Third, count how many numbers in the larger set are smaller than the largest number in the other set. The largest of Tyrell's scores is 80%. Only one of Barb's numbers is smaller—the 75%. Fourth, total up the overlapping numbers. In this case, Tyrell has one overlap and Barb has one overlap; two out of the four numbers overlap. Express this as the percentage of observations that overlap—in this case, 50%. Figure 6-1 illustrates this process.

How much overlap suggests that the differences are not convincing? In this book, I will use the rule that if more than half the numbers overlap, the difference is not convincing. This is arbi-

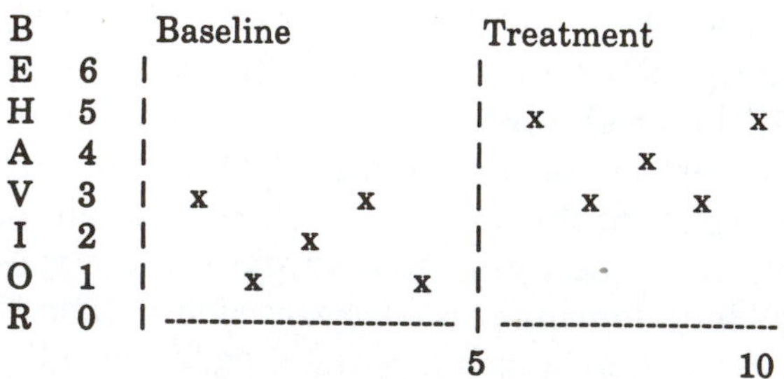

Figure 6-3. Some overlap. Two points in baseline are higher than or equal to 3, which is the lowest point in treatment. Two points in treatment are lower than or equal to 3, the highest point in baseline.

6. In Figure 6-3, the overlap is _____ out of ten. That's 40% overlap. You would probably find a difference if you took more observations.

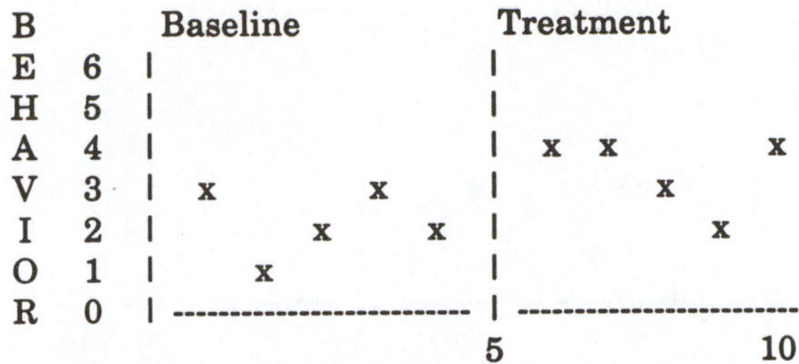

Figure 6-4. Moderate overlap.

7. In Figure 6-4, how many points in baseline are equal to or more than 2, the lowest point in treatment? ________. How many points in treatment are equal to or less than 3, the highest point in baseline? _____. That makes six in ten, or 60% overlap. You can be pretty sure that you would not find a difference if you took added observations.

```
B        Baseline               Treatment
E   6 |                         |
H   5 |                         |
A   4 |                         |
V   3 |  x           x          |  x            x
I   2 |          x              |          x
O   1 |     x            x      |     x       x
R   0 | ----------------------- | ----------------------
                                5                      10
```

Figure 6-5. Total overlap.

8. In Figure 6-5, the highest points in treatment are equal to the highest points in baseline. There is ______ percent overlap.

trary but it will give you a starting point for learning visual analysis. (See Figures 6-2 through 6-5.) Later you can learn the more subtle rules used by behavior analysts.

In summary, to find overlap, you take four steps. First, you label one condition the larger set and the other condition the smaller set. Second, you count how many observations in the smaller set are larger than the smallest number in the other set. Third, you count how many observations in the larger set are smaller than the largest number in the other set. Fourth, you add the total number of overlaps counted in the second and third steps. Express overlap as a percentage of the total numbers.

Determining Trends

To decide whether the data show a convincing difference, you should also ask if the data for each condition show an unbroken <u>trend</u> converging toward the other condition. To the extent that the numbers do not show a converging trend, a convincing difference exists. A converging trend means that their values are becoming closer. To the extent that they are trending toward each other, you cannot predict that they will continue to show a difference during additional observations. If they do not show a trend toward each other, you can predict a continued difference. You should consider trends that start before the last five observations, but they must continue to the last point in the condition.

How many points show a trend? I will use the rule of thumb that three points that differ in the same direction count as a trend. There can be points in between them that don't reverse the trend. For example, if the points are 5, 6, and 7, you would have a trend. If the points are 5, 6, 6, and 7, you have a trend, since the second 6 is a duplicate. It doesn't reverse the trend, but it doesn't confirm it either. The three numbers 5, 6, and 6 do not yet show a trend.

Be sure to understand the difference between converging and diverging trends. If two sets of numbers show a converging trend, they are becoming more alike. Finding a converging trend raises doubts about whether the numbers will continue to show a difference. The current difference will no longer be convincing. If two sets of numbers show a diverging trend, they are becoming less alike. Finding a diverging trend does not raise doubts about whether the numbers will continue to show a difference; the current differences

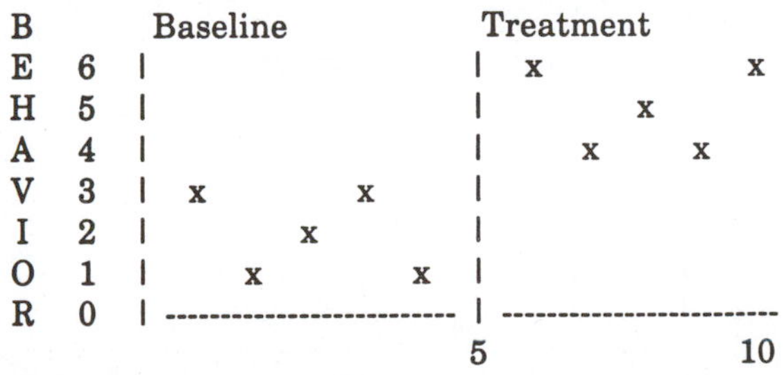

Figure 6-6. No trend. This graph shows no trend at the end of baseline or treatment. The numbers are not tending to get either larger or smaller.

10. In Figure 6-6, the converging trend shown by three points in baseline ________ (is, isn't) broken by a return to the first point. The data are stable. You can be quite confident that you would still find a difference if you gathered added observations.

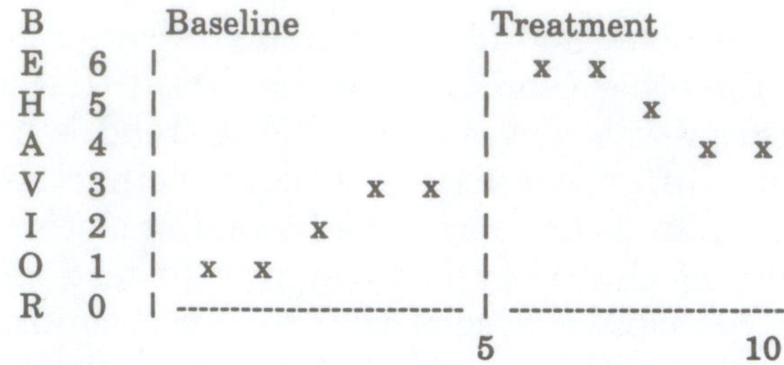

Figure 6-7. Converging trend. The baseline numbers show a trend toward treatment. The treatment numbers show a trend toward the lower values of baseline by getting smaller.

11. In Figure 6-7, the treatment trend ________ (is, isn't) converging toward baseline. You can be quite confident that you would not find a difference if you took added observations.

will be even more convincing. In Figures 6-6 through 6-9, I will show you examples of trends.

9. Because the trends are diverging, you can be quite confident that you ___________ (would, wouldn't) find a difference if you took added observations.

A trend can be broken in two ways. It can be broken by a point that returns to the starting point. For example, if 5, 6, and 7 is followed by another 5, the trend is broken. I am picking this arbitrary rule to get you started using visual analysis. (See Figure 6-10.) Later you can learn the more complex rules that behavior analysts use.

A trend can also be broken by a countertrend. This requires two additional points that return toward the starting point. For example, suppose

```
B        Baseline                 Treatment
E  6  |                          | x                 x
H  5  |                          |           x
A  4  |                          |      x          x
V  3  |                x    x    |
I  2  |           x              |
O  1  |  x    x                  |
R  0  | ------------------------ | ----------------------
                                 5                  10
```

Figure 6-8. Converging baseline. The baseline numbers are getting larger and more like the treatment numbers.

12. In Figure 6-8, the numbers ______ (do, don't) show a converging trend toward treatment. You can be quite confident that the trend would eliminate the difference if you took added observations.

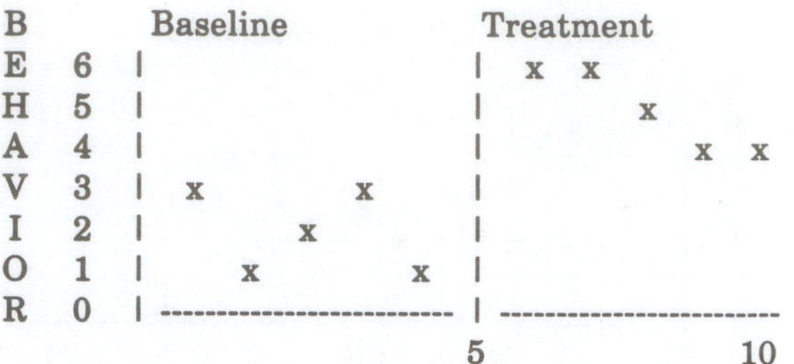

Figure 6-9. Converging treatment. The treatment numbers are getting smaller and more like the baseline numbers.

13. In Figure 6-9, the numbers ______ (do, don't) show a converging trend toward baseline. You can be quite confident that the trend would eliminate the difference if you took added observations.

the trend is 4, 6, and 9. If two additional observations are 8 and 7, the last three points 9, 8, and 7 define a countertrend. Notice that the countertrend doesn't return to the starting point of 4. Another example might be 2, 3, 6, 5, and 3. The three numbers 6, 5, and 3 define a trend counter to the original one. Countertrends can include ties. For example, in the sequence 6, 7, 13, 9, 9, and 8, the four numbers 13, 9, 9, and 8 define a countertrend. (See Figure 6-11.)

Remember, only converging trends that are still unbroken by the end of the condition suggest that future points will move toward the other condition. So a converging trend undermines your confidence in the difference between two conditions only if it continues at the end of the condition. Look for a converging trend at the end of the baseline toward the values in treatment. Look for a converging trend at the end of the treatment toward the values in baseline.

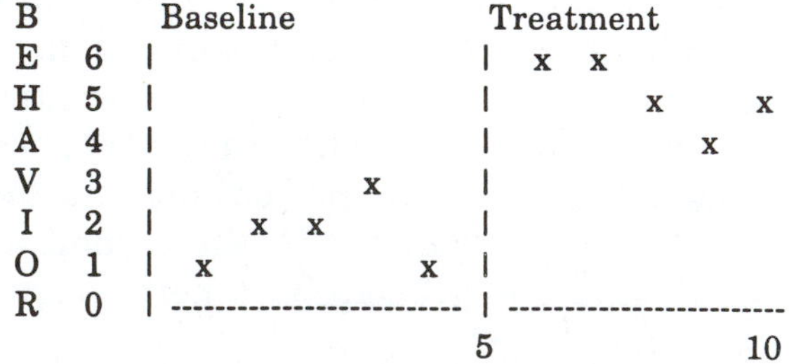

Figure 6-10. Broken trend. The first four observations show a converging trend, but the trend is broken.

14. In Figure 6-10, the trend is broken because point #5 is the same as point # ______.

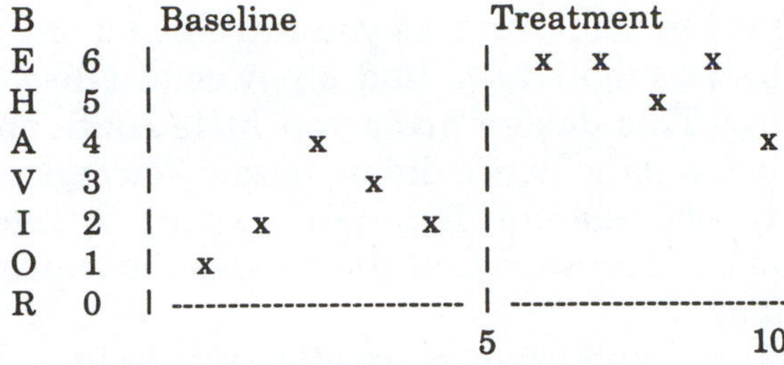

Figure 6-11. Countertrend. The first three points show a converging trend, but there is a countertrend.

15. The trend in Figure 6-11 is broken because an opposite trend is shown by points #3, #4, and # _____.

Ignoring Transition Points

When you answer the questions about overlap and trend, you should ignore any transition period. People often take time to adjust to new conditions. The first few times you walk to your new class may take longer, since you are still a bit unsure where it is. The first few times you see a new person, you may take a few moments to remember her name. After you do something a few times, you may get better at it; you find the new class quickly and remember the new friend immediately. When visually analyzing data, you should ignore overlap between the old condition and the new condition during the transition period. You can count observations during the transition period as part of a trend if it continues unbroken to the end of the condition. In general, you should ignore at least the first three observations at the beginning of a new condition. The rule of looking only at the last five points of any condition will eliminate most transition points. (See Figure 6-12.)

In summary, look at both overlap and trend when visually analyzing data. Be sure to ignore observations during the transition period when doing so. Ask if the data for different conditions overlap and if they trend toward each other. If you find little overlap and no trend, you can conclude that the data show a real difference between conditions. I will examine these questions for the three basic single-subject designs.

Visual Analysis of the Comparison Design

The visual analysis of comparison designs is simple. You look for overlap between the baseline and the treatment observations. You restrict your attention to the last five observations in each condition, to eliminate the transition period. Next, you look for trends. At the end of the baseline, you look for an unbroken trend that is moving toward the treatment values. Then, at the end of the treatment, you look for an unbroken trend that is moving toward the baseline. I will give you examples of both convincing and unconvincing data in a comparison design. I will start with an example that might convince you that a clear change of behavior occurred.

Suppose you want to know whether praising Tommy will increase the percentage of time he studies during study hall. You might select a comparison design, observing Tommy's studying for ten days without praise and ten days with praise

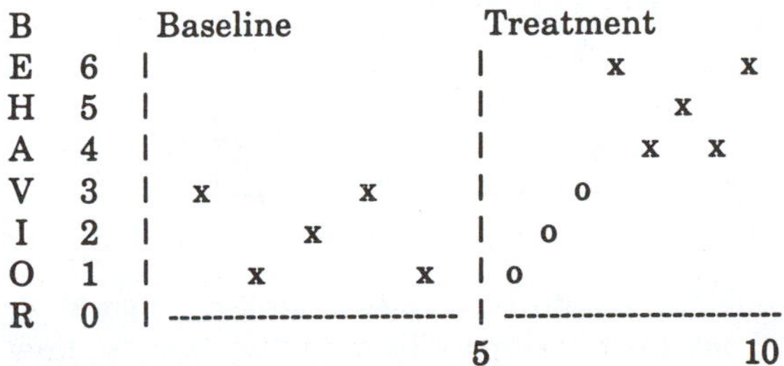

Figure 6-12. Transition. This graph seems to show over 50% overlap between baseline and the first three points of treatment (shown by o's). However, you should ignore those first three points, because the person was still learning. If you ignore these points, baseline and treatment do not overlap. You can be sure that you would still find a difference with added observations.

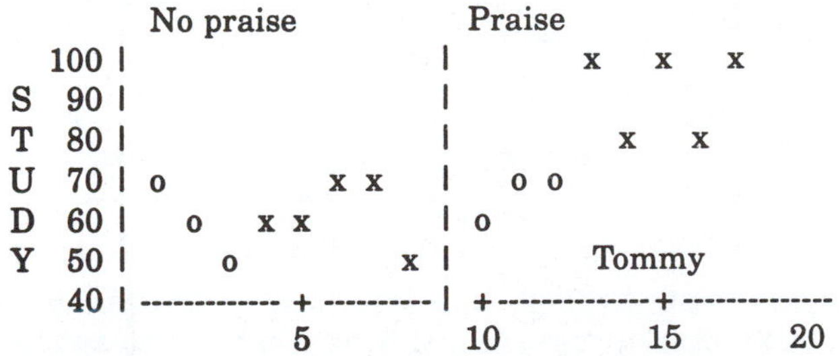

Figure 6-13. A convincing comparison design. Look for overlap. Using only the last five points (x's) in each condition, you find no overlap. Look for a trend. You find a trend toward the end of baseline starting with an "o." Notice that the last point of baseline breaks this trend. Therefore the difference between baseline and treatment is convincing because there is no overlap and no trend.

(Figure 6-13). Suppose you find that Tommy studies about 60% of the time before you praise him and about 90% of the time after you praise him. Is this convincing evidence of a difference?

To analyze Tommy's data correctly, you must ignore the first three points of the treatment condition. During those five days, Tommy is clearly learning to study more because you are praising him. During those days, his studying overlaps with baseline. In fact, 75% of his study times overlap, suggesting no difference. But once he gets it, he starts studying a lot more. He averages about 90% studying for the last five days of treatment. The overlap once he gets it is 0%. Be sure to eliminate transition periods. Focus on the last five days of each condition.

Tommy's data show a trend during points 3 through 6 of baseline: 50, 60, 60, 70, and 70. Each point is either equal to or higher than the previous point. However, the trend is broken by the seventh point, which decreases to 50 again. Notice that you should include trends that start before the last five data points. However, they must continue and remain unbroken by the end of the condition.

In summary, Tommy's data show a clear and stable difference that is convincing.

If you can rule out alternatives, then you can conclude that your praise made a difference. You can rule out individual differences because you have studied only Tommy. Unfortunately, as you already know, comparison designs do not rule out time coincidences. Some event may have happened at about the same time as you introduced praise. That event might have had a powerful effect on studying. This design gives you little confidence that such a coincidence did not occur. You can confidently conclude that Tommy's studying changed, but you can't be sure that praise was the cause of the change.

Before going on to more effective designs, let me show you an example of results with comparison designs that are not as clear. Suppose you want to know whether praising Alicia will increase her studying. You find that Alicia studies about 65% before and about 80% after. Can you be confident that this represents a real change in Alicia's studying? Let's conduct a visual analysis of the data. (See Figure 6-14.)

When analyzing Alicia's data, use only the last five points of each condition to look for overlap. These points are 80, 50, 70, 60, and 60 for baseline and 100, 60, 80, 100, and 60 for treatment. All baseline points equal to or above 60, the lowest point in treatment, overlap with treatment. There are four. All treatment points equal to or below 80, the highest point in baseline, overlap with baseline. See how many you count. Did you get three? That makes a total of seven for each condition. Seven out of ten makes 70% overlap.

In summary, her data show a stable but slight difference, with great amounts of overlap. We cannot be sure that the level of Alicia's studying has changed.

Now let's consider an example of differences that are not convincing because of a trend. Sup-

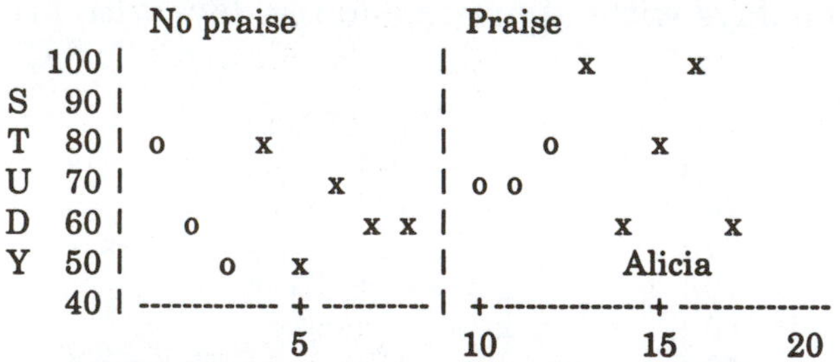

Figure 6-14. **A comparison experiment with overlap. Look for overlap; use the last five x's in baseline and in treatment.**

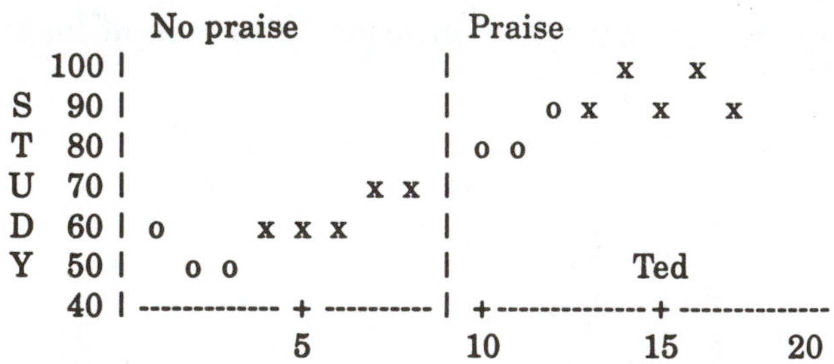

Figure 6-15. **A comparison experiment with a trend. Look for overlaps. There is 0% overlap; now look for trends.**

16. In Figure 6-14, there are _____ overlapping points in baseline and _______ in treatment. Thus, there is 70% overlap. Next, look for trends. There is no converging trend. Because of the overlap, these data do not show convincing evidence of a difference between baseline and treatment.

17. In Figure 6-15, do the last six points in baseline show an unbroken upward trend? _____. Note that this trend starts before the last five points. It suggests that studying was rising during baseline and would have continued even without the treatment. The difference is not convincing.

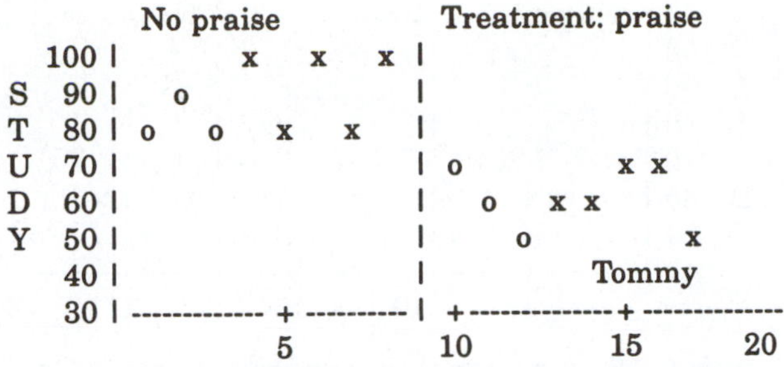

Figure 6-16. A treatment that reduces behavior. Look for overlap. You find none; now look for trends.

18. In Figure 6-16, do the last six points of treatment show an unbroken trend? _____. The difference between baseline and treatment is convincing.

Modifying Cartoonists' Behavior

Cartoons can be very influential. Two researchers noticed that many cartoonists showed their characters in cars without seatbelts; only 15% showed seatbelt usage. The researchers set out to change that. They wanted cartoonists to set a good example for children by showing seatbelt usage. They wrote a letter to eight cartoonists, asking them to do so. They sent the letter after differing amounts of time, thus creating a multiple-baseline design. After their letter, 41% of the cartoons showed seatbelt usage. Thus, cartoonists showed 26% more seatbelt usage after the letter. (Based on Mathews & Dix, 1992.)

19. To see if the difference was real would require a(n) ____________________ analysis.

pose you are studying the effect of praise on Ted's studying. You might find that he studied about 65% of the time during baseline and about 95% during treatment. (See Figure 6-15.)

You analyzed Ted's data by looking first for overlap, and you found none. Then you looked for a trend. You found a trend in the last six observations during baseline: 50, 60, 60, 60, 70, and 70. The trend started with 50 and increased to 70. It remained unbroken at the end of the baseline condition. Note again that you can include more than just the last five points in looking for a trend, but the trend must remain unbroken at the end of the condition. That is because you are looking to see whether the data for the next condition are an extension of the data for this condition.

In summary, Ted's data show a very clear difference between baseline and treatment. But the baseline was unstable and seemed to be leading to the level observed during treatment. This means that the treatment may not be the cause of the higher level of studying.

Analyzing a treatment that reduces behavior is no different from analyzing one that increases behavior—you simply reverse the process. You are now looking for the observations in baseline that are lower than the highest treatment values, instead of the other way around. Likewise, you are looking for trends at the end of baseline that decrease toward treatment. You look for trends at the end of treatment that increase back up toward baseline. (See Figure 6-16.)

In summary, here's how you visually analyze data from a comparison experiment. You ask whether the observations in baseline and treatment overlap, looking only at the last five observations to avoid transitions. If the treatment was designed to increase the behavior, you count the number of baseline observations that are as large as the smallest treatment observation. You count the number of treatment observations that are as small as the highest baseline observation. If more than 50% overlap, the difference is not convincing. You reverse the process if the treatment was designed to decrease the behavior.

After asking if points overlap, you ask if the data for either condition show an unbroken trend toward the data for the other condition. You look for three points during baseline that change consistently toward the treatment values. These points may have duplicate points in between them that don't change. You must check to see if a later point returns to the initial value of the three points. If so, this breaks the trend. You must also look to see whether the data show a countertrend. If so, this would also break the trend. You must also look to see if three points during treatment converge toward the baseline values. When examining trends, you should consider trends that start before the last five data points. If you find an unbroken trend bringing the conditions together, then the differences are not convincing.

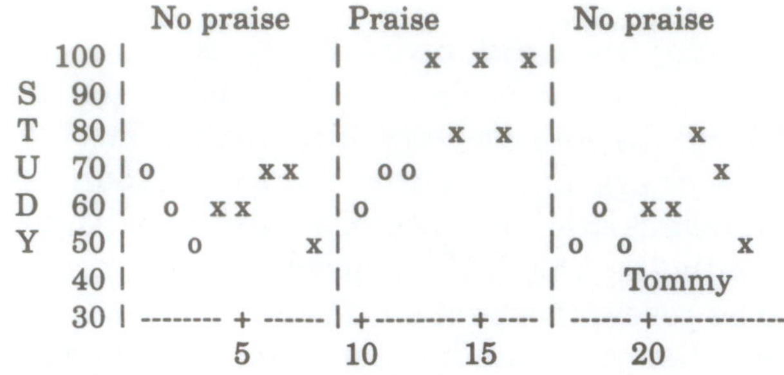

Figure 6-17. A convincing reversal design. Look for overlap.

20. In Figure 6-17, you find 0% baseline to treatment and _____ percent treatment to reversal. Look for trends. You find trends in baseline and reversal, but they are both broken. The difference between baseline and treatment and between treatment and reversal is convincing.

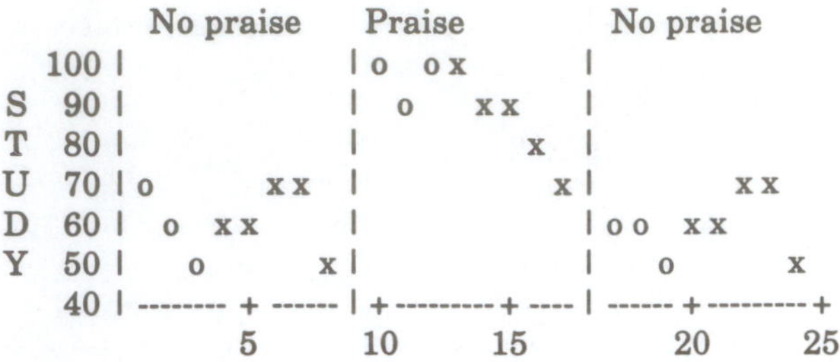

Figure 6-18. A reversal design with a trend. Can you spot the trend before reading further? Look for overlap. Baseline to treatment is 30%; treatment to reversal is 30%. Both are below 50%. Look for trends.

21. In Figure 6-18, is there a trend from baseline to treatment? _____. Is there a trend from treatment toward reversal (or baseline)? _____. We can't be confident that these data show a difference.

Visual Analysis of Reversal Designs

As you recall, reversal designs start out as comparison designs. You make them into reversal designs by adding one more condition, which is the same as the initial condition. This is called a reversal to baseline. You could easily make the comparison design for Tommy's studying into a reversal design. All you need to do is stop praising him for eight days and observe his level of studying. The visual analysis of Tommy's data is easy. You ask whether the observations in baseline and treatment overlap. Then you ask whether the observations in treatment and reversal overlap. If more than 50% overlap, then the behavior change associated with treatment is not convincing. You ask whether the observations in baseline trend toward treatment. Then you ask whether the observations in treatment trend toward reversal. If you find a trend, then the behavioral change associated with treatment is not convincing. (See Figure 6-17.)

Tommy's data show large differences with little overlap. They show no converging trend. You can be pretty sure that the level during each condition would remain the same even if you made another 100 observations. You can conclude with confidence that Tommy's amount of studying changed each time praise changed.

If you can rule out alternatives, then you can conclude that praise caused Tommy to study more. The reversal design rules out alternatives by making them unlikely. Tommy might have started studying more after day 8 because of something his mother said to him. A coincidence of that sort could happen. Tommy might have stopped studying after day 16 because the new topic was less interesting. A coincidence of that sort could happen. But it is very unlikely that such coincidences would have occurred after both day 8 and after day 16. Thus, the chance of an alternative factor accounting for both the increase and the decrease is very low. You can conclude with great confidence that praise caused the change in Tommy's studying.

Now remember, if you are still not convinced, you can always reverse once more. After day 24, you can start praising Tommy again for studying. If his studying once again increases, then you can be even more sure that praise caused the change. The chance of a third coincidence is extremely low.

Let's look at a reversal design that shows a trend. Suppose that you tried the praise experiment with Dave. He shows 60% during baseline, 85% during treatment, and 60% during reversal. (See Figure 6-18.) Can you be confident that these data show a real difference between treatment and nontreatment?

You looked at Dave's data. You found reasonable overlap. However, when you looked at the data 100, 90, 90, 80, and 70, you saw an unbroken converging trend. Each new observation showed an equal or lower number. This is a strong trend, because it consists of four decreasing values. The data tell us that praise may have had an initial effect, but then the effect disappeared. The trend suggests that Dave's level of studying would have gone to the reversal level even without stopping the praise. You can have no confidence that treatment produced more than a momentary effect.

In summary, here's how you visually analyze data from a reversal experiment. You ask whether the observations in baseline and treatment overlap; then you ask whether the observations in treatment and reversal overlap. If more than 50% overlap, then the behavior change associated with treatment is not convincing. Next, you ask whether the observations in baseline trend toward treatment; then you ask whether the observations in treatment trend toward reversal. If you find a converging trend, the behavioral change associated with treatment is not convincing.

Visual Analysis of Multiple-Baseline Experiments

Multiple-baseline designs also start out as comparison designs. You make them into multiple-baseline designs by adding a second behavioral variable. You rule out the possibility of coincidences by adding a second behavior, person, or situation. You must also start the treatment for the second behavioral variable at a different time than you started it with the first behavioral variable. You have ruled out coincidences if the behavior changes only after treatment.

You can make the comparison design with Tommy into a multiple-baseline design. All you have to do is add Marie as the second subject. You would retain the ten-day baseline with Tommy and

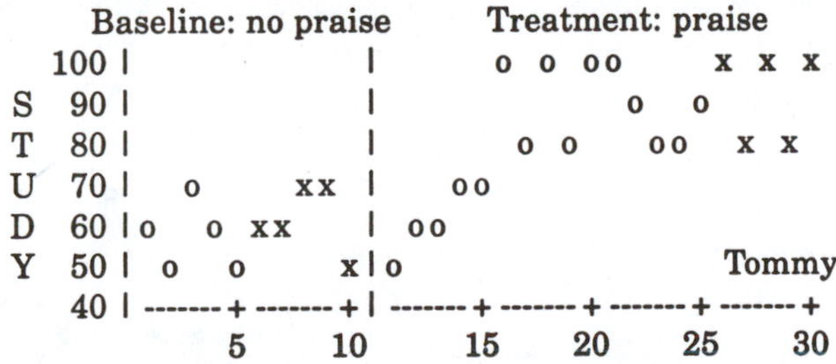

Figure 6-19. First part of a multiple-baseline experiment.

22. In Figure 6-19, what is the overlap between baseline and treatment? ________ percent. Is there a converging trend in either condition? ________. Because you find no overlap and no converging trend, Tommy's data are convincing evidence that there is a difference.

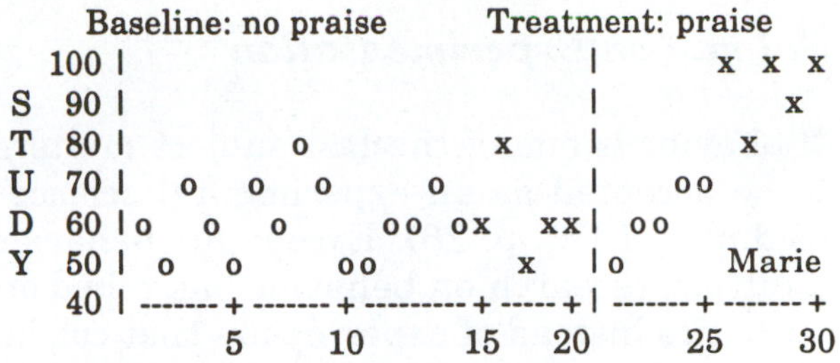

Figure 6-20. Second part of a multiple-baseline experiment.

23. In Figure 6-20, the overlap between conditions is ________ percent. Because this is not over 50%, you can conclude that there is acceptable overlap. Do you find a converging trend? ______. Because overlap is acceptable and there is no trend, you can have confidence that the treatment is different from the baseline.

introduce praise on day 11, but now you would add Marie. You would make her baseline longer than Tommy's—perhaps 20 days. Then you would introduce treatment for ten days. Notice that you would also extend Tommy's treatment condition to day 30. You would visually analyze each person's data separately, using the same approach as you used with comparison designs. See Figures 6-19 and 6-20.

You visually analyzed this multiple-baseline design by comparing the last five points of each condition. That analysis showed small overlap and no trends. You could have strengthened your analysis with one more check. If some time coincidence occurred at day 10 for Tommy, it might also occur at the same time for Marie. You can check that by looking for an upward trend in Marie's data during days 10 to 19. Her data are 50, 50, 60, 60, 70, 60, 60, 80, 50, 60, and 60. As you can see, a small trend started upward, but it was broken by a return to 50 later on. I will not insist on you making this added analysis, but it can be helpful.

Finally, let's look at ruling out alternatives. When you start praising Tommy but not Marie, only Tommy's studying increases. You could propose an alternative explanation only if it happened to Tommy but not Marie. Next, notice that when you start praising Marie and keep praising Tommy, Marie's studying increases. You could propose an alternative explanation only if it happened to Marie but not Tommy. The different timing required for both coincidences is highly unlikely.

Sidman on Experimentation

"Behavior is one of the last subject matters to be accepted as an experimental science" (Sidman, 1960: p. 26). Except for behavior analysis, research on behavior has relied on statistics instead of experiments that can be visually analyzed.

24. Behavior analysts assume that the study of behavior is an experimental science. They analyze their experiments using the principle of visual ________________.

Therefore, you can conclude that an alternative explanation is unlikely.

The data show little overlap, and they show no trend. The design and results greatly reduce the probability of an alternative explanation. Therefore, you can conclude with confidence that praise increases the studying of these two students. You have found an effective way of improving their studying time!

In summary, here's how you visually analyze data from a multiple-baseline experiment. You ask whether the observations in baseline and treatment overlap for the first behavioral variable. Then you ask whether they overlap for the second behavioral variable. If you find more than 50% overlap, then the behavior change associated with treatment is not convincing. You ask whether the observations in baseline trend toward treatment for the first behavioral variable. Then you ask whether they trend toward treatment for the second behavioral variable. If you find a converging trend, then the behavioral change associated with treatment is not convincing.

Summary

In this lesson, you learned that the fifth tactic in using the behavioral strategy is to visually analyze the data. The principle of visual analysis is to look for convincing differences. You look to see if the observations in each condition overlap by more than 50%. You look to see if there is a converging trend. If the observations do not overlap and do not show a trend toward less difference, then the results convincingly show a difference. If you have ruled out alternative explanations with a single-subject design, you can conclude that the treatment caused the difference.

Behavior Analysis Examples

(Note: Actual behavior analysis experiments are often not as neat as the hypothetical examples in this chapter. Sometimes they do not have enough points to avoid transitions and still permit you to look at five points at the end of the condition. I have therefore guided you to look at fewer points; look only at the x's.)

Changing Police Behavior

Police in Greeley, Colorado were reluctant to give tickets for failure to use child safety seats. They felt it unfair if the parents were obeying the law in every other way. Lavelle and her colleagues knew that safety seats could save children from serious injuries.

Lavelle and her colleagues convinced the police to change procedures. The new procedure permitted the police to give a coupon when they issued a ticket. Drivers could use the coupon to attend a one-hour class on child safety and to get a child safety seat. If they did, the courts would waive the $50 fine. In this way, the parents could

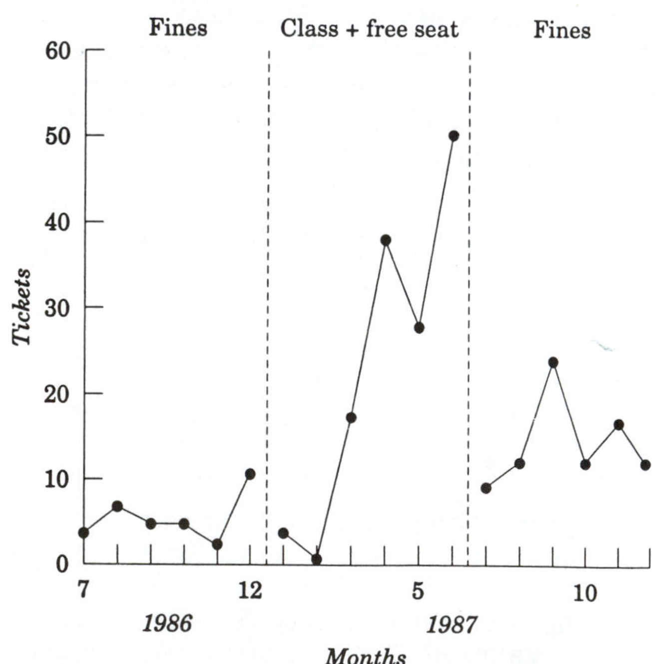

Figure 6-21. Results of an experiment to change police behavior. This shows the number of tickets for not placing infants in safety seats.

learn why safety seats are important. Also, they could get a safety seat even if they could not afford one. The police could feel better about issuing such a ticket. For the results, see Figure 6-21.

To decide whether the coupon procedure caused police to write more tickets, you must ask two questions. First, you ask if there is a convincing difference between conditions. To decide, you look for overlap among the last three points and converging trend. You find neither. Therefore, you can conclude that there is a convincing difference. Second, you ask if you can rule out alternative explanations. That is, is it likely that some other event than the coupon caused the difference? Lavelle used a reversal design that rules out alternatives. Therefore, you can conclude that other alternatives are unlikely; the coupon did cause the difference. You can be pretty sure that the coupon procedure caused the police to write more tickets. (Based on an article by Lavelle, Hovel, West, & Wahlgren, 1992. The data are rounded off to values consistent with the grid used in this figure.)

Helping the Elderly Remember

Talking with your aging relatives can be hard. They tend to ramble on; they say confusing things and ignore what you have said. Bourgeois guessed that helping their memory might improve their conversations. She made a memory booklet for six elderly people suffering from Alzheimer's. Each page of the booklet contained one fact and a relevant photo. Some pages contained facts such as name, relatives, birthplace, and dates. Other pages of the booklet contained the daily schedule and the names and photos of people who helped bathe and feed Anna. Booklets contained 20 to 40 facts. Bourgeois gave the booklets to the elderly people to use during conversations. (See Figure 6-22.)

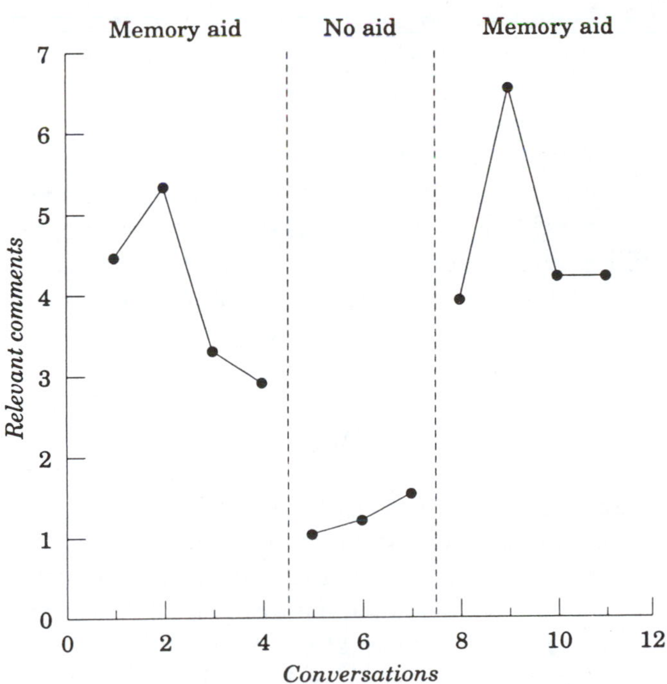

Figure 6-22. Results of an experiment helping old folks remember. The data show the number of relevant comments made by the elderly person during conversations.

Notice that this design is backward. The first condition involves the treatment. The second condition involves no treatment and is thus the baseline. The reversal returns the person to the treatment condition. Your visual analysis followed the same logic as a forward reversal design.

25. The data in Figure 6-22 show no overlap or trends. Are you convinced that there is a difference between conditions? ______. The use of a reversal design rules out alternatives. Can you conclude that the memory aid caused an increase in relevant comments? ______. (Based on Bourgeois, 1993. The data have been rounded off.)

Notes

Note #1

Most behavior analysts argue that the use of statistics has not helped find strong causal relationships. It rewards researchers for finding weak relationships. After earning a Ph.D. in social psychology, I examined the stength of statistically significant relationships reported in one journal. I found that about 100 significant relationships on the average explained only about 7% of the data (Miller, 1968). In other words, they left 93% unexplained! I soon changed my field to behavior analysis.

Statistics have not been helpful for a second reason. Researchers often use statistics to analyze correlations between variables. When they find a relationship, even if it is strong, they do not know if it is causal. If boys are more assertive than girls, there is a correlation. But the correlation doesn't provide evidence that male genes cause assertive behavior. The correlation could come from most adults encouraging assertive behavior in males and discouraging it in females. In other words, the correlation could come from other variables that the researcher has not measured. Single-subject experiments provide much stronger evidence of causality. When the researcher introduces the treatment and the behavior changes, we can be much more confident that the treatment caused the change. We can continue to turn the effect on and off until we are satisfied that the treatment is the causal agent.

26. All natural science recognizes the superiority of ________________ (experiments, correlations).

Note #2

The problem with statistics comes from what is called *inferential* statistics. Using inferential statistics, researchers infer whether two sets of data show a real difference. Descriptive statistics consist of methods to describe large amounts of data simply. These methods include means, correlations, and percent of explained variance. Behavior analysts rarely use inferential statistics, but they often use descriptive statistics.

Note #3

There are additional considerations in evaluating graphical data, beyond overlap and trend. They include variability within and between conditions, number of data points and trends within conditions, changes in trend between conditions, comparison of similar conditions, and the overall pattern of the data. Parsonson and Baer (1978) describe many of these considerations. They also present additional information on how to create and present graphical data.

27. Are overlap and trend the only considerations in visual analysis? _____

Note #4

Behavior analysts sometimes use inferential statistics to analyze their data. Sometimes these statistics can help them tease out very subtle or very complicated relationships. Some behavior analysts object to using inferential statistics even in these rare cases.

Helpful Hints

Helpful Hint #1

There are two steps in deciding whether data support the conclusion that a treatment causes a change in behavior. First, you must determine whether the data confirm a difference between conditions. You must eliminate overlap and trend to confirm a difference. In many questions, to save space, I will abbreviate questions covering this aspect of the data as "Overlap?," "Trend?," and "Convincing difference?" Second, if there is a difference, then you must decide whether the design rules out alternative explanations. If it does, then you can conclude that the treatment causes a change in behavior. I will often abbreviate that question as "Conclude cause?" to save space.

28. In order to save space in some questions, I will abbreviate questions related to the difference between conditions as follows: "Convincing ____________?" I may also abbreviate questions related to whether a treatment causes a change in behavior as follows: "Conclude ____________?"

Helpful Hint #2

Use the same approach to analyze backward designs as you would use to analyze standard designs. You still must ask if the conditions overlap and if the data for one condition trend toward those for another condition.

29. Thus, you use ___________ (a different, the same) approach for backward designs as for standard designs.

Helpful Hint #3

If you have trouble with division, be sure to use a calculator for this lesson. Otherwise, you will understand the idea but get the wrong answer. Use decimals to two digits, but do not use decimal parts of percentages (e.g., 75%, not 75.1%).

Additional Readings

Baer, D. (1977). Perhaps it would be better not to know everything. *Journal of Applied Behavior Analysis, 10*, 167–172. An excellent description of the reasons most applied behavior analysts do not rely on statistical inference to determine whether they have found an important treatment effect.

Jones, R. R., Weinrott, M. R., & Vaught, R. S. (1978). Effects of serial dependency on the agreement between visual and statistical analysis. *Journal of Applied Behavior Analysis, 11*, 277–283. This article gives the other side of the story. It suggests that visual interpretation of data is unreliable.

Kratochwill, T. R., & Brody, G. H. (1978). Single-subject designs: A perspective on the controversy over employing statistical inference and implications for research and training in behavior modification. *Behavior Modification, 2*, 291–307. A discussion of recent trends in the use of statistical inference in behavior modification. The authors argue that statistical inference is used even in *Journal of Applied Behavior Analysis* (but by less than 20% of the articles) and that it should be used more often.

Michael, J. (1974). Statistical inference for single-subject research: Mixed blessing or curse? *Journal of Applied Behavior Analysis, 7*, 647–653. A discussion of the implications of using statistical inference in conjunction with single-subject designs.

Miller, L. K. (1968). Determinancy versus risk: A critique of contemporary statistical methodology in sociology. *Kansas Journal of Sociology, 4*, 71–78. This paper describes a method for assessing the strength of relationships. It reports on all statistically significant findings in one year's *American Sociological Review*. The average strength of relationship was about 7% of the variance explained.

Parsonson, B. S., & Baer, D. M. (1978a). The analysis and presentation of graphic data. In T. R. Kratochwill (Ed.), *Single-subject research: Strategies for evaluating change*. New York: Academic Press. This article provides detailed consideration of how to conduct visual analysis. The authors consider factors in addition to trend and overlap.

Reading Quiz

77. To use the behavioral strategy: (1) create a behavioral definition, (2) use a method of direct observation, (3) check the reliability and social validity of your observations, (4) design a single-subject experiment, and (5) do a(n) ______________ (statistical, visual) analysis of your data.
8. Behavior analysts decide whether their treatment makes a difference by using ______________ (statistical, visual) analysis.
97. Analyzing the results of an experiment requires two steps. First, you decide whether the difference between conditions is convincing. Second, if it is, you decide whether the design rules out ______________ explanations. If it does, then you can conclude that the treatment caused the difference.
32. Review: Finding differences that look <u>convincing</u> is the principle of ______________ analysis.
68. The principle of visual analysis is to find differences that look ______________ (convincing, interesting).
74. To decide whether data look convincing, begin by asking if the observations in each condition have high ______________ (overlap, trend).
46. Review: Using the principle of visual analysis involves looking for high overlap in order to decide if differences are ______________.
72. Think about this question carefully. The more the observations for different conditions overlap, the ______ (less, more) different they are.
47. Review: When you are looking for overlap, look only at the last ________ observations in each condition.
73. To compute overlap between two sets of numbers, start by labeling the set with the larger numbers the larger set. Then label the other set as the ______________ set.
67. The overlap between the smaller set of 2, 3, and 4 and the larger set of 4, 5, and 6 is obviously the number 4 in each set. The number 4 in the smaller set is equal to the smallest number in the larger set. The number 4 in the larger set is equal to the ______________ (largest, smallest) number in the smaller set.
86. What numbers overlap between the smaller set of 2, 3, and 5 and the larger set of 4, 6, and 7? The number 5 in the smaller set overlaps, because it is larger than the smallest number in the larger set. The number 4 in the larger set overlaps, because it is smaller than the ______________ (largest, smallest) number in the smaller set.
87. What numbers overlap between the sets 8, 11, and 13 and 12, 14, and 16? You start by finding how many numbers in the first set are larger than the ______________ (largest, smallest) number in the other set. The 13 is larger than the 12.
88. What numbers overlap between the sets 8, 11, and 13 and 12, 14, and 16? You next find

how many numbers in the second set are smaller than the ______________ (largest, smallest) number in the first set. The 12 is smaller than the 13.

89. What numbers overlap between the sets 8, 11, and 13 and 12, 14, and 16? Once you know that the 13 in the first set and the 12 in the second set overlap, you count them to find that there are a total of __________ out of the six numbers that overlap. Finally, you divide 2 by 6 and convert to a percentage to get 33%.

11. Computing overlap is easy if the numbers are arranged from lowest to highest. Often they are not. To find the overlap between the sets 1, 5, 2, 4, and 5 and 6, 9, 5, 7, and 7, you start by finding the ______________ (highest, lowest) number in the second set. Then you count any number in the first set that is equal or higher. How many numbers is that? ______

69. The second step to find the overlap between the sets 1, 5, 2, 4, and 5 and 6, 9, 5, 7, and 7 is to find the ______________ (highest, lowest) number in the first set. Then you count any number in the second set that is equal or lower. How many numbers is that? ____

66. The final step in finding the overlap between the sets 1, 5, 2, 4, and 5 and 6, 9, 5, 7, and 7 is to count the number of numbers that overlap and divide by the number of numbers. Thus, you divide 3 by ________ and convert to a percent to get 30%.

34. Review: Suppose you are studying a low baseline and a treatment that increases behavior. Look for high overlap by counting the number of the last five observations during baseline that are ________ (higher, lower) than, or equal to, the lowest observation during treatment.

60. Suppose you are studying a treatment that increases behavior. First, look for high overlap by counting the number of the last five observations during baseline that are higher than, or equal to, the lowest observation during treatment. Second, count the number of the last five observations during treatment that are ______________ (higher, lower) than the highest observation during baseline.

10. Compute overlap between the sets 1, 3, 2, 1, and 3 and 3, 6, 5, 5, and 6 by dividing the total number of overlapping points during baseline and treatment by _______.

50. Suppose I ask you to compute the percent of numbers that overlap with the following two sets: 1, 1, 2, 3, and 3 and 3, 4, 5, 5, and 6. First, identify the high and low sets. Next, count the number of overlaps in the low set, and the number of overlaps in the high set. Then divide by the total number of numbers and convert to a percent. Overlap equals ______ percent.

35. Review: The differences between two conditions are not convincing if more than _______ percent of the observations overlap.

90. When I ask if two conditions have high overlap, I am asking whether they overlap more than what is acceptable. Specifically, I am asking whether they overlap more than _______ percent.

49. Suppose I ask you if the sets 1, 4, 2, 3, and 5 and 7, 5, 8, 7, and 9 have high overlap. You might say "yes," because both sets have a 5. However, I am asking whether they overlap more than 50%. Do these two sets have high overlap? ____

14. Do the sets 7, 9, 8, 9, and 7 and 5, 4, 6, 7, and 6 have high overlap? _____. Do the sets 12, 16, 12, 13, and 13 and 7, 9, 12, 7, and 13 have high overlap? _______. The answer to the first question is "no," because the overlap is 30%. The answer to the second question is "yes" because the overlap is 60%.

51. Suppose the baseline data are 3, 1, 2, 3, and 1, and the treatment data are 6, 4, 5, 4, and 6. The percent overlap is ______%. Do these two sets have high overlap? ____. Thus, the difference between baseline and treatment is convincing as far as overlap goes, although you still must look for a converging trend.

52. Suppose the baseline data are 3, 1, 2, 3, and 1, and the treatment data are 5, 3, 4, 3, and 5. Find the lowest treatment value. Count how many baseline values are equal to or larger. _____. Find the highest baseline value. Count how many treatment values are equal to or smaller. _____. Add those two counts together. Then divide by 10. Overlap equals _______ percent. Do these conditions have high overlap? _____. Thus, the differences are convincing as far as overlap goes, although you still must look for a converging trend.

53. Suppose the baseline data are 3, 1, 2, 3, and 1, and the treatment data are 4, 2, 3, 2, and 4. Count how many baseline values overlap with treatment. _____. Count how many treatment values overlap with baseline. _____. Add those

two counts together. Then divide by the number of numbers. Overlap equals ______ percent. Do these conditions have high overlap? ____. The difference between baseline and treatment is not convincing.

54. Suppose the baseline data are 3, 1, 2, 3, and 1, and the treatment data are 3, 1, 2, 1, and 3. Count how many baseline values overlap. ___. Count how many treatment values overlap. ____ Overlap equals _____ percent. Do these conditions have high overlap? ____. The difference between baseline and treatment is not convincing.
55. Suppose the baseline numbers are 3, 1, 2, 3, and 1, and the treatment numbers are 1, 2, 3, 6, 6, 5, 4, and 4. You might guess that treatment overlaps with baseline because of the first three numbers of treatment. However, you should exclude them from overlap and look only at the last __________ points in treatment. You should ask if those last five points overlap with baseline. Because they do not, the difference between baseline and treatment is convincing as far as overlap goes.
70. Think about this question carefully. The more the observations for different conditions overlap, the _______ (less, more) convincing their differences.
83. Using the principle of visual analysis involves looking for high overlap in order to find differences that look __________.
5. After computing overlap, the next question to ask in deciding whether data show a convincing difference is whether the conditions show a converging ____________________ (overlap, trend) toward each other.
71. Think about this question carefully. If the data in a condition show a converging trend, the differences with another condition are ______ (less, more) convincing.
84. Using the principle of visual analysis involves looking for converging trends to decide whether differences look ______________.
33. Review: I have instructed you to look for high overlap only in the last five points in each condition. Here is a question with a different number as its answer. The fewest number of points that can show a trend is _____.
3. A trend toward higher values requires that each of three (or more) numbers is _________ (higher, lower) than the previous number.
21. If each of five numbers is higher than or equal to the previous number (as with 3, 4, 4, 5, and 5), do they show a trend? _____
22. In order to be a converging trend, a trend has to continue until the ______________ (beginning, end) of a condition.
2. A trend is broken when a new observation is equal to the __________ (first, last) number in the trend.
1. A countertrend ____________ (does, doesn't) break a trend.
61. Suppose you observe 1, 2, 3, 4, and 3. Does the last 3 break the trend? ____. Suppose you observe 1, 2, 3, 4, and 1. Does the last 1 break the trend? ____
62. Suppose you observe 1, 2, 3, 4, 3, and 2. Does the last 2 break the trend? ____. Suppose you observe 1, 2, 3, 4, 2, and 3. Does the last 3 break the trend? ____
63. Suppose you observe 6, 5, 4, and 6. Is the initial downward trend broken? ____. Suppose you observe 4, 6, 9, and 5. Is the trend broken? ____
20. If a trend toward another condition is broken, you would not say that the condition has a converging trend. Only if the trend remains unbroken to the end of the condition do you say that the condition ________ (has, hasn't) a converging trend.
31. Review: Do the numbers 1, 3, 5, 6, and 4 have a converging trend toward a higher set of numbers? ____. Do the numbers 3, 5, 5, 6, and 3 have a converging trend with a higher set of numbers? _____. Do the numbers 5, 6, 7, 7, and 6 have a converging trend with a higher set of numbers? _____
29. Remember, the numbers 7, 9, 11, 12, and 7 do not have a converging trend because the trend _______ (is, isn't) broken.
93. You might think of it this way. The numbers 14, 17, 19, 19, and 14 contain some numbers that trend toward higher numbers. But because the trend is broken, the whole set of numbers _______ (does, doesn't) have a converging trend.
28. Remember that I told you to look for overlap only with the last five observations in a condition. With a trend, you should normally look only during the last five observations in a condition. However, a trend ___________ (can, can't) start before the last five numbers of the condition.

13. Diverging trends, where the values in different conditions grow apart, do not make differences less convincing. Converging trends, where values in different conditions grow together, make differences ______ (less, more) convincing.
56. Suppose the baseline numbers are 3, 3, 2, 1, and 1, and the treatment numbers are 4, 5, 5, 6, and 6. Do the baseline numbers form a converging trend? ______. Since they are steadily decreasing, they are diverging from the larger numbers.
57. Suppose the baseline numbers are 1, 1, 2, 3, and 3, and the treatment numbers are 6, 4, 5, 6, and 4. Do the baseline numbers trend toward treatment? ______. The difference between baseline and treatment is not convincing because of this trend.
58. Suppose the baseline numbers are 3, 1, 2, 3, and 1, and the treatment numbers are 6, 6, 5, 4, and 4. You look to see that the baseline numbers don't trend toward the treatment numbers. Then you look to see if the initial increase in the behavior during treatment starts to disappear over time. If it does, you can't be sure that the difference will hold up over time. Do the numbers in the treatment show a trend toward decreasing values? ____. The difference between baseline and treatment is not convincing because of this trend.
59. Suppose the baseline numbers are 3, 1, 2, 3, and 1, and the treatment numbers are 6, 4, 5, 4, and 6. Do the baseline numbers show an unbroken trend toward treatment? ______. Notice that the middle numbers (1, 2, and 3) trend toward treatment, but the last number, 1, returns to the first number. This is a broken trend. Do the treatment numbers trend toward baseline? ______. Because there are no converging trends, the differences between baseline and treatment ______ (are, aren't) convincing.
40. Review: To decide if data are convincing, ask if the observations in different conditions have high ______________ with each other or if they show a converging ______________ toward each other.
4. A visual analysis of comparison designs involves looking for high overlap and converging trends in the baseline and ____________ conditions.
85. Using the principle of visual analysis involves looking for high overlap and converging trends to decide if differences between conditions look ____________.
64. Suppose you use a comparison design to study a treatment that increases behavior. You wish to do a visual analysis of the data. Look for high overlap. Count the number of the last five observations during baseline that are higher than, or equal to, the lowest observation during treatment. Then count the number of the last five observations during treatment that are __________ (higher, lower) than or equal to the highest observation during baseline. Next, find out whether you have a converging trend between the baseline and treatment conditions.
81. Tommy's studying data are:

    Baseline: 60, 60, 70, 70, 50
    Treatment: 100, 80, 100, 80, 100

    Look for high overlap. How many baseline points overlap with the lowest treatment points? ______. How many treatment points overlap with the highest baseline point? ____. You find that the conditions overlap ________ percent.
82. Tommy's studying data are:

    Baseline: 60, 60, 70, 70, 50
    Treatment: 100, 80, 100, 80, 100

    Now look for converging trends. Do the baseline points show a converging trend toward treatment? __________. Do the treatment points show a converging trend toward baseline? ______. Do you find the values in either condition trending toward the other? ______
79. Tommy's data were:

    Baseline: 60, 60, 70, 70, 50
    Treatment: 100, 80, 100, 80, 100

    Your visual analysis found no high overlap and no converging trends. Can you conclude there is a convincing <u>difference</u>? ____. The comparison design rules out individual differences. It does not rule out ____________ coincidences. Can you conclude that the praise <u>caused</u> the differences? _____
7. Because people take time to adjust to new conditions, you __________ (should, shouldn't) consider the first few observations in a condition when asking about overlap.

6. Alicia's study data are:

Baseline:
(90, 80, 80, 60, 50), 80, 50, 70, 60, 60
Treatment:
(60, 60, 70, 70, 80), 100, 60, 80, 100, 60

Do a visual analysis. Look for high overlap. Remember to look at only the last five points in each condition (those not in parentheses). The lowest treatment point (among the last five points) is ________. How many (of the last five) baseline points are equal to or higher? ______. The highest baseline point (among the last 5) is _____. How many treatment points are as low or lower? _______. The total overlap is ______ percent. Do these data show a convincing difference? _____

65. Tyrell's study data are:

Baseline:
(50, 50, 60, 50, 50), 60, 60, 60, 70, 70
Treatment:
(70, 70, 80, 80, 90), 100, 100, 90, 100, 100

Do a visual analysis. Look for high overlap. Remember to use only the last five points (those not in parentheses). Overlap equals ______%. Look for converging trends. Remember that a trend can start before the last five points but must continue to the end of the condition. Do the baseline data show a converging trend toward treatment? ________. Therefore, these data do not show a convincing difference between conditions. Since they don't, you needn't consider whether the design rules out alternative explanations.

80. Tommy's disruptive behavior data are:

Baseline:
(100, 90, 80, 90, 80), 100, 80, 100, 80, 100
Treatment:
(90, 90, 80, 70, 60), 50, 60, 60, 70, 70

Do a visual analysis. Look for high overlap. Remember to use only the last five points. Overlap equals ______%. Look for converging trends. Remember that a converging trend can start before the last five points but must be unbroken to the end of the condition. Do the baseline data show a trend toward treatment? ____. Therefore, these data show a convincing difference between conditions.

16. Here's how you visually analyze a comparison design. Look for high ___________. Look only at the last ___________ observations in baseline and treatment. If the percent overlap is more than ____%, then the overlap between baseline and treatment is so high that the differences are not convincing.

17. Here's how you visually analyze a comparison design. After looking for high overlap, next look for converging _____________. The trend can start prior to the last five points. It must remain unbroken at the end of the condition. It must involve a minimum of ____ points that progressively change toward the values in the other condition. You must look for baseline trending toward treatment. You must also look for treatment trending toward ________________________.

75. In a comparison design, it takes two steps to decide whether treatment causes any differences found. First, decide whether the difference is convincing. This requires looking for high overlap or a converging trend. Second, if there is a convincing difference, then ask if the design rules out alternative explanations. Since it rules out individual differences but not time coincidences, you _____ (can, can't) conclude from a comparison design that a treatment causes a difference.

18. Here's how you visually analyze a reversal design. You look for high overlap between baseline and treatment. Then you look for high overlap between treatment and _____________. Next, you look for converging trends. You look to see if the baseline trends toward treatment. Then you look to see if treatment trends toward ______________. Finally you look to see if the reversal trends toward treatment.

45. Review: Tommy's study data are:

Baseline:
(60, 50, 70, 60, 50), 60, 60, 70, 70, 50
Treatment:
(50, 60, 60, 70, 70), 100, 80, 100, 80, 100
Reversal:
(90, 70, 50, 60, 50), 60, 60, 80, 70, 50

Look for high overlap. Earlier you found no overlap for baseline and treatment. Now find the treatment-to-reversal overlap. _____%. Look for converging trends. Earlier you found no converging trend from baseline to treatment. You also found no converging trend from treatment to reversal. Is there an unbroken trend from reversal back toward treatment? ________. Are the differences between baseline, treatment, and reversal convincing? ____

92. You found that the differences between Tommy's conditions are convincing. Does a reversal design allow you to rule out alternative explanations of the differences? ______. Therefore, you can conclude that the treatment caused Tommy to study ________ (less, more).

12. Dave's study data are:

Baseline:
(60, 50, 70, 60, 50), 60, 60, 70, 70, 50
Treatment:
(80, 90, 100, 90, 100), 100, 90, 90, 80, 70
Reversal:
(70, 70, 60, 60, 50), 60, 60, 70, 70, 50

Look for high overlap. Baseline to treatment is _____%. Treatment to reversal is ______%. Look for converging trends. Is baseline trending toward treatment? ___________. Is treatment trending toward reversal? ______. Is reversal trending toward treatment? ______

91. You found 30% overlap between Dave's conditions. Should you conclude that the differences are not convincing because of this much overlap? ______. You found treatment trending toward reversal. Should you conclude that the differences are not convincing because of converging trends? _____. Because you cannot be sure that there are differences, you can't conclude that treatment caused more studying.

19. Here's how you visually analyze a reversal design. Look for high ___________. Look between baseline and treatment, then between treatment and reversal. Next, look for converging ________________. Look for baseline toward treatment. Look for treatment toward reversal. Look for reversal toward treatment. If you find convincing differences, you can conclude that treatment caused them, because a reversal design rules out ________________ explanations.

94. You take two steps to decide whether a treatment caused a change in behavior within a reversal design. First, you decide whether the differences between baseline and treatment are convincing. Second, you decide whether the design rules out alternative explanations. If you are using a reversal design, you can conclude that it rules out alternative explanations. Therefore, if the differences are convincing, you can conclude that the treatment ________________ them.

26. Multiple-baseline designs start out as comparison designs. You rule out alternative explanations by adding a second ___________.

96. You visually analyze a multiple-baseline experiment by analyzing each behavior. You do two analyses to decide whether any differences are convincing. For each behavior, you look for high __________ between baseline and treatment. You look for ____________ from baseline to treatment. You repeat the process for each behavioral variable.

23. Kim is the first person in a multiple-baseline experiment involving several persons. Her studying is:

Baseline:
60, 50, 70, 60, 50
Treatment:
(50, 60, 60, 70, 70), 100, 70, 90, 80, 100

Visual analysis involves looking for high overlap (for the last five observations). The overlap is _____ percent. Does baseline trend toward treatment? ____. Does treatment trend toward baseline? ____. Can you conclude that the differences in her studying are convincing? ____

27. Reba is the second person in a multiple-baseline experiment. Her studying:

Baseline:
(70, 50, 70, 60, 50), 60, 70, 50, 60, 60
Treatment:
90, 80, 90, 80, 100

Visual analysis involves looking for high overlap. The overlap is ________%. Does baseline trend toward treatment? _____. Does treatment trend toward baseline? ______. Can you conclude that the differences in her studying are convincing? ________

78. To visually analyze the multiple-baseline experiment involving Kim and Reba, you first decide whether the differences between baseline and treatment for each person are convincing. If they are, then you can conclude that the treatment caused the differences, because the multiple-baseline design rules out ______________ explanations.

76. To decide whether a treatment causes a behavior change requires two steps. First, you decide whether the differences between conditions are convincing. Look for high _______

between baseline and treatment. Then look for ________________ in baseline and treatment. Second, you decide whether you can rule out alternatives.

25. Looking for high overlap and converging trends in order to decide whether differences look convincing is using the principle of ________ analysis.
95. You use the principle of visual analysis by looking for high overlap and converging trends in order to decide whether differences look ________________.
42. Review: To use the behavioral strategy: (1) create a behavioral definition, (2) use a method of direct observation, (3) check the reliability and social validity of your observations, (4) design a single-subject experiment, and (5) do a(n) ________________ analysis of your data.
24. Lavelle and colleagues used educational coupons to encourage police to write more tickets for child safety seat violations.

Baseline:	4,	1,	13
Treatment:	38,	28,	52
Reversal:	11,	16,	11

Do they show high overlap? ______. Do they show a converging trend? _____. Are they convincing? _____. Can you conclude that the coupons caused a difference in police behavior? ______

9. Bourgeois used a memory book to help the elderly. She used a backward reversal design. The number of relevant comments per day were:

Treatment:	5,	4,	4
Baseline:	1,	1,	2
Reversal to treatment:	6,	4,	4

Do they show high overlap? _______. Do they show a converging trend? ______. Are they convincing? ______. Can you conclude that the memory book caused a difference in relevant comments? _____

15. From Helpful Hint #1: To analyze your results, find out whether the data show a convincing difference between conditions. Then decide whether the design rules out alternative explanations. If both are true, then you can conclude that the treatment ____________ a change in behavior.
30. Review: Because people take time to adjust to new conditions, you ____________ (should, shouldn't) consider the first few observations when asking about high overlap.
43. Review: To use the behavioral strategy, you must (1) create a behavioral definition, (2) use a method of direct observation to observe the problem behavior, (3) check for reliability and social validity, (4) design a single-subject experiment, and (5) do a(n) ______________ analysis of the results.
39. Review: The principle of visual analysis is to find differences that look ______________.
38. Review: The name of the science that studies environmental events that change behavior is ____________________; the term for a statement that specifies exactly what to observe is ____________________.
41. Review: To decide whether a treatment causes a behavior change requires two steps. First, you must decide whether the data show a convincing difference between baseline and treatment. Second, you must rule out ________ explanations for the difference.
37. Review: The fourth tactic in using the behavioral strategy is to design a(n) ____________ ____________ experiment.
48. Review: You should ask two questions to decide whether data are convincing. You should ask if the observations in different conditions have high ______________ or if they show a ____________ toward each other.
36. Review: The formula for reliability between two observers is ________________.
44. Review: To use the behavioral strategy: (4) design a(n) ______________ experiment; and (5) do a ______________ analysis of the data.

Examples

1. You were eating too many fatty foods like meat, cheese, and chips. You publicly resolved to have no more than three portions a day.

Before resolution:	12, 9, 10, 15, 13, 10, 18, 13
After resolution:	14, 13, 2, 4, 3, 5, 3, 2

Did your resolution make a difference? First, look for high overlap. Remember to look only among the last 5 points. Remember that high overlap is having more than 50% of the points overlap. First, do baseline and treatment have high overlap? ____. Second, look for a converging trend. Remember that the condition does not have a converging trend if the trend of a few numbers is broken. Does baseline trend toward treatment? ____. Does treatment trend toward baseline? ____. Are the differences between conditions <u>convincing</u>? ______. Does your design rule out alternatives? ____. Notice that although the differences are convincing, your design does not rule out alternative explanations for what caused the differences. Can you conclude that your resolution <u>caused</u> the difference? ____

2. Fred's son, Tom, read a few pages every day. After getting a baseline, Fred started encouraging Tom to read more. Later Fred got sick and stopped encouraging Tom. Tom read:

No encouragement:	4,	2,	4,	5,	3,	5,	4,	4
Encouragement:	4,	5,	6,	9,	10,	11,	10,	12
No encouragement:	9,	8,	7,	6,	5,	3,	5,	4

Do the last 5 points of baseline and treatment have high overlap (more than 50%)? ____. Do treatment and reversal have high overlap? ____. Does baseline have an unbroken trend toward treatment? ____. Does treatment have an unbroken trend toward reversal? ____. Because there is no high overlap and no converging trend, can you conclude that the differences in reading are <u>convincing</u>? ____. Does the design permit you to rule out alternatives? ____. Notice that the differences are convincing, and the design rules out alternative explanations of what caused the differences. Can you conclude that Fred's encouragement <u>caused</u> Tom to read more? ____

3. Sam is learning how to tell jokes effectively. He tells ten jokes every day. At first he makes up his jokes; then he reads them from a book. His Mom laughs at the following number of jokes per day:

His own:	1,	0,	3,	0,	2					
Book:	2,	6,	10,	9,	10,	8,	6,	9,	8,	10

Sam also tells jokes to his friend Samantha without and with the book. The number of laughs by his friend:

His own:	4,	6,	3,	4,	5,	2,	4,	5,	2,	4
Book:	5,	7,	9,	8,	10					

First, do the data for Mom have high overlap? ____. Do the data for the friend have high overlap? ____. Do the conditions for Mom trend together? ____. Do the conditions for the friend trend toward each other? ____. Can you conclude that the differences in conditions are <u>convincing</u>? ____. Does the design let you rule out alternative explanations? ____. Can you conclude that reading jokes from the book <u>caused</u> more laughs? ____

4. Jamilla sometimes gives you a big smile in the morning. At first you don't give her a cheery greeting; then, for a while, you do give her a cheery greeting. Then you stop giving her a cheery greeting. Number of days per week on which Jamilla gives you a smile:

No cheery:	2,	3,	1,	2,	1,	2,	2,	1
Cheery:	2,	2,	2,	4,	3,	2,	2,	4
No cheery:	5,	4,	2,	2,	1,	2,	2,	1

Do you find high overlap (between treatment and either nontreatment condition)? ____. Do you find a converging trend (between treatment and nontreatment conditions)? ____. Can you conclude that there is a <u>convincing</u> difference? ____. Can you conclude your greeting <u>caused</u> Jamilla to smile more? ____

5. You are working on a term paper. Your professor warns you that the paper counts as half your grade. You write this many paragraphs per day:

Before warning:	11,	10,	6,	3,	1,	2,	3,	5
After warning:	6,	8,	10,	9,	11,	9,	10,	15

First, do you find high overlap (treatment and nontreatment)? ____. Do you find a converging trend (treatment and nontreatment)? ____. Can you conclude that there is a <u>convincing</u> difference? ____. Can you conclude that treatment <u>caused</u> the difference? ____

6. Doc told Bob to eat more veggies. Ounces of veggies before and after Doc's orders:

Veggies before:	1,	4,	5,	2,	6					
Veggies after:	5,	4,	6,	8,	9,	13,	14,	10,	9,	11

Doc later told Bob to eat more soybean products like tempeh and tofu. Ounces of soybean products before and after Doc's orders:

Soybeans before:	0,	0,	0,	0,	0,	0,	1,	2,	2,	3
Soybeans after:	3,	4,	3,	6,	4					

Do you find high overlap (in either behavior)? ____. Do you find a converging trend (in either behavior)? ____. Can you conclude that there is a convincing difference? ____. Can you conclude that treatment caused the difference? ____

7. Review: Kay smoked too much. After getting a baseline, she tried substituting gum for smoking. Later she ran out of gum. She had the following number of cigarettes a day:

No gum:	21,	19,	23,	15,	24,	18,	20,	22
Gum:	20,	19,	18,	17,	11,	13,	9,	12
No gum:	11,	13,	12,	16,	14,	22,	18,	19

High overlap? ____. Converging trend? ____. Convincing difference? ____. Treatment caused difference? ____

8. Review: Kim was fighting off depression. She tried to see friends but didn't do it very often. She got counseling from Dr. Hale, and he taught her why seeing friends was important. He taught her some skills to make seeing friends more fun, and also how to record data about seeing friends. She started seeing friends much more often. Even when she discontinued counseling, she continued to use her new skills and to see friends often. She felt much less depressed. The period before she got counseling is called the ______________. Counseling is called the ______________. The period after she stopped counseling is called the ______________ to baseline. Her experiment with counseling uses what single-subject design? ______________ design. This is a strong design because it rules out ______________ explanations.

9. Review: Sam checked every 15 minutes to see whether any of his students were studying. He was using what method of direct observation? ______________ recording. (Do you still remember the questions?)

10. Review: Professor George noticed that Paulo rarely talked in his classes. Starting in October, he reacted to every comment that Paulo made in Sociology. Paulo starting making more comments, but only in Sociology. Starting in November, Professor George reacted to every comment that Paulo made in Political Science. Paulo started making more comments in that class, too. Professor George used what kind of single-subject experimental design? ______________ design. (Do you remember the questions?)

11. Review: Bev wanted Bob to spend more time with their son, Bill. After a baseline period, she asked him every day to spend more time with Bill. He spent the following amount of time each day:

No requests:	14,	10,	5,	10,	5,	15,	20,	25
Requests:	73,	66,	63,	58,	51,	45,	40,	35

High overlap? ____. Converging trend? ____. Convincing differences? ____. Treatment caused differences? ____

12. Review: Melodie wrote down each time Tim attended class prior to the strike at Reagan College. If the strike is considered the treatment condition, the period before the strike is called the ______________ condition.

13. Review: Mom noticed that Sue had trouble getting up in the morning. After a baseline period, she started waking Sue. Later, Mom got sick and stopped waking Sue. Sue woke up late by the following number of minutes each day:

No Mom:	14,	21,	18,	9,	12,	15,	16,	14
Mom:	1,	2,	1,	3,	2,	4,	6,	2
No Mom:	1,	3,	2,	14,	12,	14,	10,	11

High overlap? ____. Converging trend? ____. Convincing differences? ____. Treatment caused differences? ____

14. Review: Louise observed the interrupting behavior of Archie while she was being her usual polite self. She continued to observe his interrupting behavior after she began ignoring him. She was using a design that couldn't rule out ______________ explanations for any change in his interrupting behavior. She used what type of single-subject design? ______________ design

15. Review: Ben noticed that his Mom and Dad put almost no materials into the recycling bins. The following are the number of ounces of materials Dad recycled before and after Ben had a talk with him about the health of the earth:

Recycled before: 1, 4, 5, 6, 6
Recycled after: 5, 4, 6, 8, 9, 13, 14, 10, 9, 11

Here are the number of ounces of materials Mom recycled before and after a similar talk:

Recycled before: 0, 0, 0, 0, 0, 0, 1, 2, 2, 3
Recycled after: 3, 4, 3, 6, 4

High overlap? ____. Converging trend? ____. Convincing differences? ________. Treatment caused differences? ______

16. Review: If a teacher is having trouble with his children hitting each other, an observer might note whether anyone was hitting during each 30-

second period of the class. The observer would be using what method of observing? ___________ recording

17. Review: Fred counts the number of supportive comments you make to Beth each day. Then he simply gives you feedback at the end of every day as to how many supportive comments you made. Fred also counts supportive comments to Barb during her baseline. He then also gives her feedback. Comments to Beth:

No Feedback: 1, 2, 1, 2, 0
Feedback: 5, 7, 9, 8, 8, 7, 9, 8, 7, 8

Comments to Barb:

No feedback: 2, 0, 3, 4, 3, 3, 4, 3, 5, 2
Feedback: 4, 6, 7, 8, 7

High overlap? ____. Converging trend? ____. Convincing differences? ____. Treatment caused differences? ____

18. Review: John decided that good interview behavior is "looking the interviewer in the eye and answering each question clearly and politely." The words in quotes would be called a(n) ________ ___________________.

19. Review: Tim is an avid dart player. After a baseline period, Ann gives him a tip on improving his score. Later, Tim goes on vacation and forgets the tip. He throws the following percentages of bull's-eyes:

Before tip: 8, 11, 9, 10, 14, 16, 15, 18
During tip: 19, 21, 20, 20, 24, 25, 24, 27
After tip: 18, 19, 20, 19, 24, 22, 25, 23

High overlap? ____. Converging trend? ____. Convincing differences? ____. Treatment caused differences? ______

20. Review: John kept track of the number of times his dancing partner forgot the new disco step. He counted 20 times, but she disagreed, saying it had been only 16 times. Their reliability is ______ percent. If this was a new behavioral definition, would this constitute an acceptable level? __________

LESSON

7

Review of Behavioral Methods

Behavior analysis is the modern form of behaviorism. It keeps many beliefs of early behaviorism: that we can study human action by natural science methods; that such a science must study behavior rather than mental events; that such a science can help us solve our problems. Behavior analysis has kept the optimistic and forward-looking aspects of the old behaviorism.

At the same time, it has taken a direction that has revolutionized behaviorism. It has cast off narrow behaviorism by defining behavior very broadly. It has gone beyond the stimulus-response mechanism by looking at the context of behavior (e.g., Morris, 1988; Hayes, 1988). It has cast off the involuntary reflex as the building block of complex behavior. Behavior analysis has broadened behaviorism to deal with the entire range of human activities.

Skinner's formulation of reinforcement in the 1930s let behavior analysts study voluntary, or operant, behavior. The practical use of behavior analysis has expanded greatly since 1970, helping to solve behavioral problems from shyness to creativity to autism. It has spawned such new fields as behavioral medicine and behavioral social work. This modern form of behaviorism has enjoyed widespread success.

This success comes partly from enlarging the meaning of the term *behavior.* Behavior analysts refer to obvious movements as behavior just as everyone else does. However, they extend the meaning of *behavior* beyond obvious movement. They extend its meaning slightly by including more subtle activity such as talking, looking, listening, and reading. They extend it still further to include internal events measurable by electronic devices, such as muscle tension, brain waves, and stomach acidity. Finally, they extend it radically to include private events such as thinking and feeling. In short, they apply the term *behavior* to anything that people do.

You have read in this book about many examples of this broader meaning of behavior. Behavior analysts have found useful ways to observe many obvious, but complex, behaviors. They have observed carrying out football assignments, doing cooperative household chores, recycling, disrupting dental treatment, conserving electricity, and giving traffic tickets. They have observed many subtle behaviors, such as accepting criticism

Sleeping As Behavior

You may think of sleep as "markedly reduced consciousness" (Chaplin, 1985: p. 430). How would you measure that? You might not think of observing sleep as behavior, but that is exactly what two researchers did. They provided older insomniacs with a simple device to measure sleep. The device sounded a very soft tone for one second every ten minutes. It then tape-recorded whether the insomniacs said, "I'm awake" within ten seconds. Obviously, if they replied, they were not asleep. If they did not reply, they were probably asleep. Thus, these researchers defined consciousness in terms of whether the insomniacs were responsive to their environment. That's just common sense! (Based on Lichstein & Johnson, 1991.)

1. By observing briefly every ten minutes and not observing the rest of the time, what method of observation did these researchers use to observe sleep? ________ ________________ recording

and conversing skillfully. Behavior analysts have observed other subtle behaviors involving what many would call cognitive functioning: learning, creating, studying, and remembering. They have observed internal behavior such as tension. They have found ways to get at private behaviors such as pain, attention, and thoughts. The box on page 119 shows how sleep may be observed as a behavior. Behavior analysts have observed such behaviors in order to help people change them. Examples in this book often report the success of behavior analysis at doing just that. Can anyone familiar with the richness and depth of this approach to behavior call it narrow or mechanical?

The success of behavior analysis also comes from other sources. It has solved some major problems that used to plague researchers studying human behavior. The biggest problem has been to seek the causes of behavior in private events. The problem with using private events to explain behavior is that they must still be explained.

Behavior analysis solves this problem by using the principle of public events. You use this principle when you seek the causes of behavior in environmental events. You can study these causes with the methods of natural science, thereby avoiding the problems of causes that must themselves be explained.

The success of behavior analysis also comes from its natural-science approach, which lets you apply powerful methods of inquiry to human behavior. The result is that science has at last come to human behavior. You have learned about five tactics that let you apply the behavioral strategy to solving human problems.

The Five Tactics of the Behavioral Strategy

Behavior analysis helps you find treatments for changing socially important behavior. Finding such treatments involves at least five tactics. First, you create a behavioral definition of the problem. Second, you use a method for the direct observation of the behavior. Third, you check the reliability and social validity of your observations. Fourth, you use a single-subject experiment that rules out alternative explanations. Fifth, you do a visual analysis of the data. Each of these tactics is a part of the behavioral strategy for solving human problems.

The first tactic in using the behavioral strategy is to create a behavioral definition of the problem behavior. This often requires that you translate everyday talk into behavioral language. Sometimes, everyday talk is explicitly behavioral. In this case, all you have to do is make a more explicit definition. "Crying" already has a clear behavioral referent. To define *crying*, all you have to do is specify when a vocal sound is a cry. This might involve specifying loudness. Other times, everyday talk is implicitly behavioral. "Studying" obviously describes what a person is doing. However, you must specify aspects of the behavior that are a valid part of studying. This might be as simple as the student looking at the book or answering questions about the book. It is easy to make behavioral definitions when everyday talk is already behavioral.

Often, however, everyday talk is vague. It may not seem to refer to behavior at all. For example, *understanding* seems to refer to thoughts, not to behavior. However, common sense dictates that if someone understands an idea, he or she can explain it. For example, you might want to find out whether Tom understands *reliability*. You can ask Tom to apply it to a set of behavioral observations. If he can, then you know that he understands the concept. In this way, you move understanding from an unobservable event to a behavioral event.

When you get interested in a human problem, you can search for the behaviors involved. They may be obvious, subtle, internal, or private. You can find good behavioral definitions through this search. Researchers have defined creativity (Goetz & Baer, 1973), nervous tension (Budzynski & Stoyva, 1969), and cooperative living (Miller & Feallock, 1974). Researchers will continue to look at human actions not now considered "behavioral," and you can be sure they will find ways to translate them into behavioral terms.

Once you have created a behavioral definition, you can use the next tactic: using a method of direct observation to gather information about the problem behavior. This involves using the principle of direct observation. You can use trained observers to record people's observable behavior. You can get accurate and detailed data and avoid the problems that come from people reporting their own behavior.

Direct observation solves the problem with self-reports, which are inaccurate or of unknown accuracy. When you can check up on people's self-reports, you often find that they are wrong. Too many times, you can't even check up on them, because they are about mental events that no one else can see.

You can use any of the four methods of direct observation: outcome recording if the behavior leaves a result; event recording if the behavior is uniform; interval recording if the behavior occurs for nonuniform episodes; and time sample recording to observe a sample of the behavior. Each method allows you to observe the behavior directly.

The third tactic in using the behavioral strategy is to check the reliability and social validity of your observations. You first find out if the data are reliable. If they are not, then they have no meaning or use to other people. If the data are reliable, you can use them to find a solution to the problem. You must also find out if your observations are socially valid, by seeking the advice of a panel of outside judges.

If the behavioral observations are not reliable, you have several options. You can give more training to the observers. You can revise the behavioral definition so that it is clearer. Likewise, if your behavioral definition is not socially valid, you can revise it to agree with the meaning used by your judges.

The fourth tactic in using the behavioral strategy is to design a single-subject experiment to find out whether the treatment works. You use single-subject experiments to rule out alternatives. You use this tactic when you find a treatment that seems to change the behavior. Your treatment can be anything capable of objective specification, such as a reward, a new training method, or even meditation. If you can specify the treatment, you can test to see if it really works.

Finding out whether a treatment works requires ruling out alternative explanations. You can do this by using the principle of single-subject experiments. Single-subject designs, such as comparison, reversal, and multiple-baseline, look at the behavior of <u>one person</u> at a time. The most powerful designs are the reversal design and the multiple-baseline design, both of which rule out individual differences by studying one person at a time. They also rule out time coincidences by observing behavior change at least twice. In contrast, the comparison design rules out only individual differences.

Single-subject designs solve the problem of alternative explanations. The problem with alternative explanations is that we can't be sure what actually caused any observed behavioral differences. Designs that don't rule out alternative explanations have not helped discover the <u>causes</u> of individual behavior.

The fifth tactic in using the behavioral strategy is to do a visual analysis of the data. You do this to decide whether the effect of the conditions is different. You must look for the absence of high overlap between conditions and trends in which the conditions converge. If you don't find high overlap or converging trends, you can conclude that the conditions differ. You may have ruled out alternatives with a single-subject design. If so, you can then conclude that the treatment caused the change in behavior. This approach finds powerful causes of behavior change. It is called the principle of visual analysis. It requires that you look for <u>convincing</u> effects.

Visual analysis solves the problem of finding weak effects. It finds powerful treatments that

Inner versus Outer Causes in Everyday Language

Hineline (1992) analyzed how people talk about the causes of behavior in everyday life. He suggested that people point to an inner cause when explaining unexpected behavior. When John rejects a $25,000 promotion, people say he is "a man of principle." Those people are pointing to an inner cause. Hineline suggested that people sometimes point to external causes when explaining expected behavior. If John turns down a promotion that would prevent him from helping his terminally ill wife, he is likely to say that his wife needs his help. John is pointing to an external cause. Note those places in the book when the behavioral approach of using an external cause to explain behavior doesn't sound right.

2. The behavioral approach may sound right to you when it uses an external cause to explain an expected behavior. However, it is likely to sound wrong to you when it uses an external cause to explain a(n) ______ ______________ (expected, unexpected) behavior.

cause large and important differences in behavior. These treatments have important theoretical and practical implications.

Summary

Behavior analysis uses a natural-science approach to studying human activity. It has broadened behaviorism to deal with voluntary behavior. It has solved major problems that often plague researchers wishing to study human behavior. You can use its methods to help solve human problems. I have outlined the behavioral strategy for doing so. The heart of this approach involves five tactics. First, you create a behavioral definition of the problem behavior. Second, you use a method of direct observation to gather information about the behavior. Third, you check the reliability and social validity of your observations. Fourth, you use a single-subject experiment to test the treatment. Fifth, you do a visual analysis of your data. This method can produce dramatic successes. Used by behavior analysts, it has spawned many new fields of scientific inquiry.

Glossary

You can review the ideas of this unit by reading the following definitions. The lessons of this unit taught these terms. As you review the terms, see if you can define them before looking at the definition. See if you can think of an example for each term.

Baseline is the period of an experiment without the treatment.

Behavior is anything that a person does. This implies that the activity is physical.
- This includes obvious, subtle, internal, and private events.
- Operant behavior is synonymous with voluntary behavior.

Behavior analysis is the study of environmental events that change behavior.
- The founder of behavior analysis is Skinner.
- Behavior analysis increased greatly in popularity in 1970.
- Behavior analysis doesn't deny thoughts and feelings.
- Behavior analysis isn't stimulus-response behaviorism.

A **behavioral definition** is a statement that specifies exactly what behavior to observe. Creating a behavioral definition is the first step in studying behavior.
- It makes communication clearer; it maintains consistency of observations.

The **behavioral strategy** is to define human problems as behavioral problems. It involves five tactics:
1. Create a behavioral definition of the problem behavior.
2. Use a method of direct observation to gather information.
3. Check the reliability and social validity of your observations.
4. Use a single-subject experiment to test your treatment.
5. Do a visual analysis of your data.

Comparison design involves comparing the baseline condition with the treatment condition.
- It rules out individual differences but not time coincidences.

Event recording is when you record a response when you see an instance of the behavior. You use this method when the instances of the behavior are regular or uniform.

Interval recording is when you record a response if the behavior occurs in one of a series of continuous intervals.

Multiple-baseline design introduces the treatment at different times for two or more behavioral variables. This design rules out alternatives.

Outcome recording is when you record a response when you see the result of the behavior.

The **principle of direct observation** is to use trained observers, who personally see (or hear) a behavior and immediately record it.
- **Direct observation** is personally seeing and immediately recording behavior.

The **principle of public events** is to seek the causes of behavior in environmental events.
- The problem with using private events to explain behavior is that you still must explain the private events.

The **principle of single-subject experiments** is to expose one person to the baseline and treatment.

The **principle of visual analysis** is to find differences that look convincing.
- Differences are convincing if conditions do not have high overlap and do not show a converging trend.
- A converging trend is three points increasingly closer to the values of the other condition; the trend remains unbroken at the end of the condition.
- Overlapping points are (a) those points in the smaller set that are equal to or greater than the lowest number in the larger set (b) plus those points in the larger set equal to or less than the highest number in the smaller set.
- Overlap can be expressed as the percent of points being considered that overlap; you will usually use only the last five points in each condition.
- If the sum of these counts is more than 50% of the number of observations, then you have unacceptably high overlap.

Reliability is the percentage of agreement between two independent observers. Both observers must observe at the same time and use the same behavioral definition.
- The formula for reliability is 100%xA/(A+D).
- In trial reliability, you compare each observation. You can always use trial reliability with interval and time sample recording. You can only use trial reliability with outcome or event recording of complex behaviors with a checklist.
- In frequency reliability, you compare overall frequencies. You can use frequency reliability with outcome or event recording of simple behaviors.
- Old definitions should reach 90%; new definitions, only 80%.

A **reversal design** looks at a behavior during baseline, treatment, and reversal. It can rule out alternatives.

Ruling out alternatives means showing that events other than the treatment are unlikely to have caused an observed difference.
- One alternative is that any effect is caused by individual differences.
- Another alternative is that the effect is caused by time coincidences.

Social validity is the rating of a behavioral definition by outside judges.

Time sample recording is when you record a response if one behavior occurs within one of a series of discontinuous intervals.
- This method is also used to observe multiple behaviors of one person or multiple people performing one behavior.

Treatment is the method introduced to modify the rate of a behavior.

Notes

Note #1

Baer, Wolf, and Risley (1968) propose a set of practices that characterize applied behavior analysis. They assert that applied behavior analysis research studies applied problems, defines them behaviorally, analyzes their causes, specifies the treatment so that others can use it, states the principle underlying the treatment, makes effective changes, and has generality. This article is often referred to as the classic definition of the science. See also the recent follow-up (Baer, Wolf, & Risley, 1987).

Helpful Hints

Helpful Hint #1

You can review the entire unit by working through the Practice Review that follows the Additional Readings. It has questions similar to those in a Reading Quiz; but it has many more questions. Also, it has a wide variety of questions from all of the lessons in this unit. Answering them all is an excellent way to study for the review exam on these lessons.

3. An excellent way to study for the review exam on Unit One is to answer the questions in the ________________ Review.

Additional Readings

Bachrach, A. J. (1962). *Psychological research: An introduction*. New York: Random House. This book is an easy introduction to the philosophy of behavioral research.

Bernard, C. (1957). *An introduction to the study of experimental medicine*. New York: Dover. Claude Bernard is often called the father of experimental medicine. This book is a modern release of his century-old classic. It advocates an experimental method similar to single-subject experimentation. Because the logic is applied to medical problems, it may help you understand the same logic applied to behavioral problems.

Skinner, B. F. (1958). *Cumulative record*. New York: Appleton-Century-Crofts. This book is an excellent introduction for the advanced student, to Skinner's approach to the methods of behavioral science.

Practice Review

The following material has questions on every concept studied in Unit One. By answering the questions and checking your answers, you can prepare yourself for the Review Exam. The Review Exam will contain questions from all lessons in Unit One.

57. Review: Vera wasn't getting anywhere with Juan during an initial period of knowing him. He hadn't even kissed her yet. She decided to wear musk oil perfume to see if that would increase his kissing behavior. Juan now kisses Vera on every date. What type of single-subject experimental design is this? ________ ________________

62. Review: You watch four children to see their writing behavior. You divide the one-hour writing period into 240 intervals of 15 seconds each. You watch the first child for the first 15 seconds, the second child during the next 15 seconds, and so on. Thus, you observe each child's writing for one 15-second period per minute. Your method of observing is ________ ________________ recording.

12. Review: A formal description of what to observe is called a(n) ________________________.

28. Review: Ken was interested in nervousness. He observed his professor's displays of nervous pacing during lectures by breaking the lecture period into 150 consecutive 20-second periods and recording whether any nervous pacing occurred during each 20-second period. Ken was using ________________________ recording.

40. Review: The method of observation that involves observing someone's behavior for ten seconds at several randomly scheduled times is called ________________________ recording.

26. Review: In the science of behavior analysis, any procedure designed to change the rate of a behavior is called a(n) ____________.

37. Review: The behavioral strategy is to define human problems as ________________ problems.

25. Review: If Dave observed the amount of studying that Pam did for three weeks, then started urging her to study more while continuing to observe the amount of studying she did for another three weeks, and then finally stopped urging her to study but observed her studying for another three weeks, he would be using what experimental design? ______________ design

20. Review: Behavior analysis was founded by ________________________.

58. Review: What method of observation involves observing a behavior during a series of discontinuous intervals? ________________ recording

8. Mr. Warren, a high school teacher, was quite negative in his class. Several of his students decided to observe him to find out how much of the time he was negative. They made their observations in consecutive 15-second blocks throughout the day and found that he was negative 75% of the time. What method of observation did they use? ________________ recording

52. Review: The use of outside judges to determine whether a behavioral definition is acceptable to interested parties is called determining the ________________________ of the definition.

35. Review: Suppose Diane developed a behavioral definition of assertiveness. She had an outside group rate the assertiveness of individuals observed by means of a videotape, in which some individuals exhibited a high level

of what she defined as assertive behavior and others exhibited a low level. If she compared the ratings made by the outside group with her own observations to see whether they were using a similar definition of assertiveness, she would be determining the ____________ ____________ of her definition.

48. Review: The problem with using private events to explain behavior is that we must still ____________ them.
45. Review: The principle of visual analysis is to seek differences in graphical data that look ____________.
34. Review: Suppose a behavior is observed for a period before treatment and then a period during treatment, to see whether the treatment has any effect. What single-subject experimental design is used? ____________ design
49. Review: The simplest form of the time sample method of observation involves observing behavior during a series of ____________ time intervals.
22. Review: Defining human problems as <u>behavioral</u> problems is called the ____________ strategy.
46. Review: The principle of single-subject experiments is to experiment with ____________ person(s) at a time.
53. Review: The widespread publication of behavior analysis results began in what year? ____________
5. Hineline (1992) discusses when a behavior analysis explanation of behavior by environmental events sounds right or wrong in our culture. The explanation that an employee does the job because of the pay sounds right. The explanation that a soldier saved his buddies by throwing himself on a hand grenade because of basic training and group morale may not sound as reasonable. Thus, environmental causes are more likely to sound reasonable if the behavior was ____________ (expected, unexpected).
47. Review: The principle of direct observation requires that the observer personally____________ the behavior and ____________ it at that time.
66. Two requirements of reliability are that both observers must observe at the same____________ and must use the same ____________.
60. Review: When Damon counts the number of times Janice compliments him, he is using what method of observation? ____________ recording
6. If John observes Maria's smiling during 75 consecutive time periods, each of 15 seconds duration, he is using what method of observation? ____________ recording
10. Observing a behavior during one brief interval at several times of the day would be called ____________ recording.
54. Review: Two observers are counting the number of times a person smiles. One counts 8, and the other counts 10. What is the reliability? ________ percent. Is it acceptable? ________
23. Review: Dr. Peterson developed a way to help people be nice to one another. He defined being nice as a behavior. He taught people to thank others for being nice. Dr. Peterson used a multiple-baseline design to study the success of his approach. Dr. Peterson's work would be an example of what behavioral science? ____________
36. Review: The basic formula for computing reliability is ____________.
7. John was a pretty good golfer, scoring an average of 85. He decided to see what effect daily practice would have on his score. After five weeks of practice, his scores had improved to an average of 78. He stopped practicing when school started again and noticed that his scores slowly crept up until he was averaging about 83. What single-subject experimental design was John inadvertently using? ____________ design
18. Review: Behavior analysis is the field that studies ____________ events that ____________ behavior.
30. Review: May observed Professor Brainbuster on Thursday to see how many chauvinistic comments he made. She counted 18. April observed Professor Brainbuster on Friday and found that he made 20 such comments. Can you conclude that May and April were making reliable observations of Professor Brainbuster's chauvinistic comments?____________
44. Review: The principle of public events is to seek the causes of behavior in ____________ events.
15. Review: A single-subject experimental design in which treatment is introduced at different times for two or more behaviors is called a(n) ____________ design.
38. Review: The instructor decided to count the

number of times Dale spoke in class. She found that Dale spoke 20 times during one class period. However, another observer counted only 15 times. Compute their reliability: _____ percent. If this is a new behavioral definition, is the reliability acceptable? __________

50. Review: The statement, "Assertive behavior consists of making eye contact, speaking loud enough to be clearly heard, and asking the other person to change his or her behavior," is called a(n) __________________ of assertiveness.

32. Review: One criterion for sound observations is that they be based on what the observer can personally see and immediately record. Any procedure that incorporates those features conforms to the principle of ________ ________________.

29. Review: Mary's teacher and another observer made the following observations of Mary's nearness to other children (N=near; F=far):

Teacher:
F N F F F F F N F F F F N F F N N F F

Another:
F N F N F F F N N F F F F F F F N N F F

What is the reliability of these observations? __________ percent. Is this an acceptable level if the behavioral definition is a new one? ______

39. Review: The method of observing that counts occurrences of behavior is called ________ recording.

31. Review: Name a specific single-subject experimental design that rules out both time coincidences and individual differences as alternative explanations of any observed change in behavior. ____________

51. Review: The tactics in using the behavioral strategy: first, create a behavioral definition; second, use a method of direct observation; third, check reliability and social validity; fourth, use a single-subject design; and fifth, do a(n) ______________ analysis of the data.

24. Review: If a behavior is observed during many consecutive short periods of time, the method of observation is called ____________ recording.

13. Review: A good experimental design is one that can rule out ________________ explanations of any observed behavior change.

56. Review: Vera kept a record of the number of kisses from Juan before she started to use musk oil to increase his rate of kissing. The period before she started to use musk oil would be called the ____________________ condition.

11. Professor Mills made up a checklist of behaviors that a good teaching assistant should perform every time a student came up to obtain a quiz form. The checklist included such behaviors as greeting the student by name, asking the student if he or she has a question, and so on. The professor then watched every new assistant when students came to get a quiz. She recorded each behavior as it occurred. She was using ____________ recording.

19. Review: Behavior analysts regard thoughts and feelings as physical activities that people do. Therefore, they call them __________.

67. Two young black men were observing a policeman as he covered his beat, to see how many times he called another black man "boy." They wrote their observations down immediately. What method of direct observation were they using? ______________ recording

14. Review: A group of students in the 1960s tried using sit-ins to desegregate a northern suburb. Before starting their protests, they sent ten black students into three restaurants every day for a week to test whether the owner would serve them. None were served. They began a sit-in at Restaurant A. The testers continued going to two other restaurants during this time. After ten days, Restaurant A changed its policy and served the testers. The students then repeated the procedure, first with Restaurant B and then Restaurant C. The students' experiment is an example of a(n) ______________ design.

33. Review: Reliability for new behavioral definitions should equal or exceed __________ percent.

17. Review: An experimental design that studies a behavior before the treatment, during the treatment, and after the treatment is called a(n) ______________ design.

16. Review: About one student per week joined the new compact disc buying cooperative. Then the cooperative decided to try a newspaper advertisement. As a result, about 20 students joined each week. The members concluded that advertising pays, since the ad succeeded

in getting many new members. This is not a good experimental design, because it doesn't rule out ______________ explanations of the increase (such as the approach of Christmas).

42. Review: The percent of agreement between two observers is called ______________.

65. Two observers find the following patterns for a behavior:

Observer 1:	Y	N	Y	Y	Y	Y	Y	Y	N	Y
Observer 2:	Y	N	Y	Y	Y	N	Y	Y	Y	Y

Compute their reliability. ______ percent. Is it acceptable? _______

63. Suppose behavior A is observed for 12 weeks before any procedure is used to change its rate. Suppose behavior A is observed for 24 weeks after the procedure is introduced. Suppose behavior B is observed for 24 weeks (instead of 12 weeks) before the same procedure is used, and then for 12 weeks after. The name of the experimental design is ___________ _________ design.

59. Review: What science studies environmental events that modify what people do? ______ ______________

43. Review: The period of time when behavior is observed prior to an attempt to change the rate of that behavior is called the _________ condition.

27. Review: Jenny decided to record the number of pieces of junk that her roommate piled on her desk and bed for two weeks and then confront her roommate with this information. At the end of the two weeks, she showed her roommate the data proving that an average of 12 objects per day had been left in Jenny's part of the room. Her roommate was surprised by the data; she apologized and promised to stop. If this is considered a behavioral experiment, what is Jenny's talking with her roommate called? ___________

1. Behavior analysts call anything that a person does ________________.

21. Review: Dale wasn't very kind. His favorite aunt tried to convince him to do more acts of kindness, and she praised him when he did. But then she left. His acts of kindness per day were:

Before aunt:	0,	1,	1,	0,	2
During aunt:	5,	7,	3,	5,	4
After aunt:	3,	2,	1,	0,	1

Are you convinced that he performed more acts of kindness during her visit? _____. Are you convinced that she caused the change? _______

9. Name a single-subject experimental design that does not rule out all alternative explanations of any observed change in behavior. ______________________

4. Harry didn't like to read. His teacher tried to get him to read more by offering early recess if he read most of the period. His teacher then withdrew the offer. The percent of the period Harry spent reading was:

Before recess offer:	25,	15,	30,	20,	10
During recess offer:	60,	85,	80,	95,	85
After recess offer:	55,	35,	10,	25,	15

If the third week of the experiment had not been conducted, the first and second weeks would have been an example of a(n)_________ ______________ design.

41. Review: The method that observes a result of behavior is called ________________ recording.

3. During the first week, Wade observed Tom's smiling and making positive comments. Starting the second week, Wade gave Tom frequent pep talks on the importance of smiling. He said nothing about positive comments. Starting the third week, Wade also gave frequent pep talks about the importance of positive comments. He continued to give frequent pep talks about the importance of smiling. Tom is a changed person due to those pep talks. What experimental design did Wade use to investigate the effect of his pep talks on Tom's two behaviors of smiling and making positive comments? ________________ design

64. The teacher and another observer decided to measure the amount of time John was studying. Since they weren't able to make continuous observations, they checked John every half hour and noted whether he was studying. Their observations the first day were:

Teacher:	Y	Y	N	N	N	N	N	N	Y	N
Another:	N	Y	N	N	N	N	N	N	Y	Y

What is the reliability? _______ percent. Is this acceptable for a new behavioral definition? _________

61. Review: When you do a visual analysis, you check for high ______________ between conditions and check for a converging ________.
2. Behavior analysts rarely use inferential statistics. Do they ever use descriptive statistics? ________
55. Review: Using the behavioral strategy involves: first, creating a(n) ______________________; second, using a method of direct observation; third, checking reliability and social validity; fourth, using a(n) ______________________ experimental design; and fifth, visually analyzing the data.
68. Review: Experimenting with one person at a time is called the principle of ____________ ________________ designs.

UNIT

2

The Reinforcement Strategy

LESSON 8 Reinforcement of Everyday Behaviors

Introduction to Unit Two

This unit and the rest of the units in the book introduce you to what behavior analysis has learned about environmental influences on behavior. Unit Two teaches you about reinforcement and the reinforcement strategy for solving human problems. The first lesson in this unit introduces the concept of reinforcement, which lies at the heart of environmental influences that create and maintain behavior. Other lessons in Unit Two explain additional concepts related to reinforcement, such as shaping and scheduling. Unit Three explains how reinforcement influences cognitive behavior. Finally, Unit Four explains the concept of punishment. Punishment is the opposite of reinforcement; it reduces and destroys behavior. Units Two through Four present what you might call the behavioral theory of everyday human behavior. Thus, they present an introduction to what behavior analysts have learned by using the methodology outlined in Unit One.

This lesson introduces you to reinforcement, which is at the heart of behavior analysis. Reinforcement means that people learn to repeat those behaviors that work. They learn through experience. Usually such learning helps people become happier and more productive, but it can misfire and make people less happy and less productive. Behavior analysts have found that reinforcement holds the key to understanding both results.

In this lesson, you will learn the first tactic in using the reinforcement strategy to help people solve their problems: to increase desired behavior through reinforcement.

1. The first tactic in using the reinforcement strategy is to increase desired behavior through ____________________.

Definition of Reinforcement

A **reinforcer** is any event that (1) follows a behavior and (2) increases the probability of that behavior. The first part of the definition is that a reinforcer must be a consequence—it must come after the behavior. The second part of the definition is that a reinforcer must be effective. It must cause the person to do more of the behavior. It is this second part that makes a reinforcer like a proven reward.

2. A **reinforcer** is any event that (1) __________ a behavior and (2) __________ the probability of that behavior.

Reinforcement is the procedure of using a reinforcer to increase the rate of a behavior. The procedure ensures that the reinforcer follows the behavior. Be sure you understand the difference between *reinforcer* and *reinforcement*. One is an event; the other is a procedure. You will run into this important distinction throughout the book, so be sure you understand it.

3. **Reinforcement** is the procedure of using a reinforcer to __________ the rate of a behavior.

I can illustrate these terms with respect to an obvious behavior. Suppose Mom gives Tommy a dessert for eating spinach. If Tommy eats spinach more often in the future, you call the dessert a *reinforcer*. You call the procedure of giving Tommy dessert after he eats spinach *reinforcement*.

Notice that Mom doesn't reinforce Tommy. She gives the dessert to Tommy, but she doesn't reinforce him. She reinforces Tommy's behavior of eating spinach. She doesn't strengthen Tommy, but rather a specific behavior of Tommy's. The rule for talking about reinforcement is simple. You do not reinforce people, you reinforce their behavior (Baer, 1976).

You must carefully look to see if both elements of reinforcement are present in every example. Suppose Mom gave Tommy a dessert whenever he ate his spinach, but Tommy didn't eat his spinach any more often because of the dessert. Notice that giving Tommy the dessert for eating his spinach did not produce an increase in his rate of eating spinach. Therefore, the dessert would not be an example of a reinforcer. We will call an event that follows a behavior but does not increase its rate an *unknown*.

Remember, you must carefully look to see if both elements of reinforcement are present. Suppose Mom told Tommy he had to eat his spinach from now on. Tommy might eat his spinach more often after that. Notice that the event "Mom told Tommy he had to eat his spinach" does not follow Tommy's behavior of eating spinach; it precedes it. It should be obvious to you that Mom would tell Tommy to eat his spinach before he has eaten it, not after! Therefore, her demand would not be an example of a reinforcer. Until a later lesson, we will call an event that does not follow a behavior but does increase its rate an *unknown*.

An event must have two elements to be a reinforcer. It must <u>follow</u> the behavior of interest, and it must cause that behavior to <u>increase</u> in rate. (See Figure 8-1.) If an event does not have both elements, it is not a reinforcer. I will call events that have one but not both elements *unknowns*. I will slip in examples of events that have one but not both elements, in order to teach you to look very carefully for both elements before calling an event a reinforcer.

Notice that the definition of *reinforcer* does not require that the event be "pleasant." For example, suppose Tommy burped at the table and Mom yelled at him, "That's disgusting!" Tommy might act like many little boys and burp more often as a result of Mom's reaction. Her yelling follows his burping and increases the rate of burping. Even though you might think of her yelling as unpleasant, it is still a reinforcer.

The term *reinforcer* is similar in meaning to the everyday word *reward*. <u>Reward</u> refers to any event that the speaker feels another person should like but that has not yet been proven to be a reinforcer. I can illustrate the relation between reward and reinforcer with respect to a subtle behavior.

Figure 8-1. A touchdown probably reinforces the football behavior that leads to it.

Don might reward his daughter Mary for admitting that she broke a dish. Don might reward Mary with a trip to the movies, hoping that rewarding Mary will make her more likely to tell the truth in the future. It may not; Mary may not like that particular movie. However, if the movie is a reinforcer, Mary will be more likely to tell the truth in the future.

A reinforcer is proven to modify the behavior of the person receiving it. You might think of a reinforcer as a proven reward.

Students often get mixed up between *reinforcer* and *reinforcement*. A reinforcer is an event. It is giving a piece of candy, seeing a sunset, or receiving a "Thank you." Of course, the event has to follow the response and increase its future rate. A reinforcement is a procedure. It is a rule or repeated pattern of giving a reinforcer for a particular behavior. It is giving dessert whenever Tommy eats his spinach.

4. Students often get mixed up between *reinforcer* and *reinforcement*. A reinforcer is a(n) _______. A reinforcement is a(n) ___________.

The Variety of Reinforcers

A limitless variety of events can serve as reinforcers. Social reinforcers might consist of a smile, a word of praise, agreement, or attention. Edible reinforcers might be candy, snacks, or beer. Play reinforcers might consist of toys, airplanes, or Frisbees. Some activity reinforcers would be dancing, skydiving, or jogging. Generalized reinforcers might consist of money or points. Rare and sublime events can be reinforcers, as shown by the box that follows. Some events are reinforcers for almost everyone—for example, sex, money, and food. On the other hand, some events may be reinforcers only for small groups or even single individuals. Rare art or the study of Latin might be examples. In fact, some reinforcers may even be painful; some people like others to spank or whip them.

People may deliberately contrive reinforcement, or nature may deliver it. Teachers may deliberately praise the studying of their pupils. Nature may produce a beautiful scene that increases the rate at which you go outside in the evening. (See Figure 8-2.)

You should carefully limit your use of the term *reinforcer*. Suppose you find that an event follows a person's behavior and increases his or her rate of that behavior. You should call that event a reinforcer only for that person and that behavior. You cannot be sure that the event would reinforce other behaviors of that person, although it might. Nor can you be sure that the event would reinforce the same behavior in another person. Remember the old saying, "Different strokes for different folks," and limit your use of the term *reinforcer* to an event proven for a particular person. Do not depart from this very precise use of the term, the very essence of the meaning of *reinforcer*. Applied researchers have found that this precision is essential to helping people in many situations (e.g., Mason et al., 1989; Vollmer & Iwata, 1991).

Uses of Reinforcement

Reinforcement can be applied to all human behavior, and behavior analysts use the concept to guide their help for people. They deliberately arrange reinforcing events to follow useful behav-

Reinforcers Can Be Magic Too: The Case of the Glass Meadow

You may think the term *reinforcer* applies only to events like money, praise, or candy. Perhaps you think the magic of life is excluded. One mom and dad went night-sledding with their children after a freezing rain. "I will never forget the unbelievably beautiful sight that met our eyes when we reached the meadow. The moon and stars, shining brilliantly in the clear, cold night, had turned the meadow into a lake of glass... . We left most of the sledding to our children and stayed absorbed in the dreamlike magic of this night." They learned from this magic night to go with their children to other special moments. "We have gone with them to glimpse the moment—a new calf, a robin on the lawn, a butterfly or bug" (Carpenter, 1993).

5. Because these magic moments are events, not procedures, that follow going with their children and increase the rate of going, we call them ___________ (reinforcements, reinforcers).

Figure 8-2. A beautiful scene may reinforce the subtle behavior involved in looking at it.

iors. Behavior analysts aren't alone in using reinforcement; we all use reinforcement in our everyday lives—sometimes deliberately, more often without plan.

Behavior analysts use reinforcement to teach useful behavior to people. For example, the staff of a home for elderly people taught residents to choose healthy foods by praising them when they did so (Stock & Milan, 1993). Therapists taught people with retardation simple language skills by giving them candy when they made correct responses (e.g., Garcia, Guess, & Byrnes, 1973). Therapists taught people to relax (e.g., Budzynski & Stoyva, 1969). Coaches improved swimming warmups by following them with music (Hume & Crossman, 1992). A cooperative dorm increased the amount of cleaning by giving residents rent reductions (Feallock & Miller, 1976). Coaches have improved football blocking by giving players immediate feedback (Komaki & Barnett, 1977). Reinforcement helps many types of people improve their behavior.

Behavior analysts are not the only people who use reinforcement; ordinary people often make intuitive use of it. Madeline Cartwright used reinforcement to make an inner-city school into a dynamic learning center, as the "Changing Blaine Elementary School" box illustrates.

The Basic Building Block

The significance of reinforcement extends far beyond helping people improve their behavior. Behavior analysts claim that reinforcement is the basic building block of all human behavior. People are more likely to repeat behavior that produces reinforcement, and they are less likely to repeat behavior that does not. Ultimately, people usually do that which produces reinforcement. Thus, reinforcement is the basic motor that drives all human learning and hence everything that we are and do.

Reinforcement plays a central role in children's development. Suppose Danny cleans his room thoroughly. His parents might praise, hug, and otherwise pay increased attention to him, which may make Danny more likely to clean his room in the future. If so, attention is a reinforcer for room

© 1972 McNaught Synd., Inc.
7-10
"Boy! What do you do with all that swell stuff?"

Figure 8-3. A reinforcer for one person is not necessarily a reinforcer for another person. Cartoon © 1972 McNaught Syndicate, Inc., used by permission.

Figure 8-4. Meditation leads to normalizing body functions. Muscles relax, heart rate slows down, blood pressure decreases, hands warm. These changes may reinforce the internal behaviors involved in meditation.

cleaning. Behavior analysts believe that children learn many behaviors because of parental attention. Attention may reinforce talking clearly, using new words, studying in school, bathing, wearing clean clothes, saying "Thank you," and so on. The results shape the child's personality.

Misuse of Reinforcement

Of course, the use of attention doesn't always work out so nicely. Around dinnertime, Danny might pester Mom for a snack. She might reprimand or lecture him about not eating just before dinner. Such attention, although unpleasant, may be reinforcing to Danny. This is even more likely if Mom pays little attention to him otherwise. Misused parental attention can lead to many problem behaviors in children.

Behavior analysts find that parents aren't the only people who misuse their attention. Teachers attend to disruptive behavior—almost three times more frequently than they attend to constructive behavior (Thomas et al., 1978; White, 1975). This may account for the rise of violent and disorderly behavior in public schools. Friends often express sympathy for complaints of pain, and this may cause some people to develop chronic pain behaviors (White & Sanders, 1986). Mental hospital aides often attend to the "crazy" behavior of patients (e.g., Ayllon & Michael, 1959), perhaps caus-

Changing Blaine Elementary School

When Madeline Cartwright came as the new principal of Blaine School, it was crawling with roaches and rats. The teaching staff had given up. When she left, it was sparkling with the energy of its teachers, pupils, and parents. What did she do? She created a clothing room, where children who could not afford new clothes could get good used clothing. She bought a washer and dryer and made sure the kids had clean clothes. The kids looked well-clothed and clean. By attending school, children got clean clothes. As a result, their attendance increased. She used the power of positive reinforcement to improve Blaine School (Cartwright & D'Orso, 1993).

6. Because getting clothes <u>followed</u> attending and <u>increased</u> its rate, we call these events ____________________ (reinforcers, reinforcements).

ing much of the crazy behavior in mental hospitals. Nurses may show "understanding" whenever children with autism hurt themselves (Lovaas & Simmons, 1969). This may cause much of the self-injurious behavior that is so common with hospitalized people. Parents of delinquents frequently give in to their agressive behavior (e.g., Patterson, 1977). Many well-meaning people accidentally reinforce unpleasant behavior with their attention.

> ***Oops***
>
> "Our young daughter had adopted a stray cat. To my distress, he began to use the back of our new sofa as a scratching post. 'Don't worry,' my husband reassured me. 'I'll have him trained in no time.' I watched for several days as my husband patiently 'trained' our new pet. Whenever the cat scratched, my husband deposited him outdoors to teach him a lesson. The cat learned quickly. For the next 16 years, whenever he wanted to go outside, he scratched the back of the sofa." (Reported in *Behavior Analysis Digest*, March, 1990.)
>
> 8. You would call the event of being put out a(n) ______________ (reinforcer, reinforcement) for scratching the back of the sofa.

What Behavior Can Be Reinforced?

Behavior analysts have studied the impact of reinforcement on many types of behavior. I have given a wide range of examples, spanning the range of activities constituting behavior. They include obvious, subtle, internal, and private behaviors.

I have shown how reinforcement might apply to obvious behaviors such as eating spinach, going to school, and cleaning your room. I have given examples of increasing other obvious behaviors such as choosing healthy foods, warm-ups for swimmers, cleaning a co-op dorm, and football blocking assignments. There have also been examples of increasing obvious behaviors by mistake: pestering parents, disrupting classrooms, crazy behavior, delinquent behavior, and even self-injurious behavior.

I have shown how reinforcement might apply to subtle behaviors, such as telling the truth and sharing rare moments within a family. There have been examples of increasing other subtle behaviors, such as language skills among people with retardation. Later in this lesson, I will give an extended description of increasing the subtle behavior of creative word use.

One example of reinforcement given earlier involved increasing the internal behavior of relaxation. The whole field of biofeedback suggests that therapists can reinforce many internal behaviors. In fact, behavior analysts have reinforced individual brain cell activation (Stein, Xue, & Belluzzi, 1994). These authors suggest that they may have found "atoms" of behavior.

Finally, one example indicated how reinforcement by well-meaning friends might increase the private behavior of feeling pain. Skinner has argued that the form of thought called problem solving helps us control our world in ways that are reinforcing (Skinner, 1953b). Future lessons will provide other examples of how reinforcement can affect private behavior.

Thus, behavior analysts have shown that all forms of human activity are affected by reinforcement. It applies not only to obvious behaviors, but

> ***Even Presidents Can Misuse Reinforcement***
>
> Former president Nixon and Henry Kissinger were sitting in the Oval Office discussing policy matters. King Timahoe, Nixon's Irish setter, came in and began chewing on the rug. The president commanded him to stop. King Timahoe kept right on chewing. The president commanded again. More chewing. Finally, Nixon opened his desk drawer, took out a dog biscuit and gave it to King Timahoe. "Mr. President," said Kissinger, "you have taught that dog to chew the rug." (Based on Roberts & Santogrossi, 1976.)
>
> 7. If King Timahoe chewed on the rug more often after Nixon gave him a biscuit, we would say that Nixon used the behavioral procedure called ______________ (reinforcer, reinforcement).

also to subtle behaviors, internal behaviors, and private behaviors. It affects the entire range of human activity.

Summary

The first tactic in using the reinforcement strategy is to increase desired behavior through reinforcement. Reinforcement can modify behavior, causing both desirable and undesirable outcomes. Incompetent or unscrupulous persons can use it in dangerous ways. They might try to reinforce conformity, exploitation, or even criminal behavior. Behavior analysts can help people in safe ways. The key to safety is to consult with others about when and how to use reinforcement. Behavior analysts can train teachers to reinforce children for studying. They can teach parents to reinforce their children for desirable behavior. They can teach clients who want to improve themselves how to produce reinforcement. They can train members of groups to reinforce other members for working for the common good.

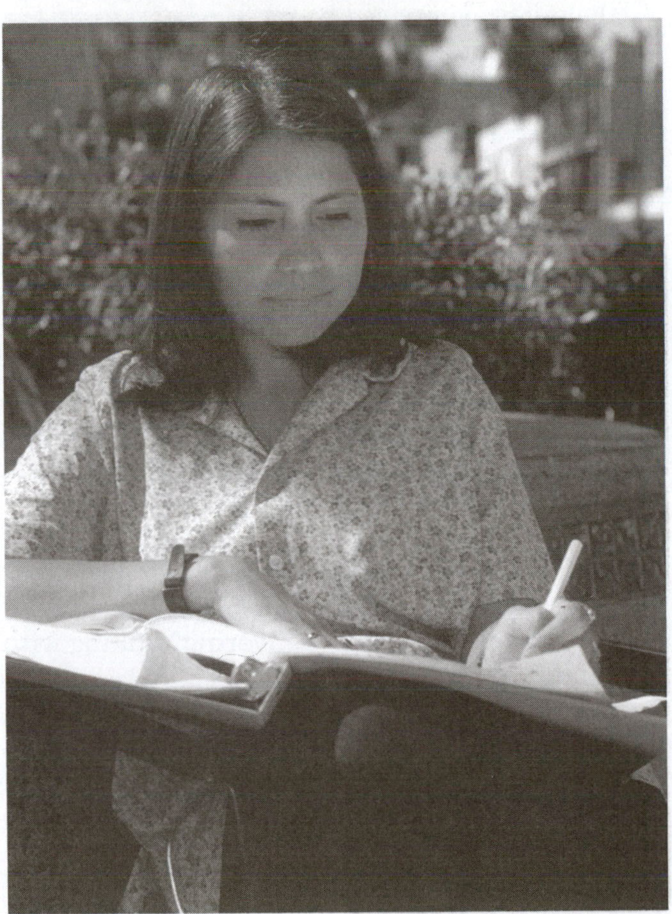

Figure 8-5. Passing your test tomorrow may reinforce the private behaviors involved in studying.

Behavior Analysis Examples

Helping Athletes

Two researchers used music to help teenage swimmers make better use of their warm-up time (Hume & Crossman, 1992). Typically these swimmers failed to stretch, run, do push-ups, or help other swimmers. Instead they ate, talked, played practical jokes, or even left practice. Kevin is a good example of this pattern; he made good use of about 10% of his time. The coach then announced that he would play music if the swimmers made better use of their time. Specifically, he set the goal of increasing good use of the warm-up period by 15%. Kevin increased his use of the warm-up period to about 45%, and the other members of the team made comparable improvements. The swimmers liked the procedure so much that they voted to continue using it.

9. Behavior analysts call the procedure of playing music only when team members make good use of the warm-up period ________________.

Creative Word Use

Researchers studied the creative use of words by fourth- and fifth-grade students (Glover & Gary, 1976). To do so, they created a game by putting the name of a new object on the blackboard every day. Suppose they wrote the word *football* on Monday. They would then give students ten minutes to list all the uses for footballs they could think of. Brad might respond, "throwing it, sitting on it, flinging it, and giving it to a friend." Suppose they wrote the word *video* on Tuesday. Brad might respond, "watching it, looking at it, writing an English paper about it, and giving it as a gift."

The researchers counted four aspects of Brad's responses. First, they counted the number of <u>different responses</u>—any use not identical to a use for another object. On Monday, Brad listed four uses for a football: throwing it, sitting on it, flinging it, and giving it to a friend. He would get a score of four different responses. Notice that even though throwing and flinging are similar, he used a different word. On Tuesday, Brad listed four uses for a video: watching, looking, writing, and giving it as a gift. He would clearly get credit for suggesting watching, looking, and writing, because these are different from the uses of a football. While he suggested giving the football as a gift, he did not word his giving of the video identically. So he gets credit for all four uses.

Second, they counted the number of different verb forms. Brad's list included watching, giving, looking, and writing about the video. They did not give him credit for watching and looking, since they have the same meaning. He would get a count of three verb forms.

Third, they counted the number of words per response. This was the number of words used by the students in explaining each use of the noun. Brad used 17 words to explain four uses, or an average of 4.33.

Fourth, they counted the number of infrequent verb forms. This was the number of verb forms students used that they had never used before. On Tuesday Brad used *watching*, *looking, giving*, and *writing*. He had not used *watching* or *writing* before (for football) but he had used *giving*, and *looking* was a duplicate form of *watching*. So he got a score of two for novel verb forms.

The researchers observed the baseline frequency of each of these behaviors daily. During treatment, the experimenter picked one behavior, such as verb forms. Each student earned a point for each new verb form. The researchers divided the group into two teams, competing against each other for the highest score. The team with the highest point total went to recess early. However, both teams could win if the lower team got 80% of the points earned by the higher team.

Figure 8-6 shows the results. During treatment, the number of different responses increased from 10 to 13; the number of different verb forms increased from 1 to 5 per day; the number of words per response increased from 3 to 13; and the number of infrequent verbs increased from 1 to 3. Each behavior decreased when the researchers removed treatment. Thus, for each aspect of creativity, when researchers awarded points, the behavior increased.

10. These data show that the event of going to recess early was a(n) ________________ for the students' creative responses.

The researchers wished to find out whether these behaviors would increase the children's creativity. They used a popular standardized test of creativity, giving the test before and after the experiment. The students' scores increased about 13% after their training. This suggests that these behaviors relate to what other psychologists consider to be creativity. Thus, the researchers' definition was socially valid.

Notes

Note #1

The definition of the term *reinforcer* requires the rate of the behavior to increase. You should be able to answer two questions about that increase. First question: The rate increases compared to what? The answer is: With respect to its baseline—in other words, compared to the period when the reinforcer does not follow the behavior. Second question: The rate increases when? The answer is: For the duration of the treatment period—for the period during which the event follows the behavior.

11. A reinforcer should increase the rate of the behavior compared to its ________________ and it should increase for the duration of the ________________ period.

Note #2

I will give you many examples in which people accidentally reinforce others for talking about their problems. Don't conclude that talking with people about their problems is harmful or that listening to their complaints is harmful. Behavior analysts always start by talking with their clients; it is the major component in many treatments. However, talking with people is like any other application of reinforcement. It can harm people if you don't know what you're doing.

12. If talking with people about their problems actually increased the rate of their complaining, the procedure of "delivering" talking with them would be called ________________.

Note #3

The definition of a reinforcer requires that you observe an increase in behavior caused by the event. Suppose you observe that the rate of a particular response increases, and the increase occurs after you start delivering some event following the response. This does not prove that the event caused the increase. Alternative events

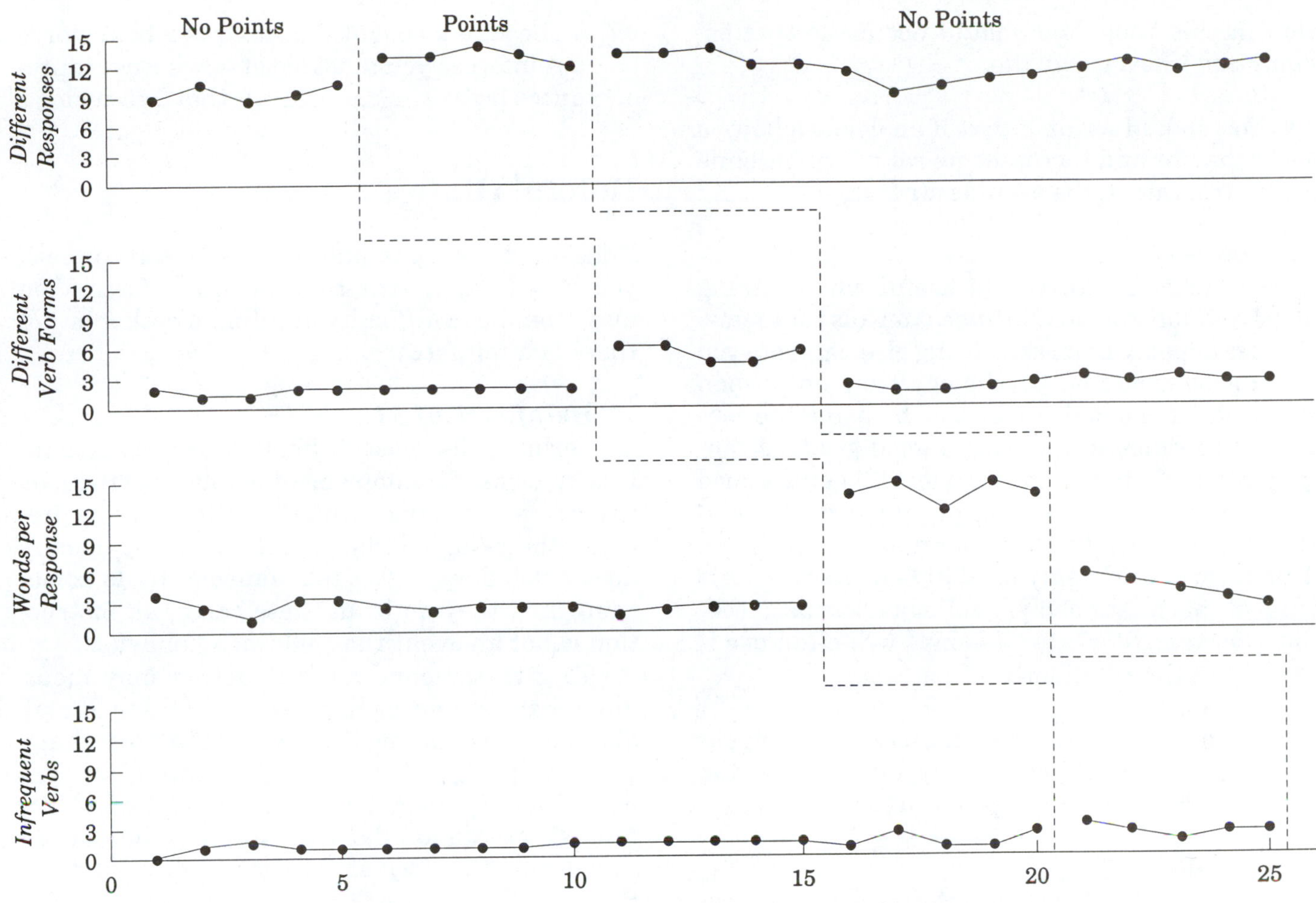

Figure 8-6. A reinforcing game can increase creative word usage. Adapted from "Procedures to Increase Some Aspects of Creativity," by J. Glover and A. Gary, *Journal of Applied Behavior Analysis,* 1976, *9,* 79–84. Copyright 1976 by the Society for the Experimental Analysis of Behavior, Inc. Used by permission.

could have caused the increase. For example, suppose the teacher gives John an M&M each time he raises his hand instead of just blurting out his question, and John then raises his hand more often. Without further research, the new behavior pattern doesn't prove that the teacher caused this increase by delivering the M&Ms. John's mother might have just told him always to raise his hand in class—or else!

The most rigorous way to prove that an event is a reinforcer is to use a reversal design. You observe the rate of a behavior during a baseline condition, then during the reinforcement condition. Suppose that it increases. Finally, you observe the rate of the behavior during a reversal-to-baseline condition. If it decreases, then you have firm evidence that the event is a reinforcer.

A slightly less rigorous way is to use a multiple-baseline design across behaviors. Suppose the rate of three behaviors increases only after each is followed by reinforcement. This is evidence that the event is reinforcing. Likewise, you could use a multiple-baseline design across different situations or different individuals.

13. To prove scientifically that an event is a reinforcer requires the researcher to use either a(n) ______________________ design or a(n) ______________________ design.

For convenience, this book assumes that an increase from baseline to treatment proves that the treatment was a reinforcer. That is, the book requires only a comparison design to prove that an event is a reinforcer. You should assume that if an event follows a behavior and increases its rate from baseline to treatment, the event is a reinforcer. However, remember that this is a convention in this book. You should not make that assumption in everyday life.

14. You should assume that if an event follows a behavior and increases its rate from baseline to treatment, the event is a(n) ____________.

Note #4

The term *contingent* is useful when talking about reinforcement. *Contingent* means that something is dependent on something else. Suppose you get a good grade on psychology tests only when you study. You can describe this by using the concept of contingency. Getting a good grade is contingent on studying. That is, you will get the good grade only if you study. A contingency is a relationship between the behavior and the reinforcer. This term is commonly used in behavior analysis to label this relationship. I will not use it as a technical term until a later lesson; I will often use it to refer to the relationship.

15. When I write that a reinforcer is contingent on a behavior, I mean that you won't get the reinforcer unless you perform the __________.

Note #5

A person's history of reinforcement often explains his or her current behavior. If Jamal has a history of reinforcement for working math problems, he is likely to use math skills now. If Rosa has a history of assertive behavior, she is likely to act assertively now. Many aspects of a person that we call personality stem from his or her history of reinforcement.

16. People's current behavior can often be explained by their past experience in receiving reinforcement for that behavior, which is called their *history of* ____________________.

Note #6

Please understand that you must observe whether an event increases behavior to be sure it is a reinforcer. One study showed that even teachers have trouble predicting what events will reinforce their own students (Dyer, Dunlap, & Winterling, 1990). Another study showed that caregivers can't predict what will reinforce people with retardation who are in their care (Green et al., 1991). Numerous studies confirm that casual observation does not lead to accurate predictions.

17. To be sure an event that follows a behavior is a reinforcer, you must observe whether it produces a(n) ____________ in that behavior.

Helpful Hints

I designed the remainder of this lesson to teach you how to apply the concept of reinforcer. You may often have difficulty deciding whether or not there is a reinforcer.

Helpful Hint #1

Perhaps the most difficult examples to analyze in terms of reinforcement involve instructions to perform a behavior. An instruction usually precedes the behavior that it influences; it usually does not follow it. You tell someone to do something, and they do it. In these cases, an instruction is not an event that follows a behavior.

To give someone an instruction may mean more than explaining how to do something. It may also mean instructing the person to do something. Thus, you might "tell," "ask," "remind," or "demand" of the person. If someone "tells," "asks," "reminds," or "demands" that another person do something, this is just another form of instruction.

The situation is murkier when an instruction follows a low-rate behavior and leads to an increase. You usually won't go wrong if you remember that an instruction can't be a reinforcer. An instruction will be labeled an unknown until later chapters, because it does not follow the behavior that it affects. Any verbal behavior is an instruction if it implies that a positive or negative consequence will follow the behavior. However, verbal behavior that follows a behavior and is not an instruction may be a reinforcer if it increases the rate of the behavior.

18. An instruction usually ______ (can, can't) be a reinforcer. If you are asked to identify an instruction in the examples, you should label it a(n) ____________________.

Helpful Hint #2

An "unpleasant" event may follow a behavior and, surprisingly, the behavior may increase in probability. For example, a person may engage in stupid arguments and be put down. Instead of shutting up, he or she may start more stupid arguments. Remember that the unpleasant event is a reinforcer, because it follows the behavior and increases its probability.

19. If an unpleasant event follows a behavior and increases the probability of that behavior, then the event would be termed a(n) __________.

Helpful Hint #3
Sometimes an event will occur concurrently with the behavior, and the rate of the behavior will increase. A teacher may watch while a child works a problem, and the rate of working problems may increase. The attention would be a reinforcer, because the word *follows* can refer to following the start of the behavior as well as its end. An event can qualify as a reinforcer if it follows the end of the behavior or if it follows the start of the behavior.

20. In other words, you should call an event that occurs at the same time as the behavior (and that increases the rate of that behavior) a(n) ______________________.

Helpful Hint #4
The situations on the following pages contain many examples of reinforcers. They also contain some examples in which only one element of these concepts is known. The example may tell you that the event follows the behavior but not whether it increases the behavior. Or you may know that the event increases the behavior but not whether it follows the behavior. You should label such an event an unknown.

21. If you know only that an event follows a behavior, you should label it as a(n) __________ in this book.

Helpful Hint #5
The book will ask you to distinguish between *reinforcer* and *reinforcement* throughout the rest of the book. Remember that a reinforcer is an event that follows a behavior and increases the rate of the behavior. Reinforcement is the procedure of delivering that event following the behavior. For example, suppose the rate of a behavior increases after an event follows it. The book may ask two kinds of questions. It might ask you, "What is the event called?" In this case, you should label it a reinforcer. The book might ask, "What behavioral procedure did Mom use to increase the behavior?" In this case, you should label it reinforcement.

22. If an event follows a behavior and increases the rate of the behavior you should call it a(n) ______________. The procedure of delivering that event following a behavior is called ______________.

Additional Readings

Allen, K. E., Hart, B. M., Buell, J. S., Harris, F. R., & Wolf, M. M. (1964). Effects of social reinforcement on isolate behavior of a nursery school child. *Child Development*, *35*, 511–518. The teacher used her attention to reinforce a shy child for playing with other children. The child played much more often with other children.

Homme, L. E., DeBaca, P. C., Devine, J. V., Steinhorst, R., & Rickert, E. J. (1963). Use of the Premack Principle in controlling the behavior of nursery school children. *Journal of the Experimental Analysis of Behavior*, *6*, 554. This article discusses an interesting use of reinforcement. It illustrates the Premack principle for finding reinforcers. "Suppose Behavior B is more likely than Behavior A. You can reinforce Behavior A by making permission to engage in Behavior B depend upon it." The authors noted that preschool children ran and screamed at a high rate. They did not often sit and look at the blackboard. The researchers gave permission to run and scream only after the children sat and looked at the blackboard, and the rate of sitting and looking increased dramatically. Another reinforcing event was kicking the wastebasket. The most reinforcing event was pushing the instructor around the room in a chair. Who says reinforcement has to be serious?

McEvoy, M. A., Nordquist, V. M., Twardosz, S., Heckaman, K. A., Wehby, J. H., & Denny, R. K. (1988). Promoting autistic children's peer interaction in an integrated early childhood setting using affection activities. *Journal of Applied Behavior Analysis*, *21*, 193–200. These researchers used affection to help integrate children with retardation into a normal classroom. They prompted the children to show affection through hugs, smiles, and words. After this show of affection, the normal children and children with retardation interacted many times more often.

Osborne, J. G. (1969). Free-time as a reinforcer in the management of classroom behavior. *Journal of Applied Behavior Analysis*, *2*, 113–118. This article reports the effective use of free time as a reinforcer. The researcher studied children in a normally rowdy classroom. He got the teacher to let them have extra free time if they stayed in their seats during study time. The number of children staying seated increased.

Reading Quiz

81. The major concept that lies at the heart of most environmental influences that create and maintain behavior is the behavioral procedure called ______________.
79. Tactic #1 in using the reinforcement strategy to solve human problems is increase desired behavior through ______________.
49. Review: Any event that <u>follows</u> a behavior and that <u>increases</u> the probability of that behavior is called a(n) ______________.
3. A reinforcer is any event that <u>follows</u> a behavior and ______________ (decreases, increases) the probability of that behavior.
4. A reinforcer is any event that ______________ (follows, precedes) a behavior and <u>increases</u> the probability of that behavior.
46. Review: A reinforcer is any <u>event</u> that ________ a behavior and ______________ the probability of that behavior.
82. The term *reinforcement* is used to refer to the <u>procedure</u> of arranging for an event to follow a behavior, knowing the event will ______________ the rate of the behavior.
67. Review: The <u>procedure</u> of delivering a reinforcer is called ______________. An <u>event</u> that follows a behavior and increases its rate is called a(n) ______________.
39. If Davey eats spinach in the future because he was given dessert after eating spinach in the past, then the dessert would be called a(n) ______________.
40. If the rate of eating spinach is increased by delivering a dessert after spinach is eaten, this <u>procedure</u> is called ______________.
69. Review: When you're talking about reinforcement, you should remember that you do not reinforce a person, you reinforce his or her ______________.
36. If an event follows a behavior and increases the rate of that behavior, you should call it a reinforcer. However, if it does not both follow and increase the behavior, then you should label it a(n) ______________ (reinforcer, unknown).
31. Here is one way an event can be similar to a reinforcer but still not be a reinforcer. If an event <u>precedes</u> a behavior and increases the rate of the behavior, you should call it a(n) ______________ (reinforcer, unknown)
88. You must distinguish closely related examples. First example: Suppose you smile everytime that Tim looks at you, and Tim then looks at you more often. Because your smile follows his looking and his looking increases, you call your smile a(n) ______________ (reinforcer, unknown).
72. Second example: Suppose you whisper "Psst" and Tim looks at you. Suppose you whisper "Psst" often, so that the rate of Tim's looking at you increases. Because your "Psst" <u>precedes</u> his looks, even though his looking increases, you call your "Psst" a(n) ______________ (reinforcer, unknown)
32. Here is the other way an event can be similar to a reinforcer but still not be a reinforcer. If an event follows a behavior and <u>doesn't increase</u> the rate of the behavior, is it a reinforcer? ______________
5. Again, you must distinguish closely related examples. First example: you're a little kid, and you've never thrown horseshoes before. You throw for a while but can't quite get the hang of it. Then you throw a ringer, the best throw possible. Your rate of throwing goes up. The event of throwing a ringer is called a(n) ______________.
73. Second example: You're a different little kid who has never thrown horseshoes before. You throw for a while but can't quite get the hang of it. Then you throw a ringer, the best throw possible. Your rate of throwing doesn't change. The event of throwing a ringer is called a(n) ______________.
30. Here are a few practice examples. Suppose Mom gave Tommy a dessert whenever he ate his spinach, but Tommy didn't eat his spinach any more often after that. Because the

dessert did not increase the rate of eating spinach, we call the event of giving the dessert a(n) ______________ in this book.

77. Suppose Mom told Tommy he had to eat his spinach from now on. Tommy might eat his spinach more often after that. Because mom's demand did not follow Tommy's spinach eating, we call the event "Mom told Tommy he had to eat his spinach" a(n) ___________ (until a later chapter).
83. Tommy burped at the table, and Mom yelled at him, "That's disgusting!" Tommy burped more often as a result of Mom's reaction. Label the event of Mom's yelling a(n) ______________.
15. Every time Tommy burped at the table, Mom calmly said "Don't do that at the table, young man!" Tommy burped no more often as a result of Mom's reaction. Label the event of Mom's calm comment as a(n) ______________.
8. Be careful about this one. As they sat down to dinner, Mom said "I know your stomach is upset. You can burp at the table tonight." Tommy burped at the table much more than usual that night. You should label the event of Mom's comment as a(n) ______________.
34. Here's a variation that many students have trouble with. Suppose Tommy apologizes for one of his burps, and his Dad gives him $5. Many students seem to assume that money will always be a reinforcer for everyone. They forget to check whether the money increases the rate of the behavior. Would you call the $5 a reinforcer if Tommy's rate of apologizing did not increase? ______
84. Johnny's Dad gave him $5 for apologizing for a burp at the dinner table. Johnny's rate of apologizing increased after that. What is the $5 called? ____________
85. Tommy's Dad gave him $5 for apologizing for a burp at the dinner table. Tommy's rate of apologizing didn't change after that. What is the $5 called? ______________
44. Remember, no matter how desirable an event may seem to you, if it doesn't increase the rate of a behavior that it follows, it __________ (is, isn't) a reinforcer.
6. An event must have two elements to be a reinforcer. It must be timed so that it ________ (precedes, follows) the behavior of interest. It must also cause that behavior to ____________ in rate.
61. Review: Remember, if an event has one, but not both, elements of a reinforcer, I will call it a(n) ______________ in this book.
42. One last point on this issue. If an example tells you only that an event increases a behavior, you should call it a(n) ____________, because you don't know if it followed the behavior.
2. A limitless variety of events, such as attention, candy, jogging, or money, might be given following a desired behavior. If they increase the rate of the behavior, then they serve as ________________________.
17. For the Mom and Dad who captured the magic of the glass meadow, similar rare and magic moments with their children are events that serve as ______________ for them.
43. People may deliberately contrive, or nature may deliver, the procedure of ____________.
60. Review: Remember, if we discover that an event is a reinforcer for a particular behavior for a particular person, we cannot conclude that it will reinforce a different __________ in the same person.
14. Behavior analysts have been guided to help individuals who otherwise would not engage in a functional behavior by the behavioral procedure called ______________.
16. Ordinary people, not just behavior analysts, often make intuitive use of events, called ______________.
9. Because Blaine School saw an increase in attendance after providing children with new, clean clothes and teacher praise, these events would be called ______________.
74. Suppose Blaine School provided children with new, clean clothes and teacher praise after they came to school, but their attendance did not increase. I want you to call these events ______________.
13. The behavior analysts claim that reinforcement is the basic building block of all human ______________.
80. The effect of parental attention on children's behavior indicates that the procedure of _____ ______________ plays a central role in children's development.
41. Nixon gave King Timahoe a biscuit after he chewed on the rug. Suppose the dog chewed on the rug no more often after Nixon gave him a dog biscuit. Check the first two sentences to see if Nixon gave the dog the biscuit preceding or following the chewing. Also check

to see if the chewing increased. Now you can confidently label the procedure that Nixon used as ______________.

51. Review: Dad put the cat out for scratching the sofa. Because it resulted in the cat scratching the sofa more often, the event of being put out would be a(n) ______________ for scratching the back of the sofa.
35. Hume and Crossman (1992) delivered music to swimmers following their increased use of a warm-up period. This procedure would be called ______________.
87. When Glover and Gary (1976) awarded points for a creative behavior, that behavior increased. The results of this multiple-baseline study showed that the points were a(n) ______________ for the students' creative word use.
28. Glover and Gary (1976) defined "number of infrequent verbs" as "the number of verbs used in describing an object that had never before been used by the student." Behavior analysts call this statement a(n) ______________ ______________.
29. Glover and Gary (1976) gave a standardized test for creativity, accepted by other psychologists, before and after their experiment. These other psychologists judged what behaviors indicated creativity when creating their test. The agreement of the standardized test with Glover and Gary's behavioral definitions showed that their definition of creativity has ______________.
22. From Note #3: We will assume in the examples given in this book that if an event that follows the behavior, and the behavior increases, the event is actually a(n) ______________, even without scientific proof.
23. From Note #4: When I write that a reinforcer is contingent on a behavior, I mean that you won't get the reinforcer unless you perform the ______________.
24. From Note #5: People's current behavior can often be explained by their past experience in receiving reinforcement for that behavior. Behavior analysts call this experience their history of ______________.
25. From Note #5: What people are currently doing can often be explained by their past history in receiving reinforcement for that behavior. Behavior analysts call this experience their ______________ of reinforcement.
26. From Note #5: What someone is doing right now is often explained by his or her past experience in receiving reinforcement for that behavior. Behavior analysts call this experience the person's ______________ of ______________.
27. From Note #6: Studies have shown that even teachers who know their students well often cannot predict what events will be reinforcers. You cannot guess about what is a reinforcer. To be sure that an event that follows a behavior is a reinforcer, you must observe whether it produces a(n) ______________ in that behavior.
18. From Helpful Hint #1: The event "Bob tells Mary to take out the garbage" may increase the rate of Mary's taking out the garbage. However, such an instruction will usually ______________ (precede, follow) actually taking out the garbage.
11. Because the event "Bob tells Mary to take out the garbage" increases the rate of Mary's taking out the garbage but does not follow it, you ______________ (can, can't) call "Bob's telling" a reinforcer.
12. Because the event "Bob tells Mary to take out the garbage" increases the rate of Mary's taking out the garbage but does not follow it, you would call "Bob's telling" a(n) ______________.
86. When do you usually tell someone to do something? Do you tell them following their behavior of doing it, or do you tell them preceding their behavior of doing it? ______________ (following, preceding)
10. Because instructions generally precede the behavior that they influence, they generally would be called a(n) ______________ rather than a reinforcer.
1. The term *instruction* refers to any talk that lets another person know you want him or her to do something. You might "tell," "ask," "remind," or "demand" of the person. If Jim demands that Jack study, and Jack then studies, is the event "Jim demands" likely to be a reinforcer? ______
37. If Ann asks Larry to make his bed every day, and he does, I want you to call this a(n) ______________ (until I teach you about instructions in a later chapter).
38. If Ann thanks Ben for cooking dinner, and he cooks dinner more often, I want you to call Ann's thanks a(n) ______________.
56. Review: If Pablo reminds Eduardo to eat brown

rice for lunch, and he does, you would label Pablo's procedure as ______________.

33. Here's a twist on what you just learned. Suppose an instruction follows an <u>incorrect</u> performance of a behavior. Suppose you observe an increase in the <u>correct</u> performance of the behavior. The instruction can't be a reinforcer for correct behavior, because it did not follow the ________________ (correct, incorrect) behavior.
64. Review: Suppose Ben fails to make his bed, and Mom tells him to make it from now on. Suppose Ben's rate of making his bed increases. You should label Mom's telling as a(n) ____________________.
76. Suppose Ben makes his bed, and Dad gives him a driving lesson. Suppose Ben's rate of making his bed increases. You should label Dad's driving lesson as a(n) ______________.
19. From Helpful Hint #2: If an unpleasant event follows a behavior and increases the probability of that behavior, then the event would be termed a(n) ______________.
62. Review: Suppose George makes a terrible face every time Wendy serves steamed broccoli for dinner. If Wendy's rate of serving steamed broccoli increases, George's terrible face would be called a(n) ______________.
75. Suppose George gives Wendy an extra $100 for fun money whenever she serves steamed broccoli for dinner. If Wendy's rate of serving steamed broccoli stays the same, the $100 would be called a(n) ______________.
63. Review: Suppose George asks Wendy to serve steamed broccoli for dinner more often. If Wendy's rate of serving steamed broccoli increases, George's request would be called a(n) ________________.
20. From Helpful Hint #3: An event can qualify as a reinforcer if it follows the end of the behavior or if it follows the start of the behavior. In other words, you should call an event that occurs at the same time as the behavior (and increases the rate of the behavior) a(n) ________________.
78. Suppose you know only that an event follows a behavior. You should label such an event a(n) ____________ in this book.
7. An event that follows a behavior and increases the rate of the behavior is called a(n) ______ ______________. The procedure of delivering that event whenever a behavior occurs is called ______________.
21. From Helpful Hint #5: An example might tell you that Tom praised Anneli every time she asked a question at the Greenpeace meeting. It might tell you that Anneli's rate of questions increased. It might then ask what a single instance of Tom's praise is called. This is like asking what the event is called. You should answer that a single occurrence of Tom's praise following Ann's questioning is a(n) ____________________.
58. Review: In the study by Glover and Gary (1976), points were awarded for creative responses. The points would be called a(n) ____________; awarding the points to increase creativity would be called ____________________.
45. Review: A reinforcer is any event that is timed to ____________________ a behavior and ____________________ the probability of that behavior.
50. Review: Behavior analysts claim that the basic building block of all human behavior is ________________.
65. Review: Tactic #1 in the reinforcement strategy may enable you to increase the rate of desired behavior through ______________.
48. Review: After every statement that Rhonda made to Kevin about her problems, Kevin expressed sympathy. If Rhonda started telling Kevin more about her problems, the procedure of delivering sympathy for her complaints would be called ______________.
59. Review: Kevin expressed sympathy every time Rhonda complained about one of her problems. Rhonda's rate of complaining remained the same. What procedure did Kevin use when delivering sympathy? ______________
68. Review: To be sure that an event is a reinforcer, you must observe to see if it actually results in a(n) ____________ in behavior.
52. Review: If an event follows a behavior and results in an increase in the behavior, that event is called a(n) ____________.
47. Review: A researcher must use either a(n) ____________________ design or a(n) ____________________ design to prove scientifically that an event is a reinforcer.
54. Review: If an instruction follows an <u>incorrect</u> performance of a behavior and leads to an increase in the <u>correct</u> performance of the behavior, it would be called a(n) ____________. (Think about this one.)

55. Review: If an unpleasant event follows a behavior and increases the probability of that behavior, the event would be termed a(n) ________________.
66. Review: Tactic #1 in using the reinforcement strategy to solve human problems is to increase desired behavior through __________.
71. Review: You know only that an event increases a behavior. You should label it in this book as a(n) ________________.
53. Review: If an event occurs while someone is making a response, it is considered to be the same as an event following the response. Therefore, if the event also increases the probability of the behavior, we would call the event a(n) ________________.
70. Review: Whenever Maggy waved at him, Tom gave her one of those wonderful smiles. Maggy started waving at him more often. What is a single smile called? ____________
57. Review: If you deliver an event following a behavior, and the rate of the behavior doesn't change, the book will always label the procedure as ______________.

Examples

1. Carla sometimes smiled at men she passed on campus. One day she smiled at a guy, and he then came right up and asked her for a date. Carla now smiles at many of the guys she passes on campus, and she frequently gets asked out for interesting dates. Check for both elements of reinforcement. First, when Carla smiled, getting a date ______________ (followed, preceded). Second, after she started getting dates, the rate at which Carla smiled ____________________ (decreased, increased, stayed steady). In this example, getting a date is an event that follows smiling and that increases the rate of smiling. Therefore, getting a date is a(n) ______________.

2. Alma liked Grant a lot, but he rarely did favors for her such as opening doors or helping her put her coat on. So she started saying "Thank you" immediately after a favor. After a month, Alma found that Grant still rarely did favors for her. Check for two elements. First, when Grant did a favor, Alma's thanks ____________________ (followed, preceded). Second, his rate of doing favors __________________ (decreased, increased, stayed steady). Because the "Thank you" followed the behavior but did not increase the rate of doing favors, it should be labeled a(n) ____________.

3. Jose's TV set went on the blink during the NFL playoffs, so he tapped it with the palm of his hand. Immediately, the picture cleared up. Now, whenever the picture goes bad, he taps the set. Check for two elements. First, when Jose tapped, picture clearing ______________ (followed, preceded). Second, Jose's rate of tapping the set ____________________. Therefore, the event of the picture clearing up is an example of a(n) ______________________.

4. Sam was a fourth-grader who liked to wander around town after school. His mother worried about him, especially after he described what the underside of a train looked like. She therefore told him to come straight home from school, and Sam started coming home earlier. Check for both elements. First, Mom told Sam to come straight home following not coming home. Therefore, Mom's telling Sam to come straight home didn't follow coming home. When Sam started coming straight home, Mom's telling ______________ (followed, preceded). Second, the rate of Sam's coming right home after school ____________ after his mother told him to. You should label Mom's telling as a(n) ____________. You could also have guessed that this cannot be an example of a reinforcer, because of the rule, "An instruction ________ (can, can't) be a reinforcer."

5. Dave was a slob; he would rip off his clothes at night and just throw them down. Shawna, his roommate, didn't like living with the resulting mess, so she asked Dave to please hang up his stuff. No result. She then started looking carefully for any time that Dave did hang up even one article of clothing. When he did so, she gave him a special hand-printed ticket that read, "This ticket is good for one special gift of your choosing." Dave started picking up all his clothes. Check for both elements. First, when Dave picked up, Shawna's ticket giving ______________. Second, the rate of Dave's picking up ____________. Therefore, you would call the event of giving a ticket a(n) ____________________.

6. Verna decided that her child Tom interrupted her too often. She tried to punish him every time he interrupted, by giving him a good spanking. She was disappointed, however, because Tom seemed to interrupt much more often than before. She concluded that punishment just doesn't work with some children. Check both elements.

First, when Tom interrupted, Verna's spanking was timed to ______________. Second, Tom's interrupting ______________ in rate. Therefore, the spanking is an unpleasant event that a behavior analyst would label a(n) ______________.

7. Elvis used to be a safe and sane driver. One day he was in a hurry to get to a movie that supposedly had a torrid opening love scene, so he drove fast. He noticed that as soon as he increased his speed, his girlfriend appeared frightened and leaned on him much more than usual. Elvis frequently drove fast after that. Check both elements. First, Elvis's girlfriend leaned on him while he was still speeding. You could say that her leaning followed the beginning of his speeding. Thus, the moment that Elvis started to speed, his girlfriend's leaning was timed to ______________. Second, the rate of Elvis's speeding ______________. Therefore, you should label the event of her leaning on him a(n) ______________.

8. As usual, Francie didn't do her homework Thursday night. The teacher firmly told her to start doing her homework. From then on, Francie did her homework all the time. Be sure to check for both elements. First, did the teacher's demand follow doing the homework? Second, did Francie's rate of homework increase? Therefore, the event "teacher demanded" is called a(n) ______________.

9. Marty was in second grade. One day during spelling, he laid his head on the desk. The teacher asked him what was the matter, and he said, "Teacher, I have a terrible headhurt." The teacher, a kind woman, soothed him by saying, "That's too bad, Marty. Why don't you just lay your head down until it feels better?" It was noted that Marty frequently complained about headaches after that, even though he had never had any in the previous year. Marty's schoolwork became much poorer. First, did the teacher's permission to rest follow Marty's complaint of a headache? Second, did Marty's rate of complaining about headaches increase? Therefore, the teacher's permission to rest is an event called a(n) ______________. The procedure of giving permission following a complaint is called ______________.

10. Linda didn't talk with her roommate Priscilla very often. However, whenever Priscilla complained about how badly life was going for her, Linda would reassure her that everything would be okay. After several months, Priscilla was talking about how awful life was even more often than before. Check: Does reassurance follow complaining? Does complaining increase? Therefore, Linda's <u>procedure</u> of reassuring complaints would be an example of ______________. The event of reassurance is an example of ______________.

11. Review: May came home from school on Monday and told her parents that she had finally beaten up the little boy who had been tormenting her every day. On Friday, May's father took her out for ice cream and told her it was a special treat for beating up the awful little boy. May now beats up the little boy more often. What is the ice cream an example of? ______________

12. Review: Bill almost never welcomed Jane home when she finished her late evening class. So Jane decided on a new approach: When Bill did welcome her, she kissed him. Naturally, Bill's rate increased. What behavioral procedure did Jane use? ______________

13. Review: Professor Reynolds was dissatisfied with his students' rate of participation in his discussion class. So he announced that he would award all students who presented good ideas during discussion with a bonus point toward their grade. They would know they got it because he would write it in his book as soon as it happened. Professor Reynolds was disheartened to discover that none of his students participated more often as a result of his new rule. What procedure did he use? ______________

14. Review: Gail felt that her 6-year-old son Jimmy did not hug her often enough. She started giving him a special treat every time that he spontaneously hugged her, and she found that Jimmy gradually hugged her more often. Gail used what behavioral procedure? ______________

15. Review: Leslie had long regretted being so remote from her parents. She had tried talking with them about it to no avail. So she decided that she would give them a really nice compliment anytime her parents shared something intimate with her. Their rate slowly increased. One of Leslie's compliments would be an example of a(n) ______________.

16. Review: Dollie was really turned off by Jim's table manners. So she asked him to request food rather than just grabbing it. To her surprise, Jim started asking her to pass food. Dollie's asking Jim to request food is an example of what behavioral procedure? ______________

17. Review: Carla sometimes went to the club for a little dancing. However, she was a super dancer and was bored dancing with most of the

guys who usually hung out there. One day Steve asked her to dance, and she found out that he was also a super dancer. She started dancing a lot more after Steve started asking her. One dance with Steve is a(n) ________________.

18. Review: John complained of problems every once in a while. One day his friend had a long talk with him. After that, John complained more often of his problems and thus had more talks with his friend. His friend inadvertently used what procedure to increase John's rate of complaining?

____

19. Review: Larry sometimes commented that he liked long hair. His friends always agreed with him, and they frequently discussed the stupidity of many older people's reaction to long hair. Larry's rate of commenting about long hair remained unchanged. What behavioral procedure did his friends' agreement exemplify? ______________

20. Review: Stuart spontaneously trimmed the front hedge around his home one day. His parents were delighted and took him out for a steak dinner to thank him for his spontaneous helping around the house. His spontaneous helping increased. What behavioral procedure did his parents use? ___________________

LESSON

9 Extinction of Everyday Behaviors

In the last lesson, you learned about reinforcement, a procedure that increases the rate of a behavior. In this lesson, you will learn about extinction—a procedure that decreases the rate of a behavior.

You can use extinction to help solve human problems when you need to decrease an undesirable behavior rather than increase a desirable one. It is very useful because it is a gentle way to decrease the rate of a behavior. You will see that you do not need to hurt, coerce, or punish people to help them reduce their unpleasant or harmful behaviors. With extinction, you simply remove the reinforcers that were maintaining that behavior. Tactic #2 in using the reinforcement strategy for solving human problems is to decrease undesired behavior through extinction.

1. Tactic #2 in using the reinforcement strategy for solving human problems is to decrease undesired behavior through ____________.

Definition of Extinction

Extinction is the procedure of (1) stopping the delivery of a reinforcer that follows a behavior and (2) finding a decrease in the rate of the behavior. You should call a procedure *extinction* only if it has both of these elements. Behavior analysts call the act of using extinction extinguishing the behavior.

2. Extinction is the procedure of (1) __________ the delivery of a reinforcer that follows a behavior and (2) finding a ____________ in the rate of the behavior.

The definition of extinction states that the event being stopped is a reinforcer. Why this connection between reinforcement and extinction? If the event is a reinforcer, its delivery must have increased the rate of the behavior. Therefore, stopping its delivery must decrease the rate of the behavior. Here is another connection. Remember that using a reversal design is the best way to find out if an event is a reinforcer. You find the rate of the behavior during baseline, the period when the event does not follow the behavior. You observe the rate again during the treatment, when the event follows the behavior. Finally, you observe the rate during reversal, when you stop delivery of the event. Therefore, we call that an extinction condition. Extinction and reinforcement include each other in their definitions.

Two elements must be present for a condition to be called *extinction*. First, you must stop the delivery of a reinforcer. Second, you must observe a decrease in the behavior. For example, suppose Mom accidentally reinforces Tommy's burping by yelling, "That's disgusting!" Tommy starts burping often during meals. Mom might realize her mistake and stop the reinforcer, and Tommy's rate of burping might then decrease. In this case, Mom stopped the reinforcer, and the behavior decreased. Since both elements are present, we would label this *extinction*. We would say that Mom extinguished Tommy's burping.

If only one element is present, you should not label the procedure as extinction. For example, suppose Mom told Tommy before he sat down for his next meal that he mustn't burp at the table anymore. Tommy might stop burping at the table. However, Mom's instruction cannot be a reinforcer. Therefore, in this case, the behavior decreased, but Mom did not stop the reinforcer. Since only one element was present, we would not label this *extinction*. I will follow the convention of calling such a situation an *unknown*.

Of course, either element might be missing. For example, suppose Mom stopped yelling, "That's disgusting" whenever Tommy burped at the table.

Tommy might not stop burping at the table. In this case, Mom stopped a reinforcer, but the behavior did not decrease. Since only one element was present, we would not label this *extinction*. You should also label this situation as an *unknown*.

Before you label any situation as *extinction*, be sure that both elements required in the definition are present. The reinforcer must be stopped, and the behavior must decrease. If either element is missing, do not label the situation as *extinction*. Label it as *unknown*.

Uses for Extinction

In the preceding lesson, I described some cases where people often reinforce undesirable behaviors. Extinction gives us a gentle but effective method for dealing with undesirable behavior. For example, most of us assume that children with retardation who hit themselves are crazy or stupid. But Lovaas and Simmons (1969) guessed that this behavior was a method to get attention from the children's attendants. To check this guess, they picked the most active self-hitting children from among several thousand in local hospitals.

John was an 8-year-old with an IQ of 24. He often struck his forehead with his fists and knuckles, giving himself bruises and contusions. Whenever John struck himself, the hospital attendants put him in restraints to keep him from hurting himself. However, they had to give him lots of attention to get him into the restraints. The researchers guessed that this attention reinforced John's behavior of hitting himself. To test this, the researchers took the restraints off John and did not put them on again. By abandoning the restraints, the researchers stopped giving John the attention involved in putting them on. At first, their approach seemed to fail. John struck himself at the rate of once every two seconds, for a total of more than 2500 times during the first hour and a half. Over the next ten days, John struck himself almost 9000 times. However, during this time, his rate gradually decreased and finally dropped to zero. By the end of ten days, John could sit in the room without restraints.

This case exemplifies extinction. The researchers stopped the delivery of a reinforcer—attention—for hitting. They saw a decrease in the rate of hitting. The example contains both elements of extinction.

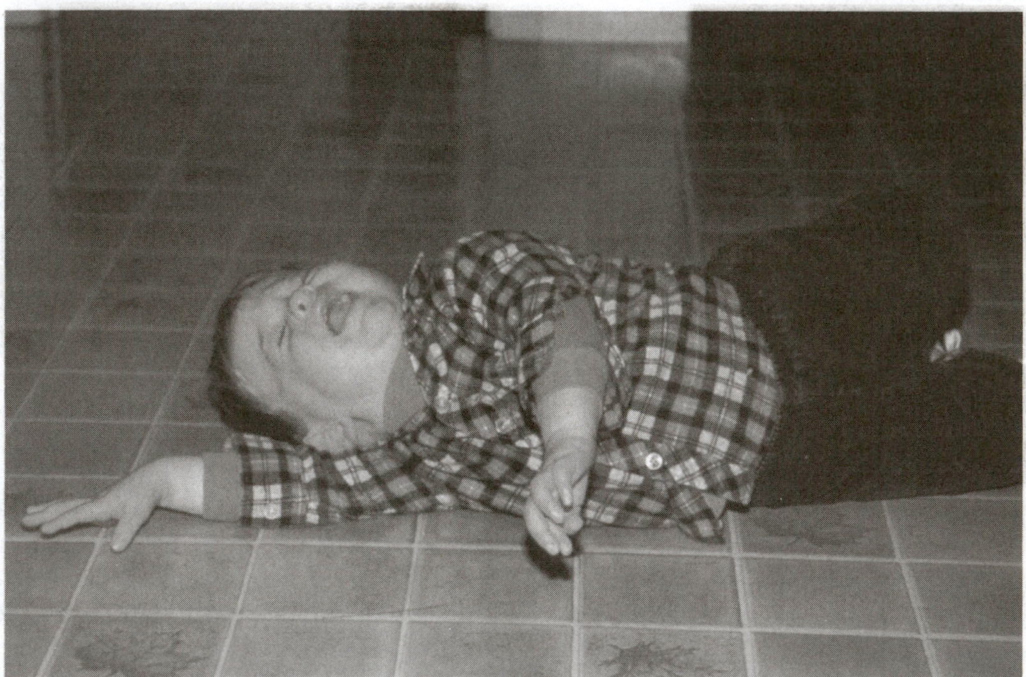

Figure 9-1. Many small children try to assert their will by throwing temper tantrums. This behavior is often reinforced by busy caregivers, who pay attention only when the child throws a tantrum. When this is the case, the behavior can often be extinguished by teaching the caregiver to stop giving attention for tantrums.

This case also illustrates another aspect of extinction, called the *extinction burst*. An extinction burst is a temporary increase in responding as soon as extinction begins. John illustrated this increase when he hit himself once every two seconds at the beginning of extinction. It is almost as if he couldn't believe that no one would pay attention when he was hitting himself. The occurrence of an extinction burst may discourage people who try to use extinction. If this ever happens to you, the solution is simply to persist until the person finishes with the extinction burst.

An extinction burst is a temporary increase in responding as soon as extinction begins.

Another researcher used a very clever way to decrease self-injury (Luiselli, 1991). She put mittens on the patient's hands so that their blows would not cause injury. This gradually reduced hitting.

Behavior analysts rarely use extinction of self-injurious behavior (SIB) by itself. People can seriously hurt themselves during an extinction burst before they stop. Therefore, behavior analysts often use punishment initially. That way, they can reduce SIB quickly before it causes much injury (e.g., Linscheid et al., 1990). They often combine punishment with extinction. Behavioral methods are the only effective way to reduce SIB; there is little scientific evidence that medical or psychodynamic methods can reduce it (Favell et al., 1982).

Williams (1959) described an example of extinction with a normal 2-year-old child who lived with his parents. The parents reinforced the child's behavior by comforting him anytime he cried after being put to bed. As a result, the child cried and raged whenever his parents put him to bed. He typically took several hours to go to sleep. Williams advised the parents to put the child to bed and then firmly ignore the crying. Figure 9-2 is a graph of the resulting crying. On the first day, the child cried for a total of 45 minutes before quitting and going to sleep. This is typical of an extinction burst. It might have discouraged the parents had the researchers not warned them to expect it. On the second day, the child did not cry at all. On successive days, the child cried for only a few minutes, finally stopping on the seventh day. An unexpected reversal (not shown on the graph) occurred when the child's aunt took care of him one night; she comforted him when he cried. The next night, the parents ignored the child's crying, and

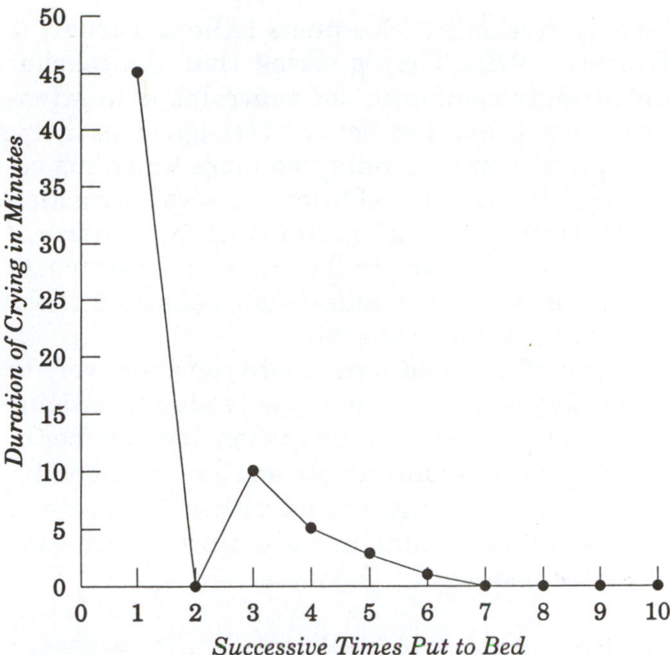

Figure 9-2. Number of minutes a chronic crier cried after being put to bed and ignored on ten successive nights. The parent previously comforted the child if he cried. Adapted from "The Elimination of Tantrum Behavior by Extinction Procedure," by C. D. Williams, *Journal of Abnormal and Social Psychology*, 1959, *59*, 269. Copyright 1959 by the American Psychological Association. Reprinted by permission.

he again showed an extinction burst. His crying lasted for almost an hour. The crying rapidly decreased and stopped in the following days.

Williams's (1959) use of ignoring is a clear case of extinction. The parents stopped their comforting, and he had reinforced crying, and the crying then decreased. Similar studies with crying at night also report success (e.g., France & Hudson, 1990; Seymour et al., 1983). Several studies have used graduated extinction (Durand & Mindell, 1990; Lawton, France & Blampied, 1991). The parents wait longer and longer before attending to crying, and the crying gradually stops. The only alternative to behavioral management of crying is drugs (France & Hudson, 1990). Drugs are not acceptable to most parents.

I noted in the preceding lesson that public school teachers pay far more attention to undesirable behaviors than to desirable ones. The widespread disruptive behavior in schools may result from this pattern of teacher attention. Researchers studied a child who had frequent tantrums lasting five minutes apiece (Allen, Turner, & Everett, 1970). They guessed that the teacher unwittingly reinforced the tantrums with attention. They convinced her to start ignoring them. From that point on, only two more tantrums occurred. The first one showed a typical extinction burst, lasting over 25 minutes. Many classroom studies have shown similar results. When teachers stop attending to undesirable behaviors, those behaviors decrease sharply.

Most of us could react more constructively to disruptive behavior in many everyday situations. For example, we may laugh when one member of our group rudely interrupts another member. Ignoring that rudeness would be likely to reduce it. This would be a sound use of extinction in everyday situations.

Misuses of Extinction

People can use extinction, like reinforcement, incorrectly. Parents may ignore a child's desirable behavior because they are "too busy." By doing so, they may decrease the probability of that behavior. Many of us have a fit of shyness and act embarrassed at compliments. By doing so, we will decrease the rate at which we get compliments. Parents may not take time to talk with their teenage child. They may thereby create a communication problem in later years, extinguishing conversational behavior with that child.

Similar problems may arise in the business world. Employers may not praise employees' good work behavior, arguing that they should not have to "baby" the worker. The worker "should want to do a good job." Perhaps that is true, but they may be extinguishing good work behavior anyway. You might guess that the worker's pay reinforces the behavior, but pay usually only reinforces showing up. You don't get more pay for doing a good job; employer praise is the major reinforcer for good work.

Similar problems may arise even in government. A government's employees and politicians may ignore the legitimate complaints of its citizens. By doing so, they may extinguish communication. They may later face open rebellion and an inability to communicate with the citizens.

Extinction, then, is a powerful tool with which to change behavior. Like reinforcement, people can use it wisely or unwisely.

Outpsyching Crazy Drivers

We hear many stories about crazy drivers these days. You try to pass them; they speed up; you speed up more; they take out a gun and shoot you! We all have encountered crazy drivers. Maybe the most common kind is the tailgater. A car comes up behind you, can't pass, and stays dangerously close. Why do they do that? What is the reinforcer? They may be reinforced by your behavior showing that they are influencing you. The National Safety Council suggests that you may be showing such an influence by slowing down or by making eye contact (in the rearview mirror). What's the best defense if you can't let them pass? Stop delivering eye contact and stop slowing down. (Based on Rodgers, 1993.)

3. If tailgating decreases, behavior analysts would call your procedure ______________ (extinction, reinforcement, unknown).

Summary

Tactic #2 in using the reinforcement strategy for solving human problems is to decrease undesirable behavior through extinction. Extinction can modify behavior. If a response no longer produces reinforcement, the person will probably stop emitting it. Behavior analysts use extinction to eliminate undesirable behavior. Everyone can use extinction to change behavior; we often do so without even being aware of what we are doing. Often the result is desirable and helpful, but extinction can be used incorrectly. We can end up extinguishing valuable behavior from other people, which can sometimes have tragic results. You can be sure you do not produce such results by learning about extinction. If you are aware when you are using extinction, you may avoid eliminating desirable behavior from others.

Behavior Analysis Examples

Helping the Elderly Communicate

Elderly people often communicate negative messages to their loved ones. They may make bizarre statements and angry accusations. We often explain this behavior as the inevitable result of growing old. Mr. Ford, a 63-year-old man who had had a stroke, spent several hours a day making wild accusations at his wife. He accused her of hiding men, staying out all night, and being a whore. Researchers found that Mrs. Ford discussed or denied the accusations 95% of the time and ignored them only 5% of the time. As a result, Mr. Ford spent over an hour a day making accusations. The researchers then taught her to ignore this behavior. She discussed or denied 14% of the time and ignored 82% of the time. This changed Mr. Ford's talk until he spent almost no time making accusations. A reversal to baseline resulted in increased accusations. (Based on Green, Linsk, & Pinkston, 1986.)

4. Mrs. Ford stopped the delivery of a reinforcer when she stopped arguing. Mr. Ford's rate of making accusations decreased. Therefore, behavior analysts would call her procedure _______________ (extinction, reinforcement, unknown).

Aggression in Young Children

Pinkston and colleagues (1973) studied Cain, the 3½-year-old son of well-educated parents. Cain was bright and often had long discussions with the teachers in his preschool. However, playing with other children was a disaster. The researchers noticed that he often stood on the edge of the play area with his fists clenched. After a few minutes, he attacked other children without reason. He bit, scratched, struck, and yelled "I hate you" at any teacher who tried to stop him.

The researchers defined aggression so that it included both physical and verbal aggression. Physical aggression was any negative behavior directed toward peers. It could also be directed at materials the peers used. They gave specific definitions for eight categories of physical aggression: choking, head pushing, biting, pinching, pushing, poking, hitting, and kicking. They also defined verbal aggression. It included threatening or ordering someone to stop an activity, as well as making negative judgments about persons, their relatives, or their property. The researchers made observations during consecutive ten-second intervals and found that reliability was 92%.

Figure 9-3 shows the results of this experiment. During baseline, teachers tried to stop aggression. Aggression averaged almost 30% of all Cain's interactions with other children during that time, indicating that attending to aggression by trying to stop it was reinforcing. During treatment, the teachers used extinction by ignoring all aggression. Aggression decreased to an average of only 6% of all interactions. During reversal, teachers again tried to stop aggression, and the rate of aggression once again rose. During the last three

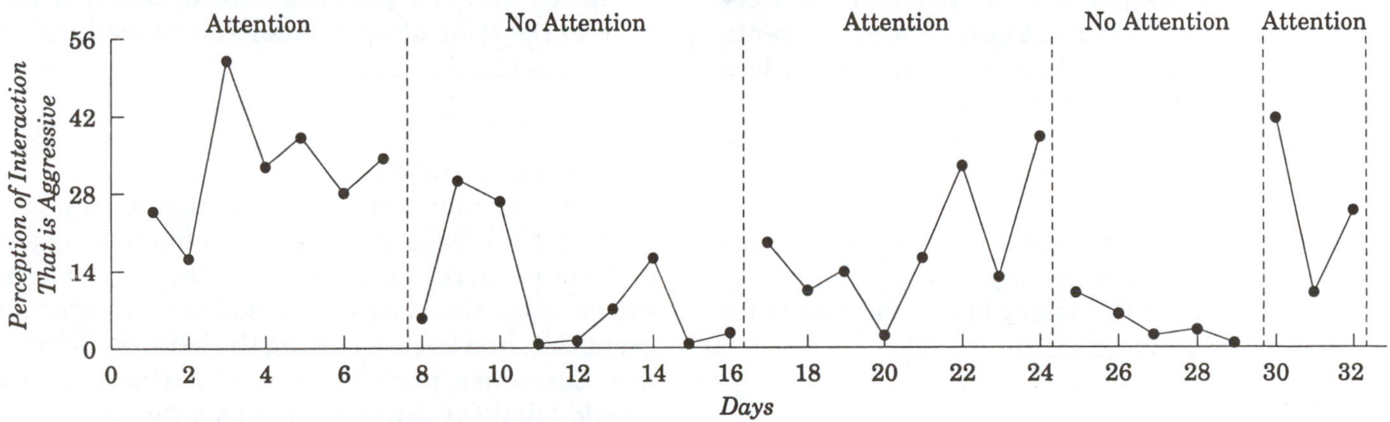

Figure 9-3. The effects of attention and elimination of attention on the aggressive behavior of Cain. Adapted from "Independent Control of a Preschool Child's Aggression and Peer Interaction by Contingent Teacher Attention," by E. M. Pinkston, N. M. Reese, J. M. LeBlanc, and D. M. Baer, *Journal of Applied Behavior Analysis*, 1973, *6*, 115–124. Copyright 1973 by the Society for the Experimental Analysis of Behavior, Inc. Used by permission.

days, it averaged about 30% again. Subsequent withdrawal of attention and reinstatement of it produced similar results. In a long period of observation not shown on this figure, the teachers continued to ignore aggressive acts. Aggression remained between 0 and 5% for 30 days.

5. This study shows that the teachers eliminated Cain's aggressive behaviors by ignoring them. Therefore, the teachers were using the behavioral procedure of ________________.

Notes

Note #1
You will find examples where someone ignores another person's complaining behavior. Don't conclude that behavior analysts solve problems by ignoring them. They use extinction only when the complaining behavior <u>is</u> the problem. That is true when the complaint is not justified. I noted in Lesson 8 that behavior analysts often listen to clients talk as part of the treatment. This lesson should lead you to be wary about listening to clients talk. Extinguishing their talk is sometimes a necessary practice.

6. Behavior analysts ignore a person's complaints only when the complaining behavior ______ (is, isn't) the problem.

Note #2
A person's history of reinforcement for a behavior may be extinction. A person whose parents never reinforced him or her for complaining is less likely to be a chronic complainer than someone with a history of receiving reinforcement for complaining.

7. If in the past a person's parents never reinforced him or her for complaining, then we say that the person's history of reinforcement for complaining is ______________.

Helpful Hints

You might confuse two types of situations where the rate of a response decreases with extinction.

Helpful Hint #1
Someone may stop giving an instruction to perform a behavior, and the rate of the behavior may then decrease. This would not be an example of extinction. The reason is that instructions do not usually act as reinforcers, so the delivery of a reinforcer is not being stopped. Just remember: <u>Stopping an instruction cannot be extinction</u>. You should label the stopping of instructions as *unknown*.

8. If an instruction to perform a behavior is stopped, and the rate of the behavior decreases, this ____________ (would, wouldn't) be an example of extinction.

To stop giving instructions refers to more than to stop explaining how to do something. To stop giving instructions can also mean to stop instructing the person to do something. So you might stop "telling," "asking," "reminding," or "requesting" that the person do something. Even if the other person's rate of doing what you stop asking them to do decreases, you are not stopping a reinforcer. You are stopping a request. Be sure to look for this kind of example. Many students notice that you are stopping something and jump to the conclusion that you are stopping a reinforcer. They incorrectly label it *extinction.* Be on the lookout for this kind of example, and be sure to label it *unknown.*

9. If someone stops "instructing," "telling," "asking," or "reminding" another person to do something, and the person's rate of doing it decreases, you should label the procedure as ________________.

Helpful Hint #2
Someone may tell another person to stop performing a behavior or threaten to stop some event if the other person does not stop the behavior. In neither situation does the person actually stop an event that had been following the behavior. Therefore, these are not examples of extinction. You should label these procedures as *unknown.*

10. If a threat is made that an event will be stopped if a behavior is not decreased, and the behavior decreases, this ______________ (would, wouldn't) be an example of extinction.

Helpful Hint #3

I will give you many examples in which a reinforcer is stopped, but the rate of the behavior does not change. I might not explicitly say it doesn't change. I might say that you stopped praising Martha for eating a good diet but that she kept eating a good diet. Look very carefully to see whether the rate of the behavior actually changes in examples where a reinforcer is stopped. If it does not, then you should label the procedure as *unknown*.

11. Suppose you stop praising someone for eating a good diet, and they keep on eating a good diet. What behavioral procedure is this an example of? ____________________

Helpful Hint #4

Remember, call the act of applying extinction to a behavior *extinguishing* the behavior.

12. The act of applying extinction to a behavior is called ______________ the behavior.

Additional Readings

Ayllon, T., & Michael, J. (1959). The psychiatric nurse as a behavioral engineer. *Journal of the Experimental Analysis of Behavior, 2*, 323–334. A series of case studies show how behavioral principles can improve the behavior of mental patients. One case involves Lucille, a person with retardation who continually entered the nurses' office and disrupted their work. The nurses had usually taken her by the hand and led her out of the office; this reaction seemed only to increase the rate of office entering. When the nurses totally ignored Lucille's visits, she stopped entering their office.

Wolf, M. M., Birnbrauer, J., Lawler, J., & Williams, T. (1970). The operant extinction, reinstatement, and re-extinction of vomiting behavior in a retarded child. In R. Ulrich, T. Stachnik, & J. Mabry (Eds.), *Control of human behavior*, (Vol. 2.) Glenview, IL: Scott, Foresman. This article shows how you can use extinction to eliminate severe behavior problems in children with retardation. In this case, a girl with retardation vomited most days when she was in a class; the teacher immediately sent her to her residence. The teacher then changed to having the child remain in the class regardless of her vomiting behavior. The teacher stopped giving her attention and stopped letting her get out of class; this eliminated the vomiting. This case shows again how easy it is to reinforce disruptive behaviors unintentionally.

Reading Quiz

64. You learned in the last lesson that <u>reinforcement</u> is a procedure that ______________ the rate of a behavior. You learned in this lesson that a procedure that decreases the rate of a behavior is ______________.
58. Tactic #2 in using the reinforcement strategy for solving human problems is to decrease undesired behavior through ______________ (reinforcement, extinction).
12. Extinction is defined (a) as stopping the delivery of a reinforcer that has followed a behavior in the past and (b) as causing a(n) ____________ in the rate of that behavior.
13. Extinction is defined as (a) ______________ (starting, stopping) the delivery of a reinforcer that has followed a behavior in the past and (b) causing a decrease in the rate of that behavior.
39. Review: Extinction can be defined as (a) ______________ the delivery of a reinforcer that has followed a behavior in the past and (b) causing a ____________ in the rate of that behavior.
1. <u>Extinguishing</u> a behavior is the term used when what procedure is applied to the behavior? ______________________
56. Students often misspell *extinguishing,* so I want you simply to copy the word to see how it is spelled. ______________________
59. The act of applying extinction to a behavior is called ____________________ the behavior.
14. Extinction is defined as <u>stopping</u> the delivery of a certain kind of event. The certain kind of event follows a behavior and increases the rate of that behavior. The label for the event that is stopped is ______________.
65. You might use a reversal design to prove that an event is a reinforcer. You would initially observe the rate of the behavior during a baseline period in which the event did not follow the behavior. Then you would observe the rate during a treatment condition in which

the event did follow the behavior. Finally, you would observe the rate during a reversal condition. During the reversal condition, you would stop delivery of the event. If you observed that the rate of the behavior decreased, you would label the reversal condition as _____________ (extinction, reinforcement).

66. You should apply the term *extinction* only when two elements are present. First, you must ___________ delivery of a reinforcer. Second, you must observe a(n) ___________ in the rate of the behavior.

30. Mom accidentally reinforces Tommy's burping by yelling, "That's disgusting!" She might realize her mistake and stop the reinforcer, and Tommy's rate of burping might then decrease. In this case, Mom would have stopped the reinforcer and would have seen the behavior decrease. If so, since both elements are present, you would label her procedure as ________________.

32. Mom told Tommy before he sat down for his next meal that he mustn't burp at the table anymore. Tommy stopped burping at the table. Because the behavior decreased, but Mom did not stop a reinforcer, you would label this procedure as ______________.

31. Mom stopped yelling, "That's disgusting" whenever Tommy burped at the table. Tommy did not stop burping at the table. Because Mom stopped a reinforcer, but the behavior did not decrease, you should label this procedure as a(n) ________________.

6. Before you label any procedure as *extinction,* be sure that both elements required in the definition are present. The reinforcer must be ________________. The behavior must ______________.

7. Some children with retardation hit themselves to get attention from their attendants. Extinction is often the best way to eliminate these behaviors, because the attendants pay attention to them and thereby inadvertently ____________________ the undesirable behaviors.

43. Review: Lovaas and Simmons (1969) found that John, a severely self-destructive child, hit himself over 2500 times in the first hour and a half of extinction. Behavior analysts call this temporary increase a(n) ___________ burst.

44. Review: Lovaas and Simmons (1969) ensured that no one attended to John's self-destructive acts. He stopped hitting himself within ten days. Removal of attention is an example of what behavioral procedure? ___________

48. Review: Suppose that Lovaas and Simmons (1969) had not eventually seen a decrease in the rate of hitting when they stopped the delivery of attention. You should then label their procedure as ____________.

3. An extinction burst is a temporary _________ (increase, decrease) in responding as soon as extinction begins.

38. Review: A temporary increase in responding as soon as extinction begins is called a(n) ___ _________ burst.

2. A temporary increase in responding as soon as extinction begins is called a(n) _________ __________.

28. In the treatment of self-injurious behavior (SIB), clients could seriously hurt themselves during extinction bursts before they stopped the problem behavior. In order to reduce the amount of self-inflicted injury, behavior analysts often combine punishment with the procedure of __________.

62. Williams (1959) consulted with a family that had comforted their child anytime he cried after being put to bed. By doing so, the family had inadvertently increased crying by using the procedure of ______________.

63. Williams (1959) proposed that the family stop attending to the child's crying. The rate of his crying decreased. The family used what procedure to get this result? ____________

25. If the parents in Williams (1959) had stopped attending to the child, but the child's crying had not decreased, you would say they used what procedure? ____________

36. Researchers often find that when teachers first stop paying attention to undesirable behaviors, the rate of those behaviors ___________ sharply.

35. Researchers found that pulse rate and subjective fear in social situations decreased when the procedure of _______________ was used.

27. Ignoring rudeness, rather than laughing at it, would be a sound use of ___________ in everyday situations.

5. Because they may increase tailgating, events such as making eye contact or slowing down would be called ___________.

10. Extinction can be used incorrectly. People may ignore desirable behavior because they are too busy. The rate of the desirable behavior may ________________ as a result.
34. Praising an employee for a job well done often results in more good work. If an employer stops praising a worker, and then the good work decreases, you should call this procedure __________.
40. Review: If an employer asks a worker to stop acting carelessly, and the worker's rate of carelessness decreases, the employer's procedure is an example of ____________.
8. By ignoring the legitimate complaints of its citizens, a government's employees and politicians may inadvertently use the procedure of ____________ to reduce communication.
11. Extinction is a powerful tool that can be used to change people's ___________.
26. If used correctly, extinction may eliminate undesirable behavior. If used incorrectly, extinction may also eliminate ____________ behavior.
9. By reducing the number of times she discussed accusations with her husband, Mrs. Ford decreased the number of accusations to almost none. This is an example of ____________.
57. Suppose Mrs. Ford had told Mr. Ford that she was no longer going to discuss his accusations, and Mr. Ford's rate of accusations then decreased to almost none. This would be an example of ____________.
29. Specifying physical aggression as "any negative behavior directed toward peers or at the materials they use" would be an example of creating a(n) ______________________.
33. Pinkston and her colleagues (1973) instructed the preschool teachers to stop paying attention to the child when he was being aggressive. If the rate of the child's aggressive acts stayed about the same, what procedure were they employing? ____________
61. When Pinkston and her colleagues (1973) instructed the teachers to attend to the child's aggressive behavior, the child's rate of aggressive behavior actually increased. What procedure were the teachers using in this condition? ________________
21. From Note #1: Behavior analysts ignore a person's complaints only when the complaining behavior ________ (is, isn't) the problem.
23. From Note #2: We say that a person's <u>history</u> of reinforcement for complaining is reinforcement if the person's parents paid attention to it. We say that a person's <u>history</u> of reinforcement for complaining is extinction if the parents _____ (did, didn't) pay attention to it.
22. From Note #2: If a person's parents stopped reinforcing him or her for complaining, we say that the person's <u>history</u> of reinforcement for complaining is ____________.
24. From Note #2: We say that a person's <u>history</u> of reinforcement for complaining is reinforcement if the person's parents paid attention to it. If the parents did not pay attention to it, we say that extinction is the person's ________ of reinforcement for complaining.
15. From Helpful Hint #1: If an instruction to perform a behavior is stopped (rather than a reinforcer), and the rate of the behavior decreases, this ___________ (would, wouldn't) be an example of extinction.
16. From Helpful Hint #1: If someone stops "instructing," "telling," "asking," or "reminding" another person to do something, and the rate of doing it decreases, you should label their procedure as ______________.
17. From Helpful Hint #2: If a threat is made that an event will be stopped if a behavior is not decreased, and the behavior decreases, this ____________________ (would, wouldn't) be an example of extinction.
18. From Helpful Hint #3: Suppose you stop praising someone for eating a good diet, and the person keeps on eating a good diet. What behavioral procedure is this an example of? ____________________
19. From Helpful Hint #3: Suppose you stop giving your spouse a kiss after he or she does a favor for you, and his or her rate of doing favors stays the same. What behavioral procedure are you using? ________________
20. From Helpful Hint #4: The act of applying extinction to a behavior is called __________ the behavior.
4. Ayllon and Michael (1959) encouraged nurses to ignore Lucille when she entered the office. As a result, the rate at which Lucille entered their office ______________.
60. The teacher sent a child with retardation home from school when she vomited, and the rate of vomiting increased. The teacher could solve the problem by using the procedure called ____________.

47. Review: Suppose you stop telling your roommates to clean the room, and they stop. This would be an example of what behavioral procedure? ______________
53. Review: When a preschool teacher stopped paying attention to Cain's aggressive behavior, and the behavior decreased, what behavioral procedure did the teacher use? ______________
67. Review: When complaining behavior is ignored, but the behavior does not decrease, what behavioral procedure is being used? ______________
49. Review: Tactic #1 in using the reinforcement strategy for solving human problems is to increase the desired behavior through reinforcement. Tactic #2 is to decrease undesired behavior through ______________.
52. Review: The definition of extinction is ______ the delivery of a reinforcer following a behavior and producing a(n) ______________ in the rate of that behavior.
37. Review: A temporary <u>increase</u> in responding as soon as extinction begins is called a(n) ______________.
42. Review: If you tell people to perform a certain behavior, and they do it, and then they stop when you stop telling them to do it, what behavioral procedure are you using? ______
51. Review: Tactic #2 in using the reinforcement strategy for solving human problems is to decrease the undesired behavior through ______________.
41. Review: If you ignore Sara's behavior of interrupting others, and her interruptions continue, this would illustrate what behavioral procedure? ______________
45. Review: Preschool teachers stopped paying attention to Cain's aggressive behavior, resulting in a decrease of that behavior. Their procedure is an example of ______________.
55. Review: You tell Fred to stop scowling. If he stops scowling, you would be using what procedure? ______________
46. Review: Remember, if you use a procedure to increase someone's behavior, and it does not increase, the book will always label the procedure as ______________. Likewise, if you use a procedure to decrease someone's behavior, and it does not decrease, the book will always label the procedure as ______________.
50. Review: Tactic #1 in using the reinforcement strategy for solving human problems is to increase desired behavior through ______________. Tactic #2 is to decrease the undesired behavior through ______________.

Examples

1. Martha's 5-year-old son Paul frequently pinched his mother for no apparent reason. When Paul pinched Martha, she explained that pinching was not nice, and asked Paul why he had pinched her. He usually said, "I don't know," and later pinched her again. Martha finally started to ignore the pinches no matter how irritating they were. She did this for several weeks and noticed that the pinching stopped. Check for two elements if you think this is extinction. First, did Martha eventually stop an event that could be a reinforcer? ____. (Note that her explanations could be a reinforcer because they followed the pinching.) Second, did the frequency of Paul's pinching decrease? ____. (Note that the fact that the behavior decreased when Martha stopped explaining provides evidence that explaining was a reinforcer.) Because Martha <u>stopped</u> paying attention to the pinches, and the rate of pinching <u>decreased</u>, ignoring pinching is called ______________.

2. Lora was taking a biology course from a rather conservative professor. Each class period, she would ask one silly question, such as "Why do dogs mate only twice a year? Don't they like it?" The professor usually got mad, turned red, and said, "That will be enough, Miss Smith." After talking with a behavior analyst, the professor started handling Lora's questions differently. He didn't get mad or turn red, he just responded, "Are there any other questions?" After 12 class periods of the professor's new technique, Lora was still asking one silly question every class period. Check for both elements. First, did the professor <u>stop</u> an event that could be a reinforcer? ________. (He no longer got mad and turned red after a silly question.) Second, did the rate of Lora's behavior <u>decrease</u>? ______. Because the professor stopped an event that could be a reinforcer, but the rate of silly questions did not change, you should label the procedure used by the professor to decrease Lora's silly questions as ______________.

3. Rasheed often whispered to his friends in English class. To stop his behavior, the teacher

told the class, "I will tolerate no more whispering in this class. I want it stopped as of today!" Rasheed never whispered in class again after that. Check for both elements. First, did the teacher stop an event that could be a reinforcer? _____. (Note that the teacher's demand could not be a reinforcer.) Second, did the rate of a behavior decrease? _____. In this example, the teacher did not stop a reinforcer. Therefore, the teacher's procedure is called _____________.

4. Mary had spent Wednesday nights with her friends for the past few months. She enjoyed their company, and they liked hers except for one habit: She interrupted the conversation (particularly when Sally was talking). She always had something interesting to say, however, so they would pay attention to her interruptions. Sally finally became angry with Mary for interrupting her all the time. She asked Mary to stop doing it, and Mary apologized and said she would stop. But she didn't, so Sally told her feelings to the other members of the group. They all agreed to ignore Mary whenever she interrupted Sally. Sally would continue to talk, and the other members would continue to pay attention to her and to ignore Mary. After several Wednesday nights of this procedure, Mary had completely stopped interrupting. Check for both elements. First, did the group stop an event that could be a reinforcer? _____. Second, did the rate of a behavior decrease? _____. In this example, the group stopped a reinforcer, and an undesirable behavior decreased. Therefore, the group's procedure is called _____________.

5. Jimmy and his Dad had trouble getting along with each other. Whenever Dad would ask him how things were, Jimmy always explained at great length how bad his life was. Not wanting to make the boy's sad state worse, his Dad always paid attention to him and tried to comfort him. One evening, Jimmy's mother suggested that Dad should stop all the attention to such sad talk. Dad stopped the attention, and Jimmy's rate of sad talk decreased. Check for both elements. First, did Dad stop an event that could be a reinforcer? Second, did the rate of a behavior decrease? In this example, Dad's procedure is called _________________.

6. James often said things to Donnell, thereby interrupting his studying. When James would say something, Donnell would answer. Eventually, Donnell did not answer James any longer, but James continued to say things to Donnell. Check for both elements: Did Donnell stop an event that could be a reinforcer? Did the rate of the behavior decrease? In this case, Donnell's refusal to answer James is an example of what procedure? _________

7. At the beginning of the semester, Gary, the new instructor of philosophy, told his students that he would give them a bonus if they handed their weekly papers in by Thursday. Everyone in the class did so. After several weeks, Gary figured that the problem of late papers was solved and stopped giving bonuses. The students stopped handing their papers in on time. Check for both elements. (Stop reinforcer? Decrease behavior?) In this example, Gary's procedure of no longer giving bonuses is called _____________.

8. Ben, the star pledge in his fraternity, was in charge of vacuuming the house. As long as Skoog, the frat president, asked him every Saturday to do it, Ben did an excellent job. However, Skoog finally stopped asking Ben to do it, feeling that Ben should be responsible enough to do it without being asked. Ben's rate of vacuuming dropped to nearly zero. Check for both elements. (Stop reinforcer? Decrease behavior?) In this case, Skoog's stopping his requests is an example of what procedure? _____________

9. Mr. Suzuki wanted to get his students to turn their papers in on time each week, so he reminded them on Thursday to be sure to have them in by Friday. Everyone did so. Midway through the semester, he stopped reminding them, and to his surprise, they stopped handing them in on time. Check both elements. What behavioral procedure did he use when he stopped reminding them? _________________

10. At first, Maria tried to be nice to Fred. But she did not like the kind of attention he gave her, so she finally just totally ignored his attentions, and he stopped paying attention to her. What behavioral procedure was she using by ignoring him? _________________

11. Review: (Note: I will start mixing in examples of reinforcement. Check first whether you think the example is reinforcement or extinction. Then check for the elements appropriate to the concept you think it may be. Remember, it may be unknown!) Connie was becoming extremely irritated with her husband's habit of throwing his clothes around. She had asked him repeatedly about this habit, but the chair in the bedroom was still his favorite storage place. One morning, Connie saw him actually hanging up his clothes, so she fixed him a large breakfast. (His usual

breakfast was oatmeal and toast.) Connie thought this was such a good idea that she made it a rule to fix a large breakfast whenever the clothes were hung up. She noticed that they were hung up most of the time from then on. What procedure did Connie use? ____________________

12. Review: Galen had finally gotten fed up with the teasing that he was getting from Ben for going to church. So he decided to ignore all teasing, and Ben continued teasing as much as before. What behavioral procedure did Galen use? ________________

13. Review: Darwin, a publicity-seeking student posing as a radical, came up with a sensational new tactic for disrupting the campus. The disruption was followed by the news media, and Darwin was interviewed on TV. He used that same tactic frequently thereafter. What behavioral procedure were the news media unwittingly applying to Darwin? ____________________

14. Review: Ward liked Bev a lot, and he went out of his way to find things about her to compliment. At first, Bev liked this and smiled and thanked him. However, after she got engaged to Tom, she felt embarrassed by Ward's compliments. She invariably ended up ignoring them, and Ward doesn't compliment her anymore. What behavioral procedure did Bev use when she ignored Ward's compliments? ______________

15. Review: Tom liked compliments a lot; anytime he got one, he beamed and profusely thanked the person for the compliment. Tom noticed that this increased the number of compliments he got from each person he had thanked. What behavioral procedure did Tom use by thanking people? ____________________________

16. Review: Willie was unhappy with the slow pace at which Sonny was carrying rocks for the wall, so he started asking Sonny to carry the rocks faster. Sure enough, Sonny did. What behavioral procedure did Willie use to increase Sonny's rate of carrying rocks? ____________

17. Review: Pat teased Carol incessantly about her weight. At first, Carol took it all very seriously. Later she stopped taking it so seriously and just laughed it off. Pat stopped teasing her. What behavioral procedure did Carol use? ___________

18. Review: Whenever Pam took Clara with her in the car, Clara would continually ask, "How long until we get there?" At first, Pam would explain carefully, but later she decided that Clara was just pestering her, so she stopped answering these questions. Clara continued to ask the question afterwards. What procedure was Pam using? ___________________

19. Review: Dan had a fantastic smile. Anyone who did a favor for him and received a "Thank you" accompanied by that smile was much more likely to do another favor for him in the future. One of Dan's smiles is termed a(n) ___________.

20. Review: Professor Jones disrupted faculty meetings with insane ideas. His colleagues used to argue vehemently with him. However, the chairman finally convinced them simply to ignore Jones, and soon Jones wasn't disrupting meetings anymore. The faculty's ignoring Jones's insane ideas is an example of what behavioral procedure? __________________

LESSON 10 Differential Reinforcement of Everyday Behaviors

You have learned two tactics in using the reinforcement strategy to solve human problems. First, when you want to increase a single behavior, you can use tactic #1: Increase the desired behavior through reinforcement. Second, when you want to decrease a single behavior, you can use tactic #2: Decrease the undesired behavior through extinction. However, there will be times when you may want to increase one behavior while decreasing other related behaviors. As you might guess, you can combine the two procedures of reinforcement and extinction to change the relative rate of two behaviors. You will learn in this lesson that this combined procedure is called *differential reinforcement*. Tactic #3 in using the reinforcement strategy to solve human problems is to increase a desired behavior relative to undesired behaviors through differential reinforcement.

1. Tactic #3 in using the reinforcement strategy to solve human problems is to increase a desired behavior relative to an undesired behavior through differential ________________.

Defining Differential Reinforcement

Differential reinforcement is a procedure in which one behavior is reinforced while other behaviors are extinguished. The ultimate goal is to increase the rate of that behavior relative to the others. The term **differential reinforcement** is applied to any procedure that has the following three elements: (1) two or more physically different behaviors occurring in one situation are involved; (2) one behavior is reinforced; and (3) the other behaviors are extinguished. All three elements must be present before the procedure can be called differential reinforcement.

2. The term **differential reinforcement** is applied to any procedure that has the following three elements: (1) two or more physically ________________ behaviors occurring in one situation are involved; (2) one behavior is ______________; and (3) the other behaviors are ____________________. All three elements must be present before the procedure can be called differential reinforcement.

Here is an example where all three elements are present. Suppose Dad wants to get Lulu to eat more vegetables and drink less pop during lunch at home. He might praise Lulu when she eats vegetables and ignore her when she drinks pop. If Lulu starts to eat more vegetables and drink less pop, then all three elements of differential reinforcement are present. First, it has two physically different behaviors: eating vegetables and drinking pop. They occur in one location: home. Second, Dad uses praise to reinforce eating vegetables. Third, Dad uses ignoring to extinguish drinking pop. This is an example of differential reinforcement, because all three elements are present.

Many situations can look like differential reinforcement but be missing one element. For example, suppose Dad wants Lulu to eat with the family more often and to eat by herself less often. He might praise Lulu when she eats with the family but ignore her when she eats alone. If Lulu starts to eat with the family at home more often, then this example is similar to differential reinforcement. It involves reinforcement and extinction, but it does not involve two different behaviors. Lulu could pick up the same food with the same fork held in the same way with the same hand and chew it in the exact same way with the family and alone. Her eating behavior might be exactly the same. So Dad is not praising one kind of eating behavior and ignoring another kind. Rather, he is praising eating behavior in one situation and ignoring the same eating behavior in a second situation. This example has one behavior in two different situations, not two different behaviors in one situation.

Other situations might look like differential reinforcement while missing other elements. For example, Dad might praise Lulu when she eats slowly and ignore her when she eats fast. If Lulu continues to eat fast just as often as before, then Dad is not using reinforcement on one of the behaviors. Thus, this would not be an example of differential reinforcement. Likewise, he might also tell her to eat slowly, while he ignores eating fast. She might then start eating slowly. But this would not be an example of differential reinforcement, because he used an instruction instead of reinforcement.

Be sure to read every example very carefully to see if it is similar to differential reinforcement but missing one element. I will include many examples both of differential reinforcement and of procedures very similar to it. You will not truly understand differential reinforcement until you can tell not only when it is present but also when it is not. As in past lessons, I will label procedures that lack one element of differential reinforcement as *unknown*.

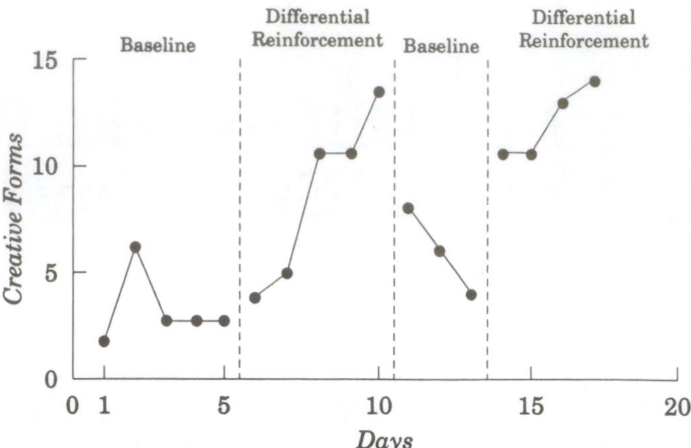

Figure 10-1. This graph shows the outcome of an experiment designed to increase 4-year-old Mary's creativity. Adapted from "Social Control of Form Diversity and the Emergence of New Forms in Children's Blockbuilding," by E. M. Goetz and D. M. Baer, *Journal of Applied Behavior Analysis,* 1973, *6,* 209–217. Copyright 1973 by the Society for the Experimental Analysis of Behavior, Inc. Used by permission.

Uses of Differential Reinforcement

Two researchers applied differential reinforcement to coaching a young girl in tennis (Buzas & Ayllon, 1981). The tennis coach previously coached Debbie by first explaining how to make the strokes. He then watched her try the strokes and pointed out her errors. She couldn't seem to get the hang of basic tennis strokes; she performed forehand, backhand, and serve correctly only 13% of the time. The researchers convinced the coach to ignore errors and praise correct strokes. Debbie improved until she was making 58% of these strokes correctly. The researchers had similar success with Sherry and Kristen.

We encountered a good example of the application of differential reinforcement in Unit One. Goetz and Baer (1973) differentially reinforced the behavior of Mary, a preschool child, for creative block building. They did this in two ways: praising any form that she had not previously built, and ignoring those forms that she had previously built. Figure 10-1 shows the result of that experiment. During the periods marked Differential Reinforcement, Mary was given social attention only when she built a new, creative structure with her building blocks. During the reversal period, Mary was reinforced only when she built noncreative forms similar to ones that she had already built. As you can see, Mary built many new forms when they were differentially reinforced; she built few new ones when they were not. This experiment suggests that creative behavior can be nurtured by using differential reinforcement.

I gave other examples of differential reinforcement in Unit One. For example, Komaki and Barnett (1977) improved the coaching of skills on a youth football team. They taught the coaches to differentially reinforce the young players, and all team members increased correct play. Budzynski and Stoyva (1969) used biofeedback to differentially reinforce relaxation; this led to a decrease in forehead tension. Differential reinforcement of relaxation may improve meditation skills (Karlins & Andrews, 1972). Thus differential reinforcement can teach such diverse skills as creativity, football plays, and relaxation. It even helped a great-grandmother cure an alleged case of possession by demons (Murphy & Brantley, 1982).

Even Carl Rogers Used Differential Reinforcement

Carl Rogers rejected behavior analysis in a famous series of debates with Skinner (Rogers & Skinner, 1956). He asserted that psychotherapists could help clients most if they expressed positive regard for them no matter what they did. Charles Truax, a colleague of Rogers, studied whether Rogers did this with his own clients (Truax, 1966). He found that Rogers expressed positive regard when his client showed insight, but not when the client showed negative feelings. As a result, insight increased and negative feelings decreased.

3. Truax concluded that Rogers used the procedure of differential ____________ on constructive behavior and ignored nonconstructive behavior.

Differential reinforcement may explain how people teach many behaviors in everyday life. For example, a skillful singing teacher might use differential reinforcement to teach her student to sing middle C. The teacher would reinforce singing middle C, but she would extinguish singing notes close to middle C but not close enough. Similarly, a skillful mother might use differential reinforcement to teach her child how to say "television." Jose might use differential reinforcement to teach you how to say "caramba." A coach might use differential reinforcement to teach a young pitcher how to throw a curveball. Dad might use it to teach Sue how to shift gears. He might praise pushing in the clutch while letting up on the accelerator; he might ignore letting up on the accelerator too fast but failing to push in the clutch.

People are often not aware when they use differential reinforcement. One researcher showed that the father of humanistic psychology, Carl Rogers, unwittingly used it to help people.

Misuses of Differential Reinforcement

In previous lessons, I pointed out that people often use reinforcement to increase problem behavior or use extinction to decrease desired behavior. You won't be surprised to learn that people often misuse differential reinforcement. For example, researchers (Gil et al., 1988) studied children with chronic skin problems affecting about 13% of the body. The children made the problem worse by scratching. The researchers found that parents paid attention to the children when they scratched and were less likely to pay attention when the children were not scratching. Thus, the parents differentially reinforced scratching. In the box below, one psychologist describes how his psychoanalyst taught him to be unhappy (Kaufman, 1991).

Differential reinforcement may also explain how people often fail to teach the desired behavior or sometimes even teach problem behaviors. For example, an unskillful singing teacher might ignore notes close to C. She might react with criticism only to those notes that differ from C. If the pupil rarely gets any kind of attention, the criticism might be reinforcing, and the singing might get worse and worse. An unskillful mother might show great sympathy when her son refuses to try

How a Therapist Taught Unhappiness

Kaufman tells this story about his psychoanalysis. "During some early sessions I moaned and groaned, incriminating myself and protesting the actions of others. As I walked toward the door in the concluding moments, the therapist often put his arm on my shoulder parentally and said, 'You're really working on it. Good session. Just stay with it.' However, on other rare occasions, I talked effusively about seeing my life as moving productively ahead. When those sessions terminated, the analyst walked me to the door and said, 'Maybe next time you'll get down to it and really work.' His message was clear. Be anxious, uncomfortable, fearful and frustrated and the session would be deemed productive and useful; be cheerful and optimistic and I would be seen as avoiding issues, the session not helpful or meaningful" (Kaufman, 1991).

4. By calling some sessions "good" and not others, the therapist differentially ______ ____________ unhappy talk by Kaufman.

Figure 10-2. Suppose Dad comforts Jenny whenever she's unhappy. He may end up paying lots of attention to Jenny when she's crying. He may figure she doesn't need Dad's help when she is happy. Which face do you think she will make most often?

saying "television," and he might start refusing even to try saying difficult words. An unskillful Spanish teacher might become annoyed when your pronunciation is wrong. If he boasted what a good teacher he is, you might delight in annoying him. An unskillful coach might ignore your good attempts, reacting only when you don't follow their instructions. Your goofs might be reinforced by these reactions. Granted, many people might not react this way. Even so, the approach of focusing on mistakes and ignoring good attempts is often an unwitting use of differential reinforcement for undesirable behavior.

Reducing Behavior with Differential Reinforcement

Differential reinforcement has two effects: to increase the rate of a desirable behavior and to decrease the rate of a competing undesirable behavior. Therefore, you can use differential reinforcement to reduce problem behavior rather than to increase desired behavior.

Researchers applied this method to Stan, a kindergarten student (Madsen, Becker, & Thomas, 1968). Stan was wild: He pushed, hit, and grabbed; he swore, stole, and broke things; he didn't do any work. The teacher tried what anyone might try: She scolded and reprimanded. As you might expect, this simply reinforced Stan's wildness. The teacher then tried another common approach: She told Stan "the rules." This didn't do any good. The researchers then suggested that the teacher ignore the wild behavior, but that didn't do any good either. Finally, they had the teacher praise Stan when he followed the rules and ignore his wildness. Appropriate behavior increased; wild behavior dropped from 80% of the time to around 30%. The researchers found similar effects with two other second-grade children. This approach has become the foundation for the behavioral approach to classroom management.

Sometimes you need to decrease problem behaviors quickly. This is particularly true when the problem behaviors are dangerous. Yet these behaviors may be very resistant to change. Perhaps the behavior analyst cannot eliminate their reinforcing consequences. For example, suppose Tom is a very aggressive preschool child. He likes to use the swing, but other children often won't let him. Tom might punch Carl to convince him to turn it over. If punching works, then it may increase in frequency. Teachers can't withdraw the reinforcer, and they also may find such punching difficult to catch. One solution is to differentially reinforce a behavior that is incompatible with hitting. They might teach Tom to tell the teacher when he asked nicely. The teachers could then check with the other child. If Tom told the truth, they could give him a strong reinforcer.

Researchers used differential reinforcement to stop the aggression of a youth with severe retardation (Mace, Kratochwill, & Fiello, 1983). The 19-year-old youth hit, scratched, and butted others with his head. The researchers reinforced him for complying with instructions (he could not comply with the instructions and aggress at the same time). During baseline, he aggressed 16 times per ten minutes. During treatment, he aggressed twice in eight months. His compliance increased from zero to over 60% of all requests.

Differential reinforcement offers a positive approach to reducing problematic and dangerous behaviors. It provides an alternative to punishment.

Summary

Tactic #3 in using the reinforcement strategy to solve human problems is to increase a desired behavior relative to an undesired behavior through differential reinforcement. Differential reinforcement can alter the relative rates of two or more behaviors. You can exert a powerful effect on the behavior of others with this process. Behavior analysts use it to help people develop more functional behavior. People often use differential reinforcement to help others even when they are not aware of it. However, they can also damage others because of a lack of awareness. You can avoid this danger by being very aware when you are using it.

Behavior Analysis Examples

Helping the Elderly Communicate

Elderly people often have trouble communicating positively. They may say things that don't make sense, or they may fail to say anything. We often explain this behavior as the result of medical conditions or simply growing old. Such was the case with Mr. Orr, who was 67 years old and had suffered a stroke. He correctly responded to questions about 30% of the time and spoke spontaneously only about once every two hours. Researchers taught Mrs. Orr to praise, smile, and touch him when he answered questions and spoke spontaneously. She ignored him when he responded incorrectly to questions. Mr. Orr's correct answers increased to about 85%, and Mrs. Orr could again talk meaningfully to her husband of many years. Even his spontaneous talk increased to about three times per hour (based on Green, Linsk, & Pinkston, 1986).

5. Mrs. Orr improved Mr. Orr's ability to talk by using what behavioral procedure? Differential ______________

Safe Garbage

One of the most unpleasant jobs in a modern urban society is that of garbage collector. The job is made worse by citizens' lack of cooperation in packaging their trash carefully. Stokes and Fawcett (1977) investigated the possibility of improving the packaging of trash by the citizens of one city. The city ordinance specified a number of rules to be followed by citizens when they put out their garbage. These rules were designed to make the work of the sanitation personnel safer and more pleasant. These rules included placing containers conveniently near the curb; not overfilling the containers; tying plastic bags and using only untorn ones; not using containers that fall apart when wet; tying yard trimmings into easily manageable bundles; and picking up loose litter at the collection point. Stokes and Fawcett developed behavioral definitions that would permit the observation of violations of these standards. They measured reliability on four days and found it to be 95%. Their observations suggested that almost half of all residences violated the standards before treatment.

They then developed a simple treatment procedure in which the households being studied were notified of the standards and told that any trash not correctly packaged would not be collected. In addition, the sanitation crews wrote out a ticket, to be placed on any container not collected, explaining the reason it was not being collected. In other words, packaging behaviors that met the city standards were followed by collection of the trash, while packaging behaviors that did not meet city standards were followed by no collection.

The experiment was conducted by studying two neighborhoods, one middle-class and the other working-class. Figure 10-3 shows that in the middle-class neighborhood, the percent of households violating one or more of the standards was about 40% under normal conditions. After five days, the noncollection policy was implemented, and the percentage of households making one or more violations fell to about 12%. In the working-class neighborhood, the percentage of violating households was about 45% under normal conditions. After ten days, the noncollection policy was implemented, and the percentage fell to 23%. Thus, for both neighborhoods, the effect of the noncollection policy was a sharp drop in packaging behaviors that violated the standards.

To determine whether the packaging standards were relevant to the sanitation crews, they were asked to rate the neighborhoods before and after the new policy was put into effect. These ratings indicated that the crews considered the packaging to be much better done after the start of the policy and that the collections were easier and safer to make. This study suggests that differential reinforcement may be relevant not only to individual skill acquisition but also to broader social change.

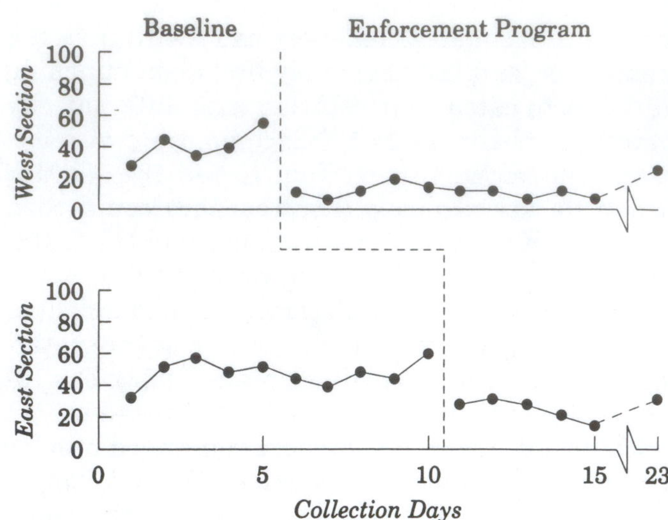

Figure 10-3. Percentage of residences violating the trash packaging standards of a Midwestern city. From "Evaluating Municipal Policy: An Analysis of a Refuse Packaging Program," by T. F. Stokes and S. B. Fawcett, *Journal of Applied Behavior Analysis,* 1977, *10*, 391–398. Copyright 1977 by the Society for the Experimental Analysis of Behavior, Inc. Used by permission.

6. The process of collecting trash when packaged properly and not collecting improperly packaged trash would be called ________________.

Notes

Note #1

A history of reinforcement may describe the differential reinforcement a person has received in the past. Suppose a person's parents reinforced reading books and discouraged watching TV. This history of reinforcement could make the person into a bookworm, which could help to explain current behavior.

7. In order to explain current behavior, it may be necessary to describe the differential reinforcement a person has received in the past, which is called the person's __________ of reinforcement.

Note #2

Behavior analysts label several types of differential reinforcement. When they use it to increase a desirable behavior among other less desirable behaviors, they simply call it differential reinforcement. When they use it to reinforce behavior incompatible with an undesirable behavior, they call it differential reinforcement of incompatible behavior, or DRI. When they use it to reinforce any behavior that is an alternative to undesirable behavior but not incompatible, they call it differential reinforcement of alternative behavior, or DRA. They call differential reinforcement of behavior other than undesirable behavior differential reinforcement of other behavior, or DRO.

8. When differential reinforcement is used to reinforce behavior that is incompatible with an undesirable behavior, the procedure is abbreviated as DRI, which stands for differential reinforcement of ________________ behavior.

Helpful Hints

Helpful Hint #1

To apply the concept of differential reinforcement to everyday situations, you must first determine whether there are at least two different behaviors involved. If not, then you can rule out the possibility that differential reinforcement is involved. This step is particularly important, because there is another behavioral procedure (presented in a later lesson) that involves the reinforcement and extinction of one behavior in differing situations. Thus, determining whether there are at least two behaviors will permit you to make a very difficult distinction. Examples of this other procedure will be introduced in this lesson to help you learn how to tell the difference. If the example involves a single behavior that is reinforced in one situation and extinguished in a different situation, you should label it as *unknown*.

Here is the best rule to remember. If one behavior is reinforced and a different behavior is extinguished in the same situation, this might be differential reinforcement (if the behavior changes). If a single behavior is reinforced in one situation and the same behavior is extinguished in a different situation, this cannot be differential reinforcement. If a procedure involving reinforcement and extinction is applied to two behaviors in one situation, the procedure might be differential reinforcement. However, if a procedure involving reinforcement and extinction is applied to one behavior in two situations, the procedure cannot be differential reinforcement. Call the second procedure *unknown*.

9. Therefore, if a single behavior is reinforced in one situation and extinguished in a different situation, you should label this procedure as ______________________.

Helpful Hint #2

To determine whether an example contains two or more different behaviors, you must analyze whether the individual makes different physical movements of his or her muscles. If the same muscles are moved in the same way, then only one behavior is involved, no matter what else may differ in the surrounding situation.

10. You should conclude that a person emits two different behaviors only if he or she makes different movements of the ______________.

The following are some common examples in which there is only one behavior.

A. Making and not making a response. Not making a response is the absence of behavior, so it cannot be considered to be a second behavior.

11. Hitting and not hitting someone ________ (are, aren't) two different behaviors.

B. The same muscles in two locations. Digging a hole in the front yard does not involve different muscular movements than digging a hole in the back yard. You don't shovel differently just because you are in the back yard.

12. Are playing tennis in Kansas and playing tennis in Florida two different behaviors? ____

C. The same muscles at different times. Pointing at a cardinal does not involve a different movement of the finger muscles than pointing at a robin.

13. Is touching a wall and touching a door a single behavior? _____

D. Reading different materials. Your eyes focus in the same way and scan from left to right no matter what you are reading. Although there may be slight differences in line length, print size, illustrations, and even type arrangement (as in a comic book), the minor variations in movement required usually do not justify regarding the behaviors as different.

14. Reading the front page and reading the editorial page ________ (are, aren't) two different behaviors.

E. Saying the same word to different people. Your vocal cords, lips, tongue, and lungs move in the same way to say "stop" to John as to Sam.

15. Are talking about the weather with Mary and talking about the same weather with Bob two different behaviors? ____

The following are examples of different behaviors.

A. The same muscles at different speeds. Sprinting and running involve similar movements of the leg muscles. However, the greater speed of sprinting clearly requires a different length of stride, a stonger push-off, and landing on a different portion of the foot.

16. Is walking up the hill a different behavior from walking down the hill? _____

B. The same muscles at different strengths. Whispering "stop" exerts the vocal muscles differently than screaming it. Driving a nail with one blow requires a longer backswing, more wrist action, and a stronger pull than driving it with ten blows.

17. Slamming a tennis ball ________ (is, isn't) the same behavior as tapping a tennis ball.

C. Talking about different topics. Talking about different topics requires the use of different words, which in turn involves different movements of the vocal apparatus. Talking about poetry would be a different behavior than talking about cars.

18. Is talking about a sunny day the same behavior as talking about a hurricane? ____

D. Pronouncing a word correctly and incorrectly. This would be the same as saying two or more different words, since differing pronunciation will result in differing sounds.

19. If a person imitates the way a New Yorker says "you all" and the way a Southerner says "you all," he or she _______ (is, isn't) performing a single behavior.

Helpful Hint #3

Verbal behavior can present problems in analysis. If two individuals are talking, it is helpful to focus on one individual's talking as a series of responses whose rate might be increased or decreased. Then the talking of the other individual can be analyzed as a possible reinforcing event for the first person. For example, if Jean talks about how tough her job is, and Larry listens sympathetically, he could well be reinforcing her. That is, each comment that Jean makes about her job (the response) may be followed by comments from Larry such as "Gee, that's too bad!" or "You ought to do something about that." If these comments by Larry increase the rate of Jean's negative job statements, they can be viewed as reinforcing events because they follow and increase the rate of Jean's comments. When you read examples involving conversations, be sure to read into the example this type of dyadic interaction between the two individuals.

20. When analyzing a discussion, it is helpful to focus on the talking of _______________ (one, both) individual(s) as a behavior whose rate may be increased or decreased by the response of the other individual.

Helpful Hint #4

Here's another way you can decide whether a procedure is differential reinforcement. Differential reinforcement teaches a person what response to make. It teaches the person to eat vegetables instead of drink pop, to stroke the tennis ball correctly, to build new instead of repeated block patterns, to answer questions correctly, to carry out football assignments, or to package garbage correctly. A procedure is likely to be differential reinforcement if it teaches someone what response to make.

Here's how to decide if a procedure is not differential reinforcement. Differential reinforcement does not teach a person when to make a response. If the procedure teaches a baby to call its father "Dada" but not any other male, then it is teaching the baby when to say "Dada." If it teaches Lulu to eat with the family rather than alone, it is teaching her when to eat. If a procedure teaches someone when to make a response, label it as an *unknown* procedure.

21. If a procedure teaches someone when to make a response, label it as *unknown*. If a procedure teaches someone what behavior to make, the procedure is likely to be _______________ _______________.

Helpful Hint #5

If the teacher reinforces the student only for a particular behavior, the teacher must be extinguishing the student for all other behaviors. Therefore, the teacher is using differential reinforcement. Please note the use of the word *only* in descriptions of examples.

22. If the teacher is reinforcing the student only for emitting a particular behavior, then the teacher must be applying what procedure to all other behaviors? _______________

Supppose you read that a teacher reinforces the student for a particular behavior. If the example does not say the student was reinforced only for that behavior, do not assume that it means *only*.

23. The procedure that the teacher would be using if he or she reinforces for a particular behavior is called ______________.

Additional Readings

Green, G. R., Linsk, N. L., & Pinkston, E. M. (1986). Modification of verbal behavior of the mentally impaired elderly by their spouses. *Journal of Applied Behavior Analysis, 19,* 329–336. This paper reports two case studies of wives using differential reinforcement to help elderly spouses communicate meaningfully.

Schwartz, G. J. (1977). College students as contingency managers for adolescents in a program to develop reading skills. *Journal of Applied Behavior Analysis, 10,* 645–655. Schwartz organized a tutorial program for 260 seventh-grade students with important reading deficits. She used 42 college students as the tutors; they gave the seventh-graders special remedial materials and wrote contracts with them to complete agreed-upon amounts of work. They awarded points to the students based on carrying out the contracts. The students advanced about two school years on a reading test. The tutors differentially reinforced them for making positive comments about reading, the learning process, and their abilities. The ratio of positive to negative comments changed from 50% positive before the program to about 85% afterwards. Differential reinforcement and effective training of reading skills improved the attitudes of the students toward reading and also toward themselves.

Reading Quiz

68. So far you have learned two methods for altering the rate of a single behavior. They are the procedures of 1) ______________ and 2) ______________.

87. You will be called on to write the word *differential* many times in this lesson. Focus on spelling it correctly. Copy the word now: ______________. Notice that you will sometimes be asked to write *differentially*. Copy that now: ______________.

80. This lesson is about the procedure called differential reinforcment, which is Tactic #3 of the reinforcement strategy. Tactic #3 is to increase a desired behavior relative to an undesired behavior through differential ______________.

86. You can use Tactic #3 of the reinforcement strategy to increase one behavior relative to another behavior through ______________ reinforcement.

77. Tactic #3 of the reinforcement strategy is to increase a desired behavior relative to an undesired behavior through ______________ ______________.

83. What procedure has the following three elements? (1) Two or more physically different behaviors occur in one situation; (2) one behavior is reinforced; and (3) all other behaviors are extinguished. Differential ______________

40. Notice that the term *differential reinforcement* starts with the word *different*. That can remind you that one characteristic of differential reinforcement is that two or more physically ______________ behaviors are involved.

78. The different behaviors occurring in an example of differential reinforcement must occur in ________ (many, one) situation(s).

1. A second characteristic of differential reinforcement is that one behavior is increased through use of the procedure of ______________.

79. The third characteristic of differential reinforcement is that another behavior is decreased through use of the procedure of ______________.

50. Review: Dad praises Lulu when she eats vegetables but ignores her when she drinks pop at home. Lulu starts to eat more vegetables and drink less pop. Notice that Dad works with two different behaviors (eating, drinking) in one situation (home). He increases eating vegetables by praise, and he decreases drinking pop by ignoring it. Because his procedure has these three elements to it, this is an example of what procedure? ______________ ______________

6. Dad praises Lulu when she eats with the family but ignores her when she eats alone. Sup-

pose Lulu starts to eat with the family more often. Notice that she could eat exactly the same way whether she is eating with the family or eating alone. Therefore, this is an example of a single behavior in two different situations. It is not an example of differential reinforcement, because it does not involve two ____________ (different, identical) behaviors. Therefore, it is an unknown procedure.

48. Review: Dad might praise Lulu when she eats slowly and ignore her when she eats fast. Lulu might continue to eat fast just as often as before. Because the praise and ignoring doesn't change the speed of her eating, Dad is using what procedure? ____________

49. Review: Dad might tell Lulu to eat slowly, while he ignores eating fast. She might start eating slowly. Because telling Lulu to eat slowly does not involve stopping or delivering a reinforcer, Dad's telling would be an example of what procedure? ____________

61. Review: To be a good example of differential reinforcement an example must have three elements. (1) It must involve at least two ____________ behaviors in the same situation. (2) It must increase one behavior through the procedure of ____________. (3) It must decrease other behaviors through the procedure of ____________.

47. Review: A situation might involve two or more different behaviors in one situation. Reinforcement might be used to increase one behavior and extinction used to decrease one or more other behaviors. If all three elements are present, then you should label this procedure as ____________.

3. Buzas and Ayllon (1981) taught a tennis coach to ignore errors by a youth and praise correct strokes. If the rate of correct strokes increased and the rate of errors decreased, the coach used what procedure? ____________

22. If an example describes a teacher praising behavior A, you should not assume that the teacher is not praising other behaviors. You must limit your analysis to Behavior A. If praising behavior A increases its rate, then you should label the use of praise as the procedure called ____________.

4. Buzas and Ayllon (1981) observed the tennis coach before they taught him to use differential reinforcement. They found that he used a self-defeating approach in which he yelled at the student whenever she made incorrect strokes. Her rate of incorrect strokes increased. Since you don't know if the coach ignored correct strokes, you don't know if his procedure included extinction. Therefore, you cannot conclude that he was using differential reinforcement. You can only analyze what he did with the errors. The coach unwittingly used what procedure to increase errors? ____________

84. When a teacher scolded and reprimanded a kindergarten student for wild behavior, the student increased his wild behavior. What procedure did the teacher use to inadvertantly increase wild behavior? ____________

19. Goetz and Baer (1973) taught preschool teachers to praise children when they built novel structures and ignore them when they built repeated structures. Children built more creative structures and less repeated structures. While the differences between creative and repeated structures may have been subtle, there must have been differences. The different structures must have involved different behaviors to build them. Therefore, the procedure is an example of ____________.

41. Other researchers might have taught the preschool teachers simply to tell the children to build more creative structures and simply to ignore repeated structures. If the children had built more creative structures compared to repeated structures, the preschool teachers would be using what procedure? ____________

37. Komaki and Barnett (1977) taught coaches to praise youth football players when they carried out their assignments and ignore them when they didn't. The procedure improved the correct carrying out of assignments. Label the procedure ____________.

76. Suppose Komaki and Barnett (1977) had taught coaches to praise the football players when they carried out their assignments and ignore them when they didn't. If the procedure had not improved the correct carrying out of assignments, what would you label the procedure? ____________

46. Researchers used a feedback device to teach adults how to relax their forehead muscles.

The device made a low-pitched sound; the adults knew this meant that their forehead was relaxed. When it made a high-pitched sound, the adults knew that their forehead muscles were tense. The adults increased the rate of relaxed muscles and decreased the rate of tensed muscles. The researchers used what procedure? ____________________

74. Students have a great deal of trouble telling whether an example involves a single behavior or different behaviors. This is the biggest cause of student errors. I am going to give a whole series of examples of same and different behaviors so you can practice telling which is which. If a procedure involves two different behaviors, it ______ (can, can't) be differential reinforcement.
39. Making and not making a response ______ (are, aren't) two different behaviors.
27. Is moving a set of muscles fast a different behavior from moving the same set slowly? ___
2. Are using a set of muscles in location A and using the same muscles in location B different behaviors? _____
82. Using a set of muscles strongly ______ (is, isn't) the same behavior as using the same set weakly.
33. Is using a set of muscles when X happens and using the same muscles when Y happens a single behavior? ____
32. Is talking about one topic the same behavior as talking about a different topic? ___
43. Reading novel A and reading novel B ______ (are, aren't) a single behavior.
21. A person pronouncing a word one way and then another way ______ (is, isn't) a single behavior.
30. Are saying the same word to person A and then to person B two different behaviors? ___
26. Is jogging a different behavior from walking? _____
67. Smiling and not smiling at someone ______ (are, aren't) two different behaviors.
42. Reading about conservation and reading about weather ____ (are, aren't) a single behavior.
31. Is talking about Fred the same behavior as talking about Jane? _____
28. Are saying "That's one" when you see a jet and saying "That's one" when you see a car a single behavior? ______
66. Screaming "No" ______ (is, isn't) the same behavior as whispering "No."
25. Are giving a high five on the football field and giving a high five at dinner two different behaviors? ___
24. If you say "Buenas dias" with a learner's accent and "Buenas dias" with perfect Spanish pronunciation, you ______ (are, aren't) performing a single behavior.
29. Are saying hello to Mary and saying hello to Bob two different behaviors? ___
35. Jane praised John when he was reading English but ignored him when he was reading physics. John started to read English more than physics. Decide whether reading different books is different behavior. What procedure did Jane use? ____________________
81. To teach the correct pronunciation of a difficult English word to a child while eliminating the incorrect pronunciation, one could use the behavioral procedure of ____________________ ____________.
5. Carl Rogers expressed positive regard when his client said insightful things, but not when she said negative things. The client's insight increased relative to her negative feelings. Carl Rogers inadvertently used the behavioral procedure of ____________________.
18. Gil and associates (1988) found that parents paid attention to children when they scratched but not as often when they engaged in behavior other than scratching. They caused the children to scratch more often. By their attention, the parents accidentally used what procedure to increase scratching? __________ ____________________
7. Dad usually pays attention if baby says "Dada" to him but he ignores it when baby says it to other males. Baby will quickly come to say it only to Dad. Before you jump to conclusions about the procedure that Dad uses, ask, "Does baby move different muscles when saying 'Dada' to Dad than when she says it to other males?" You should label the procedure that Dad uses as ____________________.
36. Kaufmann (1991) was praised by his psychoanalyst for unhappy talk and discouraged for happy talk. His talk became unhappy more often and happy less often. The psychoanalyst used what procedure? ______________ ______________
23. If you reinforce someone <u>only</u> when he or she engages in behavior A, you must not be reinforcing that person when engaging in any

other behavior. Therefore, the situation involves at least two behaviors: behavior A and every other behavior. You are increasing behavior A through reinforcement. You are decreasing all other behaviors through extinction. Therefore, you are using what behavioral procedure by reinforcing only behavior A? _______________

85. When you read that a teacher reinforces a student <u>only</u> when the student performs a certain behavior, you know that the teacher also decreases other behavior through the procedure called _______________.

75. Suppose a music teacher praises <u>only</u> notes sung close to C. That means that he ignores notes sung far from C. If your rate of singing close to C increases, what procedure has your teacher used by praising only when you sing close to C? _______________

45. Remember that *only* is an important word in describing differential reinforcement. It permits me to keep examples short. If you know that only one behavior is reinforced, you also know that all other behaviors are subjected to what procedure? _______________

8. Differential reinforcement can sometimes produce the wrong result. Remember that an unpleasant event can sometimes serve as a reinforcer. Suppose a music teacher criticizes <u>only</u> those notes that differ from C. If the student's singing gets worse, the procedure used by criticizing only mistakes is called _______________.

44. Remember, if an example states that a teacher reinforces a student for a particular behavior, that's what it means. Do not assume that it means <u>only</u>. If a teacher reinforces a student for a particular behavior, the teacher is using what behavioral procedure? _______________

9. Differential reinforcement has two effects: 1) it __________ the rate of a desired behavior; and 2) it __________ the rate of an undesired behavior.

34. It may be necessary to quickly decrease someone's problem behavior when the reinforcing consequences for that behavior cannot be eliminated. If you increase the rate of a behavior that is incompatible with the problem behavior, then you decrease the time that the person has to perform the problem behavior. You could accomplish this outcome by differentially reinforcing the behavior that is _______________ (compatible, incompatible) with the problem behavior.

38. Mace and associates (1983) stopped the aggression of a youth with severe retardation by reinforcing complying with instructions and ignoring the youth's aggression. Aggression decreased relative to complying with instructions. Notice that complying with instructions is incompatible with aggressing. These researchers used the procedure called _______________ of incompatible behavior.

10. Differential reinforcement provides a(n) _______________ to punishment.

11. Differential reinforcement can affect the relative rates of _____ or more different behaviors.

58. Review: Tactic #3 in using the reinforcement strategy to solve human problems is to increase a desired behavior relative to an undesired behavior through _______________.

20. Green and associates (1986) taught Mrs. Orr to use praise, smiles, and touch to reinforce her elderly husband's correct answers. She ignored incorrect answers. Her husband's rate of answering questions correctly increased relative to answering them incorrectly. What procedure did she use? _______________

69. Stokes and Fawcett (1977) studied the correct and incorrect packaging of trash by the residents of a city. Correct and incorrect packaging of trash _______________ (are, aren't) physically different responses.

70. Stokes and Fawcett (1977) developed a treatment procedure for trash-packaging behaviors in which packaging behaviors that met the city standards were followed by collection of trash, and packaging behaviors that did not meet the standards were followed by no collection of trash. If correct packaging increased and incorrect packaging decreased, what procedure did they use? _______________

71. Stokes and Fawcett (1977) found that correct packaging behaviors increased when they were followed by collection and that incorrect packaging behaviors decreased when they were not followed by collection. We can conclude that the event of collection is a(n) _______________ for everyone whose packaging behavior improved.

72. Stokes and Fawcett (1977) asked sanitation workers to serve as outside judges. They asked them to rate how well the garbage had been packaged before and after treatment. They compared the workers' ratings with their own observations based on a behavioral definition of good packaging. They were finding out the ____________ of their behavioral definition.
73. Stokes and Fawcett (1977) found that correct packaging behaviors increased and incorrect packaging behaviors decreased when only correct packaging was followed by collection. Therefore, their procedure would be labeled ____________.
17. From Note #1: In order to explain current behavior, it may be necessary to describe the differential reinforcement a person has received in the past, which is called his or her ________ of reinforcement.
12. From Helpful Hint #1: If a single behavior is reinforced in one situation and extinguished in a different situation, you should label this procedure as ____________.
13. From Helpful Hint #2: To determine whether a person emits two different behaviors, you must examine what movements the person makes with his or her muscles for each behavior. You should conclude that a person emits two different behaviors only if the person makes different movements of his or her ____________.
14. From Helpful Hint #4: If a procedure teaches someone what behavior to make, the procedure is likely to be ____________.
15. From Helpful Hint #4: If a procedure teaches someone when to make a response, label it as ____________.
16. From Helpful Hint #5: If the teacher is reinforcing the student only when he emits a particular behavior and that behavior increases, can you conclude that the teacher is using differential reinforcement? ________
55. Review: One of the characteristics of differential reinforcement is that one behavior is increased by using ____________.
52. Review: If a single behavior is reinforced in one situation and extinguished in a different situation, you should label the procedure as ____________.
64. Review: When one behavior is reinforced and any others are extinguished in the same situation, this is termed ____________.
62. Review: To use the reinforcement strategy for solving human problems, you may follow these tactics: (1) increase the desired behavior through reinforcement; (2) decrease the undesired behavior through extinction; (3) increase a desired behavior relative to an undesired behavior through ____________.
56. Review: Stokes and Fawcett (1977) observed that correct trash-packaging behaviors increased and incorrect ones decreased when only correctly packaged trash was collected. The behavioral procedure they used was ____________.
59. Review: Tactic #3 in using the reinforcement strategy to solve human problems is to increase a desired behavior relative to an undesired behavior through ____________.
63. Review: Two behavioral procedures that are involved in differential reinforcement are ________ and ________.
53. Review: If Fred praises May only when she works on her computer, and she starts working more on her computer and less on other activities, then Fred is using what procedure? ____________
54. Review: One characteristic of differential reinforcement is that one or more behaviors are decreased by using the method of ____________.
65. Review: If a baby says "Mama" to other females besides the mother, and the parents ignore these occurrences but pay attention to the "Mama" said to the mother, what procedure are they using? ____________
51. Review: Differential reinforcement involves three elements. First, the example must involve one situation with at least two behaviors that are ________ from each other. Second, the example must increase one behavior through the procedure of ________. Third, the example must decrease one or more behaviors through the procedure of ________.
57. Review: Stokes and Fawcett (1977) studied the effect on packaging behavior of collecting properly packaged trash and not collecting improperly packaged trash. Does the example involve two (or more) different behaviors? ________

60. Review: Tactic #3 in using the reinforcement strategy to solve human problems is to increase a desired behavior relative to an undesired behavior through ______________________.

Examples

1. A baby boy makes many vocalizations such as "ba," "glub," "goo-goo," and eventually "da" or "da-da." When parents first hear a vocalization similar to "da," they immediately pay a lot of attention to the child, pet him, hold him, make nice sounds back at him, and generally ignore "ba," "glub," and "goo-goo." As a result, the child starts saying "da" more often. Check for the elements of differential reinforcement. First, is "da" a different behavior from "ba" and "glub"? ______. Second, is one behavior increased with use of reinforcement? _____. Third, are one or more other physically different behaviors decreased with use of extinction? _____. Since the example involves two or more different behaviors, one of which is being reinforced and the others extinguished, the parents were using what procedure? ______________________________. They were teaching baby what sound to make, not when to make it.

2. A baby boy may say "Mama" to many females other than his mother. His parents, by reserving their attention for those occasions when the child says "Mama" to its mother, will eventually teach the child not to say "Mama" to any other females. Check for the elements of differential reinforcement. First, does saying "Mama" to the mother involve a behavior that is physically different from saying "Mama" to other females? _____. Because the parents are reinforcing a behavior in one situation and extinguishing the same behavior in another situation, you should label the procedure that the parents use to teach their baby to call its mother "Mama" ______________________________. They are teaching the baby <u>when</u> to say "Mama," not what sound to make.

3. Roger watched everything on TV, from cartoons to *Sesame Street*. However, his father started praising him when he watched *Sesame Street* and started ignoring him when he watched cartoons. Soon Roger was watching only *Sesame Street*. Check for the elements. First, do Roger's eyes focus differently while watching cartoons than while watching *Sesame Street*? ________. Therefore, you should label father's procedure as ______________________________. Father was teaching Roger when to watch TV, not what behavior to emit.

4. Frank's dad noticed that his son's habit of tuning the radio had changed considerably. At first his son would usually twirl the knob very quickly and then complain of not being able to find his favorite radio station. As time went on, Frank's rapid twirling of the dial decreased. However, the few times that he turned it slowly, he was able to find the station. As time went on, Frank turned the knob slowly more often. Check for elements. First, does turning the knob quickly constitute a different behavior from turning it slowly? ______. Second, does the example state any evidence that turning the knob slowly was reinforced by Frank's finding his favorite radio station? ______. Third, is turning the knob quickly extinguished by failure to find his favorite radio station? ______. The procedure being followed by the natural operation of the tuner on the radio would be called ______________________________. The radio was teaching him what behavior to emit not when to emit it.

5. Rolando was pretty good at using a hammer and screwdriver. However, his mother saw him sometimes hammer in a screw rather than using the screwdriver. Mom decided to help Rolando by praising him whenever he used the screwdriver on the screw. She ignored him when he used the hammer on the screw. Soon Rolando was using the screwdriver for the screw. Check. First, are there two or more different behaviors? ________. Second, is one behavior increased through reinforcement? ______. Third, are one or more other behaviors decreased through extinction? _____. Therefore, by praising using the screwdriver on screws and ignoring using the hammer on screws, Mom was using what procedure? ______________________________. She was teaching Rolando what behavior to emit, not when to emit it.

6. Faith was learning the language of radical politics. For some reason, she had trouble pronouncing "imperialism." So her boyfriend Imamu delighted in helping her learn the correct pronunciation. When she was right, he praised her; when she was wrong, he didn't. She soon learned to pronounce it correctly. Check for different behaviors, reinforcement of one, and extinction of others before answering the next question. What procedure was Imamu using in this example? ______________________________. He was teaching Faith what behavior to emit.

7. Garvey liked the meetings of the Young Republicans, and he also liked the meetings of the Humanists' Club. But he found that if he made his speech about the dignity of all humans, including poor people, the Republicans didn't seem too interested. On the other hand, when he made the same speech to the Humanists, they seemed overjoyed. Without even noticing it, Garvey found himself giving his speech less to the Republicans and more to the Humanists. Check elements. Between them, these organizations unintentionally applied what procedure to Garvey's speech about dignity? ______________________. They were teaching him when to talk about dignity, not what to talk about.

8. Marcie was tired of Dave watching the baseball game on TV every weekend. She told him about her feelings and asked him to stop watching it. He agreed and now no longer watches the weekend game. Check, then answer the next question. What procedure did Marcie use to reduce Dave's rate of watching the game? ______________________

9. Review: (Note: I will start mixing in examples of other procedures. Start by deciding what concept you think may be involved. Then check for the elements appropriate to that concept. Remember, it may be unknown.) Gary's parents always criticized fashion-conscious college students. During his freshman year, they made about three put-downs an hour. During his sophomore year, any time they made such a put-down, Gary started explaining to them why students need to buy the latest fashion. Gary's parents' rate of put-downs increased to nine an hour. What behavioral procedure did Gary unintentionally use to increase the parents' put-downs? ______________________

10. Review: John and Darrin were in the cafeteria having an important discussion about their social action meeting that night. Lee came over and sat down with them. John and Darrin both said hello and immediately included Lee in their conversation. After this incident, Lee sat with John and Darrin more often during lunchtime, and they always included him in their conversations. What behavioral procedure was at work in determining how often Lee sat with John and Darrin? ______________________

11. Review: Bob's coach helped him to improve his hitting. Before every at-bat, he would remind Bob to keep his eye on the ball. Bob usually did. Then the coach decided that Bob now should be able to do it on his own, so he stopped reminding him. Bob does not keep his eye on the ball very often now. What procedure did the coach use that resulted in the decrease in Bob keeping his eye on the ball? ______________________

12. Review: David Jaynes was the new psychiatrist for Mrs. Brooke. She became annoyed at Jaynes's habit of describing his own problems but never asking what help Mrs. Brooke needed. So she started ignoring all descriptions of his problems and paid attention only when he asked what she needed. He quickly changed, asking her more often what she needed and describing his own problems less often. What behavioral procedure was Mrs. Brooke using? ______________________

13. Review: Mr. Howard taught a ninth-grade geography class. It was his conviction that the students would learn more about geography if they participated in class discussion. For the most part, the students appeared to enjoy the discussion classes and to enter willingly into discussions. However, one boy, Ben, said very little. Mr. Howard decided that rather than continue to put him on the spot by constantly asking him questions, he would compliment him profusely whenever he did say anything. Pretty soon Ben was talking a lot during class. Mr. Howard changed Ben's behavior by using what behavioral procedure? ______________________

14. Review: Grace wanted desperately to learn how to do the new dance, but she didn't know the steps. Patty showed her the dance steps. Then Grace copied it, and she had learned the dance just like that. By showing her how the dance went, what method did Patty use? ______________________

15. Review: Many new parents are unhappy that their baby cries so often. For example, they may change a baby's diapers, attend to all his or her physical needs, and put him or her to bed for the night. However, they will then answer the baby's cries for hours even though there is nothing wrong with the child. They would be advised by a behavior analyst to ignore all crying after the baby is put to bed properly cared for. The child will cry a lot for the first part of a few nights but will gradually stop crying. This method of decreasing the baby's crying after he or she is put to bed is called ______________________.

16. Review: Gary found that if he smiled when he was with Jane, she would pay a lot of attention

to him. However, if he smiled when he was with Gloria, she would ignore him. Naturally, Gary started smiling a lot when he was around Jane and hardly at all when he was around Gloria. Getting attention from Jane and getting ignored by Gloria for smiling is what behavioral procedure? ______________________

17. Review: Carol had a friend who was helping her learn to jog. Whenever she took a long smooth stride, her friend praised her; when she took a shorter stride or a rougher stride, her friend made no comment. She was soon the smoothest runner around. What procedure was her friend using to teach Carol how to jog? ______________________

18. Review: If a child starts to read the comics out loud, his or her parents usually make a big fuss about this suddenly displayed reading skill. What behavioral procedure would account for any increase in the child's reading from the comics? ______________

19. Review: Faith has learned about radical politics from her friend, Imamu. After she had read parts of *Das Kapital*, Imamu would talk with her excitedly about it. After she had read parts of *The Rise and Fall of the Roman Empire*, however, he was very quiet. Faith came to read *Das Kapital* more and more often. What behavioral procedure was Imamu using? ______________________

20. Review: Kurt wanted to learn to speak German really well, but he was having trouble learning to say "ch" as the Germans do. He found that it was a gutteral sound that combined some aspects of the English "k" and the English "ch." His instructor praised him strongly when he got it right but ignored him the rest of the time. If Kurt's pronunciation of "ch" improved, what procedure was his instructor using? ______________

LESSON

11 Shaping Everyday Behaviors

You have now learned the basics of reinforcement. Any behavior that produces reinforcement will increase. That's how you and I have learned the many useful everyday skills that we have. Behavior analysts can use reinforcement to help people learn particular skills, and you can use it to increase desired behavior in other people.

Of course, reinforcement can also cause undesirable behavior to increase. However, if undesirable behavior is no longer followed by reinforcement, it will decrease. That's called extinction. Most of us don't have lots of undesirable behavior, because other people have extinguished it. (They have also punished it, but that's a story for later in the book.) Behavior analysts use extinction to help people get rid of some of the remaining undesirable behavior, and you can use it to decrease the undesirable behavior of others.

As you know, most of our behavior is the result of the combined effect of reinforcement and extinction. The world usually reinforces one behavior while extinguishing many other behaviors. Behavior analysts, you, and I can use these principles to help ourselves and others. They are powerful principles. However, as powerful as they are, they only work on existing behavior. They can't create new behavior such as that displayed by a skillful ballerina. (See Figure 11-1.)

Behavior analysts can use these principles to teach children creative block building. However, notice that the children already must know how to build with blocks. Teachers can use these principles to teach creative word use, but students must already know how to speak and write those same words. The point is that reinforcement can only increase the rate of an existing behavior. Critics often point to this limitation, claiming that behavior analysts cannot explain the origin of <u>new</u> behaviors. In this lesson, you will learn how simple it is to shape new behavior. You will learn Tactic #4 in using the reinforcement strategy to solve human problems: to create new behavior through <u>shaping</u>.

1. Tactic #4 in using the reinforcement strategy to solve human problems is to create new behavior through ____________________.

Figure 11-1. Many psychologists wonder how reinforcement could account for such a rare accomplishment as ballet dancing. After all, you can't reinforce such behavior if it doesn't exist. This lesson will show you how.

Some Examples of Shaping

The easiest way to introduce shaping is to give you an example. Suppose Danny, your 3-year-old son, fears the dark. He insists on sleeping with the light on all night. You want to teach him a new behavior: to sleep with the light off all night. Suppose you ask him to turn it off, but he refuses. If he never turns the light off, you can't reinforce that response. What do you do? You shape the new behavior of turning off the light.

The first thing you might do is to install a light dimmer. This light dimmer has ten gradations: On 10, the light is fully on; on 0, it is fully off. The dimmer permits Danny to dim the light a little bit. Now you can ask him at bedtime to dim the light to 9. If he turns it to 9 and leaves it there all night, you can praise him the next morning. If he leaves it on 10, you can ignore his behavior and say good night. If he sometimes turns it to 9, your praise may increase the rate. You can then ask him to turn it to 8. You can repeat this process until he turns it all the way off. You will have created the new behavior of sleeping in the dark. Researchers taught the parents of six children to use this procedure, and it worked with all six (Giebenhain & O'Dell, 1984).

Notice the pattern here. You first pick a starting point for the shaping—in this case, any dimming of the light. The starting point must be a behavior that the child can now do. You pick the starting point because it is related to your goal of turning the light off. You then differentially reinforce that starting behavior. At the same time, you extinguish behavior that is not related to the goal. You thereby increase the rate of the behavior that is related to the goal in proportion to that which is not. Once you have increased your starting point, you then find a next step: some behavior that is closer to the goal. In the example, it might be a setting of 8. You shift the criterion for what you will reinforce to this behavior, which is more closely related to the goal. Step by step, you get closer and closer to the goal. Finally, you reach it—you have "shaped" an entirely new behavior.

Here's another example. Suppose Ann, your infant, makes the usual baby vocal sounds. She coos, cries, gurgles, and babbles, making vowel sounds like "ah," "uh," "oh" and "eeh." Suppose you want to teach her to say "Dada." The hard part is the "d" sound, because she is already saying the "ah" sound. You start shaping by picking any sound that is remotely like the "d." When you hear it, you smile at her and praise her immediately. You might also hug, pat, or even feed her to reinforce that sound. You ignore all other sounds. You want to increase the "d" sound compared to other sounds. When she makes more "d" sounds, you start listening for "da" sounds. Again reinforce those sounds and ignore all others, including the simple "d" sounds. When she makes lots of "da" sounds, start working on repeats of "da." You might hear "da" and, a second later, another "da." Reinforce it. Keep going this way until she says "Dada." Depending on how skillful you are, you might take a few minutes or a few hours to shape an entirely new behavior. Two researchers used this method to teach a mute 4-year-old child to say "eat" (Blake & Moss, 1967).

Parents often use shaping to develop the language skills of normal children (Moerk, 1990). In fact, we all use this method to help children learn many important skills. The advantage of shaping is that it does not rely on language. People can use it to teach new behaviors to babies, infants, and individuals with retardation. Of course, once a person can speak, you can use other methods; I will teach you some of those other methods in Unit Three. However, even after we develop exquisite language skills, we continue to learn through shaping. You might be surprised just how much of your own behavior is influenced by the principle of shaping. I will give some examples later in this lesson.

Definition of Shaping

You should use the term **shaping** only when two conditions exist. (1) You have specified a target behavior. (2) You have applied differential reinforcement to a series of successive approximations to that target behavior. You can also use the term *shaping* with natural situations. It is not necessary that someone intentionally specify a target behavior. You need only observe that the successive approximations move toward some end result. You can think of that end result as an unintentional target behavior.

2. Use the term *shaping* when you have specified a target behavior and you have applied differential reinforcement to a series of successive ____________ to the target behavior.

Skinner Shaped a Critic's Behavior

Skinner told this story of what happened when a committee he was on brought in Eric Fromm as a guest. "All morning long he had easy explanations for everything. And after lunch it was the same thing. We were all seated at a big table, a couple of dozen of us. He was sitting across the table from me and he started in. 'Pigeons aren't people you know,' he told me. 'You have to realize that man is different.' He went on and on. I wrote a note saying, 'Watch Fromm's left hand. I'm going to shape a chopping motion.' I passed the note down to the chairman. I just turned toward [Fromm] and every time his hand went up, I nodded. Pretty soon he was chopping and chopping the air with his left hand as he spoke. I thought, 'Why does he say this doesn't work with people?'" (cited in Snyder, 1990: p.4).

5. Skinner's goal was to get Fromm to make a chopping motion. The chopping motion would be considered the ____________ (shaping, approximation, target) behavior of a shaping procedure.

You should use the term <u>target behavior</u> to refer to the new behavior. The target behavior is the goal of your shaping. In the earlier example, it is saying "Dada." The target behavior is any behavior that you seek to produce through shaping. It is also any behavior toward which the world unintentionally moves behavior.

3. The goal of shaping is called the ____________ behavior.

You should use the term <u>successive approximations</u> to refer to steps toward the target behavior. In the example, "d," "da," and "da... da" were successive approximations to "Dada." The shaping procedure rests on successive approximations. It involves selecting an initial approximation to the target behavior. You then differentially reinforce that approximation until it occurs frequently. Then you select a second, closer approximation and differentially reinforce that behavior until it occurs at a high rate. You then select a behavior that takes another step toward the target behavior. You repeat the process until you reach the target behavior. Each behavioral approximation to the target behavior is called a *successive approximation.*

4. You should use the term ____________ ____________ to refer to steps toward the target behavior.

Shaping Shooting an Arrow

Suppose you wish to teach your son, Fernando, how to shoot an arrow into a target from 25 feet. You teach him the first approximation—perhaps, how to draw the bow with the arrow in it. You praise him when he does it right; you overlook his mistakes. When Fernando can do it, you move on to the second approximation: You teach how to sight the target and release the arrow from 5 feet. Again, you praise him when he hits the target and

Figure 11-2. When using shaping to teach someone a new skill, you should start by differentially reinforcing behavior that the person can do successfully. Cartoon copyright 1973 King Features Syndicate. Reproduced by permission.

overlook his goofs. When he can hit the target every time, you are ready to find a third approximation. Perhaps it is to shoot from 10 feet. Again, you praise and ignore. You continue this process until he can shoot accurately from 25 feet, the target behavior. Figure 11-2 illustrates how a concerned father might start with a very easy first approximation.

Overcoming Shyness and Other Problems

Intentional shaping involves the deliberate effort of a behavior analyst to create a new behavior. A good example is the program devised by Jackson and Wallace (1974). They set out to teach a very shy 15-year-old girl to speak loudly enough to be heard. Alice had been diagnosed as extremely withdrawn since age 7. She had no social skills, had no friends, and learned little in school. She spoke in such a soft whisper that no one could hear her.

The researchers used very sensitive electronic equipment. They gave Alice a list of 100 simple words and asked her to read them. The equipment could detect when she did so in a soft whisper. Using the equipment, they immediately delivered a reinforcer for these whispers. They set the equipment to ignore very soft whispers. Thus, they differentially reinforced Alice for softly whispering the words on their list. Once she was doing that, they required a louder whisper for reinforcement. They continued to increase the loudness requirement as she mastered each stage. Eventually, she was reading the words in a normal tone of voice. The researchers then went through a series of additional steps. They reinforced her for reading words of more than one syllable in a normal voice. They reinforced her for saying things to other people. Finally, they reinforced her for talking in a classroom. After this training, Alice changed quite dramatically. She talked with other kids, did quite well in a normal classroom, and even got a job as a waitress.

Here's another example of intentional shaping. Researchers helped children accept insertion of contact lenses (Mathews, Hodson, Crist, & LaRoche, 1992). For example, they helped the parents of 2-year-old Charles. They broke insertion down to eight steps. The first step was teaching Charles to accept touching his face. Second was accepting pulling open the eyelid. Third was having the child pull open the eyelid. Fourth was accepting drops in the eye. Fifth was accepting approaching the eye with a finger. Sixth was accepting touching the eye with the finger. Seventh was accepting touching the eye with a soft lens. The target behavior was accepting touching the eye with a hard lens. That permitted insertion. The researchers reinforced Charles's acceptance of each step with praise, bubbles, food, and access to toys. They ignored nonacceptance. Charles learned to accept each step, and eventually he accepted insertion.

Another example of intentional shaping is given by Horner (1971). He taught Dennis, a 5-year-old child with moderate retardation, to walk with crutches. Dennis had moderate retardation, with a birth defect that left his legs paralyzed. His muscles functioned at the level of a 10-month-old child; he could sit up and pull himself along the floor with his arms. Horner differentially reinforced Dennis for a series of approximations to using the crutches. The first step was to have Dennis place the crutch tips on two dots on the floor. The next step was to place the crutch tips on the dots and swing his body to an erect crutch-supported position. The very gradual increase in the behavior required for differential reinforcement occurred through ten steps. Dennis finally learned to walk with the crutches. He learned to walk to and from all programs and activities in the hospital within 15 days. The treatment permitted Dennis the dignity of controlling when and where he went.

Researchers have used shaping to develop complex behaviors. They have used it where normal psychiatric or medical procedures had not worked. For instance, researchers have used shaping to teach electively mute psychotics to resume talking. The behavior analysts started by reinforcing eye contact; they then reinforced nodding in response to questions; then they moved to grunting. Finally, they reinforced verbal behavior (Isaacs, Thomas, & Goldiamond, 1960). Others have used similar procedures (e.g., Sherman, 1963).

Behavior analysts have used shaping to teach many of the skills of verbal communication to children with retardation. They have shaped the correct use of plurals (Guess et al., 1968), the correct use of adjectives (Baer & Guess, 1971), and the appropriate asking of questions (Twardosz & Baer,

> ***Giving Hou a New Personality***
>
> Hou was a female porpoise at the Sea Life Park in Hawaii. She showed little initiative, so Karen Pryor, a veteran porpoise trainer, set out to teach Hou initiative by reinforcing novel tricks. During the first sessions, Pryor did not reinforce Hou's existing tricks. Hou engaged in the highly repetitive tricks of leaping and circling. Pryor broke the pattern by differentially reinforcing successive approximations to the novel trick of tail walking. That got Hou started. She added a tail slap on her own. She did back flips, somersaults, figure eights and spins. Hou's novel tricks became so complex and rapid that Pryor could not react fast enough. Hou now shows much initiative (Pryor, Haag, & O'Reilly, 1969).
>
> 6. By differentially reinforcing successive approximations to tail walking, Pryor used what behavioral procedure to teach Hou this novel trick? ______________________ (differential reinforcement, reinforcement, shaping)

1973). They have used similar procedures in natural settings (Cavallaro & Poulson, 1985). These studies hold promise for teaching children with retardation improved language skills. They may also help us understand normal language acquisition.

Karen Pryor used shaping to train porpoises in performing many kinds of behavior. Perhaps the most heartwarming is the story of Hou, told in the accompanying box.

What Shaping Is Not

Do not apply the term *shaping* to just any gradual change related to a person's behavior. It is not shaping when the response rate gradually increases from reinforcement. Nor is it shaping when a person's behavior changes without differential reinforcement. For example, suppose Mary gradually buys more expensive books. Yet her actual buying behavior may not change. That is, she may still pick out the book, carry it to the counter, and write a check. Be sure that some physical aspect of the person's behavior changes through a series of approximations.

Natural Shaping

You can't overestimate the importance of shaping; it is responsible for much complex human behavior. We acquire many of our skills through natural shaping. We are shaped into playing a musical instrument, writing poetry, making a speech, building a house, speaking a foreign language, or pleasing a sweetheart. Virtually everything we do builds on a simple starting behavior. Shaping helps build on that behavior until we have a complex skill. Much of the building occurs through shaping without explicit verbal instruction.

The normal functioning of your environment may produce natural shaping. You might find that a light tap restores the picture on your TV. If the picture gets worse, you may find yourself pounding on it harder and harder. The normal functioning of a failing TV have shaped you into beating on your TV. You might find that a computer is very useful to you. You start by learning the basics of one program; pretty soon you learn many programs; and eventually you may learn operating systems, utilities, and even how to program. The advantages of computer use have shaped you into acquiring a very complex skill. Or you may start out jogging a few times a week, then train for a short race, and eventually run marathons. You've been shaped into running farther and harder. No one intentionally shaped any of these behaviors. The normal benefits of aerobic health and the admiration of others have shaped you into a marathon runner. No one intended to shape any of these target behaviors; the normal operation of your physical and social environment did the shaping.

People often use shaping without awareness. They may talk about it in nontechnical words. For example, Barry Neal Kaufman and his wife Samahria use words of love to describe their use of shaping. They discovered that their infant son had severe retardation and autism. When the doctors "encouraged institutionalization, we suggested love. When they advised realism, we countered with hope.... We turned to God more fervently than ever.... We decided to be happy with our son and rather than push him to come to us and conform to our world, we joined him in his.

Overcoming Autism through Shaping

Doctors told the Kaufmans that their infant son, Raun, had incurable autism. He lived in an alien world devoid of human contact. The Kaufmans worked with his existing behaviors: When he rocked, they rocked; when he flapped his fingers, they flapped theirs; when he screeched, they treated it like a song and tried to learn it. "Slowly we reached into the darkness and... built bridges of words and affection.... By taking thousands of painstakingly tiny steps with him, we taught him how to speak, interact with people and master self-help skills." They worked with him 12 hours a day, seven days a week, for three years. He "blossomed into a highly verbal, extroverted, expressive and loving youngster" with a near-genius I.Q. and graduated from college (based on Kaufman, 1991).

7. Behavior analysts call the "painstakingly tiny steps" successive ________ (approximations, targets) to the target behavior.

Since we did not judge his autistic behaviors as 'bad' or 'sick' but saw them as the best he could do for now, we used them as vehicles to communicate acceptance and to teach him about the world" (Kaufman, 1991: pp. 15–16). The box on overcoming autism shows that their miraculous efforts are actually an inspiring example of shaping.

Misuse of Shaping

Shaping can be misused just like any other behavioral principle. For example, mothers often shape obnoxious pestering behaviors in their children. A mother may give her sweet young son a cookie just before dinner the first few times he asks. Later, the mother may decide that it isn't such a good idea to do that, so she refuses to give the cookie. But the child may persist, and pretty soon the mother gives him a cookie to shut him up. At a later time, the mother may again resolve to stop this pattern, whereupon the boy may raise his voice and continue nagging, perhaps breaking down the mother's resolve. In such a situation, the mother's natural, unprogrammed response is to differentially reinforce first sweet requests, then persistent requests, then loud and obnoxious requests—each being a successive approximation to some unintended target behavior that might best be described as "brat" behavior.

Summary

Tactic #4 in using the reinforcement strategy to solve human problems is to create new behavior through shaping. Shaping involves picking a target behavior, then successive approximations to the target behavior. It involves differential reinforcement of those approximations. Researchers have used shaping to help people with many kinds of problems. They helped a normal teenager speak loud enough that others could hear her. They helped a youngster use crutches. They helped many individuals with retardation improve their language skills. Our normal environment may naturally shape many of our skills with no intentional direction. People may unintentionally shape obnoxious behavior. Overall, shaping offers the magic of creating new behavior.

Belief in the magic of shaping has made many behavior analysts into radical egalitarians who believe that any skill can be taught through shaping. Shaping specific skills requires sound behavioral definitions of the successive approximations. It also requires discovery of effective reinforcers. We may find some day that everyone has vastly greater potential than we now assume. Perhaps no one need be inferior.

Behavior Analysis Examples

Proper Use of Asthma Therapy Equipment

Renne and Creer (1976) investigated the possibility of using behavior analysis methods to help young asthma sufferers learn how to use inhalation therapy equipment properly. When properly used, the equipment gave the children immediate relief from asthma symptoms. If the children did not use the equipment properly, they frequently required additional medication that relieved their symptoms more slowly, or sometimes they even required hospitalization. Although simple instructions from a nurse usually sufficed to teach the children to use the equipment properly, a small percentage did not learn in this way. This description will focus on one of the children helped by Renne and Creer, whom we shall call David.

Renne and Creer identified three behaviors that were involved in successful use of the equipment: (1) eye fixation, which consisted of looking at the pressure gauge indicating air pressure; (2) facial posture, which consisted of holding the mouthpiece at the right angle and keeping the lips motionless and secured to the mouthpiece; and (3) deep breathing, which consisted of extending the stomach when inhaling and contracting when exhaling.

Prior to teaching David proper eye fixation, Renne and Creer observed him during three baseline trials, each consisting of 15 breaths. They counted the number of breaths during which he looked at the air pressure dial for the full duration of each breath. They found that he looked at the dial during 4, 4, and 3 breaths for these baseline trials. They then explained to him that he could earn tickets that could be applied toward a surprise gift. To earn the first ticket, he had to look at the dial without interruption for the duration of at least 4 breaths—his best baseline score. They then followed the rule that if he surpassed the criterion, they would increase it to his new best score. As you can see from Figure 11-3, he surpassed his best baseline score of 4 by looking at the dial for all 15 breaths. Except for the very next trial, he looked at the dial for all 15 breaths on every subsequent trial.

By the end of the sixth trial, it was clear that eye fixation had been taught. Renne and Creer turned their attention to teaching David correct facial posture. Prior to trial 7, they told him that to earn a ticket, he now had to do two things. First, he had to maintain his eye fixation performance, and second, he had to at least match his best baseline performance of the correct facial posture. That was easy, since his best baseline performance was maintaining the correct posture for only one breath out of 15. He maintained it for 13 out of 15 breaths on the next trial, so they changed the criterion to maintaining correct facial posture for 13 out of 15 breaths. As you can see, he improved in several trials to the point where he was maintaining the correct facial posture and eye fixation for virtually every breath.

At the end of the 12th trial, Renne and Creer told David he could now earn tickets by maintaining his performance on eye fixation and facial posture and by matching his best baseline performance for deep breathing. The figure shows that it was somewhat harder to develop correct deep breathing responses, but there was a notable improvement to an average of about 13 out of 15 correct breaths.

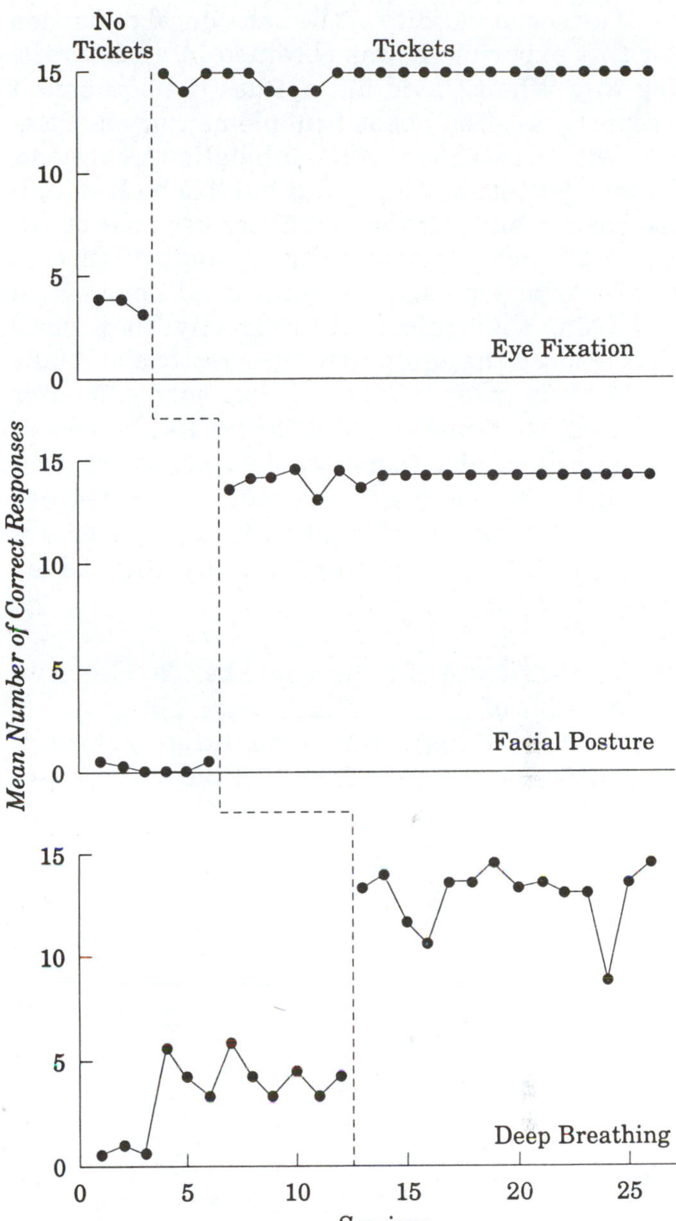

Figure 11-3. Training asthmatic children in the correct use of inhalation therapy equipment. (Note: This figure is based on the average of David and three other children.) Adapted from "Training Children With Asthma to Use Inhalation Therapy Equipment," by C. M. Renne and T. L. Creer, *Journal of Applied Behavior Analysis,* 1976, *9,* 1–11. Copyright 1976 by the Society for the Experimental Analysis of Behavior, Inc. Used by permission.

The social validity of the behavioral definition for this experiment was obtained in an interesting way. When David did not use the equipment properly, he often needed supplementary medication within two hours of the inhalation treatment. In fact, sometimes he would have to be hospitalized as a result. Renne and Creer used the occurrence of such a situation as an indication that under normal, nonexperimental conditions, David was using the equipment incorrectly. They found that he used the equipment incorrectly about 60% of the time prior to training, but only 20% after training. This suggests that the trained behaviors were those needed to use the equipment properly. The behavior analysts first required proper eye fixation to earn a prize. Then they required eye fixation and facial posture. Finally, they added deep breathing.

8. This sequence of goals would be considered an example of ______________________ (successive approximations, target behavior) with respect to correct use of the equipment.

Reducing Cigarette Smoking

Hartmann and Hall (1976) developed a behavioral procedure to help a heavy smoker, whom we shall call Paul, reduce his rate of smoking. The first step was to determine Paul's initial rate of smoking, which averaged 46 cigarettes per day. They then imposed a monetary contingency that paid Paul 10¢ for smoking one less, 20¢ for two less, 30¢ for three less, and so on. In addition, a fine was imposed for smoking more than 46 cigarettes per day. After Paul's rate had held steady at 46 or fewer cigarettes per day, Hartmann and Hall changed the criterion to 43 cigarettes per day and used the same payment schedule. They continued to reduce the criterion through a series of 21 steps, until the rate was under 15 per day. Figure 11-4 shows the gradual decrease in smoking through the first six criteria. Paul's smoking decreased from 46 cigarettes smoked per day to less than 15 per day. The entire course of treatment extended over a period of one year.

9. The procedure of reinforcing successive ap-

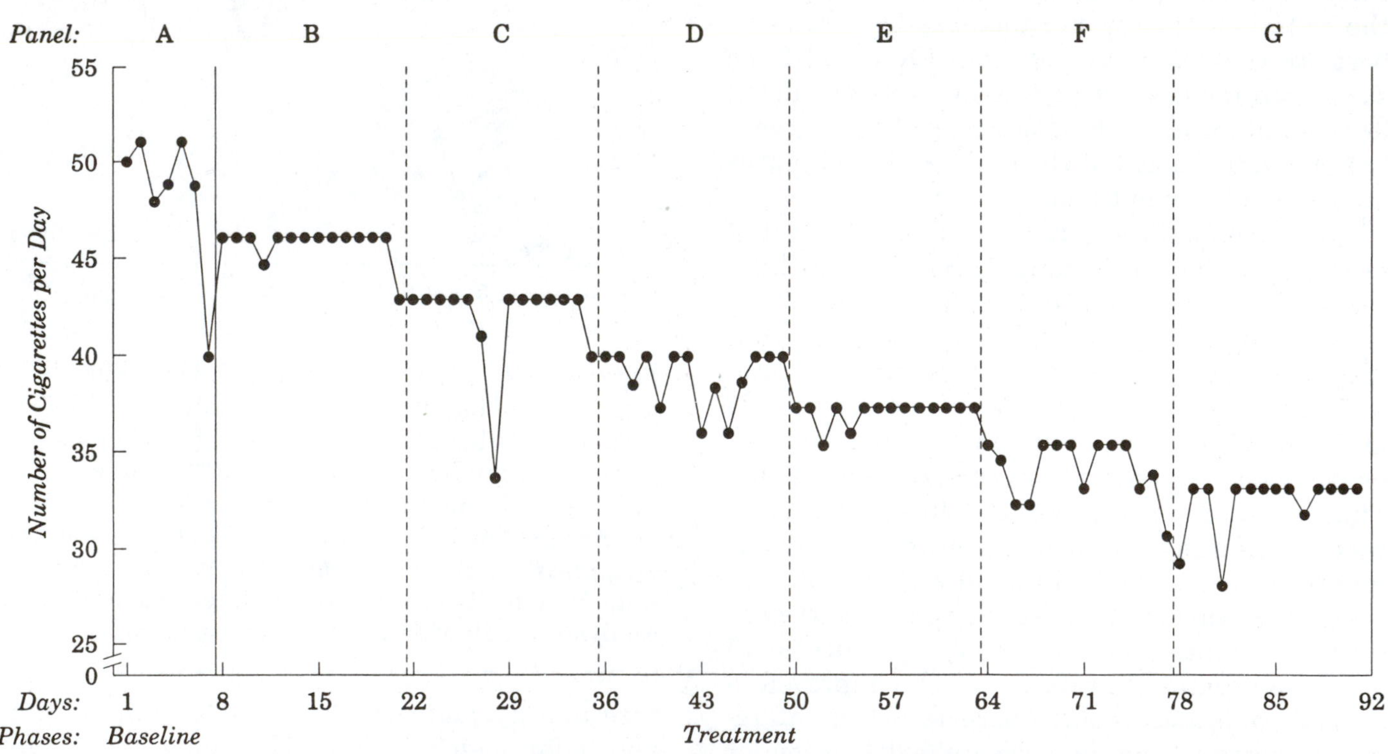

Figure 11-4. The number of cigarettes smoked per day during a shaping program designed to reduce smoking. From "The Changing Criterion Design," by D. P. Hartmann and R. V. Hall, *Journal of Applied Behavior Analysis,* 1976, *9,* 527–532. Copyright 1976 by the Society for the Experimental Analysis of Behavior, Inc. Used by permission.

proximations to smoking under 15 cigarettes per day is called ____________________ (differential reinforcement, shaping).

Notes

Note #1

Martin and Pear (1988) suggest several guidelines for effective application of shaping. First, select a target behavior that is as specific as possible and that will be maintained by naturally occurring reinforcers after it has been shaped. Second, select an appropriate reinforcer that is readily available, that can be delivered immediately after the behavior, that can be consumed quickly, and that the person won't tire of rapidly. Third, select an initial behavior that occurs at least once during the observation period and that resembles the target behavior as closely as possible. Fourth, if possible, explain to the person the goals of shaping, move from one approximation to the next after it has been performed correctly six out of 10 times, and, if the person has difficulty with a step, reassess your program—because if the program is properly designed, you can produce the new behavior.

10. Among the suggested guidelines for shaping are the following. 1. Select as your ultimate goal a target behavior that is as specific as possible. 2. Select an event that can be delivered immediately after the behavior as your ____________________.

Note #2

Shaping complex behaviors with many components is sometimes also referred to as *chaining* (see Lesson 20). For example, teaching a child to walk with crutches involves a number of components that are joined together into a smoothly functioning unit. This book will not refer to such a procedure as *chaining* but rather will conform to general usage and call it *shaping*.

11. Teaching a child to walk with crutches involves a number of components that are joined together into a smoothly functioning unit. This book will not refer to such a procedure as *chaining* but rather will conform to general usage and call it ____________________.

Helpful Hints

Helpful Hint #1

When I give examples of shaping, I will often not explicitly state the extinction part of differential reinforcement. However, if the example states that a person is reinforced <u>only</u> when he or she makes a particular response, you should assume that the person is put on extinction for all other responses. Therefore, the procedure is differential reinforcement. I will use this wording often, because it saves many words. If you fail to realize that when someone only reinforces one behavior, he or she also extinguishes all other behavior, you will often get the wrong answer.

12. If the teacher reinforces <u>only</u> when the student emits a particular behavior, you can assume that the teacher is using what procedure to increase that behavior and decrease all other behaviors? ____________________

If an example states that Tomas is reinforced when he makes a particular response, you should not assume that all other responses are extinguished. You should make that assumption if the example states that the person is reinforced <u>only</u> for that response. You should not make that assumption otherwise.

13. If a teacher reinforces a person when he or she makes a particular response, the teacher is using what procedure? ____________________

Helpful Hint #2

Many students incorrectly shorten the answer "target behavior" to "target" by itself. When a question asks you to name the ultimate goal of a shaping procedure, you should answer "target behavior," not "target." Only "target behavior" will be considered a correct response.

14. When a question asks you to name the ultimate goal of a shaping procedure, you should give the full answer of ____________________.

Helpful Hint #3

You may shorten the answer "successive approximation" to simply "approximation."

15. Remember, you can shorten "successive approximation" to ____________________.

Helpful Hint #4

When answering a question asking you to name a procedure described in an example, you may be tempted to answer "successive approximation" when several steps are involved. Do not do so! Successive approximation is an element in the procedure of shaping; it is not itself a procedure. For instance, a teacher may set correctly counting to 100 as the target behavior. The teacher may set successive approximations of counting to 10, then to 20, and so on until the student can count to 100. If I ask you to name the procedure, do not respond, "successive approximation." The best rule is this: Successive approximation is not a procedure. The teacher uses the procedure of shaping to reach the target behavior of counting to 100.

16. Remember that successive approximation is not a procedure. It is merely an element in the procedure called _______________.

Helpful Hint #5

Identifying the procedure involved in an example is often quite complex. First, you have to decide whether it is a procedure discussed in a prior lesson. Second, you must consider whether it is only similar to a procedure from a prior lesson but is actually an unknown procedure. Third, you have to decide whether it is the new procedure from this lesson. Fourth, you must consider whether it is only similar to the new procedure but is actually an unknown procedure. At first, you will have to consider each of these possibilities rather carefully. That will take time at first, but very soon you will be able to do it almost automatically.

17. Remember, when analyzing what procedure is involved in an example, do not jump to conclusions and name an old procedure before you have read the whole example. Be sure to consider that a better or fuller answer might be the _______ (new, old) procedure.

For example, suppose the example has Dad teaching his daughter to count to 100. Dad may give her pennies for correctly counting to 10, but not if she uses an incorrect number or fails to reach 10. When she can count to 10, Dad may require that she count to 20, then to 30, and so forth. You should consider past and new procedures. First, it involves reinforcement with pennies. But you can rule this out because it also involves extinction by not giving pennies for incorrect numbers. It might be differential reinforcement, because it involves both reinforcement and extinction. But the requirement changes from 10 to 20 and so forth. Finally, you must consider whether the example contains all the elements of shaping. If so, you can feel confident that it is shaping.

Additional Readings

Baer, D. M., Peterson, R. F., & Sherman, J. A. (1967). The development of imitation by reinforcing behavioral similarity to a model. *Journal of the Experimental Analysis of Behavior*, *10*, 405–416. This classic article demonstrates the use of shaping for training children with severe retardation to imitate progressively more complex behaviors demonstrated by others. Such imitation makes it possible for the children to learn new skills by observing the people around them.

Hingtgen, J. N., Sanders, B. J., & DeMeyer, M. K. (1965). Shaping cooperative responses in childhood schizophrenics. In L. Ullman & L. Krasner (Eds.), *Case studies in behavior modification* (pp. 130–183). New York: Holt, Rinehart & Winston. Six subjects diagnosed as early childhood schizophrenics were taught to engage in cooperative responses through shaping. At first, either of two children was permitted to push a button for coins whenever he wanted, then only when the signal light was on, then only when one member of the pair turned on the signal light for the other. This procedure resulted in a simple cooperative response between the two children.

Isaacs, W., Thomas, J., & Goldiamond, I. (1960). Application of operant conditioning to reinstate verbal behavior in psychotics. *Journal of Speech and Hearing Disorders*, *25*, 8–12. This article illustrates the use of shaping procedures to get mute mental patients to begin talking. The patients were reinforced with a stick of gum—first when they moved their lips, then only when they made a noise, and finally only when they imitated a word. As a result, the patients quickly learned to engage in conversation.

Skinner, B. F. (1948b). *Walden two*. New York: Macmillan. This is a utopian novel based on the principles of behavior modification. It presents how man can control his own behavior and develop a more perfect community. The use of shaping to develop new behavioral skills plays a prominent part in the novel.

Wolf, M. M., Risley, T. R., & Mees, H. L. (1964). Application of operant conditioning procedures to the behavior problems of an autistic child. *Behavior Research and Therapy*, *1*, 305–312. This paper reports the use of shaping to teach a child with severe autism to wear corrective glasses, thereby permitting him to see. The problem was that the child would not wear the glasses, would not permit anyone to touch him, and would throw the glasses down if handed them. Shaping this response proceeded from picking the glasses up, holding them, carrying them about, and bringing them toward his eyes. Food was used as the reinforcer.

Reading Quiz

24. In prior lessons, you learned that the procedure of reinforcement is used to ___________ (increase, decrease) desired behavior.
71. You also learned that when you stop reinforcing an undesirable behavior the behavior decreases. The procedure is called ___________.
62. The procedures of reinforcement and extinction can only work on ___________ (new, old) behavior.
4. Behavior analysts use shaping to create ___________ (new, old) behavior.
57. Tactic #4 in using the reinforcement strategy to solve human problems is to create new behavior through ___________.
23. In order to teach Danny the new behavior of sleeping in the dark, it was necessary to use the procedure of ___________.
27. Letting Danny gradually dim the light more and more is an example of the use of successive ___________ to the target behavior of sleeping in the dark.
72. You differentially reinforce some starting behavior that is remotely related to the behavior you want to end up with. You extinguish all other behavior. When the initial behavior is well established, you pick a second behavior that is a little more closely related to the end behavior. You differentially reinforce it while extinguishing all other behavior. This whole process of gradually increasing the rate of behaviors that more and more closely approximate the goal is the procedure called ___________.
15. From the last lesson, you learned that reinforcing an infant for making a desired sound and ignoring all other sounds is an example of ___________.
70. When you differentially reinforce successive approximations to some new behavior, you do not have to tell the other person anything. You simply give a bite of food when he or she more or less randomly emits the next approximation. The person you are helping does not need to understand language. Therefore, when you want to teach new behaviors to people with little or no language (such as babies, infants, and individuals with retardation), the ideal procedure is ___________.
66. The term *shaping* should be used only when both a target behavior has been specified and differential reinforcement has been applied to a series of successive ___________.
67. Use the term *shaping* only when you have differentially reinforced a series of successive approximations and when you have specified a target ___________.
65. Shaping has two elements. First, there must be an ultimate goal called the *target* ___________. Second, differential reinforcement must be applied to a series of intermediate goals called *successive* ___________ to that target behavior.
73. You may shorten "successive approximation" by omitting "successive." The second element of shaping is the differential reinforcement of a series of (omit "successive") ___________ to the target behavior.
41. Review: Shaping has two elements. First, the teacher must specify the ultimate goal, which is called the ___________. Second, the teacher must differentially reinforce a series of intermediate goals called ___________ ___________ to that target behavior.
46. Review: The first element of shaping is the specification of some new behavior that is the ultimate goal of the shaping program. This new behavior is called the ___________ ___________.

64. The term *shaping* can sometimes be applied even if no "teacher" has deliberately established a target behavior. Someone may be unintentionally acting as a teacher. Without planning to do so, or even knowing that they are doing so, that person may be differentially reinforcing successive approximations that will lead to an ultimate behavior. You might call the ultimate behavior an unintentional target ______________.

7. Can the term *shaping* ever be applied to situations in which no target behavior has been intentionally defined in advance? __________ (yes, no)

47. Review: The second element of shaping is that the teacher must differentially reinforce each of a series of behaviors that are progressively more similar to the target behavior. Each behavior in this series is called a(n) __________ ______________.

54. Shaping involves applying what procedure to a behavior that approximates the target behavior? ______________________

55. Shaping proceeds in a series of steps. First, you apply differential reinforcement to a first approximation to the target behavior. Once the rate of that approximation has increased, you then take a second step. You apply differential reinforcement to a second, closer approximation to the ______________________. (Use both words of the whole term.)

22. If you wanted to teach a man to shoot a bow and arrow accurately from a distance of 30 feet, you might differentially reinforce him for shooting accurately from 5 feet, on the theory that shooting from 5 feet is a first __________ ______________ to the target behavior of shooting from 30 feet.

36. Review: Jackson and Wallace (1974) differentially reinforced first soft whispers, then louder and louder whispers, in order to teach a girl with retardation to talk loudly enough to be heard. What is the name of the procedure in which they differentially reinforced successively louder talking until she "talked loudly enough"? ______________________

37. Review: Jackson and Wallace (1974) used shaping to help a 15-year-old girl learn to talk loudly enough to be heard by others. Talking loudly enough to be heard by others would be called a(n) ______________________. (Use both words.)

50. Review: Jackson and Wallace selected barely audible whispering to start with. Such whispering would be called their first __________ to talking loudly enough.

25. Jackson and Wallace (1974) selected barely audible whispering as their first approximation to talking loudly. What behavioral procedure did they use when they reinforced barely audible whispers and extinguished inaudible whispers? ______________________

69. When Mathews and his associates (1992) selected the children's accepting the insertion of contact lenses as the ultimate goal of their shaping program, they were specifying what is known as their ______________ behavior.

5. By differentially reinforcing a series of successive approximations to walking with crutches, Horner (1971) was using what behavioral procedure? ______________________

17. Horner (1971) developed a procedure to teach Dennis how to walk with crutches. The ultimate goal of having Dennis walking with crutches would be called Horner's __________ ______________.

18. Horner first differentially reinforced placing the tips of the crutches on two circles on the floor while they were attached to Dennis's hands. This would be called the first __________ ______________ to walking with crutches.

3. Behavior analysts have taught persons with retardation the correct use of plurals and adjectives, as well as appropriate question asking and other language skills, by use of the procedure called ______________.

61. The procedure of differentially reinforcing approximations to novel behavior in order to teach spontaneity to a dolphin would be termed ____________.

28. Many procedures that do not involve the differential reinforcement of approximations to a target behavior produce a gradual change in people's behavior. Therefore, if you are asked to name a procedure that produces a gradual change in a person's behavior, you ______ (can, can't) assume that it is shaping.

59. The everyday world often produces approximations to some target behavior that no individual consciously planned. The differential reinforcement of approximations to such an unintentional target behavior would still be called ______________________.

2. Beating on a failing TV, acquiring complex

computer skills, and becoming a marathon runner may be unintentional target behaviors that ______________ (can, can't) be acquired through natural shaping.

60. The Kaufmans helped their young son overcome autism by approaching his treatment as a series of painstakingly tiny steps of development. These tiny steps would be called ____________________________.
1. An example of shaping might consist of the parent developing a child's unintended target behavior of loudly and obnoxiously demanding a snack by differentially reinforcing a series of ______________________________ to that behavior.
6. By picking a target behavior and reinforcing successive approximations to the target behavior, shaping can create _______ behavior.
44. Review: Tactic #4 in using the reinforcement strategy to solve human problems is to create new behavior through ______________________ ______________.
56. Students often confuse differential reinforcement with shaping. Shaping involves a series of steps during which differential reinforcement is used to increase an approximation. If an example does not involve a series of approximations, then it ______ (can, can't) be shaping.
19. If someone reinforces one approximation and extinguishes all other behavior, then the procedure used is not shaping. Instead it is _____ ________________________.
20. If someone reinforces one approximation and extinguishes all other behavior, and then repeats the process with a new approximation, the procedure is _________________________.
21. If someone reinforces one approximation and extinguishes all other behavior, then the procedure used is __________________________.
58. Teachers need good behavioral definitions of successive approximations, and they also need effective reinforcers to use the procedure of ____________________ to create new skills.
29. Renne and Creer (1976) attempted to teach the correct use of inhalation equipment to asthmatic children. They did so by differentially reinforcing approximations to correct use. The correct use of the equipment would be called the ____________________________ in their experiment.
30. Renne and Creer (1976) identified three behaviors that could be taught in steps leading up to the goal of proper use of inhalation equipment. Those three behaviors are called ____________________________ to the target behavior.
31. Renne and Creer at first gave David a ticket good for a prize only if he looked at the dial for at least 4 breaths out of 15. They gave him the ticket only if he looked at the dial, but not if he looked elsewhere. David's rate of looking at the dial increased as a result. This was one step toward the target behavior of correct use of the inhalation equipment. While *shaping* is the name of the overall procedure used on all the steps, what is the name of the procedure that they used on this step? ________ ____________________________
63. The researchers decided to give David a prize only if he looked at the dial 4 or more times out of 15. While their ultimate target behavior is for David to look at the dial for all 15 breaths, this requirement would be called a(n) ______________________________ to that ultimate goal.
26. Later in their program, they required David to breathe deeply at least 7 of 15 times (and also to look at the dial and maintain the correct facial posture). This would be a more advanced ___________________________ to using the equipment properly.
68. When David did not use the inhalation therapy equipment correctly, he often required medication or even hospitalization. You might say that the doctors judged whether David had used the equipment properly. The agreement between the researchers' behavioral definition of correct use and the doctors' decision to medicate or hospitalize confirms the ________ ________________ (reliability, social validity) of the behavioral definition of correct use of the equipment.
16. Hartmann and Hall (1976) developed a procedure to help Paul reduce his rate of smoking from 46 cigarettes per day during baseline to 15 after treatment. In this example, 15 cigarettes per day is called the _______________ ______________.
8. For the first step, Hartmann and Hall (1976) paid Paul only when he smoked less than 46 cigarettes a day. For the second step they paid him only when he smoked less than 43 per day. They continued with many additional

steps until they reached the last step of paying him only when he smoked less than 15 per day. The researchers used what overall procedure to get from the first to the last step?

____

9. From Helpful Hint #1: If the teacher reinforces only a particular behavior, you should assume that the teacher is using what procedure for all the other behaviors of that person? ______________
10. From Helpful Hint #1: Suppose the teacher reinforces only a particular behavior. Since you can assume that the teacher extinguishes all other behaviors, what procedure is the teacher using to increase the relative rate of the desired behavior? ______________
11. From Helpful Hint #2: When a question asks you to name the ultimate goal of a shaping procedure, you should give the full answer of ______________.
12. From Helpful Hint #3: You may shorten the answer "successive approximation" to simply ______________.
13. From Helpful Hint #4: A teacher may establish correctly counting to 100 as the target behavior. The teacher may then establish successive approximations of counting to 10, then to 20, and so forth until the student can count to 100. If asked what procedure the teacher used, be sure not to answer "successive approximations." Remember that successive approximations is not a procedure. It is merely an element in the procedure called ______________.
14. From Helpful Hint #5: Remember that successive approximations is not a procedure. It is merely an element in the procedure called ______________.
40. Review: Shaping has two elements. First, the teacher must specify the ultimate goal, which is called the ______________. Second, the teacher must differentially reinforce a series of intermediate goals, called ______________ to that target behavior.
49. Review: The term *shaping* is used to denote the repeated use with approximations of what behavioral procedure that you have already studied? ______________
34. Review: By giving tickets to David only when he met a behavioral criterion related to using the inhalation equipment properly, and then changing that criterion in successive steps until completely correct use was developed, Renne and Creer were using what behavioral procedure? ______________
53. Review: When one behavior is reinforced and all others are extinguished, then another behavior that more closely approximates the target behavior is reinforced while others are extinguished, the overall process is called ______________.
42. Review: Tactic #4 in using the reinforcement strategy to solve human problems is to create new behavior through ______________.
33. Review: An approximation is a behavior that is similar to the ______________ of a shaping procedure.
39. Review: Renne and Creer (1976) defined a goal of correct use of inhalation equipment by asthmatic children. That goal would be called the ______________ of their experiment.
32. Review: A behavior that is similar to a target behavior is called a(n) ______________.
48. Review: The shaping process begins with the selection of an ultimate goal, which is called a(n) ______________.
51. Review: To use the reinforcement strategy to solve human problems is to (1) increase desirable behavior through reinforcement; (2) decrease undesirable behavior through extinction; (3) increase a desirable behavior relative to undesirable behavior through ______________; and (4) create new behavior through ______________.
45. Review: The differential reinforcement of successive approximations to a target behavior is called ______________.
38. Review: Looking at the dial 4 out of 15 breaths is called a(n) ______________ to looking at it for all 15 breaths (Renne & Carr, 1976).
52. Review: Two conditions must be met for a situation to involve shaping: (1) The teacher must specify the ______________; (2) the teacher must differentially reinforce a series of ______________.
43. Review: Tactic #4 in using the reinforcement strategy to solve human problems is to create new behavior through ______________.
35. Review: If the teacher reinforces only when the student emits a particular behavior, you can assume that the teacher is using what procedure to increase that behavior and decrease all other behaviors? ______________

Examples

(Note: Many students have difficulty telling shaping from differential reinforcement. I will give examples of shaping. I will give examples of shaping with questions about differential reinforcement. I will give examples of differential reinforcement alone. Look for the differences between shaping and differential reinforcement in the following examples.)

1. Dean taught his son Jason how to play badminton. Jason learned the rules quickly and developed a good stroke, but he kept hitting the shuttlecock right to Dean. To change this, Dean started praising Jason anytime that he hit the shuttlecock at least one step away from him. The intermediate goal of hitting it at least one step away from Dean is called the first ____________ to the target behavior. By praising Jason only when he hit the shuttlecock one step away (but not praising him when he didn't), Dean was using what procedure? ______________________. When Jason was hitting the shuttlecock one step away, Dean started praising Jason only when he hit it two steps away from him. Pretty soon Jason was hitting his shots away from Dean as often as possible. The ultimate goal of hitting the shuttlecock as far away as possible is called the ____________________________. Dean's total procedure is called ________________.

2. Charlie Brown wanted the little redheaded girl to sit by him. He decided to stop being wishy-washy and to try to get her to sit near him at lunch. At first, each time she looked in his direction, he smiled at her. After a while, he smiled only when she sat within five feet of him. Then he smiled only when she sat within two feet of him. Finally, the little redheaded girl sat right next to Charlie Brown at lunch. You should call the intermediate goals of having her look at him, sit within five feet, and sit within two feet ____________ to his ultimate goal. The ultimate goal of having the little redheaded girl sit next to him would be an example of a(n) _______________________. Reinforcing her <u>only</u> when she sat within five feet is called ______________________________. The behavioral procedure used in this example is called ________________________.

3. Mr. Baker had taken on the job of teaching Tone Deaf Tony to sing on key. He decided to start by teaching Tony to hum within half a note of middle C. He first played the note on the piano and asked Tony to hum the same note. Mr. Baker praised him when he came within a half tone of middle C. When Tony missed it, Mr. Baker ignored him and simply played the note over again. Pretty soon Tony could sing within a half tone of middle C. Mr. Baker used what behavioral procedure? ____________________________

4. Ralph was helping his brother Bob learn to hit a fastball. He started by throwing not-so-fast pitches. Each time Bob got a hit, Ralph gave him a swig of beer. After many hits, Ralph threw medium-fast pitches and continued to give Bob a swig after each hit. Finally, Ralph threw fast pitches and still gave Bob a swig of beer after every hit. Bob learned to hit a fastball pretty well in the process. But further practice had to be put off, because after 147 hits Bob couldn't stand up anymore. Hitting a fastball in this example would be called the __________________. Giving Bob a swig of beer after he got a hit increased the rate of good swings and decreased the rate of poor swings. Therefore, Ralph was using what behavioral procedure? __________________________. Hitting medium-fast pitches is a(n) ____________ to hitting fast pitches. What procedure did Ralph use to teach his brother to hit a fast pitch? __________________________

5. Janice's parents wanted her to be more assertive, so they talked with her about it and found that she too wished to be more assertive. They decided to teach her through role playing to be able to say "No thank you" firmly if a boy asked her to go to a movie she wasn't interested in. Initially they praised her if she simply said "No thank you," even if they could barely hear it. They did not reinforce her if she said nothing or shook her head. Later, they praised her only if she said "No thank you" firmly. Being able to say "No thank you" firmly would be called the ________________ ________________. Simply saying "No thank you," even if they could barely hear it, would be called a(n) _________________________________ to saying it firmly. What procedure did Janice's parents use by praising her only when she first whispered "No thank you" and later firmly said "No thank you"? _________________________

6. Tad wanted to take up jogging. He decided to build up slowly to running a mile a day in under 6 minutes. He set as his goal during the first week to run the mile under 12 minutes. When he made it he bought himself a Super Sundae. The

next week, he tried to run it under 11 minutes and again rewarded himself when he made it. Each week he lowered his goal until he was running the mile under 6 minutes. Tad's first goal of running the mile in under 12 minutes would be termed a(n) ______________________ to running it in under 6 minutes. What behavioral procedure was Tad using to get in condition to run the mile in under 6 minutes? ______________

7. Jawan decided to teach his best friend to do the new disco step—the Twirling Chicken. He always praised her when she did it correctly and said nothing when she did it incorrectly. She started doing it much better. Jawan's procedure would be an example of ______________________.

8. Sammy's mother told him to take out the garbage every night, and he did so. When he was 12, she stopped telling him to take out the garbage, and he quit doing it. What behavioral procedure did she inadvertently employ to reduce his rate of taking out the garbage? ______________

____

9. Johann complained to Mary about how his teachers treated him. Mary agreed that they treated him unfairly, and she listened with endless patience to his complaints. Johann complained more and more often. What behavioral procedure did Mary use? ______________

10. Kerr went to the New West Freedom Preschool, where he was the brat of the school. He yelled, broke things, pushed into line, spilled paint, and wet his pants. The staff had a meeting and decided that instead of paying attention to him as they had done, they would henceforth ignore Kerr's brat behavior. Unfortunately, he kept doing it. What behavioral procedure did they use? ______________

11. Review: Clarence, a skilled carpenter, remembers how he learned to hammer in a 16-penny nail with one stroke. At first, his father praised him only when he hit the nail with each tiny tap, taking many taps to drive the nail in. His father then praised him only when he drove it in with several rough raps. Finally, his father praised him only when he drove it in with one thunderous thump. What behavioral procedure was his father using? ______________

12. Review: Betty complains of illness much of the time. She didn't use to be so sickly. Her stepmother loves Betty and pays close attention to her health. At the same time, she ignores other things that Betty says. Betty complains of sickness much more since her stepmother arrived. What behavioral procedure has the stepmother used to make Betty a hypochondriac? ______________

13. Review: Five-year-old John was a loner. He never played with the other children; he preferred to play alone in a far corner of the room. Mr. Lima, John's teacher, decided to get John to play with other children. At first, Mr. Lima attended to John only when he looked toward other children. Next, he attended to him only if he moved toward other children. Finally, he attended to John only when he was actually playing with another child. After a few weeks of this special teacher attention, John was playing with other children. Name the procedure Mr. Lima employed in modifying John's play behavior. ______________________.

14. Review: Yancey wanted Fran to smile more often. Every time she smiled, he told her how good she looked. Fran didn't smile any more often, even after a month of compliments. What behavioral procedure was Yancey using? ______________

____

15. Review: Bobby was a pretty good chess player who liked to win. When he played with Dan, he won most of the time; as a result, he started playing with Dan more often. But when he played with Shelly, he lost most of the time, even when he made the same moves. As a result, he almost completely stopped playing with Shelly. What behavioral procedure accounts for Bobby playing more with Dan and less with Shelly? (Remember to check the elements.) ______________

____

16. Review: Marie helped Fred learn to not get angry over a minor annoyance. She taught him to count to 10 if an annoying event occurred. She continued to praise him whenever he counted to 10 during annoyances until he was doing it all the time. Next she would praise him only when he counted to 20, which he soon mastered. In this way she finally got him to count to 100, at which time he was no longer angry. What is the goal of getting Fred to count to 100 called? ______________

____

17. Review: Jean wanted Sam to help more often so she wouldn't have to do all the work. Every time he helped, she made sure to get him a cold beer immediately. As a result, he started helping more often. What procedure did she use?

____

18. Review: Mary wanted to teach John how to do really good, fast dancing. She decided to start

by teaching him some very slow steps. Slow dancing would be a(n) ________________ to fast dancing.

19. Review: Frank was a pretty inattentive boyfriend. Finally Marsha told him to start opening doors for her. From then on, he always opened the door for Marsha. What behavioral procedure did Marsha employ? ________________

20. Review: At first Dave swam the 100 meters in about 75 seconds. His coach praised him only when he swam it in under 75 seconds. Then his coach praised him only when he swam it in under 70 seconds. Using this same approach, the coach eventually got Dave swimming the 100 in under 50 seconds. What behavioral procedure did the coach use? ________________

LESSON

12 Reinforcer Effectiveness

Reinforcers are events that cause an increase in the rate of a behavior that they follow. You already know that an event that is a reinforcer for one person may not be a reinforcer for another. You will learn in this lesson that the same event may be a reinforcer when it is delivered in one way but not in another. Behavior analysts have learned quite a lot about how to make reinforcers effective. I will consider an event effective when it increases the rate of the behavior.

There are four main factors that cause events to be more or less effective. You must deliver an event contingent on the behavior; that means delivering it only when the desired behavior occurs. You must deliver it immediately after the behavior has occurred. You must ensure that the size (or amount) of the event is worthwhile. Finally, you must ensure that the person is deprived of the event. That means you use a reinforcer that the person hasn't had too much of.

Tactic #5 in using the reinforcement strategy to solve human problems is to use the principles of reinforcer effectiveness.

1. Tactic #5 in using the reinforcement strategy to solve human problems is to use the principles of ________________ effectiveness.

The Effect of Contingency on Effectiveness

The first factor in effectiveness is contingency. The **principle of contingency** states that you must deliver the event only when a desired behavior occurs. You must never deliver it for an undesired behavior. Consider why this is so. If you repeatedly deliver the event for some undesired behavior, the rate of that behavior will increase. That will decrease the time available for the desired behavior. In fact, it may totally crowd out the desired behavior. If you deliver events sloppily, you may reinforce undesired behaviors. Stealing an object is a classic example of an undesired behavior; if you permit a person to steal something, why would he or she work for it?

2. The **principle of contingency** states that you must deliver the event ____________ when a desired behavior occurs.

Notice that the principle of contingency does not state that you are restricted to delivering the reinforcer for only one desired behavior. Most of the time, a reinforcer will be delivered for only one desired behavior at a time, but you can deliver the reinforcer for several desired behaviors. You cannot, however, deliver it for even one undesired behavior. To do so would undermine the effect of the reinforcer on the desired behaviors. You will see examples where the reinforcer is delivered for several desired behaviors.

You will still be observing the principle of contingency if you deliver the reinforcer for more than one desired behavior. You could give your brother chocolate-covered raisins for vacuuming your room, for playing nicely with his toys, and for just being a sweet kid. You just have to ensure that he can't get them without doing the behaviors that you desire. You must ensure that he can't steal them, lie about his behaviors, or otherwise trick you into giving him the candy.

Consider an everyday example. Suppose you ask Sam, your little brother, to vacuum your room while you are at a dance. You might come home, glance at the room, and conclude that he has vacuumed it. You might give him a box of chocolate-covered raisins, his favorite candy, as thanks. But perhaps your quick glance didn't evaluate his job very well—Sam might have picked up your room without vacuuming it. Clearly, your gift would teach him the wrong lesson: He would learn that you are satisfied with a partial job. Your gift certainly would not be very effective in increasing his rate of vacuuming. Thus, the principle of contingency warns you to take care that you deliver the event only when the desired behavior occurs. You must be sure not to deliver it for undesirable responses like stealing, lying, or doing only part of the job.

Behavior analysts are careful to deliver reinforcers only when desired behavior occurs (e.g., Bourgeois, 1990). They know that if they deliver reinforcers whether or not the behavior occurs, the behavior decreases.

Behavior analysts can sometimes use the principle of contingency to understand behavioral problems. One team of researchers examined the case of Brenda (Vollmer et al., 1993). Brenda was a 42-year-old woman with profound retardation, who often deliberately banged her head very hard.

Figure 12-1. This man may have tried to steal money rather than working hard for it. Reinforcers like money will be effective only to the extent that their delivery is contingent on desired behaviors like work.

The researchers found that aides paid no attention to her except when she banged her head. Anytime she banged her head, the aides told her she would hurt herself. Without realizing it, the aides were attending to Brenda only when she banged her head. This attention was an effective reinforcer because it was contingent on Brenda banging her head.

The researchers were able to use the principle of contingency in reverse to solve the problem. They instructed each aide to give Brenda attention as often as possible. They continued to express their concern about hurting herself when she banged her head, but they often attended to her when she wasn't banging her head. Her rate of head-banging decreased from once every second to almost not at all! This shows how much noncontingent reinforcement can weaken the effect of a reinforcer. The behavior increased when attention was contingent on head-banging, even though the attention was in response to negative behavior. It decreased when it was not contingent on head-banging. These researchers sought to decrease head-banging, but you might want to *increase* a desired behavior. If so, you will be more successful if you are contingent with your reinforcement.

To decide whether the principle of contingency was followed in a specific case, ask, "Was the event given only for a desired behavior?"

3. To decide whether the principle of contingency was followed in a specific case, ask, "Was the event given ________________ for a desired behavior?"

The Effect of Immediacy on Effectiveness

The second factor in effectiveness is immediacy. Immediacy is a very powerful determinant of an event's effectiveness. The **principle of immediacy** states that you must deliver an event immediately after a desired behavior. The faster you deliver it, the stronger the effect. Remember that you wanted to shape Ann into saying "Dada." Your praise would be most effective if you gave it the instant she first said "da." In fact, you would be most successful with each successive approximation if you reinforced it immediately.

4. The **principle of immediacy** states that you must deliver an event ______________ after a desired behavior.

Consider an everyday example. You want to get Sam to vacuum your room. Suppose (miracle of miracles) he does vacuum your room. You should reinforce him immediately to have the greatest effect. Give Sam his chocolate-covered raisins just as he is finishing the job. If you wait until you get home from the dance, or maybe even until tomorrow, the gift will have less effect. In general, the event should be delivered as soon after the behavior as possible. Delivering it within seconds is the most effective timing. (I will describe two exceptions to this principle in a moment.)

Behavior analysts are usually very careful to give reinforcers immediately. For example, one researcher sought to help Alzheimer's patients to engage in meaningful conversations (Bourgeois, 1990). You may remember that she gave them a picture book to help them remember important topics. She taught husbands to praise their wives immediately when they talked about the pictures. The number of on-topic statements for one patient increased from a few per day to about 45. Immediacy is a powerful factor in reinforcer effectiveness.

Behavior analysts have found two exceptions to the principle of immediacy. The first exception is that a delayed reinforcer can be effective if you immediately signal the later reinforcement. This is not a true exception, because the signal itself becomes a reinforcer. I will describe this procedure in a later lesson. The second exception is that a delayed reinforcer can be effective if the person can describe the relation between behavior and delayed reinforcer. For example, an employer gives you your paycheck many days and even weeks after you put in your work. Yet you continue to work, even with this delay. Clearly, you can describe the relation between work and pay. If I asked you, you would say, "No work, no pay!" For the rest of the book, do not assume that the people in an example can describe a relation unless the example clearly states that they can. If the example does not state this, then assume that the principle of immediacy holds true.

To decide whether the principle of immediacy was followed, ask, "Was the event delivered within a <u>minute</u> of the behavior (or while the behavior was still occurring)?" This rule will hold true unless the recipient can describe the relation between their behavior and a delayed reinforcer.

5. To decide whether the principle of immediacy was followed, ask, "Was the event delivered within a ______________ of the behavior (or while the behavior was still occurring)?"

The Effect of Size on Effectiveness

The third factor in effectiveness is size. The amount of the event is an important determinant of it's effectiveness. The **principle of size** states that you must give a worthwhile <u>amount</u> of the event. The more you deliver at one time, the more effect it will have. Your goal is to deliver just enough of the event to be effective. You don't want to give so much that the person never has to emit the desired behavior again. This optimum amount will vary depending on such factors as the difficulty of the behavior, the amount of behavior required, and competing opportunities for reinforcement.

6. The **principle of size** states that you must give a worthwhile ______________ of the event.

Consider an everyday example. If Sam vacuumed your room, one chocolate-covered raisin probably wouldn't be effective. Maybe even a handful wouldn't be enough, but a small box of the candy might be. To decide just how many raisins might be effective, you need to decide what amount would be worthwhile to Sam. This depends on how hard it is for him to operate the vacuum, how long it takes, and whether Mom just offered him a slice of chocolate cake. In any event, this principle is based on the fact that the more of an event you deliver, the more effective it will be.

Behavior analysts have found that the amount of reinforcement is very important in helping people. For example, one researcher studied chronic smokers (Stitzer & Bigelow, 1984). I will call their average smoker Fred. They found that the more they paid Fred, the more he reduced his smoking. During baseline, Fred smoked about 12 cigarettes a day. When they paid Fred $1.50 for reducing his smoking, he smoked about 10 cigarettes. When they paid him $12, he smoked only about 5 cigarettes. Another researcher tried to help mental patients keep their teeth clean (Fisher,

1979). He found that about 60% of the patients brushed their teeth during baseline. When he gave them one reinforcer for brushing their teeth, the percent increased to 76%. When he gave them five reinforcers, the percent increased to 91%. The amount of reinforcement is clearly an important factor in effectiveness.

To decide whether the principle of size was followed, ask, "Was the amount of the event used worthwhile?"

7. To decide whether the principle of size was followed, ask, "Was the amount of the event used ______________?"

The Effect of Satiation and Deprivation on Effectiveness

The final principle involves the opposing concepts of satiation and deprivation. **Satiation** refers to how recently the person has received the event—the more recently, the more satiation. If you have just had a quart of ice cream, you are more satiated on ice cream than if you had not had it for a month. The opposite of satiation is deprivation. **Deprivation** refers to how long it has been since the person has received the event—the longer it has been, the more deprivation. If you have not had ice cream for a month, you are more deprived of it than if you have had it recently.

8. **Satiation** refers to how ____________ the person has received the event—the more recently, the more satiation. **Deprivation** refers to how ____________ it has been since the person has received the event.

The state of deprivation of the person with respect to a particular event is a powerful determinant of the event's effectiveness. The **principle of deprivation** states that you must use events that the person is deprived of. The more deprived the person is, the more effective the event will be.

9. The **principle of deprivation** states that you must use events that the person is ________ of.

This principle is important in everyday behaviors. For example, suppose Sam has not had any chocolate-covered raisins for a week. The raisins will be more effective than if he just had a box of them half an hour ago. Two researchers found such an effect with young children (Gewirtz & Baer, 1958a). They used praise to reinforce children's performance of a simple task. They deprived some children of attention by not interacting with them before the experiment. Those children responded faster. The researchers concluded that even this short deprivation increased the effectiveness of the praise. In a second study, they satiated some children with attention by interacting with them before the experiment (Gewirtz & Baer, 1958b). Those children responded slower. The researchers concluded that even this small amount of satiation decreased the effectiveness of the praise. You should carefully examine the level of deprivation for any event you hope to use as a reinforcer.

Behavior analysts make careful use of satiation and deprivation. For example, one researcher used satiation to reduce a man's hallucinations (Glaister, 1985). The man was a chronic mental patient who frequently hallucinated voices. The researcher urged the patient to sit quietly and listen to the voices. He instructed the patient to record what the voices said, how long he heard them, and so on. After 16 months, the patient was sick of hearing the voices. He stopped hearing them! The researcher suggested that by listening to the voices, the patient satiated on them.

A team of researchers studied the effects of satiation and deprivation on Rich, a man with severe retardation (Vollmer & Iwata, 1991). Rich liked to listen to music. To create satiation, they played taped music for him while he sat for 30 minutes in a waiting room. To create deprivation, they played no music while he sat for 30 minutes in the waiting room. After the 30 minutes, the researchers asked Rich to do a simple task. Every time he made six responses, they played taped music for four seconds. If he responded fast enough, he got to hear music continuously. He made ten responses per minute when he was deprived, and only about two per minute when he was satiated. Thus, he responded much faster when deprived than when satiated on music. The researchers found similar results for food and social reinforcers.

To decide whether the principle of deprivation was followed, ask, "Has the reinforcer rarely been delivered?"

10. To decide whether the principle of deprivation was followed, ask, "Has the reinforcer _______________ been delivered?"

Comparison of the Four Principles

You might easily confuse the principle of immediacy and the principle of contingency. If you deliver an event immediately after the desired behavior occurs and only after it occurs, you have used both principles. However, you can deliver the event in such a way that you use only one of the principles. For example, suppose you deliver the event within a minute after some behavior, but it is undesirable behavior. You will have used the principle of immediacy but not the principle of contingency. Your reinforcement won't increase the desired behavior. Likewise, suppose you deliver the event for the desired behavior, but long after it occurs. You will have used the principle of contingency but not the principle of immediacy. Your reinforcement probably won't increase the desired behavior.

You might also easily confuse the principle of size and the principle of deprivation. If you deliver a worthwhile amount of the event to someone who hasn't had any recently, you have used both principles. However, you can deliver the event in such a way that you use only one of the principles. For example, suppose you deliver a worthwhile amount to someone who has recently had lots of the event. You have used the principle of size, but not the principle of deprivation, and your reinforcement probably won't work. Likewise, you might rarely deliver the event to someone, but in too small an amount. You will have then used the principle of deprivation, but not the principle of size. Again, your reinforcement probably won't work.

The size principle refers to whether the amount of the reinforcer on any one given delivery is large enough to be worthwhile. The deprivation principle refers to whether the reinforcer has rarely been delivered, so that the person has not had too much of the reinforcer. Thus, the distinction is between the amount of a single delivery and the timing of deliveries.

These four principles can make the difference between success and failure. You can fail if you don't deliver reinforcers contingently and immediately. You can also fail if you use too little reinforcement or give the other person something he or she already has too much of. All four factors are important tools for improving the effectiveness of a reinforcer.

You should take several other factors into account when selecting reinforcers. For example, the reinforcers should be convenient to dispense, inexpensive, and not simultaneously available from another source. In addition, they should not generate behaviors that are incompatible with the behavior that is being reinforced. For example, you shouldn't give gum for saying words clearly.

Summary

Tactic #5 in using the reinforcement strategy to solve human problems is to use the principles of reinforcer effectiveness. Reinforcers can have powerful effects on our behavior. Their effectiveness depends on four factors. The more contingent, immediate, large, and rare the reinforcement is, the more effective it will be. When your use of a reinforcer is not effective, you may find that you failed to apply one or more of the principles of reinforcer effectiveness.

Behavior Analysis Examples

Basic research with animals revealed the importance of these four principles. The complexity of applied situations often obscures their importance. However, I have been able to find the following examples in applied behavior analysis, to give you an idea of their practical value.

Teaching Handwriting

Researchers taught kindergarten children beginning handwriting. They developed a set of materials for the children to use. However, the children made only about 50% correct responses during baseline observation. The investigators decided to give the children tokens good for a variety of fun activities. They first tried giving them tokens at the beginning of the session, regardless of the accuracy of their work. The children's accuracy decreased to around 40% correct. They then gave the tokens to the children only for accurate responses; accuracy increased until it was over 60%. Thus, when tokens were given regardless of accuracy, the accuracy decreased below baseline.

When they were given only for accurate responses, accuracy increased. (Based on Brigham et al., 1972.)

11. Giving tokens only for accurate responses is following the principle of ________________ (contingency, deprivation, immediacy, size).

Wearing Orthodontic Braces

Researchers consulted with the mother of an 8-year-old boy who needed braces to straighten his teeth. Despite the expense of about $3000 with four dentists over a period of eight years, Jerry's teeth were not any better, because he did not remember to wear his braces. Observations during baseline indicated that he was wearing them during only 25% of the five times that he was checked each day.

Hall and his colleagues suggested that the mother give Jerry 25¢ for each time he was wearing them during those five checks. A record was kept of the money owed, which was to be paid at the end of the month. This procedure increased Jerry's rate of wearing the braces to about 60%. The rate increased to nearly 100% when Jerry was given the money immediately after any check during which he was wearing them. Thus, you can see that when money was given at the end of the month, the rate was better than baseline—but not nearly as good as when the money was given as soon as the desired behavior was observed. Eight months after the study was initiated, the dentist indicated that there had been great progress in Jerry's mouth structure. (Based on Hall et al., 1972.)

12. Immediate reinforcement for wearing braces is an example of the principle of ____________ (contingency, deprivation, immediacy, size).

Towel Hoarding

A patient whom we shall call Doris had been a resident in a mental hospital for nine years. One of her behaviors was particularly bothersome to the staff: She hoarded towels. This required the staff to enter her room twice a week and remove some of the towels, which were needed for the rest of the hospital. During a baseline period lasting seven weeks, researchers observed that the patient had about 25 towels in her room even though they were continually removed.

In an attempt to solve the problem, Doris was given all the towels she wanted. Within four weeks, she was keeping over 600 towels in her room. At first she patted the towels and folded and stacked them. During the first week of this treatment, when the nurses brought her some towels, she said, "Oh, you found it for me, thank you." The second week, she said, "Don't give me no more towels. I've got enough." The third week, she said, "Take them towels away... I can't sit here all night and fold towels." The fourth week, she said, "Get these dirty towels out of here." The sixth week, she had started to remove the towels from her room herself, and she told the nurse, "I can't drag any more of these towels. I just can't do it." Within the 16 weeks, Doris had removed all the towels from her room and no longer kept them. This observation was followed by over a year during which towel hoarding never reappeared.

The nurses had felt that hoarding towels reflected a deep-seated need for love and security and guessed that this approach would not work, because it did not treat that underlying need. Not only did it work, but no one observed the development of any other problems that might have replaced hoarding. This example deliberately violates a principle of effectiveness in order to reduce the effectiveness of towels as reinforcers. They reduced the effectiveness of towels as reinforcers for hoarding behavior by not giving them <u>rarely</u>, but rather by giving them freely. (Based on Aylon, 1963.)

13. Giving Doris as many towels as she wanted is an example of violating the principle of ______ ________________ (contingency, deprivation, immediacy, size).

Helpful Hints

Helpful Hint #1

When asked a question about which principle is involved when a reinforcer is given frequently, you may be tempted to answer, "satiation." The name of the principle, however, is the principle of deprivation. Nonetheless, if a person has recently received a lot of a reinforcer, we say that the person is *satiated* with that reinforcer.

14. So remember, the name of the principle con-

cerned with how frequently a reinforcer has been given is not *satiation*. Rather, it is called the principle of ______________.

Helpful Hint #2

I have given you a major hint in this lesson. If I want you to consider the principles of contingency, immediacy, size, and deprivation, I ask you, "What principle is involved?" If I want you to consider the procedures of reinforement, extinction, differential reinforcement, or shaping, I ask you, "What procedure is involved?" Remember, when you are asked what principle is involved, don't even think about the procedures you have learned in prior lessons.

15. When answering questions that ask you to name a principle of reinforcer effectiveness, remember to think in terms of the principles of __________, __________, __________, and ______________________.
16. When asked to name a behavioral procedure that is involved, do not select from the list of principles of effectiveness. Rather, think in terms of the procedures learned in prior lessons that increase or decrease behaviors: ______________, ______________, ______________, and ______________.

Helpful Hint #3

Judging whether the size of a reinforcer is worthwhile can be very difficult. I will give you clues in the examples. The clues will be whether the people receiving the reinforcer act as though they "like" it. This might be an expression of wanting or liking it. It might be simply that it works to maintain their behavior. It might be that they were thrilled with it. Look for these clues to judge whether a reinforcer is worthwhile.

17. If an example states (or implies) that the person liked the reinforcer, you can conclude that the principle of size has been used and that the amount of the reinforcer is __________.

Helpful Hint #4

Later in this lesson, I will give you many examples of people using reinforcers. I will ask you what principles of reinforcer effectiveness, if any, are being violated. If you find any being violated, you should write the name of those principles in the blank. If none are being violated, you should enter "none" in the blank. I will mix in some questions that ask what procedure from prior lessons is involved, and some of these may have the answer "unknown." Many students end up getting confused between "none" and "unknown."

18. Remember, if a procedure is not one that you have already learned, then you should answer ______________. If an example violates no principle of reinforcer effectiveness, then you should answer ______________.

Additional Readings

Ayllon, T., & Michael, J. (1959). The psychiatric nurse as a behavioral engineer. *Journal of the Experimental Analysis of Behavior*, *2*, 323–334. Several mental patients who hoarded magazines were treated through satiation by giving them as many as they would accept. Within a few weeks, they were no longer hoarding magazines.

Schroeder, S. R. (1972). Parametric effects of reinforcement frequency, amount of reinforcement, and required response force on sheltered workshop behavior. *Journal of Applied Behavior Analysis*, *5*, 431–441. This article reports a study in which the amount of money paid to retardates for a job was increased. Unlike the expected finding that they would work harder for the larger amount, they actually worked less. No satisfactory explanation was offered for this contradictory finding.

Schwartz, M. L., & Hawkins, R. P. (1970). Application of delayed reinforcement procedures to the behaviors of an elementary school child. *Journal of Applied Behavior Analysis*, *3*, 85–96. This article reports the use of delayed feedback to teach a 12-year-old girl to use more socially acceptable behavior. The authors taught her to stop slouching and picking at her face, and to start talking loudly enough to be heard. They showed her videotape records of her behaviors in class five hours later. In spite of the lack of immediacy, the reinforcement was very effective at improving her behaviors. In addition, her self-image soared as a result. The delayed consequences may have worked in this case because of the powerful impact of videotaping.

Sulzer, B., & Mayer, G. R. (1972). *Behavior modification procedures for school personnel*. Hinsdale, IL: Dryden Press. This book contains many practical tips for teachers wishing to use behavior modification procedures. Chapter 2, "Reinforcement," reviews some of the principles covered in this lesson.

Reading Quiz

63. The effectiveness of an event as a reinforcer is defined as the extent to which it ____________________________ (decreases, increases) the rate of the behavior.
64. The extent to which a reinforcer increases the rate of a behavior is called its ____________________________ (effectiveness, ineffectiveness).
75. This lesson is about the principles of reinforcer effectiveness. Notice that the principles are not directed at making the procedure more effective but rather at making the event more effective. Thus, it is called the principle of ____________________ effectiveness.
61. Tactic #5 in using the reinforcement strategy to solve human problems is to use the principles of reinforcer ____________________ (effectiveness, ineffectiveness).
65. The fifth tactic in using the reinforcement strategy to solve human problems is to use the principles of ____________________ effectiveness.
57. Review: To use the reinforcement strategy to solve human problems, (5) use the principles of ____________________.
66. The first principle of reinforcer effectiveness is the principle of contingency. Saying that there is a *contingency* between the particular reinforcer A and the particular behavior A means that reinforcer A will be delivered only if behavior A occurs. You might guess that the principle of contingency is the general rule that the reinforcer is delivered ____________ if the person emits the desired behavior.
78. What principle states that the reinforcer must be delivered only if the person emits a desired behavior? ____________________ (contingency, deprivation, immediacy, size)
47. Review: The principle of contingency states that the reinforcer must be delivered to the person ____________________ if he or she emits the desired behavior.
69. The principle of contingency states that the effectiveness of an event will be maximized if it is delivered only when a desired behavior occurs but never when an alternative behavior that is not ____________ occurs.
40. Review: Suppose you give chocolate-covered raisins to Sam because you think, based on only a quick glance, that he did a good job of vacuuming your room. What principle of effective reinforcement may have been neglected? ____________
3. Behavior analysts observe that if people don't have to perform the behavior to get the reinforcer, they won't. Therefore, they have concluded that if a reinforcer is delivered whether or not the behavior actually occurs, the behavior ____________________ (decreases, increases) in rate.
68. The important message of the principle of contingency is that you should not give the reinforcer for any undesired behaviors. Does the principle of contingency imply that you are restricted to delivering a particular event for only one desired behavior? ______
38. Review: Of which principle do you ask, "Was the reinforcer given only if a desired behavior occurred?" ____________
52. Review: To determine whether the principle of contingency is being used, ask, "Was the reinforcer given ______ if a desired behavior occurred?"
5. Brenda, an adult with retardation, banged her head because she received attention only when she did so. The attention she got was a(n) ____________ for banging her head.
62. The aides used to give Brenda attention only when she banged her head. Then they started giving Brenda attention at other times as well. Her head banging decreased. This is an example of deliberately violating the principle of ____________ to weaken attention as a reinforcer for head banging.
73. The second principle of reinforcer effectiveness is the principle of immediacy. It states that the more ____________ (delayed, immediate) the delivery of a reinforcer, the more effective that reinforcer will be.
1. According to the principle of immediacy, a reinforcer should be delivered as ____________ (quickly, slowly) after the behavior as possible (or even during the behavior).
4. Bourgeois (1990) taught husbands to praise

their wives (who had Alzheimer's) immediately when they talked about pictures in a book to help them remember important topics. This treatment caused a(n) ___________ in the number of on-topic statements made by the wives.

23. One exception to the principle of immediacy is that a delayed reinforcer can be effective if you immediately signal that there will be a delayed ___________.

2. Another exception to the principle of immediacy is that a delayed reinforcer can be effective if the person is able to describe the relation between his or her ___________ and the delayed reinforcer.

29. Review: To determine whether the principle of ___________ was used, ask the question, "Was the reinforcer delivered within one minute of the behavior (or while the behavior was still occurring)?"

53. Review: To determine whether the principle of immediacy was used, ask, "Was the reinforcer delivered within one ___________ of the behavior (or while it was still occurring)?"

16. If an event is delivered to a person <u>while</u> he or she is performing a behavior (in other words, after he or she started performing it), the principle of immediacy ________ (is, isn't) followed.

74. The third principle of reinforcer effectiveness is the principle of size. It states that you must give a <u>worthwhile</u> ___________ of the reinforcer for it to be effective.

13. How much of the reinforcer should you give to be effective? You should give a <u>worthwhile</u> amount according to the principle of ___________ (contingency, deprivation, immediacy, size).

14. How much of the reinforcer should you give to be effective? According to the principle of size, you should give a(n) ___________ (minimal, reasonable, worthwhile) amount.

51. Review: To detect which principle do you ask, "Was the amount of the reinforcement used <u>worthwhile</u>?" to detect the principle of _____.

50. Review: To decide whether the principle of size was followed, ask, "Was the amount of the reinforcement used ___________?"

76. To decide whether the amount of a reinforcer is worthwhile, figure out whether the person ___________ (disliked, liked) it.

19. If the person liked the reinforcer, then you can conclude it was a ___________ amount.

9. Every time Jan argued with him, Jim smiled at her. She liked those smiles. Can you conclude that Jim is using the principle of size? _____ (no, yes)

39. Review: Stitzer and Bigelow (1984) paid Fred, a chronic smoker, for not smoking. When they paid him only $1.50 for reducing smoking, he didn't change much. When they paid him $12.00, he reduced by more than half. Was $1.50 a worthwhile amount to endure the agony of reducing smoking? _____. Clearly, that amount violates the principle of size. Was $12.00 a worthwhile amount to endure the agony of reducing smoking? _____. Clearly, that amount follows the principle of size.

67. The fourth principle of reinforcer effectiveness is the principle of deprivation. You violate this principle if you use a reinforcer that you have repeatedly given to someone recently. We say that the person to whom you have repeatedly given that reinforcer is ___________ (deprived, satiated) with respect to that reinforcer.

17. If someone has received the reinforcer rarely, we say that he or she is ___________ (deprived of, satiated with) that reinforcer.

45. Review: The more rarely a person has received the reinforcer, the more ___________ he or she is.

48. Review: The principle stating that the more <u>deprived</u> a person is of the reinforcer, the more effective it will be is called the principle of ___________.

49. Review: The principle of deprivation states that the more ___________ a person is of the reinforcer, the more effective it will be.

54. Review: To determine whether the principle of deprivation was followed, ask, "Has the reinforcer ___________ (rarely, frequently) been delivered?"

30. Review: Ask the question "Has the reinforcer <u>rarely</u> been delivered?" to determine whether the principle of ___________ was followed.

55. Review: To determine whether the principle of deprivation was followed, ask, "Has the reinforcer ___________ been delivered?"

34. Review: Gewirtz and Baer (1958) scheduled a period of time before a child was to perform a simple task. They withheld attention from the child during that period of time. Once they permitted the child to start performing the

task, they praised her. Making attention rare by withholding it for a period of time increases the effectiveness of the attention as a reinforcer through the principle of ______.

59. Review: When a chronic mental patient was instructed to listen as often as possible to the voices he hallucinated, the "voices" became a less effective reinforcer for listening. The instructions to listen to the voices deliberately violated a principle in order to weaken their effectiveness. By making the voices anything but rare, the researchers were instructing the patient to violate the principle of ______. (Glaister, 1985).
79. When the patient listened to his "voices" so often, he eventually became ______ with them (Glaister, 1985).
58. Review: Vollmer and Iwata (1991) used taped music to reinforce a simple task performed by Rich, a man with severe retardation. They played no music while he sat for 30 minutes in the waiting room prior to starting work on the task. Because the taped music was rare (in fact, absent) during the initial 30 minutes, we would say that Rich was ______ of music.
24. Remember, the question to ask to confirm that an example uses the principle of deprivation is: "Has the reinforcer been delivered ______ ______?" If so, the principle has been followed.
22. Let's review the questions for each principle. If a person is reinforced within a minute of his or her response, the principle of ______ is being used.
15. If a reinforcer is given only when a particular desired behavior is made, then the principle of ______ is being used correctly.
18. If the amount of a reinforcer was worthwhile, then the principle of ______ was being used correctly.
20. If the reinforcer has rarely been delivered, then the principle of ______ is being used correctly.
21. Let's review the key words for each question. Be sure to memorize them. The principle of size is being used if the amount of a reinforcer is ______.
71. The principle of deprivation is being used if the reinforcer has ______ been delivered. If you got this one wrong, be sure to memorize it, because you will use it often throughout the rest of the book!
70. The principle of contingency is being used if a reinforcer is given ______ when a particular desired behavior is emitted.
72. The principle of immediacy is being used if a person is reinforced within one ______ of the response.
28. Review: All four principles of effectiveness can make the difference between success and failure of behavioral treatments. Those principles are (1) the principle of ______, (2) the principle of ______, (3) the principle of ______, and (4) the principle of ______.
11. Giving gum for saying words clearly is an example of the mistake of selecting a reinforcer that will generate behavior that is ______ ______ (compatible, incompatible) with the desired behavior.
42. Review: The effectiveness of reinforcers depends on four factors: ______, ______, ______, and ______.
77. To use the reinforcement strategy to solve human problems, (5) use the principles of ______. (Use two words.)
6. Brigham and his colleagues (1972) delivered tokens to children whether or not they made accurate responses. They delivered the tokens within a minute of the response. The tokens bought the children a worthwhile amount of activities that they enjoyed. They got the tokens rarely enough because they could trade them for many enjoyable activities. This example clearly violated which principle of effective reinforcement? The principle of ______
7. Brigham and his colleagues (1972) delivered tokens during treatment, contingent on accurate handwriting. They then delivered them during reversal, noncontingent on correct handwriting. Which procedure produced a higher rate of accurate behaviors? ______ ______ (contingent, noncontingent)
35. Review: Hall and his colleagues (1972) gave Jerry 25 cents at the end of the month for each time during the month when he wore his braces. He got money only for the times when he was wearing his braces. He got a worthwhile amount of money because he could buy some things he wanted. He certainly got the

money rarely enough. What principle of effective reinforcement, if any, did they violate? ______________________

12. Hall and his colleagues (1972) tried two procedures for giving Jerry 25 cents for each time that he was observed wearing his braces. The first procedure involved observing him every day and paying him at the end of the month. The second procedure involved observing him every day and paying him within a minute of observing that he was wearing the braces. Which procedure would you guess produced the higher rate of wearing the braces—paying him daily or monthly? ______________.
8. Doris had hoarded towels for nine years. During those years, the attendants constantly took towels back from Doris. Ayllon (1963) violated one of the principles in order to reduce the effectiveness of towels as a reinforcer for Doris's hoarding behavior. Instead of taking towels away from her, he flooded her with as many as 600 towels, so that they were anything but rare. She started taking them out of her room herself. Ayllon violated what principle of effective reinforcement to <u>reduce</u> the reinforcing effectiveness of towels? ______________________
10. From Helpful Hint #1: When asked a question about which principle is concerned when a reinforcer is given frequently, you should not answer, "the principle of satiation." Rather, answer, "the principle of ______________."
43. Review: The fifth tactic in using the reinforcement strategy to solve human problems is to use the four principles of ______________________.
37. Review: If a person has recently received a lot of a particular reinforcer, that person is said to be ______________ with respect to the reinforcer.
60. Review: When a reinforcer is delivered only when a desired behavior occurs, the principle of ______________ is being followed.
46. Review: The principle that states that a reinforcer should be delivered as soon after the behavior has occurred as possible is the principle of ______________.
32. Review: Brigham and his colleagues (1972) delivered tokens to children whether or not they wrote a letter correctly. If delivering tokens is meant to be a way to reinforce the accuracy of writing, this procedure violates what, if any, principle of effective reinforcement? ______________
44. Review: The four factors that contribute to the effectiveness of a given reinforcer are ______________, ______________, ______________, and ______________.
56. Review: To use the reinforcement strategy to solve human problems, (1) increase desirable behavior through reinforcement, (2) decrease undesirable behavior through extinction, (3) increase a desirable behavior relative to undesirable behavior through differential reinforcement, (4) create new behavior through ______________, and (5) use the principles of ______________.
26. Review: According to the principle of contingency, the reinforcer should not be delivered after any undesired behavior. Rather, it should be delivered ______________ after a desired behavior.
36. Review: Hall and his colleagues (1972) gave Jerry 25 cents for each time he wore braces during the month. Jerry got paid only for the times he was wearing braces. Jerry got the money at the end of the month. He liked the money because it permitted him to buy things that he wanted. He got money rarely enough to always appreciate it. What principle of effective reinforcement, if any, was violated? ______________
27. Review: According to the principle of size, enough of the reinforcer should be given to the person to be ______________.
25. Review: Selecting a reinforcer according to whether the person has rarely had a lot of that reinforcer is making use of the principle of ______________.
41. Review: Tactic #5 in using the reinforcement strategy to solve human problems is to use the principles of ______________.
31. Review: Asking whether enough of the reinforcer has been delivered to be worthwhile tests the principle of ______________.
33. Review: Doris had hoarded towels for nine years. Ayllon (1963) started giving her towels only when she was in her room. After she had been given 600 towels, she started removing them from her room. Ayllon reduced the reinforcing properties of towels for Doris by using the principle of ______________.

Examples

1. Lora gave Mary one cookie for reading each of the first 99 pages. When Mary read the 100th page, Lora gave her a cookie only when she had read that page. She gave her the cookie immediately after finishing the page. Clearly, Mary considered each of the first 99 cookies worthwhile. Yet Mary stopped reading. Did Lora deliver the 100th cookie for the 100th page according to the principles of effective reinforcement? First, the principle of contingency: "Was the 100th reinforcer given ______________ when a desired behavior occurred?" Yes! Second, the principle of immediacy: "Was the 100th reinforcer given within a(n) ____________________ of reading a page?" Yes! Third, the principle of size: "Was the amount of the 100th reinforcer __________________?" Yes! Finally, the principle of deprivation: "Was the reinforcer delivered ________________ (frequently, rarely) by the 100th page?" No! What principle, if any, was violated with the 100th cookie? ________ ____________ (Write just the key word for any principle violated: "contingency," "immediacy," "size," "deprivation," or "none.")

2. Sarah tried to help her friend Juan overcome his shyness by signaling him with a wink only when he acted assertively during a social gathering. She winked at him as soon as he acted assertively. Juan was elated each time she winked at him; he never tired of earning a wink. For the principle of contingency, you should ask, "Was the reinforcer given only when a desired behavior occurred?" _____. For the principle of immediacy, you should ask, "Was the reinforcer given within a minute of the desired behavior?" __________. For the principle of size, you should ask, "Was the amount of the reinforcer given worthwhile?" ____. (Answer "yes" if he seemed to like it.) For the principle of deprivation, you should ask, "Was the reinforcer rarely delivered?" ____. What principle, if any, was ignored by Sarah when she was helping Juan become more assertive? ______________ ____________ (Remember, write either the key word or "none.")

3. Judy encouraged her son Tom to read by bringing him a delicious snack. She gave him a snack only when he was reading, never when he was not. She gave them while he was reading. Tom appreciated the snacks immensely, as they were always his favorite foods. Judy was careful never to give the snacks too often. Tom's rate of reading increased. Decide whether Judy gave the snacks only for reading: ______ (yes, no). Decide whether Judy delivered the snacks within a minute of the behavior. ______. Decide whether Judy's snacks were worthwhile. ______. Decide whether Judy rarely used the snacks. ______. What principle of effective reinforcement, if any, did Judy fail to employ? ____________________ (Write "none" if she used them all.)

4. Boz and Lancey usually went fishing all day on Saturday. They usually caught a fish every 20 casts or so. This Saturday, they went to an artificial lake that had been stocked, and they caught a fish almost every cast. Each cast took less than a minute. They quit by lunchtime, after each had caught dozens of fish. Clearly, their casting was reinforced at the beginning by catching a fish. But what principle was violated that led them to quit early? Did they catch fish <u>only</u> by casting? ____. Was the amount of each reinforcer worthwhile? ____. Did they rarely catch a fish on this day? ____. What principles, if any, were violated this Saturday by the end of their fishing, leading to a decrease in the effectiveness of catching fish as a reinforcer? _______________

5. Members of Utopian Village relied on expressions of respect to maintain work behaviors in their community. These expressions of respect were given only for work behavior and on no other occasion. They were given during or right after work behavior. Members did not seem too thrilled when they got them, but the expressions of respect were not given too often. (Ask the four questions to decide whether any of the principles were violated.) What principle of effective reinforcement, if any, was being ignored by this community when they used expressions of respect as a reinforcer? ____________________________

6. Barb had been really thoughtful to Ken. Every time he complained about how poorly his relationship with friends was going, she had listened and asked questions, hoping to help him. She listened only to his complaints and asked questions after each complaint. However, he had gotten to complaining more and more often. So she decided to just plain quit listening—in fact, she would get up and walk away when the complaining started. Barb was disappointed to find that Ken just kept right on complaining as frequently as ever. What behavioral <u>procedure</u> did Barb use? ____________ __________. (Note that the question is not about a principle, but about a procedure.)

7. Geraldo told his mother that he wanted to learn how to sew. His mother did not have a stereotyped view of children's sex roles, so she welcomed Geraldo's interest. She patted him on the head, but only when he was sewing. She patted him during his sewing or right afterwards. Geraldo didn't seem too thrilled to get a brief pat on the head. His mom rarely patted Geraldo on the head. He lost interest in sewing very quickly. What principle of effective reinforcement, if any, did his mother fail to employ? (Remember to ask the four questions.) ________________. (Remember to answer "none" if she used them all.)

8. Chester took his children for an ice cream treat only on the Sunday of any week during which they brought home a good school paper for him to see. They loved the ice cream treat, which they got rarely. (Ask questions!) What principle probably accounts for the fact that this is not an effective reinforcer for schoolwork? ____________.

9. Darell got interested in meditation and tried very brief meditation periods during the day. He felt so good after his meditation that he started doing more of them during the day. Feeling good as an event would be called a(n) ____________. for meditating.

10. Carey had Dave, the star football tackle, compose poems and hand them to her during class. She read them and wrote praise only for the good aspects of his poems. She returned them the next day during class. Surprisingly, her praise was very important to Dave. She was careful not to give him too much praise. However, in spite of her careful procedure, Dave's poetry writing did not improve. What principle of effective reinforcement, if any, did Carey fail to use? ____________. (Students have been getting this wrong because they are not asking the four questions.)

11. Review: Dad wanted to help Bobby improve his math skills, so he gave him problems orally. For example, "What is 4 times 9?" For every correct answer, Dad gave Bobby a potato chip. Bobby could not earn potato chips during this session in any other way. Dad gave the chips immediately after the correct answer. Bobby loved potato chips when he was hungry! Dad always scheduled these sessions for right after dinner. Dad's procedure didn't work too well. What principle of effective reinforcement, if any, did Dad ignore? ____________________

12. Review: Marvin was determined to teach his daughter Bee how to do math problems. He bought a math workbook. Every morning, he insisted that she do all the problems in one chapter before being allowed to play. He then graded her problems and had her correct the ones that were wrong. When she was done, she could play for the rest of the day. She could soon do the problems very rapidly but still didn't seem to know any more than before. It was then that he noticed the correct answers listed in the back of the book. If Bee was copying the answers, the delivery of the opportunity to play would violate what principle of effective reinforcement? ____________

13. Review: Señor Jimenez taught 4-year-old Janice to say his name by telling her one day to say "hee-may-nayz." From then on, she said it correctly. What behavioral <u>procedure</u> did he use? ________________

14. Review: Nguyen didn't like Timmy to play with his model cars, because Timmy usually played too rough and damaged them. One day Nguyen had the idea that he would reinforce Timmy for playing nicely with the models by giving him several M&M's. He gave Timmy M&M's only for playing nicely. He gave him the M&M's right after or while Timmy played nicely. Timmy loved M & M's. The procedure worked really well for several hours, but finally Timmy started getting too rough again. What principle of effective reinforcement, if any, would you guess had finally been violated after several hours? ____________

15. Review: He was every employee's dream. He praised you only when you did your work well (no matter what your past mistakes had been). He praised you during or right after doing good work. You always appreciated his praise. He didn't load you down with praise too often. What principle of effective reinforcement, if any, did he neglect? ________________

16. Review: Hal did not invite Dana to parties very often. On those occasions when Hal did extend an invitation, Dana would immediately say, "Thank you very much," as enthusiastically as he knew how. He did not say it when Hal failed to invite him to a party. Hal did not seem very receptive to Dana's thanks. Dana thanked Hal rarely enough to not overdo it. Hal did not invite Dana to parties any more often. What principle of effective reinforcement, if any, did Dana ignore in his attempt to get Hal to invite him to more parties? ____________. (Keep asking the questions, but I'm no longer going to put the clues in the order you learned them.)

17. Review: Bo had two really tough classes that were required for his degree. One day he went up to Professor Barnes and asked him a question after lecture. The professor was very friendly and encouraged Bo to ask his question. Bo frequently did so after that and was always greeted warmly by Professor Barnes. Bo tried the same thing with Professor Mead, but he was not at all friendly or encouraging. Bo didn't ask questions of Professor Mead very often. What behavioral procedure would be used to explain why Bo asked more questions of Professor Barnes and fewer of Professor Mead? ______________________. (Most students get this wrong. It would pay to ask the questions you learned in earlier lessons about your first guess.)

18. Review: Maria didn't like the way Vera treated her—Vera was usually very unpleasant. But Maria had heard about reinforcement and decided to try it. She kept track of any pleasant behavior that Vera engaged in for a week and then mentioned those things to her on Sunday night. She never praised Vera for unpleasant behaviors. You can be sure that Vera did not get too much praise. Vera seemed genuinely delighted at the praise, but she did not get any nicer as a result. If you could talk with Maria, what principle of effective reinforcement would you tell her she was neglecting in her method? ______________________. (Ask questions, don't assume that the clues are in the order you learned them.)

19. Review: Alice liked Abdul very much, but he was a bit reserved. So she was warm and friendly only when he at least held her hand. Then she was warm and friendly only when he held her hand and kissed her. Next she was warm and friendly only when he held her hand, kissed her, and embraced her passionately. She reached her goal of getting him to propose marriage. What procedure was she using to get there? ______________________

20. Review: Professor Brainbuster asked his students to formulate literary criticisms of the novel that they had just read. The moment Fred made a good point, the professor praised him lavishly, hoping to reward such critical thinking. Little did the good professor know that Fred was simply parroting the notes from his frat brother. Fred, knowing that his grade was going up, was very pleased about each occurrence of praise. Certainly he only rarely received praise. What principle of effective reinforcement, if any, did the professor not follow in this example? ______________

LESSON 13 Ratio Schedules

This lesson introduces you to schedules of reinforcement. In previous lessons, you learned about two generic schedules of reinforcement. In one of them, the delivery of a reinforcer is scheduled for every occurrence of the behavior. Behavior analysts call that a continuous schedule of reinforcement. In the other one, the delivery of a reinforcer is scheduled to be withheld after occurrences of the behavior. Behavior analysts call this an extinction schedule. You will learn about four additional schedules in which a reinforcer is scheduled to follow only some occurrences of the behavior. Behavior analysts call them by the generic name of intermittent schedules.

1. When the delivery of a reinforcer is scheduled for every occurrence of the behavior, behavior analysts call that a ______________ schedule of reinforcement. When a reinforcer is scheduled to follow only some occurrences of the behavior, behavior analysts call such schedules by the generic name of ______________ schedules.

In this lesson, you will learn about the sixth tactic in using the reinforcement strategy to solve human problems. Sometimes you may want a person to respond more rapidly than is possible when you give them a reinforcer after every response. Tactic #6 is to increase response rate with a ratio schedule of reinforcement.

2. In this lesson, you will learn about the sixth tactic in using the reinforcement strategy to solve human problems. Tactic #6 is to increase response rate with a(n) ______________ schedule of reinforcement.

Fixed-Ratio Schedules

Two common intermittent schedules of reinforcement are based on counting. They count the number of responses that have occurred since the last reinforcement. A **fixed-ratio** schedule requires reinforcing a person's behavior every time he or she completes a fixed number of responses. For example, if Dan is on a fixed-ratio of 3, then reinforcement occurs for every third response. A common example of this schedule is the piece-rate system of wage payments sometimes used in factories. The employer pays the worker for making a fixed number of responses. Thus, the employer might pay an assembly-line worker 25¢ for making five spot welds on an auto body. Behavior analysts call this a fixed ratio of 5. They abbreviate it FR-5.

3. A **fixed-ratio** schedule requires reinforcing a person every time he or she completes a ______________ number of responses.

Notice that a continuous schedule involves reinforcement for every single response. Thus, it is a fixed-ratio schedule. Specifically, it is a fixed ratio of 1. You can abbreviate it as FR-1. All other fixed-ratio schedules (FR-2 and greater) are intermittent schedules.

People tend to work rapidly on fixed-ratio schedules. Fixed-ratio schedules generate a higher rate of responding than do continuous reinforcement schedules. The pattern of responding involves rapid responding prior to reinforcement. After reinforcement, people tend to pause. Thus, the fixed-ratio schedule is characterized by alternating periods of responding and periods of rest.

4. The pattern of responding with fixed-ratio schedules involves rapid responding prior to

reinforcement. After reinforcement, people tend to ___________.

This pattern of rapid responding followed by rest is best displayed in a cumulative record graph. Figure 13-1 shows an example (Miller, 1968). The graph shows the response pattern of a high school boy whose vocal responding was reinforced after every 50 responses. Usually the boy made 50 vocal responses in less than 20 seconds to earn his reinforcer. Then, after he consumed it, he paused for up to 3 minutes before starting to make the vocal responses that would earn him another reinforcer.

People respond faster as you increase the ratio requirement. Thus, they respond faster when you increase the ratio from 1 to 5. They will respond even faster if you increase the ratio from 5 to 10. They will continue these increases until you reach some upper limit, at which point they will start to respond more slowly.

Stephens and colleagues (1975) found this effect when they studied the rate of learning for Sidney, a child with severe retardation. The re-

"Attention" Behavior? Part 2

In Lesson 4, I told you how Jim Holland approached attention as a behavior. He let Navy men press a button to light a dial for 0.07 seconds and told them to report the moment they saw the pointer on the dial deflect. His behavioral definition of attention was pressing the button to look for deflections. He found that the pointer deflection was a reinforcer for looking. Furthermore, the pattern of looking was controlled by the schedule of reinforcement. When the men saw a deflection only after a fixed number of looks, they worked at high rates. They often paused after a deflection. We see this pattern with fixed-ratio schedules (Holland, 1958).

5. Thus, Holland found that attention would come and go according to the pattern found with a(n) ___________ (continuous, extinction, fixed-ratio, variable ratio) schedule.

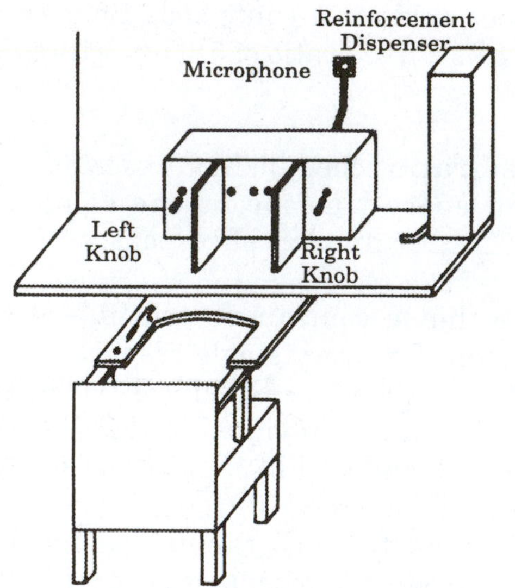

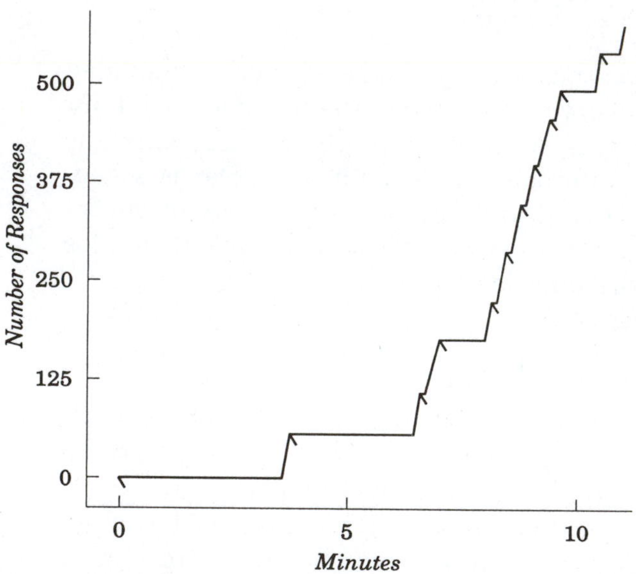

Figure 13-1. This graph shows an experiment with a fixed-ratio schedule. A high school boy made vocal responses into the microphone. These responses are shown on the cumulative record graph on the right. When he was responding rapidly, the graph went up; when he was pausing, the graph went to the right. The boy earned nickels by pulling either the right or the left knob. The right knob required a pull of 50 pounds. If he made 50 vocal responses, he was permitted to pull with the left knob for one minute. The left knob required only one pound of pull. Thus, the researcher reinforced his vocal responses by permitting him to pull the easier knob on a fixed-ratio schedule of 50. Notice that he worked at a high rate until he got the reinforcement (indicated by the slash mark). Then he paused for a while. Adapted from "Escape from an Effortful Situation," by L. K. Miller, *Journal of the Experimental Analysis of Behavior,* 1968, *11*, 619–627. Copyright 1968 by the Society for the Experimental Analysis of Behavior, Inc. Used by permission.

searchers studied the rate at which Sidney learned to name objects shown in pictures. The researchers used a complex procedure because Sidney had trouble learning. First, they taught him to look at the picture of a table. When he could do that, they said "table" and taught him to repeat it. Second, they required him to say "table" without help. Third, they required him to say "table" when they showed the picture among other already known pictures. The researchers reinforced Sidney's responses on different ratios. When they increased his ratio from 1 response per reinforcement to 5 responses per reinforcement, he learned faster. His rate increased with ratios of 10, 15 and 20, but it decreased when they increased his ratio to 25. Similar findings were obtained with four other children. This example shows the usual finding in this area of research, but other variables affect the relationship. The Additional Readings list includes several studies that illustrate some of the complexities of the area.

Pear has suggested that writing one chapter may serve as a fixed-ratio within the overall book.

Novel Writing: A Case of Fixed-Ratio Scheduling?

Irving Wallace had to write 1100 pages to complete his novel *The Prize*. Figure 13-2 shows a cumulative graph of the number of pages he wrote each day. The graph shows that he wrote less than 10 pages a day when he started but increased to over 20 pages a day near the completion of the novel. Suppose that writing a page is one response. Suppose that completing the whole book of 1100 pages is a reinforcer. If Wallace must write 1100 pages to get the reinforcer, then the specific schedule he would be on is called a fixed-ratio schedule. It took him over four months to complete the book. How would you like to be on that big a schedule? (Based on Wallace & Pear, 1977.)

6. Suppose that writing a page is one response, and completing the whole book of 1100 pages is a reinforcer. If Wallace must write 1100 pages to get the reinforcer, the specific schedule he would be on is a(n) ____________ (fixed-ratio, variable-ratio) schedule.

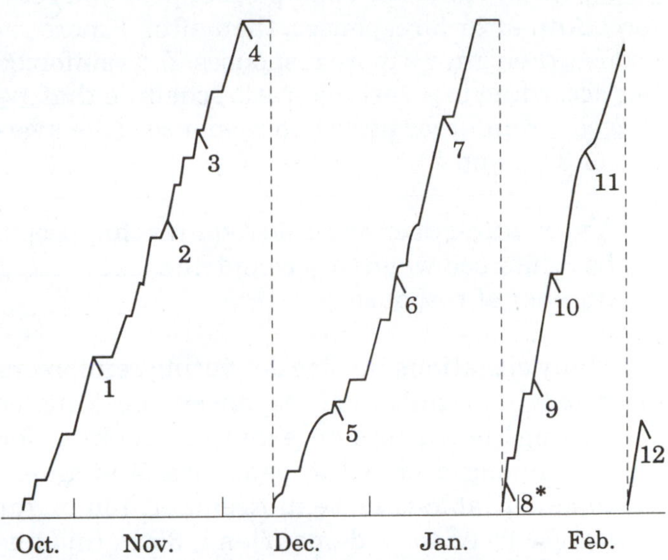

Figure 13-2. This is a cumulative graph of the number of pages written by Irving Wallace on his novel *The Prize*. He gathered the data himself, using his own self-recording diary. The number of written pages was too much for the size of the graph, so it had to be started over again. Without this convention, the graph would be three times as high. Adapted from "Self Control Techniques of Famous Novelists," by I. Wallace and J. J. Pear, *Journal of Applied Behavior Analysis,* 1977, *10,* 515–525. Copyright 1977 by the Society for the Experimental Analysis of Behavior, Inc. Used by permission.

The graph shows a pause in writing after many of the chapters were completed (for example, Chapter 1). Furthermore, the author's records indicate that he stopped writing for the day after completing all but one of the 12 chapters. (The missed one is Chapter 8, indicated by an asterisk.) This pattern suggests that each chapter served as a fixed-ratio schedule. Thus the laws of behavior extend even into that most creative and "subjective" process of writing a novel.

Variable-Ratio Schedules

Behavior analysts use another common intermittent schedule based on counting. They call it a variable-ratio schedule. A **variable-ratio** schedule requires that people be reinforced when they complete a variable number of responses. The number of responses required for reinforcement varies every time. For example, suppose you reinforce Ann after 3 responses, then after 1 more response, then after 2 more responses. You reinforced her according to a variable-ratio schedule that averages a reinforcer after two responses (the average of 3, 1, and 2).

7. A **variable-ratio** schedule requires that people be reinforced when they complete a ________ number of responses.

Many situations involve delivering reinforcers after varying numbers of responses. "Looking for something" is a common example. Looking for friends among a crowd of pedestrians is an example of variable-ratio reinforcement. You might look at 50 faces to find one friend, 35 to find another, and 65 to find a third. Your looking is on a variable-ratio schedule of 50.

Variable-ratio schedules can be useful in business situations. A lumber company found that beavers were damaging its trees and paid employees for trapping the beavers. The company compared the productivity of employees paid $1 for every beaver and that of employees paid an average of $4 for every four beavers. The employees paid on the variable-ratio of 4 schedule trapped 11% more beavers. Both schedules were more effective than an hourly rate. Other business-related studies show a similar effect (Latham & Huber, 1992).

Two researchers used a variable-ratio schedule to increase exercise (DeLuca & Holborn, 1992). Overweight kids pedaled an exercise bicycle, which kept count of turns of the pedal. The equipment awarded points on a variable ratio. The kids could turn in the points for prizes after their exercise. They greatly increased their exercise, improved their physical appearance, and enjoyed exercising.

Two other researchers used a variable-ratio schedule to increase the attention of Jamie, a deaf child (Van Houten & Nau, 1980). The teacher observed whether Jamie attended to her for each five-minute interval. If he did, the teacher let him draw one block out of a bag. One of the eight blocks was blue. Every time Jamie drew a blue block, he got a small toy. This method put Jamie on a variable ratio of 8. His rate of attending increased from about 60% of the intervals to about 90%.

Variable-ratio schedules produce the highest overall rate of responding of any schedule considered in this book. However, you should note that people respond as fast on a fixed-ratio schedule, when they are responding! The absence of pausing on variable-ratio schedules gives it the advantage over fixed-ratio schedules. The lack of a pause may be caused by the fact that the very next response might produce a reinforcer. Later in this lesson, I include a graph illustrating responding on a variable-ratio schedule in connection with a behavior analysis example.

Here is a summary. The fixed-ratio schedule delivers a reinforcer after a fixed number of responses. It produces a high rate of responding prior to reinforcement and a pause after reinforcement. The variable-ratio schedule delivers a reinforcer after a variable number of responses. It produces a high rate of responding with no pauses. Overall, the variable ratio produces a higher rate of responding because of the absence of pauses (e.g., Van Houten & Nau, 1980).

Advantages of Ratio Schedules

Ratio schedules have a number of advantages for behavior analysts, as outlined below.

Resistance to Extinction

Behavior analysts may use ratio schedules to increase a person's resistance to extinction. By *resistance* I mean the number of responses the person makes without reinforcement. For example, suppose Mary has a history of receiving a reinforcer for every response. She will stop responding pretty quickly after her responses no longer produce reinforcement. That is, she will stop responding quickly during extinction. Suppose Alice has a history of receiving a reinforcer only after some of her responses, but not after all of them. She will continue responding much longer than Mary. The basic fact is that a person will continue to respond longer during extinction if they have a history of reinforcement from an intermittent schedule.

8. Behavior analysts may use ratio schedules to increase a person's resistance to ________.

This law can be very useful. Often, the behavior analyst knows that a person's behavior will result in extinction at some point. For example, the behavior analyst may be teaching Fred to be more assertive. After the training period ends, Fred will take his new skill to his usual environment, where his new assertiveness may not pay off as often as in the training period. The behavior analyst may anticipate this transition by using an intermittent schedule during the last part of the training period. Instead of praising Fred for every assertive act, the behavior analyst may shift to praising only an average of one in three assertive acts. With this history, Fred is likely to persist with many more assertive acts even if they don't always work. The result is that his usual environment has longer to accidentally reinforce his new skill. This gives him a greater chance of obtaining enough reinforcement to keep him using the skill.

Koegel and Rincover (1977) provide a dramatic illustration of this effect. They taught children with severe retardation to imitate behaviors that a therapist demonstrated—quite an accomplishment when the children's IQs were so low that they were untestable. They then had another adult, in a different setting, demonstrate the same behavior but provide no reinforcement for imitation. They found that the children stopped imitating after 20 trials if they had a history of continuous reinforcement. The children stopped after 60 to 100 trials if they had a history of reinforcement on every other response (FR-2). However, the children showed no signs of stopping if they had a history of reinforcement on every fifth correct response (FR-5). They were still responding after as many as 500 trials! The use of a ratio schedule resulted in the children maintaining the behavior in the natural environment even with no one reinforcing that behavior. Thus, imitation was maintained in the natural environment after training with a fixed-ratio schedule.

An experiment by Kazdin and Polster (1973) also confirmed this effect. They worked with two adults with retardation who were social isolates. They reinforced every social conversation by Ted with another person in his workplace. They reinforced only one of three conversations by John. When they stopped reinforcement, Ted decreased interactions to less than one per day. John maintained the high rate of about ten interactions per day.

Here is one explanation for the greater resistance to extinction produced by intermittent schedules. People can easily recognize the change from every response producing a reinforcer to no responses producing a reinforcer. When they can be sure that their responses are not going to produce reinforcers, they are likely to quit responding. On the other hand, people may have more difficulty recognizing the change from some responses producing reinforcers to no responses producing reinforcers. Since they can't be as sure that their responses are not going to produce reinforcers, they are less likely to quit responding.

This theory leads to other predictions. For example, people may more readily recognize the change from reinforcers after a fixed number of responses to extinction than from a variable number to extinction. Indeed, research indicates that variable-ratio schedules produce <u>greater</u> resistance to extinction than do fixed-ratio schedules.

For example, Goltz (1992) suggests that individuals' history of reinforcement with investments may determine whether they persist when they should stop investing. She examined people who have a history of successful investments on a fixed-ratio schedule. She compared them with people who have a history of successful investments on a variable-ratio schedule. Those with the fixed-ratio history reduced or stopped their investments during extinction faster than did those with a variable-ratio schedule. In fact, many of those with a variable ratio history actually increased the amount of their investment during extinction.

Decreased Satiation

Ratio schedules also have the advantage that behavior analysts can use fewer reinforcers to generate the same amount of behavior. For instance, suppose a behavior analyst is delivering one reinforcer for ten responses (FR-10 or VR-10). That means she will use ten reinforcers for a hundred responses. With continuous reinforcement, 100 reinforcers would have to be delivered. Thus, ratio schedules may be used to reduce the problem of the person becoming <u>satiated</u> on the reinforcer and then no longer responding. Fixed-ratio and variable-ratio schedules of the same size are equally good at opposing satiation.

9. Ratio schedules also have the advantage that behavior analysts can use fewer reinforcers to generate the same amount of behavior, resulting in decreased ______________.

The Disadvantages of Ratio Schedules

Continuous Schedule for Shaping

When shaping a new response, you must consistently reinforce each approximation. The fastest way to increase its rate compared to nonapproximations is to reinforce it every time it occurs. Thus, behavior analysts use continuous reinforcement during shaping.

10. Behavior analysts use continuous reinforcement during ____________.

Ratio Strain

If a person's behavior is reinforced too infrequently, the behavior may fall apart and become very irregular. Normally, a ratio schedule is introduced by small steps. First the person is reinforced for every response, then for every other one, then for one of five, and so on. Using this gradual approach, behavior analysts can gradually build up very sizable ratios. However, at some point, no matter how gradually the schedule is changed, the ratio simply becomes too large to maintain responding. There is no predictable point at which this happens, because it depends on how effortful the response is, how valuable the reinforcer is, how much is delivered, and how gradually the behavior analyst increased the ratio requirement. Thus, at some point, ratio strain sets in. **Ratio strain** occurs when the people are placed on such a large ratio that they aren't reinforced often enough to maintain responding.

11. When people are placed on such a large ratio that they aren't reinforced often enough to maintain responding, ratio ______________ occurs.

Summary

Tactic #6 in using the reinforcement strategy for solving human problems is to increase response rate with a ratio schedule of reinforcement. You are using a ratio schedule when you reinforce varying numbers of responses. Ratio schedules are intermittent schedules. You are using an intermittent schedule when you do not reinforce every response. You are using a fixed-ratio schedule when you deliver reinforcement for a fixed number of responses. This produces a pattern of pausing after reinforcement followed by a high rate until reinforcement. You are using a variable-ratio schedule when you deliver reinforcement for a varying number of responses. This produces a pattern of high and uniform responding. You would use a ratio schedule to increase resistance to extinction and to reduce problems from satiation. You would not use one for shaping or where you are concerned about ratio strain.

Behavior Analysis Examples

Pay for Performance

Businesses usually pay workers by the hour. A few companies pay workers for each piece of work completed. Economists call this *piece rate* wages. Lincoln Electric uses piece rate to manufacture welding equipment and electrical motors. It has been in business since 1895 (Handlin, 1992). You can think of piece rate as a fixed ratio of 1. Some research demonstrates that workers are more productive with the piece rate than with hourly pay (Latham & Huber, 1992).

12. Because it continuously reinforces whenever there is a response, fixed ratio of 1 is also known as the generic schedule called a(n) ______________ (continuous, extinction, intermittent) schedule of reinforcement.

Teaching Reading

Staats, Finley, Minke, and Wolf (1964) developed a behavioral approach to teaching reading under controlled conditions so that the process could be carefully studied. They first attempted to analyze the process of reading acquisition from a behavioral point of view. They determined that acquiring a reading response meant that people could name the word they were looking at. In order to acquire it, they had to begin by looking at the word. Next they had to either hear how that word sounded or sound it out for themselves. They then had to repeat that sound. Finally, they had to distinguish that word from other words and say its name. Each step involves a response on the part of the learner. Staats could increase the probability of each response by reinforcing it. Based on this analysis, Staats developed an apparatus that permitted the observation of each component response. It also allowed reinforcement of the total reading acquisition response.

Figure 13-3. The Staats apparatus for studying the reading acquisition process. From "Reinforcement Variables in the Control of Unit Reading Responses," by A. E. Staats, J. R. Finley, K. A. Minke, and M. M. Wolf, *Journal of the Experimental Analysis of Behavior,* 1964, 7, 139–149. Copyright 1964 by the Society for the Experimental Analysis of Behavior, Inc. Used by permission.

Figure 13-3 shows the apparatus that Staats developed to study the children's reading acquisition behaviors. It consisted of a working area facing the child and a reinforcer area to the right.

Here is how a child named Sally might proceed. Sally would begin learning a word by pressing a button on the table. The apparatus then projected the word onto the square window. The experimenter said the word. Sally then named that word out loud while pressing that window. Pressing the window ensured that she looked at the word. The press also provided a way to observe her looking response. Next, Sally repeated the word and pressed the rectangular windows below that contained the same word. This step required her to practice naming the word without the help of the experimenter. It also required her to notice the difference between that word and other similar words.

If Sally made the wrong response, the experimenter required her to repeat the sequence. If she made the correct response, she received a marble from the dispenser on the right. She could apply that marble toward the purchase of any of the toys on the right by placing it in the tube below her choice. When the tube was filled, she earned the toy.

Staats and his colleagues have undertaken many experiments to investigate the development of reading behavior. These studies included an examination of different schedules of reinforcement. Figure 13-4 shows a cumulative graph of responding under two conditions. The bottom record shows the rate of responding when Staats reinforced Sally for every correct response. The top record shows the rate when he reinforced her on a variable-ratio schedule of five correct responses (VR-5). This experiment demonstrates that Sally's rate of responding was more rapid with variable ratio than with continuous reinforcement. The series of experiments illustrates that as complex a human behavior as the acquisition of reading behavior occurs according to behavioral principles.

13. Under which schedule of reinforcement was Sally's rate of responding more rapid? ______________________ (continuous, extinction, fixed-ratio, variable-ratio)

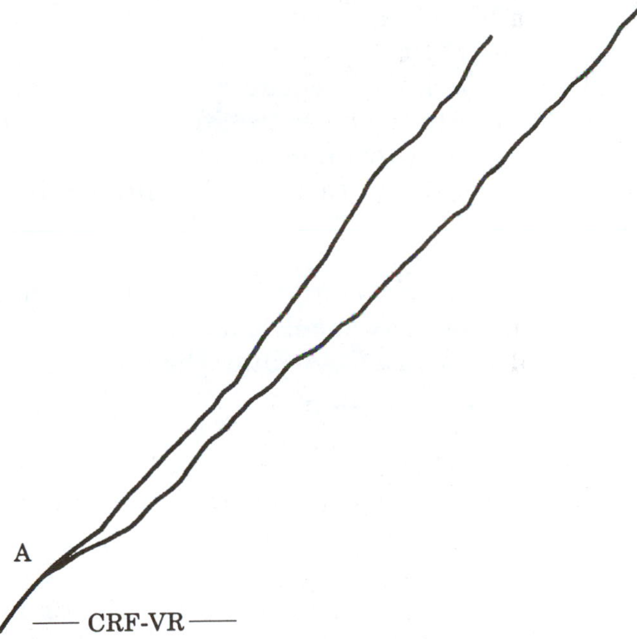

Figure 13-4. A cumulative graph of reading acquisition responses in the Staats experiment. The line on the left shows the rate of reading responses when every fifth correct response on the average was reinforced; the one on the right shows the rate of reading responses when every correct response was reinforced. From "Reinforcement Variables in the Control of Unit Reading Responses," by A. W. Staats, J. R. Finley, K. A. Minke, and M. M. Wolf, *Journal of the Experimental Analysis of Behavior,* 1964, 7, 139–149. Copyright 1964 by the Society for the Experimental Analysis of Behavior, Inc. Used by permission.

Notes

Note #1

Notice that the number of responses for a reinforcer and the size of the reinforcer interact. Suppose your boss pays you $10 to load 5 trucks; you can view this as a fixed ratio of 5. Suppose your boss pays you $2 for each truck you load; that is continuous reinforcement. In terms of the amount of work you have to do for each dollar, you earn the same either way. You can vary the amount of work per dollar either by changing the size of each reinforcement or by changing the size of the ratio. Behavioral economics calls the relation between amount of work and amount of monetary reinforcement the *unit price* (e.g., Bickel et al., 1991). This concept unifies the two separate concepts of reinforcer size and ratio size.

Helpful Hints

Helpful Hint #1

When asked what schedule describes a situation, always use the most specific name. If a person is reinforced every five responses, describe the situation as a fixed-ratio, not an intermittent, schedule.

14. If a person is reinforced for every 30 responses, would the book label it as an intermittent schedule or as a fixed-ratio schedule? ______ ________________

Helpful Hint #2

Do not abbreviate any of the schedules of reinforcement except when also giving its numerical value. If you want to show off, you may abbreviate a fixed ratio of 10 responses as "FR-10" and variable ratio of 15 response as "VR-15." These abbreviations are widely used by behavior analysts. Always spell out the words if you are not identifying a specific numerical value.

15. If you read that Jose was praised for every 5 math problems he got correct, you may abbreviate the schedule as ________________.
If you read that Katrina the beggar scored money from an average of only one passerby in 53, you may abbreviate the schedule as ________________________.

Helpful Hint #3

You can assume that if the reinforcer is delivered after an <u>average</u> of 14 responses, it is delivered after varying numbers of responses. This will point to a variable-ratio schedule.

16. You can assume that if the reinforcer is delivered after an <u>average</u> of 14 responses, it is delivered after ____________________ (fixed, varying) numbers of responses.

Helpful Hint #4

If every response is reinforced, the response is on a continuous schedule of reinforcement. That is the answer the book will prefer. However, the book will also list FR-1 as a correct answer, but it will not list fixed ratio. That is too general for this case.

17. If a response is reinforced every time it occurs, the book will not list as the answer the general response of "fixed ratio." The best answer is that it is the generic schedule called a(n) ________________ schedule.

Helpful Hint #5

I have again narrowed the possibilities you have to consider in answering a question. In past lessons, I used "What procedure?" to ask about reinforcement, extinction, differential reinforcement, and shaping. I used "What principle?" to ask about contingency, immediacy, size,and deprivation. During this lesson, I will continue using those words. In addition, I will use "What schedule?" to ask about continuous, variable-ratio, fixed-ratio, and sometimes extinction. I will never ask "What procedure?" to ask about a schedule.

18. If I ask you "What procedure was used?", can the answer ever be variable-ratio? ______

Helpful Hint #6

I will often use the word *generic* to refer to continuous reinforcement, extinction, and intermittent reinforcement. If I ask for the generic schedule, I am asking for one of these three schedules. However, if the context makes it clear, I will not always refer to them as generic. If I do not ask for the generic schedule, you should not rule out these three schedules.

19. If I ask you for a generic schedule, you know I am asking you about either ________________ ________________, or ________________.

Additional Readings

Ferster, C. B., & Skinner, B. F. (1957). *Schedules of reinforcement*. New York: Appleton-Century-Crofts. This advanced book is the original and most comprehensive source of information on schedules. It is the "bible" of behavior analysis.

Lovitt, T. C., & Esveldt, K. A. (1970). The relative effects on math performance of single versus multiple ratio schedules: A case study. *Journal of Applied Behavior Analysis*, *3*, 261–270. This study involved a disturbed child having problems learning math. The researchers found that his response rate did not increase when the schedule was changed from an FR-5 to an FR-20.

Schroeder, S. R. (1972). Parametric effects of reinforcement frequency, amount of reinforcement, and required response force on sheltered workshop behavior. *Journal of Applied Behavior Analysis*, *5*, 431–441. Schroeder found that individuals with retardation made more electrical components per hour when reinforced on a higher fixed-ratio or variable-ratio schedule (up to FR-600), but only if the effort required in making the response was easy. If the effort was great, then they worked more slowly the higher the ratios.

Reading Quiz

90. This lesson introduced another tactic. Tactic #6 in using the reinforcement strategy for solving human problems is to increase response rate with a(n) ________________ (extinction, ratio) schedule of reinforcement.

35. My first goal is to teach you what I mean by a *generic* schedule. The generic schedule of reinforcement in which a reinforcer is delivered after every response is called a(n) ____________ (continuous, extinction, intermittent) schedule of reinforcement.

84. The generic schedule of reinforcement in which the delivery of a reinforcer is stopped for any responses is called a(n) ____________ ________________ (continuous, extinction, intermittent) schedule.

85. The generic schedule of reinforcement in which a reinforcer is delivered after only some of the responses is called a(n) ____________ (continuous, extinction, intermittent) schedule of reinforcement.

19. If I ask you which generic schedule involves reinforcing only some responses, the answer will not be a specific schedule like fixed-ratio or variable-ratio; it will be ________________ (continuous, extinction, intermittent).

20. If I ask you which generic schedule involves reinforcing no responses, the answer will be ________________ (continuous, extinction, intermittent).

21. If I ask you which generic schedule involves reinforcing every response, the answer will not be a specific schedule like fixed-ratio or FR-1; it will be ________________ (continuous, extinction, intermittent).

18. If I ask you for a generic schedule, you know I am asking you about either ____________, ____________, or ____________.

55. Review: The first topic is fixed-ratio schedules. A fixed-ratio schedule requires that the person be reinforced when he or she completes a(n) ____________ number of responses.

25. If you deliver a reinforcer after a <u>fixed</u> number of responses, the schedule is called a(n) ____________ ratio schedule.

67. Since the continuous schedule involves reinforcement for every single response, it is also known as a fixed ____________ schedule of 1.

86. The name of the schedule in which a reinforcer is delivered after a fixed number of responses is a(n) ________________ schedule.

22. If Jose is reinforced after every five responses, he is said to be on a fixed-ratio schedule of 5. When answering a question to identify this schedule, you could answer either spelled out ________________ or abbreviated as FR-5.

3. A fixed-ratio schedule usually produces a ________________ (higher, lower) rate of responding than does a continuous schedule.

4. A fixed-ratio schedule causes people to respond at a high rate prior to reinforcement, but they tend to ____________ (pause, work) immediately after reinforcement.

95. When the high school boy was reinforced for every 50 responses, he made the responses in less than 20 seconds. Then, after he had consumed the reinforcer, he ________________ for up to 3 minutes.

57. Review: The pattern of pausing after reinforcement is associated with the ____________

schedule. (Spell out the whole phrase. Hint: Use the abbreviation only when you can also give the numerical size of the ratio.)

8. Behavior analysts usually find that people's response rates ______________ as the ratio requirement increases (up to some limit).

53. Review: Stephens and his associates (1975) found that children with retardation learned to name pictures. He reinforced them on schedules of continuous reinforcement and fixed-ratio reinforcement. On which schedule did they respond more rapidly? ______________ ______________

74. Suppose every fifth response of Jim's is reinforced. If I ask you what generic schedule Jim is on, you know the answer must be continuous, extinction, or intermittent. Since every response is not reinforced but some are, Jim is on what generic schedule of reinforcement? ______________

76. Suppose every tenth response of Eric's is reinforced. If I ask you what schedule Eric is on, you should give me the specific, not the generic intermittent schedule. Eric is on what schedule of reinforcement? ______________

75. Suppose every seventh response of Kathy's is reinforced. If I ask you what generic schedule Kathy is on, you should not give me the specific schedule: fixed-ratio or FR-7. Kathy is on what generic schedule of reinforcement? ______________

88. The second topic is variable-ratio schedules. What schedule delivers reinforcement after a variable number of responses? ______________ ______________ (fixed-ratio, variable-ratio)

5. A variable-ratio schedule produces reinforcement after a(n) ______________ (fixed, variable) number of responses.

58. Review: The schedule that delivers reinforcement after a variable number of responses is called a(n) ______________ schedule.

23. If Jose is reinforced after an average of five responses, he is said to be on a variable-ratio schedule of 5. When answering a question to identify this schedule, you could spell out the schedule with two words as ______________ ______________ or you could abbreviate with a numerical value as ______________.

28. In learning to distinguish between fixed-ratio and variable-ratio schedules, it is very important that you note whether an example states that the schedule produces the reinforcer after every 7 responses or on the average of 7 responses. If it produces reinforcement on the average of every 7 responses, then it might first produce reinforcement after 6 responses and then after 8, for an average of 7. If a schedule produces reinforcement on the average of every 7 responses, should you assume that it produces reinforcement after every seven responses? ______ (yes, no)

17. If a reinforcer is delivered after seven responses on the average, the schedule is a(n) ______________ ratio schedule. If the reinforcer is delivered after every seventh response, the schedule is a(n) ______________ ratio schedule.

24. If the reinforcer is delivered after every eleventh response, the schedule is a(n) ______________ ratio schedule. If a reinforcer is delivered on the average of seven responses, the schedule is a(n) ______________ ratio schedule.

44. Review: If you look at 50 faces to find one friend, 35 to find another, and 65 to find a third, your looking is on a(n) ______________ ______________ schedule. (Remember that if you abbreviate, you must give a numerical value.)

37. One group of lumber company employees was paid $4 for varying numbers of beavers, averaging four. What schedule were they on? A(n) ______________ schedule

38. Overweight kids pedaled an exercise bicycle, earning points after varying numbers of pedal responses. The schedule of reinforcement is known as a(n) ______________ schedule.

94. When Jamie drew a blue block (good for a prize) out of the bag on the average of one out of every eight times, he was on a(n) ______________ ______________ schedule.

72. Suppose an average of one in five of Jim's responses is reinforced. If I ask you what generic schedule Jim is on, you know that the answer must be continuous, extinction, or intermittent. Since every response is not reinforced but some are, Jim is on what generic schedule of reinforcement? ______________

77. Suppose that on the average, Eric must make ten responses for reinforcement. If I ask you what schedule Eric is on, you should give me the specific (not the generic "intermittent") schedule. Eric is on what schedule of reinforcement? ______________

78. Suppose that on the average, every seventh response of Kathy's is reinforced. If I ask you what generic schedule Kathy is on, you should not give me the specific answer of fixed-ratio or FR-7. Kathy is on what generic schedule of reinforcement? ______________

79. Suppose that on the average, every 15th response of Ken's is reinforced. Ken is on what specific schedule of reinforcement? ______________

7. As part of the distinction, you should learn about the rate and pattern of responding on both ratio schedules. Does the fixed-ratio schedule produce rapid responding alternating with pauses? ______

9. Does a variable ratio usually produce a pause after reinforcement? ______________

39. People do not pause after reinforcement with the variable-ratio schedule. They do pause after reinforcement with the fixed-ratio schedule. Which of these two schedules produces the highest rate of responding? ______________

89. The variable-ratio schedule produces a uniform and ______________ (high, low) rate of responding.

68. Imagine a stair-step pattern of responding with the fixed-ratio. The person pauses after a reinforcer and then works really hard. Imagine a uniform rate of responding with the variable ratio: The person works really hard all the time. Which schedule will produce the higher rate of responding? ______________

27. In general, the more responses you require before delivering a reinforcer, the faster the person works. How would you guess that the rate of a person working on a continuous schedule (also known as a fixed ratio of 1) will compare with the rate of a person working on a fixed ratio of 10? The continuous schedule will produce a ________ (higher, lower) rate.

33. Let's summarize. Which schedule produces the higher and more uniform rate? The ______________ schedule. Which schedule produces the stair-step pattern of working and pausing? The ______________ schedule. Which generic schedule produces the slowest rate? The ______________ schedule

87. The next topic is the benefits of ratio schedules. I will start with increased resistance to extinction. Ratio schedules may be used to reduce satiation and also increase a person's resistance to ______________.

6. After a behavior analyst has helped change clients' behavior, the clients must return to their everyday life. If they don't receive reinforcement for the new behavior, it will extinguish. Behavior analysts often create greater resistance to extinction in their clients by shifting them to the generic schedule called a(n) ______________ (continuous, extinction, intermittent) schedule near the end of training.

30. Koegel and Rincover (1977) found that, at the request of an adult who never reinforced them, children with retardation would imitate for much longer when they had been trained on what type of schedule—continuous or fixed-ratio? ______________

29. Kazdin and Polster (1973) found that an individual who was reinforced for one in three interactions maintained a high rate of interaction when reinforcement was discontinued, compared to another individual who had been reinforced for every interaction. Thus, they found that intermittent reinforcement leads to greater resistance to ______________.

80. Suppose you have been reinforcing a man for every response he makes. Suppose you then stop reinforcing any of his responses. Because the change from a reinforcer after every response to no reinforcers after any responses is so obvious, you would expect his rate of responding to decrease ______________ (quickly, slowly).

81. Suppose you have been reinforcing a woman for every tenth response. Suppose you then stop reinforcing any of her responses. The change from a reinforcer after every tenth response to no reinforcers after any responses is not as obvious at the change from every response. Therefore, you would expect the rate of responding to decrease (for fixed-ratio compared to continuous reinforcement) more ______________ (quickly, slowly).

82. Suppose you have been reinforcing someone for every tenth response on the average. Suppose you then stop reinforcing any responses. The change from a reinforcer after varying numbers of responses averaging ten to no reinforcers after any responses is not as obvious as the change from every tenth response. Therefore, you would expect the rate of re-

sponding during extinction to decrease (for variable-ratio compared to fixed-ratio) even more ______________ (quickly, slowly).

97. Which of the following schedules produces the greatest resistance to extinction: continuous, fixed-ratio, or variable-ratio? ______________ ______________

73. Suppose Daddy Warbucks often emits the response of making a financial investment, and his investment response is reinforced by making money. Suppose he makes money on a fixed-ratio schedule. Now compare his resistance to extinction with Little Orphan Annie, who makes money on a variable-ratio schedule. Would his investment responding extinguish __________ (faster, slower) than Little Annie's?

36. One benefit of ratio schedules is that they increase resistance to extinction. Here is a second benefit from ratio schedules: They produce more responses per reinforcement than continuous schedules. Therefore, using them reduces the number of reinforcers you have to give someone. In other words, reinforcers occur more rarely. This fact makes them useful in combatting the decrease in reinforcer effectiveness due to ______________ (deprivation, satiation).

83. The generic schedule that produces greatest resistance to extinction and that combats the decrease in reinforcer effectiveness due to satiation is a(n) ______________ schedule.

40. Remember, intermittent schedules produce greater resistence to ______________ and they combat the decrease in reinforcer effectiveness due to ______________.

16. I will next cover two drawbacks to ratio schedules. The generic continuous schedule of reinforcement is the most effective schedule when shaping a(n) __________ (old, new) response.

98. You are shaping a new response. You are differentially reinforcing the first approximation to the target behavior. This first approximation doesn't happen very often. Do you think the subjects would learn to make that approximation more quickly if they were reinforced only some of the time or if they were reinforced every time they performed it? They would learn more quickly if they were reinforced __________ (sometimes, every time).

64. Review: Using a ratio schedule for shaping new responses does not produce good results. What type of schedule should be used when shaping a new response? ______________

93. When a person stops responding because the ratio has become very high, you might say that the ratio has strained his or her ability to respond. You might call such an event by the name ratio ______________.

65. Review: When a ratio is made so high that the person receives few reinforcers, his or her responding may be so strained that it breaks down. This occurrence is not extinction, because reinforcers are still delivered. Rather, this occurrence is known as ______________.

2. A drawback to ratio schedules called *ratio strain* comes if you make the ratio too ________ (big, small).

26. If you make the ratio of responses to reinforcers too large, then you risk reducing responding, in what is called ______________.

91. Two drawbacks of ratio schedules are that they don't work very well when you are ______________ new behavior, and you can set a ratio so large that you decrease behavior—which is called ______________.

92. Using a ratio schedule for shaping doesn't work very well. What generic schedule is best? ______________

32. Let's summarize. The benefits of ratio schedules are that they combat the decrease in reinforcer effectiveness from ______________, and they increase resistance to ______________ ______________.

34. More summary. The drawbacks to ratio schedules are that they are not very effective for ______________ new behavior, and you can set the ratio so high that you weaken behavior through ______________.

31. Let's summarize from the earlier material on rates. Which schedule produces the higher and more uniform rate? The ______________ schedule. Which schedule produces the stairstep pattern of working and pausing? The ______________ schedule. Which of the generic schedules produces the slowest rate? The ______________ schedule

96. When you do not deliver reinforcement for every response, you are using a(n) ______________ ______________ (continuous, intermittent) schedule. When you deliver reinforcement for a fixed number of responses (greater

than one), you are using a(n) ______________ ______________ schedule. When you deliver reinforcement for a variable number of responses, you are using a(n) ______________ ______________ schedule.

46. Review: Intermittent schedules produce an increased resistance to ______________. They also help combat the decreased effectiveness of reinforcers due to ______________.
1. Piece rate wages are defined as giving a set amount of money for each repetition of a job completed. For example, you might be paid 50 cents for each sales prospect you call and tell about a special sale. Every response (such as a phone call) produces a set reinforcer. Piece rate wages may be said to be the generic schedule called a(n) ______________ schedule.
59. Review: The sixth tactic in using the reinforcement strategy for solving human problems is to increase response rate with a(n) ______________ schedule of reinforcement.
15. Here's a review from Unit One. Staats and associates (1964) defined an attending response as "pressing a window with a word displayed on it." This statement of what to observe would be called a(n) ______________ ______________ of the behavior "attending."
52. Review: Staats and associates (1964) found that reading-acquisition responses could be increased in rate by delivering a marble after every response. What generic schedule of reinforcement were they using? ______________ ______________
69. Staats and associates (1964) delivered a reinforcer after a varying number of reading-acquisition responses that averaged 5. What is the name of the schedule that they were using? ______________
70. Staats and associates (1964) studied the rate of making reading-acquisition responses for two schedules: (a) when children were given a reinforcer after every response and (b) when they were given a reinforcer after varying numbers of responses that averaged 5. Which schedule produced the highest rate of responding? ______________
71. Staats and associates (1964) sometimes delivered reinforcers after every response and sometimes after an average of five responses. Which one of these two schedules would have been least likely to satiate the child? ______________ ______________ schedule
10. From Helpful Hint #1: The book uses the most specific label for a schedule as the answer to questions. If a person is reinforced for every 30 responses, would the book label it as an intermittent schedule or as a fixed-ratio schedule? ______________
11. From Helpful Hint #2: Fixed-ratio of five may be abbreviated as ______________. Variable ratio of ten may be abbreviated as ______________.
12. From Helpful Hint #3: You can assume that if the reinforcer is delivered after an <u>average</u> of 14 responses, it is delivered after ______________ (fixed, varying) numbers of responses.
13. From Helpful Hint #4: If a response is reinforced every time it occurs, the book will not list as the answer the general response "fixed ratio." The best answer is that it is the generic schedule called a(n) ______________ schedule.
14. From Helpful Hint #5: If I ask you what procedure was used, can the answer ever be "variable ratio"? ______________
62. Review: To use the reinforcement strategy for solving human problems, (1) increase the desired behavior with reinforcement; (2) decrease undesired behaviors with extinction; (3) increase desired behavior relative to undesired behaviors through differential reinforcement; (4) create new behavior through shaping; (5) use the principles of effective reinforcement; (6) increase the rate of responses through a(n) ______________ schedule.
66. Review: When a reinforcer is delivered after every response, the schedule is referred to by the generic label: a(n) ______________ schedule. When a reinforcer is delivered after only some responses, the schedule is referred to by the generic label: a(n) ______________ schedule. When a reinforcer is never delivered after a response, the schedule is referred to by the generic label: a(n) ______________ schedule.
60. Review: The specific schedule in which you deliver a reinforcer after different numbers of responses each time is called a(n) ______________ ______________ schedule of reinforcement.
42. Review: If a student is complimented every 13 times she just says "No," what schedule of reinforcement are the student's responses on? ______________
47. Review: Name a ratio schedule that produces alternating periods of responding and paus-

ing: ____________ schedule. Name the schedule that produces a high and uniform rate of responding: ____________ schedule

50. Review: One advantage of ratio schedules is that they produce greater resistance to ____________. They also use fewer reinforcers, so they combat decreased reinforcer effectiveness due to ____________.
51. Review: One disadvantage of ratio schedules is that they are not as good as a continuous schedule when ____________ a new response. Another disadvantage is that if you use too high a ratio, you may produce ____________.
63. Review: To use the reinforcement strategy for solving human problems, (1) increase the desired behavior through reinforcement; (2) decrease undesired behaviors through extinction; (3) increase desired behavior (relative to undesired) through differential reinforcement; (4) create new behavior through shaping; (5) use the principles of reinforcer ____________; (6) increase the rate of response through a(n) ____________ schedule.
48. Review: Name the generic schedule of reinforcement usually used with shaping. A(n) ____________ schedule
61. Review: The specific schedule on which reinforcement is delivered after different numbers of responses each time is called the ____________ schedule. The specific schedule on which reinforcement is delivered after the same number of responses each time is called the ____________ schedule.
56. Review: The highest and most uniform rate of responding is produced by the ____________ schedule.
49. Review: Name the schedule of reinforcement that most increases the length of time for a response to be extinguished after reinforcement is stopped. ____________
45. Review: If you use too high a ratio, the person often stops responding in the middle of a ratio or responds erratically. This is known as ____________.
43. Review: If Hal receives reinforcers for an average of one out of three responses, what generic schedule is he on? An ____________ schedule
41. Review: A person whose responses are never reinforced is on a(n) ____________ schedule.
54. Review: Tactic #6 in using the reinforcement strategy for solving human problems is to increase response rate with a(n) ____________ schedule.

Examples

1. Johnny found that if he did enough favors for his mother, she would eventually give him a cookie. Sometimes she gave it to him only after he had asked for it 20 times, but other times she gave it to him the first time he asked. Mom reinforces Johnny's favors on a(n) ____________ schedule of reinforcement. Would Johnny's rate of favors be higher (a) if she continued to give him a cookie after varying numbers of favors or (b) if she gave him a cookie every time he did a favor? ____________. If his mother wanted Johnny to continue doing favors after she ran out of cookies, should she (c) give him a cookie after varying numbers of favors or (d) after every time he did a favor? ________

2. When Mr. James was reinforcing Karna's studying after every 5 problems, he was using what schedule? ____________. Would Karna work her problems faster (a) when praised after every problem or (b) when praised after every five problems?____. Father wants Karna to continue working longer when he is not around to praise her. Should he (c) praise her after every problem or (d) praise her after every five problems? ____. When Father is praising Karna's work after every five problems, what would she do right after the praise for the fifth problem? ____________ (pause, work). Suppose Mr. James checked Karna's problems after different numbers of problems, averaging five. Would Karna work faster on this schedule compared to the one described in the example? ____________

3. Angie seemed to have a hearing problem. She never answered a question the first time it was asked of her. She always said "What?" and then would answer the question the second time it was asked. Because Angie answered every second question, what schedule of reinforcement did she put the questioner on? ____________

4. When Tom got home from work, he would always check to see if there was any mail, because he loved to receive mail. He found that there was

mail on the average of one day in three. What schedule of reinforcement is he on for finding mail? ________________. If he started finding mail only once in 30 days, his looking might become somewhat strained. What is the name for this phenomenon? ____________

5. Julio praised and hugged his infant daughter Lou when she tried to say "Dada." At first he praised her only when she said something that started with "da"; later only when she said both the "da" and a following "da." Teaching her to say "Dada" is called the ____________________. By teaching her through a series of steps, Julio is using what procedure to get Lou to say "Dada"? ____________________________. What schedule of reinforcement would you recommend that Julio use when he tries to teach Lou to say "Dada"? ____________________

6. Jeanie, a 6-month-old baby, was just learning to feed herself with a spoon. Since she was a bit clumsy, she dropped an average of three out of four spoonfuls. Fortunately, Jeanie kept trying. What intermittent schedule of reinforcement was Jeanie on for operating her spoon? ____________ ____________. (Ask yourself if the reinforcement occurred after a fixed number of spooning responses or after a varying number of spooning responses.)

7. Professor Brainbuster required Ken to turn in an essay on ancient history every week. Professor Brainbuster never returned any of Ken's essays, nor did he tell Ken what his grade was. Ken's essay-writing behavior is on what schedule of reinforcement? ____________________

8. Marge let little Timmy earn some money by pulling weeds. She paid him a penny for each weed that he told her he pulled. She gave him the money as soon as he told her how many weeds he had pulled that day. Timmy never had any money, so his earnings were welcome to him. The pay of one penny per weed seemed to add up fast enough that Timmy wanted to tell her he had pulled a lot of weeds. However, one day his mother looked at Timmy's weeding and found that he had not done as much as he had told her. The effectiveness of Marge's reinforcer was undermined because she had ignored the principle of ____________.

9. When Don was 14, he was always reading science fiction stories. His father was also a science fiction fan, so when Don had finished reading a chapter, he would immediately go to his father and describe all the interesting events in that chapter of the story. Don's father seemed to have endless interest in hearing about the latest adventures in Don's books. Assuming that his father's attention is a reinforcer and that one chapter is one response, what generic schedule of reinforcement is Don on? ______________. Suppose Don's father started listening to his accounts of the science fiction stories only when Don had completed a whole book. Because the books contain different numbers of chapters, Don's chapter reading would be on a(n) ________________ schedule of reinforcement.

10. Rico had talked Fran into washing the windows of their house, but Fran needed encouragement. At first Rico made it a point to come by every window Fran completed. Soon, however, Rico just didn't have the time, so he came by after Fran had completed 3, 1, 8, and 4 windows. Fran seemed to finish the windows faster then. What schedule was Fran on for her last 16 windows? __________ ____________________

11. Review: In Dr. Smith's course, each student used to take a daily quiz with six questions. Any student who got all six questions correct advanced one step toward an A. Having to make six correct responses for one step toward an A is an example of what schedule? ______________

12. Review: Walter's mother was teaching him to sew. At first, she praised him for any kind of job that he did. After that, she praised him only when he made the right kind of stitch and made it well. Finally, she praised him only when he cut his own pattern and then sewed it properly. This is an example of what behavioral procedure? __________ ____________

13. Review: Jake always says "Sure" when his friends offer him a beer. His friends buy him one after 2, 5, 4, 6, or 3 (an average of 4) agreements. On what schedule of reinforcement is his saying "Sure"? ____________________

14. Review: Sam thanked his roommate for taking a phone message, and his roommate's message-taking increased as a result. What behavioral procedure did Sam use to increase message-taking? ____________________

15. Review: Andre lived near the phone in the dorm, so he had to answer it much of the time. Most of the dorm members didn't bother to thank him for answering it; on the average, he got thanked once in every four times that he answered the phone. His phone answering is on what schedule of reinforcement? ______________

16. Review: At first, Horace's teacher praised him lavishly whenever he wrote a short poem. He wrote several poems one stanza long. Later, she praised him only when he wrote a poem two stanzas long and paid no attention to his shorter poems. By this method, the teacher eventually got him writing 20-stanza poems. What behavioral procedure did the teacher use to teach Horace to write 20-stanza poems? ______________

17. Review: Have you ever played "the dozens"? "The dozens" involves trading insults in a funny way. After you say something such as "You know, Joe is the ugliest person I ever saw," the other person says "Who's Joe?" You answer, "Joe Momma (your Momma)." The reinforcer is that everyone laughs. Then it's his turn to insult you. After playing for a while, everyone gets tired of getting laughs this way. Getting tired of the laughs just means that the effectiveness of laughs has decreased as a result of ______________.

18. Review: Mr. Potts couldn't decide whether to reinforce his son's behavior every time he took out the trash or only after every 5 times. Under which of these two schedules would his son continue longest to take out the trash if he was never again reinforced? ______________ (continuous, fixed-ratio)

19. Review: One criticism of the idea that most of what people do is because of reinforcement is that most people are constantly doing all kinds of things without reinforcement. One possible explanation for why they do things without reinforcement lies in resistance to extinction. Perhaps they are doing things without reinforcement because, in the past, they were on the generic schedule called a(n) ______________ schedule of reinforcement.

20. Review: Many people try to use reinforcement without success. One reason may be that they deliver their reinforcer long after the response has occurred. If they delay their reinforcer, they are violating the principle of ______________.

LESSON

14 Interval Schedules of Reinforcement

The last lesson described the concept of an intermittent schedule of reinforcement. It defined two intermittent schedules based on counting. Both the fixed-ratio and the variable-ratio schedules count the person's responses to determine when to deliver the reinforcer.

This lesson describes two intermittent schedules based on the passage of time. Behavior analysts call them interval schedules. Tactic #7 in using the reinforcement strategy for solving human problems is to reduce reinforcer frequency with an interval schedule.

1. Tactic #7 in using the reinforcement strategy for solving human problems is to reduce reinforcer frequency with a(n) ______________ schedule.

Definition of Fixed-Interval Reinforcement

The simplest interval schedule is a fixed-interval schedule. A **fixed-interval** schedule is one in which the person must (1) wait for a fixed time to pass (during which responses are not reinforced) and (2) after that time, make a response that will be reinforced.

2. A schedule in which the person must (1) wait for a fixed time to pass (during which responses are not reinforced) and (2) after that time, make a response that will be reinforced is the ______________ schedule.

For example, suppose we reinforce Tom for the first response after five minutes and continue to reinforce him for the first response after each additional five minutes. We say that Tom is on a fixed-interval of five minutes. Tom could wait for the passage of five minutes without making any responses at all; he could then make a single response for the reinforcement. Of course, Tom would have to know in advance how long the interval was, and he would have to time it accurately. This is seldom possible. Be sure to notice that Tom will not receive a reinforcer simply for the passage of the five minutes. He must make a response after the five minutes has passed.

Behavior analysts find that fixed-interval schedules produce a "scallop" pattern of responding (e.g., Ferster & Skinner, 1957; Weiner, 1969). The word scallop refers to a pause after reinforcement followed by a gradual increase in rate prior to the next reinforcement.

3. A pause after reinforcement followed by a gradual increase in rate prior to the next reinforcement is called a ______________.

Tom would probably show a scallop pattern during his five-minute fixed interval. He would probably work at an increasing rate as the five minutes passed. He would end up working at a high rate at the moment of reinforcement. Then, after reinforcement, he would pause for a while. The pattern is similar to a fixed-ratio pattern: Both patterns alternate between responding and resting. However, the overall rate of a fixed-interval schedule is lower. This is because the fixed-interval schedule shows a gradual increase in rate. It does not show the abrupt increase of the fixed-ratio schedule.

Waiting for a friend might be on a fixed-interval schedule. Suppose Jean arrives in the student union every day at 12:50 and waits for Bill, who always arrives at 1:00 P.M. If Jean is reading a book, she will probably stop reading and look for Bill from time to time. Furthermore, if Jean is like most of us, she will look up only infrequently at first (say, until 12:55). After that, she will start looking more often. If Bill is on time, the first look that Jean takes after 1:00 will be reinforced by the sight of Bill.

In this example, Jean's looking will not be reinforced by the sight of Bill until the ten-minute period of time has passed. Bill's arrival will reinforce her first look after that time.

Note that this is not an example of a fixed-ratio schedule. No fixed number of looks will somehow produce the sight of Bill. Jean cannot cause Bill to appear sooner by looking more often; she must wait for ten minutes to pass.

This schedule occurs frequently in the natural environment, so behavior analysts don't have to arrange for it to happen. For example, one researcher studied the betting behavior of chronic horse-racing gamblers (Dickerson, 1979). He found that they tended to place their bets in the last two minutes before a race started. He argued that this was a clear case of fixed-interval scalloping.

Even Congress Obeys the Laws of Behavior

Two researchers investigated the rate at which Congress passed bills. Congress passes very few bills at the beginning of a legislative session, and the rate gradually increases as adjournment approaches. Figure 14-1 shows this pattern on a cumulative graph for the years 1951, 1952, 1953, and 1954. The researchers suggested that finishing the legislative session and going home was the reinforcer. The members of Congress can do this by passing the last bill before them by the last day of the session. Since the interval between the first and last days is always the same, Congress is on a fixed-interval schedule of reinforcement. This schedule should produce a pattern of passing bills that starts out at a low rate. The rate of passing bills should then increase as the interval passes, and this is exactly what happens. Note that this same pattern occurs for pigeons responding for food reinforcement. (Based on Weisberg & Waldrop, 1972.)

4. Since the interval between the first and last days is always the same, Congress is on a(n) _______________ interval schedule of reinforcement.

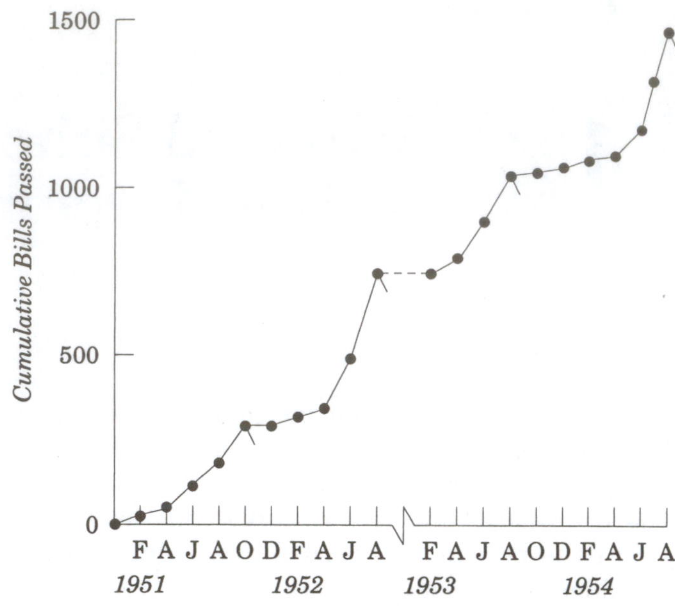

Figure 14-1. The cumulative number of bills passed by Congress in four years. The diagonal deflections indicate adjournment of Congress. Adapted from "Fixed Interval Work Habits of Congress," by P. Weisberg and P. B. Waldrop, *Journal of Applied Behavior Analysis,* 1972, *5,* 93–97. Copyright 1972 by the Society for the Experimental Analysis of Behavior, Inc. Used by permission.

Figure 14-1 shows another example of a naturally occurring fixed-interval schedule. It graphs the legislation passed by Congress. The researchers interpret the resulting scallop as the product of a fixed-interval schedule of reinforcement.

Behavior analysts sometimes use this schedule to help people. For example, two researchers studied how to help obese children to exercise more (DeLuca & Holborn, 1985). They reinforced pedaling an exercise bicycle on a fixed-interval. The first rotation of the pedal after the end of the interval resulted in a reinforcer. This schedule resulted in increased exercise for the children.

Definition of Variable-Interval Schedule

Behavior analysts call the other common interval schedule a *variable-interval schedule*. A **variable-interval** schedule is one in which the person (1) must wait for a variable time to pass (during which responses have no effect) and (2) after that time, must make a response that will be reinforced. For example, suppose we reinforce Ann for the first response after three minutes had passed. We might then reinforce her for the first response after seven minutes had passed. Then we might reinforce the first response after five minutes had gone by. Ann's responding would be on a variable-interval schedule averaging five minutes. Theoretically, Ann could wait for the passage of each of these differing intervals. She could then make only one response per interval and receive reinforcement. Of course, she would have to know in advance how long each interval was, and she would have to time it accurately. Clearly, this would not usually happen. Note that Ann will not receive the reinforcer simply after the passage of time; she must respond after the time has passed.

5. A **variable-interval** schedule is one in which the person (1) must wait for a ______________ ________ time to pass (during which responses have no effect) and (2) after that time, must make a ______________________ that will be reinforced.

Typically, people on a variable-interval schedule work at a uniform rate. They do not stop working after reinforcement. The next interval may be very short, so any response may produce reinforcement. Similarly, they do not work faster as they near the end of the interval. They can't, because the end of the interval is not predictable. The rate of responding is considerably lower than for a variable-ratio schedule.

6. Typically, people on a variable-interval schedule work at a ________________ rate.

I described how Jean's looking for Bill might be reinforced on a fixed-interval schedule. Actually, looking for a friend is more likely to be reinforced on a variable-interval schedule. For example, suppose Ted waits for Jen in the student union every day from 12:50 on. Jen arrives after five minutes the first day. Ted may look up from his paper from time to time to see if Jen is coming. He will probably look up fairly often right from the beginning, since Jen could show up at any time. But on this day, only his first look after five minutes will see her. If, on the following days, Jen arrives after one, then ten, then eight minutes, Ted is on a variable-interval schedule that averages six minutes.

Note that this is an example of a variable-interval schedule, not a variable-ratio schedule. Ted cannot cause Jen to appear sooner by looking more often. On the first day, he must wait for five minutes to see her; no amount of looking will cause her to arrive sooner.

This schedule occurs in the natural environment. The box on attention describes how such a schedule affects attention. This box describes more of the research by Jim Holland on human attending. He showed that seeing what you are looking for can reinforce the looking. If what you are looking for appears on a fixed- or a variable-interval schedule, looking will show the patterns typical of those schedules. When the deflections appeared on a fixed-interval schedule, the rate of looking scalloped. When the deflections occurred on a variable-interval schedule, the rate of looking was uniform.

Behavior analysts sometimes use a variable-interval schedule to help people change. For example, researchers used variable-interval rein-

***Is "Attention" Behavior?* Part 3**

Jim Holland found that the deflection of a pointer reinforced Navy men for looking at a dial. When deflections of a pointer on the dial occurred after a fixed number of looks, they looked steadily. When deflections never occurred, they stopped looking. Holland also studied the effect of deflections for the first look after a fixed time. He found that the Navy men seldom looked during the start of the interval, but they looked often toward the end. This is the pattern typical of fixed-interval schedules. When the deflections occurred after variable periods, the men's attention was on a variable-interval schedule. On this schedule, they looked steadily. Holland showed that the schedule of reinforcement increases the private behavior called *attention* just like any other behavior. He took attention out of the mysterious realm of the mind. It is just something that people do—it is behavior. (Based on Holland, 1958).

7. When the deflections occurred after variable periods, the men's attention was on a(n) ________________ interval schedule. On this schedule, they looked steadily.

forcement with Dan, a fourth-grader who didn't study very much during class (Martens, Lochner, & Kelly, 1992). During baseline, he studied about 45% of the time. The researchers praised Dan according to a variable-interval schedule. When they praised his first academic responses after an average of two minutes, his studying increased to 94% of the time. His rate of studying was quite uniform during the school period.

Advantages and Disadvantages of Interval Schedules

Interval schedules have advantages similar to ratio schedules. You can use them to reduce the problem of satiation, as well as to produce increased resistance to extinction. They also have similar disadvantages. You will not find them to be useful in shaping a new response. You may find that they deliver too little reinforcement to maintain responding. This results in a breakdown of responding similar to ratio strain.

Comparison of Basic Intermittent Schedules

Figure 14-2 illustrates the patterns and comparative rates of the four simple schedules of reinforcement. As you can see, a variable-ratio schedule produces the fastest rate of responding, with fixed-ratio somewhat less. The two interval schedules produce response rates that are lower than the ratio schedules. Notice that the variable-interval and variable-ratio schedules both produce uniform rates of responding. The fixed-ratio and fixed-interval schedules both produce pauses after reinforcement. However, the fixed-interval schedule tends to produce a brief pause that switches very gradually to high-rate responding. This pattern is called a *scallop*.

Research has confirmed these comparisons. For example, researchers reinforced reading acquisition on interval and continuous schedules (Staats et al., 1964). The interval schedule produced response rates below those of continuous reinforcement. Other researchers reinforced pedaling an exercise bicycle according to fixed-interval and fixed-ratio schedules (DeLuca & Holborn, 1990). They found that the fixed-ratio schedule produced faster pedaling. These same researchers reinforced pedaling on a variable-ratio schedule (DeLuca & Holborn, 1992). This produced the highest overall rates that they observed. Thus, these comparisons apply to common everyday behavior.

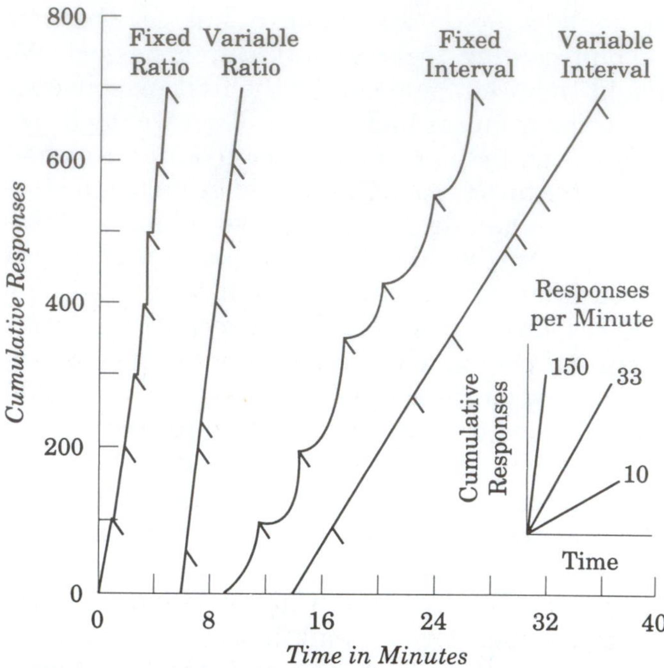

Figure 14-2. Stylized cumulative graphs of the patterns of responding produced by the four simple schedules of reinforcement. The diagonal slash marks indicate the delivery of reinforcement. From *Operant Learning: Procedures for Changing Behavior,* by J. L. Williams. Brooks/Cole Publishing Company, 1972.

Laws of Behavior

The unique patterns of responding associated with each schedule are immensely important to behavioral science. They provide powerful examples that behavior is lawful. In fact, behavior analysts describe these patterns as behavioral laws applicable to many species and many behaviors. As you have seen, these laws apply to many complex forms of human behavior. They may even apply to the passing of Congressional legislation and the writing of novels.

Summary

Tactic #7 in using the reinforcement strategy for solving human problems is to reduce reinforcer frequency with an interval schedule. Interval schedules are another kind of intermittent schedule, based on time rather than counting. You are using a fixed-interval schedule when you reinforce the first response after a fixed period of time. This produces a scallop pattern: pausing after reinforcement, then a gradual increase in rate leading up to reinforcement. You are using a variable-interval schedule when you reinforce the first response after variable periods of time. This produces a uniform pattern of responding. Interval schedules produce lower response rates than ratio schedules. Interval schedules increase resistance to extinction and reduce problems from satiation. They are not useful for shaping. They may lead to too little reinforcement and thus something like ratio strain. The patterns produced by ratio and interval schedules are basic laws of behavior. They control many kinds of behavior, including private behavior and the actions of Congress.

Behavior Analysis Example

Study Behavior

One research team taught a class in which the reading material was available only in a library room. They kept track of the total amount of time that each student had the material for study in that room. At first, they scheduled a test for each day of the class. As the cumulative graph in Figure 14-3 shows, during this portion of the semester, the students studied the material for a roughly equal amount of time each day. The researchers then shifted to a schedule of testing every three weeks. The students studied very little for the first part of the three-week period but gradually started studying more and more as the time of the test approached. The researchers next reversed to daily tests and found equal studying each day. Finally, they once again tried a three-week testing period. Although there was a less dramatic effect, they once again found little studying at the beginning of the period and an increasing rate as the test date approached.

8. Because the researchers' testing was based on time rather than counting, this is an example of a(n) ____________ (interval, ratio) schedule.

This experiment produced a pattern of responding that is like that in fixed-interval studies. It is possible to view the test as a reinforcing event that can be scheduled in different ways. When the test is scheduled daily, it approximates

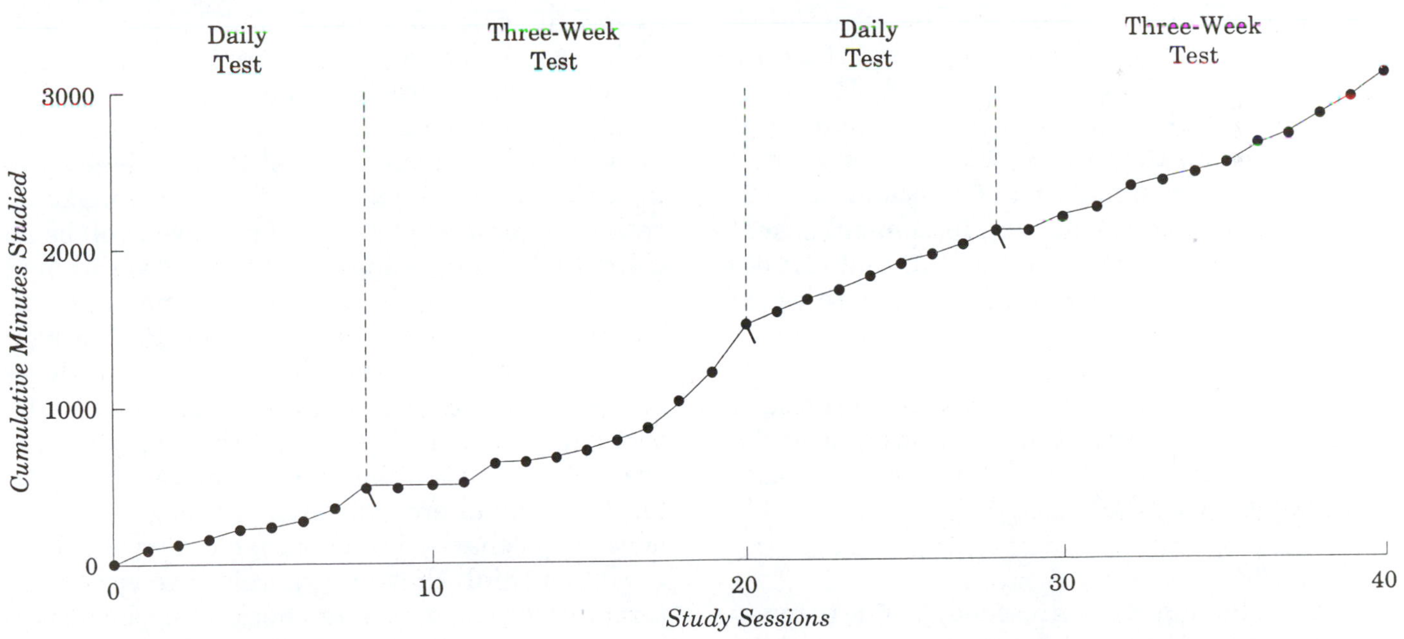

Figure 14-3. The cumulative study hours by college students. The experiment compared the effects of testing on a fixed interval one-week versus testing on a fixed interval three-weeks schedule. Adapted from "A Comparison of Students' Studying Behavior Produced by Daily, Weekly, and Three-Week Testing Schedules," by V. T. Mawhinney, D. E. Bostow, D. R. Laws, G. J. Blumenfeld, and B. L. Hopkins, *Journal of Applied Behavior Analysis,* 1971, *4,* 257–264. Copyright 1971 by the Society for the Experimental Analysis of Behavior, Inc. Used by permission.

a continuous schedule of reinforcement. A continuous schedule produces uniform responding. When the test is scheduled after long intervals, it is similar to a fixed-interval schedule, which produces a scalloped rate of responding. These results indicate that even the complex intellectual behavior involved in studying follows predictable and lawful patterns observed in other behaviors. (Based on Mawhinney et al., 1971.)

9. When the researchers tested every three weeks, they were using a(n) ______________ (fixed, variable) interval schedule.

Notes

Note #1

If a person is reinforced after a fixed period of time, no matter what he or she is doing at the time, the situation is called <u>superstitious reinforcement</u>. This situation was named by Skinner (Skinner, 1948a), who delivered food to pigeons for 5 seconds every 15 seconds, no matter what the pigeons were doing. The pigeons developed a variety of superstitious behavior—such as turning in a full circle, swaying the body like a pendulum, and hopping from one foot to the other. These behaviors were called *superstitious* because the pigeons acted as if their behavior caused the reinforcement, even though it did not. People display many superstitious behaviors—like swearing at their cars when they won't start—that may well be caused by the same kind of coincidental reinforcement. Superstitious reinforcement differs from fixed-interval reinforcement in that it is delivered after a fixed period of time regardless of whether the person emits a specified behavior.

10. If a person is reinforced after a fixed period of time, no matter what he or she is doing at the time, would this be an example of a fixed-interval schedule? ____

Note #2

The scalloping of Congress may be due to many factors in addition to the fixed-interval schedule. Other factors include instructions, history, time-correlated stimuli, observation of response, other schedules, response cost and effort, "limited hold," interval duration, and aversive consequences (Poppen, 1982).

Helpful Hints

Helpful Hint #1

This section is intended to teach you how to distinguish between interval and ratio schedules when they occur in everyday situations. When a behavior analyst is arranging the delivery of a reinforcer according to a predetermined schedule, distinguishing between them is quite simple. You must find out his or her rule and determine whether it requires the person to make a number of responses before it is delivered, or whether it requires the passage of time before the reinforcer is delivered for the next response.

In everyday situations, however, the distinction is a lot harder to make, since we do not have someone to put the rule into words. Suppose, for example, you are operating a slide projector and looking at slides that you took (only a few of which are interesting and therefore reinforcing). What type of schedule is your slide advance response on? Some responses will be reinforced when you see one of the few interesting slides; most will not be. Is your advancing of the slides reinforced after the passage of time? Or is it reinforced as a function of making a number of responses?

Here's how you should analyze this. You must realize that the slides are in some unknown sequence, in which you may have to advance many slides before coming to an interesting one. Suppose the first interesting one occurs after seven slides. Waiting some amount of time before your next advancing response will not suddenly produce the interesting slide. In fact, if you make no responses for a fixed period of time, you will be no closer to the interesting slide than you were when you started. Thus, the passage of time is not involved in getting to the reinforcer. Rather, you must advance the slide projector past seven slides before you get to the reinforcer. You must make those responses before the interesting slide arrives. Because the number of uninteresting slides until the next interesting slide will vary, your slide-advancing behavior is on a variable-ratio schedule.

If you think that an example involves an interval schedule, you may check your conclusion by asking the question, "If the person makes no response at all, will there eventually arrive a time at which <u>one response</u> will produce the reinforcer?"

If you think that an example involves a ratio schedule, you may check your conclusion by asking, "If the person makes the responses very rapidly, will the next reinforcer arrive sooner (than if the responses are made slowly)?" In other words, the rapidity of reinforcement for an interval schedule is time-controlled (although the person must still make at least one response), while for a ratio schedule it is response-controlled.

11. When you are advancing slides to find an interesting one, the passage of time does not determine when you get to the reinforcer. Furthermore, if you advance them quickly, you will get to the next interesting one sooner. Therefore, your slide-advancing behavior would be on a(n) ________________ (interval, ratio) schedule.
12. To summarize, then, you can ask two questions to decide whether an example involves a ratio or an interval schedule. If you think that an example involves a ratio schedule, you can check your conclusion by asking, "If the person makes the responses very rapidly, will the next reinforcer arrive ________________ (sooner, later) than if the responses are made slowly?"
13. If you think that an example involves an interval schedule, you can check your conclusion by asking the question, "If the person makes no response at all, will there eventually arrive a time at which _____ response will produce the reinforcer?"

Helpful Hint #2

The slide projector example can also be analyzed from the point of view of people watching slides that are being advanced by someone else. In that case, the watcher's looking response would be reinforced by the sight of an interesting slide only after the passage of the amount of time that it takes the operator to get around to advancing the projector seven slides. Thus the viewer, unlike the operator, is on a variable-interval schedule. Watching a movie would be analyzed in a similar manner. Remember to determine whether the person's response advances the slide or whether it involves looking at a slide whose delivery depends on someone else.

Watching a slide show where someone else is advancing the slides is also like watching a movie, or TV, or any events controlled by someone else. You can't change when anything happens. All you can do is act at the right time. Thus, all of these examples involve interval schedules.

Operating a slide show is like turning the pages of a book to read, or flipping through photographs, or sorting slides. They are like any activity in which you are in charge of the pace. The faster you advance slides or pages, the faster you flip photos or sort slides, the sooner you find the reinforcers. Thus, these activities all involve ratio schedules.

14. When watching slides being advanced by someone else, you as the viewer, unlike the operator, are on a(n) ________________ (interval, ratio) schedule.

Helpful Hint #3

You may not abbreviate the schedule of reinforcement unless you also give its numerical value. If you want to show off, you can enter the exact schedule, including the time. In this case, you must abbreviate fixed-interval or variable-interval and state the amount of time until the next response produces the reinforcer. If it is a variable-interval schedule, you can state the average time until the next response produces a reinforcer. These abbreviations are widely used by behavior analysts. If you do show off, be sure to abbreviate the schedule with the length of time. However, do not include whether the unit of time is seconds, minutes, or hours. The book will show two correct answers. For example, if the average interval is two minutes, the book will show "variable-interval" as one answer and "VI-2" as an alternative answer. It will not show "variable-interval of 2," or "VI-2 minutes," or "VI" as answers.

15. If you are labeling a fixed-interval schedule where the first response after three minutes will be reinforced, the correct answer for the full name would be ________________ schedule (abbreviated as ____________).

Helpful Hint #4

If the book tells you that the first response after an average of 2 minutes will be reinforced, you can assume that each interval will be variable. They might be 2, 3, 1, and 2 minutes long, but they will average 2 minutes. Thus the schedule will be a variable-interval, not a fixed-interval, schedule.

16. If the first response is reinforced after intervals that average 2 minutes in length, then you should conclude that it is not a fixed-

interval schedule but rather a(n) __________ interval schedule.

Helpful Hint #5

Throughout the book, I have introduced various "helper terms" that refer to a group of concepts. The terms include *method* for the methods of observation and *schedule* for the generic and the specific schedules of reinforcement. Students sometimes confuse the interval method of observation with the fixed-interval schedule of reinforcement. If you notice whether a question asks for a method or a schedule, you can avoid this mistake.

17. If an example refers to "intervals every five minutes" and then asks, "What method of observation was used?", you might guess which of the following: time sample or fixed-interval? ____________________

Additional Readings

Bentall, R. P., & Lowe, C. F. (1987). The role of verbal behavior in human learning: III. Instructional effects in children. *Journal of the Experimental Analysis of Behavior, 47*, 177–190. This article shows how instructions affect the pattern of fixed-interval responding for young children. It raises the issue of how reinforcement and verbal behavior interact to determine behavior.

Holland, J. G. (1958). Vigilance. *Science, 128*, 61–67. Also reprinted in R. Ulrich, T. Stachnik & J. Mabry (Eds.). (1966). *Control of human behavior* (Vol. 1). Glenview, IL: Scott, Foresman. This article reports one of the earliest demonstrations of schedule effects with human subjects. Holland showed that the looking response is one that is influenced by its consequences (that is, seeing a reinforcing scene) and that, depending on the schedule of seeing what one is looking for, the pattern of looking will vary.

Reese, E. P. (1978). *Human behavior: Analysis and application*. Dubuque, IA: William C. Brown. This book is a fine introduction to operant psychology applied to the analysis of human behavior. It contains an excellent description of schedule effects and many citations to research illustrating these effects.

Reading Quiz

75. The seventh tactic in using the reinforcement strategy for solving human problems is to reduce reinforcer frequency with a(n) __________ (interval, ratio) schedule.
5. First, I want to contrast ratio and interval schedules. The fixed-ratio and variable-ratio schedules that you learned about in the previous lesson deliver reinforcers based on ____ ____________ (counting, timing) responses.
68. The fixed-interval and variable-interval schedules that you learned about in this lesson deliver reinforcers based on __________ (counting, timing) responses.
83. When the behavior of someone is being reinforced on a fixed-interval schedule, not every response is reinforced. Therefore, the person is being reinforced according to the generic schedule called a(n) ____________________ (intermittent, continuous) schedule.
70. The most important fact about fixed-intervals is that the simple passage of time does not produce a reinforcer. The person must do more than wait; he or she must also make a <u>response</u>. So remember, a fixed-interval schedule is one in which the person must (1) wait for a fixed period of time to pass and then (2) make a(n) ______________ after that time.
2. A fixed-interval schedule is one in which the person must wait for a fixed period of time to pass. Is it true that (a) the person automatically gets the reinforcer at the end of the period, or (b) the person has to make a response after the period is over to get the reinforcer? ____
3. A fixed-interval schedule is one in which the person must make some response after a(n) ________________ period of time has passed.
76. Theoretically, a person on a fixed-interval schedule of reinforcement could wait for the passage of the fixed-interval without making any responses. However, the person would then have to make one ________________.
84. Will a person on a fixed-interval schedule be reinforced at the end of the fixed-interval even if he or she does not respond? __________
37. Review: A fixed-interval schedule is one in which the person must (1) wait for a(n) _____ ____________ period of time to pass and then (2) make a(n) ______________ after that time.
58. Review: The name of the schedule on which

the person must (1) wait for a fixed period of time to pass and then (2) make a response is called a(n) ______________ schedule.

22. If Jose is reinforced for responding after every 5 minutes, he is said to be on a fixed-interval schedule of 5. When answering a question to identify this schedule, two forms of answer are correct. First, you can spell out the whole name but omit the actual time: ______________. Second, you can "show off" with the abbreviation (with the actual time): ______.

80. Typically, the behavior of someone on a fixed-interval schedule of reinforcement "scallops." That means that the person pauses just after reinforcement and then, as the time for reinforcement nears, the rate of responding ______________ (increases, decreases).

79. Typically, someone on a fixed-interval schedule of reinforcement pauses just after reinforcement and then, as the time for reinforcement nears, the rate of responding increases. Behavior analysts call this pattern a(n) ______________ (reinforcer, scallop).

4. A scallop is the typical pattern for which schedule? The ______________ schedule.

41. Review: Behavior analysts call the pattern in which someone pauses, and then their rate of responding gradually increases a(n) ______________.

69. The fixed-interval schedule produces a pausing and working pattern. Another schedule that you learned about in the lesson on ratio schedules also produces a pausing and working pattern. The name of that schedule is the ______________ schedule.

47. Review: Jean arrives in the student union at 12:50 every day and waits for Bill. She must always wait ten minutes, because Bill arrives at 1:00. What schedule is Jean on if seeing Bill is a reinforcer? A(n) ______________ schedule.

27. It is easy to confuse interval and ratio schedules. A schedule is a ratio schedule if responding rapidly produces the reinforcer sooner. A schedule is an interval schedule if the person can wait without responding until a time comes when ______________ response(s) will produce the reinforcer.

20. If Jean looks more often while waiting for Bill, she will not see him any sooner. He will get there at 1:00 no matter what she does. However, at 1:00 she must make the single response of looking for him to see him. Therefore, she is not on a(n) ______________ (interval, ratio) schedule.

42. Review: Dickerson (1979) found that horse-racing gamblers did not place their bets right after the last race. Rather, their probability of placing the bets slowly increased. Most gamblers placed their bets in the last two minutes before a race started. The reinforcer was the chance to win the bet. He argued that this pattern was the result of a fixed-interval schedule. Therefore, the pattern should be labeled a(n) ______________.

81. Weisberg and Waldrop (1972) pointed out that Congress passes legislation during the ten-month-long period of time set for a legislative session, and that the members' behavior is then reinforced by adjournment. If legislative sessions are always of the same length, passing legislation is on what schedule of reinforcement? ______________

82. When DeLuca and Holborn (1985) compared not reinforcing with reinforcing obese children for pedaling an exercise bicycle on a fixed-interval schedule, the result was a(n) ______ (increase, decrease) in exercise.

35. Remember this. Suppose a person is on a fixed-interval schedule of three minutes. If at the end of three minutes, the person does not make a response, he or she ______________ (will, won't) get a reinforcer.

74. The second topic is to learn about variable-interval schedules. Remember, with a fixed-interval schedule, a person must wait for a fixed period of time before earning the reinforcer. With a variable-interval schedule, a person must wait for a(n) ______________ period of time before earning the reinforcer.

19. If a person's behavior is being reinforced according to a variable-interval schedule, not every response is reinforced. Therefore, the behavior is being reinforced according to the generic schedule called a(n) ______________ (continuous, intermittent) schedule.

39. Review: A variable-interval schedule is one in which the person must (1) wait for a(n) ______________ time to pass and (2) make a(n) ______________ after that time.

77. Theoretically, if a person's responses are reinforced on a variable-interval schedule, he

or she could wait for the passage of the time without responding and then be reinforced for making ________ (how many?) response(s) after that time.

85. Will a person on a variable-interval schedule be reinforced at the end of the different-length intervals even if he or she doesn't respond? ________________

57. Review: The name of the schedule in which a person (1) waits for a variable period of time and then (2) makes a response is the ________ ________________________ schedule.

21. If Jose is reinforced for responding after an average of five minutes, he is said to be on a variable-interval schedule of 5. When answering a question to identify this schedule, two forms of answer are correct. First, you can spell out the full name (without the time): ____________________. Second, you can abbreviate (and include the time): ________.

53. Review: On what schedule do people typically work at a uniform rate for the entire period of time the schedule is in effect? __________ ________________________

63. Review: Typically, people on a variable-interval schedule work at a(n) ____________ rate for the entire period of time the schedule is in effect.

73. The pattern of uniform responding for the variable-interval schedule is similar to the pattern for a ratio schedule you studied in a prior lesson (not counting continuous reinforcement): ________________

43. Review: If Ted waits in the student union every day from 12:50 on to see Jen, who arrives within an average of six minutes, what schedule of reinforcement is Ted on if seeing Jen is a reinforcer? ________________

28. It is essential that you tell the difference between ratio and interval schedules. In the previous example, Ted cannot cause Jen to appear sooner by looking more often. He must wait until the interval passes, and then he must make one response. Therefore, his looking response is on a(n) ________________ (interval, ratio) schedule.

87. You can tell the difference by asking two questions. One question is: "If the person makes no response at all, will there eventually arrive a time at which one response will produce the reinforcer?" If the answer is "Yes," the schedule is based on time, and you can be sure that it is a(n) ______________ (interval, ratio) schedule.

71. The other question you can ask is: "If the person makes the responses very rapidly, will the next reinforcer arrive sooner than if the responses are made slowly?" If the answer is "Yes," the schedule is based on counting, and is a(n) ________________ (interval, ratio) schedule.

23. If the person can make the reinforcer arrive sooner by responding rapidly, then it is a(n) ______________ schedule. If the person must simply wait for passage of time until one response will produce the reinforcer, it is a(n) ______________ schedule.

78. These questions are the key to telling the difference between ratio and interval schedules. So remember that the schedule is an interval schedule if the person must simply wait for the passage of time until _______ (how many) response(s) will produce the reinforcer. But it is a ratio schedule if the person can respond rapidly and make the reinforcer arrive ______ ________.

29. Jim Holland (1958) found that when deflections of a pointer used to reinforce Navy men appeared on a fixed-interval schedule, the rate of looking showed a(n) ________________ (scallop, uniform) pattern as reinforcement approached. When the deflections occurred on a variable-interval schedule, the rate of looking was more of a(n) ________________ (scallop, uniform) pattern.

59. Review: The Navy men looked at a steady, uniform rate when deflections of the pointer occurred on a(n) ________________ schedule.

30. Martens and associates (1992) found that variable-interval reinforcement helped increase study time for a fourth-grader from 45% to 94%. Under this interval schedule, his rate of studying showed a(n) ___________ (scallop, uniform) pattern.

46. Review: Interval schedules don't deliver reinforcers after every response. They therefore have many of the advantages of ratio schedules. They can be used to combat the decrease in reinforcer effectiveness due to ________. They can also increase resistance to _______.

24. Interval schedules also have many of the disadvantages of ratio schedules. Interval schedules are not suitable for use when ________

__________________ a new response. Interval schedules may not maintain responding when, as in ratio strain, they deliver too few __________________.

33. People can control how rapidly they earn a reinforcer on a ratio schedule, unlike on an interval schedule. People usually earn reinforcers as fast as possible. Therefore, when they are on a ratio schedule, they work __________________ (faster, slower) compared to an interval schedule.
26. Is the responding rate higher in a variable-ratio schedule or a variable-interval schedule? __________________ schedule
86. Would you guess that the overall rate of responding is higher for a fixed-interval schedule or a fixed-ratio schedule? __________________
32. Pauses after reinforcement and then faster response rates are characteristic of the response pattern produced by what two schedules of reinforcement? __________________ and __________________
72. The pattern of responding that is produced by a fixed-interval schedule (pause after reinforcement and then a gradually increasing response rate) is called a(n) __________________.
25. Interval schedules produce __________________ (higher, lower) response rates than ratio schedules.
67. Scientists refer to a constant relationship as a *law*. One behavioral law describes the relationship between fixed-interval schedule and pattern of behavior. The law is that the person pauses after reinforcement and then slowly increases the rate of responding as the moment of reinforcement approaches. Behavior analysts label this lawful pattern of responding produced by fixed-interval schedules a(n) __________________.
18. Here's another example. The variable-ratio schedule produces a uniform, high rate of responding. This relationship between variable-ratio schedule and pattern of responding always occurs. Because the relationship is constant, it is like a physical law. Such a constant relationship is called a behavioral __________.
1. A common feature of fixed-interval and fixed-ratio schedules is that not every response is reinforced. Therefore, both those schedules are examples of the generic schedules called __________________ schedules.
55. Review: Tactic #7 in using the reinforcement strategy for solving human problems is to reduce reinforcer frequency with a(n) __________ schedule.
31. Mawhinney and associates (1971) tested students every three weeks. If passing a test is a reinforcer, then the students' study behavior was on what schedule of reinforcement? __________________
17. From Note #1: If a person is reinforced after a fixed period of time, no matter what he or she is doing at the time, this would be called __________________ (fixed-interval schedule, superstitious reinforcement).
6. From Helpful Hint #1: In order to determine whether an interval or a ratio schedule is being used by a behavior analyst, you must find out whether it requires the person to make a number of __________________ before delivery of the reinforcer, or whether it requires the passage of __________________ before the next reinforcer.
7. From Helpful Hint #1: When you are advancing slides to find an interesting one, the passage of time does not determine when you get to the reinforcer. Therefore, you would be on a(n) __________________ (interval, ratio) schedule.
8. From Helpful Hint #1: If you think that an interval schedule is involved, ask, "If the person makes no responses, will a time arrive when only __________ response will produce the reinforcer?"
9. From Helpful Hint #1: If you think that a schedule is a ratio schedule, ask, "If the person makes responses very rapidly, will the next reinforcer arrive __________________ (sooner, later) than if the responses are made more slowly?"
10. From Helpful Hint #1: In which type of schedule is the rapidity of reinforcement response-controlled? __________________ (interval, ratio). In which type is it time-controlled? __________________ (interval, ratio).
11. From Helpful Hint #2: Suppose you are watching slides being advanced by someone else, and your looking response is reinforced by finding an interesting slide. The amount of time it takes to get to an interesting slide depends on the amount of time taken by the operator to advance each slide. Also, that time will be different, because not all slides are in-

teresting. Therefore, you as the viewer, unlike the operator, are on a(n) ______________ schedule.

12. From Helpful Hint #2: Operating a slide show is like turning the pages of a book to read, or flipping through photographs, or sorting slides. They are like any activity in which you are in charge of the pace. The faster you advance slides or pages, the faster you flip photos or sort slides, the quicker you find the reinforcers. Thus, these activities all involve ______________ (interval, ratio) schedules.
13. From Helpful Hint #2: Watching a slide show where someone else is advancing the slides is also like watching a movie, or TV, or any event controlled by someone else. You can't change when the reinforcer arrives. All you can do is look or act at the right time. Thus, all of these examples involve ______________ (interval, ratio) schedules.
14. From Helpful Hint #3: Fixed interval may be abbreviated as _____ and variable-interval as _______.
15. From Helpful Hint #3: Suppose the book tells you that the reinforcer is delivered for the first response after an average interval of two minutes. If you wish to show off and include this average time, the book will show the correct answer as ______.
16. From Helpful Hint #4: If the first response is reinforced after intervals that average two minutes in length, you should conclude that it is not a fixed-interval schedule but rather a(n) ___________ interval schedule.
34. Read this question very carefully. Depending upon which exact word is used in the question, either "time sample" or "fixed-interval" could be the correct answer. If an example refers to "intervals every 5 minutes" and then asks "What method of observation was used?", you might guess which of the following: time sample or fixed-interval? ______________
61. Review: To use the reinforcement strategy for solving human problems, (6) increase response rate with a ratio schedule; (7) reduce reinforcer frequency with a(n) ______________ schedule.
50. Review: Most people keep reading books, hoping that a really exciting scene or passage will soon come along. Such a scene may occur on an average of once in 20 pages. Because they can control how fast they find these scenes by their reading rate, their reading behavior is on what specific schedule? A(n) ______________ ______________ schedule. (Warning: many students get this wrong.)
65. Review: Which intermittent schedule studied in this or in prior lessons produces the highest sustained rate of responding? ______________ ______________
48. Review: Mawhinney and associates (1971) might have given tests unannounced but occurring either (a) on the average of every three weeks or (b) exactly every three weeks. Which schedule of test-giving would result in a more uniform pattern of studying? ________
54. Review: People maintain a uniform but low rate of responding in which interval schedule? ______________ schedule. (Give the full name)
60. Review: To determine whether an example involves an interval schedule, you should ask, "If the person makes no response at all, will there eventually arrive a time at which ______ response will produce the reinforcer?"
62. Review: To use the reinforcement strategy for solving human problems, (6) increase response rate with a(n) ______________ schedule; (7) reduce reinforcer frequency with a(n) ______ schedule.
51. Review: Name the interval schedule in which people respond at a gradually increasing rate, called a *scallop*, as the time for the reinforcement approaches. ______________
44. Review: If the climactic scenes are placed too far apart in a book, readers might quit reading even though they were being reinforced occasionally. That is, they might find themselves on a rather large ratio schedule. If their responding stopped or became erratic, this would be an example of ______________.
66. Review: You have learned three generic schedules in which responding is reinforced always, never, or sometimes. They are the ______________ ______________, ______________, and ______________ schedules.
49. Review: Mawhinney and associates (1971) observed students' study patterns in relation to tests. Suppose that passing a test is a reinforcer. Then Mawhinney used two schedules of reinforcement: (a) students were tested daily and (b) student were tested at consistent three-week intervals. If the professor suddenly stopped reinforcing studying with tests

but didn't tell the students, which schedule would lead to students studying longer on their own? ________

64. Review: When determining whether an example involves a ratio schedule, ask, "If the person makes the response very rapidly, will the next reinforcer arrive ____________?"
40. Review: Although only an average of one in ten jokes in a joke book is hilarious, most people rapidly read through all the jokes looking for the good ones. What schedule of reinforcement is the joke reader on? ___________ ___________ (Ask whether the person can make the reinforcer arrive sooner.)
52. Review: Name two types of intermittent schedules that produce a tendency for people to stop responding after reinforcement (stair-step or scallop). ______________________ and ______________________
38. Review: A variable-interval schedule of reinforcement is one in which the person is reinforced for the first response after __________ periods of time.
36. Review: A fixed-interval schedule is one in which the person is reinforced for the first response made after a(n) __________ period of time passes.
56. Review: Tactic #7 in using the reinforcement strategy for solving human problems is to reduce reinforcer frequency with a(n) ________ schedule.
45. Review: If you can make the reinforcer arrive <u>sooner</u> by responding rapidly, then it is a(n) ____________ schedule; if you must simply wait for the passage of time until <u>one</u> response will produce the reinforcer, then that is a(n) ____________ schedule.

Examples

1. Diego meets Doris for lunch at the corner of Market and Fifth every day. Doris is supposed to show up at 1:00, but she comes anywhere from ten minutes early to ten minutes late. Suppose Diego looks at each passerby to see if he or she is Doris. Suppose that seeing Doris reinforces his looking. Guess what schedule his looking behavior is on. Suppose you guessed it is a ratio schedule. You could check your guess by asking, "If Diego looks more often at people, will Doris arrive <u>sooner</u>?" Notice that the question isn't whether he will see her sooner, but whether she will arrive sooner. The answer is ____. Because his response does not speed up the reinforcer, you know it's not a ratio schedule. You might then guess that it is an interval schedule. You could check this by asking, "If Diego does not look at all, will there eventually arrive a time when <u>one</u> looking response will sight Doris?" The answer is ____. Because one response is ultimately all that's needed, you know it's an interval schedule, but which one? Because Doris comes at different times each day, you can conclude that Diego's looking is on a(n) __________ ____________________ schedule.

2. Ron and Betty are watching a movie that contains a few scenes showing dancing. Since they are interested in learning some new steps, these scenes are the only ones that are of interest to them. Suppose the scenes are 2 minutes long, and the first one occurs after 15 minutes have elapsed, the second after another 5 minutes, the third after another 25 minutes, and the last after another 15 minutes. You guess that this may be a ratio schedule. To check your guess, you should ask, "If Ron and Betty look at the movie more often, will the dancing scenes arrive <u>sooner</u>?" The answer is _____. You would now change your guess to an interval schedule. You should again check your answer. Ask, "If Ron and Betty do not look for a time, will there eventually arrive a time when making <u>one</u> looking response will result in seeing the dancing?" The answer is _____. Since the time between scenes varies from 5 to 25 minutes, this example illustrates a(n) ____________________ schedule.

3. Martha works on an assembly line at the Ford plant. It is her job to tighten 13 nuts on each car frame. She gets paid 50 cents for every 13 nuts tightened. To determine whether this is a ratio schedule, ask, "If Martha makes the response very fast or very often, will the next reinforcer arrive <u>sooner</u>?" The answer is _____. It is usually wise also to check to see whether this might be an interval schedule by asking, "If Martha makes no response at all, will there eventually arrive a time at which one response will produce the reinforcer?" The answer is _____. Because Martha must make 13 responses per reinforcer, her work is on a(n) ____________________ schedule of reinforcement.

4. George works in a factory. His supervisor comes by to check on him every 30 minutes. (Assume that the supervisor reinforces his working.) To check whether this is a ratio schedule, ask, "If

George works faster, will the supervisor arrive sooner?" The answer is ____. To check whether this is an interval schedule, first ask, "If George does not work at all for a time, will there eventually arrive a time when one response will result in the supervisor seeing him working?" The answer is _____. Since the supervisor comes by every 30 minutes, this is an example of a(n) ____________ schedule.

5. When reading a book, one might find many passages or scenes that are boring. However, most people keep reading with the hope that a really exciting passage will come along soon. Such a scene may occur on an average of once every 20 pages. This can be a confusing example, because you might think it is like watching a movie. However, the movie goes on whether you look or not. Unless you are going to skip pages, which will destroy the plot and make no passages exciting, you must read on. If you guess that it is an interval schedule, you should check by asking, "If the person does not read for a period of time (and does not turn pages), will there arrive a time when reading only one page will produce the reinforcer (the exciting passage)?" The answer to this question for reading a book must be ____. If you change your guess to a ratio schedule, ask, "If you read fast, will the reinforcer arrive sooner?" The answer is ____. Therefore, reading a book for exciting passages is on a(n) ____________________ schedule.

6. Jamal is very clothes-conscious. He likes to have on his hip clothes whenever anyone stops by his room to visit. On an ordinary day, Jamal has a visitor on the average of once every 93 minutes. The visitors come between 7:00 and 11:00 P.M. Having a visitor come in when he has his hip clothes on reinforces wearing hip clothes. Ask: "If Jamal makes the response more often (for example, by staying in his hip clothes for the full four hours), will the next reinforcer arrive sooner?" By asking the question, "If Jamal does not make the response for a time, will there arrive a time when he can dress in his hip clothes and produce the reinforcer?", you can determine whether this is a(n) ________________ schedule. In this example, Jamal's dressing in hip clothes is being reinforced according to a(n) ____________________ schedule. (Name the specific schedule.)

7. Marty's teacher wanted him to do more math problems for less reinforcement. She decided to reinforce him an average of once every five times that he completed a problem. She kept track of where he started and then she complimented him after he completed 3, 8, 5, and 4 problems. The teacher was giving out compliments on a(n) ____________________ schedule. (Check your answer by asking both questions.)

8. Believe it or not, Gloria is a peeper. She can see into Dave's room from her own room. She starts watching his room at 11:30 every night. Dave comes into his room and starts undressing at exactly 11:40 every night. What schedule of reinforcement is Gloria's peeping behavior on? ____________________ (Check your answer by asking both questions.)

9. John was trying to teach his son to bring his plate into the kitchen and put it in the sink immediately after dinner. During the first month, John gave his son an ice cream dessert each time he brought his plate into the kitchen. In the second month, John started giving his son an ice cream dessert when he brought his plate to the kitchen for several meals in a row, averaging four. What schedule of reinforcement was the son on during the second month? ____________

10. Alice was a radar scanner in Alaska. She was supposed to scan the radar screen continually for an eight-hour period, looking for unidentified (and possibly hostile) planes. She spotted an average of two unidentified planes per night; usually they were American planes that were off course. What schedule of reinforcement was Alice's scanning on? ____________________ (Be sure to ask the questions.)

11. Review: Chester took his children for an ice cream treat only when they brought home a good school paper for him to see. He gave them the treat on the Sunday of any week that they brought home a good paper. It seemed like they would do anything for such a treat. They did not get ice cream treats too often. What principle of effective reinforcement accounts for the fact that Chester's treat did not result in higher grades for his children? ____________________

12. Review: Darlene's clock radio always woke her at exactly 6:45. As she dressed, she would listen to see if the 7:00 news had come on yet. What schedule of reinforcement was her listening behavior on? ____________________

13. Review: Daisy continued to cry every night after being put to bed. Her parents would go into her room to see what was the matter, and they always spent some time comforting her. They

never found any physical problems such as wet diapers. After some months, they decided that they should simply ignore the crying. They found that within several days Daisy no longer cried after being put to bed. What generic schedule of reinforcement did her parents place her crying on by ignoring her crying? ______________________

14. Review: Stan wanted everyone around him to be happy and cheerful. Anytime Susan said something cheerful, he was happy and smiled. Anytime she said something gloomy, he was unhappy and glum. Susan began saying cheerful things more often. What behavioral procedure did Stan unconsciously apply to Susan's behavior to increase happiness relative to unhappiness? ________________

15. Review: The Kramers had a light switch that didn't work right. The first time you moved the switch, the lights did not come on. In fact, you had to turn the switch three times before the lights would come on. Operating the light switch was on what schedule of reinforcement? ______________ ______________________________

16. Review: Porno Pete had reduced the writing of pornographic books to a science. He had a chart that told him how many pages to wait before creating one of the filthy scenes for which he was famous. He made his reader wait for 1 page to get to the first one, then 11, then 5, then 23 more, and so on. If reading a page is one response, what schedule of reinforcement is that response on? ______________________________

17. Review: Timmy discovered that if you hold a magnifying lens between an ant and the sun, and focus it properly, the ant will burn up with a popping sound. Timmy's rate of focusing the magnifying glass on ants increased dramatically after this discovery. The event "frying ants" is called a(n) ______________________.

18. Review: Kayla was always thrilled when she saw a deer. She used to sit for hours on her favorite hill waiting to see one. What schedule of reinforcement was her deer-looking behavior on? ______________________

19. Review: Willis was fascinated by comets. He watched patiently to catch sight of Alpha 13, which was visible at 4 A.M. on August 24 every two years. What schedule of reinforcement was his watching for Alpha 13 on? ________________ ______________

20. Review: Tillie was difficult to engage in a conversation. In particular, it was difficult to get her started talking about herself. Francisco found out that if you asked her enough questions about herself, she would eventually open up. Sometimes it took only a couple of questions, but at other times it took many more. What schedule of reinforcement was Francisco's questioning on if Tillie's opening up is the reinforcer? ________________

LESSON

15 Review of Reinforcement

This unit focuses on reinforcement. The lessons mention many reinforcers, most of which stem directly from the behavior of other people. Such reinforcers include attention, encouragement, and compliments. The lessons have also discussed many desirable and undesirable behaviors that may result from reinforcement, including studying, talking about problems, and nagging.

Positive Reinforcement Is Magic!

Here is a love story about the power of reinforcement. Larry and Jo Ann were an ordinary couple who fought and complained about each other. Then one day, Larry thanked Jo Ann for washing his socks. Naturally, Jo Ann suspected that Larry wanted something. A few days later, he thanked Jo Ann for recording a check in their ledger. She wondered what had gotten into him, but she became more careful of recording check numbers. Then he thanked her for a great dinner and for cleaning the house. Then (gadzooks!) he complimented their teenage daughter's appearance. Another day he washed the dishes. Jo Ann started to get used to the praise, and she liked it. One day, Jo Ann surprised herself by thanking Larry for bringing home a paycheck. Positive reinforcement from one person led to positive reinforcement from the other. Maybe if we all used a little more, the world would be a better place. (From Larsen, 1991.)

1. The procedure Larry used is ______________ ______________.

Reinforcement Can Help

Most reinforcement arises from how people treat each other. Under the best of circumstances, the behaviors of two people (whether spouses, friends, or roommates) are mutually reinforcing. The benefits to each person help maintain the relationship. Reinforcement can be magic!

Reinforcement Can Harm

Sometimes we don't fully understand the concept of reinforcement, so we may engage in self-defeat-

Santa Didn't Save the Day

Barry Kaufman tells the following story. He was waiting in the checkout line of a grocery store during the Christmas season. A 2-year-old girl wanted to eat snacks her mother had put in the cart. The mother refused. The girl screamed, and still the mother refused. Other shoppers demanded that the mother do something. Suddenly Santa Claus appeared, saying, "Ho! Ho! Ho!" He gave her a red and white striped candy cane. She immediately stopped crying and smiled through her tears. One shopper remarked, "Santa saved the day." Kaufman's 13-year-old daughter laughed and said, "Santa didn't save the day. He just taught that little girl that unhappiness pays. If you scream and cry, you get candy. I'll bet she does the same thing in the next store." (From Kaufman, 1991.)

2. If the 13-year-old is right, what would you call the candy? A(n) ______________

ing behaviors. If we give in to a nagger to stop the nagging, we thereby ensure that the nagger will keep nagging. We listen to complainers to avoid confronting them, so the complainers continue to complain. We let shirkers have the same privileges as those who do their share of the work, increasing the probability that the shirkers will continue to avoid doing their share. We may even teach people to be unhappy!

Reinforcement Is Everywhere

Reinforcement occurs constantly in personal interactions. I have recounted numerous anecdotes about it. Larry thanked Jo Ann for being a loving wife; Santa gave candy to a screaming child; a special family shared a magic ice storm. The principal provided clothes, praise, and hope to children in an inner-city school. A president gave his dog a biscuit for chewing on the rug, and a husband taught his cat to scratch up the furniture. I have described studies showing that teachers inadvertently reinforce disruptive behavior. Friends reinforce pain behaviors. Mental hospital aides, nurses, and parents teach people to act crazy, to hit themselves, and to engage in violence. None of these people planned to use reinforcement in those ways, but they used it without understanding it. Surely they would not reinforce undesirable behavior if they understood what they were doing.

Psychologists often make deliberate use of reinforcement to help people. They help students, elderly people, adults, and individuals with retardation. They help swim teams, dorms, and football teams. They help people become more creative, healthier, more cooperative, smarter, and even happier! Behavior therapists use reinforcement to help individuals solve their own problems (Cautela, 1969). Behavioral sociologists use reinforcement to set up more cooperative dorm meetings (Welsh, Miller, & Altus, 1994). Psychologists use reinforcement to teach individuals to apply behavioral principles to solving their own problems (Watson & Tharp, 1972).

Reinforcement is a powerful part of any social system. When group members reinforce desirable behavior and extinguish undesirable behavior, they help to create a happy and comfortable situation. Skinner's novel *Walden Two* illustrates how people might use reinforcement to create a better community. The novel emphasizes how we can use reinforcement to modify our own behavior in ways agreeable to all. As the box indicates, behavior analysts have analyzed how reinforcement affects college basketball teams.

Behavioral Momentum in College Basketball

Behavior analysts find that people generate a high rate of responding if they have recently been reinforced frequently. They call this *behavioral momentum.* Researchers applied this to college basketball games, recording three types of events for seven games. First, they recorded events that were probably reinforcers, including scoring baskets and having the other team turn the ball over. Second, they recorded adversities such as fouls, missed shots, and turning the ball over to the other team. Third, they recorded responses to adversities: the outcome of the first possession after an adversity. They found that teams responded more favorably to adversities if they had received more reinforcers during the preceding three minutes. (Based on Mace, Lalli, Shea, & Nevin, 1992.)

3. This behavioral momentum is the result of having received many recent __________ ____________________.

Reinforcement Works in Every Age and Culture

The effect of reinforcement is not restricted to the United States, nor to modern Western civilization. Researchers have shown that reinforcement influenced ancient cultures. The liberal use of reinforcers sharply increased the musical activities of orphans in 17th-century Venice, leading to the development of world-famous orchestras and performers (Kunkel, 1985b). Other researchers found that reinforcement helped reduce disruptive behavior in African second-graders (Saigh & Umar, 1983). Anthropologist Allan Holmberg changed the centuries-old behavioral patterns of 1700 Peruvian peasants (Kunkel, 1985a). They became very hard workers, adopted new agricultural practices, and began attending school. One researcher has

> ***Behavioral Principles Are Universal Laws***
>
> Sociologist John Kunkel studied 17th-century Venice and Peruvian Indians. He concluded that "Behavioral principles... operate in the open society of other cultures and historical epochs. These principles are not the reflections of 20th century America" (Kunkel, 1985b: p. 457).

shown the value of reinforcement in Latin America and Indonesia (Elder et al., 1991; Elder et al., 1992). John Kunkel summarizes what we know about the generality of reinforcement in the box on universal laws.

Reinforcement Works with All Behavior

Behavior analysts have used reinforcement to modify all types of behavior. They have used it to modify obvious behavior, such as playing tennis and making football plays, and subtle behavior such as studying or relaxing. They have used it to modify internal behavior, such as brain waves characteristic of meditation, and private events such as attention. The box below left is the last of a series on understanding "attention" as a behavioral event. Reinforcement is not some mechanical and trivial part of life; it is the very foundation on which human beings learn to conduct their lives.

> ***Is "Attention" Behavior?* *Part 4***
>
> Jim Holland found a way to study "attention" as a behavior. Navy men looked at a dial for deflections of a needle. Their pattern of looking was a function of the schedule on which deflections occurred. The attention of radar observers is vital to our national defense around the world, 24 hours a day. They look for unexpected planes, ships, or missiles. When they pay attention, we are safer; when they don't, we are more vulnerable! Holland's work suggests that we must reinforce them for continuing to attend. The military could supply false signals to the radar on an intermittent schedule. If the observers reported the false signals promptly, the computer could thank them. If they failed to report them, the computer could let them know it (Holland, 1958).
>
> 4. If the military used schedules of reinforcement to maintain attending by vital radar operators, which schedule would produce a constant rate of attending? ________________ (fixed-interval, variable-inverval)

The Reinforcement Strategy

In Unit One, you learned how to use the behavioral strategy to solve a human problem. The essence of the behavioral strategy is to view a human problem as a behavioral problem. You can then use one or more of the five tactics. You can define it behaviorally, observe it, check reliability and social validity, design an experiment, and/or visually analyze the results. You may find that just defining it behaviorally will be enough to solve the problem. The solution may be obvious once it is clearly defined. Or you may have to use other tactics. The essence of the behavioral strategy is that it allows you to react to a problem in a pragmatic, nonmystical way. Many problems will require more specific treatment than that.

If the behavioral strategy does not solve the problem, you can try the next strategy. In Unit Two, you learned about the reinforcement strategy. The essence of this strategy is to change the way in which reinforcers follow desirable and undesirable behaviors. Doing so lets you change the rate of those behaviors. You learned seven tactics for applying this strategy in various ways.

The first tactic is to increase desirable behavior through <u>reinforcement</u>. If the problem is simply that a desirable behavior is not occurring often enough, all you have to do is find a way to reinforce it. Often simply paying attention to the behavior is all that is required. However, you may need more powerful reinforcers if the behavior is very difficult or if other factors are discouraging it. You can be sure, however, that if you do find a reinforcer, the behavior will occur more often.

The second tactic is to decrease undesirable behaviors through <u>extinction</u>. If the problem is that an undesirable behavior is occurring too often, all you have to do is identify the reinforcer and remove it. Very often the reinforcer will be the ill-advised attention of yourself or others to that behavior. You can be sure that this approach will work if you can find and remove all the reinforcers for the undesired behavior. However, often the reinforcers are controlled by other people, who will not stop delivering them, or by the physical world. Drugs like alcohol and nicotine are always going to produce potentially reinforcing effects. As long as the person can get them, you can't stop those effects.

The third tactic is to increase a desirable behavior relative to undesirable behavior through differential reinforcement. If the problem is more complex than a single desirable or undesirable behavior, you may need to use this tactic. You reinforce the desirable behavior at the same time as you extinguish the undesirable behavior. For this tactic to work, you must find an effective reinforcer for the desirable behavior, and you must also identify and stop the reinforcers for the undesirable behaviors. If you can do both parts of the tactic, you can be sure that the desirable behavior will increase in rate compared to the undesirable behavior.

The fourth tactic is to create new behavior through shaping. If the problem is the total absence of a desirable behavior, you will never get a chance to reinforce the behavior. The solution is differential reinforcement of an approximation to the desired target behavior. You then define successive approximations to that target behavior and continue differentially reinforcing them until you reach the desired behavior. You must find workable successive approximations, as well as reinforcers for them. If you do, you will be able to shape the new behavior.

The fifth tactic is to use the principles of reinforcer effectiveness. If the problem is that the reinforcer is simply not doing the job, one possibility is that you are not using it in an effective manner. To do so, you must ensure that the reinforcer is delivered contingent on the desired behavior, that it is delivered immediately, that the amount of the reinforcer is worthwhile, and that delivery of the reinforcer is rare enough to maintain interest. If you use these principles, your reinforcer should work.

The sixth tactic is to increase response rate with a ratio schedule of reinforcement. If the problem requires more behavior per reinforcement, you can deliver fewer reinforcers per response. With ratio schedules, you deliver the reinforcer after you have counted some number of responses. The fixed-ratio schedule will produce a pause after reinforcement and then a high rate of responding. The variable-ratio schedule will produce a high and steady rate of responding. The drawbacks of these schedules are that they may lead to ratio strain and that they are not suitable for shaping.

The seventh tactic is to reduce reinforcer frequency with an interval schedule of reinforcement. If the reinforcer occurs on a time basis, you will have to use this schedule. The fixed-interval schedule produces a scalloped pattern of responding. The variable-interval schedule produces a uniform but moderate rate of responding.

These seven tactics provide you with many tools to solve human problems. If the problem stems from inadequate or misplaced reinforcement, one or more of these tactics should be able to solve it.

You may find that the behavioral problem is too complex to solve with these tools. For example, the problem may be that the desired behavior does not occur in the proper circumstances. The infant may say "Dada" to all males, not just its father. People may not follow instructions very well even though they are capable of doing so. Someone may reinforce undesired behaviors. These problems involve what behavior analysts call *stimulus control*. You will learn the stimulus control strategy in the next unit.

You may find that the behavioral problem presents dangers that must be eliminated more quickly than is possible with reinforcement procedures. You would then turn to the use of punishment. You will learn about this in Unit Four, which presents the aversive control strategy.

If the behavioral strategy does not work, you can try the reinforcement strategy. If that doesn't work, then you can try the stimulus control strategy. If that doesn't work, then you can try the aversive control strategy as a last resort.

The Ethics of Reinforcement

You need not manipulate others to use reinforcement. You can use reinforcement to change your own behavior. Usually you should arrange the program through a second person. Otherwise, you might find it more immediately reinforcing simply to adjust the rules for giving yourself reinforcement rather than changing your behavior. Democratic groups can also use reinforcement to establish a successful social system.

To be sure, reinforcement can be used to manipulate others. For instance, suppose someone will not voluntarily change a behavior that is annoying to you. You are then faced with a decision. You can tolerate the behavior, avoid the person, leave the situation, or attempt to modify the behavior. Or suppose an enemy tries to control your behavior. By understanding the principles of reinforcement, you have a better chance of not being controlled.

Reinforcement always involves the problem of *countercontrol*. Countercontrol occurs when one person resists the control of another person. For example, if the owner of a factory uses reinforcement principles to make workers work harder and faster, how can workers fight that control? The traditional tool of the worker has been the labor union, but unions are sometimes weak and incapable of resisting the control of owners. One possibility is that workers might use behavioral principles to develop a stronger resistance. Thus, a knowledge of behavioral principles can potentially help any group resist control by another group (Skinner, 1953b).

Behavior analysis is not manipulative; people are manipulative. Reinforcement is simply a tool. People and groups can use it to modify their social environment. Using it, they may be able to create a happier and more productive life.

Summary

Sometimes people use reinforcement to help others. At other times, they misuse it to harm others, usually by accident. Reinforcement is involved in everything we do. It works in all ages and cultures, and with all behaviors—from obvious to private. Six tactics will help you design a successful program. Specify the target behavior. Discover a reinforcer. Use the principles of effectiveness. Shape new behavior. Select a schedule. Evaluate the result. Reinforcement is not in itself good or bad.

Helpful Hints

Helpful Hint #1

In past lessons, I have introduced helper words that help you know which group of terms I am selecting from. I have used the word *methods* to refer to the methods of observation, the term *designs* to refer to experimental designs, and the word *procedures* to refer to the ways of increasing or decreasing the rate of a behavior (e.g., reinforcement). I have used the term *principles* to refer to the principles of effective reinforcement and the word *schedules* to refer to the generic schedules and the specific ratio and interval schedules. Be sure to notice when I start a question with a phrase like "What principle?" You can narrow the concepts that you must consider to answer the question. Be sure to notice whether a question contains a helper term such as *principle*, *procedure*, *method*, or *schedule*.

5. If the question asks for a method, which of the following terms might be the correct answer: (a) fixed-interval, (b) reinforcement, or (c) interval recording? ________

Helpful Hint #2

The definitions of all terms introduced in this unit of the book are presented in the following glossary. You can review the unit and prepare for your exam by testing yourself on the definitions and related facts presented for each term. You might use a piece of paper as a mask and leave only the term exposed; see if you can formulate a reasonable definition and remember any other important facts about that term. Then move the mask and check on yourself.

Glossary

A (successive) **approximation** is any behavior similar to a target behavior; it is usually one of a series of behaviors differentially reinforced in a program of shaping toward the goal of producing the target behavior.

Continuous reinforcement is a schedule of reinforcement in which every response is reinforced.

- This schedule is usually used when a person is first learning a behavior, particularly in shaping procedures.

Deprivation is the frequency with which a person has received a particular reinforcer in the recent past—the less frequent the reinforcer, the more deprived the person is.

Differential reinforcement involves two or more physically different behaviors. One behavior is reinforced, and all others are extinguished.

Extinction is the procedure by which an event that followed a behavior in the past is stopped, and probability (or rate) of the behavior decreases.
- An extinction burst is a temporary increase in responding as soon as extinction begins.

In a **fixed-interval** schedule, a person is reinforced for the first response after a fixed period of time has passed since the previous reinforcement.
- This schedule usually produces a scallop pattern of responding, in which people tend to pause after a reinforcer and then gradually increase their response rate until they are working at a high rate at the moment they receive the next reinforcer.

In a **fixed-ratio** schedule, people are reinforced for making a response only after they have made a fixed number of those responses without reinforcement.
- This schedule usually produces a stair-step pattern, in which people pause after reinforcement and then work at a very high rate until the next reinforcer.
- The overall rate is higher than with continuous reinforcement but lower than with a variable-ratio schedule.

Intermittent reinforcement applies to schedules of reinforcement in which only some responses are reinforced; ratio and interval schedules are common examples.
- A person trained on an intermittent schedule of reinforcement will have greater resistance to extinction, as he or she will continue making a response during extinction for a longer period of time than a person trained on a continuous schedule.
- Intermittent reinforcement also produces more responding for fewer reinforcers, thus reducing the problem of satiation.

The **principle of contingency** states that a reinforcer will be maximally effective if the reinforcer is delivered only when the desired behavior has occurred.
- To decide whether this principle has been followed, ask the question, "Was the reinforcer given only when the desired behavior occurred?"

The **principle of deprivation** states that the more deprived a person is of a certain reinforcer, the more effective that reinforcer will be.
- To decide whether the principle has been followed, ask "Has the reinforcer rarely been delivered?"

The **principle of immediacy** states that the more immediate the delivery of the reinforcer after the occurrence of the behavior, the more effective the reinforcer will be.
- To decide whether this principle has been followed, ask the question, "Was the reinforcer delivered within one minute of the behavior (or while the behavior was still occurring)?"

The **principle of size** states that you must give a worthwile amount of any single reinforcer for it to be effective.
- To decide whether the principle has been followed, ask the question, "Was the amount of reinforcement worthwhile?"

Ratio strain refers to the fact that a behavior that is seldom reinforced (for instance, once every 1000 responses) may slow or stop altogether.

A **reinforcer** is any event that follows a behavior and increases the probability (or rate) of that behavior.

Reinforcement is the procedure of using a reinforcer to increase the rate of a behavior.

The **reinforcement strategy** consists of seven tactics:
1. Increase desirable behavior through reinforcement.
2. Decrease undesirable behavior through extinction.
3. Increase a desirable behavior relative to undesirable behavior through differential reinforcement.
4. Create new behavior through shaping.
5. Use the principles of reinforcer effectiveness.
6. Increase response rate with a ratio schedule.
7. Reduce reinforcer frequency with an interval schedule.

Satiation is the opposite of deprivation. The more frequently a person has received a particular reinforcer in the recent past, the more satiated he or she is.

Shaping is the use of differential reinforcement on a series of successive approximations to a target behavior.

A **target behavior** is the ultimate goal of a program of shaping.

Unknown is the term used in this book to describe a behavioral procedure or event for which a name and definition have not yet been taught.
- Any instruction occurring prior to the behavior.
- Any attempt to use a method that is unsuccessful.
- A situation in which a person is reinforced for emitting a behavior in one situation and extinguished for emitting the same behavior in another situation.

In a **variable-interval** schedule, a person is reinforced for the first response after a varying period of time has passed since the previous reinforcement.
- This schedule usually causes a person to respond at a uniform rate.

In a **variable-ratio** schedule, people are reinforced only after making a varying number of responses.
- This schedule usually causes people to work at a high and uniform rate of speed.
- It produces the highest rate of responding of the simple schedules.

Additional Readings

Wheeler, H. (Ed.). (1973). *Beyond the punitive society*. San Francisco: W. H. Freeman. This book is a collection of writings by economists, philosophers, and social scientists on the social and political aspects of behavior analysis.

Practice Review

The following material has questions on every concept studied in Unit Two, as well as review questions from Unit One. By answering the questions and checking your answers, you can prepare yourself for the Review Exam, which will contain questions from both units.

57. Review: To use the reinforcement strategy to solve human problems: (1) Increase desirable behaviors through reinforcement. (2) Decrease undesirable behaviors through extinction. (3) Increase a desirable behavior relative to undesirable behavior through differential reinforcement. (4) Create new behaviors through shaping. (5) Use the principles of reinforcer effectiveness. (6) Increase response rate with a ratio schedule. (7) Reduce reinforcer frequency with a(n) ______________ schedule.
8. From Helpful Hint #1: Be sure to notice whether a question has a helper term in it like *principle, procedure, method*, or *schedule*. If the question asks for a method, which of the following terms might be the correct answer: fixed-interval, reinforcement, or interval (as in interval recording)? ______________
23. Review: An event that follows a behavior and leads to no change in the rate of that behavior is always called a(n) ______________.
68. The record of a behavior prior to the treatment is called the ______________.
10. Here is a question that most students have repeatedly gotten wrong earlier in the book, as well as in this review. Think long and hard about this one. Ask the questions that help you decide whether it is what you think it is. If a person is reinforced for emitting a behavior in one situation and is extinguished for emitting it in another situation, his or her behavior is being modified by what behavioral procedure? ______________
50. Review: Pam told the other members of her sorority that they were far too interested in material things like clothes, money, and cars. At first her sisters ignored her, but later they started arguing with her. As a result, her rate of making such comments increased. Her sisters' arguments as events would be called ______________.
6. Compute the reliability of these two observations:

Observer 1:	X	O	X	O	O	O	O	O	X
Observer 2:	O	O	X	O	O	O	O	O	X

Reliability: ______________ percent. Is it acceptable? ____________

35. Review: If a behavior produces a reinforcer every second time it occurs, the behavior is said to be reinforced on a(n) ____________ ____________ schedule. (Name the specific schedule.)
54. Review: The behavioral procedure of extinction is being used if the delivery of a reinforcing event is ____________ and the rate of the behavior ____________.
40. Review: If people are reinforced only when they emit a specified behavior, which principle of reinforcer effectiveness is being followed? The principle of ______________
26. Review: Ben and Sue were building up their endurance for the disco marathon. They began by setting the goal of dancing continuously for 3 hours. When they got so they could do that, they set their goal at 4 hours. They were aiming for 35 hours. Dancing for 3 hours straight is called a(n) ______________ ____________ to dancing for 35 hours.
80. To use the reinforcement strategy to solve human problems: (5) Use the principles of reinforcer ______________.
47. Review: Jaime and Pedro had trouble getting along even though they were brothers. Jaime kept teasing Pedro, who would get upset and cry. One day, Pedro realized that his brother was simply trying to get him to cry. So he decided he would never again cry when he was teased. Jaime teased Pedro just as often. What behavioral procedure did Pedro use on Jaime? ______________
61. Review: What specific schedule of reinforcement produces the highest average rate of responding? ______________
27. Review: Ben and Sue were building up their endurance for the dancing marathon. They began by setting the goal of dancing for 3 hours. When they could do that, they set their goal at 4 hours. They were aiming at 35 hours. Dancing for 35 hours would be called the ______________.
84. What two intermittent schedules produce a uniform rate of responding rather than pausing and then responding? ______________ and ______________
74. To use the reinforcement strategy to solve human problems: (4) create new behaviors through ______________.
67. The overall name for any of the many procedures (such as reinforcement, extinction, or shaping) used in an experiment to either increase or decrease a given behavior is a(n) ______________.
25. Review: Behaviors that successively approximate a target behavior are differentially reinforced in the procedure called ____________.
48. Review: One factor that increases the effectiveness of a reinforcer is having the reinforcer occur as soon as possible after a response has been made. This is called the principle of ______________.
12. Interval recording involves observing a behavior during a series of continuous intervals. Time sample recording, on the other hand, involves observing a behavior during a series of ______________ intervals.
64. Sarge decided to find out once and for all how often Beetle was asleep. So he observed "the amount of time that Beetle did not move—whether or not his eyes were open." The words in quotes are called a(n) ______________.
65. Suppose someone fails to do something that he or she has agreed to do. If you then tell the person to do it and he or she does, what behavioral procedure are you using? ____________
51. Review: Sam's teacher tried to come by his desk after different periods of time to see if he was working on his spelling lesson. If it was reinforcing for Sam to be found working, what schedule was his studying on? ____________ ______________
38. Review: If one behavior is extinguished and another behavior is reinforced, we say that the procedure of ______________ is being used.
15. John was interested in finding out whether he would get more compliments if he reinforced compliments that he got. He observed the rate of compliments that he got for several weeks when he did not reinforce them. He then started reinforcing compliments from Mary, while still not reinforcing them from Bev. After two more weeks, he started reinforcing them from Bev also. He found large increases after he had started using reinforcement. What experimental design did he use? ______________ design
28. Review: Bernie told Professor Jacobs that he studied so hard in sociology because he was terribly interested in social problems, al-

though he had never explained it that way before. The professor nodded in agreement and then spent a long time discussing social problems with Bernie. After that, Bernie always explained his extensive studying of sociology as resulting from his interest in it. What behavioral procedure did the professor use (probably without realizing it) to increase Bernie's rate of explaining his studying as resulting from a strong interest in sociology? ______________

36. Review: If a person is reinforced after differing numbers of responses, he or she is on a(n) ______________ schedule of reinforcement.
85. Review: To determine whether the principle of deprivation was followed, ask "Has the reinforcer ________ been delivered?"
82. Two observers counted the number of times Fearsome Freddy hit another child. Observer 1 counted 15 hits, while Observer 2 counted 20 hits. Compute their reliability: ________ percent. Is this acceptable if it is a new definition? ________
13. Interval recording involves dividing the observation period into a series of ________ ________ time intervals.
46. Review: Intermittent schedules of reinforcement reduce the probability of satiation and create a greater resistance to ________ than do continuous schedules.
69. The science of behavior analysis examines ______________ events that ______________ behavior.
75. To use the reinforcement strategy to solve human problems: (6) Increase response rate with a(n) ______________ schedule.
14. John counted the number of times Professor Brainbuster said the word *orthogonal*, because he was interested in the professor's tendency to use big words that his students did not understand. What method of observation was he using? ______________ recording
39. Review: If only some responses are reinforced, the behavior is said to be on the generic schedule called a(n) ______________ schedule of reinforcement.
1. Alice was a third-grader who liked to take long bike rides after school. Her father worried about this, particularly after Alice described how she almost got run over by a heavy truck. He therefore told her to come straight home after school. She started coming straight home after that. What behavioral procedure did her father use to increase her rate of coming right home? ______________
5. Claire was interested in whether ignoring complaining behavior would reduce it. She observed the rate of complaints uttered by Bill for three weeks, during which she tried to appear sympathetic. She then totally ignored complaints for three weeks. Finally, she again appeared sympathetic to his complaints for three weeks. She noted a substantial drop during the time when she ignored them. What experimental design was she using? ________ design
29. Review: Dave found that he could get a date for dancing if he asked enough single women outside the discoteque. Sometimes the first woman he asked agreed to go dancing; at other times, he asked as many as 30 before having success. What schedule of reinforcement is his date-asking behavior on? ______________ ______________
59. Review: What schedule of reinforcement produces a stair-step pattern, with a pause after reinforcement and then very rapid responding until the next reinforcement? ________ ______________
33. Review: If a behavior is reinforced every time it occurs, what generic schedule of reinforcement is it on? ______________
76. To use the reinforcement strategy to solve human problems, (1) increase desirable behaviors through ______________.
21. Professor Clark wanted her students to turn in a two-page essay every Friday, so for the first part of the semester she reminded them every Thursday to hand in an essay by Friday. Midway through the semester, she stopped reminding them, and to her surprise they stopped handing them in on time. What behavioral procedure did she use to decrease their rate of handing their essays in on time? ______________ (Think about this one!)
63. Review: Willa helped her friend Sarah learn to be more assertive by providing her with feedback during parties. Anytime Sarah was properly assertive, Willa nodded her head so Sarah could see. She nodded her head immediately after Sarah was assertive and only when she was assertive. Sarah seemed to like the nods and certainly never got too many

nods from Willa. What principle of reinforcement, if any, did Willa neglect in her procedure? ______

22. Review: An event is called a reinforcer only if it is timed to ______ a behavior and also ______ the rate of the behavior.
72. The use of outside judges to determine whether a definition is valid is called investigating its ______.
49. Review: One way to increase the effectiveness of a reinforcer is to make sure the person doesn't receive any of that type of reinforcer for a long time. This technique involves the principle of ______.
45. Review: In Unit 1, you learned the ______ strategy for solving human problems. In Unit 2, you learned the ______ strategy.
30. Review: Differential reinforcement involves two basic behavioral procedures. They are ______ and ______.
34. Review: If a behavior becomes erratic, or even stops, after it has been placed on a very high ratio of responses to reinforcers, we say that ______ has occurred.
19. One experimental design involves determining the effect of a treatment on two or more behaviors at different times. This is called a(n) ______ design.
44. Review: If you stop telling someone to do something and he or she stops, what behavioral procedure is this an example of? ______
73. Time sample recording involves observing whether a behavior is occurring during each of a series of ______ intervals.
81. Two intermittent schedules of reinforcement that produce a high rate of responding prior to reinforcement and a pause just after reinforcement are the ______ and ______ schedules.
11. If an event that usually follows a behavior is stopped and there is no change in the rate, the procedure involved is ______.
70. The term we use to refer to the procedure of delivering an event following a behavior that will increase the rate of the behavior is ______. The term that is used to refer to the event itself is ______.
56. Review: The swallows come back to Capistrano on exactly March 21 every year. Mr. Peterson watches all year round for their return. What schedule of reinforcement is his swallow-watching behavior on? ______
62. Review: When Damon was first learning to play ping-pong, he hit many shots too hard. Those shots didn't hit the table. He also hit a few shots softly, and those shots hit the table. If the rate of hard shooting decreased while the rate of soft shooting increased, what behavioral procedure would this be an example of? ______
71. The use of a second observer to determine whether your observations are in agreement is called ______. The use of outside judges to determine whether your definition is in agreement with theirs is called ______.
37. Review: If a person is reinforced for many responses in a row, the effectiveness of the reinforcer may decrease because the person has been ______ with respect to that reinforcer.
9. Harvey (the con man) Miller once told Jim a fantastic story about how he could arrange for Jim to buy a small jet airplane worth $100,000 for only $5000 if he could just get the money the same day. Jim believed him and got the money. Naturally, Harvey took the money and left town, never to be heard from again. He told many such stories to other suckers from then on. The money is clearly a(n) ______ for Harvey's con jobs.
77. To use the reinforcement strategy to solve human problems: (3) increase a desirable behavior relative to undesirable behavior through ______.
32. Review: Fran tried to increase the amount of study time put in by her daughter Melanie. She looked in on Melanie often and gave her a snack at bedtime if she had been studying more than a half hour. She gave her a snack only if she was sure that Melanie had been studying all that time. Melanie loved the snack and never seemed to get too much of it, but she didn't increase her studying. What principle of effective reinforcement, if any, did Fran fail to employ? ______
55. Review: The principle of size states that you must give a worthwhile ______ of a reinforcer.

24. Review: At first, little Janie called everyone "Mama." But her parents hugged and petted her when she called her mother "Mama" and ignored her when she called anyone else "Mama." Gradually, Janie called only her mother "Mama." What behavioral procedure did her parents use to teach her to call only her mother by the name "Mama"? ______________________________ (Warning: Most students get this wrong, so ask the questions.)
18. Mr. Davis helped his daughter with her homework by checking her work after every seven problems. If having her homework checked is a reinforcer, what schedule is doing homework on? ______________________
3. At the Freedom Food Co-op, the bookkeeper's work was observed by auditing his books. Assuming his entries in the books are the results of the behavior of interest, what method of observation is this? ______________ recording
83. What generic schedule of reinforcement should be used when shaping a new response? ______________
16. Les had long regretted that he was so distant from his parents. He had tried talking with them about the problem to no avail. He decided to give them a really nice compliment anytime they shared something intimate with him. Their rate of intimacy did not change. What behavioral procedure was Les using? ______________________
41. Review: If the old reinforcer for a behavior is no longer delivered, and the rate of the behavior decreases, what generic schedule is the behavior on? ______________
42. Review: If you reinforce the first response that occurs after varying periods of time, the behavior is on a(n) ______________________ schedule.
17. Most researchers aim for a reliability figure that is ________ percent.
31. Review: Differential reinforcement involves two or more physically ___________ behaviors.
78. To use the reinforcement strategy to solve human problems, (7) reduce reinforcer frequency with a(n) ______________________ schedule.
2. At first, Kevin liked to have Alice hang around him all the time, and he always tried to be friendly. Finally, however, it got to be a drag, so he stopped being friendly to her. To his surprise, she kept hanging around him anyway. What behavioral procedure was Kevin using to try to decrease Alice's hanging around? ______________________
7. Computing the agreement between two independent observations results in a measure of the ______________________ of the observers.
60. Review: What schedule of reinforcement produces very rapid and uniform responding? ______________________
58. Review: Wanda rarely did any work at the Freedom Food Co-op. If you worked at the Co-op, your hours were immediately recorded on the bulletin board; if you had five hours a month, you could buy food at the wholesale price. Wanda needed the financial savings and could never get enough money. However, anyone could just write up the number of hours he or she worked, and many people cheated. Wanda found that she could work an hour and record five hours. What principle of effectiveness was at work weakening the privilege of buying at wholesale as a reinforcer for working for the Co-op? ______________
66. Suppose you wanted to engineer a classroom in which ghetto children learned basic skills more effectively. If they didn't possess those skills at all, you might find some skills they did possess that were related to your target skills. You could then differentially reinforce these simpler skills and gradually progress to the more difficult skills. This behavioral procedure would be called ______________ the complex skills.
43. Review: If you reinforce the first response that occurs after a fixed amount of time has passed, you are following a(n) ______________ schedule.
20. One experimental design involves studying a behavior before the treatment has been introduced and while the treatment is in effect. Such a single-subject design is called a(n) ______________________ design.
52. Review: Shaping involves the differential reinforcement of a series of behaviors that are ______________________ to a target behavior.
53. Review: Shaping involves the differential reinforcement of a series of behaviors that are successive approximations to a(n) ____________ ______________________.

4. Can you name all of the tactics based on the reinforcement strategy to solve human problems? (1) Increase desirable behaviors through ________________. (2) Decrease undesirable behaviors through ________________. (3) Increase a desirable behavior relative to undesirable behavior through ________________. (4) Create new behavior through ________________. (5) Use the principles of ________________ (6) Increase response rate with a(n) ________________ schedule. (7) Reduce reinforcer frequency with a(n) ________________ schedule.

79. To use the reinforcement strategy to solve human problems, (2) decrease undesirable behaviors through ________________.

UNIT 3

The Stimulus Control Strategy

LESSON

16 Stimulus Discrimination and Everyday Behavior

Introduction to Unit Three

This unit looks at the principles of how stimulus situations affect behavior. These principles govern the development and maintenance of stimulus control. What is stimulus control? Let me contrast it with another major factor controlling behavior. In Unit Two, you learned that reinforcement control is the increase in behaviors from an event that follows the behavior. By contrast, stimulus control is the increase in behavior from an event that precedes the behavior. Some events that might precede a behavior and influence the person's behavior include questions, commands, the sight of a person or object, or being present in a room or at a football game. Behavior analysts call the effect of such events on behavior *stimulus control*. Sidman suggests that the term *cognitive* refers to behavior under stimulus control (Sidman, 1978).

The emphasis in this unit changes from looking at what happens after you behave—reinforcement or extinction—to looking at what happens before you behave. The concept of stimulus is central. A **stimulus** is any physical event, or object, related to a person's behavior. The plural of *stimulus* is *stimuli*. Stimuli might be objects such as doors, windows, other people, parts of one's own body, clothing, or hair. They might be vocal sounds such as words, sighs, or laughter, or visible configurations such as words on a page, colors, length, and width. The term also refers to broader situations such as an entire room. In that case, we then often use the term *stimulus situation*. As you can see from this definition, reinforcers are also stimuli. A reinforcing stimulus is one that follows a behavior. This unit will deal primarily with stimuli that precede a behavior.

2. A stimulus is any physical event, or object, related to a person's ______________.

This unit deals with how people learn to behave in ways that work for their current stimulus situation. The lessons in this unit teach concepts relating to the influence of the stimulus situation on behavior. This lesson deals with distinguishing among different situations, a process known as *discrimination*. The next lesson deals with grouping similar situations into general categories, a process known as *generalization*. Future lessons deal with simple aspects of verbal behavior. In general, this unit describes a behavioral approach to intellectual behavior.

Stimulus control is present in everyday situations. By understanding stimulus control, you can better understand your own behavior as well as that of friends, family, and coworkers.

Behavior analysts use stimulus control to solve people's problems. They turn to it when the behavioral strategy and the reinforcement strategy aren't enough. Behavior analysts may be able to define the problem in behavioral terms and differentially reinforce desirable behavior, but the behavior may not occur in the appropriate situa-

Behavioral Approach to Cognition

"Behavior under stimulus control is essentially the field of cognition.... Terms like cognition or knowledge refer to the control of behavior by its environmental context, by events which, unlike consequences, precede or accompany the behavior; here, it is sometimes said that our behavior expresses meaning or comprehension" (Sidman, 1978: p. 265).

1. The field of cognition involves behavior under ______________ (reinforcement, stimulus) control.

tions. They may then turn to the stimulus control strategy. I have placed the unit on stimulus control third to suggest that behavior analysts turn first to the other strategies.

This unit will describe five tactics in using the stimulus control strategy. They include using discrimination and generalization training; fading and programming; imitation and instruction; and conditioned or generalized reinforcers. This lesson introduces Tactic #1, using discrimination training. The first tactic in using the stimulus control strategy is to narrow stimulus control through discrimination training.

3. The first tactic in using the stimulus control strategy is to narrow stimulus control through ______________ training.

Discrimination Training

People act differently in the presence of different stimulus situations. They act differently toward the friendly professor than they do toward the pompous one, differently in a library than in a car, and differently when driving toward a red light than toward a green light. There is a basic process at work in developing these behavioral differences. The process involves reinforcement of a behavior in the presence of one stimulus and extinction of the same behavior in the presence of another stimulus. Behavior analysts call this procedure *discrimination training*.

Discrimination training consists of reinforcing a behavior in the presence of a particular stimulus and extinguishing it in the presence of another stimulus. Examples of discrimination training in everyday life are common. Consider the story of Sam, a professor's 6-year-old son. Sam visits his Mom in the large campus building where she teaches. He often leaves without his Mom so he can get home for dinner. How did he learn to get out of the building? Each time Sam went through a door with the sign "Exit" over it, he got out. Each time he went through doors marked with signs such as "Women," "Library," or "223," he did not. He soon learned to look for doors with "Exit" signs over them. In this example, Sam's response of going through doors with an "Exit" sign was reinforced by getting out. His response of going through other doors was extinguished. Therefore, this is an example of discrimination training.

4. Discrimination training consists of ______________ a behavior in the presence of a particular stimulus and ______________ it in the presence of another stimulus.

Behavior analysts call the stimulus associated with reinforcement the *discriminative stimulus*. They abbreviate it SD. The D stands for *discriminative* and the S stands for *stimulus*. A **discriminative stimulus** (or SD) is a stimulus in whose presence a particular behavior produces reinforcement. For example, the sign "Exit" indicates that the behavior of going through the door will be reinforced by getting out of the building.

5. A stimulus in whose presence the behavior produces reinforcement is called a ______________ ______________.

Behavior analysts call the stimulus associated with extinction the *S-delta*. An **S-delta** is a stimulus in whose presence the behavior will be extinguished. For example, the sign "Library" would indicate that the behavior of going through that door will not be reinforced by getting out of the building.

6. A stimulus in whose presence the behavior will be extinguished is called the ______________.

If discrimination training is successful, it will cause a behavior to occur more frequently in the presence of the SD than in the presence of the S-deltas. Behavior analysts call that behavior *discriminated behavior*. **Discriminated behavior** is a behavior that is more likely to occur in the presence of the SD than in the presence of the S-delta. Sam's behavior of going through doors marked "Exit" is discriminated behavior. Before he learned to go through exit doors, his behavior was not discriminated behavior. We would call a single instance of the behavior a *discriminated response*. Thus, when Sam went through the exit door last Sunday, he made a discriminated response.

7. A behavior that is more likely to occur in the presence of the SD than in the presence of the S-delta is called a ______________ behavior.

Behavior analysts refer to the effect of the SD on the behavior as *stimulus control*. **Stimulus**

control is the increased probability of a discriminated behavior produced by a stimulus (SD). Thus, behavior analysts call the increased probability that Sam will go through a door marked "Exit" *stimulus control*. The "Exit" sign literally controls his behavior. We usually say that the stimulus exerts stimulus control over the behavior.

8. Stimulus control is the increased probability of a discriminated behavior produced by a ________________.

Thus, if you wish to refer to the behavior that results from discrimination training, you would designate it as discriminated behavior. A single instance of the behavior is a discriminated response. If you wish to talk about the effect of the stimulus involved in discrimination training, you would call it stimulus control.

Simple Examples of Discrimination Training

Many everyday examples of discrimination training are easy to analyze. For example, history teachers use discrimination training to increase the probability of their students giving the correct answers. They will reinforce students for answering, "December 7, 1941" when asked, "When did the Japanese bomb Pearl Harbor?" However, they will attempt to extinguish that response when asking, "When did the Japanese formally surrender in World War II?" Behavior analysts call the question "When did the Japanese bomb Pearl Harbor?" the discriminative stimulus (SD), or cue, for "December 7, 1941." They call most other questions the S-delta for that response. They call the correct answer a discriminated behavior. If a student is more likely to answer "December 7, 1941" in response to the question, they say that the question exerts stimulus control over that answer.

Here are some other simple examples based on discrimination training. You might learn to call the blonde person "Laverne" but not the brunette person. The blonde person reinforces you by looking at you when you call her Laverne. She is a discriminative stimulus, or SD, for that name, because she will reinforce you for calling her by that name. The brunette person ignores you if you call her Laverne. She is an S-delta for that name, because she will extinguish you if you call her Laverne. When you learn the difference, your use of "Laverne" is a discriminated response. Your increased probability of calling the blonde person "Laverne" is called *stimulus control*. You might say that the blonde person exerts stimulus control over your use of her name.

You might learn to yell at a football game but not in a library. Other people join you when you yell at the football game but not when you yell in the library. If having others yell with you is reinforcing, then what would you call the stimulus situation of the football game? You would call it an SD, because yelling is reinforced at the game. If having others not yell with you is extinguishing, what would you call the stimulus situation of the library? You would call it an S-delta, because yelling is extinguished in the library. Thus, the library is the S-delta, and the game is the SD. What would you call the process of having yells reinforced at the game and extinguished in the library? It is discrimination training, because yelling is reinforced at the game and extinguished in the library. What would you call the effect of being at the game on your probability of yelling? It is stimulus control. What would you call the behavior of yelling? It is discriminated behavior, because it is more likely to occur at the game than in the library.

Suppose that the question, "What is 9x9?" has come to exert stimulus control over your behavior. That means that you are more likely to answer "81" when the teacher asks you that question than when she asks you another question. Other questions, such as "What is 8x8?", will serve as S-deltas for that answer. You will be less likely to answer "81" when asked, "What is 8x8?" The answer has become a discriminated behavior. Presumably this happens because the teacher uses a form of discrimination training to teach you the difference. She may smile and say, "That's right" when you answer "81" to "What is 9x9?" but not when you answer "81" to "What is 8x8?"

These examples share two basic components. First, the training is for only one behavior (saying "Laverne," yelling, or answering "81"). Second, the behavior is reinforced in the presence of only one stimulus situation (the blonde person, a football game, or "What is 9x9?"). It is not reinforced in the presence of other stimulus situations (brunette persons, libraries, or other questions).

You may feel a bit overwhelmed by all the new

terminology that I have introduced. I have done so because I need the new terms to talk about the elements of discrimination training. I need to talk about the behavior that results from discrimination training. You know by now that behavior analysts call the resulting behavior *discriminated behavior*. I also need to talk about the stimulus associated with reinforcement for the discriminated behavior. You know by now that behavior analysts call the stimulus associated with reinforcement the *discriminative stimulus*. But it is easier just to call it the SD. I also need to talk about the stimulus associated with extinction for the discriminated behavior, which behavior analysts call the S-delta. Finally, I need to talk about the whole process by which some stimuli increase the probability of certain behaviors. Behavior analysts call that increased probability *stimulus control*. I need each term. So hang in there; you will soon find using them as natural as using *reinforcement* and *extinction*.

Sometimes you may be tempted to confuse the behavior with the stimulus. For example, reading Freud's *Interpretation of Dreams* may seem like a different behavior from reading Skinner's *Walden Two*. However, reading is the same behavior, no matter what you read. You hold a book open, look at the page, and move your eyes to the next word or phrase. Therefore, learning to read historical novels instead of science fiction is an example of developing a discriminated behavior. Reading behavior is occurring in the presence of one kind of book but not the other. The same analysis applies to watching TV or movies. The same looking behavior occurs in the presence of different stimulus situations.

Realistic Examples of Discrimination Training

Discrimination training is usually more complex than the preceding examples imply. It usually involves some modification of the stimuli. Suppose you show Nan two pictures: The one on the right is a cat, and the one on the left is a dog. If you always ask Nan to point to the cat, all she has to remember is to point to the picture on the right. She doesn't even have to look at it. However, if you switch the sides on which the cat and dog appear, Nan must look at the pictures to point to the cat. Even simple discrimination training requires that you switch the order of the stimuli.

Discrimination training usually involves more than switching the order of the stimuli. It usually involves learning multiple discriminations at the same time. For example, the teacher wants you to answer "81" to "What is 9x9?" But she wants you to do more than *not* answer "81" to the other question. She wants you to give the correct answer to every question. You learn the whole times table, not just one correct answer. Likewise, you not only learn the blonde person's name; you also learn other people's names. Similarly, you not only learn not to yell in the library; you learn what to do there.

One study provides a behavior analysis example. Two researchers taught a 4-year-old child to discriminate four industrial objects (Mann & Baer, 1971). The researchers named one object and asked the child to point to it. When correct, the child earned chips that could later be exchanged for a toy. When wrong, the child lost a chip. The researchers did not repeatedly name one object. Rather, they randomly named each of the four objects. Thus, the child was learning the name of four objects rather than just one, undergoing four discrimination training programs at the same time. When the researchers named object #1, it became an SD for that name. But it was also an S-delta for the other three names. Thus, this training situation was no longer a simple discrimination training procedure. Even so, the child learned the four discriminations in about 300 trials.

Researchers have used similar methods to teach other discriminations. They have taught 4-year-old children to discriminate letters (Tawney, 1972). They have taught teachers to discriminate correct use of behavior analysis in their teaching (Koegel, Russo, & Rincover, 1977). They have taught baseball players to discriminate curveballs and thus hit them better (Osborne, Rudrud, & Zezoney, 1990). They have even taught individuals with severe retardation to discriminate complex forms (Rodgers & Iwata, 1991). In each case, the researchers taught multiple discriminations at the same time.

Two researchers taught male trainees to discriminate females' level of interest (Azrin & Hayes, 1984). They trained the males with films of couples conversing. They might show a conversation where the female later said she was "very interested." They asked the trainee to guess her level of inter-

Helping Batters Discriminate Curveballs

Researchers guessed that a batter must discriminate the spin of a pitched baseball for effective batting. Seeing the spin allows batters to adjust the speed and location of their swing. "Different types of pitches have differing rates and directions of spin. A curveball spins in a downward direction. . . . A batter must decide whether or not to swing within 0.13 seconds after the delivery of the pitch." The researchers taught hitters to discriminate the spin on a curveball by adding ¼-inch-wide orange highlighting to the seams of the ball. This made it easier for the hitters to see the spin on the ball. The percentage of well-hit curveballs increased from about 40% to about 50% with the addition of the orange highlighting. (Based on Osborne, Rudrud, & Zezoney, 1990.)

9. When a batter adjusts his or her swing depending on the spin of the ball, we say that the spin is exerting ______________ (reinforcement, stimulus) control.

est and then informed him of her true level of interest. Presumably, if the trainee guessed "very interested," the feedback that she was indeed very interested would reinforce his guess. If he guessed "uninterested," the feedback that she was very interested would extinguish his guess. The training consisted of 24 conversations. The trainees improved in the accuracy of their guesses by 50% as a result of the feedback. They thus became more socially sensitive. Using the new terminology, you could say that this sensitivity has become discriminated behavior. The subtle cues of the females were now exerting stimulus control over the males' guesses about the females' level of interest.

Researchers have taught several health-related discriminations. One researcher taught a woman to discriminate the temperature of her hand (Gainer, 1978). A lower temperature is a warning of an impending migraine headache. This training led to a marked reduction in migraine headaches. Another research team taught college students to discriminate their blood pressure (Cinciripini, Epstein, & Martin, 1979). The researchers asked the students to guess their blood pressure. They then measured it and gave them feedback. This led to improved guesses. The researchers suggest that this skill might improve the ability of individuals with high blood pressure to manage their disease better. Another team taught diabetics to discriminate their blood-sugar level (Gross et al., 1983). They asked diabetics to guess their level and then provided feedback. This may help diabetics to manage their disease better. Each example illustrates that internal events can become SD's for people.

Behavior analysts often use discrimination training. They use it with educational behaviors, particularly in programmed instruction. They use it to teach simple skills to children with retardation and autism, such as imitation and following instructions. They use it to get behaviors to occur outside the training situation. The methods used to teach these skills involve the basic discrimination-training procedure. I will describe them in greater detail in succeeding lessons.

Improving Supervision with Marked Items

Cities often hire youths to pick up the litter in an area. They pay them for each bag of trash that they turn in. Unfortunately, their supervisor can't tell whether the youths picked up the trash from the ground or from a garbage can. One solution is to place marked pieces of trash on the ground in the target area. If the youths don't know which items are marked, they must pick up all litter to be sure of getting the marked items. Three researchers tried this procedure. They paid the youths 25 cents for each marked item. This approach reduced litter as much as 90%, resulting in a much cleaner neighborhood. The marked items permitted the supervisors to discriminate when the youths were actually picking up litter from the area. (Based on Hayes, Johnson, & Cone, 1975.)

10. Because the supervisor's seeing a marked item comes <u>before</u> paying the youth, a marked item is called a(n) ______________ (reinforcer, SD) for the supervisor to pay the youth.

Establishing Stimulus Control

Sometimes behavior analysts can create stimulus control without explicit training. The procedures seek to establish a "right" time and place to emit problematic behaviors. When the procedures are successful, the behaviors become discriminated behaviors and occur at a more functional rate in this more restricted situation. The "right" situation becomes the SD that controls the behavior.

For example, researchers helped a group of worriers decrease their worrying (Borkovec et al., 1983). They told the worriers to note but otherwise ignore their worries during most of the day. The worriers were then to do all their worrying during a half-hour "worry period" once a day. The worriers reported considerably less worrying as a result.

Researchers helped overweight people lose weight (Carroll & Yates, 1981). They told these people to eat in only one room, use only one chair, and eat at the same times each day. They told them to do nothing else while eating—no reading or watching TV. They told them to keep food out of sight—no fruit or candy in bowls. They even told them to store food in the refrigerator in opaque bowls. These rules greatly reduced the stimuli that would lead to eating. They led to better maintenance of weight loss.

Researchers have used similar methods to combat insomnia (Espie et al., 1989). Other researchers have helped normal adults maintain exercise programs (Keefe & Blumenthal, 1980).

Intelligence Can Be Taught

Educators test for "intelligence" by giving students analogies, jumbled sentences, and verbal math problems. Recently educators have begun teaching "intelligence" by teaching the behaviors involved in solving such problems. Xavier, a small black college, has increased the number of its graduates going to medical school from 5 to 74 a year by teaching "intelligence" behaviors. Washington, DC schools increased their Merit Scholars from none in 1988 to four in 1995 by teaching the steps in solving problems. Intelligence is knowing how to take these steps when faced with a problem. Being faced with a problem is the SD for taking the steps. Taking the steps when faced with a problem has become a discriminated behavior. Being able to define low intelligence as a behavioral problem may mean that we don't have to "condemn the educationally disadvantaged to a life of wretchedness" (Cose, 1995).

11. The increased probability of taking the right steps when faced with a problem is called ______________ (reinforcement, stimulus) control.

Summary

Everyday people frequently use discrimination training. Behavior analysts often use it to help people. It involves reinforcing a behavior in the presence of one stimulus and extinguishing it in the presence of other stimuli. Behavior analysts call the stimulus associated with reinforcement a *discriminative stimulus* or SD. They call the stimulus associated with extinction the S-delta. When the behavior occurs with the SD but not the S-delta, they call it *discriminated behavior*. They say that the SD exerts stimulus control. Tactic #1 of the stimulus control strategy is to narrow stimulus control through discrimination training.

Behavior Analysis Examples

Teaching Reading to a Culturally Deprived Chicano

Carlos was a 14-year-old Chicano boy who read at a second-grade level. He had a long history of school failure; he had never passed a course in school. Carlos was a persistent behavioral problem for his teachers.

Staats and Butterfield (1965) used behavior analysis to help Carlos learn to read. They gave him training consisting of four stages. First, they taught him new words; second, they had him read stories out loud using those words; third, they had him read the same stories to himself and then answer questions about them; and fourth, they reviewed his new words every 20 lessons.

They used a set of stories starting at the first-grade reading level and progressing to a higher level. Each story ended with a set of test questions. They reinforced reading behavior with toys, special events, and money.

For stage one, they taught Carlos any new words appearing in the next story. They gave him a reinforcer when he read a new word correctly. When he did not, they corrected him and gave him another chance.

For stage two, they had Carlos read the story out loud after he had mastered the new words. They gave him a reinforcer each time he read a paragraph with no errors. When he made an error, they corrected him and gave him another chance later.

For stage three, they gave him the whole story on a single page, along with the test questions. They instructed him to read it silently and answer the questions. They reinforced him on a variable-interval schedule averaging 15 seconds when he was looking at the story, gave him a reinforcer when he completed the questions, and told him of his errors and let him reread the story.

For stage four, they presented him with a review of all his newly learned words after every 20 stories. They gave him a reinforcer for each correct answer on the review.

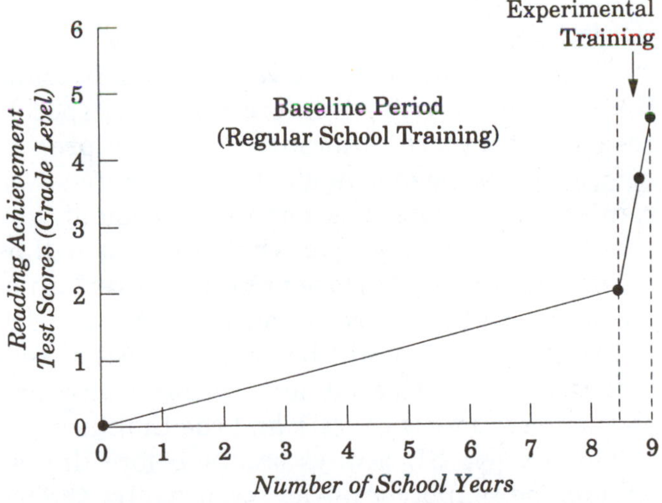

Figure 16-1. The reading achievement level of Carlos with regular school training and special training using discrimination training methods. Adapted from "Treatment of Non-reading in a Culturally Deprived Juvenile Delinquent: An Application of Reinforcement Principles," by A. W. Staats and W. H. Butterfield, *Child Development,* 1965, *36,* 925–942. Copyright 1965 by The Society for Research in Child Development, Inc. Used by permission.

The training resulted in remarkable improvement in his reading. Figure 16-1 shows the results of reading achievement tests given to him. Carlos had attained a second-grade reading level after 8½ years in public school. In just six months of special training, he improved to a grade level of 4.3. During that term, he passed all of his courses—the first time that he had passed even one course! Also, his misbehavior in the classroom had decreased to near zero. Behavior analysis helped Carlos more in 40 hours than had public school methods in more than 8 years.

As mentioned earlier, Skinner guessed that at least 50,000 responses must be reinforced to learn basic arithmetic. Carlos made a total of about 65,000 oral responses to words during his training period. This experiment shows that Carlos was not stupid; he couldn't read because his parents and teachers had not reinforced enough reading responses. When behavior analysts reinforced his reading responses, he learned to read.

12. The first stage of teaching Carlos involved showing him a written word and asking him to say that word. For example, if Carlos said "car" when they showed him the word *car*, they reinforced him. If he said "car" when they showed him the word *cat*, they did not reinforce him but rather corrected him. Because they reinforced a behavior in the presence of one stimulus and extinguished it in the presence of another stimulus, the researchers were using discrimination ____________ (behavior, training).

The Effects of Different Adults on a Child's Behavior

Redd and Birnbrauer (1969) studied the effects of Bill and Bob on the cooperative play behavior of Paul, a 14-year-old boy with retardation. The researchers selected Paul because he did not engage in cooperative play. They had Bill reinforce cooperative play, while Bob did not. They studied whether Paul would play differently around Bob than around Bill.

The researchers brought Paul and four other children into a playroom containing a wide variety of toys. Two observers sat behind a one-way mirror. They recorded whether Paul engaged in cooperative play every 2½ seconds. With no adults in the room, Paul engaged in no cooperative play.

Bill then proceeded to shape cooperative play. He gave Paul reinforcers contingent upon approximations to cooperative play. The reinforcers consisted of saying "Good boy" plus an M&M, a bite of ice cream, or a sip of Coke. Paul learned to play cooperatively. Bill then gradually reduced the reinforcement to a fixed-interval schedule of 45 seconds. That schedule maintained cooperative play.

Bob came into the room at times when Bill was not there. He gave as many reinforcers as did Bill, but not contingent on cooperative play.

Paul soon adopted a very distinctive pattern of cooperative play. If neither adult was in the room, he did not engage in cooperative play. If Bill came into the room, he immediately started playing cooperatively and continued as long as Bill remained. If Bill left the room, Paul stopped playing cooperatively. When Bob came into the room, Paul did not play cooperatively. Thus, Bill became a "signal" to play cooperatively.

The researchers wanted to make sure that this finding was not the result of some personality difference between Bill and Bob. So they had them exchange roles. Bob now awarded reinforcers contingently for cooperative play, while Bill did not. With this reversal, Paul started to play cooperatively the moment Bob entered the room. He stopped when Bill entered the room.

This study shows that the cooperative play behavior of Paul underwent only a very limited change. Paul's behavior changed only in the presence of the adult who reinforced him; it did not change more generally than that. Paul had not learned to play cooperatively with other children in general. The next lesson will discuss procedures for producing such general changes.

This study has everyday implications for all of us. Suppose your friend Stanley never compliments you but often compliments Kay. You might conclude that he doesn't like you very much, or that he isn't a very positive person. But it may be that you simply don't reinforce his compliments. You may act shy or look embarrassed. Giving compliments is like any other behavior. If others stop reinforcing your giving compliments, you will stop doing it.

13. If Bob's presence prompted Paul to play cooperatively, then his presence exerted ________ ________ (reinforcement, stimulus) control over Paul's cooperative play.

Notes

Note #1

The ability of humans to use language may explain our extraordinary success as a species. Sidman may have discovered the behavioral foundation for language. He found that "stimulus equivalence" may emerge from discrimination training (Sidman, 1971). It works this way. A discrimination based on a visual stimulus may become equivalent without training to an auditory stimulus. For example, suppose you teach Pat to point to the picture of a cat when you say the word. Suppose you then teach Pat to point to the written word *cat* when she sees the picture. Without further training, she may also point to the written word *cat* when you say the word. Further, she may even say the word when you show her the written word. Numerous experiments have demonstrated that spoken and written words and the objects or pictures that they stand for become equivalent with the right kind of training (e.g., Sidman & Tailby, 1982; Saunders & Spradlin, 1990; Hayes, Kohlenberg, & Hayes, 1991).

14. The term *stimulus equivalence* refers to people responding as though one stimulus is ________ ________ (different from, equivalent to) another unrelated stimulus.

Note #2

The SD, or discriminative stimulus, is sometimes confused with a reinforcer. For any specific response, they are different. The SD is present <u>before</u> the response is made. It is associated with reinforcement, but it is not reinforcement. You should view it as a cue to what behavior will be reinforced. To hear "Please pass the butter" is not a reinforcer. It is a discriminative stimulus (SD) indicating that you will be reinforced (thanked) for passing the butter but not for passing anything else. The request is the SD, and the thanks is the reinforcer. The SD always occurs <u>before</u> the behavior. The reinforcer always occurs <u>after</u> the behavior.

15. The SD always occurs ________________ (after, before) the behavior.

Note #3

Dinsmoor (1995) argues that discrimination between two stimuli is the result of increased observing responses. That is, people learn to look more frequently for the discriminative stimulus because that tells them when to make the response leading to reinforcement. He argues that this can happen even when the S-deltas have never been extinguished. This is a fascinating area for further research. I have used the established definition of discrimination training in this lesson, pending the outcome of that further research.

Helpful Hints

Helpful Hint #1

As you have probably guessed by now, discrimination training is the procedure mentioned in an earlier lesson that is easy to confuse with differential reinforcement. At the time, the book had you label it as unknown. From this lesson on, you should label it as discrimination training. Remember, differential reinforcement involves two or more different behaviors; you reinforce one and extinguish the others. This happens in the presence of only one stimulus. Discrimination training involves two or more different stimuli; you reinforce a behavior in the presence of one stimulus and extinguish that same behavior in the presence of the other stimulus. You should also label complex cases involving two or more stimuli and two or more behaviors as discrimination training.

16. If you reinforce a behavior in one situation and extinguish it in others, the name of the procedure is ________________________.

Additional Readings

Barrett, B. H., & Lindsley, O. R. (1962). Deficits in acquisition of operant discrimination and differentiation shown by institutionalized retarded children. *American Journal of Mental Deficiency*, *67*, 424–436. Also reprinted in L. P. Ullman & L. Krasner (Eds.). (1965). *Case studies in behavior modification.* New York: Holt, Rinehart & Winston. This article reports the use of operant psychology to measure the ability of children with retardation to rapidly form a variety of discriminations.

Dinsmoor, J. A. (1995). Stimulus control: Part 1. *BehaviorAnalyst, 18,* 51–68. For the advanced student, this is an excellent introduction to current issues in stimulus control. It contains an excellent discussion of the role of observing responses in discrimination training.

Hayes, S. C., & Wilson, K. G. (1993). Some implications of a contemporary behavior-analytic account of verbal events. *BehaviorAnalyst, 16,* 283–301. This article presents a behavior-analytic theory of verbal behavior called *relational frame theory*. It is based on stimulus equivalence. This article is for the advanced student who wishes to understand how the meaning of language arises from discrimination processes.

Neale, D. H. (1963). Behavior therapy and encopresis in children. *Behaviour Research and Therapy, 1,* 139–149. Discrimination training was used as part of the procedure for treating four disturbed children with encopresis (the children defecated in their pants rather than in the toilet). The success of the procedure permitted the children to be released from the hospital and develop normal lives.

Rodgers, T. A., & Iwata, B. A. (1991). An analysis of error-correction procedures during discrimination training. *Journal of Applied Behavior Analysis, 24*(4), 775–781. The standard discrimination training procedure simply ignores errors made by the trainee. This study compares the effect of the standard procedure with a variation: presenting the same discrimination problem to the person until he or she gets the right answer. The study found that this variation improved the performance of some trainees.

Simmons, M. W., & Lipsitt, L. P. (1961). An operant discrimination apparatus for infants. *Journal of the Experimental Analysis of Behavior* 1961, *4*, 233–235. Chimes were used as a reinforcer to teach a 10-month-old girl a simple discrimination.

Staats, A. W., Staats, C. K., Schutz, R. E., & Wolf, M. M. (1962). The conditioning of textual responses using "extrinsic" reinforcers. *Journal of the Experimental Analysis of Behavior, 5*, 33–40. This article describes a procedure for systematically teaching young children to discriminate written words from one another through a complex discrimination training procedure. This procedure provides a systematic way to teach young children to read.

Reading Quiz

30. I first need to introduce the idea of stimulus control. The increase in a behavior caused by an event that follows it is called *reinforcement control*. The increase in behavior from a preceding event is called ___________ (reinforcement, stimulus) control.
90. Sidman suggested that the field of cognition studies behavior that is under ___________ control.
32. If an event such as a question influences someone's behavior, it _______ (is, isn't) an example of a stimulus.
140. You will need to know that *stimuli* is the plural of ___________.
8. Any physical event or object in a person's environment that is related to his behavior is termed a(n) ___________.
117. The plural of *stimulus* is ___________.
60. Remember that a reinforcer is an event that follows a behavior and increases its rate. A reinforcer can be a stimulus. A reinforcer is a stimulus that ___________ (follows, precedes) the behavior.
123. This unit on stimulus control _____ (is, isn't) about intellectual and cognitive behavior.
2. A brief introduction to the third strategy: When behavior does not occur in the appropriate situations, behavior analysts turn to the ___________ (behavioral, reinforcement, stimulus control) strategy.
141. You will need to know that the third strategy for solving human problems is called the stimulus ___________ strategy.
61. Remember that the third strategy for solving human problems is called the ___________ control strategy.
73. Review: Narrowing stimulus control through <u>discrimination training</u> is the first tactic in the ___________ strategy.
128. To use the stimulus control strategy for solving human problems, (1) narrow stimulus control through discrimination ___________.
129. To use the stimulus control strategy for solving human problems, (1) narrow stimulus control through ___________ training.
82. Review: The first tactic in using the stimulus control strategy for solving human problems is to narrow stimulus control through ___________.
110. The first major topic is discrimination training. Behavior analysts call the procedure of <u>reinforcing</u> a behavior in the presence of one stimulus and <u>extinguishing</u> it in the presence of another stimulus ___________ training.
20. Discrimination training consists of reinforcing a behavior in the presence of one stimulus and ___________ that same behavior in the presence of another stimulus.
15. Behavior analysts use the term *discrimination training* to refer to the procedure of extinguishing a behavior in the presence of one stimulus and ___________ it in the presence of another stimulus.
13. Behavior analysts call the procedure of extinguishing a behavior in the presence of one stimulus and reinforcing it in the presence of another stimulus ___________.
99. Suppose Mom praises Benny when he calls his father "Dada" but ignores him when he calls his uncle "Dada." Benny may learn to call his father "Dada" but no one else. Mom is reinforcing Benny for saying "Dada" in the presence of his father and extinguishing saying the same word in the presence of his uncle. She is using the procedure called ___________.
121. This is discrimination training because Mom is using the procedure of reinforcement to increase Benny's saying "Dada" in the presence of his father and using the procedure of ___________ to decrease saying the same word in the presence his uncle.
49. Mom is working with how many behaviors? _____. The presence of Benny's father is one situation; the presence of his uncle is another situation. Mom is using reinforcement and extinction with how many situations? ___
39. In order to apply discrimination training, you will need to learn the several technical terms for the different parts of the procedure. I will start with *discriminative stimulus*. Any <u>stimulus</u> that precedes the behavior and is present only if reinforcement will occur for that behavior is called a *discriminative* ___________.
51. Notice that the name of the procedure, *discrimination training*, ends with the suffix "ion," but the name of the stimulus, *discriminative stimulus*, ends with the three letter suffix _______.

139. You will be reading and writing the word *discriminative* many times in the rest of the book. Many students have trouble spelling it at first. Practice spelling *discriminative* right now. I would suggest that you try to memorize it with your eyes closed, check to see if you are right, and if so, then write it without looking. _______________

10. Any stimulus that precedes the behavior and is present only if reinforcement will occur for that behavior is called a(n)_______________ stimulus.

120. The term *discriminative stimulus* is a mouthful. Behavior analysts abbreviate it in an unusual way: as though the term were *stimulus, discriminative*. They abbreviate it with the first letter of each of those words, in that order. Thus the abbreviation is the two letters __________.

1. SD is a widely used abbreviation for the term _______________ *stimulus*.

79. Review: The abbreviation for a stimulus that precedes the behavior and is present only if reinforcement will occur for that behavior is the two letters ________.

44. Let's go back to Mom and Benny. Mom reinforces Benny's saying "Dada" in the presence of his father. The father is a stimulus in the presence of which saying "Dada" is reinforced. Thus, it is a stimulus that is discriminative of reinforcement for that response. Therefore, behavior analysts call the father a(n) _______________. (Give the full term, do not use the abbreviation.)

14. Behavior analysts define a discriminative stimulus as "any stimulus that precedes the behavior and is present only if reinforcement will occur for that behavior." In what sense does the father precede the behavior? In the sense that the father must already be present in the room for Benny to call him "Dada." Thus, the father is a stimulus that _______________ (follows, precedes) the behavior, and only if he is present will Mom reinforce that behavior.

21. Don't confuse SD with reinforcer. Both are stimuli, and both increase the rate of a behavior. If an event occurs before the behavior and increases the rate of the behavior, it is a(n) _______________. If it occurs after and increases the rate of the behavior, it is a(n) _______________.

41. In the case of Mom and Benny, Mom's praise is delivered after Benny says "Dada" in the presence of the father. If the stimulus of praise increases the rate of "Dada," then you should call it a(n) _______________. Mom praises Benny's "Dada" only if the father was already in the situation. If the praise is a reinforcer, you should call the father a(n) _______________. (You may abbreviate.)

28. Here's another way to look at an SD. We know that an SD (discriminative stimulus) is a stimulus that precedes a behavior. We know that this stimulus is associated with reinforcement for a particular behavior. When his father is there, Benny knows that saying "Dada" will be reinforced. You might say that the SD "signals" that the particular behavior will be _______________.

7. Another term you will need to know is *S-delta*. While SD stands for a stimulus that increases behavior because it is associated with reinforcement, S-delta stands for a stimulus that decreases behavior because it is associated with _______________ (extinction, reinforcement).

68. Review: Any stimulus that precedes a behavior and is present only if extinction will occur for that behavior is called a(n) _______________.

11. Back to Mom and Benny again. Benny's father is an SD. Benny's uncle is an S-delta. Mom extinguishes Benny's saying "Dada" in the presence of his uncle. The uncle is a stimulus in the presence of which Mom reduces saying "Dada" by applying the procedure of _______________ to saying "Dada."

47. Mom extinguishes Benny's saying "Dada" in the presence of his uncle. Because his uncle is a stimulus in the presence of which Mom extinguishes saying "Dada," behavior analysts call the uncle a(n) _______________ for saying "Dada."

125. To tell the difference between SD and S-delta, you have to find out what response we are talking about. So read past the blanks. Because Benny is reinforced for saying "Dada" only when his father is around, his father is a(n) _______________ for saying "Dada." Because Benny is extinguished for saying "Dada" when only his uncle is around, his uncle is a(n) _______________ for saying "Dada."

57. A quick summary of terms so far. The name of the procedure of reinforcing a behavior in the presence of one stimulus and extinguishing it in the presence of another stimulus is ________________ training. The full name of the stimulus associated with reinforcement is ________________ stimulus. It is abbreviated as ________. The name of the stimulus associated with extinction is __________.

138. You must be vigilant about the difference between a reinforcer and an SD. Both are stimuli. Both increase the rate of the behavior. If the stimulus occurs after the behavior, it is called a(n) __________, but if it occurs before the behavior, it is called a(n) ________________.

16. Benny may not say "Dada" all day. But when his father comes home from work and Benny sees him, he is likely to say "Dada" a bunch of times. He sees his father before saying "Dada." Seeing his father increases his rate of saying "Dada." Therefore, father is a(n) ________________ for saying "Dada."

31. If a stimulus <u>precedes</u> a behavior and increases the rate of the behavior, the stimulus is a(n) ________________; if a stimulus <u>follows</u> a behavior and increases the rate of the behavior, the stimulus is an event called a(n) __________.

27. Here's another term you will need to know to apply discrimination training. *Discriminat<u>ed</u> behavior* is the name of behavior that has a higher probability of occurring in the presence of an SD than it does in the presence of an S-delta. Notice that the name of the behavior ends with the two-letter suffix ________.

137. You learned about discriminat<u>ion</u> training. Then you learned about discriminat<u>ive</u> stimulus. Now you are learning about discriminat<u>ed</u> behavior. Memorize these endings. If a behavior has a higher probability of occurring in the presence of an SD than it does in the presence of an S-delta, that behavior is called ________________ behavior.

43. Let's find out how discriminated behavior applies to Mom and Benny. We would call the behavior of saying "Dada" discriminated behavior once Benny was ________ (more, less) likely to say "Dada" in the presence of his father than in the presence of his uncle.

54. Once Benny is more likely to say "Dada" in the presence of his father than in the presence of his uncle, we would call the behavior of saying "Dada" ________________ behavior. You could now say that Benny has learned to call his father "Dada."

50. Notice that the name of the procedure (discrimination training) uses the three-letter suffix ________. The name of the stimulus (discriminative stimulus) uses the three-letter suffix _____. And the name of the behavior (discriminated behavior) uses the two-letter suffix ______.

124. It's time to remember the exact terms with the right endings. If a behavior has a higher probability of occurring in the presence of an SD than it does in the presence of an S-delta, then it is called ________________ behavior.

9. Any stimulus that precedes the behavior and is present only if reinforcement will occur for that behavior is called a(n) __________ stimulus. (Don't use the abbreviation.)

118. The procedure in which a behavior is reinforced in the presence of one stimulus and extinguished in the presence of another stimulus is called ________________ training.

25. Here is a small variation on one of these new terms. You learned in an earlier lesson that behavior analysts call a single instance of a behavior a <u>response</u>. Thus, they call a single instance of a discriminated behavior a *discriminated* __________.

46. Let's say that Benny's father comes home from work on Thursday evening. Benny might see his father and say "Dada." Because this is a single instance of discriminated behavior, you should call it a *discriminated* ______.

24. Here is a review of a term learned at the beginning of the lesson. Remember that *stimulus control* refers to the ____________ (decreased, increased) probability that a discriminated behavior is evoked by the SD.

112. The increased probability of a discriminated behavior that is produced by the stimulus (SD) is called __________ control.

133. When referring to the effect of the stimulus on a behavior (as a result of discrimination training) we say that the stimulus <u>exerts</u> stimulus __________ over the behavior. When referring to the behavior that occurs

more frequently in the presence of the SD than the S-delta, we call it ______________ behavior.

107. The behavior that results from discrimination training is ________________ behavior. A single instance of the behavior is a(n) discriminated ________________; and the effect that a stimulus exerts on the behavior is called ____________ control.

69. Review: I want to emphasize how important it is to not confuse reinforcer and SD. If an event that increases behavior occurs before the behavior, you should call it a(n) _______ __________________________; if it occurs after the behavior, you should call it a(n) ______________________________.

84. Review: The next few items summarize the terms you need in order to apply discrimination training to everyday situations. To firm up your mastery of each term, I will have you write out the whole term. The increased probability that a discriminated behavior will occur in the presence of the SD is called ______________________.

111. The full name of the stimulus associated with reinforcement is ___________________ ______, which is abbreviated as _____. The name of the stimulus associated with extinction is ______________________________.

113. The name of a behavior that is more likely to occur after the SD than after the S-delta is ______________________________. The name of a single instance of that behavior is __________________________.

114. The name of the procedure in which a behavior is reinforced in the presence of one stimulus and extinguished in the presence of another stimulus is __________________.

70. Review: I will give you a bunch of examples of the terms you have just learned. This will help you master those terms for use throughout this unit. Suppose Mrs. Jones teaches American history. Her lesson today involves important dates in World War II. She wants to teach when the war started. In case you don't remember, December 7, 1941 is the day the Japanese bombed Pearl Harbor. Suppose she asks two questions. When did the Japanese bomb Pearl Harbor? Second, when did Franklin Roosevelt die? (This happened near the end of the war.) If she reinforces you for answering December 7, 1941 for the first question but extinguishes you for the same answer to the second question, she is using what procedure? __________________

119. The question "When did the Japanese bomb Pearl Harbor?" would be called a(n) _______ for the answer "December 7, 1941." (Use the abbreviation.)

12. Be sure to read to the end of the sentence, or you may get this one wrong. The question "When did President Franklin Roosevelt die?" would be called a(n) ___________________ with respect to answering "December 7, 1941."

136. When you are more likely to give the answer "December 7, 1941" when asked about Pearl Harbor and less likely when asked about Roosevelt's death, we would call your answer ____________________ behavior.

134. When the question "When did the Japanese bomb Pearl Harbor?" evokes the response "December 7, 1941," we say that the question <u>exerts</u> _______________ control over the behavior.

71. Review: If the brunette person ignores you when you call her Laverne, she is considered a(n) _________________________ for that name.

29. However, if that same brunette person smiles at you when you call her Sally, she is considered a(n) _________________________ for that name.

88. Review: When being present at a football game exerts stimulus control over your yelling behavior, yelling has become a(n) _______ __________ behavior.

72. Review: If the question "What is 9x9?" results in a greater probability that you will answer "81," it is said to exert ____________ __________________ over your answering behavior.

58. Reading historical novels more often than science fiction is an example of developing a(n) _________________ behavior.

53. Now that you know that some of those "unknown" examples were discrimination training, you can finish learning to distinguish differential reinforcement. Dad praises Lulu when she eats vegetables but ignores her when she drinks pop at home. Lulu starts to eat more vegetables and drink less pop. Because Dad is increasing the rate of one behavior and decreasing the rate of another in the same situation, you know that Dad is

using the procedure called ______________

______________.

19. Dad praised Lulu when she waited until after eating her vegetables to have dessert but ignored her when she had her dessert first. Pretty soon, Lulu waited until after eating her vegetables before having her dessert. Because Dad was increasing the rate of eating dessert in one stimulus situation (after eating veggies) and decreasing the same behavior in another stimulus situation (before eating veggies), you know that this time Dad was using the behavioral procedure called ______________.

97. Suppose Dad praised Lulu when she called their big loud vehicle "truck" but ignored her when she called their smaller vehicle "truck." If Lulu came to call only the big loud one a truck, what procedure was he using? ______________

98. Suppose Dad praised Lulu when she called the picture of the airplane "airplane" but ignored her when she called it "truck." If Lulu came to call the picture "airplane," what procedure was he using? ______________

____

35. If you praise Timothy when he drinks pop but ignore him when he drinks whiskey, and if his rate of drinking pop increases, you are using what procedure? ______________

36. If you praise Timothy when he puts on a suit to go to a business meeting but ignore him when he puts on a suit to eat dinner at home, what procedure have you used? ______________

____

33. If Mr. Jones looks pleased when Martha says, "I don't like that idea" about physics but ignores her when she says, "I don't like that idea" about the way he grades the class, he is using what procedure? ______________

37. If you reinforce desirable behavior in one situation and ignore undesirable behavior in the same situation, and if the rate of desirable behavior increases, you are using what procedure? ______________

38. If you reinforce desirable behavior and ignore undesirable behavior in the same situation, and if the rate of desirable behavior increases, you are using what procedure? ______________

116. The next topic is <u>complex</u> discrimination training. When discrimination training involves only one behavior in two stimulus situations, I will call it simple discrimination training. When discrimination training involves two behaviors in two stimulus situations, I will call it complex ______________ training. I will also call discrimination training involving more than two behaviors and/or more than two stimuli *complex*. You do not have to learn the term *complex*. Just recognize it when you see it.

91. Simple discrimination training involves learning only one <u>discriminated</u> behavior. Complex discrimination training involves learning multiple ______________ behaviors at the same time.

101. Suppose you reinforce one response in the presence of Stimulus #1 and extinguish it in the presence of Stimulus #2. Suppose you reinforce a second response in the presence of Stimulus #2 and extinguish it in the presence of Stimulus #1. Notice that this is discrimination training that involves two behaviors and two stimuli. Would this be an example of complex discrimination training? ______________

126. To understand complex discrimination training, let's go back to Mom and Benny. Suppose Mom starts reinforcing Benny for calling his uncle "Unk" and extinguishing calling his father "Unk." Mom is now using a second instance of what procedure? ______________

____

48. Mom is now applying discrimination training to the behavior "Dada" at the same time that she is applying it to the behavior "Unk." What she is doing is a perfect example of ______________ (complex, simple) discrimination training.

115. The next few items cover what is a very difficult and arbitrary point. Suppose Mom reinforces Benny for calling his father "Dada" and extinguishes him for calling his father "Uncle." Because this example involves using reinforcement and extinction with two different behaviors in the same situation, you would properly call Mom's procedure ______________.

52. Now suppose the example also tells you that Mom reinforces Benny for calling his uncle "Unk" but extinguishes him for calling his uncle "Dada." The situation is different. You could describe the example a different way.

Mom reinforces Benny for calling his uncle "Unk" but extinguished him for calling his father "Unk." She also reinforces Benny for calling his father "Dada" but extinguishes him for calling his uncle "Dada." Because in both cases Mom is using reinforcement and extinction with one behavior in two situations, you could properly call either case the procedure of ______________________________.

22. Finally, I can get to the point! Mom is working with a complex procedure involving two behaviors and two situations. Behavior analysts have (pretty much arbitrarily) decided not to call such a complex combination *differential reinforcement*. Instead, they call it ______________________________.

100. Suppose Dad praises Tommy when he puts plastic in the recycling bin for plastic but ignores him when he puts paper in the same bin. Suppose Tommy's rate of putting in plastic increases, and putting in paper decreases. Because this involves reinforcing one behavior and extinguishing another in the same stimulus situation, you would label the procedure ______________________________.

18. Dad might later add a recycling bin for paper. Suppose Dad continues to praise Tommy when he puts plastic in the recycling bin for plastic and to ignore him when he puts paper in the bin for plastic. But now suppose Dad also praises Tommy when he puts paper in the bin for paper but ignores him when he puts plastic in the bin for paper. Suppose Tommy's rate for both correct responses increases relative to mistakes. We now have a situation that is more complex. What should you label Dad's procedure now? ______________________________

102. Suppose you reinforce Timothy for wearing a suit to a business meeting but ignore him if he wears casual clothing to a business meeting. Suppose you reinforce him for wearing casual clothing to eat dinner at home but ignore him for wearing a suit to eat dinner at home. What procedure are you using? ______________________________

103. Suppose you thank Bev for telling you to lighten up when you are looking very tense but ignore her for telling you to lighten up when you are simply looking busy. If she starts saying it only when you look tense, what procedure are you using? ______________________________

104. Suppose you thank Bev for telling you to lighten up when you are looking very tense but ignore her for telling you, "It will be OK" when you look tense. If she starts saying, "Lighten up" when you look tense, what procedure are you using? ______________________________

105. Suppose you thank Bev for telling you to lighten up when you are looking very tense, but you ignore her when she asks, "Can I help?" when you look tense. Suppose you also thank Bev for asking, "Can I help?" when you are looking busy, but ignore her if she tells you to lighten up when you look busy. If she starts saying, "Lighten up" when you look tense, and "Can I help" when you look busy, what procedure are you using? ______________________________

3. A child learning the names of four objects rather than just one is an example of complex discrimination training. The teacher must use discrimination training for each of the four objects versus the other three. Thus, the child is undergoing four ______________ training procedures at the same time.

142. Your next task is to apply these concepts to actual behavioral research examples. Researchers added orange highlighting to help batters see the spin on a pitched ball. The increased hits indicated that the spin had come to exert greater ______________________ over the batters' hitting.

130. Two researchers taught male trainees to discriminate females' level of interest (Azrin & Hayes, 1984). Suppose a trainee guessed "very interested" and was then told his guess was correct. If the feedback increased the rate of correct guessing, you would call the event a(n) ______________.

106. Teaching people to discriminate the temperature of their hand, their blood pressure, or their blood-sugar level involves reinforcing guesses when they match measurements of their physiological signs (the SD) and extinguishing the same guesses if they do not match the measurements (the S-delta). Teaching these behaviors are health-related examples of the procedure of ______________.

56. Placing marked pieces of trash into the target area helped permit supervisors to tell

when youths hired to pick up trash were actually picking up litter from the area. A marked item was a(n) ________________ for the supervisor to pay the youth.

131. What procedure have behavior analysts often used to develop educational behavior? ________________

93. Sometimes behavior analysts can create stimulus control without explicit training by establishing a right time and place to emit problematic behaviors. When successful, the right situation becomes a stimulus in whose presence the behavior leads to reinforcement. Behavior analysts call that stimulus the ________________.

135. When worriers were limited to worrying during a half hour "worry period" once a day, the worriers reported considerably ________ (less, more) worrying during the rest of the day (Borkovec et al., 1983).

62. Researchers told overweight people to eat in only one room, use only one chair, and eat at the same times each day (Carroll & Yates, 1981). They also were to do nothing else while eating and to keep food out of sight. This "right" situation reduced eating and led to reinforcers in the form of weight loss. You can say that the right situation came to exert ________________ over their eating.

5. A mini-review. Increasing the probability of a behavior in one situation through reinforcement and decreasing its probability in another situation through extinction is called ________________.

42. Increasing the probability of a behavior in one situation through reinforcement and decreasing the probability of a second behavior in the same situation through extinction is called ________________.

94. Staats and Butterfield (1965) presented Carlos with the written word *whenever* and gave him a token if he said that word. The written word *whenever* would be called a(n) ________________ for the spoken word *whenever*; it would be called a(n) ________________ for any other spoken word.

95. Staats and Butterfield (1965) repeatedly presented any written word to Carlos that he got wrong until he could say its name correctly. Of course, he must also not say that word when some other word was on the card. The increased probability of saying the written word would be called ________________ control.

96. Staats and Butterfield (1965) reinforced the behavior of saying the name of the word on the card. If that behavior was more likely to occur in the presence of the word on the card than it was in the presence of some other word, then we would call the behavior ________________ behavior.

77. Review: Staats and Butterfield (1965) gave Carlos a token when he said "inspect" if that was the word on the card. They gave him nothing when he said "inspect" if any other word was on the card. What procedure were they employing? ________________

6. After eight years of school, Carlos had a second-grade reading level. After six months (40 hours) of training by Staats and Butterfield, he had a reading level beyond the fourth-grade level. This shows the power of their procedure called ________________ training.

17. Carlos made a total of about 65,000 oral responses to words during his training period. This suggests that he hadn't been able to read because his parents and teachers ________ (had, hadn't) reinforced enough reading responses earlier.

26. Here's a review question. Bill gave Paul reinforcers contingent upon approximations to cooperative play (Redd & Birnbrauer, 1969). By differentially reinforcing closer and closer approximations to the target behavior of cooperative play, he was using the behavioral procedure called ________________.

59. Redd and Birnbrauer (1969) studied the results of having one behavior analyst give a child with retardation edibles when he played cooperatively with other children, while a second behavior analyst did not. The child learned to play cooperatively when the adult who reinforced him was present but not when the other adult was present. What procedure accounts for this result? ________________

109. The child with retardation is observed to play cooperatively in the presence of an adult who reinforces him for such play but not play cooperatively in the presence of a second adult. We say that the first adult exerts ________________ over the child's play behavior.

132. When Bob gave praise and edibles to Paul for cooperative play, his presence became a(n) ______________________ for cooperative play.

4. A child with retardation was observed to play cooperatively in the presence of an adult who reinforced such play but not in the presence of a second adult who did not. We say that cooperative play has become ________ behavior.

23. Giving compliments is like any other behavior. You will stop giving them if others stop ______________ them.

40. In past units, you have learned some tactics that are part of the behavioral strategy and the reinforcement strategy. The third strategy for solving human problems is called the ______________ strategy.

127. To use the stimulus control strategy for solving human problems, (1) narrow stimulus control through ______________________.

45. Let's review an important distinction you have learned in this lesson. If a stimulus increases the probability of a behavior and occurs before the behavior, that stimulus is called a(n) ______________________. If a stimulus increases the probability of a behavior and occurs after the behavior, the stimulus is called a(n) ______________.

108. The biggest difficulty for most students is telling the difference beween discrimination training and differential reinforcement. One behavior might be reinforced and one or more other behaviors extinguished in one stimulus situation. The name of that procedure is ______________________. (Check your answer!)

55. One behavior might be reinforced in one situation and extinguished in a second situation. You should label the procedure as ______ ______________________.

92. Thus, if reinforcement and extinction are applied to one behavior in two situations, the procedure is called ______________, but if reinforcement and extinction are applied to two or more behaviors in one situation, the procedure is called ____________ ______________. Notice that the key is the number of situations.

34. If reinforcement and extinction are applied to behaviors in one situation, the procedure is ______________________; if in two situations, the procedure is ____________ ______________.

122. This simple distinction applies even to complex discrimination training. In complex discrimination training, reinforcement and extinction are applied to behaviors in two or more stimulus situations. So if reinforcement and extinction are applied in two or in more than two stimulus situations, the name of the procedure is always ______________ ______________.

78. Review: Staats and Butterfield (1965) showed Carlos a card with the word *inspect* on it; they gave him a token if he said "inspect," but nothing if he said any other word. They repeated this for about 700 new words. What procedure did they use? ______________ ______________

80. Review: The first tactic in using the stimulus control strategy for solving human problems is to narrow stimulus control through ______________________.

83. Review: The increased probability of a discriminated behavior produced by a stimulus (SD) is called ______________________.

67. Review: An SD (discriminative stimulus) is a stimulus that precedes a behavior. It "signals" that the behavior will produce ______________________.

89. Review:The question "What is 2+2?" always gets Ward to say "4." Therefore, the question exerts ______________ over his behavior.

64. Review: A particular behavior that is more likely to occur in the presence of the SD than in the presence of the S-delta is called a(n) ______________________.

63. Review: "What does 2+2 equal?" is called a(n) ______________________ for the answer "4."

81. Review: The first tactic in using the stimulus control strategy for solving human problems is to narrow stimulus control through ______________________.

75. Review: Reinforcing one behavior while extinguishing a second behavior in the presence of one stimulus and extinguishing the first behavior while reinforcing the second behavior in the presence of a second stimulus is considered to be an example of what procedure? ______________________

74. Review: Redd and Birnbrauer (1969) studied the results of having one behavior ana-

lyst give a child with retardation edibles when he played cooperatively with other children, while a second behavior analyst did not. The child learned to play cooperatively when the first adult was present but not when the second adult was present. The behavioral procedure that accounts for this result is called ______________.

76. Review: Reinforcing one behavior while extinguishing a second behavior in the presence of one stimulus and seeing a relative increase in the reinforced behavior is the procedure labeled ______________.

65. Review: A stimulus occurring before a behavior that increases the rate of the behavior is called a(n) ______________. A stimulus occurring after a behavior that increases the rate of the behavior is called a(n) ______________.

66. Review: A stimulus that precedes a behavior and is associated with extinction is called a(n) ______________.

87. Review: Two procedures involve both reinforcement and extinction. If reinforcement and extinction occur with different stimuli (i.e., two or more stimuli), then the procedure is called ______________, but if reinforcement and extinction occur with the same stimulus (i.e., one stimulus), then the procedure is called ______________.

86. Review: To use the stimulus control strategy for solving human problems (1) narrow stimulus control through ______________ ______________.

85. Review: The third strategy for solving human problems is called the ______________ ______________ strategy.

Examples

1. Ms. Yablonski asks Ward, "What does 2+2 equal?" and praises him when he says "4." When she asks, "What does 2+3 equal?", she ignores him when he answers "4." Ward learns to say "4" to answer the first question but to not say "4" to answer the second question. Clearly, this example involves reinforcement and extinction. But both discrimination training and differential reinforcement involve reinforcement and extinction. Differential reinforcement would require that one behavior be reinforced while a second behavior was extinguished. It requires that there be two behaviors and one stimulus situation. This example talks about the answer "4." How many behaviors are there? ____ (1, 2). The relevant stimuli are the questions that might call forth his answer. How many stimuli are there? ________ (1, 2). Because the response "4" is reinforced with one stimulus and extinguished with the other, this example must involve what procedure? ______________

2. Sammy had trouble pronouncing dates in his American history class. He just couldn't seem to say "1492" clearly. When the teacher asked him "When did Columbus discover America?", Sammy would answer, "Forty nineteen two," "Forty-nine two," or "Fourteen nineteen two." The teacher ignored Sammy when he made these responses. Sometimes Sammy answered, "Fourteen ninety-two", and the teacher immediately praised him. Sammy soon learned to say the date correctly. This procedure involves reinforcement of one behavior and extinction of all others. Again, the relevant stimulus is the question that called forth his answers. How many stimuli (not behaviors) were reinforcement and extinction used with? _____. How many answers, correct and incorrect, did Sammy give at different times? ______ (1, 2, 3). Because the example involves reinforcement of one answer and extinction of all other answers in a single stimulus situation, the procedure involved was ______________.

3. Jeff swears by saying "X@#" a lot around the dorm, and his friends pay a lot of attention to it. When Jeff goes home, his parents ignore his "X@#." As a result, Jeff does not say "X@#" much at home. In this example, the relevant stimuli are the locations where he says "X@#." How many stimuli does this example involve? ________ (1, 2). How many types of behavior occur in the example? ______ (1, 2). Because his swearing is reinforced in one situation but not the other, what procedure is being applied to him? ______________ ______________

4. When Jeff was around Gerry, he often loudly and angrily said "gosh" and "X@#." Gerry ignored "gosh" but paid attention when he said "X@#." Gradually, Jeff said "X@#" more often than "gosh." Be careful not to think of the words "X@#" and "gosh" as stimuli. They are words that he said, not stimuli that set the stage for the words. How many stimulus situations were there in which Jeff could swear? _______ (1, 2). How many behaviors does this example involve? ______ (1, 2). Because

one word was reinforced in the the dorm but the other word is extinguished in the same situation, this is an example of what procedure? ______________________

5. Mr. Campbell frequently asked Daryl multiplication questions. When Mr. Campbell asked, "What does 7x8 equal?", he praised Daryl for answering "56" but ignored him for saying "18." When Mr. Campbell asked "What does 3x6 equal?" he praised Daryl when he said "18" but ignored him when he said "56." In this example, how many stimuli called forth Daryl's answers? _____ (1, 2). How many behaviors did Daryl perform as answers? _____ (1, 2). Since Mr. Campbell praised Daryl when he answered "56" but not "18" to the first question and also praised him when he answered "18" but not "56" to the second question, Mr. Campbell was using what procedure? ______________________. I hope you remembered that this was a complex situation.

6. Johnny's parents ignored most of the "baby noises" he made when they were around. However, when Johnny first said "Dada," his parents paid a lot of attention to him, but they ignored "goo goo." As a result, Johnny said "Dada" at a much higher rate than "goo goo." How many stimulus situations does this example involve? ________ (1, 2). How many of Johnny's behaviors does this example involve? ______ (1, 2). What procedure were the parents using to increase "Dada" relative to "goo goo"? ______________________

7. When Johnny first said "Mama," his father showered him with attention. Soon afterwards, father praised him when he said "Mama" to his actual mother and ignored him when he said "Mama" to anyone else. As a result, Johnny started saying "Mama" only to his mother. The relevant stimuli in this case are those that signaled him he would get reinforced or extinguished for saying "Mama." If his mother was there, would father reinforce him for saying "Mama"? ______. So the presence of his mother was one relevant stimulus. If his mother was not present, would his father reinforce him for saying "Mama"? ______. You could count mother as one relevant stimulus and then many additional people as additional stimuli. Therefore, this is an example of what procedure? ______________________

8. Johnny's parents paid a lot of attention when he called his mother "Mama" but ignored him when he called his mother "Dada." Of course, they paid a lot of attention when he called his father "Dada" but ignored him when he called his father "Mama." Count how many stimuli were associated with reinforcement and extinction. What procedure were Johnny's parents using? ______________________ (Check your answer on this one!)

9. Martha had two teachers in her kindergarten class. Ms. Chang praised Martha anytime she was appropriately assertive around the other children, while Mrs. Mansur ignored Martha's assertive behavior. Pretty soon Martha was assertive when Ms. Chang was around but was not when Mrs. Mansur was around. The two teachers were unwittingly using what procedure with respect to Martha's assertive behavior? ______________________

10. Mary's father started going into her room to see what she was reading. If she was reading archaeology books, he got very interested and held long discussions with her. If she was reading anything else, he usually went off to read the paper. She started reading many more archeology books than other kinds of books. Since reading occurred more frequently in the presence of archaeology books, we would say that archaeology books exerted ______________________ over Mary's reading behavior.

11. Review: When Frank started hanging around with the gang, he found that the tall redheaded guy answered when called Bob but didn't if called Jim, Ken, or Dave. Similarly, the short muscular dude answered when called Jim but not when called anything else. What procedure was at work in this group situation affecting Frank's choice of names for each person? ______________________

12. Review: Doris usually acted in a happy mood around Fran, because Fran got into the spirit and they had a good time together. Doris usually did not act in a happy mood around Kay, because Kay remained serious and did not get into the happy mood. In this situation, we would say that Fran exerted ______________________ over Doris's happy behavior.

13. Review: When Flora first moved into the sorority, she found that she could get to the bathroom by going down her hall and turning left at the corner. If you consider the corner of the hall to be a stimulus, then it would be considered a(n) ______________________ for turning left to get to the bathroom.

14. Review: When Karen was learning how to use this book, she discovered that the answers to

the Example questions could be found in the back of the book by looking under the heading "Examples" rather than under the heading "Text." If looking up an Example answer under "Examples" produced reinforcement, while looking up an Example answer under "Text" produced extinction, the book is applying what procedure to where she looks up Example answers? ______________________________

15. Review: Bob tried to boogie with Alice every chance he had, because she was such a good dancer. She easily followed any complicated turn that Bob tried, which increased his rate of complicated turns. But she often missed the dips that he tried, thus decreasing his dips. He gradually came to perform many complicated turns but no dips when dancing with Alice. What procedure accounts for the increase in turns and decrease in dips? ______________________

16. Review: If Carol smiled at Lenny, you would guess that this would be a(n) ___________ for asking her out for a date; but if Carol frowned at Lenny, you would guess that this would be a(n) ___________ for asking her out for a date.

17. Review: Barb showed little Wanda a picture of a dog and praised her when she said "doggy," but not when she said "kitty." Of course, Barb also showed Wanda pictures of cats, snakes, and gila monsters and followed the same procedure. What procedure did Barb use to teach Wanda the names of the animals? ______________________________

18. Review: Frank always stops his car at any red, octagonal sign that reads "STOP." He does this because Dad praises him when he stops at this sign and ignores him when he stops at other signs. Behavior analysts say that the stop sign exerts ____________________ over his stopping behavior.

19. Review: Mrs. Niles praised her son Larry for using unusual words when describing events. Unfortunately, his friends ignored him when he used unusual words around them. In this situation, we would call Mrs. Niles a(n) ___________ for using such words and Larry's friends a(n) ____________________ for using such words.

20. Review: Dennis was sometimes out past the 11:00 P.M. curfew. A few times, he was stopped by a policeman. He learned to act courteously and apologize for losing track of time. When he did that, the policeman would let him go. He did not act this way at other times. His polite behavior was more likely to occur when talking to a policeman, so it is referred to as ______________ behavior.

LESSON

17 Generalization Training of Everyday Behaviors

Discrimination training increases behavior in one situation and decreases it in other situations. In a sense, it draws a boundary between two situations, so that the behavior does not spread from one to the other. The person learns the difference between situations. This lesson introduces generalization training, which does just the opposite. It eliminates boundaries between situations so that the behavior spreads from one situation to the other. The person learns the similarity between situations. Discrimination training and generalization training are related but opposite concepts (Stokes, 1992). Tactic #2 of the stimulus control strategy is to broaden stimulus control through generalization training.

1. Tactic #2 of the stimulus control strategy is to broaden stimulus control through ____________ ____________ training.

Definition of Generalization Training

Suppose Dad teaches Kay to call animals of a certain shape *dogs*. Dad might point to Bowser and ask Kay to say "dog." Of course, he would reinforce her when she says it. Suppose Kay learns to call Bowser a dog. How does Dad get her to do the same with all dogs? Obviously, he doesn't want to repeat his lesson for every single dog in the world. What he needs is a way to give her the idea. He can do so by teaching her to label a few animals as dogs. From there her naming can spread to all dogs without further teaching. Behavior analysts use generalization training to accomplish this goal.

Generalization training is reinforcing a behavior in each of a series of situations until it generalizes to other members of that same stimulus class. This book is full of examples of this procedure. For example, I wanted you to "get the idea" of extinction, so I presented a series of stories exemplifying extinction. With the first stories, I taught you to label the procedure as extinction. Then I asked you to identify added stories as extinction on your own. Right now you could probably correctly label as extinction any new story I gave you. You would not need further generalization training to do so. By using this procedure, the boundaries between examples of extinction are eliminated so that your labeling spreads to most of them.

2. Generalization training is reinforcing a behavior in each of a series of situations until it generalizes to other members of that same ______ ____________________.

A key term in defining generalization training is *generalization*. **Generalization** is the occurrence of a behavior in the presence of a novel stimulus. A novel stimulus is any stimulus in whose presence the person's behavior has not been reinforced. In this book, new stories of extinction are novel stimuli, because you have not already been reinforced for identifying them as extinction.

3. The occurrence of a behavior in the presence of a novel stimulus is called ________________.

Another key term in the definition of generalization training is *stimulus class*. A **stimulus class** is a set of related stimuli. For example, stories of extinction are all related, because they conform to the definition of extinction. Other examples of related stimuli would be red objects, behavior analysts, differential equations, or students.

5. A stimulus class is a set of related ____________.

The Importance of Generalization

"A child who is learning to talk may speak his first words in the presence of his mother, who usually has more opportunities than other people to reinforce this behavior. He soon 'speaks' to other members of the family and to strangers. When he is taken to a strange place, speaking usually generalizes to the new surroundings. All of which is fortunate. Without generalization, we would probably spend most of our time relearning the same few skills in each new situation, and be able to develop only the most limited behavioral repertoires" (Reese, 1978: p. 26). This quote is about generalization, the occurrence of a behavior in the presence of a novel stimulus.

4. If a child has never been reinforced for speaking to Jim, then Jim is a novel stimulus. Therefore, if the child speaks to Jim for the first time, it is an example of ______________________ (generalization, generalization training).

I can't overemphasize the importance of generalization and generalization training. Without generalization, you would have to learn whether every possible story was or was not extinction. You would not "understand" the concept; you would only memorize individual instances of it. Without generalization, human behavior would come to a virtual standstill. We would be helpless in the face of constant bombardment by novel stimuli.

Don't get me wrong; generalization is not magic. You won't always be reinforced when your behavior generalizes to a novel situation. You might call someone's infant a pretty girl just because it is wrapped in a pink blanket. That might be very embarrassing if the parents are particularly proud of their handsome little baby boy. This process is sometimes called *overgeneralization*. It is a real, but undesirable, instance of generalization. It can be counteracted through discrimination training. Therefore, behavior analysts often use the procedures of discrimination training and generalization training together.

Generalization of behavior change is important in behavior analysis. Suppose Jim wishes to become more assertive. A behavior analyst may present Jim with situations requiring assertive behavior and praise Jim for behaving assertively. However, Jim's assertiveness may remain on extinction by his friends and family. Jim might learn to discriminate when others will reinforce him for behaving assertively. His new behavior may occur with increased frequency only with the behavior analyst. This wouldn't be worth much, since Jim undoubtedly wants to learn to be assertive in his everyday life. Many behavior analysis studies study this problem. After treatment, they measure assertive behavior in the person's normal situations to see whether the behavior has generalized to people and situations outside training.

Behavior analysts have used many strategies to achieve generalization (Stokes & Baer, 1977). I will review several common strategies.

The "Train and Hope" Method

The most frequent approach to generalization by behavior analysts has been dubbed by Stokes and Baer (1977) "train and hope." The behavior analyst trains the desired behavior and hopes that it generalizes to everyday situations. The "train and hope" approach usually results in failure to produce generalization, although it sometimes produces limited success. For example, researchers studied racial integration in a first-grade classroom (Hauserman, Walen, & Behling, 1973). They measured social contacts between 5 black children and 20 white children. Then they reinforced any child who sat with a new friend during lunch. Figure 17-1 shows that this increased the rate of integrated seating in the lunchroom from about 20% to about 60%. Surprisingly, it also increased the amount of playing together on the playground. More playing together on the playground is an example of generalization, because such playing was not reinforced. Unfortunately, this generalization stopped when sitting together in the lunchroom was no longer reinforced.

Other studies have also shown some limited success with the "train and hope" approach. Researchers treated four couples with distressed marriages (Behrens, Sanders, & Halford, 1990). They taught the couples communication and problem-solving skills. They assessed the couples' skills by observing them discussing difficult issues and found that negative comments decreased sharply.

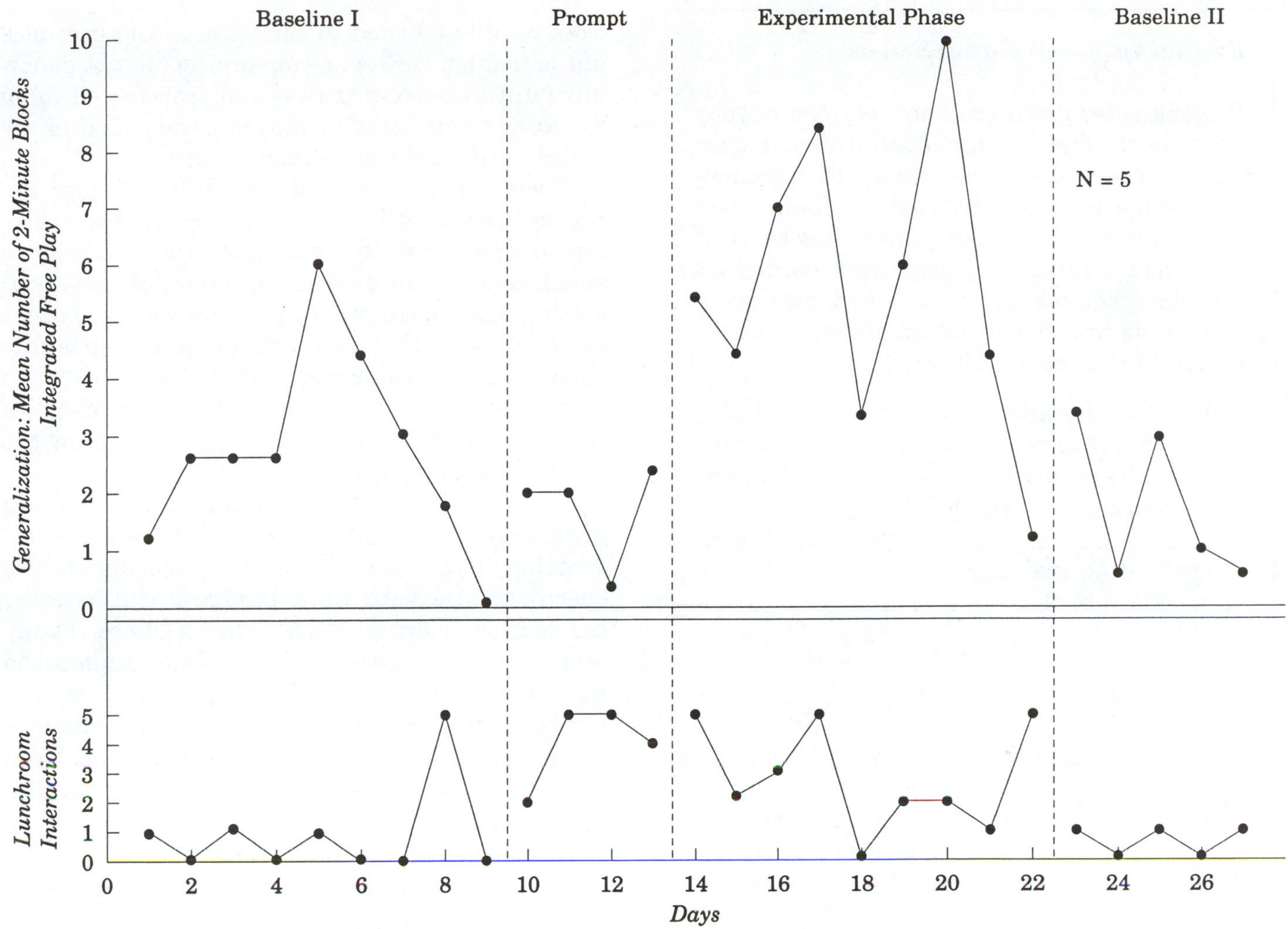

Figure 17-1. The amount of social interaction between 5 black and 20 white first-graders. Children were given snacks for sitting with "new friends" (of either race) in the lunchroom during the "prompt" and "experimental phase," but nothing for playing together on the playground during free play. Adapted from "Reinforced Racial Integration in the First Grade: A Study in Generalization," by N. Hauserman, S. R. Walen, and M. Behling, *Journal of Applied Behavior Analysis,* 1973, *6,* 193–200. Copyright 1973 by the Society for the Experimental Analysis of Behavior, Inc. Used by permission.

They also scored audiotapes of the couples discussing touchy issues at home and found that they made few negative comments at home after training. Thus, the improved communications generalized to the home.

Researchers reinforced nondepressed behavior emitted by depressed individuals (Hersen et al., 1973). Several of them continued emitting a small amount of nondepressed behavior even after the reinforcement program was stopped. Thus, the nondepressed behavior generalized to the everyday situation without reinforcement.

Researchers showed that biofeedback training reduced migraine headaches (Sturgis, Tollison, & Adams, 1978). They found that the reduction continued after biofeedback training was stopped. They also observed decrements in headaches at home even though the training occurred in a psychological clinic. Thus, the headache reduction generalized to the home.

I have reviewed several studies in which the "train and hope" method produced generalization. These studies are in the minority, however, because most studies using "train and hope" show little or no generalization. In general, researchers must use some systematic approach to produce generalization if they are to produce it with any consistency.

Reducing Video Game Stress

Playing video games can stress you out; your heart beats faster, your blood pressure goes up, and your hands get clammy. Researchers gave some kids biofeedback for their heart rate while playing video games. This lowered their heart rate. The lower rate continued after biofeedback and also stayed low during the novel stimulus situation of mental arithmetic (Larkin et al., 1992).

6. Because the kids had not been reinforced to lower their rate during mental arithmetic, its occurrence in the presence of that novel stimulus is called ______________ ______________ (generalization, generalization training).

Generalization Training

Generalization training appears to be the most effective method to produce generalization (Horner, McDonnell, & Bellamy, 1986). In fact, it may be the underlying principle in other generalization methods (Kirby & Bickel, 1988). Researchers used this approach to teach a child with retardation to greet people (Stokes, Baer, & Jackson, 1974). They taught the child to greet one experimenter. That training did not cause the child to greet others. However, after they taught the child to greet a second experimenter, the behavior generalized. The child greeted other staff members and even visitors without having been trained to do so.

Remember the researchers who taught males how to discriminate females' interest level? They showed the males videotaped scenes of conversations involving several females (Azrin & Hayes, 1984). As you remember, the males learned to discriminate interest indicated by these females. The researchers then observed the males in role-playing situations with new females. They found improvements in the males' ability to discriminate the interest level of these new females. Thus, the males' sensitivity generalized to new (i.e., novel) females.

Another researcher taught two children with retardation to converse (Garcia, 1974). The children readily learned to converse in the presence of the trainer. However, conversing did not generalize until a second trainer also reinforced them for conversing. They produced generalization by training the children across trainers.

Two researchers used a slightly different approach (Griffiths & Craighead, 1972). They reinforced a 30-year-old woman with retardation to speak clearly, training her in a special classroom setting. She continued to speak unclearly in other settings. Next, they also reinforced her speaking clearly at her residence, and she then began to speak clearly in all situations. The researchers in this study produced generalization by training the woman across settings.

You might think that intelligent adults would generalize important skills by themselves. A researcher taught two fourth-grade teachers to use specific praise with their pupils during reading instruction (Horton, 1975). The teachers readily learned to use specific praise. They understood how this helped the children learn, but they did not begin to use specific praise in math and language arts until they were trained to do so. Even then, they did not use specific praise in health or social science.

Beating Up Black Bears

Kenneth Markley was awakened by a noise in the middle of his vacation in Canada. He found a huge black bear raiding the refrigerator in his cabin. He grabbed a lawn chair and hit the bear over the head. "That made him mad and he started snapping. His old teeth was just a-popping. He was growling and swinging his head and coming right at me. I hit him two or three times on the head, but the last time I got him on the nose." The hit on the nose caused the bear to bolt out the door (based on a story in the Lawrence *Journal World*, Sept. 1, 1995).

7. If, before taking on the bear, Ken had won fights by hitting several big humans, the bear might simply be a novel stimulus for hitting. If so, Ken's hitting the bear would be an example of ______________ (discrimination, generalization).

Figure 17-2. Trever Stokes and Don Baer wrote the "classic" article on generalization. They convinced applied behavior analysts that studying and producing generalization is important. They described a number of strategies for producing generalization.

The Similar-Stimuli Method

Behavior analysts use other methods to increase generalization. One common method is the similar-stimuli strategy. This method ensures that stimuli similar to those present in the training situation are also present in the everyday situation. Reinforcement always occurs in the presence of one or more specific stimuli. For example, suppose that Kay learned to say "dog" in the presence of many stimuli. Bowser was one stimulus; Dad was another. Others might include the lawn, the house, Dad's clothing, and the doghouse. The presence of any of those stimuli might increase the chances that Kay would label a second animal a dog. In general, a response reinforced in the presence of one stimulus will tend to occur spontaneously in the presence of similar stimuli (Skinner, 1953a). Those stimuli that are common to both situations assist generalization.

The similar-stimuli method involves trying to maximize the similarity between the training situation and everyday situations. One way to do this is by training in everyday situations. Another is to structure the training situation so that it is similar to everyday situations. For example, two researchers worked with severely disruptive elementary school children (Walker & Buckley, 1972). They trained them in a special classroom to engage in appropriate behavior. These children increased their rate of appropriate behavior from about 40% in their regular classroom to about 90% in the special classroom. The researchers arranged for some elements of the regular classroom to be similar to the training classroom for half of the children; but not for the others. The children who were returned to similar classrooms maintained over 50% of their improved behavior, while the other children maintained only about 30% of their improvement.

Generalization of Extinction

Generalization training may be used in connection with many behavioral procedures other than reinforcement. Thus, an undesirable behavior could be extinguished in a series of situations to produce generalized extinction. For example, one researcher used this approach to reduce 8-year-old Ben's penguin talk (Allen, 1973). Ben fantasized about penguins for up to eight hours a day. While at summer camp, Ben talked constantly about penguins. He frequently talked about his imaginary pet penguins "Tug-Tug," "Junior Polkado," and "Super Penguin." The researcher used a multiple-baseline analysis. He told the camp counselors to ignore Ben's penguin talk while walking on a trail. Ben stopped his penguin talk on the trail, but he didn't talk about penguins any less in other settings. The counselors next ignored Ben's penguin talk in the dining hall. Ben immediately talked less about penguins in the dining hall. At this point, Ben stopped talking about penguins in his cabin and in his classroom. Thus, extinguishing the behavior in two settings produced generalized extinction in other settings.

Concept Formation

A particularly important behavioral process occurs when discrimination training is generalized so that a person can make a discrimination as to whether a stimulus is within or outside of a stimulus class. The outcome of this is called *concept formation*. It is one basis of complex intellectual activity, thinking, and ideas. Any type of understanding beyond memorizing must involve this process. Miller and Weaver (1974) showed how this book's use of discrimination and generalization produced concept formation.

> ***You Don't Generalize; Your Response Generalizes***
>
> "Generalization is not an activity of the organism; it is simply a term which describes the fact that the control [over a behavior] acquired by a stimulus is shared by other stimuli with common properties" (Skinner, 1953a: p. 134). Thus, don't say, "You generalized," but rather, "Your behavior generalized."
>
> 8. A behavior analyst wouldn't say, "You generalized," but rather, say, "Your __________ generalized."

Summary

Generalization is the occurrence of a response in a novel situation. "Train and hope" sometimes produces generalization, but generalization training is more certain to do so. Behavior analysts have used generalization training to increase greeting behavior and speech clarity among individuals with retardation. They have used it to increase social sensitivity and use of specific praise with normal adults. Teaching people to emit these behaviors in enough situations leads to generalization to many similar situations. Such generalization is crucial to human behavior. Without it, we would be endlessly learning the same few behaviors in new situations. Tactic #2 of the stimulus control strategy is broadening stimulus control through generalization training.

Behavior Analysis Examples

Teaching Assertiveness

Researchers sought to help Jane, a very passive 8-year-old girl (Bornstein, Bellack, & Hersen, 1977). She had difficulty relating to her peers, didn't express anger even when it was appropriate, was unable to refuse unreasonable requests, was oversensitive to criticism, and rarely volunteered in class.

The researchers taught Jane three assertive behaviors. They defined <u>eye contact</u> as looking at the other person while speaking. They defined <u>loudness of speech</u> on a scale of 1 to 5, where normal was 5. They defined <u>requests for new behavior</u> as asking other people to change their behavior. They computed reliability for each measure; it ranged from 85% to 100%.

The researchers used a role-playing scene to teach Jane the assertive behaviors. They told Jane to imagine the following scene: "You are part of a small group in science class. Your group is trying

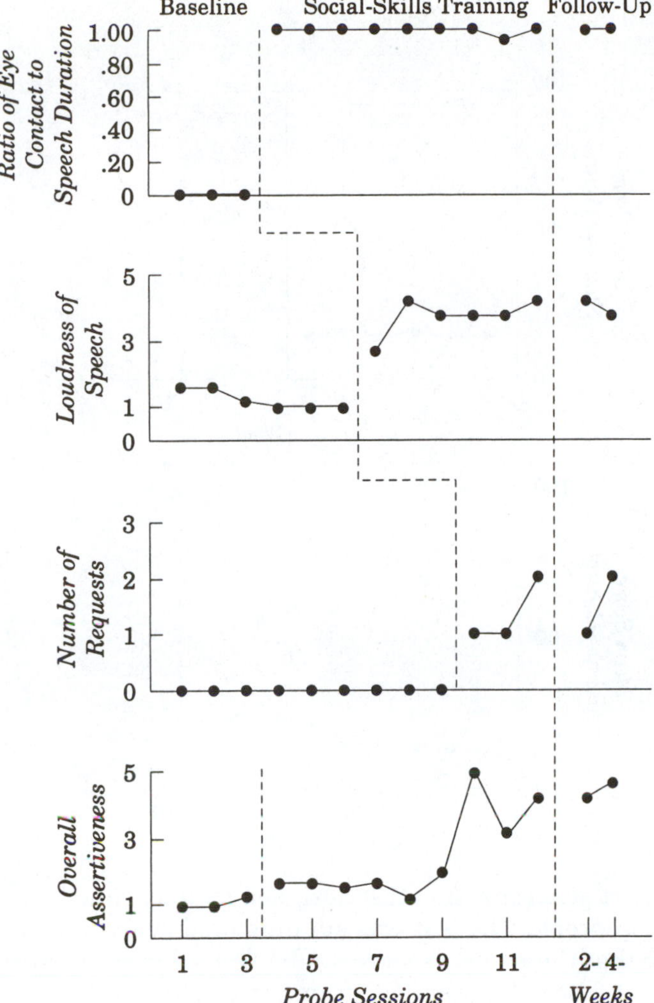

Figure 17-3. The amount of three assertive behaviors observed in Jane. The bottom graph reports the overall assessment of "assertiveness" by outside judges not aware of the experimental treatment. Adapted from "Social-Skills Training for Unassertive Children: A Multiple-Baseline Analysis," by M. R. Bornstein, A. S. Bellack, and M. Hersen, *Journal of Applied Behavior Analysis,* 1977, *10,* 183–195. Copyright 1977 by the Society for the Experimental Analysis of Behavior, Inc. Used by permission.

to come up with an idea for a project to present to class. You start to give your idea when Amy begins to tell hers also." Then an actor pretended to be Amy. She said, "Hey, listen to my idea." The researchers asked Jane to react to Amy's interruption. Afterwards, they gave Jane feedback for one target behavior. For example, they might say, "Jane, you failed to look at Amy for the whole time." Then they discussed the situation with Jane and modeled the correct behavior for her. Finally, they instructed Jane how to perform the target behavior. They replayed the scene, with Jane performing the target behavior. Training continued until Jane performed the target behavior correctly. The researchers used six different everyday scenes during training.

For the experiment, the researchers used three novel scenes. Figure 17-3 shows the results. Jane's eye contact increased from near zero to 100% after training. Her loudness increased from very low to close to normal. Her requests increased from zero to two out of three. Jane maintained her new assertive behaviors two and four weeks later.

Two independent judges rated Jane's behavior as very unassertive before treatment. Figure 17-3 shows the results. They rated it slightly higher after Jane learned to make eye contact. They rated it slightly higher after she increased her loudness. Finally, they rated it much higher when she started to request changes in the other person's behavior. The final ratings were "moderately" to "very" assertive. The researchers replicated these results with three other unassertive children.

These results indicate that behavioral training can increase assertive behaviors in untrained situations. The judges' ratings suggest that everyday people call these three target behaviors assertive.

9. Behavior analysts call the increase in assertive behaviors in the novel scenes ____________ ____________.

Understanding

Hal Weaver and I studied the effect of an early version of this book as a generalization training program (Miller & Weaver, 1974). We observed whether readers' responses generalized from examples in the book to other novel stories. We made up a test, with 48 novel stories unrelated to any examples in the book. The test had four parts, each defining a baseline for each unit of the book. We gave this test at the beginning of every week during the semester and computed the percentage of correct responses for each baseline.

We used a multiple-baseline design. The reading material in each unit was the treatment condition for each of the four baselines.

Figure 17-4 shows the results of the experiment. After reading the Research Methods unit,

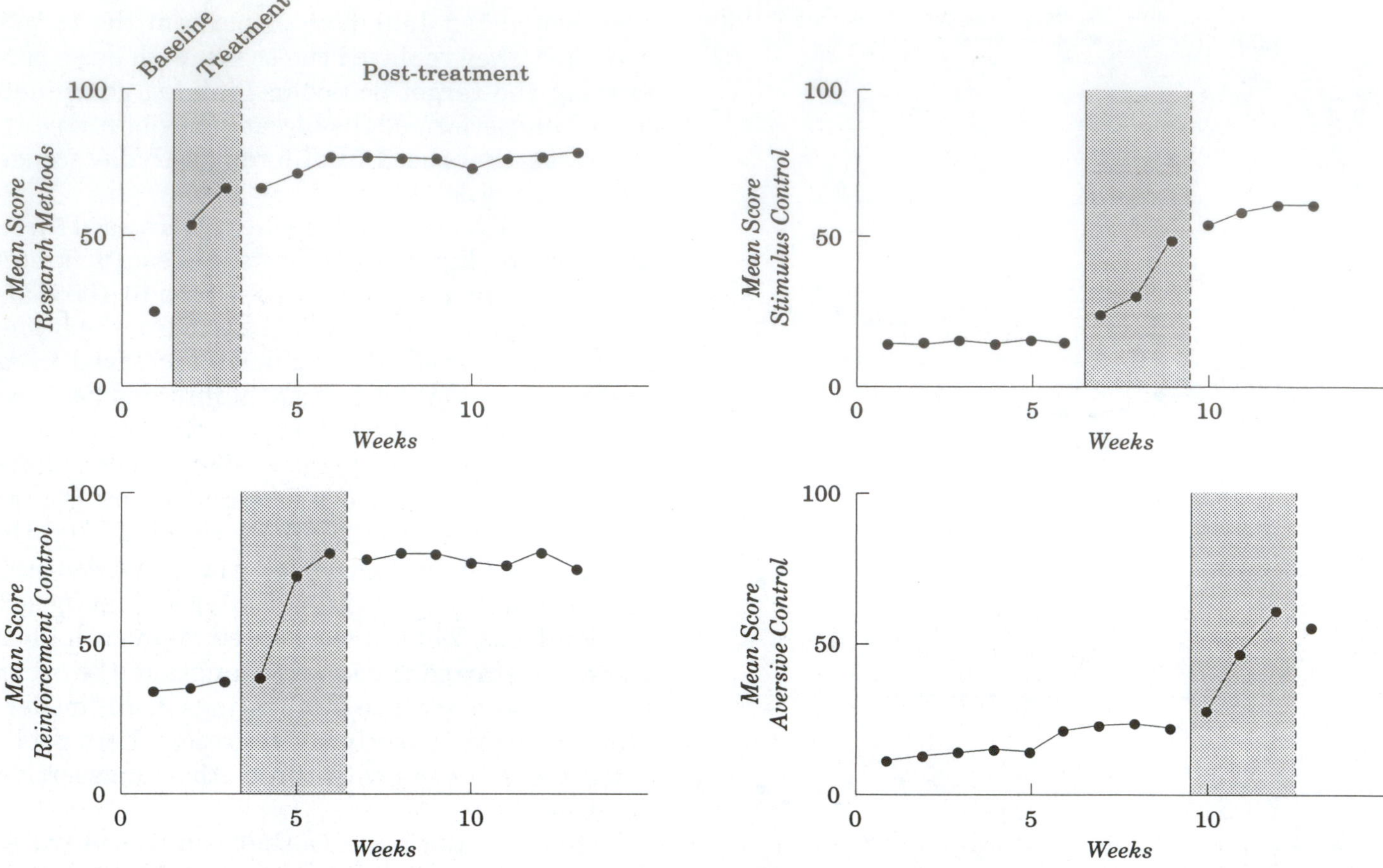

Figure 17-4. The average scores of 50 students on a four-part generalization test designed to determine whether each unit in the book assisted students in forming concepts. The test was administered every week of the semester. The striped bars represent the period of time that the students were studying each unit designed to teach them the concepts in that part of the test. From "The Use of 'Concept Programming' to Teach Behavioral Concepts to University Students," by L. K. Miller and F. H. Weaver. In J. Johnston (Ed.), *Behavior research and technology in higher education.* Copyright 1974 by Charles C Thomas, Publisher. Reprinted by permission.

scores for that baseline increased. However, they did not increase at that time for the other three baselines. After reading the Reinforcement Control Strategy Unit, only scores for that baseline increased. The same effect was present for each baseline.

10. The book reinforces responses to a series of similar stories. For example, it reinforces the response "satiation" to stories about too frequent reinforcement. These stories about frequent reinforcement are members of the same stimulus class. This research suggests that the response generalized to novel stories about satiation. Thus, the reinforcement of the response to many stories of satiation would be an example of ______________________________ training.

Notes

Note #1

Behavior analysts use additional strategies to facilitate generalization to everyday situations (Stokes & Baer, 1977). They train loosely, with varying stimuli, so that discrimination doesn't occur. They use contingencies in training that can't be discriminated from everyday contingencies. They teach people to talk about the generalization. They train a generalized skill of "generalizing."

11. Each method is a strategy for promoting _____ _______________ to novel stimuli.

Note #2

Reports concerning generalization have become standard in applied behavior analysis. For example, almost 50% of all studies of child and adolescent therapy from 1978 to 1989 reported whether generalization occurred (Allen, Tarnowski, Simonian, Elliott, & Drabman, 1991). Between 1976 and 1990, 70% of all studies of social skill training with children reported on generalization (Chandler, Lubeck, & Fowler, 1992).

12. Almost 50% of all studies of child and adolescent therapy from 1978 to 1989 reported whether _______________ to novel stimuli occurred.

Note #3
Generalization may also occur among behaviors. For example, when teaching someone to make positive statements to other people, one might begin by teaching first one positive statement, then another, and another. At some point, the individual will generalize to the class of all positive statements. This process is often referred to as *induction* or *response generalization*.

13. Generalization occurring among behaviors, such as a person making positive statements, is often referred to as *induction* or *response* _______________.

Helpful Hints

Helpful Hint #1
When you are asked to identify instances of generalization and generalization training, remember the following: Generalization is a process, and generalization training is a behavioral procedure. Therefore, you would label "reinforcing a behavior in each of a series of situations until it generalizes to other members of that same stimulus class" as the procedure of generalization training. You would label "the occurrence of a behavior in the presence of a novel stimulus" as the process of generalization.

14. Remember that one of the terms refers to a procedure and one refers to a process. Which term refers to a process? _______________ _______________. Which term refers to a procedure? _______________

Helpful Hint #2
Students often mix up discrimination training and generalization training. Here's how you can always tell the difference. If the procedure increases the behavior in the presence of one stimulus but not in the presence of another stimulus, then it is discrimination training. The person is learning to discriminate between the situations. If the procedure increases the behavior in the presence of many related stimuli, then it is generalization training. The person is learning to generalize to novel stimuli. So you can tell whether an example is discrimination training or generalization training by asking whether it uses reinforcement in the presence of one stimulus or in the presence of many stimuli.

15. If the procedure increases the behavior in the presence of many related stimuli, then it is _______________ training, but if the procedure increases the behavior in the presence of one stimulus but not in the presence of another stimulus, then it is _______________ training.

Helpful Hint #3
Always consider the possibility that a complex example is differential reinforcement (or shaping). I will give you many such examples so that you can learn to tell the difference between differential reinforcement, discrimination training, and generalization training. You can tell the difference by asking whether the example involves two behaviors and one stimulus or one behavior and two stimuli.

16. Always ask whether a complex example involves differential reinforcement. You can tell whether it does by asking if it involves _____ (1, 2) behavior(s) and _____ (1, 2) stimulus (stimuli).

Additional Readings

Chandler, L. K., Lubeck, R. C., & Fowler, S. A. (1992). Generalization and maintenance of preschool children's social skills: A critical review and analysis. *Journal of Applied Behavior Analysis*, *25*(2), 415–428. This review reports on generalization with a select set of studies. It examines only studies of children learning social skills and reports the success of different strategies in producing generalization of those skills.

Houlihan, D. D., Sloane, H. N., Jones, R. N., & Patten, C. (1992). A review of behavioral conceptualizations and treatments of child noncompliance. *Education and Treatment of Children, 15*(1), 56–77. This article reviews studies of how to modify child noncompliance from 1968 to 1990, examining the methods used to increase compliance. It reports how effectively these methods promote generalization of increased compliance to everyday situations.

Stokes, T. F., & Baer, D. M. (1977). An implicit technology of generalization. *Journal of Applied Behavior Analysis, 10*, 349–367. This is the "classic" treatment of generalization in applied behavior analysis. It reviews 270 behavior analysis studies to establish what is known about generalization. The authors suggest nine strategies for promoting generalization. The article has been widely influential, leading to a great increase in attempts to produce generalization.

Reading Quiz

69. The second tactic in using the stimulus control strategy is to broaden stimulus control through ________________ (discrimination training, generalization training).
24. Let's start by learning the difference between discrimination training and generalization training. Remember Mom and Benny from an earlier lesson? Mom praised Benny for saying "Dada" in the presence of his father but not in the presence of his uncle. She was teaching Benny to draw a "boundary" for whom to call "Dada." Discrimination training ________ (draws, eliminates) boundaries between two or more stimulus situations.
83. Unlike discrimination training, generalization training ____________ (draws, eliminates) boundaries between stimulus situations.
13. Dad teaches Kay to call Bowser a dog. He then teaches her to label a few animals as dogs. From there he wants her naming to spread to all dogs, with a minimum of further teaching. Dad's procedure is an example of generalization training, because it ________________ (draws, eliminates) boundaries between different dogs.
64. The first goal is to learn to define and apply the concept of generalization training. What is the name of the procedure that has the following three elements? It reinforces the same behavior (1) in a series of situations until (2) the behavior generalizes to (3) other members of the same stimulus class. ________________ ________________ (discrimination training, generalization training)
78. To talk about the first element of generalization training, I refer to a series of situations. Because you must reinforce the same behavior in more than one situation, I refer to a(n) ________________ (single, series of) situation(s).
76. To produce generalization with the procedure of generalization training, you must reinforce the same behavior in a(n) ____________ of situations until it generalizes to other members of that stimulus class.
79. To talk about the second element, I refer to the process in which the behavior generalizes to other stimuli. Because your goal is for the behavior to occur in the presence of novel stimuli in the same stimulus class, I talk about when the behavior ________________ (discriminates, generalizes).
77. To produce the process of generalization with the procedure of generalization training, you must reinforce the same behavior in a series of situations until it ____________ to other members of that stimulus class.
80. To talk about the third element, I refer to a stimulus class. Because you want the behavior to generalize only to relevant stimuli, I talk about other members of the same ________ class.
72. The three elements of the procedure of generalization training are that you reinforce the same behavior (1) in a series of situations until (2) the behavior generalizes to (3) other members of the same ________________.
73. The three elements of the procedure of generalization training are that you reinforce the same behavior (1) in a series of situations until (2) the behavior ____________ to (3) other members of the same ____________.
54. Review: The three elements of the procedure of generalization training are that you reinforce the same behavior (1) in a(n) ________ ________ of situations until (2) the behavior ____________ to (3) other members of the same ____________.
58. Review: What is the name of the procedure in which you reinforce the same behavior (1) in

a series of situations until (2) the behavior generalizes to (3) other members of the same stimulus class? ______

29. Notice that I always refer to generalization training as a(n) ______ (procedure, process) and generalization as a(n) ______ ______ (procedure, process).
66. The procedure of generalization training involves generalization. The process of generalization involves making a response in the presence of a novel stimulus. A novel stimulus is a stimulus in whose presence a particular response ______ (has, hasn't) previously been reinforced.
39. Review: Everyday speech would use the term *novel stimulus* to refer to a stimulus that the person has never seen or heard before. In this book, I will use the term in a slightly more specific way. I will call any stimulus in whose presence the person's behavior has not been reinforced a(n) ______ stimulus.
68. The process in which a behavior occurs in the presence of a novel stimulus is called ______ ______ (generalization, generalization training).
51. Review: The process of generalization is the occurrence of a behavior in the presence of a(n) ______ stimulus.
2. A child who is learning to talk may be reinforced for speaking to her mother. There may be a time when she has spoken to her mother but not to her father. Naturally, she will not yet have been reinforced for speaking in the presence of her father. Therefore, speaking to her father for the first time is an example of the behavioral process called ______.
67. The procedure of generalization training involves the behavior generalizing to other members of a stimulus class. A stimulus class is a set of ______ (related, unrelated) stimuli.
5. A set of stimuli that are related by some common element like color, species, or name is called a(n) stimulus ______.
8. All those animals we call dogs form a stimulus class, because they are a set of stimuli that are ______ by common elements like barking, having four legs, and having a tail.
11. Because cats are a set of stimuli related by such common elements as meowing, fur, and claws, they are called a(n) ______ ______.
62. Suppose Kay learns to call Bowser "dog." Suppose she sees Blackie for the first time and calls him "dog." Because she has never been reinforced for calling Blackie "dog," Blackie would be called a(n) ______ stimulus.
10. Because Blackie is a novel stimulus in the same stimulus class as Bowser, having Kay call Blackie a dog would be an example of the process called ______.
34. Review: A set of related stimuli is called a(n) ______. When a behavior occurs in the presence of a novel stimulus, the process is called ______.
6. A stimulus class is a set of ______ stimuli. Generalization occurs in the presence of a(n) ______ stimulus in the same stimulus class.
20. Generalization is the process whereby a behavior occurs in the presence of a(n) ______ stimulus. A set of related stimuli is called a(n) ______.
74. The three elements of the procedure called generalization training are that you reinforce the same behavior (1) in a(n) ______ ______ of situations until (2) the behavior ______ to (3) other members of the same ______.
87. You may find it easy to confuse generalization training with discrimination training. As you recall, discrimination training consists of reinforcing a behavior in the presence of a particular stimulus and ______ it in the presence of another stimulus.
84. We saw how generalization training might help Kay call both Bowser and Blackie "dog." Dad might also reinforce Kay for calling their dog Bowser but extinguish her for calling the neighbor's dog Bowser. Dad would be using what behavioral procedure? ______ ______
60. Suppose Dad praised Kay whenever she called their cat, Fluffy, "cat." If Kay's rate of calling Fluffy "cat" increased, what procedure would Dad be using? ______
61. Suppose Dad praised Kay whenever she called a series of four cats that they saw around the neighborhood "cat." If Kay then called a fifth cat "cat," what procedure would Dad be using? ______
63. Suppose Kay then called a rat "cat." Suppose Dad ignored her when she called the rat a cat and reinforced her when she called Fluffy a

cat. If Kay came to call only Fluffy "cat," then Dad used what behavioral procedure? ____________

85. When Dad reinforced Kay for making the same response in the presence of more and more stimuli, he was using what behavioral procedure? ____________. However, when he reinforced Kay for making the response in the presence of one stimulus but (through extinction) not other stimuli, he was using what behavioral procedure? ____________
86. Without generalization, human behavior would come to a virtual standstill, because we would have to learn what to do all over again every time we encountered a(n) ____________ stimulus.
32. Responding in the presence of a novel situation doesn't always produce reinforcement. When it doesn't, we call it *overgeneralization*. Overgeneralization is the occurrence of generalization to a novel situation in which it ____________ (does, doesn't) lead to reinforcement.
25. Many behavior analysis studies have measured the behavior after treatment or in other settings to see if the process of ____________ has occurred to these novel situations.
65. The next topic is to learn what strategies produce generalization. With the first strategy to obtain generalization, behavior analysts <u>train</u> the desired behavior and <u>hope</u> that it generalizes to everyday situations. This strategy is called the "train and ____________" strategy.
75. The "train and hope" strategy sometimes shows limited success in producing ____________.
46. Review: Researchers gave some kids biofeedback for their heart rates while playing video games. This lowered their heart rates. The heart rates also stayed low during mental arithmetic. What behavioral process occurred? ____________
30. Researchers showed that biofeedback training reduced migraine headaches. They also observed decrements in headaches at home. Thus, the headache reduction ____________ to the home.
4. A second strategy uses generalization training. To produce reliable generalization of behavioral change, it is necessary to reinforce the response in a series of situations until it has generalized to other stimuli in the same stimulus class. That is, you must employ what behavioral procedure? ____________.
59. Review: Researchers reinforced males when they correctly guessed the interest level of females shown in a series of videotaped conversations. They then found that the males more often correctly guessed the interest level of other females in role-playing situations. What behavioral procedure accounts for this result? ____________
81. Two children with retardation readily learned to converse in the presence of one trainer. However, a second trainer had to reinforce them for conversing before this response ____________ to other people.
21. Griffiths and Craighead (1972) reinforced a 30-year-old woman with retardation for speaking clearly in a special classroom setting. They also reinforced her speaking clearly at her residence, and she then began to speak clearly in all situations. What behavioral procedure did the researchers use to get her to speak clearly in all situations? ____________
31. Researchers taught two fourth-grade teachers to use specific praise with their pupils during reading instruction. The teachers did not begin to use specific praise in math and language arts until they were trained to do so. The researchers had to reinforce the use of specific praise in math and language arts because the praise did not ____________ to those subjects without further training.
7. A third strategy is called the *similar-stimuli strategy*." Generalization is likely to occur from situation A to situation B to the extent that more of the stimuli in both situations are ____________ (different, similar).
26. Maximizing the similarity between the training situation and the everyday situation is called the ____________ stimuli strategy.
9. Allen (1973) produced generalized extinction of penguin talk in a little boy by extinguishing his behavior in ____________ (more than one, one) situation.
1. <u>Concept formation</u> is a process resulting from discrimination training and generalization training. First, a teacher teaches someone to discriminate between stimuli A and B. Second, she teaches the person to generalize from

stimuli A and B to all related stimuli. The process of the person's learning this "generalized discrimination" is called ______________ formation.

3. A person does not generalize. Rather, his or her ______________ generalizes.
70. The second tactic in using the stimulus control strategy is to broaden stimulus control through generalization ______________.
71. The second tactic in using the stimulus control strategy is to broaden stimulus control through ______________ training.
52. Review: The second tactic in using the stimulus control strategy is to broaden stimulus control through ______________.
23. If a person's behavior is changed in one situation, the procedure for ensuring that the change appears in other situations would be ______________.
22. Here's a review from an earlier lesson. The statement "Eye contact is looking the other person in the eye while speaking" would be an example of a(n) ______________.
12. Bornstein and associates (1977) taught Jane to be assertive in response to being interrupted by another person. They then taught her to be assertive in several other types of situations. When they tested her assertiveness in three other untrained situations, they found her to be quite assertive. What behavioral procedure did they use? ______________ ______________
37. Review: Bornstein and his colleagues (1977) used six teaching situations and three testing situations. Because they had never reinforced Jane for being assertive during the three test situations, the test situations would be called ________ stimuli.
82. Two outside judges rated Jane's behavior as very unassertive before treatment. After treatment, the final ratings were "moderately" to "very" assertive. The judges' ratings served to establish the ______________ of the treatment.
27. Miller and Weaver (1974) reinforced students for correctly labeling the examples contained in this book. They then observed that the students could correctly label examples that they had not seen before. The occurrence of the students' labeling behavior in the presence of the new examples would be called ______________.
28. Miller and Weaver (1974) reinforced students for correctly labeling successive examples of extinction in this book. They then observed that the students could correctly label examples that they had not seen before. What behavioral procedure did they use to produce this result? ______________
43. Review: Miller and Weaver (1974) showed students a series of examples of extinction. Because they are related by virtue of all being examples of extinction, the collection of examples would be termed a(n) stimulus ______________.
17. From Note #1: Behavior analysts use strategies such as training loosely, using contingencies that can't be discriminated from everyday contingencies, teaching people to talk about generalization, and training the generalized skill of generalizing. Each method is a strategy for promoting ______________.
18. From Note #2: Almost 50% of all studies of child and adolescent therapy from 1978 to 1989 reported whether ______________ occurred (Allen et al., 1991).
19. From Note #3: <u>Generalization</u> occurring among behaviors, such as making positive statements, is often referred to as *induction* or *response* ______________.
14. From Helpful Hint #1: Which one of the two terms *generalization* and *generalization training* refers to a process? ______________ ______________. Which term refers to a procedure? ______________
15. From Helpful Hint #2: If a procedure increases the behavior in the presence of many related stimuli, then call it ______________ ______________, but if the procedure increases the behavior in the presence of one stimulus but not in the presence of another stimulus, then it is ______________.
16. From Helpful Hint #3: Always ask whether a complex example involves differential reinforcement. You can tell whether it does by asking if it involves ______ (1, 2) behavior(s) and ________ (1, 2) stimulus (stimuli).
33. Review: A procedure in which a behavior is reinforced in each of a series of situations until it generalizes to other members of that stimulus class is called ______________.
50. Review: The procedure in which a behavior comes to occur more frequently in the presence of one stimulus but less frequently in the presence of other stimuli is called ______________ ______________.

38. Review: Bornstein and associates (1977) taught Jane to be assertive in response to being interrupted by another person. They then taught her to be assertive in several other types of situations. When they tested her assertiveness in three novel situations, they found her to be quite assertive. What behavioral procedure did the researchers use? ______________
35. Review: A set of related stimuli is called a(n) ______________.
56. Review: To use the stimulus control strategy, (1) narrow stimulus control through discrimination training; (2) broaden stimulus control through ______________.
48. Review: The increased probability of a discriminated behavior that is produced by a stimulus is called ______________.
40. Review: Generalization is defined as a behavior occurring in the presence of a(n) ______________ in the same stimulus class.
47. Review: The collection of stimuli that share being tall, woody, leafy, and plants would be an example of a(n) ______________.
55. Review: The three elements of generalization training are that you reinforce the same behavior (1) in a(n) ______________ of situations until (2) the behavior ______________ to (3) other members of the same ______________.
36. Review: Any stimulus in whose presence a behavior has not previously been reinforced is called a(n) ______________ stimulus.
42. Review: I may ask you what process is involved when a behavior occurs in the presence of some stimulus not previously associated with reinforcement. Because I used the word *process*, you can guess that the answer is ______________.
49. Review: The occurrence of a behavior in the presence of a novel stimulus is what we call ______________.
53. Review: The second tactic in using the stimulus control strategy is to broaden stimulus control through ______________.
41. Review: Generalization training is defined as reinforcing a behavior in each of a series of situations until it ______________ to other members of that same stimulus class.
45. Review: Reinforcing Kay for saying "4" when asked "What is 2 plus 2?" and extinguishing her for saying "4" when asked "What is 8 plus 3?" would be the procedure of ______________.
44. Review: Miller and Weaver (1974) reinforced students for correctly labeling the examples contained in this book. They then observed that the students could correctly label examples that they had not seen before. What process is responsible for the students' labeling behavior in the presence of the new examples? ______________
57. Review: To use the stimulus control strategy to help people, (1) narrow stimulus control through ______________ and (2) broaden the stimulus control through ______________.

Examples

1. Professor Brainbuster had a talent for bringing students into his discussions. He was so successful that he even managed to get Sweet Sue to talk in class and express her opinions. Ken thought that this was great, that the professor was making an important change in Sue's behavior. Lisa disagreed, however, pointing out that Sue still didn't express her opinions in other classes. If Sue's talking occurred in other classes after Professor Brainbuster had reinforced her, this would be an instance of what behavioral process? ______________. All university classes would be called a(n) ______________ because they are related stimuli. If someone had wanted badly enough to change Sweet Sue's talking behavior in all classes, he or she could have tried arranging for several professors to reinforce her talking in class. What procedure would be used by the combined group to increase her talking in all classes? ______________

2. Steve began speaking with a beautiful rhythm and sound to his words when he was around Marcia, and she loved it. When Steve was around Ken, he started to speak the same way, but Ken looked at him really funny and split. Eventually Steve spoke poetically around Marcia but not around Ken. The first instance of poetic speaking in the presence of Ken would be an example of the process of ______________. Because Steve's poetic speaking was reinforced in the presence of Marcia but extinguished in the presence of Ken, the combined reaction of Ken and Marcia is an example of what procedure? ______________

______________________. If Ken had also praised Steve's poetic speaking, then the combined reaction of Ken and Marcia would have been an example of what procedure to produce poetic talking in Ken for many situations? ______________ ______________________

3. Dave showered Bad Bertha with attention when she was being nice to him. He ignored her when she was bad. Dave mentioned to several friends how nice Bertha was. They thought Dave was crazy, since they showered her with attention only for her tough behavior. Because gentle behavior was reinforced in Dave's presence, what kind of stimulus would he be for her acting gently? ______________________. In his friends' presence, Bertha's gentle behavior was extinguished. What kind of stimulus would their presence be for gentle behavior? ______________. Between them, Dave and his friends were using what behavioral procedure to encourage Bertha to act gently in one place and tough in the other? ______________________________. If Dave convinced all his friends to change their reaction to Bertha and to reinforce gentleness, they would be using what behavioral procedure to make Bertha into a gentle person? ______________

4. Arnie Smith teased the family's dogs. He chased them and sprayed them with water. This behavior upset Mrs. Smith, who yelled at him and pleaded with him to stop. Arnie continued to tease the dogs. Finally, in desperation, Mrs. Smith listened to the advice of a behavior analyst. He told her to ignore Arnie's behavior completely. After a month, Mrs. Smith discovered that Arnie had indeed stopped teasing their dogs. She bragged about this one night at a cocktail party given by Mrs. Jones, a neighbor. Mrs. Jones told Mrs. Smith that Arnie hadn't stopped teasing the Joneses' dogs, even though she had chased him away and pleaded with him. The Joneses inadvertently reinforced Arnie's teasing with attention, while the Smiths extinguished it. The combination of the Joneses' reinforcement of Arnie's teasing and the Smith's extinction of it is an example of what procedure? ______________________________. Instead, they should have arranged for a series of families to extinguish Arnie's behavior until extinction generalized to everyone's pet. They would have been using what behavioral procedure? ______________________

5. Calvin was undergoing training as a salesperson for a company that makes and sells encyclopedias. After explaining to him the virtues of the product and how to be a good salesperson, the trainers had him enter a special room that looked like someone's living room. A trainer played the role of the homeowner, and Calvin tried to sell the trainer a set of encyclopedias. The trainer had a checklist of behaviors that Calvin was supposed to perform, which he quietly checked off as they went along. Calvin was told about any steps he might have forgotten. This training was repeated until Calvin did it right three times in a row. Then a different trainer was brought in—one who was a "harder sell." Again the training was repeated until Calvin got it right. Several other trainers were then brought in as the final part of the process. The training room was made to look like a living room so as to increase the probability that Calvin's selling ability would ______________ to real living rooms. What procedure was the company using by employing a series of trainers? ______________________

6. Professor Forsyth taught his classes that imperialism was one country intervening in the affairs of another country. He gave as an example the Soviet Union's intervention in Lithuania in 1939. He then asked Juan to give three other examples. Juan delighted the professor by citing the Soviet Union's intervention in Czechoslovakia in 1948, and he also won approval for citing North Korea in 1945. But then he suggested that American intervention in Vietnam was imperialism. The professor ignored Juan. The occurrence of labeling the Vietnam intervention as imperialistic would be an example of what behavioral process? ______________________. The professor reinforced Juan for labeling as imperialism any intervention by a communist country. He did not reinforce Juan for using the label when the United States intervened. By reinforcing Juan when he labeled communist intervention as imperialism and extinguishing him when he labeled U.S. intervention as imperialism, the professor was using what behavioral procedure? ______________ ______________________

7. Ms. Lucci is an eighth-grade English teacher. She taught her students the meaning of the word *alliteration*—the repetition of a sound beginning several words in a row. She asked Michael to label the sentence, "Peter Piper picked a peck of pickled peppers." She praised him profusely when he said, "alliteration." Several days later, she asked Michael to label Poe's line, "In the

clamor and the clangor of the bells!" He said, "alliteration." Michael's second response is an example of what behavioral process? ____________________________. If his behavior had not generalized after one reinforcement, Ms. Lucci could have introduced more examples and reinforced his behavior many times. She would then be using what behavioral procedure? ______________________________

8. Margo complained when Danny wouldn't go out because he was studying, and she complained when Danny wouldn't go out because he was going to a football game. Danny decided that she had a right to complain when he put football ahead of her, but not when he put studying ahead of her. He explained his conclusions to her. Thereafter, every time she complained that he wouldn't go out with her because of a football game, he canceled plans to attend the game and went out with her instead. However, when she complained about his studying, he totally ignored her. After six months, Margo was complaining about his putting football ahead of her, but not about his putting studying ahead of her. By going along with her when she complained about football but ignoring her when she complained about studying, what procedure did Danny use? ______________________________

9. A self-control procedure for studying used by many students is to set aside a specific place to do schoolwork. They make sure that no other behavior is reinforced there. Thus, they never bring magazines, food, a radio, or other potential reinforcers to their study area. By ignoring nonstudy behavior in the study area, the study area becomes a stimulus associated with extinction for nonstudy behavior. Such a stimulus is called a(n) ______________________________. By restricting the study area to studying, you would hope that the student's study behavior gets reinforced. Thus, the study area becomes a stimulus associated with reinforcement for studying. Such a stimulus is called a(n) ______________________________. If study behavior began to occur in the study area and nowhere else, we would say that the study area exerted ______________________________ over study behavior.

10. One day Corbin complained to his mother about his unhappiness. She listened sympathetically and told him that he didn't have to do his chores that day. Corbin frequently complained to her about his unhappiness after that, and she let him stop any chores that he was doing. Corbin complained to his teacher one day that he was unhappy. What behavioral process describes Corbin's complaining about his unhappiness to his teacher? ______________________________

11. Review: Raney was in the second grade. One day during spelling, she laid her head on the desk. The teacher asked her what the matter was, and she said, "Teacher, I have a terrible headhurt." The teacher soothed her by saying, "That's too bad, Raney, why don't you just lay your head down until it feels better?" Raney frequently complained of headhurts after that. She also complained of headhurts to her third-grade teacher the next year, but that teacher didn't buy it. She gave Raney an aspirin and told her to get back to work. These two teachers were combining to apply what procedure to Raney's complaints of headhurts? ______________________________

12. Review: Diane has many friends: Ann, Mary, Fred, Kenny, David, Helen, and John, to mention a few. If we consider Diane's friends as stimuli, then the collection consisting of all her friends is called a(n) ______________________________.

13. Review: Janice swears in the presence of her friends but not in the presence of her parents. Because her swearing behavior occurs more often with her friends, it is called ______________________________ behavior.

14. Review: Abdul made a joke when asked by his English teacher to define "noun" and everyone in class laughed uproariously. As a result, he made a joke the next hour in his social studies class, where he had never been reinforced for telling a joke. The occurrence of his joking behavior in the second class is an example of what behavioral process? ______________________________

15. Review: The taxonomy class was interesting but terribly difficult for Clara. She got a correct score when she remembered to apply the term *invertebrate* to a crab but not to a rat. Likewise, she got a correct score for applying the term *vertebrate* to a rat but not to a crab. The course instructor was applying what behavioral procedure to her behavior? ______________________________

16. Review: Janice carefully typed a course paper for the first time in college. She received her first A ever for that paper. She then typed a paper for another course, and got another A. This happened in several other courses. What procedure were those course instructors unknowingly

applying to Janice's typing behavior to increase its occurrence in many other courses? ____________________

17. Review: After much trial and error, Janice learned to call the big planet Jupiter and the little one Venus, but not vice versa. Her behavior of calling the big planet Jupiter but not the little one would be called ____________________ behavior.

18. Review: Janice learned to call a picture of the biggest planet Jupiter. Behavior analysts say that the picture exerted ____________________ over her planet-naming behavior.

19. Review: Dr. Feelgood reacted positively when Felix thanked him for a compliment but ignored him when he did not. Gradually Felix learned to thank Dr. Feelgood for his compliments. What behavioral procedure did Dr. Feelgood employ to teach Felix to thank him for compliments? ____________________

20. Review: Grant was usually pretty stingy with his favors. However, every time he did something nice for Alma, she immediately thanked him and often did something even nicer for him. His rate of doing favors for Alma gradually increased. One day he did a very nice thing for Karen, and she was so surprised that she thanked him profusely. This same pattern occurred with several of Grant's other friends. He gradually started doing favors for many people. What behavioral procedure was being unknowingly employed by Grant's friends to increase his rate of doing favors for everyone? ____________________

LESSON

18 Programming and Fading

This lesson introduces the two behavioral procedures of fading and programming. Behavior analysts turn to these two procedures to develop stimulus control with a novel stimulus when the person they are training never responds to that stimulus. Because the person does not respond to the novel stimulus, behavior analysts can never reinforce them for doing so. Both procedures use an added stimulus whose control is already established to evoke responding in the presence of the novel stimulus.

Fading and programming add to the novel stimulus an existing discriminative stimulus that already exerts control over the desired response. They call this added stimulus a *prompt*, because it prompts the person to make the desired response. The behavior analyst then slowly eliminates the prompt until the person is responding to the novel stimulus alone. The use of the prompt produces new discriminated behaviors.

Behavior analysts turn to fading and programming as they sometimes turn to shaping. They use shaping when the target behavior does not exist. Likewise, they use fading and programming when the discriminated behavior they want to work with does not exist.

Fading uses an added prompt to produce a single discrimination. Programming uses many added prompts to produce generalization. Tactic #3 in using the stimulus control strategy is to create new stimulus control by using prompts.

1. Tactic #3 in using the stimulus control strategy is to create new stimulus control by using ______________.

Prompts

Both procedures that are introduced in this lesson temporarily add a prompt to a novel stimulus. For example, you want to teach baby Jane to say "Dada" when you point to her father. If she never spontaneously says "Dada" when you point to her father, you can't reinforce her for saying it. Now suppose baby Jane will imitate "da" if you say it. In the language of discrimination training, your saying "da" is an existing SD in whose presence she will say "da." It can therefore serve as a prompt.

The procedures used in this lesson depend on being able to withdraw the prompt in such a way that Jane's father becomes the SD. The tactic is to point to her father and say "da." If that gets her to start saying "da," you can reinforce her for saying "da" when you point to her father plus say your prompt. You then try to gradually withdraw your prompt. For example, she might still say "da" even if you only make the "d" sound. If so, you would reinforce her "da." She may then say "da" if you only whisper the "d" sound. Again you reinforce her "da." You may then be able to mouth "d" silently. Eventually baby Jane will be saying "Dada" when you point to her father without the prompt. You have taught her to respond correctly to her father alone, so you no longer have to give her the prompt. Thus, a **prompt** is an added stimulus that increases the probability that a person will make the correct response in the presence of a novel stimulus. It is usually withdrawn as soon as practical.

2. A prompt is an added ______________ that increases the probability that a person will make the correct response in the presence of a novel stimulus.

Fading

The first procedure that uses a prompt is called *fading*. Behavior analysts use fading when the person never makes the desired response in the presence of some novel stimulus.

Fading is the temporary use of a prompt to establish a specific discrimination. You gradually withdraw the prompt. Your goal is for the person to discriminate without the prompt. Fading solves a problem that may arise when teaching a discrimination. The problem is that the behavior may never occur in the presence of the SD. When that happens, you can never reinforce the behavior to begin discrimination training. However, you may be able to get the behavior to occur by using a prompt. You can prompt the behavior in the presence of the SD so that you can reinforce it. By gradually eliminating the prompt, you shift stimulus control solely to the SD.

3. The temporary use of a prompt that is gradually withdrawn to establish a specific discrimination is the procedure of ______________.

For example, you might use a prompt to teach Patty to label colors. You might show her a red spot and ask, "What color is this?" If she can't answer, you might give her a hint such as "Is it red?" or "Say red." You would use a prompt to get the behavior started. Then you can reinforce it. Since you don't want to have to give her hints all the time, you gradually withdraw the hint.

You must understand that fading is a particular kind of discrimination training—a kind that involves the use of a prompt. Everything else about the discrimination training procedure remains the same. However, stimulus control may develop more rapidly.

Examples of Fading

Examples of prompts and fading abound in everyday life. Each time parents give a hint to a child and then gradually withdraw it, they are using prompting and fading. For example, they may show Suzie a picture of a cow. Then they may ask, "What is this, Suzie? You know, moo." The "moo" is a prompt. They may show Suzie a picture of a dog and ask, "What is this, Suzie? You know, bowwow." They are again using a prompt. They use these prompts to help Suzie make the discrimination between the cow and the dog.

Once the initial discrimination is established, the parents may start to eliminate the prompts. For example, the next time they show Suzie the picture of the cow, they may only say "moo." The time after that, they may silently mouth the "moo" sound. Finally, they may eliminate the prompt, so that the child responds solely to the visual stimulus of the cow. The gradual elimination of the "bowwow" prompt for the dog is also an example of fading. While it is not spelled out in either example, you should understand that the parents must reinforce the prompted behavior.

Notice that the parents use prompts to establish a discrimination between two distinct pictures. They use prompts to establish a discrimination.

Fading will be ineffective if a prompt is used with a single stimulus. If the parents always showed Suzie the dog, she would not need a prompt. She could just remember to say "dog." However, if they alternate the dog with the cow, remembering only "dog" would not work. The hint then helps the child learn which animal is which. The general rule is always to use at least two stimuli when trying to teach a child to label an object. In fact, you should always use at least

Helping Hitters Discriminate Curveballs: Part 2

Remember the team of sports psychologists who helped batters discriminate curveballs? They added a 1/4-inch-wide stripe of orange to the seams of pitched curveballs. This helped batters hit better. But how could this help the batters learn to hit unmarked balls better? The team used fading to help the batters learn. They faded the width of their stripe from 1/4 inch to 1/8 inch, and the batters hit almost as well with the narrower stripe. Unfortunately, the season ended at that point. Could the researchers fade the stripe out altogether while maintaining the improved hitting? You'll have to wait until next year, sports fans! (Based on Osborne, Rudrud, & Zezoney, 1990.)

4. Because it is an added stimulus, behavior analysts call the orange stripe a(n) ______ ______________ in a fading procedure. (Hint: The answer starts with the letter "p.")

two stimuli when teaching any discriminated behavior.

Researchers used a fading procedure to overcome children's fear of the dark (Giebenhain & O'Dell, 1984). "BL," an 11-year-old, would not sleep unless his parents left his lights on all night. They could never get him to sleep in the dark. Therefore, they could never reinforce him for sleeping in the dark. The researchers approached the dark as a novel stimulus and the light as an added stimulus. The researchers put a dimmer on BL's bedside light so that he could control the amount of light. They marked the dial of the dimmer from full illumination (11) to no illumination (0). During baseline, BL set the dimmer at about 8, which provided lots of light. The parents started playing a fear reduction game at bedtime. They encouraged BL to relax and make positive statements, such as "I am brave when I'm in the dark." They suggested to BL that he set the dimmer lower. They reinforced staying the whole night with the dimmer ½ number lower than the previous night. They gave him praise, hugs, toys, and treats. BL faded the light to 0 in less than three weeks. He now sleeps without the light on. Now he is brave when he's in the dark!

Researchers used fading to teach non-shy preschoolers to play with shy children (Odom et al., 1992). I will describe their procedure with Pete, who wasn't shy. Pete made virtually no initiations to the shy children. To change this, the teacher first taught Pete five ways to initiate play. He could share his play with the other child, ask to share the other child's play, organize play, assist the other in their play, or simply persist in his efforts. Next, whenever Pete did not initiate to the other child, the teacher prompted him to use one of the methods every 30 seconds. The teacher also posted a happy face every time Pete initiated. Pete's rate of initiating increased to 20 initiations every five minutes. Next, the teacher faded her prompts. She changed from prompting a specific method to prompting Pete to get the other child to play. She stopped prompting but kept the happy face. Finally, she stopped the happy face. Pete continued to initiate about 15 times in 5 minutes. Both Pete and the shy child benefited.

Researchers use fading to teach other skills as well. They teach arithmetic skills (e.g., Paine et al., 1982). They teach nearsighted people to see better (Pbert et al., 1988). They teach children with insomnia to go right to sleep when they go to bed (Piazza & Fisher, 1991). They teach smokers to gradually change to low tar and nicotine cigarettes (Prue, Krapfl & Martin, 1981).

Throw Away Your Glasses and See

Most nearsighted people wear glasses. Without glasses, their eyes bring an image into focus in front of the retina rather than on the retina. This is because their muscles make the eyeball too long. Evidence suggests that this reflects a history of reinforcement for close work. Making the eyeball long produces the reinforcer of clear focus on their on close work. Many studies now indicate that discrimination training with fading can change that habit. Case studies show that some people no longer need glasses after such training. Behavior analysts regard the muscular response of making the eyeball a different length depending upon the distance of the SD as a behavior (Rosen, Schiffman, & Cohen, 1984).

5. Because that behavior becomes more likely after fading, behavior analysts call the behavior a ________________ behavior. (Hint: The answer is one word that starts with "d" and ends with "ated.")

Programming

Programming is a more complex use of prompts. **Programming** is the temporary use of prompts to establish a generalization. You gradually withdraw the prompts. Your goal is for the behavior to generalize without the prompts.

6. Programming is the temporary use of prompts to establish a ________________.

Programming is necessary when you teach a generalization but the behavior never occurs in the presence of the novel stimulus. You can use a prompt to start the behavior. Once started, you can reinforce it in the presence of the novel stimulus. Then you can begin to withdraw the prompt. The result is that the person learns to perform the behavior solely in response to the (once novel) stimulus. The procedure becomes programming if you reinforce the same behavior in the presence of a series of novel stimuli until it generalizes to other members of the stimulus class.

For example, suppose Suzie calls a big round object, but nothing else, a ball. You might use a prompt to start her generalization to other round objects. You might hold up a golf ball and ask, "What is this?" If you get no response, you might ask, "Is it a ball?" or you might say, "Say 'ball.'" You must, of course, reinforce the resulting response. By slowly withdrawing the prompt, you may get Suzie to call the golf ball a ball with no prompting. You might do this with several other balls until she generalizes to all balls.

Programming occurs often in everyday life. Remember the parents' teaching Suzie to discriminate between a cow and and a dog? Suppose they used several pictures of each animal. The cows might differ in color, size, and location. The parents could use prompts to establish the label "cow" or "dog" for each picture. They would then gradually withdraw the prompts. If they used different cows and dogs, they would be using programming. If they used enough different animals, this procedure might produce generalization to all cows (or dogs).

Picking a prompt and programming its withdrawal are largely unspecified and intuitive processes at this time. You must withdraw the prompt so that the novel stimulus gradually develops stimulus control. Transferring stimulus control from the prompt to the SD is the hardest aspect of withdrawing the prompt. You must get the person to gradually shift his or her attention from the prompt to the SD. If the prompt is totally unrelated to the SD, this can be even more difficult (Schreibman, 1975).

You should understand that programming is a particular kind of generalization training—a kind that employs prompts. Everything else about the two procedures is the same.

Be sure you know the difference between fading and programming. Fading uses prompts to establish a <u>discrimination</u> between two specific stimuli. Programming uses prompts to teach <u>generalization</u> to a class of stimuli.

7. Programming uses prompts to teach <u>generalization</u> to a class of stimuli. Fading uses prompts to establish a ______________ between two specific stimuli.

Figure 18-1 illustrates an innovative program designed to teach German by reading short stories by Edgar Allan Poe. The program simply replaces some English words with the German word of the same meaning. The program uses the nearby English words to make it easy to guess at the meaning of the German words. The English words are prompts for translating the German words into the correct English words. The program gradually withdraws the prompts over the course of three stories. English words make up 90% of the

> True!—nervous, very very dreadfully nervous, *ich*, had been, and am; but why will you say that *ich* am mad? The disease had sharpened *mein* senses—not destroyed, not dulled them. Above all was *der* sense of hearing acute. *Ich* heard all the things in *dem* heaven and *der* earth. I heard many things in hell.

> *Der* second *und* third day went by *und* yet showed himself *mein* tormenter *nicht*. Again could *ich* as a free man breathe. *Das* monster was apparently in great terror ran away! Never again would *ich es* see!

> *Die* slope *seiner Wande wurde von Moment zu Moment* smaller, *und der* bottom *der Vortex* seemed *sich* gradually *zu* lift. *Der* sky *war klar, die Winde Hatten sich* died, *und der* moon went brightly *im Westen* down, *als ich mich auf dem* surface *des Ozeans* facing *die* coast *von Lofden* found, exactly *über der* place,...

Figure 18-1. Illustrations of three phases used in teaching German by replacing redundant words in three short stories by Edgar Allan Poe. In phase one, "skeletal" words *(a, the, and, but, in, out, have)* are replaced by their German equivalents in those places where the student can guess their meaning from the context of the story. In phase two, few new words are introduced, but the sentences are couched in the grammatical structure of German. In phase three, common words (such as *table, boy, floor,* and so on) are introduced into sentences containing skeletal words cast in the German grammatical structure. Using this method the student learns German while reading an entertaining short story. From "A Vocabulary Program Using 'Language Redundancy,'" by H. H. Schaefer, *Journal of Programmed Instruction,* 1963, *2,* 9–16.

words in the first story, 75% in the second story, but only 30% in the third story. This is a program, because the student learns to recognize each word in many novel contexts. For example, the German word *ich* appears in five different contexts in this illustration. Thus recognition of it may generalize to other contexts.

Programmed instruction is a common form of programming. It consists of a series of statements requiring a written response. Typically, these statements are sentences with one word left out. Sometimes longer units of reading (such as a paragraph) are used before the fill-in sentence occurs. Skinner suggests that three features are particularly important. (1) Programmed instruction requires a written response. This response tells the author if the student understands the statement. (2) Programmed instruction provides immediate feedback on the accuracy of each response. This feedback may serve as a reinforcement for correct responses. (3) Programmed instruction uses small steps. The program asks the student to learn only a small amount of new information at one time. Programmed instruction usually teaches complex verbal behavior. People have used it to teach children reading, arithmetic, and writing. They have used it to teach college students foreign language, algebra, history, and psychology.

8. Programmed instruction (1) requires a written ______________, (2) provides immediate ______________ on the accuracy of each response, and (3) uses small ______________.

Figure 18-2 shows a simple sequence from *Programmed Reading* (Buchanan, 1973). This sequence teaches children to write the word *bag*. Initially it gives the children the prompt "ba" to draw their attention to the "g." Then it shortens the prompt to "b." Next it omits the "b," so the

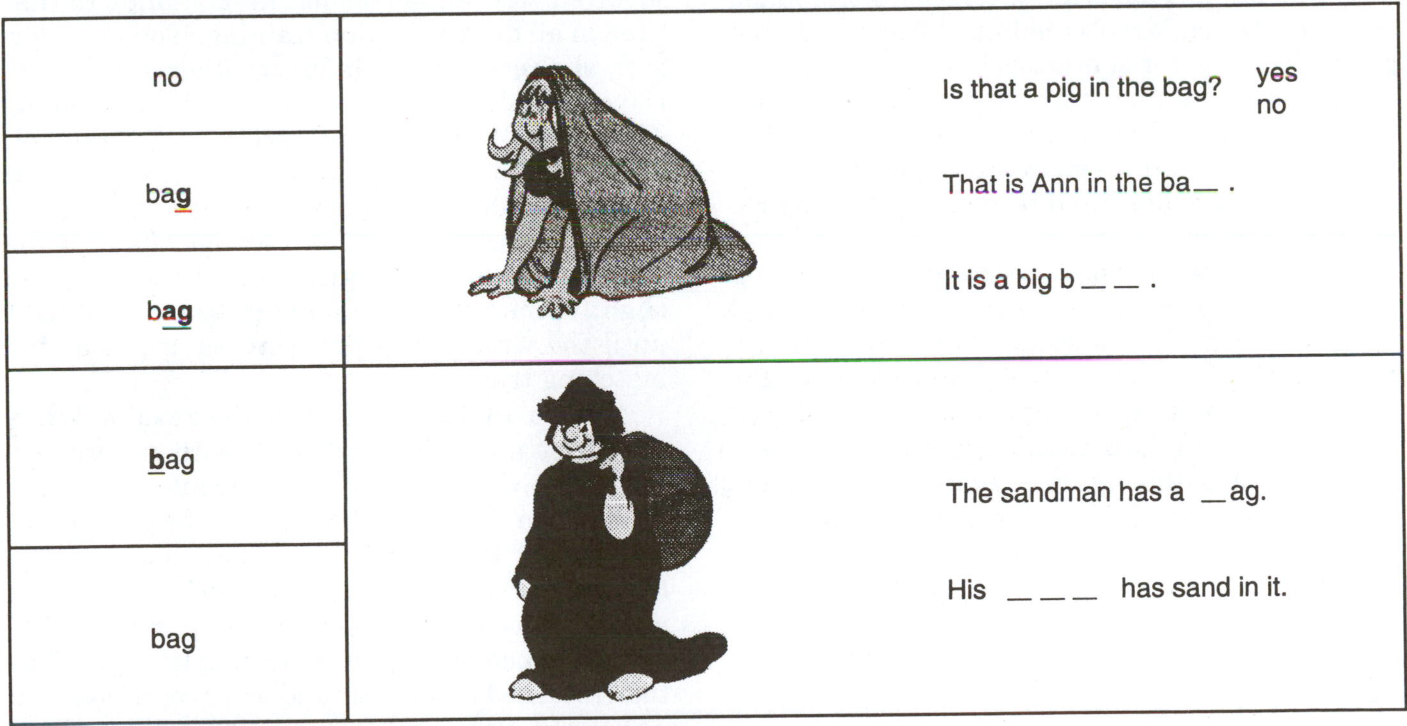

Figure 18-2. Five items from a sequence designed to teach the word *bag*. The children use this program by covering the answers on the left with a mask. They then circle either "yes" or "no" in answering the first question, move the mask down far enough to reveal the answer to that question, and proceed to the next question. This sequence is taken from the second of 23 books designed to teach children with no prior reading ability how to read. The last books involve reading complete stories at the sixth-grade level and answering questions about them. These books have been demonstrated to be extremely effective in teaching reading to all children; they are particularly useful in teaching reading to children who do not respond to traditional teaching methods. For example, they can produce gains in low-income children that are equivalent to or even greater than those attained by middle-class children using traditional reading instruction materials. From *Programmed Reading, Book 2* (3rd ed.), by W. Sullivan and C. D. Buchanan. Copyright 1973 by McGraw-Hill, Inc. Reprinted by permission.

children write out the whole word. Of course, they can still see the complete word in previous questions, so that part of the prompt still remains. At a later stage, they will fill in the whole word with no prompts. By then they will have a pretty good grasp of the word and its meaning.

Programmed reading has the features of programmed instruction. The children must make a written response. They can obtain immediate feedback by looking at the correct answer on the left. They learn only the amount contained in each of the small steps. Your first reaction might be that they will never learn very much with such a method. In fact, the program takes them from no reading skill to a sixth-grade reading level, and it teaches reading faster than alternative teaching methods. Interestingly, this method works extremely well even with children who have severe learning disabilities.

Figure 18-2 would be an example of fading if it showed a picture of a bag and stated, "This is a ba -," and later, "This is a - - -." In such a simplified situation, the children's reading of "bag" might not generalize to other sentences or other pictures of bags. They would be learning a simple discrimination (labeling this picture "bag" and not other pictures). The example shown in Figure 18-2, since it does teach a generalized response, is an example of programming.

The implications of fading and programming are revolutionary, not only for our educational system but also for our society. One implication is that specific intellectual skills can now be taught to segments of society that seemed incapable of learning by standard teaching methods. For example, these methods have been used to teach new skills to preschool children (Moore & Goldiamond, 1964), children with retardation (Birnbrauer et al., 1965), and low-income children (Miller & Schneider, 1970).

Summary

Fading and programming both use existing SD's as prompts. The prompt is added to a novel stimulus that has no effect on behavior. Then the prompt is slowly withdrawn until the novel stimulus has become an SD. The influence exerted by the prompt has then been transferred to the novel stimulus. This teaches the person the discrimination. Behavior analysts use this very powerful teaching technique to teach very difficult discriminations. Tactic #3 of the stimulus control strategy is to create new stimulus control by using prompts.

Behavior Analysis Example

Teaching Toddlers Triangles

Researchers used fading to teach 3-year-old Sarah to match triangles (Moore & Goldiamond, 1964). The researchers showed Sarah a sample triangle; they then showed her three other triangles. One of the triangles was oriented exactly like the sample triangle, and the other two were rotated to different angles. If Sarah pressed the button below the matching triangle, she was given an edible treat. If she pressed the button below the other two triangles, she was given nothing.

The researchers tried two ways of teaching Sarah to find the matching triangle. One approach involved trial-and-error learning similar to that used in all discrimination training. If she was correct, she received a reinforcer; otherwise she received nothing. The other approach was fading. They lit up the matching triangle as a prompt, but they did not light up the nonmatching triangles. Sarah always picked the lit triangle. The researchers then faded this prompt by lighting the two nonmatching triangles. At first they lit them slightly; then they gradually increased the light until the wrong triangles were as bright as the matching triangle.

Figure 18-3 is a graph of the results. When they first used trial-and-error with no prompt, Sarah got the correct answer about 20% of the time. When they used the prompt, she got the correct answer 100% of the time. They then partially faded the prompt until the nonmatching triangles were 60% as bright as the matching triangle. Sarah continued picking the matching triangle. They then returned to the trial-and-error condition with no prompt. Sarah got less than 20% correct. They returned to the prompt, and again Sarah got mostly right answers. They then completely faded the prompt, and Sarah still got the correct answer 90% of the time. Finally, they eliminated the prompt. Because of the training with the prompt, Sarah could now always pick the correct triangle. She made many errors while learning poorly through trial and error. She made almost no errors while learning through fading.

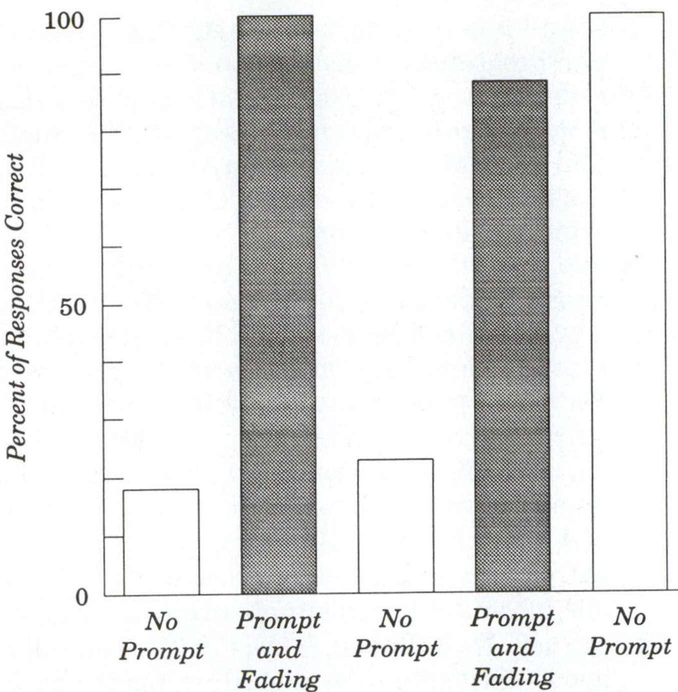

Figure 18-3. Sarah's accuracy in matching triangles when no prompt was given and when a prompt was used but gradually faded out. The last bar shows the performance after the prompt had been completely faded out. Without the prior use of the prompt and fading, this performance would have been only about 20% accurate. Adapted from "Errorless Establishment of Visual Discrimination Using Fading Procedures," by R. Moore and I. Goldiamond, *Journal of the Experimental Analysis of Behavior,* 1964, 7, 269–272. Copyright 1964 by the Society for the Experimental Analysis of Behavior, Inc. Used by permission.

These results are similar to other results often obtained when using fading or programming procedures. They suggest that learning can be faster and almost error-free when prompts are used to assist learning.

9. Behavior analysts call lighting up the correct triangle a(n) ________________. (Hint: The answer is a short word that starts with the 16th letter of the alphabet.)

Notes

Note #1

Programming has a rather unfortunate history. It was first developed by B. F. Skinner in the mid 1950s and showed great promise of improving educational technology. Skinner wrote a series of articles promoting its use (e.g., Skinner, 1954). The idea, particularly in the form of teaching machines, was picked up by book publishers. Many psychologists and educators who did not understand behavior analysis developed programs. The publishers promoted these programs without ensuring that they were properly developed (Sulzer & Mayer, 1972). The results were disastrous. Many educators exposed to these products concluded that programs were boring and ineffective. It may be many years before the ill effects of this history are overcome.

10. What behavioral procedure did B. F. Skinner invent in the mid-1950s to help students learn? ________________

Note #2

The book will ask you to identify several examples of programmed instruction. In these cases, you may label the example either as programmed instruction or simply as programming, since programmed instruction is a type of programming.

11. You may label an example of programmed instruction either as programmed instruction or simply as programming, since programmed instruction is a type of ________________ (fading, programming).

Helpful Hints

Helpful Hint #1

Students often have trouble telling the difference between fading and programming. Both procedures involve the use of prompts added onto an underlying procedure. Fading is the use of prompts with discrimination training. Programming is the use of prompts with generalization training. To tell whether an example involves fading or programming, first decide whether the underlying procedure is discrimination training or generalization training.

12. If a prompt is used with generalization training, the procedure is called ________________; if a prompt is used with discrimination training, the procedure is called ________________.

Helpful Hint #2

Shaping and fading are sometimes confused. Shaping involves gradually changing behavior. The stimulus situation remains the same, but the rules of reinforcement, and therefore the behaviors, are changed. Fading involves gradually changing the stimulus. The behavior stays the same, but the prompt is gradually withdrawn, and the stimulus situation is changed. Fading is used to gradually change the stimulus; shaping is used to gradually change the behavior.

13. Shaping is a procedure that involves the gradual changing of the ________________; fading is a procedure that involves the gradual changing of the ________________.

Helpful Hint #3

You are now learning about many behavioral procedures that are quite complicated. Within each lesson, I have given you hints to help you distinguish between the procedures covered by that lesson. But you must also distinguish between the procedures covered in different lessons. I will ask you from now on about differential reinforcement, discrimination training, generalization training, fading, and programming. You must keep all of them separate.

14. Remember to read each example to find out whether it involves reinforcing one behavior and extinguishing other behaviors in the same situation. If it does, the procedure is called ________________.

Additional Readings

Birnbrauer, J. S., Bijou, S. W., Wolf, M. M., & Kidder, J. D. (1965). Programmed instruction in the classroom. In L. P. Ullman and L. Krasner (Eds.), *Case studies in behavior modification*. New York: Holt, Rinehart & Winston. This describes the use of programmed instruction to advance the academic scores of children with retardation who had no previous record of academic achievement. Gains were made in the children's writing, reading, and math skills.

Holland, J. G. (1960). Teaching machines: An application of principles from the laboratory. *Journal of the Experimental Analysis of Behavior*, *3*, 275–287. This article is an early description of the principles of teaching machines and programmed instruction.

Lumsdaine, A. A., & Glaser, R. (1960). *Teaching machines and programmed learning*. Washington, DC: National Education Association. This book collects early articles that discuss programmed instruction.

Markle, S. (1969). *Good frames and bad: A grammar of frame writing*. New York: Wiley. This is a programmed how-to-do-it book. It explains in simple language how to write programmed materials, gives many examples, and then requires the reader to try his or her knowledge.

Miller, L. K., & Schneider. R. (1970). The use of a token system in Project Head Start. *Journal of Applied Behavior Analysis*, *3*, 213–220. An early study using fading procedures to teach low-income children simple printing skills.

Newsom, C. D., & Simon, K. M. (1977). A simultaneous discrimination procedure for the measurement of vision in nonverbal children. *Journal of Applied Behavior Analysis*, *10*, 633–644. Psychotic children with severe retardation often do not receive proper vision testing and need eyeglasses because they don't follow the instructions necessary in such testing. To test such children adequately, a procedure was devised in which they were reinforced with an edible (such as an M&M) for selecting one of two cards that could be discriminated only if their vision at that level was adequate. A fading procedure was used, initially training them to select one type of card.

Schreibman, L. (1975). Effects of within-stimulus and extra-stimulus prompting on discrimination learning in autistic children. *Journal of Applied Behavior Analysis*, *8*, 91–112. This study demonstrates that it is possible to teach severely psychotic children to make very fine discriminations, without errors, through the use of fading. However, the prompts must be integrally related to the discriminative stimuli rather than simply unrelated prompts.

Skinner, B. F. (1954). The science of learning and the art of teaching. *Harvard Educational Review*, *24*, 99–113. Also reprinted in the Lumsdaine and Glaser (1960) book referenced above. This is the earliest statement by Skinner of the concepts underlying programmed instruction.

Vargas, E. A., & Vargas, J. S. (1991). Programmed instruction: What it is and how to do it. *Journal of Behavioral Education*, *1* (2), 235–251.

This paper describes the current state of programmed instruction.

Wulbert, M., Nyman, B. A., Snow, D., & Owen, Y. (1973). The efficacy of stimulus fading and contingency management in the treatment of elective mutism: A case study. *Journal of Applied Behavior Analysis*, *6*, 435–441. This study concerns a 6-year-old child who did not speak or follow instructions in kindergarten. However, she reacted normally at home in the presence of her mother. The mother was used as a prompt to maintain normal responding, and an experimenter was faded into the situation in gradual steps until the child responded normally in her presence. This was repeated with five experimenters until the child responded normally to the sixth and to her teacher. At this point, the mother's presence was not required, and the child became a well-adjusted student in her class.

Reading Quiz

35. Review: Let's start by learning about the new tactic. Creating new stimulus control by using <u>prompts</u> is the third tactic in using the stimulus ____________ strategy for solving human problems.
62. The third tactic in using the stimulus control strategy for solving human problems is to create new stimulus control by using ________ (prompts, shaping).
63. The third tactic in using the stimulus control strategy suggests that when you must create new stimulus control, you try using ____________.
1. Another introductory point: Fading and programming are procedures that use a <u>prompt</u> to develop ________ (new, old) discriminated behaviors.
27. Review: An added stimulus that increases the probability that a behavior will occur in the presence of a novel stimulus is called a(n) ____________.
56. The first goal is to learn about fading. The gradual withdrawal of a prompt used to establish a <u>specific</u> discrimination is called ____________ (fading, programming).
31. Review: Fading is teaching a specific discrimination by the gradual withdrawal of an added stimulus called a(n) ____________.
33. Review: If the correct behavior never occurs in the presence of the SD during discrimination training, then you can try to increase its probability by using a(n) ____________.
54. Suppose when you ask Patty the question "What color is this?", she never answers correctly. If you gave her the hint "Is it red?" when asking the question, this added stimulus would be an example of a(n) ____________.
3. Fading is a particular kind of ____________ (discrimination, generalization) training that employs prompts.
43. Review: Suppose you show a young child a picture of a dog and ask her, "What is this? You know, bowwow!" "You know, bowwow" would be called a(n) ____________.
47. Review: The gradual elimination of a prompt such as "bowwow" while one is teaching a discrimination between a cow and a dog is called ____________.
45. Review: The behavioral procedure of fading is used to establish a specific ____________ between two distinct stimuli.
44. Review: Suppose you show Debby a picture of a dog (interspersed with pictures of a cat) many times during the day. You ask her what it is and reinforce her when she calls this picture "dog" but ignore her when she calls the cat "dog." What behavioral procedure would you be using if you first added "You know, bowwow," next added it more softly, then only silently mouthed the "bowwow," and finally omitted it altogether? ____________
60. The orange stripe added to baseballs to help batters discriminate curveballs is an example of a(n) ____________.
10. Giebenhain and O'Dell (1984) helped "BL" to overcome his fear of the dark. His parents praised him when he slept in the dark but ignored him when he slept with his light on all night. They used a dimmer to permit low light as a prompt for sleeping in less than full light. They encouraged him to gradually dim this light from full light (11) to no light (0). Gradually reducing this prompt to teach him to sleep in the dark is an example of what behavioral procedure? ____________
15. Odom and associates (1992) helped a preschooler named Pete to play with shy children. They praised him when he played with shy children and ignored him when he played with normal children. As part of the procedure, the teacher suggested one of five ways of playing

every 30 seconds. Each suggestion would be called a(n) ______________.

66. When you add a temporary prompt and gradually withdraw it to assist with discrimination training, you are using the procedure called ______________.

4. Fading is the use of a temporary prompt that you should gradually withdraw to assist with ______________ training.

61. The second goal is to learn about programming as a kind of generalization training. For review, remember that reinforcing a behavior in each of a series of situations until it generalizes to <u>novel</u> stimuli from that same stimulus class is the procedure called ______________ training.

57. The goal of generalization training is for the behavior to occur in the presence of ______________ stimuli from the same stimulus class.

59. The occurrence of a response in the presence of a novel stimulus is the process that's called ______________.

58. The gradual withdrawal of prompts to establish a specific discrimination is called fading. The gradual withdrawal of prompts to establish a <u>generalization</u> is called ______________ (fading, programming).

21. Programming is the gradual withdrawal of prompts during generalization training to establish a(n) ______________ (discrimination, generalization).

11. If the correct behavior never occurs in the presence of a novel stimulus during generalization training, you can try to get it to occur by using a(n) ______________.

51. Review: When you use prompts to help in training a generalization, you are using what procedure? ______________

55. Suppose you are ready to praise Suzie when she calls a basketball a ball, but she never does. You might then use a prompt to get her to call it a ball and praise her lavishly when she does. You might gradually withdraw your prompt until she calls the basketball ball without any prompting. Suppose you use, and then withdraw, a prompt to teach her to call a golf ball a ball. If she now calls a novel ball a ball, her behavior illustrates the process called ______________.

42. Review: Suppose Peggy's parents show her a series of pictures of dogs, some big, some small. To get her started, they say, "What is this? You know, bowwow," and praise her when she says "dog." Suppose they gradually eliminate the "bowwow" for all of the pictures. What behavioral procedure are they using to teach Peggy to call even novel pictures of dogs a "dog"? ______________

68. When you use programming, your goal is to have the behavior continue to occur in the presence of the novel stimulus even after you have completely withdrawn the ______________.

9. Generalization training that temporarily employs prompts is called ______________.

22. Programming is using a prompt to establish a(n) ______________.

65. Using a prompt to establish a <u>generalization</u> is called ______________; using a prompt to establish a specific <u>discrimination</u> is called ______________.

23. Programming is using a prompt to establish a(n) ______________; fading is using a prompt to establish a(n) ______________.

53. Schaefer (1963) used the German word *ich* to replace the English "I" in several short stories by Poe. The context of redundant sentences was enough to serve as an effective prompt for correct translation. Presumably, understanding the sentence and ultimately the story was the reinforcer. Schaefer withdrew the prompt by selecting a series of sentences that were not as redundant. By seeing *ich* in a series of different sentences, students learned to translate that word in many novel sentences. What behavioral procedure did Schaeffer use to teach the meaning of *ich*? ______________

16. Programmed instruction is a common procedure that uses prompts to establish many generalizations. Therefore, it is a use of what behavioral procedure that is based on prompts? ______________

17. Programmed instruction involves three important features: (1) It requires a written <u>response</u>; (2) it provides immediate <u>feedback</u> about whether the response is correct; and (3) it requires the student to take only one ______________ (large, small) <u>step</u> at a time.

18. Programmed instruction (1) requires a written <u>response</u>; (2) provides immediate <u>feedback</u>; and (3) requires the student to take only a small ______________ at a time.

19. Programmed instruction (1) requires a written <u>response</u>; (2) provides immediate ______________ about whether the response is

correct; and (3) requires the student to take only small steps.

20. Programmed instruction (1) requires a written ______________; (2) gives immediate feedback; and (3) uses small steps.
37. Review: Programmed instruction involves three important features: (1) It makes the student give a written ______________; (2) it gives immediate ______________; and (3) it uses small ______________.
50. Review: What form of programming has these three characteristics: (1) It requires a written response; (2) it gives immediate feedback; (3) it uses small steps. Programmed ______________
12. In programmed reading, the child is shown a picture of a bag and is then required to fill in a blank: "That is Ann in the ba-." Showing one or more letters contained in the correct answer would be called a(n) ______________.
46. Review: The book called Programmed Reading has the following characteristics. (1) The children must make a written response. (2) They can obtain immediate feedback by looking at the correct answer on the left. (3) They learn only the amount contained in each of the small steps. This program is an example of what type of programming? ______________ instruction
25. Programming may contain fading within it. As part of teaching the child to call any bag a bag, the child might be shown a picture of a bag with the statement "This is a ba-," and later "This is a b- -," and still later "This is a - - -." The procedure of teaching the child to label the same picture as a bag by using the added stimulus of the word and then gradually showing fewer letters in the word is called ______________.
13. In an earlier lesson, you learned that behavior analysts can teach physical skills to many people who seemed incapable of learning with conventional teaching methods by using shaping. In this lesson you learned that behavior analysts can teach specific intellectual skills to many people who seemed incapable of learning with conventional teaching methods by using the procedures of ______________ and ______________.
2. Fading and programming both add an existing SD to a novel stimulus. Behavior analysts call an existing SD added to the novel stimulus a(n) ______________. Then the prompt is slowly withdrawn until the novel stimulus alone evokes the correct response. Because it is a stimulus in the presence of which the correct response will be reinforced, the novel stimulus becomes a(n) ______________.
24. Programming is using a prompt to establish a(n) ______________; fading is using a prompt to establish a(n) ______________.
67. When you add a temporary prompt and gradually withdraw it to assist with generalization training, you are using the procedure called ______________. When you add a temporary prompt and gradually withdraw it to assist with discrimination training, you are using the procedure called ______________.
14. Moore and Goldiamond (1964) made the correct answer light up while the incorrect answers remained dark. They then gradually increased the brightness of the incorrect answers until they were as bright as the correct answer. The brightness of the correct answer is an example of a(n) ______________.
52. Sarah made many errors when trying to match the unlit triangles through trial-and-error learning. She made ______________ (many, few) errors while learning through fading (Moore & Goldiamond, 1964).
26. Research results suggest that learning can be faster and almost error-free when prompts are used to assist learning with the two behavioral procedures of ______________ or ______________.
5. From Helpful Hint #1: Fading is the use of a temporary prompt to help ______________ training, whereas programming is the use of a temporary prompt to help ______________ training.
6. From Helpful Hint #2: When you use fading, you gradually withdraw a prompt. You might say that fading changes the stimulus. When you use shaping, you successively approximate the target behavior. So you might say that shaping, unlike fading, will change the ______________.
7. From Helpful Hint #2: When you use shaping, you successively approximate the target behavior. You might say that shaping changes the behavior. When you use fading, you gradually withdraw the added stimulus called a prompt. So you might say that fading changes the ______________.

8. From Helpful Hint #2: Shaping is a behavioral procedure that involves the gradual changing of the ______________; fading is a behavioral procedure that involves the gradual changing of the ____________.
48. Review: To use the stimulus control strategy, (1) narrow stimulus control through discrimination training; (2) broaden stimulus control through generalization training; (3) create new stimulus control by using ____________, as in fading or programming.
28. Review: Behavior analysts call an added stimulus that increases the probability of making the correct response a(n) __________.
29. Review: Behavior analysts call the procedure that involves the gradual withdrawal of a prompt to establish a specific discrimination ______________.
36. Review: Moore and Goldiamond (1964) had the correct answer light up while the incorrect answers remained dark. They then gradually increased the brightness of the incorrect answers until they were as bright as the correct answer. What behavioral procedure were they using by changing the brightness to teach this specific discrimination? ______________ ____________________
39. Review: Programming temporarily uses prompts to reinforce the same response in the presence of a series of stimuli from the same stimulus class. Therefore, programming is a particular kind of ______________________ training that temporarily employs prompts.
30. Review: Discrimination training that temporarily employs prompts to establish a specific discrimination is called ________________.
41. Review: Schaefer (1963) used the German word *ich* to replace the English *I* in several short stories by Poe. The context of redundant sentences was enough to serve as an effective prompt for proper translation. By placing the German word in many different sentences, students learned to recognize the word even where the sentence was not an effective prompt. What behavioral procedure did Schaefer use to teach the meaning of *ich* in many sentences? ____________________
38. Review: Programmed instruction requires a written response, provides immediate feedback on the correctness of the response, and uses small __________.
64. The third tactic in using the stimulus control strategy for solving human problems is to create new stimulus control by using __________.
40. Review: Programming is the temporary use of a prompt during generalization training to establish a(n) ________________.
34. Review: In programmed reading, the child is shown a picture of a girl in a bag and then required to fill in the blank: "That is Ann in the ba-." Showing one or more letters from the correct answer is called a(n) ___________.
32. Review: Gradually eliminating a prompt during discrimination training is called ________.
49. Review: To use the stimulus control strategy, (1) narrow stimulus control through discrimination training; (2) broaden stimulus control through ______________________; (3) create new stimulus control by using ____________.

Examples

1. Professor Smith was trying to teach 18-month-old Tracey the concepts of "above" and "below." She placed her hand over the table and asked, "Where is my hand? You know, above," and gave Tracey a spoonful of applesauce if she repeated it. Next time, she asked, "Where is my hand? You know, abuh," not pronouncing the "v" sound. Again she reinforced Tracey for saying "above." She gradually taught Tracey to say "above" without hints. (She ignored any time Tracey said "above" when the hand was below the table.) In several days, Tracey could answer the question correctly with no hints. The phrase "You know, above" is an added stimulus that is called a(n) ____________. Because Professor Smith was using a prompt to teach Tracey to say "above" when her hand was over the table but not when it was under the table, the procedure is called ____________________.

2. Professor Smith wanted Tracey to learn to use "above" correctly for any situation, so she next placed her hand over a dish and asked Tracey, "Where is my hand? You know, above," and gave Tracey a bite to eat if she repeated "above." She then gradually eliminated the hint. Next, she put a ball over the dish and asked Tracey, "Where is the ball?" To her surprise, before she could give the hint, Tracey blurted out "above." Professor Smith tried placing the dish on top of the ball and asking where it was. Again Tracey said "above." From then on, Tracey could always tell you whether an object was above or below. When

Tracey saw the ball over the plate for the first time, it was a novel stimulus. Saying "above" for the new situation, in which the ball was over the plate, is an example of what process? ________________________. Because the prof used a prompt to teach Tracey to tell when one object was over another in a series of situations until she could tell even with a new situation, she was using the behavioral procedure called ________________.

3. Mr. Franklin had just about given up on teaching his ninth-grade students the principles of algebra. Then he heard about a new type of book that required the students to write answers, gave them immediate feedback on their responses, and presented one small step at a time. He tried it and found that his students really started to learn algebra well. The new type of book is an example of programming called ________________.

4. Terry looked up the definition of every unknown word that she came across. First, she referred to the full definition while writing several sentences using the word. Second, she referred to a shortened version of the definition while writing several sentences. Third, she looked at a definition consisting only of a synonym or key word. Finally, she wrote sentences with no help from a definition. After this process, she could use the word correctly in both speech and writing. Terry's goal was to be able to use the new word in any novel situation that might come along. Her production of the word in a novel situation is an example of the process called ________________. The written definition served as a(n) ________________ for correct use of the new word. Next, decide whether this temporary use of prompts was fading or programming. To do so, decide whether she was using discriminaton training or generalization training with each word. Because Terry was using prompts to learn use of the word in a series of sentences until she could use it in novel sentences, this is an example of what behavioral procedure? ________________

5. Mom showed Maria a card with the word *rejoice* on it. She said "What is this word? You know, rejoice." She praised Maria if she said "rejoice." Mom then said "rejoice" more and more softly until Maria said "rejoice" just from looking at the word alone. Mom also used the same procedure with the word *exhaust*. Mom praised Maria when she said "rejoice" when that was the word on the card but ignored her when the word on the card was *exhaust*. Because Mom was using a prompt to teach Maria to read the word on each card, her procedure is called ________________.

6. Can you tell the difference between programming and generalization training? James held up a tennis ball for his sister to see and asked her what it was. When she said "ball," he gave her a big smile and praised her. After she had learned to call the tennis ball a ball, he showed her a basketball and asked her what it was, again repeating the same procedure used on the tennis ball. After she had learned to call it a ball, he showed her a golf ball, and she immediately said "ball." Note that he used no prompts. His procedure involved reinforcing the word *ball* for a series of many different balls until his sister applied the word *ball* to novel types of balls. You call his procedure ________________. If he had given her a hint that he gradually withdrew for each ball, what behavioral procedure would he have been using? ________________

7. Fred learned the definition of *reinforcer* from a specially designed book. In the book, he was first given a specific definition of *reinforcer*. The first question had the same words but gave a hint with two possible answers in parentheses: "An event that follows a behavior and increases its probability is called a(n) ________________ (reinforcement, reinforcer)." When the question was presented again, the choices in parentheses were left out. The second version of the question used different words but meant the same: "An event that occurs after a behavior such that its frequency increases is called a(n) ________________ (reinforcement, reinforcer)." Next time, the parenthetical hints were left out. The book reinforced him for using the word *reinforcer* with a series of different versions of the question. After that, Fred could correctly supply the term *reinforcer* whenever the wording had the same meaning, even if he had never seen that wording before. What behavioral procedure did the book use to develop this skill? ________________

8. Here's another review example to help you keep concepts from past lessons distinct from current concepts. Ken's goal was to get Roger to say "television" correctly. At first, Ken reinforced Roger only when he said the "tel" part of "television" correctly. Then he reinforced him only if he got the "e" sound also. Then he reinforced him only when he added "viz." Finally, Ken reinforced Roger only when he also said the "ion" distinctly. Notice that Ken was not gradually changing a prompt

but rather gradually changing the behavior that he would reinforce. Therefore, Ken used what behavioral procedure to teach Roger to say "television" correctly? ________________

9. Darlene held up the picture of a crow, asked her daughter, "What is this?" and then said, "This is a large bird." Later she simply said "large"; still later she made a movement with her hands to indicate "large"; and finally she did nothing. If the child said "crow," Darlene praised her lavishly. However, if Darlene held up the picture of a blackbird and the child said "crow," Darlene ignored her. The daughter quickly learned to call the larger bird a crow but not the smaller one. What behavioral procedure was Darlene using? ________________ ________________. If Darlene did not provide the hint about size, what procedure would she be using? ________________

10. Mr. Janes taught Roberto to draw a map of Kansas by first praising any rectangle that was twice as long as it was high. He then praised the map only if the Missouri River was shown, and finally he praised the map only if Wichita, Kansas City, and Topeka were shown. The behavioral procedure by which Mr. Janes taught Roberto to draw a map with all the basic features of Kansas on it is called ________________.

11. Review: Professor Smart pointed to a complex differential equation and asked Mary, "What is that?" Mary immediately said, "That is a differential equation," and she was rewarded with a broad smile from the professor. In the presence of the differential equation, the response "that is a differential equation" is reinforced. Therefore, it is called a(n) ________________ for that response. But an algebraic equation in whose presence that same response would be extinguished would be called a(n) ________________ for that response.

12. Review: Professor Smart pointed to a linear equation ($12x+7=y$), which no one had seen before. He asked Jane what kind of equation it was. She said, "That is a linear equation." The occurrence of her correct response in the presence of this novel equation is an example of the process called ________________.

13. Review: Mr. Jones tutored his son Pete in the identification of football plays. He showed Pete diagrams of many kinds of plays and asked him to name them. He praised Pete for calling the first one a "power sweep" but not a "flea flicker." He praised Pete for calling the second diagram a "flea flicker" but not for calling it a "power sweep." Because Dad reinforced Pete for applying each name to the corresponding diagram but not to other diagrams, this procedure is an example of complex ________________. If Dad used temporary prompts, what behavioral procedure would he be using? ________________

14. Review: The coach praised Bruiser Bob for tackling the practice dummy low, but ignored him when he tackled it high. Soon, Bob only tackled it low. What behavioral procedure was the coach using? ________________ (Ask questions to identify what procedure was used. Many students get this one wrong.)

15. Review: A special tutor was used to teach Bruiser Bob, not the smartest of students, to learn his blocking assignments for the power sweep and end run. At first the tutor let Bob read from a crib sheet "power sweep—block opposing tackle to left." Later he had him use a crib sheet that said only "power sweep-tackle"; and later, no crib sheet. The tutor praised him when he said he was supposed to block the tackle when the play was a power sweep. The tutor ignored him if he gave the same answer when the play was flea flicker. Bruiser learned his assignment perfectly. What behavioral procedure did the tutor employ? ________________

16. Review: Mrs. Livermore taught her kindergarten pupil, Francie, to label a large circular line as a circle by asking, "Francie, what is this? You know, a circle" and praising her when she said "circle." Next, she gave as a hint only "You know, a cirk" but did not say the "l." Pretty soon, Francie could label the drawing as a circle with no hint. Then Mrs. Livermore showed Francie a small solid circle and used the same procedure. Mrs. Livermore had used a hint to help Francie label a series of circles correctly until she could label new circular patterns as circles. What behavioral procedure did Mrs. Livermore use to teach that skill? ________________

17. Review: Carol was taught to add by a teacher who let her see two sets of matchsticks that corresponded to the addition problem. When he asked "How much is 4+7?" the teacher would arrange a pile of four matches and a pile of seven matches. He praised her when she said "11" for this problem but ignored her if she said "11" for other problems. As Carol learned to answer the question, the teacher would gradually move the match piles out of sight. Eventually, Carol could add 4+7 without the help of the matches. What

behavioral procedure did the teacher use? ______________

18. Review: Rahim was a loner, never playing with the other preschool children. Ms. Gray started praising Rahim whenever he was playing with Jane. After several days, he started playing quite a bit with Jane. Then she started praising Rahim when he was playing with Billy. In a few days, he was playing with Billy and Jane. In addition, without further praise, Rahim started playing with Mary. What behavioral method had Ms. Gray used to produce this result? ______________

19. Review: Eleanor praised her daughter for saying "dog" when shown a picture of a dog and ignored her for saying "dog" when shown a picture of a cat. What behavioral procedure was she using? ______________

20. Review: Suppose Dad asked Lulu what to call their big loud vehicle. If she said "truck," he praised her, but he ignored her when she called their smaller vehicle "truck." When he started, he made a big-truck sound of "vrooommm" to help her remember to call it a truck. After a while, he made the sound more quietly, and then he quit altogether. If Lulu came to call only the big loud vehicle a truck, what procedure was Dad using? ______________

LESSON

19 Imitation and Instructions

This lesson introduces two widely used procedures for modifying behavior: imitation training and instructional training. Imitation training involves demonstrating to another person how to perform a behavior. Instructional training involves describing to another person how to perform a behavior. In everyday life, both procedures can be very complex. The Quakers' path of "bearing witness" to their faith through exemplary behavior may be a very complex example of imitation training. Academic courses are an everyday example of complex instructional training.

Tactic #4 in the stimulus control strategy is creating complex stimulus control through imitation training and instructional training.

1. Tactic #4 in the stimulus control strategy is creating complex stimulus control through ________________ training and instructional training.

Definition of Imitation Training

Imitation training consists of three parts. (1) The teacher shows what to do. This is the imitative stimulus. (2) The learner copies the teacher. This is the imitative behavior. (3) The teacher reinforces the learner's imitative behavior. For example, a teacher says "gut"—the German word for "good," pronounced "goot." That is the imitative stimulus. The learner copies the teacher's "gut." The teacher reinforces the correct response.

2. Imitation training consists of three parts. (1) The teacher shows what to do. This is the ___________ stimulus. (2) The learner copies the teacher. This is the ________________ behavior. (3) The teacher ______________ the learner's imitative behavior.

Notice that imitation training is a specific type of discrimination training. The teacher reinforces the learner for saying "gut" only when the imitative stimulus is "gut." The teacher does not reinforce the learner for saying "gut" when the imitative stimulus is "der." The teacher saying "gut" becomes an SD for the learner's saying "gut." The teacher saying other German words becomes an S-delta for the learner's saying "gut."

People frequently use imitation training in everyday situations. When Dad shows Debby how to hold a football, has her hold it, and praises correct holding, he uses imitation training. When Mom shows Paul how to sauté onions, has him do it, and praises good sautéing, she uses imitation training. People who do not fully understand behavioral principles may use only part of the procedure. They may show Debby how to hold the football (the imitative stimulus) but not have her hold it. Thus, Debby won't be reinforced for actually making the response. This short form of imitation training is not as sure to work. Behavior analysts sometimes call this short form *modeling* and, when it works, *observational learning*.

Uses of Imitation Training

Behavior analysts use imitation to help change many behaviors. Researchers have used imitation to increase spontaneous speech by children with autism (Ingenmey & Van Houten, 1991). Japanese researchers used it to increase conversations by a child with autism (Inoue & Kobayashi, 1992). Researchers used it to overcome phobias in children (Love, Matson, & West, 1990). Behavior analysts often use imitation training with individuals who have little or no language. They can demonstrate more effective behaviors even if the learner can't understand instructions or explanations. Research suggests that imitation training is the most acceptable treatment for persons with developmental disabilities (Davis & Russell, 1990).

Behavior analysts often use very complex imitation training. For example, researchers sought to change the food buying habits of 20 families in Blacksburg, Virginia (Winett et al., 1988). They showed the families a videotape of a family changing its food habits. This family modeled discussing the issues. They then modeled making a healthy shopping list, shopping, and preparing more nutritious meals. The researchers presented a complex set of imitative stimuli in this videotape. They obtained shopping reports from the families. They gave them feedback about the nutritional value of their choices. The families changed their buying habits; for example, they reduced fat calories by 7%.

Teaching How to Imitate

You might imagine that everyone knows how to imitate. You might even feel that imitating another person is "human nature." Unfortunately, many people do not naturally imitate others. People with developmental disorders, autism, and other disabilities often do not imitate. Psychologists have difficulty influencing the behavior of people who neither speak nor imitate. If you can't talk to them and you can't show them, how can you help them? Therefore, behavior analysts have tried to learn how to teach the general skill of imitating.

Researchers taught the skill of imitating to a child with profound retardation, whom I'll call Fran (Baer, Peterson, & Sherman, 1967). Bob trained Fran at meal time by reinforcing her imitations with bites of the meal. Bob first taught Fran to imitate him when he raised his left arm. Bob said, "Do this," and then raised his arm. Initially, Bob had to prompt Fran by raising her arm for her. He then gave her a bite of her meal. He gradually faded his help until, when he raised his arm, Fran raised her arm by herself. This required about 60 meals.

Bob next taught Fran to imitate him when he tapped the table with his left hand. Fran learned this second imitation more quickly than the first. Bob proceeded to teach additional imitations. Bob noticed that Fran gradually started imitating some behaviors on the first trial. In fact, she gradually came to imitate behaviors with no reinforcement; Fran had learned how to imitate. Bob gave her a basic skill which he and others could use to help her. Bob had taught Fran how to imitate in general by teaching her to imitate many specific behaviors. His procedure is an example of generalization training. The complete analysis of this procedure involves generalization to the class of responses called *imitative*, a process that we will not study in this book (Baer & Deguchi, 1985).

Other studies have used generalized imitation to develop language skills in several individuals with developmental disabilities (Goldstein & Mousetis, 1989). Researchers have noted both gestural imitation (Poulson & Kymissis, 1988) and vocal imitation (Poulson, Kymissis, Reeve, Andreatos, & Richards, 1988) in infants. These studies suggest that generalized imitation leads to human language learning (Kymissis & Poulson, 1990). It seems that generalized imitation is a common process in the everyday development of children.

Definition of Instructional Training

Instructional training also consists of three parts. (1) The teacher provides a <u>verbal description</u> of the desired behavior. (2) The learner produces the <u>instructed behavior</u>. (3) The teacher <u>reinforces</u> the instructed behavior. For example, Mr. Jones says to Leo, "Pass the butter." Leo passes the butter. Mr. Jones says, "Thank you," or gives an even stronger reinforcer.

3. Name the procedure that consists of these three parts—(1) a <u>verbal description</u> of the desired behavior; (2) performance of the <u>instructed behavior</u>; (3) the instructed behavior is <u>reinforced</u>. ______________ training

The training procedure for teaching by instruction is also usually a discrimination training procedure. The teacher reinforces the learner for putting the ball on the table only if the instruction was "Put the ball on the table." The teacher does not reinforce the learner for putting the ball on the table if the instruction was "Put the ball on the floor." Thus, the instruction is an SD for the described behavior.

People frequently use instructional training in everyday situations. When Dad tells Jane how to start the car, has her do it, and praises correct starting, he uses instructional training. When Mom tells Pedro how to change channels with the remote control, has him do it, and praises correct changing, she uses instructional training. People who do not fully understand behavioral principles may use only part of the procedure. They may tell Jane how to start the car but not have her try starting it. Thus, Jane won't be reinforced for actually making the response. This short form of instructional training is not as sure to work.

Uses of Instructional Training

Behavior analysts use instructional training as part of almost all treatment programs. One widely adopted procedure increases the rate at which patients keep medical appointments (Ross, Friman, & Christophersen, 1993). Researchers had the staff at a clinic mail reminders to patients one week before their appointments. They then called the day before. These patients were more likely to cancel rather than simply not show up than patients who were not reminded. The researchers did not reinforce keeping appointments. Presumably the patients had a history of intermittent reinforcement that was sufficient to maintain following instructions.

Instructional training is probably the most widely used form of behavior modification employed in everyday settings. We are all constantly engaged in talking and telling people what to do, when to do it, how to do it, and why to do it. Unfortunately, those who are not behavior analysts frequently fail to follow through by observing the instructed behavior and then supplying reinforcement. As a result, following instructions is often placed on a schedule of extinction.

Researchers showed the importance of reinforcement for following instructions (Ayllon & Azrin, 1964). Figure 19-1 shows that long-term psychotics rarely bothered to use eating implements during baseline—not even when eating soup. The researchers tried instructing the patients to use implements. About one-third of the patients complied. The researchers then awarded tokens to those patients who followed the instructions. Virtually all patients started following the instructions to use implements at that point. The researchers found that reinforcement can be crucial for maintaining instruction following.

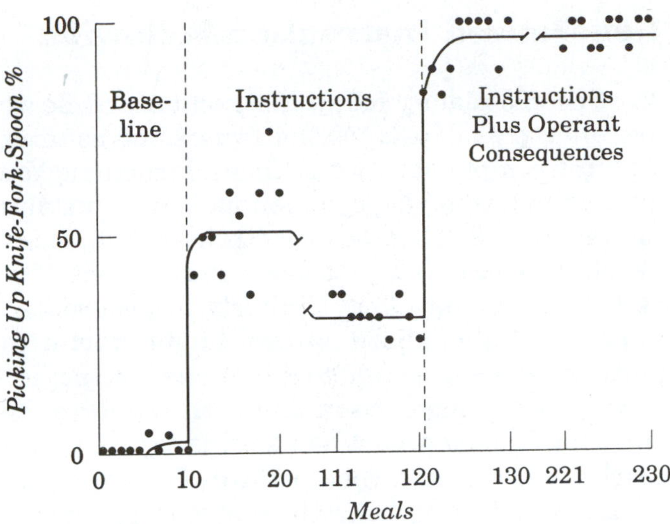

Figure 19-1. Chronic schizophrenic patients in many mental hospitals eat their food with their hands (including soup). This figure shows the number of patients who picked up the knife, fork, and spoon during a baseline period, during a period when they were instructed to pick these items up, and then during a period when they were instructed plus reinforced for picking them up. Notice that instructions helped but tended to lose their effect over time. Also notice that when reinforcement was added, almost all the patients always picked up the implements. This example shows the necessity of using reinforcement along with instructions in many applications of instruction training. Adapted from "Reinforcement and Instructions with Mental Patients," by T. Ayllon and N. H. Azrin, *Journal of the Experimental Analysis of Behavior*, 1964, 7, 327–331. Copyright 1964 by the Society for the Experimental Analysis of Behavior, Inc. Used by permission.

Behavior therapists have explored an interesting implication of instructional training. Normal adults with problems frequently report repeating the same instructions to themselves. For example, they may constantly tell themselves that they must have something to eat. They may literally instruct themselves to become fat. Such instructions may be implicated in alcoholism, depression, anxiety, drug dependence, and many other problems. Behavior therapists regard these instructions as behavior. Looking at self-instructions as behavior suggests that they can be influenced by reinforcement, extinction, and punishment. Modifying the instructions this way may be very successful—perhaps more successful than looking for the causes in the person's childhood.

Generalized Instruction-Following

Most people readily follow instructions. While we are all wary of instructions from some sources, we often comply with most other instructions. You might think that this common pattern is just human nature. But again, as with imitation, many people do not know how to follow instructions. This skill probably develops similarly to generalized imitation. An idealized pattern might start with parents teaching a child to follow one instruction. They give the instruction and then reinforce the child for following it. When that is learned, they teach a second, and then a third. The child's instruction-following behavior starts to generalize to all instructions. The child will then follow most instructions as long as some of them are reinforced. They will also learn some conditions under which instructions will not lead to reinforcement. They will learn to resist such instructions (Riegler & Baer, 1989).

Imitation and Instructions Combined

Many researchers use both procedures combined. For example, researchers used both procedures in a public health project. They wanted to encourage "safe sunning" at swimming pools (Lombard et al., 1991). They used signs and flyers to inform swimmers about the connection between sunburn and skin cancer. They described how swimmers could protect themselves. They had lifeguards model safe sunning (that is, they provided an imitative stimulus). The lifeguards wore T-shirts, sunglasses, hats, zinc oxide, and sunscreen. In addition, they equipped lifeguard stands with an umbrella for shade. Imitation and instructions increased the number of swimmers protecting themselves from the sun.

Imitation and Instructional Training Are Efficient

Instructional training is simpler and more direct than relying on reinforcement alone. For example, a teacher may wish to increase students' talking in class. Telling them to talk more is faster than waiting for them to talk and reinforcing them. Telling people to hit their ping pong shots softly is quicker than reinforcing soft shots and extinguishing hard shots. Perhaps most important, instructional training is an alternative to shaping. You may be able to instruct someone to do something in a brief time that would take an extended period to teach by shaping.

You cannot use instructional training with people who lack basic verbal skills. For example, you may not be able to use it with infants, people with retardation, or children with autism. Their verbal skills often do not permit instructions. Training someone to sing is another type of exception. You cannot describe behaviors like singing well enough to teach them to another person using only verbal instructions. Imitation training can often be used with such behaviors.

Summary

Imitation training and instructional training are forms of discrimination training. You can use them to modify many behaviors easily. They are most effective with people who have generalized skills of imitating or following instructions. These generalized skills can themselves be taught through generalization training. Imitation may be basic to learning language. Tactic #4 of the stimulus control strategy is to create complex stimulus control through imitation training and instructional training.

Behavior Analysis Example

Teaching a College Graduate How to Get a Job

Researchers used imitation and instructional training to teach people how to interview for jobs (Hollandsworth, Glazeski, & Dressel, 1978). They helped an extremely nervous college graduate to obtain a job. Herbert did not find a job for five months after graduating with a general business degree. He had participated in over 60 job interviews without a single offer. In desperation he finally accepted a part-time sales job in a men's clothing store at minimum wage.

The researchers guessed that Herbert was extremely nervous when being interviewed. His speech was incoherent, he lost his train of thought, and he stared silently into space for long periods. They therefore specified three behaviors to improve his interview performance. First, make focused responses to the interviewer's questions. Second, use coping statements, such as "Excuse me" and "Let me start over," to be made when he goofed. Third, ask questions requesting additional information, feedback, or clarification.

The researchers designed a role-playing situation to teach these three skills. One of them played the role of an interviewer, while another observed the interview. Herbert's baseline performance level for each of the three interviewing behaviors was very poor.

The researchers taught Herbert a simple method for making focused answers to an interviewer's questions after session 6. They started with instructions. They defined "clear responses" and explained their importance. They then explained how to make clear responses. This involved using a pause-think-speak paradigm. "Pause" referred to breaking eye contact and pausing when the interviewer asked him a question. "Think" referred to picking out one or two key words in the question and then deciding on one or two key words for his answer. Finally, "speak" referred to making eye contact and stating a clear answer to the interviewer's question.

Next, the researchers used modeling. They showed Herbert a videotape of an actor using the pause-think-speak method for making focused responses to interview questions. They then asked Herbert to practice what he had learned. The interviewer asked him five questions commonly asked by job interviewers. The trainer provided feedback on his performance. After practice, Herbert appeared very natural using pause-think-speak. Herbert's performance improved dramatically after training for focused responses.

Next, the researchers used a similar procedure to teach Herbert how to make coping statements. They taught this prior to session 12, and he made a modest improvement in his use of coping statements. Before session 17, the researchers taught him how to ask questions. This produced a dramatic increase in performance. Figure 19-2 shows that all three behaviors increased convincingly after treatment and showed no downward trends. The multiple-baseline design ruled out alternative interpretations, so the researchers concluded

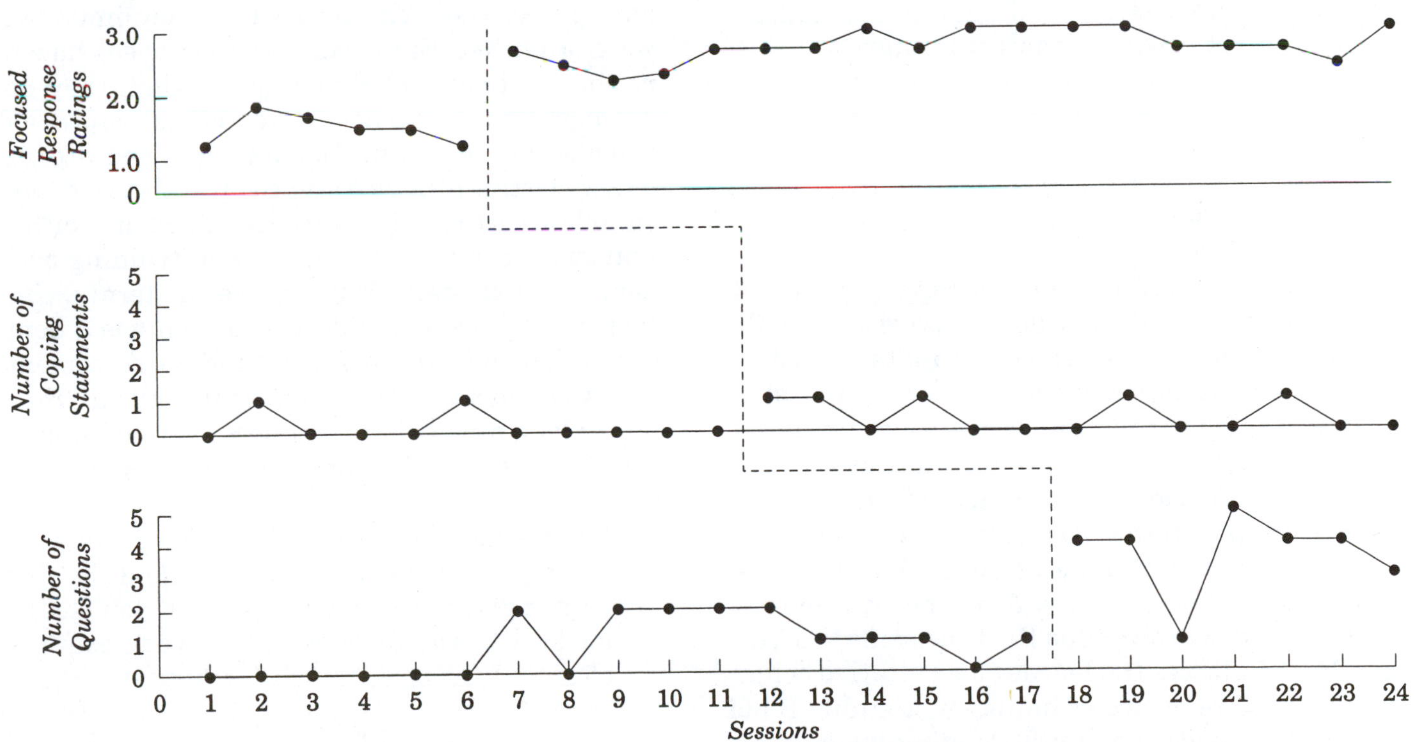

Figure 19-2. The average rating of focused responding, frequency of coping statements, and questions for Herbert during training for job interviews. From "Use of Social Skills Training in the Treatment of Extreme Anxiety and Deficient Verbal Skills in the Job Interview Setting," by J. G. Hollandsworth, R. C. Glazeski, and M. E. Dressel, *Journal of Applied Behavior Analysis,* 1978, *11,* 259–269. Copyright 1978 by the Society for the Experimental Analysis of Behavior, Inc. Used by permission.

that the imitation training caused Herbert to engage in the behaviors more often.

The researchers gathered additional data during the experiment. They measured the number of stutters that he made during each role-playing session, as an indication of nervousness. Stutters decreased from a baseline level of about 20 per session to about 2 or 3.

The most important outcome of the experiment was that Herbert went for three interviews after training and was offered three jobs. He took one as an administrative assistant in a hospital for about triple the minimum wage.

After much practice with feedback, Herbert became quite natural with the pause-think-speak behavior. Interview questions became an SD for pause-think-speak behavior. When that happened, behavior analysts would call his pause-think-speak behavior discriminated behavior.

4. The researchers produced the appropriate behavior by showing Herbert a videotape of an actor demonstrating pause-think-speak behavior, asking him to role play the behavior, and giving him praise for engaging in the behavior. The researchers used ________________ (imitation, instructional) training.

Notes

Note #1

Imitation training sometimes appears to be differential reinforcement. Such cases arise when the teacher reinforces the learner for imitative behavior A but extinguishes the learner for imitative behavior B in the presence of imitative stimulus A. However, people rarely present imitative stimuli singly. Rather, they teach the learner several imitative stimuli. In that case, the teacher reinforces the learner for imitative behavior A in the presence of imitative stimulus A but not in the presence of imitative stimulus B. At the same time, the teacher reinforces the learner for imitative behavior B in the presence of imitative stimulus B but not in the presence of imitative stimulus A.

5. In complex situations like this, the procedure could be interpreted either as differential reinforcement or discrimination training. As I have told you before, behavior analysts have arbitrarily agreed to call the procedure in such complex cases ________________.

Note #2

Programming and fading may involve imitation training prior to the withdrawal of the prompt. For example, if a fading sequence involves asking the question, "What is this, a tree?" the person can simply imitate the word *tree*. However, since that imitative stimulus is eventually withdrawn, this would not be classified as an example of imitation training. So in any example involving the withdrawal of an imitative stimulus used as a prompt, the only acceptable answer is programming or fading.

6. When teachers use an imitative stimulus as a temporary prompt during discrimination training, you should not label the procedure as imitation training but rather as ________ ________________.

Note #3

People often use imitation training and instructional training in everyday situations. Parents praise their children when they imitate a word or phrase. Employers tell employees how to perform a task and thank them when they do. Teenagers say a hip new word and act impressed when others repeat it. People describe how to use a new electronic device and congratulate a friend on following their instructions. People use either imitation training or instructional training accidentally or casually. You can use the term *imitation training* as long as the situation has a demonstration, imitative behavior, and reinforcement. Likewise, you can use the term *instructional training* as long as the situation has a verbal description, instructed behavior, and reinforcement.

7. If someone "accidentally" demonstrates a behavior, another person copies it, and the first person gives praise for copying it, you can refer to the procedure as an everyday example of ________________ training.

Helpful Hints

Helpful Hint #1

Students sometimes confuse imitation training and instructional training. In both cases, the teacher engages in some form of behavior designed to influence another person. The distinction lies in whether the teacher's behavior is identical to the desired behavior. If it is identical, then the teacher is using imitation training. If the teacher's behavior is different, but somehow describes the desired behavior, then the teacher is using instructional training. For example, if the teacher says "Guten Tag" and reinforces the student for saying "Guten Tag," then the technique used is imitation training. If the teacher says, "Say the German phrase for 'Hello'" and reinforces the student for saying "Guten Tag," the technique used is instructional training. Usually you can clarify which type of training is involved by asking, "Did the teacher describe the correct behavior (instruction), or did the teacher demonstrate the correct behavior (imitation)?"

8. If you think that an example is imitation rather than instructional training, you may check your analysis by asking the question, "Did the teacher ________________ the correct behavior?"

Helpful Hint #2

Be careful to use the correct forms of "imitation" when labeling the procedure and its respective parts. Imitation training is the procedure that consists of the teacher providing an imitative stimulus and then reinforcing the student for performing the imitative behavior.

9. Practice this now by filling in the appropriate terms in the blanks. The procedure in which the teacher demonstrates the desired behavior is __________ training. The teacher provides the ____________ stimulus, and the learner performs the ________________ behavior.

Helpful Hint #3

Be careful to use the correct forms of "instruction" when labeling the procedure and its respective parts. Instructional training is the procedure that consists of the teacher providing a verbal description and then reinforcing the student for performing the instructed behavior.

10. Practice this now by filling in the appropriate terms in the blanks. The procedure in which the teacher describes the desired behavior is called ________________ training. The teacher gives a verbal description and the learner performs the __________ behavior.

Helpful Hint #4

With this lesson, your task of identifying the procedure in an example becomes harder. You must still decide whether the example involves differential reinforcement. If it doesn't, you must consider two more stimulus control procedures. The examples now may involve discrimination training, generalization training, programming, fading, imitation training, or instructional training. Your job will be to figure out which procedure the example is based on. You will increase your chances of picking the correct label if you analyze the example systematically.

The first step is to decide whether the example is based on differential reinforcement or whether it involves a stimulus control procedure. If the example involves one stimulus and two or more behaviors, then it must involve differential reinforcement. Be sure to consider whether the differential reinforcement involves successive approximations. If so, then the procedure is shaping. If the example involves two (or more) stimuli and one behavior, then you know that you are dealing with some form of stimulus control, such as discrimination training. You must decide what type of stimulus control procedure is involved. If you think the example involves stimulus control, you need to ask questions to label the specific procedure.

First, ask whether the example involves either an imitative stimulus or a verbal description. If it does, you know that the procedure involves either imitation training or instructional training. You already know how to tell the difference.

Second, ask whether the procedure involves a prompt. If it does not, you can label it as discrimination training or generalization training. You already know how to tell the difference. If it involves a prompt, then the procedure is either fading or programming. You can check this conclusion by asking whether the prompt is gradually withdrawn. If the example involves a prompt that is withdrawn, you already know how to tell whether it is fading or programming.

In summary, if you think the procedure involves stimulus control, you can ask two questions. First, ask whether the procedure involves an imitative stimulus or a verbal description. Second, ask whether the procedure uses prompts. These two questions will help you pinpoint the procedure used in the example.

11. If the given example involves one stimulus and two or more behaviors, then it must involve ______________________.

Helpful Hint #5

People sometimes use imitation training and instructional training at the same time. For example, Mom might ask Jimmy, "What is the name of that animal? Say 'cat.'" She verbally describes what she wants Jimmy to say, but she also says the word so that Jimmy can copy it. Since her description is really only an imitative stimulus, I will always label this type of example as imitation training.

12. Mom might ask Jimmy, "What is the name of that animal? Say 'cat.'" I will always label this type of example as ______________ training.

Helpful Hint #6

People sometimes use either an imitative stimulus or a verbal description as a prompt in fading or programming. You have encountered examples in which Mom points to the cat and asks, "What is that? Say 'cat.'" If she then fades out "cat" by saying "ca" and then "c," she is using an imitative stimulus. However, because she eventually fades it out, I will consider this an example of fading, not imitation training. In general, if a procedure uses either an imitative stimulus or a verbal description as a temporary prompt, I will consider the correct label for the procedure to be either fading or programming.

13. If a procedure uses an imitative stimulus as a temporary prompt to train a specific discrimination, I will consider the correct label for the procedure to be ______________.

Additional Readings

Bandura, A. (1971). *Psychological modeling: Conflicting theories*. Chicago: Aldine-Atherton. This is an excellent source book for a broader understanding of imitation training and various psychological theories of imitation.

Brawley, E. R., Harris, F. R., Allen, K. E., Fleming, R. S., & Peterson, R. F. (1969). Behavior modification of an autistic child. *Behavioral Science, 14*, 87–97. Systematic reinforcement procedures were used to strengthen appropriate behaviors, such as talking and following instructions. Extinction was used to weaken inappropriate behaviors, such as the child's hitting himself and throwing a tantrum. These procedures were used with effectiveness in therapy sessions three times a week. Generalization was programmed by involving ward personnel in the reinforcement and extinction procedures.

Garcia, E., Guess, D., & Byrnes, J. (1973). Development of syntax in a retarded girl using procedures of imitation, reinforcement, and modeling. *Journal of Applied Behavior Analysis, 6*, 299–310. This article describes the effectiveness of using imitation training for developing complex speech patterns in a person with severe retardation.

Kennedy, D. A., & Thompson, I. (1967). The use of reinforcement techniques with a first-grade boy. *Personality and Guidance Journal, 46*, 366–370. In this case report, a child taught to pay attention in a counselor's office also paid attention more closely in the classroom. This example involved spontaneous generalization, in that the behavior modifier did not have to reinforce the child for paying attention in the classroom.

Reading Quiz

25. Let's deal with the new tactic first. The fourth tactic in using the stimulus control strategy to help solve human problems is to create complex stimulus control through imitation training and instructional ______________________ (stimuli, training).
56. The fourth tactic in using the stimulus control strategy to help solve human problems is to create complex stimulus control through imitation training and ______________________ training.
42. Review: The fourth tactic in using the stimulus control strategy to help solve human problems is to create complex stimulus control

through ________________ training and ________ training.

57. The fourth tactic involves two procedures. The first procedure this lesson presented for modifying behavior involves demonstrating to another person how to perform a behavior. You call this procedure __________ (imitation, instructional) training. The second procedure this lesson presented involves describing to another person how to perform a behavior. You call that procedure ____________ training.

80. Your first goal is to learn about imitation training. You call the act of showing a learner how to perform a behavior the *imitative stimulus*. You then ask the person to perform the behavior. You call the person's behavior the *imitative behavior*. You then reinforce that imitative behavior, if the person performs it. You call the procedure that presents an imitative stimulus, looks for an imitative behavior, and reinforces it _________________ training.

86. You need to learn about each of the three elements of imitation training. The first element involves showing a person how to do something. You call the behavioral demonstration the ______________ (imitation, imitative) *stimulus*.

72. When the teacher demonstrates how to do something, the teacher's behavior becomes a stimulus for the learner. That is why you call the teacher's behavior the *imitative* ______.

73. When the teacher demonstrates how to do something, you call the teacher's demonstration the ___________ *stimulus*.

13. Dad shows Jimmy how to throw a curveball. Call his demonstration of how to throw the curveball the ____________________.

81. You have now learned the first element of imitation training. (1) It involves demonstrating a behavior to the learner. You call this demonstration the _____________________. (2) The learner then copies the demonstration. You call that copy the imitative behavior. (3) The teacher then reinforces the correct behavior.

59. The second element of imitation training is the learner's copying of the teacher's demonstration. You call the learner's copying of the demonstration the __________ (*imitation, imitative*) *behavior*.

79. You call the demonstration of how to perform a behavior during imitation training the *imitative* _________; you call the copying of that performance by the learner the *imitative* __________.

67. When Jimmy copies Dad's demonstration of how to throw a curveball, you call Jimmy's behavior the ____________________.

82. You have now learned both elements of imitation training. (1) It involves demonstrating a behavior to the learner. You call this demonstration the *imitative stimulus*. (2) The learner then copies the demonstration. You call that copy the _______________. (3) The teacher then reinforces the correct behavior.

62. The third element of imitation training is reinforcement. After the teacher provides the imitative stimulus and the student provides the imitative behavior, the teacher can then __________ the imitative behavior (assuming it is correct).

2. After Dad demonstrates for Jimmy how to throw a curveball and Jimmy copies the demonstration by throwing a curveball himself, Dad must _____________ Jimmy's throw.

83. You have now learned the third element of imitation training. (1) It involves demonstrating a behavior to the learner. You call this demonstration the *imitative stimulus*. (2) The learner then copies the demonstration. You call that copy the *imitative behavior*. (3) The teacher then ______________ the correct behavior.

47. Review: What procedure has the teacher demonstrate a behavior, the learner copy the demonstration, and the teacher reinforce correct copies? ________________

17. Here is a summary of the three elements. (1) The teacher provides the ____________ ______________, (2) the student provides the ____________________, and (3) the teacher then ___________ the imitative behavior (assuming it is correct).

53. Suppose the learner is reinforced for producing imitative behavior #1 in the presence of imitative stimulus #1 but not in the presence of imitative stimulus #2. This form of imitation training would be an example of what behavioral procedure? ______________ (discrimination, generalization) training

63. When a father demonstrates to a child how to hold a football in order to throw it, the father is producing a(n) ______________ stimulus.

27. Notice the two elements of imitation training start with "imitat" and end with "ive," while the name of the procedure ends with ____.
20. If a father shows his daughter how to hold a football but does not have her hold it, the procedure is called *modeling* or *observational learning*. This procedure is a shortened form of ______________ training.
48. Review: Winett and colleagues (1988) showed families a videotape of a family changing its food habits in hopes of changing the viewers' food-buying habits. The family on videotape made a healthy shopping list, went shopping, and prepared more nutritious meals. Because the videotape demonstrated how to eat healthily, it would be called a(n) ______________.
52. Some people do not naturally imitate others. Behavior analysts have solved this by prompting the person's imitation of one behavior, then reinforcing it, and then gradually withdrawing the prompt. They repeat this cycle with additional imitations until the person spontaneously imitates a novel behavior. This spontaneous occurrence of imitation in a novel situation is an example of the process called ______________. (Note: The answer has nothing to do with imitation training.)
10. Bob trained Fran to imitate him when he raised his left arm. Initially, Bob had to raise Fran's arm as a prompt for her to do it. He gradually withdrew his help until, when he raised his arm, Fran raised her arm by herself. The withdrawal of this physical prompt is an example of the procedure of ________ ____________ (Baer, Peterson, & Sherman, 1967).
9. Bob taught Fran how to imitate in general by teaching her to imitate a series of behaviors until her imitating generalized to novel behaviors. Because he used temporary prompts with each imitative stimulus, Bob's procedure is an example of what type of generalization training? ______________
44. Review: The second goal is to learn about instructional training. When you explain to someone how to perform a behavior and then reinforce him or her for doing so, you are using the behavioral procedure of instructional ______________.
24. Instructional training has three elements. First you describe the behavior. You call this description the <u>verbal description</u>. Second, the learner performs the behavior. You call his or her performance <u>instructed behavior</u>. Third, you <u>reinforce</u> correct instructed behavior. You call this procedure ______________ (*imitation, instructional*) *training*.
55. The first element of instructional training involves describing to someone how to do something. Because the teacher gives a <u>description</u> of the desired behavior, you call the first element a *verbal* ______________.
74. When the teacher explains how to do something, the teacher's behavior is <u>verbal</u>. That is why you call the teacher's explaining behavior the ____________ *description*.
12. Dad explains to Jimmy how to square a number: "You multiply the number by itself." Dad's explanation is called a(n) ______________.
84. You have now learned the first element of instructional training. (1) The teacher provides a(n) ______________. (2) The learner performs the <u>instructed behavior</u>. (3) The teacher <u>reinforces</u> correct instructed behavior.
60. The second element of instructional training is the person following the instructions correctly. His or her instruction-following behavior is called *instructed* ______________.
5. After the teacher provides the verbal instructions, the student performs the ____________ behavior.
3. After Dad explains how to square a number, Jimmy then might square 8 and get 64. His squaring of the number would be called ______________.
85. You have now learned the second element of instructional training. (1) The teacher provides a <u>verbal description</u>. (2) The learner performs the ______________. (3) The teacher <u>reinforces</u> correct instructed behavior.
54. The explanation of how to perform a behavior in instructional training is called the ________ *description*. The performance of that behavior by the learner is called ____________ *behavior*.
61. The third element in instructional training is reinforcing the student for correct instructed behavior. After giving the verbal description, a trainer using instructional training must be sure to ______________ the person's correct responses.
4. After Dad explains to Jimmy how to square a number and Jimmy correctly squares 8, Dad

must be sure to ______________ Jimmy's response.

38. Review: Instructional training involves explaining to someone how to perform a behavior. You call the explanation a(n) ______________ ______________. You call the learner's correct performance the ______________. The teacher then must ______________ the instructed behavior.

77. When you explain to someone how to perform a behavior and then reinforce him or her for doing so, you are using the behavioral procedure of ______________.

75. When you demonstrate how to perform a behavior and then reinforce your student for correctly copying your demonstration, you are using what behavioral procedure? ______________. When you explain to someone how to perform a behavior and then reinforce him or her for doing so, you are using what behavioral procedure? ______________

16. Here are a few items to sharpen your ability to tell the difference between imitation training and instructional training. Mom explains to Pete how to use the TV remote control and then reinforces him when he does it correctly. She is using what procedure? ______________ training

28. Pete shows Mom how to draw a box with the computer mouse and then reinforces her for doing it correctly. What procedure is Pete using? ______________ training

70. When Pete shows Mom how to grill a marshmallow and then reinforces her for doing it, he is using what procedure? ______________ training

69. When Mom tells Pete how to fry an egg and then reinforces him for doing it, she is using what procedure? ______________ training

66. When Bob tells Ann how to outline a chapter, you should label his telling as a(n) ______________ ______________

68. When Karen writes out the solution to the same set of differential equations as Professor Brainbuster had demonstrated on the blackboard, you should label what she writes as the ______________.

22. Imitation training involves demonstrating a behavior to the learner. You call this demonstration the ______________.

71. When Professor Brainbuster shows how to solve a set of differential equations on the blackboard, you should label what he writes on the blackboard as a(n) ______________.

65. When Ann outlines a chapter in the way that Bob had told her to, you should label her outlining as the ______________.

64. When a teacher provides an imitative stimulus, a learner emits an imitative behavior, and the teacher reinforces the correct behavior, the teacher is using what procedure? ______________ ______________

26. Notice that behavior analysts refer to the teacher's behavior in imitation training as a *stimulus*. That is because it serves as a stimulus for the student. Notice that behavior analysts refer to the copying by the student of the teacher's behavior as *imitative* ______________.

23. In imitation training, then, the teacher's behavior is called the *imitative* ______________ while the student's behavior is called the *imitative* ______________.

37. Review: In the presence of verbal description #1, the learner will be reinforced for performing instructed behavior #1. In the presence of verbal description #2, the learner will be extinguished for performing instructed behavior #1. This is a kind of discrimination training. In discrimination training, you would call verbal description #1 what kind of a stimulus? It is a(n) ______________ for instructed behavior #1.

18. Here's a question based on an earlier lesson: If the teacher describes to learners how to do something and watches them try to do it, but fails to reinforce them, what schedule of reinforcement is the learner's instructed behavior on if his or her rate of imitating decreases? ______________

6. Ayllon and Azrin (1964) instructed long-term mental patients to pick up and use eating utensils at meals. This was largely ineffective until they gave tokens for following instructions. Most patients then began using utensils. Because giving tokens increased the rate of instructed behavior, the token is called a(n) ______________.

7. Behavior therapists have diagnosed many of the problems experienced by normal adults as resulting from faulty self-instructions that they repeat to themselves. Since telling yourself what to do is itself doing something, behavior analysts regard self-instructions as ______________.

8. Behavior therapists regard self-instructions as verbal behavior. Therefore, they assume that ignoring undesirable self-instructions will reduce their frequency as an example of the behavioral procedure called __________.
1. Parents teach a child to follow one instruction. They give the instruction and then reinforce the child for following it. When the child learns that first instruction, they teach a second and a third instruction. The child soon starts to follow most new instructions even without immediate reinforcement. Because the parents have reinforced instruction-following in a series of situations until it occurs with a novel instruction, the parents have used what procedure? ________________ ________________
40. Review: Lombard and associates (1991) told swimmers how they could protect themselves from sunburn. You would label the explanation as giving a(n) ________________. The lifeguards demonstrated how to avoid sunburn by wearing T-shirts, sunglasses, hats, zinc oxide, and sunscreen. You would label their demonstration as a(n) ____________ ________________.
11. Both imitation training and instructional training increase the probability that learners will perform the desired behavior by including as the third element the procedure of ____________________ for correctly performed behavior.
21. Imitation training and instructional training are forms of ________________ training. These procedures are most effective with people who imitate novel imitative stimuli and follow novel verbal instructions. People can be taught to imitate novel imitative stimuli and to follow novel verbal instructions through ________________ training.
78. When you show someone how to perform a behavior and then reinforce him or her for copying you, you are using the behavioral procedure of ____________ training.
76. When you describe to someone how to perform a behavior and then reinforce the person for following your instructions, you are using the behavioral procedure of ________________ training.
58. The fourth tactic in using the stimulus control strategy to help solve human problems is to create complex stimulus control through ____________ training and ____________ training.
32. Review: Hollandsworth and his colleagues (1978) provided Herbert with a verbal description of how to make clear responses to interview questions. They then observed his performance in a simulated interview session and reinforced correct performance. The behavior analysts used what behavioral procedure? ________________________
19. Hollandsworth and colleagues (1978) demonstrated for Herbert how to ask questions designed to clarify interview questions. They then watched his ability to ask questions in a simulated interview situation and reinforced correct performance. What behavioral procedure were they using? ________________ ________________
15. From Note #1: Here is a very tricky item. Suppose Mom shows Jimmy how to fry an egg and reinforces him when he does it correctly but ignores him when he does not. Suppose she also shows Jimmy how to soft-boil an egg and reinforces him when he does it correctly but ignores him when he does not. Behavior analysts label this very complex procedure as ____________________.
14. From Helpful Hint #1: If you think that an example is instructional training rather than imitation training, you may check your analysis by asking the question, "Did the teacher ____________________ (demonstrate, describe) the correct behavior?"
50. Review: You can use the stimulus control strategy to help solve human problems by (3) creating new stimulus control by using prompts; (4) creating complex stimulus control through ____________ training and ____________ training.
35. Review: If an instructor provides a behavioral demonstration of what another person is supposed to do, the instructor's behavior is called the ____________________.
30. Review: A teacher describes a behavior that he or she would like a learner to produce; this description would be called a(n) ____________ ________________________ (not an instruction).
33. Review: If a learner produces a behavior that someone else describes verbally, the learner's behavior is an example of ________________ behavior.

41. Review: Remember that imitation training is a type of discrimination training. Because an imitative stimulus is associated with reinforcement for the imitative behavior, the technical term for that imitative stimulus is _______________.
36. Review: Imitation training and instructional training will be effective only if the person's imitative or instructed behavior is _______________.
43. Review: The fourth tactic in using the stimulus control strategy to help solve human problems is to create complex stimulus control through _______________ training or _______________ training.
34. Review: If a learner copies the behavior of another person, you call the learner's behavior _______________ *behavior*.
29. Review: A person can learn from a lecture in two ways: (1) by doing what the lecturer tells him to do, which would be an example of _______________ training, and (2) by repeating arguments and information contained in the lecture, which would be an example of _______________ training.
45. Review: The three parts of imitation training are the _______________, the _______________, and reinforcement.
31. Review: Demonstrating to other people how to perform a behavior, watching them do it, and then reinforcing successful performance is using what behavioral procedure? _______________
49. Review: You call the use of verbal descriptions of behavior and reinforcement to teach a new behavior _______________.
39. Review: Instructional training is a particular kind of discrimination training. Because the verbal description is associated with reinforcement for the instructed behavior, the technical term for a verbal description is _______________.
46. Review: The three parts of instructional training are a(n) _______________, the _______________, and reinforcement.
51. Review: You can use the stimulus control strategy to help solve many human problems by (3) creating new stimulus control by using _______________; and (4) creating complex stimulus control through imitation training or _______________ training.

Examples

1. One night at dinner, Tiny Tim's father said, "Pass the salt." Since Tiny Tim did not yet speak very well, his father was surprised when Tim passed the salt. But he managed to say "Thank you" and act pleased enough to make Tim feel like a hero. After that, Tiny Tim always passed the salt when asked, and he always looked very grown up and pleased about doing so. When Father said, "Pass the salt," he gave a verbal _______________ of the desired behavior. By passing the salt, Tim performed the instructed _______________. His father's pleased reaction clearly served as a(n) _______________ for Tim. This is an example of instructional training, because Father _______________ (demonstrated, described) the desired behavior.

2. Tiny Tim got a wooden puzzle involving different geometric shapes. However, he wasn't able to put the shapes into the right holes, so his mother showed him where to put each piece. She took the piece from Tim, put it into the right hole, and then gave it back to Tim. Tim put the right piece into the right hole immediately. Mother beamed at him, gave him a kiss, and said, "Good, Timmy." She continued this procedure with each piece. This example of imitation training consists of three parts. (1) Mother shows Tim where to put the puzzle piece; this is called the _______________ *stimulus*. (2) Tim's putting the puzzle piece in correctly; this is called the _______________ *behavior*. (3) Tim's mother beamed, kissed him, and praised him; this is called the _______________. This is clearly an example of imitation training, because Mom _______________ (demonstrated, described) the desired behavior.

3. The first time Tom heard Judy say "cool," he didn't pay any attention. But after she said "cool" a few more times, he started saying "cool" and found that she listened to him a lot more closely. When Judy said "cool," she demonstrated a new behavior. Tom copied her behavior. Judy then listened more closely when he said "cool." Therefore, you would call Judy's saying "cool" a(n) _______________ for Tom's copying behavior. You would call Tom's saying "cool" an example of _______________. The fact that Judy started listening more closely to Tom might be a(n) _______________ for saying "cool." Judy accidentally used what behavioral procedure to teach Tom to say "cool"? _______________

______________ (Did Judy demonstrate the behavior, or did she describe it?)

4. Marcia came from a small rural farm to start college. She looked square and never got any dates. Amy, her roommate, gave Marcia informal instructions about what clothing styles were "in" and how to apply makeup. Marcia followed Amy's instructions by buying some new clothes and putting on makeup. She looked much more collegiate, and Amy told her how nice she looked. Marcia had succeeded in changing her look to fit college. She got many dates. Amy's instructions would be called a(n) ______________ of the new behavior. Marcia's behaviors of buying new clothes and applying makeup are examples of ______________. Amy's compliment and Marcia's getting dates would be an example of two ______________ that kept Marcia following Amy's instructions. Amy accidentally used what procedure to change Marcia's behavior? ______________

5. Dr. Morris always worked an example of the latest type of math problem on the board before she asked her students to work any problems. By doing this, she taught them how to organize their work—where to write the different parts of the answer and how much of the answer to show. She then gave the students an assignment of similar problems to work in class. As they worked, she walked around the room and indicated to them whether they were doing the problems correctly. This procedure of teaching the children how to organize their answers would be called ______________. (Hint: Did she demonstrate or describe how to work the problems?) The children's behavior is called ______________.

6. Tiny Tim's mother showed him a picture of a robin and asked him, "What is that? Is it a bird?" Tim agreed and said "bird," to his mother's obvious delight. She showed him the picture of the robin later and repeated the question but said "bird" much more softly. Tim said, "That's a bird." He could still identify the picture as a bird after his mother stopped saying "bird." She then showed him a picture of a bluejay and repeated the same procedure. After she had stopped giving the hint, Tim could still identify the bluejay as a bird. His mother then showed him many other pictures of birds, and he always labeled them as birds. Tiny Tim's mother used temporary hints to teach him to label a series of birds as birds. She reinforced him for his response until he labeled novel birds as birds. Because she used prompts to teach him, you should call her procedure ______________.

7. John had never used the table saw. John asked his father if he could use it to make a doghouse for his new collie. His father cut the first piece of wood for him. In the process, his father demonstrated how to measure the wood, how to set the saw blade at the right height, how to guide the wood through safely, and several other aspects of correct use of the saw. John then cut a piece with his father watching. His father praised John's efforts and left him to cut the rest of the wood. By showing John how to use the table saw, Father used what procedure to train him to use the power saw? ______________ (Ask whether Dad demonstrated or described.)

8. Jan wanted some new clothes for her vacation trip. She asked her mother to show her how to use the sewing machine. Her mother didn't have time to show her but did explain in some detail how to use it. Jan followed her mother's explanation and sewed several articles of clothing for her vacation. What procedure did Jan's mother use to change Jan's behavior with respect to the sewing machine? ______________. Successfully sewing the clothing would probably be a(n) ______________ for Jan's following her mother's explanation. The mother's explanation would be called a(n) ______________.

9. Henri was writing a book. He typed a rough draft of each chapter himself and then gave that copy to a typist to produce a polished copy. However, he found that the polished copy wasn't always perfect. If he left any abbreviations in the copy that he gave the typist, the typist did not complete the abbreviation (as a whole word) but just copied it. Thus, he found that he had to type the entire word if he wanted it to appear in the final copy. Henri started typing the entire word and stopped using abbreviations. Because Henri's use of abbreviations led to an abbreviation in his polished copy, and his rate of using abbreviations decreased, you would say that Henri's use of abbreviations was on what schedule of reinforcement? ______________. Because his typing full words led to full words in his polished copy, and his rate of typing full words increased, you would say that Henri's typing full words was on what schedule? ______________. Henri's typing behavior changed in that he started typ-

ing whole words and stopped typing abbreviations. What behavioral procedure accounted for this change? ______________

10. Children often learn cursive writing by seeing examples of the properly formed letters and words. Then the children are required to copy these letters over and over again. The teacher usually praises correct copies. The examples of properly formed letters that the children copy would be called ______________. Showing the children examples and praising good copies is an example of what procedure for teaching writing? ______________

11. Review: I am going to give you some complex examples to help you tell the difference between all the procedures. This will help you on your test. Here's the first complex example. Ada was a little league baseball coach. She had the children hit ground balls to her while she demonstrated the essential elements of fielding them. These elements included getting her body in front of the ball, kneeling, and keeping her eyes on the ball. Then she hit some ground balls and had the children try to field them. When they fielded the ball correctly, she praised them. What procedure was Ada using when she showed them how to field ground balls and then praised them when they fielded correctly? ______________

12. Review: Ada had a lot of trouble teaching Billy to field the ball. He kept taking his eyes off the ball. Ada hit several balls right to him. When he kept his eyes on the ball, she praised him. When he took his eyes off the ball, she did not praise him. Billy started keeping his eyes on the ball more and more often. What procedure did Ada use by praising Billy when he kept his eyes on the ball and ignoring him when he did not? ______________

13. Review: Sam was the best pitcher on the team, but he tended to take his eye off the catcher's mitt when he was throwing. This behavior often led to his missing the strike zone. So Ada patiently explained to Sam exactly where to look when he was pitching. She then had him throw several pitches while she was watching and praised him when he did it right. What procedure did Ada use by explaining where to look and praising him when he did? ______________

14. Review: Gordie was a good hitter, but Ada felt that he could be much better. His main problem was that he swung at bad pitches—pitches that were not thrown over the plate. So Ada got out on the mound and threw several pitches. Sometimes she threw pitches right over the plate, and sometimes she threw bad pitches. She had Gordie stand at the plate and call "strike" for the good ones. She praised him when he called strike in the presence of a good pitch and ignored him when he called strike in the presence of a bad pitch. She hoped that this procedure would teach him which pitches were worth swinging at. What procedure was she using to teach Gordie to call "strike" only for the good pitches? ______________

15. Review: Tiny Tim's mother often showed him a picture of a sailboat and asked him, "What is that?" She praised him when he said "boat." She later showed him a picture of the Queen Mary and asked him what it was. She praised him when he said "boat." Later she showed him a picture of many novel boats, and he always labeled them as boats. What behavioral procedure had she used? ______________

16. Review: Arnelle took Billy to the zoo and showed him an owl and a chicken. She pointed to first one and then the other and asked him, "What is that?" She praised him when he said "owl" when looking at the owl but ignored him when he said "chicken" while looking at the owl. She also praised him when he said "chicken" while looking at the chicken but ignored him when he said "owl" while looking at the chicken. You call the owl a(n) ______ for Billy's behavior of calling it an owl. However, you call the chicken a(n) __________ for Billy's behavior of calling it an owl.

17. Review: Mrs. Price praised Gladys for saying "81" when asked, "What does 9 to the second power equal?" but not for saying anything else. She also praised Gladys for saying "49" when asked, "What does 7x7 equal?" but not for saying anything else. What complex behavioral procedure did Mrs. Price use? ______________

18. Review: Mrs. Price asked Gladys, "What does 8 squared equal?" She also asked, "What does 4 squared equal?" She praised Gladys when she answered "64" to the first question but ignored her when she said "64" to the second question. To help her, she showed Gladys a set of eight rows of eight dots. Over time, Mrs. Price permitted Gladys to look at dots that were harder and harder to see. Eventually Gladys "knew" that 8 × 8 was 64 even without looking at the dots. What behavioral

procedure did Mrs. Price use to teach Gladys the value of 8 to the second power? ______________

19. Review: After Gladys had learned the value of 7, 8, and 9 squared, Mrs. Price asked her, "What is 10 squared?" Gladys thought a moment, realized that she had simply multiplied 7 × 7 to get the value of 7 squared and that she had done the same for 8 and 9, and simply multiplied 10 × 10 to get 100. The occurrence of Gladys multiplying the number by itself to find its square for a new number is an example of what behavioral process? ______________________________

20. Review: Turning around while on skis can be a very complicated process unless you know how to do it. Debby showed Felix how. First you take your right ski and kick it in the air right in front of you with the back end dug into the snow. Then you pivot it to the right so that the tip is pointing backward and you are standing with your right foot pointed backward. Then you simply bring your left ski around and place it parallel to your right ski, and you are turned around. Felix tried it. Turning around so easily reinforced using this method. Debby used what behavioral procedure to train Felix to turn around on skis? ______________
(This is a situation where imitation training is far superior to instructional training, as you now realize.)

LESSON 20 Conditioned Reinforcers and Everyday Situations

Reinforcing events rooted in our biological nature influence our behavior from birth. Behavior analysts call these events *primary reinforcers*. They include food, water, sex, and reasonable temperatures. The events that serve as primary reinforcers tend to be pretty much the same for everyone.

Reinforcing events other than primary reinforcers also influence our behavior. These events grow out of our experience. Behavior analysts call these events *conditioned reinforcers*. They might include such events as our mother's smile, the opportunity to wear blue jeans, or first prize in a contest. The list of such events varies enormously from person to person and society to society. Behavior analysts study conditioned reinforcers. Many behavioral problems result from the absence of appropriate conditioned reinforcers. Behavior analysts solve this problem by creating them. This lesson introduces you to three behavioral procedures designed to create conditioned reinforcers.

Tactic #5 in the stimulus control strategy is making reinforcement more practical by creating conditioned reinforcers.

1. Tactic #5 in the stimulus control strategy is making reinforcement more practical by creating _______________ reinforcers.

Definition of Primary and Secondary Reinforcer

A **primary reinforcer** is any reinforcing event that loses its effectiveness only temporarily through satiation. In other words, a primary reinforcer is any event that is always reinforcing unless someone has had too much of it recently. The effectiveness of such reinforcers is not based on learning, but rather on the unlearned biological effects they produce in us.

2. Any reinforcing event that loses its effectiveness only temporarily through satiation is known as a(n) ____________________ reinforcer.

Behavior analysts often use primary reinforcers to teach new skills. For example, researchers used food to teach children to hold still for brain scans (Slifer et al., 1993). Researchers taught teenagers with retardation to name a snack item by giving them bites of that item (Schussler & Spradlin, 1991). Food is the most common primary reinforcer used by behavior analysts.

Behavior analysts observe that the reinforcing effect of some events is less durable than that of primary reinforcers. These events start out as "neutral" events, which have no reinforcing power. They become reinforcers after being paired with other reinforcers. If a mother always smiles at her baby before feeding him, her smile may become as effective as the milk itself. Basic researchers have not fully established the necessary and sufficient conditions that create these reinforcers (Kelleher & Gollub, 1962; Williams, 1994). One hypothesis is that any event that "signals" the delivery of another reinforcer will become reinforcing itself (Rachlin, 1976). In any event, the pairing of an existing reinforcer and a neutral event is a necessary part of the process. They call these events *conditioned reinforcers*.

A **conditioned reinforcer** is any reinforcing event that permanently loses its effectiveness when presented unpaired with backup reinforcers. Earlier you learned about an experiment designed to treat a woman who hoarded towels (Ayllon & Michael, 1959). Why did the towels reinforce hoarding behavior? The researchers guessed that the towels were paired with attendants' coming to take them back. They knew that the attendants rarely gave the patients any attention otherwise. They solved the problem by instructing the attendants to give the woman all the towels she wanted, and they no longer picked them up. This stopped the pairing of attention and towels. Hoarding towels was no longer reinforcing. This is a good example of the mechanism underlying the establishment and elimination of events as conditioned reinforcers.

3. A conditioned reinforcer is any reinforcing event that permanently loses its effectiveness when presented ________________ with backup reinforcers.

Behavior analysts call the reinforcer that is paired with a conditioned reinforcer a **backup reinforcer**. The person receives this event after delivery of the conditioned reinforcer. So it "backs up" the conditioned reinforcer and makes it effective. The effectiveness of the towels as conditioned reinforcers depended on its being backed up by the attention of the attendants. Often you can think of "spending" the conditioned reinforcer to "buy" the backup reinforcer. Although it is strained to talk about the towel hoarder spending her towels to buy attention from the attendants, you will encounter many examples in which the analogy is quite helpful.

4. Behavior analysts call the reinforcer that is paired with a conditioned reinforcer a(n) ______ ______________ reinforcer.

Behavior analysts usually use conditioned reinforcers. They often select events that they can give immediately after a desired response. Probably the most common conditioned reinforcers are social. For example, researchers used immediate praise to teach naming snack items to children (Schussler & Spradlin, 1991). They then gave a bite of the snack item itself. The bite served as the backup reinforcer for the praise. Other researchers praised children whenever they sounded out the spelling of words (Gettinger, 1993). They used no specific backup reinforcers. Other researchers used points to teach an autistic boy to maintain eye contact (Koegel & Frea, 1993). He could spend his points to "buy" time playing video games. You can see that conditioned reinforcers can be backed up with primary or other conditioned reinforcers. They may also be used without backups.

The effectiveness of a conditioned reinforcer is affected by the person's deprivation with respect to the backup reinforcer. If the person is not deprived of the backup reinforcer, the conditioned reinforcer won't work. For example, suppose the attendants gave attention to the towel hoarder for many other behaviors. Hoarding towels would not be the only response that led to more attention. The woman would be relatively satiated with attention, so the towels would not be as effective a reinforcer.

Conditioned reinforcers are often events that occur immediately after the person has made a response. Often they are not very powerful events, but they are associated with the delivery of delayed events. Thus, they can be effective because of their immediacy. Behavior analysts take advantage of this immediacy by creating conditioned reinforcers that help bridge the gap to delayed reinforcers. Behavior analysts often give praise immediately after a desired behavior and later deliver the more valuable backup reinforcer.

Surprisingly, primary reinforcers sometimes are not very effective. Many children refuse food, to the point of suffering weight problems. Researchers often use other kinds of reinforcers to teach eating. Researchers used praise to teach children to swallow food (Greer et al., 1991). Others refuse some foods, which threatens their nutrition. Researchers had parents use contingent attention to teach their children to eat foods they had to chew (Werle, Murphy, & Budd, 1993). Behavior analysts had to use conditioned reinforcers to teach children to consume primary reinforcers! In other words, the conditioned reinforcers were stronger than the primary reinforcers.

At other times, the very strength of primary reinforcers is the problem. Psychoactive drugs presumably are such effective reinforcers because of their biological effects. Researchers worked with two cocaine addicts (Budney et al., 1991). They tested these men for drug use weekly. When they were "clean," the researchers reinforced them with purchased items such as movie tickets, sporting goods, and dinner certificates. This procedure produced evidence of stopping cocaine use five months after treatment. It is ironic that the researchers used conditioned reinforcers to overcome the effects of primary reinforcers.

Definition of Generalized Reinforcers

Behavior analysts create and use very powerful reinforcers called *generalized reinforcers*. A **gen-**

eralized reinforcer is any conditioned reinforcer that is paired with many backup reinforcers. A generalized reinforcer depends for its effectiveness on its backup reinforcers; it would lose its effectiveness if it were no longer paired with those backups. It also loses its effectiveness for a person who is satiated on all of its backups. Money is the most obvious example of a generalized reinforcer. It is backed up with any reinforcer that can be purchased. If you could no longer purchase desired items, it would permanently lose its effectiveness. Such a calamity occurred when the money issued by the Southern Confederacy lost its value after the Civil War. You can always talk about spending a generalized reinforcer to buy its backup reinforcers.

5. A generalized reinforcer is any conditioned reinforcer that is paired with ________ (many, one) backup reinforcer(s).

Generalized reinforcers are more uniformly effective than other conditioned reinforcers. You usually remain deprived of at least one backup reinforcer. As long as you are deprived of at least one backup, the generalized reinforcer will remain effective. Even if you satiate on food after dinner, you might still buy a drink, a movie, or a new car. Generalized reinforcers differ in this respect from primary reinforcers. You can easily satiate on any primary reinforcer and not be reinforced by it again until you are deprived of it. Generalized reinforcers differ in the same way from other conditioned reinforcers. You can satiate on the backup reinforcer for a conditioned reinforcer and not be reinforced by it again until you are deprived. You are less likely to become satiated on all of the reinforcers backing up a generalized reinforcer. Thus the saying, "You can't have too much money!"

Social approval is a more subtle example of a generalized reinforcer. If someone approves of you, you can expect a wide variety of favors from that person. These might include loans of money, invitations to parties, general assistance, and even sexual favors. Because social approval is associated with so many backup reinforcers, it is a generalized reinforcer. In a way, you spend some of the person's approval to buy specific favors from them. If you ask for too much, you may find that you haven't built up that much good will.

Another advantage of generalized reinforcers is that they can be delivered immediately after the behavior occurs. The various backup reinforcers usually cannot be delivered immediately. Therefore, the generalized reinforcer can enhance the effectiveness of the backup reinforcers by utilizing the principle of immediacy.

Figure 20-1. Ted Ayllon developed the most influential token economy in the early 1960s. His work led to the use of token economies by numerous other behavior analysts.

Behavior analysts frequently use token systems. (See Figure 20-1.) A token system is a local monetary system. A teacher may give students tokens for performing desirable behaviors. The students can spend their tokens at a fixed rate to buy backup reinforcers. Researchers have used this system to encourage boys to use an exercise bicycle (DeLuca & Holborn, 1992). By exercising, the boys earned points and could spend them on a kite, a flashlight, a model car or plane, a puzzle, or comic books. Their rate of exercise doubled because of this point system.

Behavior analysts have used token systems to solve many behavioral problems. Researchers used tokens to help 8-year-old deaf children to improve

A Point System in the 19th Century

Alexander Maconochie used a point system to run a 19th-century British penal colony. He found the penal colony "a hell but left it an orderly and well regulated community." Each prisoner started his time owing a number of points, based on the seriousness of his crime. He earned points for good behavior and lost them for breaking prison rules. When he paid off what he owed, he went free. As Maconochie put it, "When a man keeps the key of his own prison, he is soon persuaded to fit it into the lock." Maconochie's superiors were disturbed by his unorthodox method and openly repudiated his successes, soon replacing him as head of the penal colony. Because the points would lose their effectiveness if prisoners could not spend them to buy release from prison, they are not primary reinforcers. (Based on Pitts, 1976.)

6. Because the points were backed up by only one reinforcer, they were ________ (conditioned, generalized) reinforcers.

The Achievement Place Point System for Delinquent Youths

How to earn points		*How to spend points*	
300	Watching/reading news	Get allowance	1000
500	Cleaning room	Use bicycle	1000
500	Keeping self clean	Watch TV	1000
5	Reading books	Play games	500
20*	Helping houseparents	Use tools	500
500*	Doing dishes	Eat snacks	1000
100*	Dressing for dinner	Go downtown	1000
500*	Doing homework	Stay up	1000
500*	Getting a good report card	Come home late	1000

*Minimum (maximum is up to 1000)

Figure 20-2. Instead of reform school, youths go to Achievement Place, where teaching parents teach them basic responsibility. The youths earn privileges by behaving responsibly. (Based on Phillips, 1968.)

their social skills (Rasing & Duker, 1992). Others used them to assist chronic mental patients in learning self-care and productive work behaviors (Ayllon & Azrin, 1965). They were also used in settings such as institutions for children with severe retardation (Birnbrauer et al, 1965). Researchers have used them to help poor people remain involved in self-help groups (Miller & Miller, 1970).

Point systems are like a credit-card economy. No actual token changes hands, but someone records points earned and spent and maintains a running balance for each person. Point systems have been used in a variety of settings, such as Achievement Place, a family-style alternative to reform school for delinquent youths (Phillips, 1968). Figure 20-2 outlines the point system used by Achievement Place. Youths who watched the news on TV (300 points), read 20 pages of a book (200 points), and did their homework (500 points) earned points. They could then spend the points to buy a privilege, such as permission to come home late from school (1000 points). Numerous experiments have shown that this system encourages the delinquent youths to engage in a wide range of constructive behaviors. Delinquents treated with this system did well in school, stayed out of trouble, and got jobs that led to a constructive and law-abiding role in the community (e.g., Fixsen et al., 1976; Kirigan et al., 1982).

A systems of generalized reinforcers is an extremely powerful tool for producing behavioral change. The tokens or points maintain their effectiveness as reinforcers because they can buy a wide range of other reinforcers. They are simple to use with large numbers of individuals. They can be backed up with enough different events to ensure that almost everyone in the group will remain deprived of some potential reinforcer.

Groups can use a system of generalized reinforcement to develop a structure for their social environment. They can use this tool to develop behavior that they themselves define as desirable, thereby creating democratically controlled systems of reinforcement. For example, welfare recipients have used tokens to pay people to attend meetings and to help themselves (Miller & Miller, 1970).

Students have used a point system to create cooperative residences that really work. They used points to pay members to clean the house, to prepare food, and to keep the house repaired (Miller & Feallock, 1975). They used points to pay members to participate in managing the residence (Johnson et al., 1991). They used points to pay members to participate in democratic meetings that members like and use (Welsh et al., 1989; Welsh, Miller, & Altus, 1994).

You're Sending Me to the Principal's Office? Great!

Can you imagine a high school student saying "Great!" to that news? Well, they do at Pequea Valley High School in Kinzers, Pennsylvania. Teachers look for students who spontaneously pick up trash, help others carry books, or perform other commendable activities. They write down the student's name and send it to the office. The teachers also send the names of students making outstanding academic achievements. These students are then sent to the principal's office, but instead of punishment they receive praise. In addition (on a variable-ratio schedule) they get athletic tickets, McDonald's coupons, and other free prizes. (Reported in *Behavior Analysis Digest*, March, 1990.)

7. The teachers tell the students, "I'm sending you to the principal's office." Because this comment is backed up by many reinforcers rather than just one, we call it a(n) ________________ (conditioned, generalized, primary) reinforcer.

Comparison of Different Types of Reinforcers

The book has already asked you to classify points in a penal colony, and you will be asked to classify many more examples of reinforcers. You need to know how to classify these examples so as to understand fully the three kinds of reinforcers. Here are some considerations in the proper use of the three labels: conditioned reinforcer, generalized reinforcer, and primary reinforcer.

Primary reinforcers are pretty easy to spot; we all react to pretty much the same primary reinforcers. If you wish to classify an event that you think is a primary reinforcer, ask whether it has a biological base. Ask whether that event is likely to always be a reinforcer except when the person has had too much of it recently. If you are pretty sure that it will always be a reinforcer because of its biological function, then it is probably a primary reinforcer.

Generalized reinforcers are also pretty easy to spot. Their power depends on their being paired with more than one other reinforcer. I have mentioned several generalized reinforcers. Obviously, money can buy many different reinforcers. Social approval usually leads to many other reinforcers. Token or point systems permit a person to trade for many backup reinforcers. If you think an event is a generalized reinforcer, just make sure that it is paired with many backup reinforcers.

The trickiest label to use may be *conditioned reinforcer*. The definition requires that a conditioned reinforcer lose its effectiveness if it is no longer paired with its backup reinforcer. So a ticket to a football game is a reinforcer as long as you can go to the game (or sell the ticket). If you slept through the time of the game, the ticket is no longer worth anything. It is no longer backed up with being able to attend the game. Therefore, the ticket is a conditioned reinforcer only while it is still valid. If the ticket had more than one backup, you would call it a generalized reinforcer. When I ask you to classify an event as to type of reinforcer, I will always use the label *generalized reinforcer* for an event backed up by many reinforcers. I will always use the label *conditioned reinforcer* for an event backed up by only one reinforcer.

Stimulus/Response Chains

Up to this point in the book, I have analyzed the occurrence or nonoccurrence of responses. However, most of our behavior is far more complex; we usually make many related responses in some kind of sequence. We don't take just one step; we walk somewhere. We don't say just one word; we engage in conversations. We don't just hit a baseball; we hit the ball, run toward first base, watch where the ball goes, and maybe try for second base. Thus, in most situations, we don't engage in just one response over and over again. We engage in a series of responses, each of which is influenced by the prior response.

Behavior analysts call sequences of related responses *stimulus / response chains* (often shortened to just *chains*). A **stimulus/response chain** is a sequence of two or more responses. The last response produces a reinforcer. The result of each prior response produces an SD for the following response. Suppose Pam reads a verbal math problem. She translates it into an equation by writing "2+2=." Then she writes "4." The first response in the chain is reading the verbal problem. This is the SD for writing the second response, "2+2=." Writing "2+2=" is the SD for writing the third response, "4." The "4" may produce praise from the teacher.

8. A sequence of two or more responses, in which the last response produces a reinforcer and the result of each prior response produces an SD for the following response, is called a *stimulus / response* __________.

Virtually all verbal behavior consists of long chains of individual responses. An example might be singing "The Star Spangled Banner." If Ted sings "Oh say can you...," these words serve as an SD for the next word, "see." These words may be an effective SD for "see" because they start at the beginning. A word picked out of the middle may not be as effective. For example, do you immediately know what word comes right after "early" in "The Star-Spangled Banner"? Most people have to go back and start from the beginning to remember.

Many other types of behavior are chains also. For example, walking is a chain of individual steps: Each step serves as an SD for the next step. If you get off course, your next step may correct the error. The reinforcer is getting someplace. Another example is the movements a ballet dancer makes in a particular dance.

Each response in a chain produces an effect on the environment that acts as a conditioned reinforcer for that response. Getting closer to where you are going reinforces each step you take. Each response moves you closer to the final response that produces the reinforcer. Thus, each response is reinforced by its increasing nearness to the goal. For example, opening a refrigerator, taking out some milk, filling a glass, and drinking constitute a four-response chain. The last response in the chain, drinking, is obviously reinforced by consumption of the milk. However, you can't drink the milk unless the milk is in the glass. Therefore, the full milk glass is a discriminative stimulus for drinking. But it is also a conditioned reinforcer for the filling response, because it brings you a step closer to drinking the milk.

Summary

Many kinds of reinforcers influence people's behavior. Behavior analysts classify some as primary reinforcers: reinforcers that weaken only temporarily due to satiation. They classify other events as conditioned reinforcers, which can weaken through satiation and through no longer being paired with other reinforcers. They call the paired

Figure 20-3. One dancer's role in a ballet is a very long and complex stimulus/response chain.

reinforcer a backup reinforcer. They classify still other events as generalized reinforcers—conditioned reinforcers that are paired with many backup reinforcers. Finally, behavior analysts define a stimulus/response chain as a sequence of two or more behaviors. Each response in such a chain produces conditioned reinforcement for the prior response and it also produces a discriminative stimulus for the next response. Tactic #5 in the stimulus control strategy is to make reinforcement more practical by creating conditioned reinforcers.

Behavior Analysis Examples

Modifying Teacher Behavior

The personalities of students and teachers often clash. Researchers worked with Jean, an eighth-grade girl (Polirstok & Greer, 1977). The Spanish teacher, who had an M.A. degree and 15 years of experience, regarded Jean as a discipline problem. The teacher sent her to the principal for disciplinary action about five times per week and referred her for more serious offenses on an average of twice a month. Her achievement level was about a year behind her grade placement.

The researchers taught Jean to approve the teacher's desirable behaviors, hoping to increase those behaviors. They taught Jean how to do this in two steps. They asked Jean what were desirable teacher behaviors and had her role-play approving of them. They gave Jean a tape player that frequently cued her to show approval. The researchers gave her tokens each day after class, based on how many approvals she had given out. She could spend the tokens for popular music tapes, extra gym, lunch with a favorite teacher, and extra English credit.

Figure 20-4 shows the results. Prior to the tokens, Jean averaged about 6 approvals per class. Under the token system, Jean averaged 13 approvals per class. When they stopped giving her tokens, Jean's rate of approval fell to a little more than 8 per day. When tokens were again awarded, Jean averaged 13 approvals per class once again.

The researchers also taught Jean to withhold disapproval of the Spanish teacher, and her rate of disapproval decreased. At the same time, the Spanish teacher's behavior also changed radically. He showed more approval and less disapproval of Jean. The researchers had Jean use this same procedure on three other teachers, with similar results. After the experiment, Jean often commented on how nice her teachers had become. Her teachers indicated that they were pleased with her remarkable socialization and new-found maturity. They referred her for discipline only once after the experiment. The researchers concluded that they had broken a mutually unpleasant interaction pattern and created a mutually pleasant one. The nicer teacher behavior then sustained Jean's behavior even after the experiment had finished. (This final phase is not shown on the graph.)

9. Jean could spend the tokens for many backups such as popular music tapes, extra gym, lunch with a favorite teacher, and extra English credit. Because the tokens had many backup reinforcers instead of just one backup, behavior analysts call the tokens ________ (conditioned, generalized, primary) reinforcers.

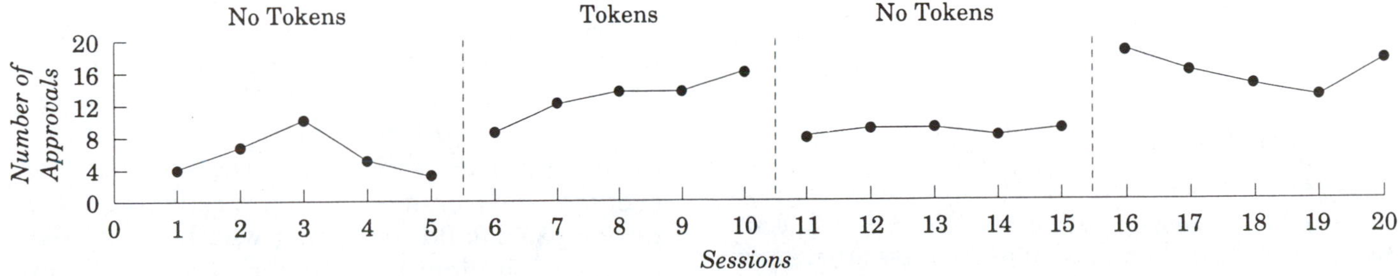

Figure 20-4. The number of approvals Jean directed per day at her Spanish teacher. Jean was given tokens during two experimental conditions to reinforce such behavior. As a result, the teacher was much more approving (and less disapproving) of Jean. Adapted from "Remediation of Mutually Aversive Interactions Between a Problem Student and Four Teachers by Training the Student in Reinforcement Techniques," by S. Polirstok and R. D. Greer, *Journal of Applied Behavior Analysis,* 1977, *10,* 707–716. Copyright 1977 by the Society for the Experimental Analysis of Behavior, Inc. Used by permission.

A Token Economy for Self-Control

Researchers used a token economy to help a college student control his own behavior (Whitman & Dussault, 1976). James was a 21-year-old undergraduate who had trouble organizing his time. He had a part-time job, a full class load, and a girlfriend. He began spending more time on his job and with his girlfriend at the expense of school. This led him to feel "guilty and depressed." He lost 20 pounds in six months, and his personal habits, such as bathing, were deteriorating.

The researchers suggested that James use a token system to organize his own behavior. James specified a large number of desirable behaviors. He assigned them points according to how important they were. He earned 20 points by studying for one of his courses at least 4 to 6 hours a week; 20 points for attending classes for all his courses; 20 points for writing home; 5 points for washing dishes once a day; and 10 points for washing his hair once a week. He could buy a visit to his girlfriend for 25 points per day, watching TV for 10 points, and walking for pleasure for 5 points. James recorded all points as he earned them. He agreed not to obtain any reinforcers unless he had previously earned sufficient points to afford them. Figure 20-5 shows that James achieved about 30% of his goals during a baseline period of observation. However, once the token system was introduced, he steadily improved until he was achieving about 70% of his goals. A reversal to baseline and subsequent reversal to the token economy confirmed the impact of the token economy on his behavior.

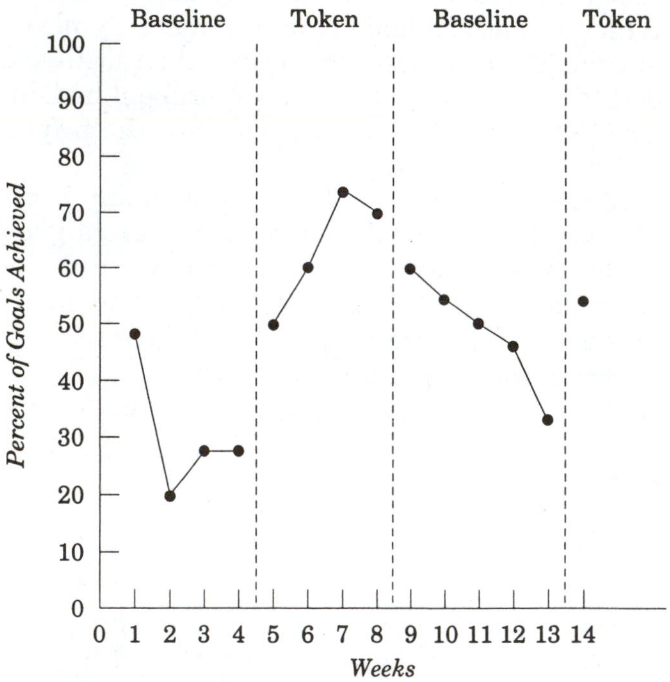

Figure 20-5. The percent of goals earned by a student having trouble maintaining studying, class attendance, and personal cleanliness. He used a token system to balance these goals with seeing his girlfriend and other reinforcing activities. From "Self Control Through the Use of a Token Economy," by T. L. Whitman and P. Dussault, *Journal of Behavior Therapy and Experimental Psychiatry,* 1976, *7,* 161–166. Copyright 1976, Pergamon Press, Ltd. Reprinted by permission.

James formulated his personal goals in terms of how many points he should earn for achieving them. He formulated his reinforcing activities in terms of how much they were worth to him. He could then keep records that permitted him to balance these two aspects of his life more judiciously.

10. James spent his points for many backups such as visiting his girlfriend, watching TV, and walking. Therefore, behavior analysts would classify the points as _______________ (conditioned, generalized, primary) reinforcers.

Notes

Note #1

Token economies have sometimes been criticized because they do not always lead to permanent behavioral change. The behavioral change does not generalize to other situations or even the same situation without the tokens (Levine & Fasnacht, 1974). This, of course, is built into the very concept of reinforcement of any kind. If you stop reinforcing a behavior, and there is no other source of reinforcement, the behavior will eventually disappear. A token economy may help to teach someone a desired behavior. If the everyday environment reinforces the behavior, removal of the token system will not stop the behavior. If the everyday environment does not reinforce the behavior, you should reconsider whether the behavior is socially significant. If not, a socially significant target behavior should be selected. However, if the behavior is socially significant and the everyday environment does not maintain it, that environment must be redesigned. One way to redesign it is to make the token economy a permanent part of that environment.

Note #2

Stopping the delivery of the backup reinforcer while continuing the delivery of the conditioned reinforcer isn't an example of extinction. Stopping the delivery of both the backup and the conditioned reinforcer is an example of extinction.

11. Can you label stopping the delivery of a backup reinforcer but not stopping the delivery of the conditioned reinforcer as *extinction*? ______

Note #3

Some behavior analysts argue that it is futile to classify reinforcers in terms of their biological origins or other causes (Schoenfeld, 1978). Note that the classifications primary, conditioned, and generalized are purely descriptive. Behavior analysts classify reinforcers as primary purely in terms of whether they permanently lose their effectiveness. They do this whether or not the reinforcer has a biological origin. They classify reinforcers as conditioned solely in terms of whether they permanently lose their effectiveness when unpaired from their backups. The distinctions between primary, conditioned, and generalized reinforcers made in this lesson are widely accepted by applied behavior analysts. These distinctions appear to help them select or create reinforcers that are useful in solving practical problems.

Helpful Hints

Helpful Hint #1

Students sometimes confuse *generalization* and *generalized reinforcer*. Remember that the occurrence of a behavior in a novel situation is called generalization. A reinforcer that is paired with many other reinforcers is called a generalized reinforcer. Be sure to distinguish carefully between these two concepts.

12. Would it be correct to refer to a reinforcer that is paired with many backup reinforcers as a generalization? ______. What is the correct label for such a reinforcer? ______ reinforcer

Helpful Hint #2

Students sometimes fail to distinguish properly between a conditioned reinforcer and a generalized reinforcer. When I ask you a question concerning one of these concepts, be sure to give the most specific answer. If I ask you the name of a reinforcer that is paired with many other reinforcers, use the more specific label (generalized reinforcer) rather than the more general label (conditioned reinforcer). If I ask you the name of a reinforcer that is paired with only one other reinforcer, you can answer "conditioned reinforcer." If the example does not specify that it is paired with many reinforcers, you should answer "conditioned reinforcer." The book will consider your answers wrong if you answer in any other way.

13. If praise is used as a reinforcer that is backed up by a ticket to a basketball game, the praise is what type of reinforcer? ______. If praise is used as a reinforcer that is backed up by tickets, food, and other privileges, praise is what type of reinforcer? ______

Helpful Hint #3

Students often have trouble figuring out which event is the conditioned reinforcer and which is the backup reinforcer. The simplest difference is that the conditioned reinforcer comes first and the backup reinforcer comes later. You earn the money and then you buy the goodies. The goodies are the backups because you can't get them until you get the money. You get the praise and then you get the favors. You can't get the favors until you've gotten on someone's good side by earning his or her praise.

14. First you get the ______ (backup, conditioned) reinforcer; then you get the ______ (backup, conditioned) reinforcer.

Additional Readings

Ayllon, T., & Azrin, N. H. (1965). The measurement and reinforcement of behavior of psychotics. *Journal of the Experimental Analysis of Behavior*, *8*, 357–383. This classic article describes the first token economy. It reports experiments using a token system to develop self-help behaviors among chronic psychotics.

Ayllon, T., & Azrin, N. H. (1968). *The token economy*. Englewood Cliffs, NJ: Prentice Hall. This book was designed as a handbook on token economies. It contains a great deal of practical information. It gives rules for how to select and define target behaviors and how to select reinforcers. It discusses other important aspects of designing and using a token economy.

Glynn, S. M. (1990). Token economy approaches for psychiatric patients: Progress and pitfalls over 25 years. *Behavior Modification*, *14*(4), 383–407. This article reviews what is known about token economies. It suggests that use of token economies has declined and discusses why.

Kazdin, A. E. (1977). *The token economy: A review and evaluation.* New York: Plenum. This book reviews what is known about token economies. It expands and updates the Ayllon and Azrin book.

Kelleher, R. T., & Gollub, L. R. (1962). A review of positive conditioned reinforcement. *Journal of the Experimental Analysis of Behavior*, *5*, 543–597. This is a highly technical review of the concept of conditioned reinforcement. It discusses many of the theories about the conditions necessary to make an event into a conditioned reinforcer.

Reading Quiz

23. I want you to get familiar with the wording of the fifth tactic. The fifth tactic in using the stimulus control strategy is to make reinforcement more practical by creating ______________ (conditioned, primary) reinforcers.
68. The fifth tactic in using the stimulus control strategy is to make reinforcement more practical by creating ______________ reinforcers.
71. The first goal is to learn about primary reinforcers. Reinforcing events that are rooted in our biological nature influence our behavior from birth. They lose their effectiveness only through satiation. Behavior analysts call these events ______________ (conditioned, generalized, primary) reinforcers.
79. We call a reinforcer *primary* because it comes first in a person's life. Primary means "first." You are born with some biological reinforcers such as food, air, water, and warmth. They come before you can learn any other reinforcers. An event that is one of your first reinforcers is called a(n) ______________ reinforcer.
38. Review: A primary reinforcer is a reinforcing event that loses its effectiveness only temporarily through ______________.
13. Behavior analysts frequently use food to reinforce children and severely impaired persons. Food loses its effectiveness only if a person has had too much recently. What kind of reinforcer is food? A(n) ______________ reinforcer
32. One kind of reinforcer gains its power from its biological function for people, not from being paired with other reinforcers. What is the name of that kind of reinforcer? ______________ reinforcer
76. The second goal is to learn about conditioned reinforcers. A conditioned reinforcer ________ (does, doesn't) gain its effectiveness by being paired with other established reinforcers that back it up.
6. A time sequence will help you understand conditioned reinforcers. First, someone performs a desirable behavior. Second, you give him or her a conditioned reinforcer to increase the rate of the desirable behavior. Third, you back up that conditioned reinforcer by giving the person an established reinforcer. The established reinforcer that you give as a backup comes ___________ (after, before) the conditioned reinforcer.
63. Since many students confuse which is the conditioned and which is the backup reinforcer, I will emphasize the point. When you see a desired behavior, you immediately deliver a conditioned reinforcer. You then maintain the effectiveness of the conditioned reinforcer by pairing it with an established reinforcer, delivered afterwards. Because it comes later and backs up the conditioned reinforcer, you call this established reinforcer a(n) __________ __________ reinforcer.
1. A <u>conditioned</u> reinforcer is an event whose effectiveness depends on being paired with an established reinforcer that you deliver later and that backs it up. You might say that pairing with the backup reinforcer is a "condition" for the newfound effectiveness of the event. That is why behavior analysts call the newly effective event a(n) ______________ reinforcer.
81. When a neutral event is paired with an established reinforcer delivered later, it may make the neutral event into an effective reinforcer. The event is effective because it is backed

up by the established reinforcer. In this case, we call the newly effective event a *conditioned reinforcer*. Because you deliver it after the conditioned reinforcer, you call the established reinforcer the ________________ reinforcer.

61. Notice that any established reinforcer can back up a conditioned reinforcer. The established reinforcer can be another conditioned reinforcer, a generalized reinforcer, or a primary reinforcer. Does the established reinforcer that backs up a conditioned reinforcer have to be a primary reinforcer? ____

73. The name for all reinforcers that gain their effectiveness by being paired with one backup reinforcer is ________________ reinforcers.

2. A conditioned reinforcer is any reinforcer that loses its effectiveness permanently if it is repeatedly presented unpaired with established reinforcers that are called ________________ reinforcers.

8. An effective conditioned reinforcer must be paired with a backup reinforcer. However, a conditioned reinforcer loses its effectiveness permanently if it is repeatedly presented ____________ with its backup reinforcers.

46. Review: An established reinforcer that is paired with a conditioned reinforcer to make the conditioned reinforcer effective is called a(n) ____________________ reinforcer.

17. For example, towels were no longer hoarded by the woman when they were no longer paired with attention from the attendants. Because the towels came first and led to attention, attention was the backup reinforcer. The towels were the ________________ reinforcer.

35. Remember, a conditioned reinforcer is any reinforcer that loses its effectiveness permanently if it is repeatedly presented __________ with backup reinforcers.

16. Behavior analysts use conditioned reinforcers much more often than primary reinforcers. However, they often make the conditioned reinforcers effective by pairing them with a primary reinforcer. They pair them by first giving the conditioned reinforcer and then later giving the primary reinforcer. When they pair a primary reinforcer with a conditioned reinforcer, you would call the primary reinforcer a(n) ___________________ reinforcer.

29. Note that a conditioned reinforcer will no longer be effective if the person has had so much of the backup reinforcer recently that the primary reinforcer has temporarily lost its effectiveness due to the person being __________ with it.

84. You can often create a conditioned reinforcer that you can deliver as soon as the behavior occurs. This gives you the advantage of delivering the reinforcer according to which principle of reinforcer effectiveness? The principle of ________________

18. For example, you may want to give your daughter a lesson riding her new bike for correctly saying "refrigerator." But you would have to get her dressed, bring her outside, and give the lesson. This may take five minutes between saying the word and getting to the bike. A better idea is first to say, "You just earned a lesson on your new bike!" If you back your words up with the lesson, the words will be an effective conditioned reinforcer. The advantage of the words is that you can deliver your reinforcer ______________.

36. Researchers often use conditioned reinforcers to teach eating. What is odd about this is that eating is reinforced by a primary reinforcer. For some children that primary reinforcer does not maintain eating. In these cases, the conditioned reinforcers are stronger than the ______________ reinforcer of food.

49. Review: Budney and associates (1991) worked with two cocaine addicts. When the men tested "clean," they were reinforced with movie tickets, sporting goods, and dinner certificates. Since the reinforcers were effective because they were backed up with pleasant activities, they would be labeled ________________ reinforcers.

25. It often helps to think of "spending" the conditioned reinforcers, after you get enough of them, to "buy" the backup reinforcer. With this analogy, the reinforcer that you can buy is called the ______________ reinforcer.

28. My third goal is to teach you about generalized reinforcers. A generalized reinforcer is one type of conditioned reinforcer, because it would lose its effectiveness if it were presented to a person ____________________ (paired, unpaired) with already established reinforcers.

24. In other words, a generalized reinforcer would lose its effectiveness if you could no longer "buy" what behavior analysts call the __________ reinforcers.

3. A generalized reinforcer is a reinforcer that is paired with ________ (one, many) backup reinforcer(s).
5. A reinforcer that is paired with either a conditioned reinforcer or a generalized reinforcer by being delivered afterwards is called a(n) ________________ reinforcer.
12. Because you can use it to get so many backup reinforcers, what is the most obvious example of a generalized reinforcer? ____________
4. A primary reinforcer loses its effectiveness when you are satiated with it. A conditioned reinforcer loses its effectiveness when you are satiated with its one backup reinforcer. But a generalized reinforcer doesn't lose its effectiveness until you are satiated with ________ (all, some) of its many backup reinforcers.
66. Taking into account the probability of satiation, which of the following reinforcers is most likely at any given time to be effective? ________________ (primary, conditioned, generalized)
26. Let me put the same idea in another way. A primary reinforcer will be effective as long as the person is deprived of it. A conditioned reinforcer will be effective as long as the person is deprived of its backup. But a generalized reinforcer will be effective as long as the person is <u>deprived</u> of at least ____ backup reinforcer(s). (How many?)
54. Review: One reason a generalized reinforcer is so effective is that the person is likely to be ________________ of at least one of the backup reinforcers.
64. Since social approval is paired with many other backup reinforcers, it should be considered a(n) ________________ reinforcer.
11. Because they can be delivered right after the behavior occurs, generalized reinforcers can enhance the effectiveness of the backup reinforcers by utilizing the principle of ________.
14. Behavior analysts frequently use a local monetary system of reinforcement called a(n) ____________ system.
74. The points in a point system are not always generalized reinforcers. Maconochie ran a penal colony that used a point system by which prisoners could earn their freedom. Prisoners could use the points for only one backup: to get out of prison. In this case, the points were a(n) ________________ reinforcer.
7. Achievement Place youths can earn points for doing homework, washing dishes, watching news, or getting a good report card. They could spend points for an allowance, watching TV, riding a bike, or staying up late. The points are what kind of reinforcer? A(n) ______________ reinforcer
15. Behavior analysts frequently use token systems or point systems to reinforce desired behaviors. The points or tokens are usually what type of reinforcer? ______________ reinforcers (Be specific.)
22. Groups of poor people and students have created democratically controlled systems of reinforcement using token economies. The tokens are usually effective reinforcers because they are paired with ________ (many, one) backup reinforcer(s).
57. Review: Students at Pequea Valley High School are sent to the principal's office when they perform commendable activities or make outstanding academic achievements. When they get there, they get athletic tickets, McDonald's coupons, and other free prizes (*Behavior Analysis Digest*, March 1990). Because the prizes are paired with being sent to the principal's office and make it a more effective conditioned reinforcer, you call the prizes that students receive ____________ reinforcers.
34. Remember, you call a reinforcer that you can spend to buy only one backup a(n) ________ reinforcer. You call a reinforcer that you can spend to buy many backups a(n) ________ reinforcer. You call the reinforcers that you can buy ____________ reinforcers.
72. The fourth goal of the Reading Quiz is to teach you about stimulus/response chains. Behavior analysts call a <u>sequence</u> of two or more responses, in which each response produces an <u>SD</u> for the next response and the last response leads to a <u>reinforcement</u>, a *stimulus/response* ______________.
9. An example of a stimulus/response chain is singing "The Star Spangled Banner." Each word appears in a <u>sequence</u> from beginning to end. Each word is an <u>SD</u> for the next word. The last word leads to the <u>reinforcement</u> of applause. Thus, singing "The Star Spangled Banner" is called a stimulus/ ______________ chain.
10. Another example of a stimulus/response chain is walking from point A to point B. Each step occurs in a <u>sequence</u>, starting with the step at point A and ending with the step at point

B. The first step puts you at a location where you must make a step in the right direction to continue to point B. This location is an SD for the step in the exact direction. Finally, the last step leads to the reinforcement of arriving at point B. These three elements define a(n) ______________ /response chain.

65. Suppose a behavior has the following three elements. (1) It is composed of a sequence of responses. (2) Each response in the sequence is an SD for the next response. (3) The last response leads to reinforcement. The behavior that has those three elements is called a(n) ________________________________.

83. You can abbreviate the term *stimulus / response chain* (using the last word) simply as a(n) ______________.

69. The first element of a stimulus/response chain is that it is a sequence of responses. A stimulus/response chain involves multiple responses that follow one another in a specific order or ______________________.

77. "The Star Spangled Banner" is a chain because singing it involves singing many words in a specific __________________.

75. The second element of a chain is that each response in the sequence is an SD for the word that follows. For example, when you sing "Oh" to start "The Star Spangled Banner," that word is a stimulus associated with reinforcement for the correct next word, "say." If you sang "can" next, that would be the wrong word, and you would not get reinforced. Because "Oh" is a stimulus in whose presense "say" will be reinforced, we call "Oh" a(n) _____ for "say."

30. Notice that "Oh" is both the initial response in the chain and also a stimulus that precedes the second response. It is a stimulus that is discriminative for the correct response, "say." Because each response in a chain is both a stimulus and a response, the whole unit of behavior is called a(n) __________ / __________ chain.

70. The first element of a chain is that it is a sequence of two or more behaviors. The second element is that each response is a(n) __________ for the next response.

78. The third element of a chain is that the last response is followed by the procedure of _____ __________________.

27. Let's review. The first element of a chain is that it is a(n) _______________ of behaviors.

86. The first element of a chain is that it is a sequence of two or more behaviors. The second element of a chain is that each response in the chain is a(n) ______________________ for the next response.

89. The first element of a chain is that it is a sequence of two or more behaviors. The second element of a chain is that each response in the chain is an SD for the next response. The third element is that the last response leads to the procedure of ________________.

87. Singing "The Star Spangled Banner" is a chain because it is (1) two or more responses that form a(n) ___________________; (2) each response is a(n) ________________________ for the next response; (3) the last response is followed by the procedure of ________________.

88. Any sequence of two or more responses in which each response serves as an SD for the next response and whose last response is followed by reinforcement is called a(n) ________ _____________________. (You may abbreviate.)

33. Probably the hardest part for students to remember is that a chain is a sequence of responses in which the last response leads to reinforcement and each response produces a(n) _________________________ for the following response.

80. What does saying "Each response produces an SD for the following response" really mean? It usually means that you ____________ (can, can't) do the second response until you have done the first one.

51. Review: For example, popping the top of a brew is one response. The opened can makes it possible to pour the brew into the mouth. Pouring the brew into the mouth is the following response. Pouring the brew into the mouth leads to tasting and relaxing. Popping the top is the first response. The opened can is a stimulus in whose presence pouring the brew into the mouth will work and lead to reinforcement. Therefore, you would call the opened can a(n) ________________________ for pouring.

53. Review: Notice that the opened can is likely to be a reinforcer for popping the top. Since an empty can is also open, the open can must be backed up by a can full of brew to be a reinforcer. Thus, the open can is what kind of reinforcer? A(n) _______________ reinforcer.

85. You need not write the full name of the term *stimulus/response chain*. You may use the last word only. So when asked what you call any sequence of responses where each response produces an SD for the following response and the last response produces reinforcement, you need write only __________.

31. Review: Walking is an example of a chain of individual steps. Each step serves as a(n) ______________________ for the next step.

56. Review: You can call the recitation of "The Star-Spangled Banner" without looking at the words a(n) ______________________.

48. Review: Behavior analysts define primary reinforcers as those that weaken only temporarily due to ______________. Conditioned reinforcers are those that weaken through satiation and through being ______________ with backup reinforcers. Conditioned reinforcers that are paired with many backup reinforcers are classified as ______________________.

45. Review: A stimulus/response chain is defined as a sequence of two or more behaviors. Each response in the chain is a(n) ______________ for the next response. The last response is followed by the procedure of ______________.

58. Review: The fifth tactic in using the stimulus control strategy is to make reinforcement more practical by creating ______________ reinforcers.

55. Review: Polirstok and Greer (1977) gave Jean a token for each approval she directed at her teachers. She could use tokens to buy music tapes, extra gym, lunch with a favorite teacher, or extra credit in English. These tokens would be ______________________ reinforcers.

82. Whitman and Dussault (1976) helped James set up a point system in which he earned points by such behaviors as studying and attending class, and he spent them on such activities as visiting his girlfriend and watching TV. Because he could spend his points on visits to his girlfriend and on watching TV, these activities are ______________________ reinforcers for the points.

21. From Hint #1: A reinforcer that is paired with many backup reinforcers is a(n) ______________ reinforcer. The occurrence of a behavior in the presense of a novel stimulus illustrates the process of ______________________.

19. From Helpful Hint #3: Suppose I tell you only two things. I will give you reinforcer A if you study. When you have ten reinforcer A's, I will give you one reinforcer B. Which reinforcer is the backup reinforcer? __________

20. From Helpful Hint #3: Which comes first, the backup reinforcer or the conditioned reinforcer? The ______________________ reinforcer.

41. Review: A reinforcer paired with only one backup reinforcer is called a(n) ______________ reinforcer.

60. Review: To use the stimulus control strategy, (4) create complex stimulus control through imitation training and instructional training; (5) make reinforcement more practical by creating ______________ reinforcers.

52. Review: If a conditioned reinforcer remains associated with a backup reinforcer, a decrease in the conditioned reinforcer's effectiveness will happen when the person has received too much of the backup reinforcer recently and is ______________ with respect to the backup reinforcer.

47. Review: Any reinforcer that loses its effectiveness permanently through being presented unpaired with other reinforcers is called a(n) ______________ reinforcer.

42. Review: A reinforcer that is associated with many other reinforcers you should call a(n) ______________ reinforcer.

43. Review: A sequence of responses that leads to reinforcement, and in which each prior response is a discriminative stimulus for the following response, is called a(n) ______________________.

39. Review: A reinforcer that loses its effectiveness only temporarily through satiation is called a(n) ______________ reinforcer.

59. Review: To use the stimulus control strategy, (4) create complex stimulus control through imitation training and ______________ training; (5) make reinforcement more practical by creating ______________ reinforcers.

50. Review: Conditioned reinforcers have one major advantage over their backups with respect to their effectiveness as reinforcers. Conditioned reinforcers can easily be delivered according to the principle of ______________.

37. Review: A generalized reinforcer is one that is associated with ______________ other reinforcers.

62. Review: What kind of reinforcer is most likely always to be an effective reinforcer even after you have earned some? ______________ reinforcer.

40. Review: A reinforcer that is paired with a conditioned reinforcer and that is responsible for the conditioned reinforcer's effectiveness is called a(n) ________________ reinforcer.
44. Review: A sequence of responses in which the results of one response serve as an SD for the next response, and in which the last response leads to a reinforcer, is called a(n) ________________.
67. The fifth tactic in using the stimulus control strategy is to make reinforcement more practical by creating ____________ reinforcers.

Examples

1. When Harry does something pleasant for the family, his father awards him reinforcer A. Harry can trade in reinforcer A for cookies later on. If reinforcer A is unpaired with cookies, it permanently loses its effectiveness (until again paired with cookies). Since reinforcer A loses its effectiveness permanently when unpaired with cookies, call it a(n) ________________ reinforcer. Call the cookies ________________ reinforcers for reinforcer A. You should be aware that the effectiveness of reinforcer A would also temporarily decrease if Harry were to eat many cookies and become ________________ with them.

2. When Harry reads the daily news or a good book, his father delivers reinforcer B, which can be traded in for a trip to the movies, allowance, a late-night snack, or a game of frisbee with his father. Since reinforcer B is paired with so many reinforcers, call it a(n) ________________ reinforcer. Call such events as a trip to the movies or a game of Frisbee ________________ reinforcers for reinforcer B. One advantage of reinforcer B is that Harry is likely at any given time to be ________________ of at least one of its backup reinforcers. Another advantage of reinforcer B is that Dad can deliver it right after Harry has done some reading. It will thus be more effective (due to the principle of ________________) than its backup reinforcers.

3. When Harry does household chores, his father gives him reinforcer C. Reinforcer C is always an effective reinforcer for Harry, except temporarily when he gets too much of it. Since reinforcer C loses its effectiveness only when Harry gets too much of it, call it a(n) ________________ reinforcer.

4. Marla signed her checks "Marla Petty Jones." If each of her names is a response, is her whole name a sequence? ______. When she has written "Marla," that is all that is on the paper. If she looked away to answer a question, when she looked back the "Marla" would tell her that the correct next response is "Petty." Therefore, "Marla" is called a(n) ____________ for "Petty." When she makes the final response of writing "Jones," the signature on her check is valid and will allow her to take home her purchase. If that increases the probability of her signing her name correctly to checks, you would call the event of taking home her purchase a(n) ________________. What is the name of the behavior of signing her name to a check called? ________________

5. Bobby was a menace to the preschool because he always left his toys strewn around after he was through playing with them. The teachers got together to figure out how to teach Bobby to pick up his toys. They decided to give him a poker chip each time he picked up a toy after playing with it. Bobby could use poker chips to buy a snack, to have a teacher tell him a story, or to go for a long walk outside. Bobby learned to pick up his toys within a week. The poker chips seemed to always be reinforcing to Bobby. Because the poker chip was associated with many other reinforcers, call the poker chip a(n) ________________ reinforcer. The poker chip was effective because it could buy many other events, called ________________ reinforcers. The poker chip was likely to be an effective reinforcer most of the time because Bobby would probably be in a state of ________________ with respect to at least one of the reinforcers associated with it. The poker chips would probably lose their effectiveness if they were not ________________ with the backup reinforcers.

6. Six-year-old Sarah was a big eater. She always ate at a rapid rate for the first ten minutes of a meal. Then she would relax, as though she knew she would get enough to eat that night, and finish the meal slowly. As Sarah ate a meal, she gradually stopped making eating responses. This decrease in response rate occurred because she had become ________________ with respect to food. Because food lost its reinforcing ability only temporarily through <u>satiation</u> and always regained the effectiveness that it had lost, food would be classified as a(n) ________________ reinforcer.

7. Carey had not learned to read at the fourth-grade level during the regular school year. To avoid

repeating the grade, her parents volunteered to get her to finish three books in the Sullivan Reading Series during the summer. Her parents gave Carey one point for each page she completed, and she could exchange ten points for an ice cream cone. Carey read about five pages a day in her reading book, averaging one ice cream cone every other day. The points might become ineffective in two ways. Her parents might no longer let her exchange them for their backup, the ice cream. Or, if her parents gave Carey so many points that she could have ten ice cream cones a day, her reading might decrease because she would become ______________ with the ice cream. Because the points in this example could be exchanged only for ice cream, they would be an example of a(n) ____________________ reinforcer. If her parents allowed Carey to exchange the points for ice cream, watching TV, or visiting a friend, the points would be an example of a(n) ______________ reinforcer.

8. Sociology 71 was a unique course. Instead of working for a grade, the students earned "credits" by reading materials for the course. The credits could be exchanged for a variety of learning experiences, including movies, guest speakers, discussions, field trips, parties, and special meetings with the instructor. The instructor found that 50% of the students earned enough credits to "buy" several learning experiences. Because the "credits" were paired with many fun learning experiences, you call the credits ____________________ reinforcers. The events, such as movies, guest speakers, and discussions, backed up the credits and made them effective. Therefore, you call them __________________________ reinforcers.

9. Kim decided to hike along the railroad track to the old abandoned station 5 miles away. She thought that she might find interesting old artifacts at the station, and it seemed like an interesting way to spend a slow summer day. To keep track of her progress, she wore a pedometer, which measured the distance she walked. Walking (by itself) usually isn't too reinforcing, but walking to go somewhere interesting can be reinforcing. In this case, the pedometer measured the rate at which Kim was walking somewhere interesting. Clicks of the pedometer might have been an effective reinforcer, because they indicated to Kim that she was getting closer to the abandoned station. You might say that Kim was "buying" the event of getting to the abandoned station by taking steps that made the pedometer click. You would call getting to the station a(n) ____________________ reinforcer for the pedometer clicks. The pedometer clicks would be an example of what type of reinforcer? ________________________

10. Teachers give grades for a course long after the students have studied. Likewise, grades for tests are given days after the studying takes place. Teachers can help overcome this long delay by arranging for conditioned reinforcers to occur immediately after the behavior. For example, students sometimes get study guides containing questions that they can answer as soon as they finish studying. Getting the correct answer to a question in a study guide may be a conditioned reinforcer. A student who gets the correct answer to the study guide question will probably get the correct answer to a similar test question. Thus, the correct answer on the study guide is paired with the correct answer on the test. Therefore, you call getting the correct answer to the study guide question a(n) ________________________ reinforcer. Because it comes after getting the correct answer on the study guide, you call the correct answer on the test the __________________ reinforcer. Getting the correct answer to the study guide question probably is effective due to the principle of ______________________.

11. Review: Willie's mother, Fay, encouraged Willie to do at least one thoughtful act a day. When she noticed him doing something particularly thoughtful, she would immediately say "Thank you" and, as soon as possible, give him an M&M. Willie did many thoughtful things each day with this kind of reinforcement. One week, however, disaster struck. The grocery store was out of M&M's and there were no more at home. Fay decided to continue reinforcing thoughtful acts by saying "Thank you." She noticed that Willie gradually did fewer and fewer thoughtful things around the house, and by the end of the week he was doing almost none. Because the M&M was paired with the "Thank you," you would call the M&M a(n) ________________ reinforcer. (Did it come first or second?) The effectiveness of the "Thank you" decreased due to the fact that it was presented ____________________ with the M&M's. Therefore, the "Thank you" is considered to be a(n) ______________________________ reinforcer.

12. Review: Here's a review. John found that if he talked about politics when he was with Mary, she would get involved in a conversation with him, but if he talked about politics with Carol, she ig-

nored him. Pretty soon he talked about politics a lot when he was with Mary but not at all when he was with Carol. What behavioral procedure did Mary and Carol unwittingly use to affect when John talked about politics? ______________ ______________ (Remember to ask some questions.)

13. Review: Martin wore a wrist counter to record the number of times he said something positive to someone. On any day that he counted at least 15 positive statements, he permitted himself to have a beer with dinner. The counts on the counter would probably be a(n) ______________ reinforcer, and the beer would be a(n) ______________ reinforcer.

14. Review: Berry's teacher asked him to complete the sentence, "Any event that follows a response and increases the future probability of that response is called...?" She reinforced him when he answered "reinforcer." Because the sentence signaled that "reinforcer" was the correct answer, this sentence would technically be called a(n) ______________ for the response "reinforcer."

15. Review: When somebody has been reinforced to make a response in the presence of a series of similar stimuli, he or she will sometimes emit that same response in the presence of a novel stimulus. This is the process known as ______________.

16. Review: Claire wanted to learn to study from 4 to 6 every afternoon after getting home from high school. So she made a giant sign for her room that said, "If you study from 4 to 6, you can take a bike ride." She reinforced studying with the bike ride and extinguished nonstudying. She left her giant sign up until she was studying every day from 4 to 6. Then she made a smaller sign for her desk saying the same thing. When she found that she was still studying from 4 to 6, she took all signs away and found that she still studied from 4 to 6. What behavioral method was involved in the use of the signs and their gradual elimination? ______________

17. Review: It took a long time for Ed to learn how to shift smoothly. First he had to take his foot off the accelerator at the same time that he pushed the clutch in. Second, he had to move the lever from one gear position to the next. Third, he had to let the clutch out while he again depressed the accelerator. What is the name of the sequence of behaviors that he learned? ______________

18. Review: For every 15 minutes of chores, Calvin was given one point by his mother. At the end of the week, Calvin could turn the points in for allowance at the rate of 25 cents per point. What type of reinforcer are the points? ______________ ______________ (Check!)

19. Review: If a chronic stutterer were reinforced by his best friend for saying complete words and sentences without stuttering, his "cure" might carry over to other friends and acquaintances. We would call the process by which his nonstuttering behavior with his best friend carried over to others ______________.

20. Review: Flora was careful always to thank anyone who did her a favor. Unlike many people, she eventually backed up her thanks with any one of a number of return favors. Therefore, we would refer to her "Thank you" as what kind of a reinforcer? ______________

LESSON 21 Review of Stimulus Control

In this unit, you have learned about stimulus control. The unit has described ways in which stimulus situations come to influence a person's behavior. This influence is often extremely complex, subtle, and difficult to observe. Also, the influence is based on past events that led to reinforcement or extinction of the behavior. Therefore, the cause of the influence can no longer be observed. In the absence of easily observed causes, many people attribute the cause to inner events. Thus, they explain attention by inventing possible mental mechanisms (see the box). Likewise, they attribute language, complex sequences of behaviors, and intellectual behavior to mental and cognitive events.

> ***Does the Mind Control Attention?***
>
> "We can listen to a particular instrument... in part by suppressing our responses to the other instruments and we are said to do so with various mental mechanisms.... [The mind is considered] a kind of gatekeeper—a loyal servant who admits wanted stimuli and defends his master against unwanted.... We have not explained anything, of course, until we have explained the behavior of the gatekeeper.... [Behavior analysis explains attention by] the contingencies underlying the process of discrimination. We pay attention or fail to pay attention to a lecturer or a traffic sign depending upon what has happened in the past under similar circumstances. Discrimination is a behavioral process: the contingencies, not the mind, make discriminations" (Skinner, 1974: 116–117).
>
> 1. Discrimination results from reinforcing a response in one situation and ____________ ____________ (extinguishing, reinforcing) it in another.

Behavior analysts have rejected explanations of cognitive behavior based on private events. They have not turned to the mind as a kind of gatekeeper but rather sought public causes of cognitive behavior. They gain an important advantage once they find such public causes: They can use them to help people become more skilled. This unit has presented numerous examples of using public events to change cognitive behavior. It is hard to imagine how anyone could gain control over private events, like the hypothetical gatekeeper, in order to help people improve their cognitive behavior.

Take the "concentrated attention" that a baseball player must give to a pitched curveball (Osborne, Rudrud, & Zezoney, 1990). Researchers did not somehow improve the behavior of a mental gatekeeper who eliminated distractions. Yet they did improve the hitters' concentration, as evidenced by their improved hitting. Researchers used discrimination training, assisted by coloring the seams of the baseball. They explain their results directly, without reference to causes arising from private events. They simply note the way in which the training was set up with the colored seams. They can still refer to "improved concentration," refering to private behavior whose existence is best proven by the players' improved hitting. The training procedure caused both it and the better hitting.

Take the "sensitivity" of male clients to women's interest in talking with them (Azrin & Hayes, 1984). To help these clients, researchers did not change some inner mechanism that you might call sensitivity. Instead, they showed the clients videotapes of females talking with other males. They trained their clients to discriminate interest from lack of interest. They did so in a way that would generalize to real females in real conversations with them. The training is sufficient to explain the increased ability of the clients to guess when females are interested in talking with them; no mental mechanism is needed.

Take the children who learned how to identify and name industrial objects (Mann & Baer, 1971). You do not need to assume some deep structure of language to explain their learning. The use of discrimination training seems to explain the learning fully.

Or take the teachers who learned how to use specific praise (Horton, 1975). You need not point to a better "understanding" of praise to explain the results. The teachers used specific praise at first only with the students for whom they were trained to use it. After they were trained in additional subjects, their use generalized. The generalization training explains their new usage of specific praise. They may indeed understand better, but this private event is not the cause of more specific praise. Rather, both the use of specific praise and the better understanding are the result of generalization training.

Take the boy who overcame fear of the dark (Giebenhain & O'Dell, 1984). He did so because of a fading program that let him earn reinforcement for tiny steps toward sleeping in the dark. His parents did not change some cognitive structure to make him a braver person. Rather, they reinforced behavior that approximated sleeping in the dark. He may now have a feeling that he identifies as braveness. If so, that feeling is not the cause of his sleeping in the dark; rather, sleeping in the dark and that feeling are the result of the fading program.

These examples may help you understand how behavior analysts see private behavior. They do not deny the existence of feelings of fear, or of understanding, sensitivity, or attention. They simply regard thoughts, feelings, and cognitive processes as private behavior. They often find that environmental events cause this private behavior just as they cause the observable behavior that is more accessible to us. In fact, the same environmental event that causes the batter to pay better attention to the curveball also accounts for the batter hitting the ball better. Behavior analysts claim that trying to explain the observable behavior by the private behavior does not lead to an understanding of all the causes. Nor does it lead to the identification of causal events that people can use to change their behavior.

Behavior analysts repeatedly find that the most powerful procedures for changing cognitive behaviors depend on reinforcement. For example, researchers found that psychotics do not follow instructions unless reinforced for doing so (Ayllon & Azrin, 1964). All of these examples, from improving vision to learning how to talk, depend on reinforcement. Remember that the reinforcement need not be continuous. Just because you observe many instances in which behavior is not immediately followed by reinforcement does not mean that reinforcement is not involved. For example, you read about one study in which intermittent reinforcement of some imitations was enough to maintain all imitations.

You learned how conditioned reinforcers can permit immediate reinforcement. Because tokens, praise, and other conditioned reinforcers can be delivered immediately, they aid learning.

All of these procedures occur naturally in our everyday lives. They account for most of the influence that complex situations have on our behavior. They may well be the source of cognitive behavior. Behavior analysts use these procedures to help people solve their problems. Their first strategy is to define the problem in terms of behavior; sometimes that alone solves the problem. Their second strategy is to reinforce the desired behavior. If these strategies don't solve the problem, the next strategy they try is stimulus control.

The Stimulus Control Strategy

Stimulus control is the basis for the third strategy of applied behavior analysis. The stimulus control strategy is to ensure that the person emits the target behavior when it will produce reinforcement. We want Mary to act assertively when Dave interrupts her, but we don't want her to act assertively toward a defensive boss who then fires her!

The first tactic in developing stimulus control is discrimination training. Discrimination training is the basic behavioral process that teaches people when to emit a particular behavior. It occurs everywhere we turn. Behavior in one situation produces reinforcement; the same behavior in another situation does not. The stimuli in the first situation become SD's for that behavior, while the stimuli in the second situation become S-deltas.

The second tactic is generalization training, which enlarges the situations in which people emit

Improving Study Behavior with Stimulus Control

Bev felt sleepy every time she tried to study. The researcher set out to make her desk an SD for studying. He told her to install a brighter light for her desk, to turn her desk so she could not see her bed while studying, and to do nothing but study at her desk. If she wished to write letters, do it at her dining table. If she wished to read a comic book, do it in her kitchen. If she wished to daydream, do it away from her desk. By the end of the semester, she had been studying three hours a day for four weeks. Presumably her newfound success with studying was the reinforcer. (Based on Goldiamond, 1965.)

2. The desk became an SD for studying, and other places became S-deltas for studying. Because studying was more likely at her desk, you call it a(n) ________________ behavior.

the target behaviors. Generalization occurs throughout all aspects of our life. If a particular behavior in one situation produces reinforcement, it is likely to produce reinforcement in similar situations. But we don't have time to teach the person to emit that behavior in every one of those other situations. Therefore, we teach the person to emit it in enough of them so that it generalizes to all of them.

The third tactic is using extra prompts to make learning easier. Fading and programming make it possible to teach discrimination and generalization quickly and with few errors. Behavior analysts use these procedures to teach material that people might not otherwise learn. They have used these procedures to teach children in normal schools, as well as children with behavioral and cultural deficits. They have used them to teach college students everything from foreign languages to English composition to behavior analysis.

The fourth tactic is to use imitation and instructional training. These two methods are also important tools for behavioral change. For example, behavior analysts have taught children with severe retardation how to imitate other people (Baer, Peterson, & Sherman, 1967). By being able to imitate, those children can learn new behaviors much more easily. They will have an important skill for surviving in a normal environment. Similarly, behavior analysts have taught oppositional children to follow instructions (Baer, Rowbury, & Baer, 1973). They have taught adult schizophrenics to follow instructions (Ayllon & Azrin, 1965)—a crucial step toward operating in a normal environment. Undoubtedly, people need many other skills to function in a reasonably normal manner. However, being able to imitate and being able to follow instructions are certainly of great importance.

The fifth tactic is to use conditioned reinforcement to improve learning. Conditioned reinforcement permits behavior analysts to use reinforcement more effectively. Most of our everyday behavior does not produce immediate primary reinforcers—or even immediate conditioned reinforcers of major importance. We work at least a week for our paycheck. We scheme many hours to get a date with a special person. We work for years to gradu-

The Family Contract Game

When Timmy and his mother discussed chores, they attacked one another. To reduce antagonistic behavior, they tried playing a game. The first square told Mrs. Smith to draw a problem card stating, "Timmy never washes dishes." The next square told her to tell Timmy, "Wash the dishes every Monday and Tuesday." The next square told Mrs. Smith to "contract" for how she would reinforce Timmy: "Let him stay up an extra half hour." The next square asked Timmy if he agreed: "Sure." Other squares told Timmy and Mom to draw humorous bonus cards if they agreed or risk cards if they didn't. Timmy's antagonism decreased from 60% during baseline to 10% during treatment. It increased to 40% during reversal. Mom's antagonism showed an even greater change. (Based on Blechman, Olson, & Hellman, 1976.)

3. Because Mom and Timmy tended to ignore each other's antagonistic behavior during the game, the game became a(n) __________ (SD, S-delta) for antagonistic behavior.

ate from high school or college. We buy groceries on Friday to have a meal on Sunday.

Instead of delayed major reinforcers, we are often influenced by immediate but less important reinforcers. We watch TV instead of studying. We get tasty snacks from a vending machine instead of nutritious food. We enjoy a cigarette instead of avoiding lung cancer. A major task of behavior analysts is to counteract the lure of immediate reinforcers so that important but delayed reinforcers influence desired behaviors. Conditioned and generalized reinforcers are powerful tools for doing this.

Stimulus Control and Other Cognitive Behaviors

The premise of this unit has been that the concept of stimulus control is the basis for a behavioral approach to cognitive behavior. The lessons have given a wide array of examples of what this means. For example, most people would regard listening to music as a cognitive behavior. Skinner (1974) suggested that listening to music is a discriminated response. If we have been reinforced for listening to a particular kind of music in the past, then we are more likely to listen to it now. Of course, the reinforcement may arise from the structure of the music itself, or it may arise from the reaction of our parents to our listening. In either event, the complex stimulus that we call music has come to exert control over our listening behavior.

You have read many more concrete examples of the stimulus-control approach to cognitive behavior. By manipulating stimuli and reinforcement, behavior analysts have been able to help people improve their cognitive functioning. The mechanism has been similar. Curveballs came to exert more control over batters' hitting (Osborne, Rudrud, & Zezoney, 1990). We would say that the batters' concentration improved. How females reacted to males came to exert more control over what guys said to them (Azrin & Hayes, 1984). We would say that the guys' sensitivity improved. Pupils' reaction came to exert control over teachers' use of specific praise (Horton, 1975). We would say that the teachers' understanding improved.

Recently two behavior analysts have extended the stimulus-control approach to cognitive behavior even further. Donahoe and Palmer (1994) have presented detailed analyses of even more complex cognitive behaviors. They show how behavioral concepts related to stimulus control can account for problem solving, verbal behavior, and memory. I will illustrate their approach only for memory.

They distinguish between two types of remembering. The simplest is based on the functioning of SD's. When you respond because of an SD, you might say that the stimulus "reminded" you to perform the behavior. Your roommate writes you a note that a friend called. You stick the note in your pocket. When you see the note later, it reminds you to call your friend. The note is a stimulus in whose presence you will be reinforced for calling your friend. Seeing it again "reminded" you to call. This is clearly a simple example of memory explained easily by stimulus control. Another example might be trying to remember how to get to a friend's house. You can't remember whether to turn right or left, but then you see the huge oak tree on the street to the left. Last time, all you

A Behavioral Approach to Remembering

Supppose someone asks you what you had for breakfast. You might actively behave in ways that increase the likelihood that you will come in contact with SD's reminding you what you ate. You might look at the dishes in your sink for clues that suggested you had eggs and toast. If your sink is clean, you might say, "I can see myself rinsing egg yolk and crumbs off the plate, so I must have had eggs and toast." You might call such active behaviors as visualizing your dirty dishes and talking about them *remembering behaviors*. They are behaviors that have been reinforced in the past by producing reminders that aid your memory. They suggest that memory is a behavioral process that might even be improved by behavioral intervention. (Based on Shull, 1995.)

4. If the question "What did you have for breakfast?" increases the probability of such remembering behaviors, we would say that the question exerts ____________ ________________ over those behaviors.

had to do was follow the street with the oak tree, and you were there. The oak tree exerts control now based on its leading you to your friend's house last time. The oak tree "reminded" you to turn left. Our behavior is full of examples in which stimulus control, exerted through simple SD's, reminds us of the correct behavior.

But we also remember in much more active ways as well. Not only do stimuli remind us to behave, but we also actively remember. The box on remembering illustrates how even this kind of memory may be viewed as a behavioral process. While an interpretation of this sort does not prove that behavior analysis can be usefully extended even into the highly cognitive arena of memory, it certainly suggests that it can. Donahoe and Palmer have done a service by showing us this possibility. We may have seen only the barest beginnings of the behavior analysis of cognitive phenomena!

Summary

Stimulus control is the influence that a stimulus situation has on a behavior. The cause of this influence lies in environmental events. Environmental causes are just as important for cognitive behavior as any other behavior. Procedures based on environmental events in general and reinforcement in particular make the stimulus control strategy possible. That strategy is to ensure that people emit target behavior when it will produce reinforcement. We have outlined five relevant tactics. The first tactic is teach people basic discriminations about when the behavior will produce reinforcement. The second is to teach additional similar situations until generalization occurs. The third is to use prompts to improve teaching. The fourth is to use imitation and instructional training. The fifth is to use conditioned reinforcers to overcome delayed delivery of important reinforcers.

Glossary

The definitions of all terms introduced in this unit of the book are presented below. You can review the unit and prepare for your exam by testing yourself on the definitions and related facts presented for each term. You might use a piece of paper as a mask to leave only the term exposed; then see if you can formulate a reasonable definition and any other facts about that term. Remove the mask and check on yourself.

A **backup reinforcer** is any reinforcing event that makes a conditioned reinforcer or a generalized reinforcer effective.

- When a person obtains a conditioned or generalized reinforcer, he or she can exchange it for other reinforcers. These reinforcers are called backups.

Chain is the most commonly used term for stimulus/response chain.

A **conditioned reinforcer** is any reinforcing event that loses its effectiveness permanently through unpaired presentations—that is, presentation of the event without its being associated with any other reinforcers.

- Behavior analysts generally assume that conditioned reinforcers are caused by a previously nonreinforcing event being frequently paired with a reinforcing event. This may happen when the nonreinforcing event serves as a discriminative stimulus.

Discriminated behavior is a behavior that is more likely to occur in the presence of the SD than in the presence of the S-delta. Discriminated behavior occurs as a result of discrimination training.

Discrimination training is the procedure in which a behavior is reinforced in the presence of one stimulus and extinguished in the presence of another.

- It is also used to label more complex situations. Complex situations may be viewed as two or more simultaneous discrimination-training situations. One behavior is reinforced during stimulus A and extinguished during stimulus B. Another behavior is extinguished during stimulus A and reinforced during stimulus B. Be careful—it is easy to identify such complex situations incorrectly as differential reinforcement.

Fading is the procedure by which an added stimulus (prompt) is gradually withdrawn.

- Fading is used to help establish a simple discrimination.

Generalization is the process whereby a behavior occurs in the presence of a novel stimulus.

- A novel stimulus is any stimulus in whose presence the person's behavior has not been reinforced. Usually the novel stimulus is similar to the SD in a discrimination-training procedure.

Generalization training is the reinforcement of a behavior in a series of stimulus situations until it generalizes to other members of that stimulus class.

A **generalized reinforcer** is a conditioned reinforcer associated with many other reinforcers.

- This kind of reinforcer is effective because the person is usually deprived with respect to at least one of the backup reinforcers.

Imitation training consist of three parts. (1) The teacher demonstrates what behavior the learner is to engage in. Behavior analysts call this the imitative stimulus. (2) The learner copies the imitative stimulus with a similar behavior. Behavior analysts call this the imitative behavior. (3) The teacher reinforces the imitative behavior.

- The imitative stimulus is an SD for the imitative behavior. All other imitative stimuli are S-delta for the imitative behavior.

Instructional training consists of three parts. (1) The teacher provides a verbal description of the desired behavior. (2) The learner produces the instructed behavior. (3) The teacher arranges for some form of reinforcement for the instructed behavior.

- The verbal description is an SD for the instructed behavior. Other verbal descriptions are S-delta for the instructed behavior.

A **primary reinforcer** is any reinforcing event that loses its effectiveness only temporarily through satiation.

Programming is the use of prompts to establish a generalization.

- Programmed instruction is a form of programming involving three features: (1) it requires a written response, (2) it gives immediate feedback, and (3) it uses small steps.

A **prompt** is an added stimulus that increases the probability that a person will make the correct response in the presence of a novel stimulus.

SD is the abbreviation for *discriminative stimulus*. It is a stimulus that precedes a behavior and is associated with (or indicative of) reinforcement of a particular behavior in discrimination training.

An **S-delta** is a stimulus that precedes a behavior and is present only if extinction will occur for a particular response.

A **stimulus** is any physical object or event in the environment that affects the person's behavior.

A **stimulus class** is a set of related stimuli.

Stimulus control is the increased probability of a discriminated behavior that is produced by a stimulus (SD).

The **stimulus control strategy** is the strategy of teaching people when to emit the desired behavior. The strategy includes five tactics:

1. Narrow stimulus control through discrimination training.
2. Broaden stimulus control through generalization training.
3. Create new stimulus control by using temporary prompts.
4. Create complex stimulus control through imitation training and instructional training.
5. Make reinforcement more practical by creating conditioned reinforcers.

A **stimulus response chain**, or simply a chain, is a sequence of two or more behaviors. Each behavior produces a result that is the discriminative stimulus for the next behavior. Each behavior also reinforces the previous behavior. The last behavior is reinforced. Most of our behavior consists of such stimulus/response chains.

Practice Review

The following material has questions on every concept studied in Unit Three, as well as review questions from Units One and Two. By answering the questions and checking your answers, you can prepare yourself for the Review Exam, which will contain questions from all three units.

22. Review: Generalization training involves reinforcing a behavior in each of a series of situations until ________________ occurs to other members of that same stimulus class.
23. Review: Harold's mother praised him when he was good. When he had been praised many times in a day, she would arrange for a special event, such as a trip to the zoo or ice cream. Mother's praise is a generalized reinforcer. Therefore, these special events are called ________________ reinforcers for the praise.
42. Review: When you reinforce one behavior in one stimulus situation and extinguish the same behavior in another stimulus situation, you call the procedure ________________. When you reinforce one behavior and extinguish another in the same stimulus situation, you call the procedure ________________.
32. Review: Martha's mother frequently explained how to do chores around the house. If Martha did them, her mother always reinforced her. Describing how to do the chores and then reinforcing the doing of them is an example of what behavioral procedure? ________________
24. Review: If a behavior occurs more frequently in the presence of the SD than the S-delta, it is called ________________ behavior.
31. Review: Maria listened to Lefkowitz when he referred to female persons as women but ignored him when he called them chicks. However, she listened to him when he referred to baby chickens as chicks and ignored him when he called them women (naturally). What behavioral procedure was she using? ________________
53. When analyzing an example, always check to see whether it involves two behaviors in only one stimulus situation. If it does, then the procedure is from an earlier unit. The procedure is ________________.
34. Review: One reason a generalized reinforcer is so effective is that the person is likely to be ________________ with respect to at least one of the backup reinforcers.
44. Review: Tactic #1 of the stimulus control strategy is to (1) narrow stimulus control through ________________.
12. If you wanted to increase a person's resistance to extinction, you would use what type of reinforcement? ________________ (continuous or intermittent)
16. Review: A reinforcer that is paired with a conditioned reinforcer and that is responsible for the conditioned reinforcer's effectiveness is called a(n) ________________ reinforcer.
5. Danny held up one object and gave Marty an M&M when he said "one"; Danny held up two objects and ignored Marty when he said "one." What behavioral procedure was Danny using? ________________
7. Fading is a method of gradually changing the ________________ in a situation. Shaping is a method of gradually changing the ________________ in a situation.
11. If an event follows a behavior and the rate of the behavior ________________, the event is called a reinforcer.
25. Review: If a person learns a certain behavior in one situation and later emits that behavior in a new situation without being trained to do so, ________________ is said to have occurred.
1. "Yassou" means "Hi" in Greek. When Eli said "Yassou" to Lou, he wanted Lou to answer "Hi." He praised Lou when he replied "Hi" to "Yassou" and ignored him when he replied "Hi" to any other word. So when Eli said "Yassou," he also waved at him. Adding the waving to "Yassou" got Lou to say "Hi." Then Eli gradually withdrew the wave by delaying it for a longer period until Lou said "Hi" before he waved. What behavioral procedure was Eli using, by gradually delaying his waving, to teach Lou to say "Hi" when greeted with "Yassou"? ________________
46. To use the stimulus control strategy: (1) narrow stimulus control through discrimination training; (2) broaden stimulus control through ________________.
40. Review: When dealing with a sequence of two responses, if the result of the first response serves as a discriminative stimulus for the second, and if the last response is reinforced, we have what is called a(n) ________________.
10. If a teacher starts the semester by making class attendance optional and later makes it required to see what difference it makes, he or she would be using a(n) ________________ design.

33. Review: One procedure for attempting to produce generalization of a behavior involves the temporary use of prompts. You use generalization training and use a prompt to get the behavior started in a new stimulus situation. The use of temporary prompts with generalization training is called ________________.
29. Review: Kay didn't give compliments to people very often. One day, however, she complimented Alice, and she was delighted by Alice's positive response. As a result, she frequently complimented Alice from then on. A bit later, she complimented Norma. The occurrence of Kay's complimenting behavior around a new person, Norma, would be an example of what behavioral process? ________________
36. Review: Suppose you stop all of the many backup reinforcers for tokens, and the rate of responding previously maintained by the tokens declines. What kind of conditioned renforcers are the tokens? A(n) ________________ reinforcer (Use the most specific term.)
52. What two types of intermittent schedules produce a tendency for people to work at a uniform rate? ________________ and ________________
47. To use the stimulus control strategy, (2) broaden stimulus control through generalization training; (3) create new stimulus control by using temporary ________________.
37. Review: Suppose you are not sure whether a specific example is imitation training or instructional training. If the teacher described what to do, then it is ________________ training; if he or she demonstrated what to do, then it is ________________ training.
35. Review: Suppose a teacher touches the top of her head, Danny touches the top of his head, and the teacher reinforces him. You call the teacher's touching the top of her head the ________________ stimulus.
38. Review: When a discriminated behavior is more likely to occur in the presence of a discriminative stimulus, you say that the SD exerts ________________.
9. If a person is required to make a high number of responses for each reinforcement, his or her responding may become erratic or decrease because of what is called ________________.
19. Review: A stimulus associated with extinction for a particular response is called a(n) ________________.
21. Review: An added stimulus used by behavior analysts to increase the probability that a person will make the correct response in the presence of a novel stimulus is called a(n) ________.
26. Review: If Gloria peeps only when the light in Todd's room is on, then we say that the light exerts ________________ over Gloria's peeping.
48. To use the stimulus control strategy, (3) create new stimulus control by using temporary prompts; (4) create complex stimulus control through ________________ training and ________________ training.
8. Fran and Will observed how often someone played a game in the lounge. They used 60-second intervals and recorded the following:

Fran: XXXOXXOXXXXXOOXXOOXX
Will: XOXOXXXXXXOXOOOXOOXX

Compute their reliability: ________________ percent. Is it acceptable if this is a new behavioral definition? ________________
13. In the process of teaching Marty to say "one," Danny would show Marty how to say "one" by saying it himself. Danny would then reinforce Marty if he correctly said "one." The method that Danny used to teach Marty to say "one" is called ________________ training.
20. Review: A stimulus/response chain consists of several related responses in which the results of one response serve as a(n) ________________ for the next response.
18. Review: A set of related stimuli is called a(n) ________________.
3. Dan gets pleasantly high after different numbers of beers. Sometimes it only takes one, but other times it takes two, three, or four; once it took 47! If getting pleasantly high is a reinforcer, what specific schedule is Dan's beer drinking on? ________________
30. Review: Many people can say the Lord's Prayer from beginning to end. Because each word in the verse's sequence is the SD for the next word, and the last word leads to reinforcement, you call such a verbalization a(n) ________________.
6. Every time Tabby came up to them, Sally asked her baby son, Marty, "What is that? Is that a kitty?" and praised him if he said "kitty." Each time, she said the word "kitty" a bit

softer until Marty could identify Tabby as a kitty with no help. She then followed the same procedure with a series of cats until Marty could identify any new cat that happened to come up to them. What behavioral procedure did Sally use? ______________

15. Review: A primary reinforcer is a reinforcing event that loses its effectiveness only through ______________.
49. To use the stimulus control strategy, (4) create complex stimulus control through imitation training and instructional training; (5) make reinforcement more practical by creating ______________ reinforcers.
51. Two procedures for modifying behavior that use discriminative stimuli (SDs) in the form of demonstrations or descriptions produced by another person are ______________ training and ______________ training.
28. Review: If the tall guy will answer you only when addressed as Marvin, and the short guy will not answer you when addressed as Marvin, we would call the tall guy a(n) ______________ for the response "Marvin."
14. Review: A generalized reinforcer is one that is associated with ______________ other reinforcers.
2. Believe it or not, Shecky counted every step that Tom took while jogging and praised him after every 100th step. What schedule of reinforcement was Tom's running on? ______________
39. Review: When a person copies the demonstration of a behavior, his or her copying behavior is called ______________ behavior.
41. Review: Mrs. Keller held up two marbles and asked "How many?" She gave Janie a cookie if she said "two." When Janie could answer the question every time, Mrs. Keller did the same training with two pencils and a series of pairs of objects. Finally, without reinforcement, Janie could answer the same question when Mrs. Keller held up two books. From then on, she could answer that question no matter what kind of objects were held up. What behavioral procedure did Mrs. Keller use? ______________
27. Review: If Kelly answers "5" when asked "4+1=?" but not when asked "4–1=?", then we call her behavior of answering "5" ______________ behavior.
45. The stimulus control strategy includes five tactics: (1) narrow stimulus control through ______________ training, (2) broaden stimulus control through ______________ training, (3) create new stimulus control by using temporary ______________, (4) create complex stimulus control through imitation training and ______________ training, and (5) make reinforcement more practical by creating ______________ reinforcers.
4. Danny asked Marty to say "elephant." Every time Marty said "elephant," Danny immediately said "very good." Danny's praise obviously pleased Marty very much. Danny praised Marty only when he said "elephant." At first Marty said "elephant" over and over again. Then he slowed down, and finally he quit altogether. Marty probably quit because by using praise so often, Danny violated what principle of effective reinforcement, if any? ______________
43. Review: Which type of reinforcer gains its effectiveness through pairings with one other reinforcer? A ______________ reinforcer.
54. You call an added stimulus that increases the probability of a person's making the correct response in the presence of a novel stimulus a(n) ______________.
17. Review: A reinforcing stimulus occurs ______________ (after, before) the response; a discriminative stimulus occurs ______________ (after, before) the response.
50. Tom was teaching Mona to play the guitar. He first praised her only when she held it correctly, then only when she strummed it correctly, and finally only when she strummed a particular chord. What behavioral procedure was Tom using? ______________

UNIT 4

The Aversive Control Strategy

LESSON

22 Punishment by Contingent Stimulation

Introduction to Unit Four

The last unit of this book discusses the topic of aversive control. The term aversive control refers to the use of what behavior analysts call punishment and negative reinforcement. The unit's three lessons will examine punishment, escape, and avoidance. These behavioral procedures have a profound influence on daily behavior. Understanding them is important to understanding everyday behavior.

People make extensive use of aversive control in everyday life. Parents spank and withhold privileges from their children. Employers reprimand, dock the pay of, and even fire employees. Teachers scold pupils and keep them after school. Police arrest criminals, and judges sentence them to prison or even death. People punch each other out. The military makes war on whole countries. Aversive control is all around us; Skinner asserts that "it is the commonest technique of control in modern life" (Skinner, 1953a: p. 182).

Aversive control often stops unwanted behavior immediately. However, it does so at a price, often producing undesirable side effects (Sidman, 1988). It may cause the person to dislike and perhaps avoid the person giving the punishment. It may cause him or her to try to countercontrol that person through violent means (Mace, 1994). It may cause a variety of negative emotional responses. Furthermore, when the punishment stops, the behavior often resumes. For that matter, if people can "get away with" the behavior without being detected, they will. The immediate beneficial effects of aversive control are offset by these undesirable long-term effects.

Skinner felt that the discovery of reinforcement makes aversive control less necessary (Skinner, 1972). He felt that parents could reinforce children for cleaning their room rather than hurting them for not doing so. Employers could praise workers for good work rather than complaining about shoddy work. Teachers could give privileges for studying rather than withholding them for making noise.

Skinner did not believe that we could completely eliminate aversive consequences. The physical world will certainly continue to deliver them: Close your eyes and you will bump into a wall; step off a cliff and you'll fall; speed and you may drive off the road. We cannot replace these consequences with reinforcement. Skinner simply proposed that people can influence each other through reinforcement rather than through pun-

Progress from Punishment to Reinforcement

"Civilized man has made some progress in turning from punishment to alternative forms of control. Avenging gods and hell-fire have given way to an emphasis upon heaven and the positive consequences of the good life. In agriculture and industry, fair wages are recognized as an improvement over slavery. The birch rod has made way for the reinforcements naturally accorded the educated man. Even in politics and government the power to punish has been supplemented by a more positive support of the behavior which conforms to the interests of the governing agency. But we are still a long way from exploiting the alternatives.... Direct positive reinforcement is to be preferred because it appears to have fewer objectionable by-products" (Skinner, 1953a: p. 192).

1. You might infer that Skinner defines civilization in part as reducing the use of punishment or aversive control and increasing the use of positive ________________.

ishment. His ideas may be of value in an increasingly violent world.

Behavior analysts turn to aversive control as a last resort (Iwata, 1988). They do so when they fail to make positive procedures work and the behavior endangers the person or others. Consider behaviorally disturbed individuals in institutions. These people often hit themselves repeatedly. They sometimes break bones, cause bleeding, blind themselves, or knock out teeth. They sometimes die. Psychologists call this *self-injurious behavior* or SIB. Sometimes behavior analysts rely on punishment to stop SIB (e.g., Linscheid et al., 1990).

I have placed the unit on aversive control at the end of the book to emphasize that it is a last resort. It is the fourth strategy for changing behavior: the aversive control strategy. The first tactic in using the aversive control strategy is to decrease undesirable behavior through punishment as a last resort.

2. The first tactic in using the aversive control strategy is to decrease undesirable behavior through ________________ as a last resort.

Figure 22-1. Nathan Azrin conducted a brilliant series of experiments on punishment in the 1950s and 1960s. He examined type of stimulus, intensity and frequency, and the schedule maintaining the behavior. He also examined many side effects of punishment.

Definition of Punishment

People usually think of punishment as doing something unpleasant to others to stop some behavior they dislike. This is not a scientifically useful definition, because people often disagree about what is unpleasant. Behavior analysts define punishment more technically. **Punishment** is the procedure in which a punisher is administered contingent on an undesired behavior. A punisher is an event that (1) follows a behavior and (2) decreases the frequency of that behavior. It is the opposite of a reinforcer (Azrin & Holz, 1966). An event that you consider unpleasant may not be a punisher for someone else. An event that you consider pleasant may be a punisher for someone else.

3. A punisher is an event that (1) ____________ a behavior and (2) ____________________ the frequency of that behavior. It is the opposite of a reinforcer.

There are two types of punishment. You can deliver an aversive event, or you can take away a reinforcer. This lesson will deal only with the delivery of an aversive stimulus contingent on behavior. Behavior analysts refer to this form of punishment as *punishment by contingent stimulation*. The next lesson will deal with punishment by taking away a reinforcer.

You can use both punishment and extinction to reduce the rate of a behavior. These two methods are easily distinguished. You are using punishment by contingent stimulation when you deliver an aversive event contingent on a behavior. You are using extinction when you stop delivering a reinforcing event.

For example, suppose Bobby throws a tantrum if his mother won't give him a cookie just before dinner. His mother has reinforced this behavior in the past by eventually giving him the cookie. She might decide to eliminate his behavior by

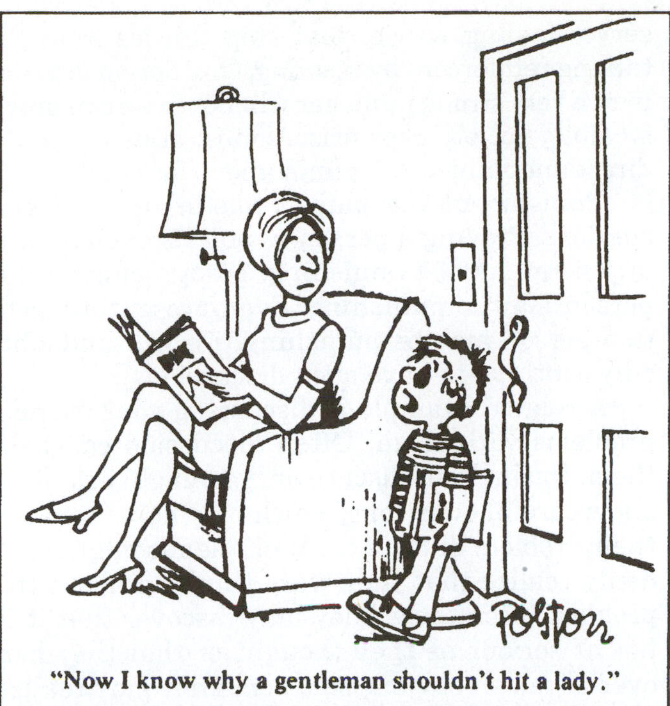

"Now I know why a gentleman shouldn't hit a lady."

Figure 22-2. Teaching little gentlemen to stop hitting ladies is an excellent example of the use of punishment. Cartoon copyright 1973 by Cartoon Features Syndicate. Reproduced by permission.

spanking him each time he throws a tantrum. This would be an example of contingent punishment. She would be delivering an aversive event after the behavior. She also might decide to eliminate the behavior by never giving him a cookie at that time. This would be an example of extinction because she has stopped delivery of the reinforcing event.

Another example of punishment might occur if Tommy often hits Sally. Sally might turn around and give Tommy a black eye. The results are shown in Figure 22-2.

The Use of Punishment

The everyday world punishes much of our physical behavior. For example, if you forget to take your finger out of the door, closing the door will serve as a punisher. If you don't look where you're going, an approaching wall might deliver a punisher.

Behavior analysts resort to strong punishment to eliminate dangerous behaviors. For example, researchers treated Diane, a 22-year-old with severe retardation and autistism, for head-banging (Linscheid et al., 1990). She had an extensive medical history of trauma to her head, face, and shoulders. She hit her head hard enough to detach a retina and produce cataracts. Doctors gave her numerous drugs to reduce her head-banging, without success. Other treatments included dance, music and play therapy, and physical restraint. Behavioral treatments included extinction and differential reinforcement. Even with these treatments, she continued head-banging. She also injured attendants by aggressively striking them with her head. Diane's physician felt that continued head-banging would produce loss of eyesight.

Researchers resorted to punishment with Diane. They used a device called Self-Injurious Behavior Inhibiting System (SIBIS). The device consisted of a helmet worn by Diane that electronically sensed when she banged her head. It instantly gave her a brief electric shock. These shocks quickly eliminated almost all of her head-banging. As a further benefit, Diane began to participate in social activities.

Stopping Diane from Injuring Herself

Diane Grant was a woman with autism. She often hit her face and head hard enough to break bones; once she almost severed an ear. No treatment of her head-banging seemed to work. Finally her parents built an electronic helmet that sensed head-banging and delivered an immediate shock. The helmet rapidly eliminated Diane's head-banging, but it was heavy and uncomfortable to wear. The Grants asked a research team at the Johns Hopkins Applied Physics Laboratory to build a lighter helmet. The helmet helped Diane live a more normal life, and it may help many others who injure themselves and who are not helped by present treatments based on positive reinforcement. Nevertheless, the inventors remain committed to searching for improved approaches based on positive reinforcement. (Based on Iwata, 1988.)

4. Behavior analysts call the procedure of delivering shock to reduce head-banging ______________ (reinforcement, punishment).

Behavior analysts can often eliminate dangerous behaviors with milder punishers. For example, researchers treated a 7-year-old boy with severe retardation (Bailey, Pokrzywinski, & Bryant, 1983). This boy bit his hands. The researchers treated hand-biting by spraying a fine mist of water in his face; this mild treatment completely stopped his self-injurious behavior. Other researchers used lemon juice to stop a child from throwing up its meals and eating them again (Glasscock et al., 1986).

Behavior analysts also use punishment to eliminate behaviors that endanger others. For example, researchers used electric shock to eliminate severely aggressive behavior (Foxx et al., 1986). Other researchers used mild punishment to treat a 4-year-old fire setter (Carstens, 1982). They required him to do one hour of hard labor for each fire-setting episode. This produced immediate and complete elimination of fire setting. Other researchers treated convicted child molesters with mild shock (Quinsey, Chaplin, & Carrigan, 1980).

Behavior analysts have used strong punishers to help people change harmful behavior. For example, some clients have volunteered to have shock treatment in an attempt to quit smoking (Azrin & Powell, 1968). Since this early study, however, researchers have turned toward much milder approaches to reducing smoking (e.g., Axelrod, 1991; Singh & Jin-Pang Leung, 1988).

Behavior analysts use mild forms of punishment in many situations. For example, one researcher used feedback to treat absenteeism of employees at a mental hospital (Ford, 1981). Each employee was required to report his or her sick leave to a supervisor. The supervisor simply described to the employee the number of other sick leaves and the number of staff left to meet work responsibilities for that day. This procedure reduced sick leave hours by about 50%. Other researchers punished hyperactivity in a girl with mild retardation by distorting the TV picture she was watching (Green & Hoats, 1969).

Everyday Use of Punishers

People will probably continue to use punishment to counteract strong reinforcement. For example, stealing may produce very strong reinforcers. Because of its very nature, we usually cannot observe stealing, so we can't stop thieves from obtaining reinforcers by stealing. One option is to deliver a very strong punisher whenever we can prove stealing. Society uses prison; most of us use more direct and immediate punishment for stealing.

Punishment also plays a role in everyday discussions. Proving a person wrong through logical argument may be punishing. Disagreeing with a person may be punishing. Even presenting facts to a person may be punishing. We will undoubtedly continue to have such discussions.

A related example is discussing your friends' problems with them. Often discussion can help them. During your discussion, you might ask them a few careful questions, which may help them see their problem differently. Your friends might suddenly realize that they were thinking about the problem incorrectly. They may discover that it is not as serious as they thought or that they had overlooked an obvious solution. They may realize that they had a silly hang-up. They might even come to laugh at the problem. Much good can come from a gentle and loving discussion of your friends' problems. By asking a few questions, you may eliminate their complaints about the problem. In

***Why Do Battered Women Stay with Their Abusers*?**

Domestic violence occurs in 28% to 55% of all marriages in any given year. A puzzling question is "Why do battered women remain in the marriage?" Here is one possible explanation. Basic researchers have shown that a punisher can sometimes increase behavior. If the punisher is paired with the delivery of a reinforcer, then punishment can become a conditioned reinforcer. It can then increase the behavior that produces it. Thus, it is possible that abuse could reinforce staying with the abuser if the abuse leads to reinforcement. Typically, after an abusive incident, the abusers apologize, buy gifts, and generally offer love and affection. (Based on Long & McNamara, 1989.)

5. Because of its pairing with gifts, love, and affection, abuse can become a ________________ (primary, conditioned, generalized) reinforcer.

spite of the gentleness of your questions, you have used punishment, because their behavior decreases in rate as a result of your action.

Every response has its own built-in punisher. One researcher showed that adults made 100 to 200 responses per minute when effort was close to 0 pounds (Miller, 1970). Their rate decreased as the effort increased. When it required 50 pounds to make the response, the rate decreased to less than 5 per minute. The experiment showed that effort is a punishing stimulus. Thus, every response we make has a punishing element to it. Punishment is always with us!

Giving Punishment Is Reinforcing

One of the dangers of punishment is that its use is too reinforcing. It can be very reinforcing to the person administering it! If you punish Bert for nagging, he is likely to stop immediately. Your punishment would have produced instant reinforcement for you, in the form of no more nagging. Its effectiveness is enhanced through the principle of immediacy, since the positive results of punishment are immediate. Furthermore, the negative results, such as Bert not liking you as much, are delivered later. It is a wonder that we do not always resort to punishment.

Contrast this immediacy of effectiveness with the delayed effects of reinforcement. Suppose you praise Bert for playing nicely instead of nagging. Bert continues playing nicely. His behavior does not change immediately and thereby reinforce your praise. No obvious event reinforces praising him. In fact, since you have to take time away from whatever you are doing, praising creates a slight negative outcome. No wonder so few people learn to reinforce desired behavior rather than punishing undesired behavior.

Social Validity of Punishment

Researchers have examined the social validity of various punishment procedures. They generally find physical punishment least acceptable. For example, researchers found that adults rated mild punishment procedures most acceptable (Blampied & Kahan, 1992). They rated reprimands and physical punishment as least acceptable. Other researchers found that mothers rated reinforcement and time out as more acceptable than spanking or drugs (Heffer & Kelley, 1987). Researchers found that staff preferred to be managed through education and reinforcement rather than punishment (Davis, Rawana, & Capponi, 1989; Davis & Russell, 1990). These results are consistent with using strong punishment only as a last resort.

The Ancient Greeks Understood Behavior Analysis

Thales was known as the "father of Greek mathematics." He may have understood the principle of punishment long before the time of Skinner. He was carrying several large sacks of salt by donkey to a nearby town. The donkey slipped and fell when crossing a shallow river. Some of the salt dissolved in the water, resulting in a lighter load. When the donkey came to a second river, it purposely fell to further lighten its load. Thales noticed this and bought a load of sponges to load on the donkey's back. When the donkey went into its stumbling act at the next water crossing, the sponges soaked up water, and the donkey then had a much heavier load of water-laden sponges to carry. Needless to say, it did not stumble at any more water crossings. (From Talsma, 1976.)

6. Because the heavier load of water-soaked sponges followed stumbling and reduced the rate of stumbling, it is an event called a ______________ (punisher, reinforcer).

Analogues between Punishment and Reinforcement

Many of the concepts associated with reinforcers have analogues with punishers. Some punishers seem to have a biological basis for their effectiveness—for example, shock, hitting, pinching, and extreme heat or cold. Some punishers seem to gain strength from association with other punishers. There are even punishers that seem to gain strength from association with many other punishers. Punishment effects may or may not generalize; if you punish Bert's nagging in the kitchen, he may still nag in the dining room.

A **primary punisher** is one that loses its effectiveness only through satiation. When referring to punishment, behavior analysts commonly call this adaptation. This effect is temporary. Primary punishers include events such as a spanking, an electric shock, or a beating. These events are effective for most people most of the time. However, if a person is subjected to these stimuli frequently in a short period of time, the stimuli may lose part of their effectiveness. The effectiveness can be regained, however, after a period of time without the punishment. This effect is analogous to the effects of satiation and deprivation with reinforcing stimuli. This book will refer to it by these terms.

7. A punisher that loses its effectiveness only through satiation is called a(n) ____________ punisher.

A **conditioned punisher** is one that loses its effectiveness through repeated unpaired presentations. Unpaired presentations occur when the conditioned punisher is not paired with another punisher. The loss of effectiveness is permanent. One example of a conditioned punisher is saying "No!" when Bert starts to tease his sister. Saying "No!" is a conditioned punisher that gets its strength by being paired with a spanking or other established punisher. The word "No" will permanently lose its effectiveness if it is never paired with another punisher. It may also temporarily lose its effectiveness if you repeat it too often in a short time.

8. A conditioned punisher is one that loses its effectiveness through repeated ____________ presentations.

A **generalized punisher** is a conditioned punisher that is associated with many other punishers. Generalized punishers are events, such as social disapproval, in which the person stands to have many punishing things happen as a result of the disapproval. Generalized punishers are effective as punishers, because usually one or more of the "backup" punishers will be effective for the person.

9. A conditioned punisher associated with many other punishers is known as a(n) ____________ punisher.

Punishment can also enter into discriminative processes. It is possible for a stimulus to be consistently associated with punishment so that it becomes a discriminative stimulus for punishment. We will refer to such a stimulus as a **discriminative stimulus for punishment** or an SP. The function of an SP in discrimination training is similar to that of the S-delta. They both produce a low rate of responding as compared with the SD, which produces a high rate of responding.

10. A stimulus that is consistently associated with punishment is called a *discriminative stimulus for punishment*, or ________ for short.

Discriminative stimuli for punishment can be used in a punishment-based form of instructional training. A teacher may describe an undesirable behavior. If the teacher punishes that behavior each time it occurs, this is an example of instructional training. In fact, people will often stop making a response just on the basis of the description. This may result from a long history of reinforcement for following instructions and punishment for not following them. For example, you might tell Bert to stop nagging. If you then punish nagging, your instruction can become an SP.

Verbal stimuli can act as instructions or, more generally, as SP's. They can also act as punishers. The phrase "Don't talk" could be either an SP or a punisher, depending on when it is used. If you say it before a behavior that will be punished, it is an SP. If you say it right after the behavior, and the rate of the behavior decreases, it is a punisher. Researchers have used signs to decrease illegal parking in handicapped parking spaces (Cope, Allred, & Morsell, 1991). These signs are paired with police action for violation. Thus, they are SP's.

Finally, the principles of effective reinforcement also apply to punishment. A punisher will be more effective if it is contingent on the behavior (Gibbs & Luyben, 1985). It will be more effective if it follows the response immediately (Abramowitz & O'Leary, 1990). It will be more effective if the person is deprived of the punisher. It will be more effective the greater the size (i.e., the intensity) of the punisher.

Summary

The fourth strategy for modifying behavior is the aversive control strategy, which is used if positive control fails. It is the strategy of last resort. The first tactic in using the aversive control strategy is to use punishment. Punishment is a procedure to reduce the rate of a behavior. The stimulus used in the procedure is a punisher. Punishment is very common in everyday situations. In fact, in the form of effort, it is a part of every response we make. Behavior analysts resort to strong punishers to reduce dangerous behaviors when other methods do not work. They sometimes use mild punishers such as feedback or reprimands. Some punishers are primary, some conditioned, and some generalized. Punishment can be used in differential reinforcement and discrimination training. Punishment is most effective when it is contingent, immediate, infrequent, and large.

Behavior Analysis Examples

Self-Injury

One researcher developed a very mild method to punish self-injury (Van Houten, 1993). He helped Tom, a 10-year-old boy with severe developmental disabilities and autism. Tom slapped his face hard enough to bruise it, slapping an average of about five times per minute. The problem became severe enough that he was forced to wear a protective helmet. Functional analysis ruled out social reinforcement for face-slapping. The researcher treated this behavior by making it more effortful for Tom to slap his face. The treatment was to put 1.5-pound wrist weights on each wrist. Tom had to lift the weights in order to slap himself. This totally eliminated the face-slapping, but it did not affect his playing with toys or engaging in other desirable behaviors.

11. The greater effort required when wearing wrist weights was a stimulus. It occurred while making the slapping response and reduced that response. Therefore, the greater effort was a stimulus called a ________________ (punisher, reinforcer).

Classwork

Strong punishment is usually used only as a last resort with dangerous behavior. Mild punishment is often used with undesirable behavior. This mild punishment of undesirable behavior is often combined with reinforcement of desirable behavior. Researchers helped underachieving first- through third-graders to increase their on-task behaviors (Pfiffner & O'Leary, 1987). They started with positive reinforcement, including praise, comic books, work breaks, and toys. They gave the reinforcement contingent on the kids being on task. They found that the kids worked about half the time. They then added brief, firm, specific reprimands for off-task behavior. They found that this decreased off-task behavior to 20%. They were then able to fade the reprimands so that they were very rare. On-task behavior remained high.

12. Because the reprimands followed the off-task behavior and decreased its frequency, behavior analysts call the procedure of delivering the reprimands ________________ (punishment, reinforcement).

Shoplifting

Shoplifting is a major problem. In 1973, shoplifting cost the average American family $150 in hidden costs. Researchers developed a way to reduce shoplifting (McNees et al., 1976). They invented an ingenious system for counting the number of shoplifted women's pants. The system involved stapling a yellow tag on the back of the price tags for every pair of women's pants in stock. The store clerks then tore off the yellow tags when they sold an item. The researchers counted the yellow tags in stock at the end of every day to find out how many were missing. They then compared the number missing with the number that store clerks tore off upon selling a pair of pants. The difference was the number stolen. They used the same system for women's tops.

The researchers observed the number of women's pants and the number of women's tops stolen. Figure 22-3 shows the results of these observations. Tops were taken at the rate of 0.66 per day, and pants were taken at the rate of 0.50 per day. After 34 days, a sign was posted in the clothing department: "Attention shoppers and shoplifters. The items you see marked with a red star are items that shoplifters frequently take." Stars were about five inches across; six were mounted on the pants racks. After 47 days, six red stars were also posted on racks containing young women's tops. The rate of shoplifting dramatically decreased for both items.

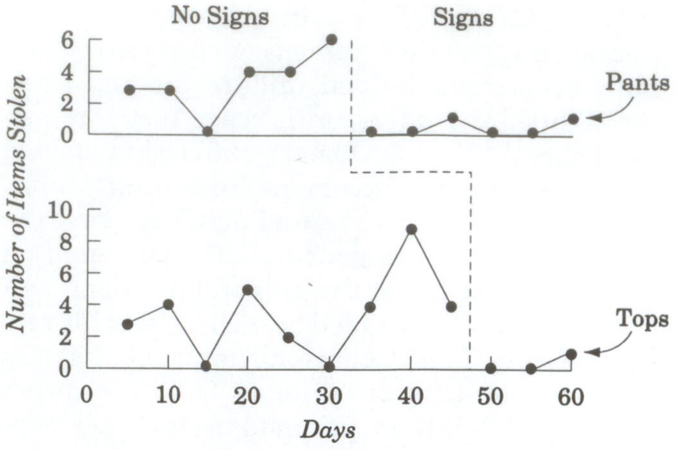

Figure 22-3. Number of women's pants and tops shoplifted. Adapted from "Shoplifting Prevention: Providing Information through Signs," by M. P. McNees, D. S. Egli, R. S. Marshall, J. F. Schnelle, and T. R. Risley, *Journal of Applied Behavior Analysis*, 1976, *9*, 399–406. Copyright 1976 by the Society for the Experimental Analysis of Behavior, Inc. Used by permission.

You may have difficulty labeling the treatment in this study. The researchers did not directly apply punishment to shoplifting. Rather, they posted a warning. Shoppers probably had a history of similar warnings leading to punishment when ignored.

13. Behavior analysts call the posted warning a discriminative stimulus for ________________ (punishment, reinforcement), which is abbreviated as ____.

Note

Note #1

Punishment can be used in place of extinction in many procedures. For example, it might be used in differential reinforcement. A desirable behavior might be reinforced while an undesirable behavior is punished. The use of punishment can speed up the reduction in the undesirable behavior. Doing so would ordinarily be a last resort.

Punishment can also be used in place of extinction in discrimination training. A behavior might be reinforced in one situation and punished in another situation. Again, the use of punishment in the second situation may speed up the reduction in the behavior in that situation.

You can discriminate between the procedures in the same way you do when extinction is used to reduce the behavior. If you note that reinforcement and punishment are being used with two behaviors in one situation, you know it is differential reinforcement. If you note that reinforcement and punishment are being used with one behavior in two situations, you know it is discrimination training. We call the use of reinforcement and punishment with two behaviors in two situations *discrimination training*.

14. If you reinforce a desirable behavior while punishing an undesirable behavior, you are using the procedure of ________________.

Helpful Hints

Helpful Hint #1

You will be given many examples of procedures that decrease the rate of a behavior. You will be asked to figure out what procedure is being used. The first question to ask is whether the procedure involves an event that immediately precedes the behavior. If an event decreases behavior and precedes the behavior, then the event must be a discriminative stimulus for punishment. Do not confuse it with a punisher.

You may be given an example in which the behavior decreases, but the event does not immediately precede the behavior. You must then distinguish between punishment and extinction. To tell the difference, you must ask a second question. "Does some usually reinforcing event no longer follow the behavior?" If an event no longer follows the behavior, the behavioral procedure involves extinction. If an event does follow the behavior, then the procedure is punishment by contingent stimulation.

To summarize, if an example involves a decrease in behavior, ask two questions. First, does the procedure involve an event that precedes the behavior? If so, then the event is a discriminative stimulus for punishment. If the event does not precede the behavior, then ask a second question. Second, does the procedure involve no longer delivering a reinforcer? If so, the procedure is extinction. If it involves delivering a punisher, then it is punishment.

15. If an example involves a decrease in behavior and the delivery of an event that follows the behavior, the procedure is ________________.

Helpful Hint #2

A discriminative stimulus for punishment will often be an instruction not to perform a behavior. Such an instruction is usually not a punisher. I will revise the general rule suggested for reinforcers and instructions to apply to punishers. The new rule is: "An instruction (usually) cannot be either a reinforcer or a punisher." The only exception is when an instruction quickly follows a behavior and decreases its rate. For example, suppose Jimmy pushes his brother and Dad says, "Don't push your brother." If Jimmy stops, you should label Dad's statement as a punisher. This distinction should be clear if you ask the first question: "Does the procedure involve an event that immediately precedes or follows the behavior?" If it precedes the behavior it is definitely not a punisher.

16. An instruction usually cannot be either a reinforcer or a(n) ______________.

Helpful Hint #3

Remember, a punisher is an event (or stimulus), whereas punishment is a procedure. The distinction is exactly the same as that between a reinforcer and reinforcement.

17. If a question asks for a procedure in which a stimulus follows a behavior and decreases its rate, you know from the word *procedure* to answer ______________. If a question asks for an event that follows a behavior and decreases its rate, you know from the word *event* to answer ______________.

Helpful Hint #4

As with previous lessons, when an example describes an event or procedure that does not change the rate of a behavior, it should be labeled *unknown*.

18. If I give you an example in which an event follows a behavior and the rate of the behavior does not change, you should label the event as a(n) ______________.

Helpful Hint #5

Suppose Dad spanked Jerry when he talked back to him, but Jerry's rate of talking back increased. You might be tempted to call this an unknown, because the spanking did not decrease Jerry's talking back. In other words, you might argue that Dad tried to punish but it didn't work, so it's an unknown. The trouble with that argument is that regardless of what Dad wanted to do, his spanking did increase Jerry's rate of talking back. You learned in an earlier lesson to call any event that <u>follows</u> a behavior and <u>increases</u> the rate of that behavior a reinforcer. Continue applying that label. The intention to punish does not in any way change what actually happens.

19. Call any event that follows a behavior and that increases the rate of that behavior a(n) ______________.

Additional Readings

Alford, G. S., & Turner, S. M. (1976). Stimulus interference and conditioned inhibition of auditory hallucinations. *Journal of Behavior Therapy and Experimental Psychiatry*, *7*, 155–160. A 32-year-old woman, who was hospitalized because she frequently heard voices and responded to them, was given an apparatus with which she could give herself a shock when she heard the voices. This procedure resulted in the woman no longer reporting hearing the voices and no longer responding to them. She was dismissed from the hospital and has lived a normal life since.

Flanagan, B., Goldiamond, L., & Azrin, N. H. (1958). Operant stuttering: The control of stuttering behavior through response-contingent consequences. *Journal of the Experimental Analysis of Behavior*, *1*, 173–177. Chronic stutterers read from a book into a microphone while an observer counted the number of disfluencies. When every disfluency was followed by a blast of noise delivered to the stutterers through earphones, their rate of stuttering decreased markedly.

Green, R. R., & Hoats, D. L. (1969). Reinforcing capabilities of television distortion. *Journal of Applied Behavior Analysis*, *2*, 139–141. A hyperactive girl of 18 with mild retardation was seated in a room watching TV. Her hyperactivity was observed, and during baseline it averaged about 22 responses per minute. During treatment, the TV picture was mildly distorted contingent on her hyperactive behavior. Her rate decreased to an average of about 3 responses per minute. Thus, the distortion served as a successful punisher of hyperactive responding.

Holz, W. C., & Azrin, N. H. (1966). Punishment. In W. K. Honig (Ed.), *Operant behavior: Areas of research and application*. New York: Appleton-Century-Crofts. This article provides an excellent overview of the concept of punishment, the side effects of using punishment, a comparison of punishment with other methods for reducing behavior, and the ethical considerations involved in using punishment.

McFadden, A. C., Marsh, G. E., Price, B. J., & Hwang, Y. (1992). A study of race and gender bias in the punishment of school children. *Education and Treatment of Children*, *15*(2), 140–146. This article reports the effects of race on the use of punishment in one school district. The authors found that blacks received more physical punishment and were more often suspended from school. Further, the referral rate for blacks was disproportionately higher than for whites.

Powell, J., & Azrin, N. H. (1968). The effect of shock as a punisher for cigarette smoking. *Journal of Applied Behavior Analysis*, *1*, 63–71. Individuals who wished to stop smoking were given a harness device that was hooked up to a special cigarette case. Each time they opened the pack, they were shocked. This procedure decreased their smoking, but the individuals began to wear the harness only for short periods of time.

Risley, T. R. (1968). The effects and side effects of punishing the autistic behaviors of a deviant child. *Journal of Applied Behavior Analysis*, *1*, 21–34. A hyperactive child with autism frequently engaged in climbing behaviors that resulted in falls and serious physical damage to the child (such as knocking out teeth). To eliminate such behaviors, shock punishment was used at the start of each climbing episode. This eliminated the dangerous climbing behavior.

Tate, B. G., & Baroff, G. S. (1966). Aversive control of self-injurious behavior in a psychotic boy. *Behavior Research and Therapy*, *4*, 281–287. A psychotic boy engaged in such serious head-banging behavior that he was in danger of losing his eyesight. The use of electric shock contingent on the head-banging response quickly eliminated this self-injurious behavior.

Wilson, G. T., Leaf , R. C., & Nathan, P. E. (1975). The aversive control of excessive alcohol consumption by chronic alcoholics in the laboratory setting. *Journal of Applied Behavior Analysis*, *8*, 13–26. Shock was used to punish the consumption of alcohol by chronic alcoholics. The alcoholics were permitted to drink as much as they wished. During baseline, they drank over 20 ounces of alcohol per day; during treatment, they were shocked each time they took a drink. This resulted in nearly complete elimination of drinking.

Reading Quiz

91. This whole unit is about aversive control. The use of punishment and negative reinforcement to control behavior is called __________ (aversive, reinforcement, stimulus) control.

90. The use of punishment and negative reinforcement are two types of ______________ control.

8. Be very careful not to equate "unpleasant" with "aversive" or "punisher." When studying reinforcers, you learned that events you consider unpleasant, if they follow behavior and increase the rate of that behavior, are called ______________________. People often work to earn events that other people consider unpleasant.

67. Skinner calls aversive control the __________ (least, most) common technique of control in modern life.

6. Aversive control may cause a person to try to countercontrol another through violence. It may cause a person to experience a variety of negative emotional responses. These are two examples of possible ______________ (desirable, undesirable) side effects of aversive control.

3. A dream of behavior analysts is to create a world in which the need for ______________ (aversive, reinforcement, stimulus) control is minimized.

65. Skinner asserted that the behavioral procedure that "is to be preferred because it appears to have fewer objectionable by-products" is positive ________________.

66. Skinner did not believe that we could completely avoid aversive consequences. He simply proposed that people can influence each other through reinforcement rather than through ________________________.

94. When institutionalized people hit themselves repeatedly and break bones, cause bleeding, blind themselves, or knock out teeth, psychologists call this *self-injurious behavior* which is abbreviated (using the first letter of those three words) as ______.
86. The fourth strategy for changing human behavior is the ______________ (aversive, reinforcement, stimulus) control strategy.
62. Review: Which strategy is the last resort for changing behavior? The ______________ control strategy.
55. Review: Tactic #1 in using the aversive control strategy is to decrease undesirable behavior through ______________ as a last resort.
84. The first goal of this quiz is to teach you about punishers. A punisher is an event that (1) follows a behavior and (2) ______________ (decreases, increases) the frequency of that behavior.
36. Review: A punisher is an event that (1) ______________ a behavior and (2) ______ the frequency of that behavior.
71. Suppose Baby Ann spits her applesauce on the floor. Mom might yell "Don't!" The event of yelling "Don't" follows Baby Ann's spitting. You should call it a punisher if it also has what effect on the rate at which Baby Ann spits out her food from then on? __________ the rate.
7. Baby Ann spits her applesauce, and Mom yells "Don't!" Baby Ann spits her applesauce less often after that. If you wish to label the procedure that Mom uses, call it *punishment*. If you wish to label the event of Mom yelling "Don't!", call it a(n) ______________.
15. Every time Baby Ann spits her applesauce, Mom yells "Don't!" Baby Ann spits her applesauce less often after that. If you wish to label the procedure that Mom uses, call it ______________.
42. Review: Behavior analysts call an event that (1) follows a behavior and (2) decreases the frequency of that behavior a(n) ______________.
11. Behavior analysts call delivering a punisher that follows a behavior the procedure of __________.
52. Review: Punishment is the procedure in which a(n) ______________ is administered contingent on some undesired behavior.
81. Suppose you read about an event that (1) follows a behavior and (2) doesn't change the frequency of that behavior. You have not learned about such events. Such an event is not a punisher, because a punisher decreases the rate of the behavior. Such an event is not involved in extinction, because with extinction, you stop an event and see a decrease in rate. If you are asked about an event that doesn't meet the definition of any terms you have learned about, you should call that event a(n) ______________.
72. Suppose Mom delivers the "unpleasant" event of yelling "Don't!" at Baby Ann after she spits her applesauce. This unpleasant event clearly follows spitting. However, it would be a punisher only if it also ______________ the rate of spitting.
73. Suppose Mom delivers the "unpleasant" event of yelling "Don't!" at Baby Ann after she spits her applesauce, but the rate of Baby Ann's spitting does not decrease. You should label this procedure as ______________.
63. Should you assume that an "unpleasant" event delivered contingent on a behavior must be a punisher? ______
70. Suppose Baby Ann smiles sweetly at Mom, and Mom delivers a spoonful of applesauce to Baby Ann. Suppose Baby Ann's rate of smiling then decreases. Because delivery of the spoonful of applesauce follows the smile and decreases its rate, you have no choice but to label this apparently pleasant event as a(n) ______________.
64. Should you assume that a "pleasant" event delivered contingent on a behavior cannot be a punisher? ________
26. In this lesson and the next, you will learn that punishment can arise in two ways. You have just learned the definition of one of those ways. One type of punishment is to deliver a punisher that is contingent on (i.e., follows) a behavior and decreases the rate of that behavior. This procedure is called ______________ (punishment, reinforcement) by contingent stimulation.
14. Does *punishment by contingent stimulation* refer to punishment in which (a) a punisher is delivered contingent on a behavior or (b) a reinforcer is removed contingent on a behavior? ____
88. The procedure of extinction ______________ (decreases, increases) the rate of a behavior.

89. The procedure of punishment _______________ (decreases, increases) the rate of a behavior.
93. Two procedures for reducing the rate of a behavior are _______________ and _______________.
21. If Mother spanks Bobby each time he pesters her for a cookie, and his rate of pestering decreases, the use of spanking is an example of what behavioral procedure? _______________
22. If Mother spanks Bobby each time he pesters her for a cookie, and his rate of pestering doesn't change, her spanking is an example of what behavioral procedure? _______________
23. If Mother spanks Bobby each time he pesters her for a cookie and his rate of pestering increases, the use of spanking is an example of what behavioral procedure? _______________ _______________
76. Suppose Mother ignores Bobby rather than pays attention to him each time he pesters her for a cookie. If his rate of pestering decreases, then ignoring him would be an example of what behavioral procedure? _______________ _______________
68. Students sometimes interpret "Mom ignores Bobby" as a punisher. Their idea seems to be that ignoring is an insult. They are assuming that ignoring can be considered an event because it is doing something. When I tell you that Mom ignores Bobby, I mean that Mom does nothing. There is no event. Thus, even if her ignoring decreases Bobby's pestering, it _______________ (can, can't) be an event called a punisher.
95. When you learn that Mom ignores Bobby, you should interpret ignoring as not giving him the attention that he got before. Thus, if Bobby's rate of pestering decreases, Mom is using the procedure of _______________.
74. Suppose Mom used to look annoyed every time Bobby pestered her, but now she maintains a neutral look when he pesters. If his pestering decreases, what procedure is she using? _______________
31. Remember, when someone ignores another person, maintains a neutral look, and doesn't reinforce him or her, but the behavior decreases, this is not an example of punishment. Such examples usually tell you that the person ignores instead of paying attention, looks neutral instead of annoyed or pleased, or doesn't reinforce instead of reinforcing. Thus, such examples involve stopping delivery of a reinforcer and therefore use the procedure called _______________.
83. The everyday world punishes much of our physical behavior. If you forget to take your finger out of the door, closing the door will be an event called a(n) _______________.
12. Behavior analysts often need to eliminate dangerous or self-injurious behaviors more quickly than is possible with extinction. In such a case, they may resort to the procedure called _______________, using very strong physical stimulation.
69. Suppose a behavior modifier delivered a very brief and mild shock each time a severely disturbed boy with autism attempted to injure himself. If the rate of such self-injury decreased, what behavioral procedure would the administration of shock be an example of? _______________
79. Suppose that when the behavior modifier delivers the shock, the rate of self-injury doesn't change. What behavioral procedure is the shock? _______________
24. If the delivery of immediate, brief shocks following dangerous head-banging reduces that behavior, the shock delivery is an example of what behavioral procedure? _______________
9. Behavior analysts can often eliminate dangerous behaviors by delivering events, milder than shock, following those behaviors. These milder events are called _______________.
32. Researchers required a 4-year-old fire-setter to do one hour of hard labor for each fire-setting episode. The fire setting was eliminated. Behavior analysts would label this procedure _______________.
80. Suppose you required the 4-year-old fire-setter to do one hour of hard labor following a fire-setting episode, and the rate of fire setting did not change. You would label this procedure _______________.
77. Suppose any hyperactivity from a girl with mild retardation is followed by distorting the TV picture she is watching, resulting in a decrease in her hyperactivity. Then the procedure of using the distortion is a form of mild _______________.
78. Suppose any hyperactivity from a girl with mild retardation is followed by distorting the TV picture she is watching, resulting in no change in her hyperactivity. Then the procedure of using the distortion is _______________.

13. Behavior analysts use punishers to decrease behavior that endangers the person. Often they must also eliminate behaviors that may harm others. If they deliver an event following a harmful behavior and the rate of such behaviors decreases, the event is called a(n) ______________.
19. If a person's undesirable behavior is strongly reinforced by events whose delivery you cannot personally stop, you cannot use extinction to reduce that behavior. What behavioral procedure could you use? ______________
96. When you prove Barry wrong in a discussion, your proof follows his assertion. If your proof reduces the rate at which he makes that assertion, then you have used what behavioral method? ______________
98. You discuss a putdown with Kay. She helps you see that labeling it as a problem is incorrect and even laughable. Your rate of labeling the putdown as a problem decreases. Kay's gentle help is an example of what behavioral procedure? ______________
41. Review: Because every response requires an effort that follows the start of the response, and because effort reduces the rate of any response, effort is a stimulus called a(n) ______________.
4. After an abusive incident, the abusers apologize, buy gifts, and generally offer love and affection. Because of its pairing with gifts and love, the physical abuse could become a(n) ______________ reinforcer.
5. An important danger of punishment is that it produces results right away. These results may turn out to be a very effective reinforcer for the person who is punishing, due to the principle of ______________
29. Punishment immediately eliminates undesirable behavior. Reinforcement may not immediately establish desirable behavior. Predict which procedure people would learn more quickly. ______________
30. Punishment immediately eliminates undesirable behavior. Extinction gradually eliminates undesirable behavior. Predict which procedure people will learn more quickly. ______________
2. A donkey carrying salt was reinforced for falling into rivers by the lightening of its load. Its owner loaded sponges on its back. The next time the donkey fell into the water, the sponges filled with water, creating a much heavier load. If loading the sponges decreased falling in the river from then on, the weight of the sponges was an event called a(n) ______________.
25. In examining the social validity of punishment procedures, physical punishment is generally rated ________ (least, most) acceptable.
97. Will punishment in one situation definitely result in the behavior decreasing in many other situations, as in generalization? ________
35. Review: A primary punisher is one that loses its effectiveness only through ______________.
53. Review: Spanking will always be a punisher unless it has been used too often recently. Therefore, behavior analysts classify it as a(n) ______________ punisher.
33. Review: A conditioned reinforcer may develop when an event is repeatedly paired with another punisher. Therefore, a conditioned punisher loses its effect permanently through ______________ presentations.
47. Review: Initially, when Mom tells Jimmy "No" and spanks him immediately after he does something dangerous, he may stop. Suppose she unpairs "No" from its backup of spanking (by never giving him a spanking after she says "No"), and "No" permanently loses its effect. You should classify her "No" as a(n) ______________ punisher.
34. Review: A generalized punisher is one that is associated with ______________ other punishers.
46. Review: If Dad tells May "No" every time she pinches him, she may stop pinching him for a time. Sometimes he backs up his "No" with a light swat, other times by pushing her away, and still other times by grabbing her roughly. Because he pairs his "No" with three other punishers, you should classify his "No" as a(n) ______________ punisher.
58. Review: Three types of punishers: ______________, ______________, and ______________ punishers.
10. Behavior analysts call a stimulus associated with reinforcement for a particular behavior a <u>discriminative</u> stimulus for reinforcement. They call a stimulus associated with punishment for a particular behavior a(n) ______________ stimulus for punishment.
1. A <u>stimulus</u> associated with punishment for a particular behavior is called a discriminative ______________ for punishment.

37. Review: A stimulus associated with punishment for a particular behavior is called a(n) ______________ stimulus for punishment, abbreviated _____.
75. Suppose Mom warns Davey, "Don't go near the edge," and then spanks him whenever he does. Behavior analysts call the phrase "Don't go near the edge" a discriminative stimulus for ______________.
99. You have learned in previous lessons that instructional training can be used to increase a desirable behavior by describing the behavior and then reinforcing instances of that behavior. You can also decrease undesirable behavior by describing the behavior and then using what procedure when the person performs that behavior? ______________ training
20. If a teacher explains that the student should not perform an undesirable behavior and then punishes that behavior each time it occurs, this is an example of ______________ training.
100. You must look carefully to find out whether an event precedes or follows a behavior. You learned to do this for reinforcers; now you must learn to do it for punishers. If an event <u>follows</u> a behavior and decreases it, call that event a(n) ______________.
44. Review: If an event <u>precedes</u> a behavior and decreases it, call that event a(n) ______________ stimulus for punishment. You may abbreviate it in the rest of the book as _____.
38. Review: A stimulus that decreases the rate of a response that it <u>precedes</u> is called a(n) ______________; a stimulus that decreases the rate of a response that it quickly <u>follows</u> is called a(n) ______________.
92. To have maximum effectiveness, when should a punisher occur in relation to the behavior? ______________ after it.
87. The greater effort of wearing wrist weights is a stimulus that occurs following the start of the slapping response, resulting in a reduction of that response. Therefore, that stimulus is called a(n) ______________.
28. In differential reinforcement, mild punishment is sometimes used in place of extinction. In this form of differential reinforcement, you combine the procedure of reinforcement of desirable behavior with the procedure of mild ______________ of undesirable behavior.
27. McNees and his associates (1976) posted stars identifying clothing items that were often stolen. Customers stole much less after the posting than before. Because the star was present before anyone stole rather than after, and because it decreased the rate of stealing, it is called a(n) ______________.
82. Tactic #1 in using the aversive control strategy is to decrease undesirable behavior through ______________ as a last resort.
85. The fourth strategy for changing human behavior is the ______________ control strategy.
101. From Note #1: In many procedures, punishment can be used in place of ______________ to decrease behaviors.
17. From Note #1: If you reinforce a desirable behavior while punishing an undesirable behavior in one situation, you are using the procedure of ______________.
18. From Note #1: If you reinforce a behavior in one situation while punishing it in another situation, you are using the procedure of ______________.
16. From Helpful Hint #3: If a question asks for a procedure in which a stimulus follows a behavior and <u>decreases</u> its rate, you know from the word *procedure* to answer ______________. If a question asks for an event that follows a behavior and <u>decreases</u> its rate, you know from the word *event* to answer ______________.
54. Review: Tactic #1 in using the aversive control strategy is to decrease undesirable behavior through ______________ as a last resort.
59. Review: Three types of punishers are: (1) ______________; (2) ______________; and (3) ______________.
51. Review: Punishment is most effective when the following four principles are followed: ______________, ______________, ______________, and ______________.
40. Review: Call an event that decreases the rate of a behavior that it follows a(n) ______________.
49. Review: Punishers and reinforcers are events that differ in one way but are similar in another. They differ in that punishers decrease behaviors, while reinforcers increase behaviors. They are similar in that both must be timed to ______________ a behavior.

60. Review: To use the aversive control strategy, (1) decrease undesirable behavior through ______________ as a last resort.
39. Review: A stimulus that occurs before the behavior and is associated with punishment of the behavior is called a(n) ______________ ______________.
61. Review: When a certain behavior is punished, it will decrease in that situation. The name for the process in which the same behavior decreases in other situations without punishment is ______________.
50. Review: Punishment and extinction both affect a behavior in the same way. They both produce a(n) ______________ in the frequency of the behavior.
43. Review: If a punisher's effectiveness is permanently eliminated when no longer paired with another punisher, what type of punisher is it? ______________
48. Review: Ken gave Jan a withering look every time she suggested that he go on a diet. Because Jan is still suggesting that Ken go on a diet, Ken's withering look is an event called a(n) ______________.
45. Review: If an event follows a behavior and reduces the future probability of that behavior, it is called a(n) ______________.
57. Review: The use of punishment to control behavior is called ______________ control.
56. Review: The fourth strategy for changing human behavior is the ______________ control strategy.

Examples

1. Tito's rate of teasing his sister decreased when Mom spanked him every time he teased her. Ask: did Mom's spanking precede, not follow, Tito's teasing behavior? _____. The spanking is not an SP. Ask: Did she stop delivering a reinforcer for teasing his sister? _____. The spanking is not extinction. Since Mom's spanking followed the teasing and decreased its rate, it is an example of the procedure called ______________.

2. Mary got very hungry during the afternoon. By the time her mother was fixing dinner, Mary felt as if she would die of hunger, so she would beg her mother for a snack. Her mother would tell her she couldn't have a snack because it would spoil her dinner. Then Mary would nag her mother. Soon her mother would scream "No!" every time Mary asked for a snack. Her mother thought that a scream would punish Mary for asking. However, Mary continued to beg and nag for a snack even when her mother screamed at her for asking. Before you start asking questions, decide whether the example involves a decrease in Mary's behavior. Does it? _____. Is Mom's screaming "No!" an example of punishment? _____. One way Mary's mother could have made her "No!" an effective punisher of Mary's request would be for her to always follow her "No!" with another, more powerful ______________.

3. Fred's repeated racial slurs were annoying to the other members of the Harmony Group. They simply ignored his comments, but the comments didn't decrease. One day he commented to Dick, another member, "Look at that black boy! He's the tallest guy I've ever seen." Dick rebuked Fred by saying, "It's disrespectful of black people to call them 'boys.'" Fred looked surprised, but he never used that word again around other group members. Make sure there's a decrease. Ask: Did Dick's rebuke precede, not follow, Fred's saying "boy"? _____. Ask: Did Dick stop delivering a reinforcer for saying "boy"? _____. Since Dick's rebuke followed and decreased Fred's use of "boy," it is an example of what procedure? ______________

4. Mr. Tubbs got mad at Jerry for whispering with his friend one day. So before class the next day, Mr. Tubbs told him not to whisper to his friend anymore. Jerry never whispered in Mr. Tubbs's class again. To analyze this example, notice that Mr. Tubbs's instruction did not follow Jerry's whispering right away. Did Mr. Tubbs's instruction precede Jerry's next chance to whisper? _____. Is his instruction a punisher? _____. You could also remember the rule: "An instruction usually is neither a reinforcer nor a(n) ______________." If Mr. Tubbs's instruction was really a warning that Jerry would be punished for whispering, the warning would technically be called a(n) ______________.

5. Professor Brainbuster wanted his students to discuss only really important ideas. As a result, he would immediately ridicule most comments from students. Within two weeks, most students stopped making comments in the class discussion. Make sure there's a decrease in comment. Ask: Did the ridicule precede the comments? If not, did the professor stop delivering a reinforcer for making comments? Since Brainbuster's ridicule followed the comments and decreased them,

it is an event called a(n) __________. One semester, Brainbuster gave everyone an A at the beginning of the semester. To his surprise, he found that the students no longer shut up after he ridiculed them. Many argued back, and some even ridiculed him! The fact that his ridicule, when unpaired with the potential for poor grades, no longer decreased comments indicates that ridicule is what kind of a punisher? A(n) ______________ punisher

6. Lou frequently insulted people with comments such as "That was a dumb idea," or "That is a terrible-looking shirt." Lou's friends apparently reinforced his insulting behavior by looking annoyed when he issued his insults. One day, several of Lou's friends decided that they had had enough of his insults. They agreed to not look annoyed when Lou insulted them. Lou's rate of insults decreased quite rapidly when his insults no longer produced looks of annoyance. Ask: Was there a decrease? Did the friends' reaction precede Lou's insults? Did they stop delivering a reinforcer for his insults? Were Lou's friends delivering a punisher or stopping delivery of a reinforcer after his insults? When Lou's friends stopped looking annoyed after his insults, what behavioral procedure were they using? ________________

7. The cooperative dorm had a written rule: No complaining about dinner during the dinner period. Bob complained one night about the dinner, and Lou immediately responded by saying, "Hey, stop that." Bob never broke that rule again. To figure out what procedure Lou used to decrease Bob's complaining, ask: Was there a decrease? Did Lou's reaction precede Bob's complaints? Did Lou stop delivering a reinforcer for the complaints? Was Lou delivering a punisher or stopping delivery of a reinforcer after the complaints? Once you have answered those questions, you can see that Lou used the behavioral procedure called

________________.

8. Barbara broke the rule that there would be no complaining about dinner during the dinner period. Another member immediately responded by saying, "Stop complaining, Barbara." Barbara continued to break the rule from time to time. Several members became annoyed enough with Barbara's complaining to bring the problem up at the next dorm meeting. Someone suggested that the reminder that the other members were giving Barbara when she complained wasn't strong enough; Barbara (or any other complainer) should be fined $1 whenever she complained during dinner. If the reminder served as a punisher when it was associated with the $1 fine but quickly lost its effectiveness when it was not paired with the fine, it would be classified as a ______________ punisher.

9. Carol told her little son, Lenny, not to touch the steering wheel while she was driving. The next time he touched the steering wheel, she spanked him. He rarely touched the wheel after that and always got a spanking when he did. Spanking is an event that followed touching the steering wheel and decreased its rate. This event is called a(n) ______________. The procedure of giving a spanking after touching the steering wheel is called __________.

10. Jane was teaching Queenie to count to ten. Queenie said, "one, two, three, five." Jane said, "No, that's wrong." Queenie never made that mistake again. Jane said, "No, that's wrong" right after Queenie said "five" instead of "four." Therefore, Jane used what behavioral procedure to decrease saying "five" after "three"? ____________. Notice that although this procedure stopped Queenie from making that specific error again, she still might make other errors. Notice that punishment did not directly encourage her to repeat any of the correct responses. To increase the rate of correct responses, Jane should use ____________ for correct responses.

11. Review: Abdul ran a red traffic light one day when he was in a hurry to get to class. A police officer caught him and gave him a ticket. Abdul didn't go through a red light again after that. By asking your questions, you can see that the event of getting the ticket was an example of a(n) ____________. Getting the ticket might help make the red light a(n) ____________ for driving through the intersection.

12. Review: Yvonne told everyone in class that she didn't think President Bush should have gotten us into the Persian Gulf War unless we were going to defeat Iraq completely. Several people immediately gasped, "Yvonne, you can't mean that!" Yvonne never mentioned her feelings about the war again in class. The reactions of Yvonne's classmates to her remark would be an example of what behavioral procedure? ____________

13. Review: Bob's father usually greeted his ideas with encouragement. But when Bob mention to his Dad that poor people in this country are treated badly, his father ignored him. Bob never brought the subject up again. Bob's de-

creased rate of talking about the problems of poor people was the result of what behavioral procedure? ______________

14. Review: Professor Young encouraged his sociology students to express ideas about U.S. social problems, but he ridiculed them if they talked about abstract theory. Professor Old encouraged his students to express ideas about abstract sociological theory and scolded them if they expressed ideas about actual social problems. Dan was a student of both professors. He soon learned to talk about social problems in Professor Young's class and not to talk about them in Professor Old's class. The changes in Dan's behavior were the result of what behavioral procedure? ______________

15. Review: Donny frequently made disparaging remarks about Dale's figure in front of their friends. As soon as they were alone, Dale always became very angry at Donny's remarks. However, Donny continued to make such remarks in front of their friends. What principle of punishment may have reduced the effectiveness of Dale's anger as a punisher? ______________

16. Review: Donnell was always arguing. His friends started paying attention when he made reasonable arguments but ignored unreasonable arguments. Donnell's rate of unreasonable arguments decreased drastically; his rate of reasonable arguments increased. What behavioral procedure accounts for the relative increase in reasonable arguments? ______________

17. Review: Sam hit Bobby a few months ago because Bobby was being a terrible pest. Bobby immediately started acting nice to Sam. Since then, Sam's rate of hitting Bobby whenever he was being a pest has increased. For the following question, focus on Sam's behavior, not Bobby's. The <u>increase</u> in the rate of Sam's hitting response is a result of what behavioral procedure? ______________

18. Review: Gladys sometimes spanked Danny for bothering her, but she immediately felt sorry for him. She gave him an ice cream cone to stop his tears. If Danny started bothering her more, rather than less, we might guess that the ice cream cone was more reinforcing than the spanking was punishing. Furthermore, whenever Danny got spanked, he knew that Gladys would then give him an ice cream cone. Therefore, a spanking by Gladys was backed up with ice cream. The spanking could become a ______________ (conditioned, generalized, primary) reinforcer.

19. Review: Instructional training was defined in earlier lessons as asking someone to do something (instructions), observing the requested behavior (instructed behavior), and reinforcing that behavior. In this lesson, you learned a broader definition. If a person is asked to stop doing something, then instructional training would consist of requesting a stop to the behavior, observing the undesired behavior, and then ______________ it rather than reinforcing it.

20. Review: Terry was the newest member of the food co-op's staff. During the regular Thursday staff meetings, Terry would frequently launch into a discourse on the evils of the local merchants. Needless to say, this subject had nothing to do with what order the food co-op was going to place next week or who was going to work what hours. Consequently, the other staff members paid no attention to Terry's irrelevant rhetoric. After a month, he had stopped his digressions. What behavioral procedure was at work decreasing Terry's rate of irrelevant comments? ______________

LESSON

23 Punishment by Contingent Withdrawal

This lesson introduces a second type of punishment. A reinforcer for some behavior other than the undesirable behavior is taken away from someone each time he or she emits an undesirable behavior. For example, treating a pinball machine too roughly will cause a "tilt" light to go on. This takes away the privilege of playing the machine any longer. Yelling at your mother may cause her to "ground" you. You can't leave the house. Behavior analysts call this form of punishment *punishment by contingent withdrawal*.

Definition of Punishment by Contingent Withdrawal

Behavior analysts define **punishment by contingent withdrawal** as withdrawing an event contingent on a behavior and producing a decrease in the rate of that behavior.

1. Behavior analysts define punishment by contingent withdrawal as ______________ an event contingent on a behavior and producing a ______________ in the rate of that behavior.

An event may be withdrawn permanently or only temporarily. One example of a permanent loss is a judge fining a person for speeding. The person permanently loses $50. Another example is a parent requiring a child to pay to replace a window broken through careless use of a BB gun. Another example is a person breaking off a friendship after learning that the other person was lying to him or her. These examples involve permanent losses. They would be examples of punishment if speeding, careless shooting, and lying decreased for these individuals.

On the other hand, it is a temporary loss if Mom won't let Gwen go out to play after school today because she ate ice cream without permission. Another example might be if the teacher makes Jack sit in the corner for five minutes because he pulled Ann's pigtail. If Gwen's eating of ice cream without permission and Jack's pigtail pulling decrease, these procedures would be punishment by contingent withdrawal. Behavior analysts frequently call this form of punishment *time out*. The name comes from making the person take time out from a reinforcing activity.

I will not ask you to distinguish between permanent and temporary forms of punishment by contingent withdrawal, but I will ask you to use the label *time out* in some examples.

Uses of Punishment by Contingent Withdrawal

Punishment by contingent withdrawal is not as severe as physical punishment. Therefore, behavior analysts prefer it to punishment by contingent stimulation when they need to use punishment as a last resort. Sometimes they use it in combination with reinforcement. They then fade it out if possible.

Behavior analysts often use fines as part of a token or point system. For example, one researcher used fines as part of a token system for chronic mental hospital patients (Winkler, 1970). During baseline, he observed rates of physical violence, including attacks on staff. Sometimes these attacks were so violent that staff members required medical care. The baseline rate decreased by about half solely as a result of using tokens to reinforce desirable behaviors. Using token fines for aggression reduced the rate much further. Because they withdrew the tokens (through fines) contingent on aggression, and the aggression decreased, the fines are punishment by contingent withdrawal. The nurses reported that the ward was a much nicer place to work as a result.

Other researchers withdrew tokens when teenagers interrupted a class (Sprute, Williams, & McLaughlin, 1990). This produced a large reduction in interruptions. Other researchers punished teenagers for coming late to dinner by taking away points (Phillips et al., 1971). The teenagers' lateness decreased. In both these cases, the token withdrawals were contingent on a behavior that decreases, so they were examples of punishment by contingent withdrawal.

Researchers used a similar approach to help a 65-year-old man quit smoking (Belles & Bradlyn, 1987). He agreed to donate money to an organization he didn't like at the end of any week during which he failed to reduce smoking. Over a two-year period, he reduced his smoking from 82 cigarettes a day to 5! Other researchers have found this same approach to be effective (Singh & Jin-Pang Leung, 1988). Another researcher used a similar approach to reduce eating (Mann, 1972). One subject lost over 100 pounds! This procedure is punishment by contingent withdrawal because people lost money contingent on a behavior, and the behavior decreased. It is clever because they not only lost it but also gave it to causes that they disliked.

Figure 23-1 gives an interesting example of an everyday use of punishment by withdrawal. The phone company began charging customers 20¢ for each local call for information made in Cincinnati in 1973 (McSweeny, 1978). The charge followed the call, and the rate of such calls decreased. Therefore, this is an example of punishment.

Uses of Time Out

Behavior analysts often use time out from a reinforcing activity to punish behavior. Researchers used brief time out to get children to hold still for brain scans (Slifer et al., 1993). Any slight motion of the head interrupted a cartoon for three seconds. The interruption is a brief withdrawal of the cartoon presentation. Because the children's move-

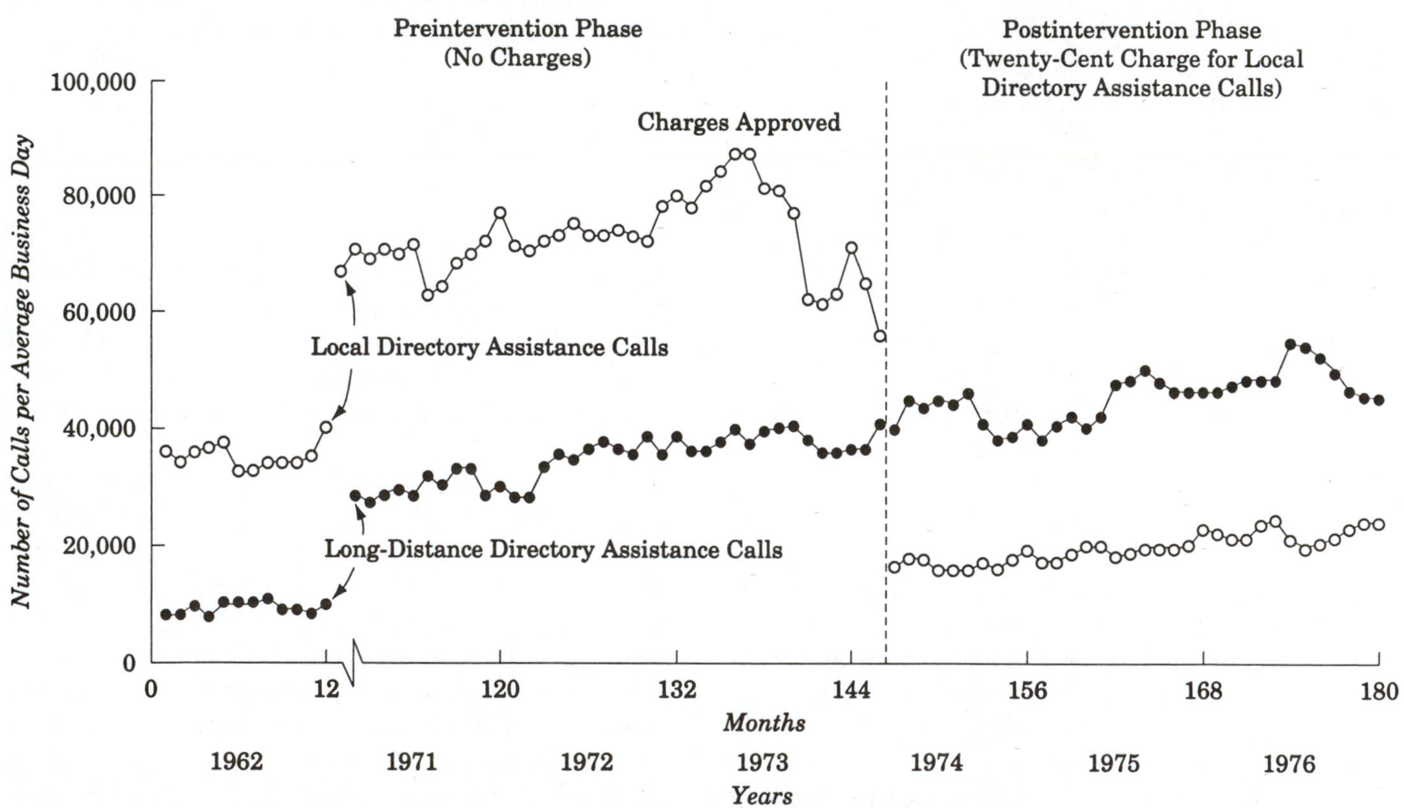

Figure 23-1. The number of information calls made in Cincinnati. The graph compares calls made before and after introduction of a charge for such calls. The charges amount to withdrawing an amount of money for the behavior. Therefore, they constitute punishment by contingent withdrawal. From "Effects of Response Cost on the Behavior of a Million Persons: Charging for Directory Assistance in Cincinnati," by A. J. McSweeny, *Journal of Applied Behavior Analysis,* 1978, *11*, 47–51. Copyright 1978 by the Society for the Experimental Analysis of Behavior, Inc. Used by permission.

ments decreased, this is an example of punishment by contingent withdrawal. Another researcher reduced thumb-sucking behavior in young children by interrupting a cartoon when the children sucked their thumbs (Baer, 1962). Other researchers reduced whining, crying, and complaining in a 5-year-old by withdrawing attention (Hall et al., 1972).

Another type of time out involves making the person watch but not participate in a reinforcing activity. For example, researchers helped the teacher of fourth- and fifth-grade physical education classes (White & Bailey, 1990). The kids didn't obey, they hit each other, and they threw things. The teacher briefly removed disruptive children from the activity, permitting them only to watch it. This brief withdrawal of the right to participate resulted in a 95% reduction of disruptive behavior.

Another form of time out involves removing people from the reinforcing environment when they emit the undesirable behavior. For example, parents used this approach to reduce the aggressive behavior of a child. They simply removed him from the room. They placed him in a specially modified room that had no toys in it (Zeilberger, Sampen, & Sloane, 1968). They kept the child in the time-out room for two minutes. If he continued screaming, they kept him there for an additional two minutes. This type of isolation may seem unusually harsh. However, the child's aggressive behavior was also extreme: It consisted of hitting, kicking, throwing, biting, and scratching.

Behavior analysts pick the duration and form of time out depending on the behavior. They needed only a brief time out from cartoons to change weak behavior like head movement or thumbsucking. They needed a longer time out to change children's disruptive play behaviors. They needed to actually remove a very aggressive child from the room to reduce aggression. Other studies have looked at the length of time out, showing that moderate time out is often effective (Roberts & Powers, 1990).

Problems with Punishment

Behavior analysts are sometimes faced with individuals who resist time out. Researchers tried several methods to deal with the resistance of oppositional children (Roberts & Powers, 1990). In this research, the mothers gave their children explicit instructions to do some tasks. The mothers praised their children when they complied and warned them when they did not. The mothers confined their children to a chair for two minutes whenever they disobeyed, requiring them to remain sitting for the full two minutes. Some children mildly resisted this time out by crying. The mothers punished this resistance by not releasing their children until they were quiet for 15 seconds. Other children resisted more strongly by leaving the chair before the time was up. The mothers punished this resistance by either putting them in another room for 60 seconds or spanking them. Both forms of punishment eliminated resistance to the time out.

Behavior analysts may also be faced with individuals for whom time out is reinforcing. Researchers found that the inappropriate behavior of two children actually increased when followed by time out (Plummer, Baer, & LeBlanc, 1977). Other researchers replicated this finding (Solnick, Rincover, & Peterson, 1977). This finding reminds us that the same events can be reinforcing for some people and punishing for others. We must never assume that an event that we think is unpleasant must be a punisher for another person. We must always see whether it decreases behavior.

Adding Punishment to Reinforcement

Some studies suggest that adding punishment to reinforcement can improve performance. In the last lesson, I described a study testing this theory (Pfiffner & O'Leary, 1987). The researchers showed that punishment helped teach kids to reduce off-task behavior. They found that they could fade out the punishment once they had reduced the off-task behavior. Another researcher found that token fines reduced violent behavior more than token reinforcement of desirable behavior alone (Winkler, 1970). Other research is confirming the benefits of supplemental punishment (e.g., Sullivan & O'Leary, 1990). Often you can stop punishment once desirable behaviors have replaced undesirable behaviors.

Be very careful when you think about these results. They do not mean that we should punish more. Punishment does not by itself create desirable behavior; it only eliminates undesirable behavior. We usually help the person more if we teach them more desirable behaviors that produce reinforcement. For example, two researchers worked with children with retardation who emitted challenging behavior toward their teachers (Durand & Carr, 1992). Analysis suggested that teachers reinforced these behaviors by attending to them. For some children, the researchers punished challenging behavior with time out. The researchers taught other children how to ask for attention. They were taught to say, "Am I doing good work?" Both methods reduced challenging behavior. However, the children treated by time out reverted to challenging behavior with new teachers. The children who knew how to ask for attention did not, because they had learned a more desirable way to produce reinforcement. The others had not learned a more desirable behavior.

You Only Punish Making a Response

One final point about punishment should be made. Behavior analysts do not speak of punishing somone for not making a response. For example, suppose Mom spanks Tommy when he forgets to let the dog out. Can you label the spanking (if it reduces Tommy's failures to let the dog out) as punishment? No. Tommy is not making the response of letting the dog out. You might be tempted to say that Tommy's response is forgetting to let the dog out. But forgetting is not itself a response, but rather the absence of a response. Behavior analysts are very precise on this point. You will get very confused in the next lesson if you label spanking Tommy for forgetting to let the dog out as punishment. Behavior analysts call this an *avoidance* schedule. I will introduce this term in the next lesson. For now, just remember the rule: Do not speak of punishing someone for not making a response.

2. Behavior analysts do not speak of punishing someone for ________________ (making, not making) a response.

Who Decides What Is Undesirable Behavior?

These two lessons on punishment raise ethical issues. You may have wondered what gives behavior analysts the right to decide what behavior is undesirable. That's an excellent question. In my opinion, they have no more right than anyone else to decide what behavior is undesirable. In fact, they usually don't decide. People consult with them about practical behavioral problems. Doctors ask them how to stop persons with retardation from injuring themselves. Parents ask them how to stop their child from throwing tantrums in public places. Teachers ask them how to stop underachieving students from wasting their time. If behavior analysts agree that they can ethically help solve a problem, they help these people. They do not decide on their own what behavior is so undesirable that it warrants punishment.

Here's a related question. What gives a behavior analyst the right to actually punish someone's behavior? I have simplified most of the examples in this book to imply that the researchers administer the punishment. Actually, they rarely do. They simply advise the doctor, parent, or teacher how and when to do it. They rarely punish anyone's behavior.

Summary

Punishment can occur by withdrawing a reinforcing event contingent on an undesirable behavior. The withdrawal can be permanent, as in a fine. Or it can be temporary, as in loss of a privilege or time out. One problem with punishment is that people may resist it. This may require further punishment to control. Also, time out may be reinforcing for some people. Punishment by withdrawal is often used as a very mild corrective procedure. It may even be used temporarily and then faded out. Behavior analysts do not take the right to punish people; they consult with others. They may advise punishment when nothing else seems to work.

Behavior Analysis Examples

Tantrums

Children often misbehave when they are in public with their parents. Some children develop extreme behaviors in public. This can develop when parents don't apply punishment because other people are around. Two researchers invented a way to eliminate tantrums in public (Rolider &

Van Houten, 1985). Michael was a 10-year-old child who threw tantrums while taking the taxi to school with his mother. He screamed demands, cried loudly, and threw himself on the floor, yelling and screaming. He engaged in this behavior 39% of the time.

During treatment, the mother tape-recorded Michael's tantrums. She played the recording of one of his tantrums at home, with the father present. The parents then placed Michael in a very restrictive time out. They made him stand in the corner without moving for 20 seconds. His rate of tantrums in the taxi decreased to 8% of the time. They repeated this treatment in a multiple-baseline design for the bus and for the bus station. In each situation, the baseline level decreased sharply when the treatment was started. The tape recorder helped bridge the delay between the tantrum and the treatment. Standing in the corner followed the tantrums.

3. Standing in the corner followed the tantrums. The tantrums decreased in frequency. Therefore, standing in the corner is a ______________ (punisher, reinforcer).

Rule-Following in a Recreation Center

Researchers found a way to increase rule-following in an urban youth center (Pierce & Risley, 1974). Young black males aged 7 to 25 went to this center. The center offered pool, ping-pong, and table games for two hours at night. The youth did not keep the center clean. They broke pool cues, fought, and threw trash around.

The director posted a list of rules. Each rule specified a group penalty, consisting of closing the center 1 to 15 minutes early per violation. The director strictly enforced the more severe violations. Problems like fighting, breaking equipment, and crowding into line stopped. However, the director did not consistently enforce less severe violations. He explained, "I'm here to help the kids. I want to show them that I'm a nice guy." Three weeks later, he agreed that they had to be enforced also.

The director enforced rule violations by walking through the center every 15 minutes and looking for violations. For every violation that he observed, he wrote it and a penalty on the blackboard. He then followed through by closing the center by the number of minutes of accumulated penalties indicated on the blackboard. Thus, the individuals attending the center lost the privilege of using the center when one or more of their group violated the rules.

An observer walked through the center every 30 minutes to count violations. The observer never enforced the rules or showed his observations to the director. At various times, a second observer

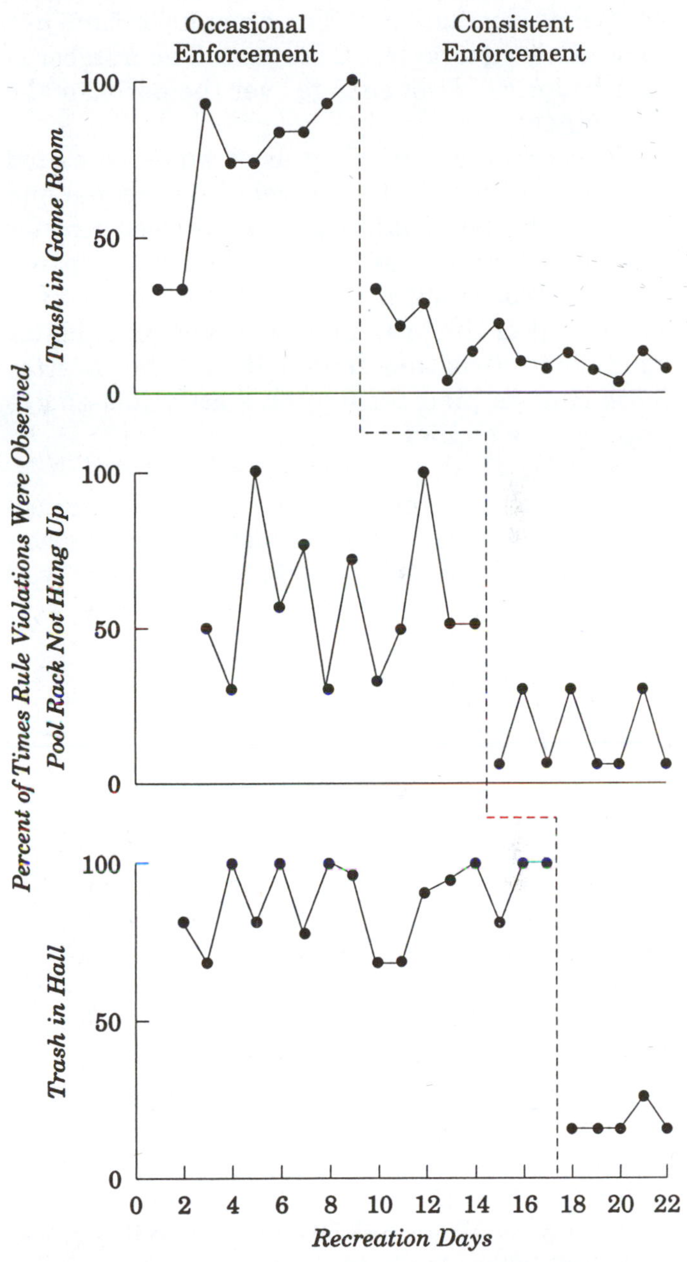

Figure 23-2. The effect of consistent rule enforcement on disruptive behavior in an inner-city recreational facility. Adapted from "Recreation as a Reinforcer: Increasing Membership and Decreasing Disruptions in an Urban Recreation Center," by C. H. Pierce and T. R. Risley, *Journal of Applied Behavior Analysis*, 1974, 7, 403–411. Copyright 1974 by the Society for the Experimental Analysis of Behavior, Inc. Used by permission.

recorded rule violations at the same time, but independently of the primary observer. Reliability averaged 96%.

Figure 23-2 shows the results of the study. When the rules were enforced only occasionally, each rule was broken most of the time. After the director consistently enforced rules, violations decreased dramatically. The amount of time lost in penalties averaged 10 minutes. The number of participants did not change over the period of the experiment.

The group contingency used was well suited to this situation. It did not require personal and possibly abrasive confrontations between director and participants. Instead, the older participants prompted the younger ones not to break the rules. The result of the procedure was a cleaner, better operating recreation center. It left the director more time to plan constructive activities and to improve the facility.

4. When a participant broke a rule or let someone else break a rule, he lost time in the center. This contingency reduced the rate of violations. The event of losing time is a(n) ______________.

Helpful Hints

Helpful Hint #1

It is not necessary to use the full label describing which type of punisher or punishment is involved. Simply label the procedure as punishment and the event as a punisher.

5. If you decide that a procedure is punishment by contingent stimulation or punishment by contingent withdrawal, you should label it as ______________.

Helpful Hint #2

Do not confuse punishment by withdrawal with extinction. Extinction is stopping the delivery of the reinforcer that caused the behavior. Punishment by withdrawal is the withdrawal of any reinforcer that did not cause the behavior. When Mom stops paying attention to Tommy's pestering, she is no longer reinforcing his pestering. She has stopped the reinforcer that caused his pestering in the first place. When Mom sends Tommy to his room for pestering her, she is sending him away from many reinforcers, but being out of his room is not the reinforcer that caused his pestering.

6. If you think a procedure that decreases the rate of a behavior might be extinction, ask whether it stops the reinforcer that caused the behavior. If it is, then the procedure is ______________.

Helpful Hint #3

Remember to distinguish between punishment and punisher in all questions. If you are asked about a procedure, the answer is punishment. If you are asked about an event, the answer is punisher.

7. The procedure of using a punisher should be labeled ______________.

Helpful Hint #4

I will continue to give you examples that do not include all elements required for a behavioral term. You can continue to refer to the procedure in these examples as "unknown." For example, you may find examples of events whose withdrawal follows the behavior but does not decrease it. However, if the behavior increases, it is reinforcement, not "unknown." You may find examples of the withdrawal of an event following the nonoccurrence of a behavior, and a subsequent decrease in the nonoccurrence of the behavior. Behavior analysts do not call this procedure punishment. They use a term that I will introduce in the next lesson. Until then you should label the procedure as unknown.

8. You may find examples of the withdrawal of an event following the nonoccurrence of a behavior, and a subsequent decrease in the nonoccurrence of the behavior. Behavior analysts do not call this procedure punishment. They use a term that I will introduce in the next lesson. Until then you should label the procedure as ______________.

Additional Readings

Baer, D. M. (1962). Laboratory control of thumbsucking by withdrawal and representation of reinforcement. *Journal of the Experimental Analysis of Behavior*, *5*, 525–528. Thumbsucking children were shown a cartoon movie. Whenever they sucked their thumbs, the movie was interrupted for as long as they sucked their thumbs. When they pulled their thumbs from their mouths, the cartoon was turned on again. The rate of thumb-sucking was drastically reduced by this procedure.

Clark, H. B., Rowbury, T., Baer, A. M., & Baer, D. M. (1973). Timeout as a punishing stimulus in continuous and intermittent schedules. *Journal of Applied Behavior Analysis*, *6*, 443–455. Time out was used to suppress the rate of extremely disruptive behaviors (including physical aggression) in a child with retardation. The article also contains references to many other studies using time-out procedures.

Hall, R. V., Axelrod, S., Tyler, L., Grief, E., Jones, F. C., & Robertson, R. (1972). Modification of behavior problems in the home with a parent as observer and experimenter. *Journal of Applied Behavior Analysis*, *5*, 53–64. Elaise, a 5-year-old girl, took an average of over three hours to get dressed in the morning during baseline. Treatment consisted of withdrawing TV-watching privileges if she took longer than 30 minutes. This reduced her dressing time to an average of 23 minutes.

Winkler, R. C. (1970). Management of chronic psychiatric patients by a token reinforcement system. *Journal of Applied Behavior Analysis*, *3*, 47–55. Chronic psychiatric patients were fined by loss of tokens for tantrums, screaming, and acts of violence. These behaviors increased rather sharply when the fines were discontinued.

Reading Quiz

70. The first thing you should know is that this lesson does not introduce a new tactic for the aversive control strategy. This lesson introduces punishment by contingent withdrawal, but the first tactic covers that type of punishment. Thus, remember that Tactic #1 of the aversive control strategy is to decrease undesirable behavior through ______________ as a last resort.

81. Your first goal in this section is to learn about punishment by contingent withdrawal. Behavior analysts call the form of punishment in which a reinforcer is withdrawn each time someone emits an undesirable behavior *punishment by contingent* ______________ (stimulation, withdrawal). (Be sure to spell your answer correctly.)

6. Behavior analysts call decreasing the rate of a behavior by withdrawing an event when a person emits the behavior ______________ (punishment, reinforcement) by contingent withdrawal.

29. Punishment by contingent withdrawal is a procedure that decreases the rate of a behavior by the ______________ (presentation, withdrawal) of an event contingent on the occurrence of the behavior.

30. Punishment by contingent withdrawal involves the same two elements as punishment by contingent stimulation. An event must be withdrawn following an undesirable behavior. The rate of the behavior must then ______________.

59. Suppose Mom won't let Karen use her bicycle for a day because she broke the rules. If Karen's rule breaking decreases after that, you should call Mom's procedure ______________ by contingent withdrawal.

32. Remember to label a procedure that doesn't work as "unknown." Suppose Mom won't let Karen use her bicycle for a day because she broke the rules. If Karen's rule breaking does not change from then on, you should call Mom's procedure ______________.

31. Punishment by contingent stimulation involves the presentation of an event following an undesirable behavior. Punishment by contingent withdrawal involves the ______________ of an event following an undesirable behavior.

79. You learned in the last lesson that behavior analysts refer to punishment by contingent stimulation by the single word punishment. You will probably not be surprised to learn that they refer to punishment by contingent withdrawal by the single word ______________.

60. Suppose Mom yells at Karen for riding her bicycle in the street. If Karen's street riding decreases after that, you should call Mom's procedure by the single word ______________.

61. Suppose Mom yells at Karen for riding her bicycle in the street. If Karen's street riding doesn't change after that, you should call Mom's procedure by the single word ______________.

15. I will use the same convention I have used before. If I ask you what procedure Mom used to decrease Karen's street riding, you should

answer "punishment." If I ask you to name the <u>event</u> of Mom's not letting Karen ride her bike for a day, you should answer ________.

57. Suppose Ken looks away whenever Alice puts down recycling. Suppose Alice's putdowns decrease after that. The event of looking away is an example of a(n) ________________. by looking away following Alice's putdowns, Ken is using what procedure? ____________

58. Suppose Ken looks away whenever Alice puts down recycling. Suppose the rate of Alice's putdowns doesn't change. By looking away following Alice's putdowns, Ken is using what procedure? ____________

1. A minor goal is to learn about the form of punishment called *time out*. A judge fines a person $50 for speeding. A fine is an example of a withdrawal that is a(n) ____________ (permanent, temporary) loss.

26. Mom grounds Jenny for the day. In other words, Mom withdraws from Jenny the privilege of playing with her friends. Grounding is an example of a withdrawal that is ____________ (permanent, temporary).

77. When punishment by withdrawal is temporary, the person is taken <u>out</u> of a reinforcing situation for a <u>time</u>. This form of punishment is called time ____.

36. Review: If a person is taken <u>out</u> of some reinforcing situation for a <u>time</u> when he or she emits a behavior, and the rate of the behavior decreases, this is a form of punishment by contingent withdrawal that is called ________ ____________.

4. Always keep in mind that time out is a form of the procedure called ________________.

68. Suppose Mom won't talk to Jimmy for ten seconds whenever he interrupts her, and the rate of his interruptions decreases. Because Mom has temporarily denied Jimmy access to talking with her when he interrupts her, this is the form of punishment called ________ ____________.

10. Belles and Bradlyn (1987) helped a 65-year-old man quit smoking. Any week in which he failed to reduce smoking, he permanently lost money by donating it to an organization that he didn't like. His smoking decreased from 82 cigarettes per day to 5. The behavioral procedure used in this case was ____________. (Remember that you don't have to specify which kind.)

45. Review: Phone company customers permanently lost 20¢ for each local call for information made in Cincinnati starting in 1973. The charge followed each call, and the rate of such calls decreased. This is an example of the procedure of ____________.

7. Behavior analysts do not have a special name for the form of punishment in which people permanently lose a reinforcer. You may refer to this form simply as punishment, because it is the name of the procedure. They do have a special name for the form of punishment in which people temporarily lose a reinforcer. When asked what <u>form</u> of punishment involves a temporary loss, the best answer is ________________ (punishment, time out).

54. Sometimes I will want you to identify the specific form (time out) and sometimes only the procedure (punishment). When I ask what behavioral <u>procedure</u> is involved when the rate of a behavior is decreased through the temporary withdrawal of a reinforcer, do not answer "time out." Rather, label the behavioral procedure as ____________.

9. Behavior analysts use two terms to refer to the temporary withdrawal of a reinforcer contingent on a behavior, when the rate of that behavior then decreases. When they refer to the general name of the <u>procedure</u>, they call it ______________. When they refer to the specific <u>form</u> of punishment, they call it ______ ______________.

35. Review: Decreasing an undesirable behavior by interrupting a cartoon temporarily when the behavior occurs is an example of what <u>form</u> of punishment by contingent withdrawal? ______________

74. When a child plays too roughly with others, a teacher might use a very mild form of time out. The teacher might have the child watch the other children play but not let him or her participate. If this reduced the child's rough play, the teacher would be using what <u>procedure</u>? ____________

3. A stronger form of punishment by withdrawal involves removing people from the reinforcing environment when they emit the undesirable behavior. If doing so decreases the behavior, then the specific name for this <u>form</u> of punishment is ________________.

72. Time for an overview. Suppose Mr. Jones yells at Mabel when she whispers to Lamar, and

Mabel continues whispering just as often. What procedure is Mr. Jones using? ________________

62. Suppose Mr. Jones keeps Mabel after school when she whispers to Lamar, and Mabel never whispers again. What do you call the event of keeping Mabel after school? ________________
63. Suppose Mr. Jones keeps Mabel after school when she whispers to Lamar, and Mabel never whispers again. What form of punishment is keeping Mabel after school for whispering? ________________
64. Suppose Mr. Jones keeps Mabel after school when she whispers to Lamar, and Mabel still whispers often. What procedure is Mr. Jones using? ________________
65. Suppose Mr. Jones keeps Mabel after school when she whispers to Lamar, and Mabel then does not whisper as often. What procedure is Mr. Jones using? ________________
12. Here are a few minor points. When individuals resist time out, behavior analysts may seek to decrease the behavior of resistance by using the procedure of ________________.
71. There are individuals for whom time out is reinforcing. We must never assume that an event that we think is unpleasant will be a(n) ________________ for another person. We must always find out what happens when the event follows an undesirable behavior. It is a punisher only if it actually ________________ the rate of that behavior.
76. When punishment by contingent withdrawal is used by behavior analysts to assist reinforcement, they ________ (do, don't) stop using it if possible.
53. Some studies indicate that adding punishment to the procedure of reinforcement can improve performance. Once desirable behaviors have replaced undesirable behaviors, we can usually stop using the procedure of ________________.
11. Clearly, punishment can eliminate undesirable behavior. Does punishment by itself create desirable behavior? ________
80. You may be able to stop a person from emitting one undesirable behavior that produces a particular reinforcer. However, the person may then develop another undesirable behavior that produces that same reinforcer. Better than using punishment to prevent undesirable behavior is to increase the rate of a desirable behavior that will produce the same reinforcer by using what behavioral procedure? ________________
13. Here is a very important, although minor, point. Behavior analysts call the procedure in which a punisher follows the occurrence of a behavior *punishment*. However, you should be very clear that they ________ (do, don't) call the procedure of having a punisher follow the nonoccurence of a behavior *punishment*.
66. Suppose a researcher decreases the nonoccurrence of a behavior by interrupting a cartoon temporarily when the behavior fails to occur. Until the next lesson, you should label that procedure as ________________.
18. If mother grounds Tommy for kicking the dog, and his rate of kicking the dog decreases, mother's grounding is an example of what behavioral procedure? ________________
22. If mother spanks Tommy for the nonoccurrence of brushing his teeth, and his rate of not brushing his teeth decreases, mother's spanking is an example of what behavioral procedure? ________________
16. If mother grounds Tommy for throwing the ball in the house, and the rate of throwing the ball in the house decreases, mother's grounding would be what form of punishment? ________________
17. If mother grounds Tommy for not feeding the dog, and the rate of not feeding the dog decreases, mother's grounding Tommy would be an example of what behavioral procedure? ________________
19. If mother sends Tommy to his room for teasing his sister, and teasing his sister increases, mother's sending him to his room would be an example of what behavioral procedure? ________________
20. If mother sends Tommy to his room for not studying, and the rate of not studying decreases, mother's sending him to his room would be an example of what behavioral procedure? ________________
67. Suppose Mom sends Tommy to his room for forgetting to study. That ________ (is, isn't) just another way of saying that she sent him to his room for not studying.
21. If mother sends Tommy to his room for forgetting to study, and the rate of forgetting decreases, mother's sending him to his room would be an example of what behavioral procedure? ________________

5. Another minor point is the role of the behavior analyst in punishment. Behavior analysts __________ (often, rarely) decide on their own what behavior warrants punishment.
8. Behavior analysts themselves __________ (often, rarely) punish anyone's behavior.
42. Review: If you withdraw a <u>reinforcer</u> contingent on an undesirable behavior, and the rate of the behavior decreases, then you are using what behavioral procedure? __________
51. Review: You can punish an undesirable behavior by withdrawing a(n) __________ contingent on that behavior.
2. A mother tape-recorded her son's tantrums in public places and played them at home, with the father present. The father then made the son stand in the corner without moving for 20 seconds. His rate of tantrums decreased (Rolider & Van Houten, 1985). The procedure used by the parents in this case is called __________.
52. Review: You have learned to classify punishers depending on how they arise. You learned to call events that arise from biological factors and lose their effectiveness only temporarily __________ punishers. You learned to call events that are paired with another punisher and may lose their effectiveness permanently __________ punishers.
46. Review: Pierce and Risley (1974) posted the number of minutes that a recreation center would close early each time a rule violation was observed. This procedure reduced rule violation dramatically. If these posted numbers were no longer paired with actual early closing of the center, they would probably lose their effect. If they did, what type of punisher would they be? __________ punisher
75. When Pierce and Risley (1974) posted a list of rules with the penalties for breaking them, but did not always enforce the penalties, the rate of rule-violating behavior __________ (did, didn't) decrease.
28. Pierce and Risley (1974) withdrew the privilege of playing in the recreation center when a rule was violated. The rule-violating behavior decreased dramatically. What behavioral procedure did they use? __________
14. Here is the second major goal of this section. You must learn to discriminate punishment by contingent withdrawal from extinction. If you stop delivering a reinforcing event that used to cause an undesirable behavior, and the rate of the behavior decreases, then you are using the procedure called __________.
56. Suppose that every time Baby Annie throws her vegetables, you give her some fruit because you know she won't throw it. You may be reinforcing throwing her vegetables. If you stop giving her fruit when she throws her veggies, she may stop throwing them. If so, you have used what procedure? __________
69. Suppose you withdraw any reinforcer other than the one that causes the undesirable behavior when the person makes the response. If the rate of the behavior decreases, what procedure is involved? __________
55. Suppose Baby Annie throws her vegetables. Perhaps you don't have a clue why she throws them. One way to stop her throwing involves finding some reinforcer for any of her behaviors. It doesn't have to be connected with throwing her veggies. Maybe she looks at you often when you are smiling; her looking is reinforced by your smiling. You may be able to decrease her throwing by withdrawing that reinforcer following her throwing. If she throws, you stop smiling and look away for a few seconds. If this procedure decreases her throwing, then you should call it __________.
25. Mom can't concentrate on her bill-paying because Tommy is banging on a pot. Mom yells at him to stop. He does for a moment and then starts again. Suppose one day Mom stops yelling at him, and his rate of banging gradually decreases. Because she has stopped reinforcing him with her yelling, you would call her procedure __________.
73. Tommy is banging on that pot again. Ignoring him by no longer yelling at him doesn't work today. He stays downstairs. Events like your reaction, getting soda from the refrigerator, reading the Sunday funnies, and watching the TV, all reinforce his behavior of staying downstairs. Suppose that anytime he bangs, you send him up to his room for 15 minutes. You are temporarily removing him from all those reinforcers. If his rate of banging decreases, you have used what procedure? __________
78. With extinction, you are stopping the delivery of the reinforcer that is causing the undesirable behavior. With punishment by withdrawal, you are temporarily withdrawing reinforcers

that ______ (are, aren't) causing the undesirable behavior.

27. Mr. Jones asks David a question about the American history homework. David makes a wisecrack. Mr. Jones keeps him after school, making him miss football practice. David never makes a wisecrack again to Mr. Jones. What procedure has Mr. Jones used? ______
24. Kenny pouted when no one asked how his day was. This got started because whenever Dad saw his pout, he would immediately ask Kenny how his day was. Starting a week ago, Dad no longer asks the question when Kenny starts to pout. Kenny rarely pouts now. What procedure did Dad use to decrease Kenny's pouting? ______
23. Kenny often pouted. Mom ignored his pouting, and after a week, Kenny was still pouting. What procedure did Mom use? ______
37. Review: If an event follows a behavior and decreases the rate of that behavior, you call the event a(n) ______; if an event precedes a behavior and decreases the rate of that behavior, you call the event a(n) ______.
33. Review: A <u>punisher</u> is any event produced or withdrawn that is timed so that it ______ (when?) a behavior and ______ the rate of the behavior.
49. Review: The procedure of withdrawing an event following a behavior, resulting in a decrease in the behavior, is called ______.
50. Review: To decide whether a procedure that decreases a behavior is extinction, you ask, "Did the procedure stop the reinforcer that caused the behavior?" If so, the procedure is ______.
43. Review: Kay doesn't talk to Kevin when he gets drunk and makes a fool of himself. Kevin gets drunk and makes a fool out of himself just as often as before. What behavioral procedure has Kay used? ______
40. Review: If Mom told Kenny he couldn't have dessert tonight because of his pestering, and his rate of pestering became less, what procedure did Mom use? ______
41. Review: If Pierce and Risley (1974) ignored all rule-violating behavior, and the rate of such behavior decreased, what procedure would they have been using? ______.
48. Review: The first tactic in using the aversive control strategy is to use ______ as a last resort.
39. Review: If delivering an event when a person does <u>not</u> emit a particular behavior causes the rate of not emitting the behavior to decrease, the procedure is called ______.
38. Review: If any reinforcer in a person's environment is taken away whenever the person emits a particular behavior, and if the rate of that behavior decreases, the procedure would be an example of ______.
34. Review: A form of punishment by withdrawal that involves the temporary loss of a privilege contingent on the occurrence of a particular behavior is called ______.
47. Review: Pierce and Risley (1974) withdrew the privilege of playing in the recreation center when a rule was violated. The rule-violating behavior decreased dramatically. What behavioral procedure did they use? ______
44. Review: Mr. Barnes docked Joe's pay $5 because he forgot to lock the money drawer. Joe never forgot again. Mr. Barnes used what behavioral procedure to decrease Joe's forgetting? ______ (Be careful with your answer here.)

Examples

1. Bobby treated his toys roughly. He would make his toy soldiers have war and break them into little pieces, or break his toy cars by crashing them into one another. Bobby's parents decided to teach him to stop being destructive. Every time Bobby played too roughly with his toys, his parents took the toys away for about 15 minutes and explained why. After 15 minutes, Bobby would get his toys back again. Within 2 weeks, he had almost stopped his destructive play. If you think the parents used extinction, ask: Were the toys the reinforcers that caused his destructive behavior? ______. Therefore, because the toys were not the cause of Bobby's destructive behavior, but their removal decreased his destructive behavior, this is an example of what procedure? ______ by contingent withdrawal

2. Dora was mean to her little brother Rickie all the time. She grabbed toys away from him and wouldn't let him have them back. She called him names and humiliated him in front of other children. Dora's parents were upset about her behavior. They felt that her meanness was harmful to

Rickie, so they decided to put a stop to it. Each time they caught her being mean to her brother, they took away her outside play privilege by keeping her indoors for an hour. Soon Dora had almost stopped being mean to her little brother. If you think that Dora's parents used extinction, ask: Did her outside play privilege cause her to be mean to Rickie? ______. Because her parents took away her outside play privilege, and Dora's rate of being mean decreased, they were using what procedure? ______________

3. John's gripes about bad food were disgusting. When the fraternity served a meal that he didn't like, he likened the food to every undesirable form of organic material he could think of. Naturally, this had a terrible effect on everyone's appetite. One day several members decided that they had been reinforcing John's gross griping by their outraged reactions. They decided not to act outraged any more. John's rate of griping gradually decreased over a period of six weeks, and members could eat their meals in peace again. If you think the group might be using extinction, ask whether their acting outraged caused his griping. ______. Because they stopped delivering the reinforcer that caused his griping, the group was using what procedure? ______________

4. Every time Paco pouted, his parents took away some of his play time by immediately sending him to his room for ten minutes. At the end of the ten minutes, they would go to his room and tell him his time was up. They usually had a useful discussion about Paco's pouting at that time. His pouting went on at about the same rate for the next few months. In this case, because their procedure did not decrease the pouting, his parents used the procedure called ______________.

5. Mary frequently burped at the dinner table. Her parents usually admonished her and explained that it wasn't polite to burp at the dinner table. Recently, however, Mary's parents decided that they had been encouraging Mary's burping behavior by admonishing her when she burped. Mary has been burping less and less since her parents instituted their new policy of not admonishing her. If you think that this procedure might be extinction, ask whether admonishing Mary caused her burping. Once you can answer that question, then you will know that they used the procedure of ______________.

6. Clarence frequently gossiped about the other members of the group—which ones got drunk, who was sleeping with whom, and who didn't like whom. At first the members of the group listened to Clarence and took his gossip seriously, but later they decided that it was creating bad feelings. They therefore decided to suspend him from membership for a week each time he gossiped. Clarence gossiped just as much as before. What behavioral procedure is this an example of? ______________ (If necessary, ask the question.)

7. Fran argued that technology would save the world from global warming. Marcie disagreed with Fran's argument so convincingly that Fran stopped making it. The decrease in Fran's rate of proposing that technology will save the world is the result of what behavioral procedure? ______________

8. Barbara was both the school artist and the school bully. She did beautiful art, but she tended to beat up her schoolmates whenever she felt like it. The teachers felt that Barbara's behavior severely disrupted the recesses and class periods, so they decided to take action. Every time they caught Barbara fighting, they immediately told her that she could not take part in the art period that day. They observed that Barbara's rate of fighting decreased. What procedure did the teachers use to decrease Barbara's fighting behavior? ______________

9. Bud had the bad habit of griping about the evening meal almost every night, no matter what food was served. The other members of the cooperative dorm became increasingly annoyed by this behavior and tried to explain to Bud why his griping was bad for the group (especially the cooks). But Bud persisted in his griping. Finally everyone decided to stop explaining to Bud why he shouldn't gripe. Each time Bud started to gripe about the food, everyone just acted as though he hadn't said anything. Bud's griping gradually disappeared. The decrease in Bud's griping is an example of what behavioral procedure? ______________

10. Bo used to flirt with all the women he met. This greatly angered Keesha, who finally decided to withhold all affection from him on any day that he flirted with someone else. Bo no longer flirts with other women. What behavioral procedure did Keesha use to stop his flirting? ______________

11. Review: Fred was a radical and Ruth was a liberal. Both of them were very aggressive in arguing their points of view. In spite of their dif-

ferences, however, Fred and Ruth got along beautifully. One rule that helped them get along was that they never talked about politics. Right from the first, Ruth obeyed the rule all the time, but Fred frequently broke it. She taught Fred to obey the rule by getting mad at him whenever he started a political harangue or made a political joke. Within two weeks, Fred was obeying the no-politics rule. The decrease in Fred's political talk is the result of what behavioral procedure? ______________

12. Review: Larry often took extreme positions just for the sake of an argument. When he did so, Jim gave him a certain kind of look that made Larry feel very uncomfortable. The rate at which he took extreme positions decreased as a result of Jim's looks. What behavioral procedure did Jim use? ______________

13. Review: Larry took extreme positions with Frank just for the sake of an argument. Later Frank just ignored all such arguments. Larry's rate of taking extreme positions for the sake of an argument decreased. What behavioral procedure did Frank use? ______________

14. Review: Larry took extreme positions with Teresa just for the sake of an argument. Teresa always broke off the conversation in a very gentle way as soon as this started to happen. Larry's rate of taking extreme positions with Teresa decreased soon afterwards. What behavioral procedure did Teresa use? ______________

15. Review: Fred decreased Larry's rate of argumentative behavior with him by stopping any conversation as soon as Larry started arguing. Tom was the next one to reduce Larry's arguing by stopping conversations. Finally, Mary also reduced Larry's rate of arguing in the same way. After Mary, Larry stopped being argumentative with other people. This is an example of using punishment (instead of reinforcement) in a series of situations until the lack of arguing spreads to other situations in the same stimulus class. What procedure involving punishment did Fred, Tom, and Mary collectively use to make this lack of arguing occur in the presence of other people who had not punished Fred? ______________

16. Review: Dr. Brunner met with Tim three times a week to help him learn to stop forgetting to study. Whenever Tim forgot to study, Dr. Brunner asked him "Why?" Tim never had an answer. Tim's rate of forgetting to study decreased. What behavioral procedure did Dr. Brunner use to decrease the rate of Tim's forgetting to study? ______________

17. Review: When Steve and Maria were talking, Maria usually looked directly at Steve with a nice little smile. However, anytime Steve talked about Maria's belief in God, she stopped looking at him for at least a minute. Pretty soon Steve stopped talking about Maria's beliefs. What behavioral procedure did Maria use? ______________

18. Review: Anytime Steve criticized socialism, Maria argued with him. However, recently she decided that she would not argue with Steve anymore. She would just ignore his comments until he changed topics. Steve does not bring up that issue much anymore. What behavioral procedure did Maria use to reduce Steve's rate of discussing socialism? ______________

19. Review: Little Kathy sometimes threw a temper tantrum if she could not have a cookie when she wanted it. When she threw a tantrum, her father carried her upstairs to her room and made her stay there until well after she had finished her tantrum. Kathy no longer throws temper tantrums when she can't have a cookie. What behavioral procedure did her father use? ______________

20. Review: Little Kathy sometimes threw temper tantrums when she couldn't stay up late. Her parents, wanting to be kind, would usually let her stay up late. Lately, however, they have ignored her tantrums, and Kathy has stopped throwing them. What behavioral procedure did her parents use to eliminate tantrums? ______________

LESSON

24 Negative Reinforcement

This lesson introduces a new kind of reinforcer—the negative reinforcer. Negative reinforcers require a person to enagage in some behavior to get rid of an event. It is a form of aversive control. Negative reinforcement exists widely in everyday life. Examples include brushing your teeth to avoid cavities, closing a window to keep out heat or cold, and drinking alcohol to tune out your problems. Behavior analysts often use negative reinforcement to get someone to emit a behavior when positive reinforcement has failed. Negative reinforcement is part of the aversive control strategy. Tactic #2 of the aversive control strategy is to increase desirable behavior through negative reinforcement as a last resort.

1. Tactic #2 of the aversive control strategy is to increase desirable behavior through __________ reinforcement as a last resort.

Definition of Negative Reinforcement

Negative reinforcement is the procedure of following a behavior with a negative reinforcer. A **negative reinforcer** is any event that meets two criteria. It is terminated or prevented by a behavior, and it causes the rate of that behavior to increase. We call it negative because you take it away rather than give it. In this case, *negative* means that a person will try to terminate or prevent the event. We call it a reinforcer because any behavior that is followed by its termination or prevention will increase. A simple example would be closing your eyes to terminate the sight of a gruesome accident. Another would be wearing a rain hat to prevent rain from wetting your head. Our everyday lives are full of negative reinforcers.

2. Negative reinforcement is the procedure of following a behavior with a negative reinforcer. A negative reinforcer is any event that meets two criteria: (1) It is terminated or __________ by a behavior, and (2) it causes the rate of that behavior to __________.

A more complex example of a negative reinforcer might be the crying of a child who doesn't stop until his mother picks him up. The mother's behavior of picking him up terminates the crying. The crying would be a negative reinforcer if the mother picks him up more often for crying from then on.

You should be able to distinguish a negative reinforcer from a positive reinforcer. A positive reinforcer is any event whose delivery following a response increases the rate of that behavior. A negative reinforcer is any event whose termination or prevention following a response increases the rate of that behavior. In everyday terms, people usually think of a positive reinforcer as a pleasant event. They think of a negative reinforcer as an unpleasant event. However, as I have warned you many times, an event that seems pleasant to you may function as a punisher for someone else. The reverse is also true! Both positive and negative reinforcers are reinforcers because they increase the rate of a behavior that they follow.

People who are not behavior analysts sometimes speak of "punishing" another person for not emitting a desired behavior. The other person can terminate or prevent the "punishment" by emitting that behavior. Behavior analysts reserve the term *punishment* for events that decrease behavior. However, the effect of "punishing not emitting behavior" is to increase the rate of the desired behavior. Therefore, they refer to this arrangement as a form of reinforcement. Reinforcement, including negative reinforcement, increases behavior.

For example, suppose Mother spanks Tommy because he didn't clean up his room. She is creating a situation in which Tommy can prevent such a spanking by cleaning his room next time. If Tommy's rate of room cleaning increases because it prevents the spanking, the spanking would be a negative reinforcer. Thus, what many people refer to as "punishing" the nonoccurrence of a behavior, behavior analysts call *negatively reinforcing* the occurrence of that same behavior.

Here is a way to decide whether an event that follows a behavior is a punisher or a negative reinforcer. Ask "Did the rate of the behavior increase, or did it decrease?" If it increased, you are dealing with a reinforcer. If it decreased, you are dealing with a punisher.

Remember, a negative reinforcer is not a punisher. Many psychologists equate the two, emphasizing the "negative" in *negative reinforcer*. Behavior analysts, however, emphasize the "reinforcer" in *negative reinforcer*. The central term here is *reinforcer*. Whether modified by "positive" or "negative," it always refers to an event that increases the rate of a behavior.

Uses of Escape and Avoidance

Behavior analysts distinguish between terminating the negative reinforcer and preventing it. They name the form of negative reinforcement in which the person <u>terminates</u> the negative reinforcer *escape*. They call the response an *escape response*. They use the term *avoidance* to refer to the form of negative reinforcement in which someone <u>prevents</u> the negative reinforcer from occurring. They call the response an *avoidance response*.

3. The form of negative reinforcement in which the person terminates the negative reinforcer is called *escape*. The term *avoidance* refers to the form of negative reinforcement in which someone _______________ the negative reinforcer from occurring.

With an escape response, the negative reinforcer is physically present in the environment until the response is made. Thus, the response terminates the negative reinforcer. For example, if Dad lends his son Jim $5 but Jim fails to thank him, Dad might scowl until Jim thanks him. As soon as Jim says "Thanks," Dad stops scowling. Jim escapes the dirty look.

Researchers taught a dentist to use escape with uncooperative children (Allen, Loiben, Allen, & Stanley, 1992). For example, 4-year-old Jenny engaged in excessive disruptive behavior during dental treatments. She pulled away from the dentist, cried, moaned, and complained during about 70% of the visit during baseline. Jenny's behavior was maintained by escaping from the dental work. The dentist modified Jenny's behavior with a behavioral treatment based on escape. The treatment was to stop letting Jenny escape when she engaged in disruptive behavior. Instead, they taught her to cooperate in order to escape: They told her, "When you are calm, and quiet, and lying still, I will stop for a rest break." Her rate of disruptive behavior fell from 70% to about 10%. The dentist rated her as "cooperative," giving social validity to the behavioral definition. The dentist got equally good results with three additional children.

Researchers used escape to increase people's frequency of taking pills at the right time (Azrin & Powell, 1969). They developed a timed pill-holder that caused a loud buzzer to sound when it was time to take a pill. The buzzer could be turned off by turning a handle, which dispensed a pill. The patients usually took the pills if dispensed in this manner. The patient could terminate the buzzer by dispensing the pill—a good example of escape behavior.

With an avoidance response, the negative reinforcer is not physically present at the time of the response. However, if the person fails to make the response, it will occur. Thus, the response prevents the negative reinforcer from occurring. For example, suppose Jim immediately thanked Dad for the $5. His "Thanks" would be an avoidance response because it prevented Dad from scowling. Of course, we must have some knowledge that Dad would have scowled if Jim had not thanked him. Figure 24-1 shows a more humorous example of avoidance.

Researchers devised a treatment for three severe burn victims (Hegel et al., 1986). Severe burn victims must actively practice stretching, to prevent the burned areas from contracting. Otherwise they will lose a great deal of flexibility in their everyday movements. The problem is that stretching burned areas is extremely painful. Thus, stretching is punished by the pain of moving. Before the treatment, the three victims were losing flexibility in burned joint areas. The treatment involved setting up a highly structured rehabilitation program. The victims could avoid that

Figure 24-1. Work is a negative reinforcer for some people. Notice the avoidance response! Cartoon copyright 1973 King Features Syndicate. Reproduced by permission.

program by complying with a very flexible self-exercise program. The treatment was very successful. The trends were reversed, and the patients had the chance to resume normal lives as a result.

Researchers used avoidance to increase the social interaction skills of chronic schizophrenics (Fichter et al., 1976). I will call one of the patients whom they helped "Joe." Joe spoke too softly to be easily heard, made the briefest possible comments, and bit his fingernails. They taught him better social skills by having simple conversations with him. They nagged him if he failed to engage in more skillful behaviors. The nagging consisted of instructing him to engage in those behaviors. They didn't nag him if he engaged in those behaviors during the conversations. Thus, Joe could prevent the occurrence of the nagging by engaging in the behavior. This is a good example of avoidance behavior.

Researchers used avoidance to treat children with cystic fibrosis (Stark et al., 1993). These children were very underweight because they did not eat enough. To change this pattern, the researchers had the parents help the children set calorie goals for each meal. Children lost privileges when they did not meet the goals. The children soon started meeting the goals for most meals; they made substantial improvements in eating and body weight as a result.

Escape and avoidance are often combined to produce a more powerful effect. Researchers used such a procedure to teach improved posture to normal adults (Azrin et al., 1968). People wore a simple device that detected slouching during their normal daytime activities. By keeping good posture, they could prevent the device from sounding a loud buzzer. Thus, keeping good posture was an avoidance behavior. If, a person slouched, the buzzer sounded and could be terminated only by the person's adopting good posture. Thus, adopting good posture was also an escape behavior. The result was that these people looked better to others and also reduced the probability of back problems that often result from slouching.

Side Effects of Using Negative Reinforcement

Many behavior analysts have argued against the use of punishment and negative reinforcement as treatment procedures. A major reason is that their use produces harmful side effects, including negative emotions, escape from the treatment procedure, and dislike of the therapist. Fichter and his colleagues found exactly this reaction when they used nagging to increase one patient's social skills. They noted that Joe's "last interaction before [leaving the treatment] unit was to tell one staff member how much he disliked the unit and the staff" (Fichter et al., 1976, pp. 384–385). Iwata (1987) points out that this dislike means Joe probably did not continue to use his improved social skills. He didn't like his teachers or the way they taught him. This is the danger of using aversive control.

4. If Joe sought to escape from the unit, then you can guess that the unit was a ________ ________ (negative, positive) reinforcer.

Do Efforts to Help Sometimes Hurt?

"It is important for us to identify how environments that we create may provide negative reinforcement for undesirable behaviors. When faced with situations in which our students and clients are disruptive, we should immediately examine the antecedent as well as the consequent conditions.... If we conclude that our clients and students exhibit bizarre and potentially dangerous behaviors to terminate instruction, we might question whether or not our well-intentioned efforts to teach are in our clients' best interest; at the very least we must question one or more aspects of our teaching technique" (Iwata, 1987).

5. If a person responds in such a way as to terminate a lesson, then the lesson is called a ________________ (negative, positive) reinforcer.

How to Respond to Coercive Behavior

All of us are often faced with unpleasant and coercive behavior by others. We often maintain such behavior by responding in ways that escape or avoid it. However, in the process, we reinforce the use of such behavior. What should we do? How should we respond to coercive behavior? How can we best help people who use coercive behavior?

For example, Kim might cry at bedtime unless we comfort her. Kim is controlling us through negative reinforcement. If we comfort her, she will stop crying. If we comfort her, we can escape from her crying. She is using negative reinforcement to get us to comfort her. Unfortunately, by comforting her we are teaching her to control us and others through crying. We may even be teaching a generalized behavior of controlling others by coercive behavior. We may think that we are being kind and loving, but we may in fact be creating a lifetime problem. What are we to do? You may remember from the lesson on extinction an example in which the parents ignored their child's crying for a little while, and it stopped (Williams, 1959). We help our children, our family, and even our community by extinguishing coercive behavior whenever possible.

Studies show that many unpleasant behaviors are maintained by others trying to escape from them. This includes teachers who pay attention to disruptive student behavior (Thomas et al., 1978; White, 1975). This teacher attention often involves aversive control. The teacher attention may involve demands, reprimands, or even sending the student to the principal. The teacher may be intending to punish the disruptive behavior and only unintentionally reinforcing it. Furthermore, the attention may terminate the disruptive behavior for the moment, but it is likely to make the problem worse in the future. What should teachers do? Often they cannot ignore the behavior, because it is disruptive to other students. Behavior analysts generally advise reinforcing desirable behaviors (e.g., Hall, 1991). The idea is to increase the rate of desirable behaviors, leaving less time and motivation for disruptive behaviors. Reinforcing desirable behaviors gives the disruptive student an alternative way to get attention. We help people by noticing when they behave in desirable ways.

I noted earlier that mental hospital staff make a mistake if they pay attention to patients only when they act "crazy" (Ayllon & Michael, 1959). The staff teach the patients many of their crazy behaviors. This is another case in which reinforcing desirable behavior could teach alternative ways to get social contact with other people.

Teachers of persons with retardation often let them skip difficult tasks if they act aggressively (Carr, Newsom, & Binkoff, 1980). The teachers unintentionally teach the person with retardation that coercion pays! In this case, the teachers are trying to help the person with retardation learn life skills. In the process, however, the person with retardation fails so often that the situation becomes aversive. The person reacts by finding ways to terminate it. Behavior analysts are pioneering many ways to make the learning situation more positive for persons with retardation. One way is to teach the person with retardation more acceptable ways to ask for a break in the situations (e.g., Reichle & Wacker, 1993). Other ways include increasing the rate of "success," and starting with very easy tasks and only gradually increasing their difficulty (Iwata et al., 1994).

Behavior analysts have learned much about how to respond to coercive behavior. The most important rule is not to reinforce it, but it is also important to find alternative behavior that lets the person obtain social reinforcement. Finally, seek to make the situation less aversive for the

Parents Teach Delinquents That Coercion Works

For 30 years, Gerry Patterson has observed hundreds of families in their own homes. He concludes that children learn coercive behavior through thousands of similar episodes that have three steps. First, the parent intrudes. Mom might complain about Dave not doing his chores. Second, Dave counterattacks by arguing, yelling, whining, or claiming that Mom always picks on him. Third, Mom withdraws. Dave's counterattack punished Mom's parenting. By withdrawing, Mom reinforces Dave's coercion. Patterson suggests that by repeating this process many times, Mom teaches Dave to control her behavior coercively. Similar experiences with other relatives and with friends will put Dave well on his way toward bullying and violent behavior. (Based on Patterson, 1993.)

6. Mom could extinguish Dave's coercive behavior by not withdrawing. She could also increase his desirable behavior through ____________________ (punishment, reinforcement).

person. You might say that this approach combines toughness with "having a heart."

Analogues between Positive and Negative Reinforcement

You can use negative reinforcement in place of positive reinforcement in any of the procedures that you studied earlier in the book. For example, stopping the termination or prevention of a negative reinforcer and observing a decrease in the rate of the behavior is an example of extinction. If you remember that positive and negative reinforcement are both reinforcement, then it should be clear that any procedure or principle that applies to positive reinforcement also applies to negative reinforcement. There follows a brief review of the major reinforcement procedures from the point of view of negative reinforcement.

Extinction of behavior maintained by a negative reinforcer. Stopping the withdrawal or termination of an event following a behavior and observing a decrease in the behavior is called *extinction*. For example, if the father no longer stops scowling when the son borrows $5 and thanks him, the son's thanking behavior is on extinction.

Differential reinforcement using negative reinforcement. Behavior analysts call the procedure in which one behavior is followed by a negative reinforcer, while other behaviors are not, *differential reinforcement*. For example, suppose Dad stops scowling only if Jim says "Thank you, sir," but not if thanked in any other way. Dad is differentially reinforcing the behavior of saying "Thank you, sir."

Shaping with the use of negative reinforcement. If each of a series of successive approximations to a target behavior is differentially reinforced with a negative reinforcer, behavior analysts call the procedure *shaping*. For example, Dad might be the kind of person who wants a very formal "Thank you" for lending Jim some money. Suppose Dad terminated his scowl initially only if Jim said "Thanks." Dad might ignore other comments like "I sure need the money." Jim would eventually learn to say "Thanks." Dad might then stop scowling only if Jim said "Thank you." Finally, he might stop scowling only if Jim said "Thank you, sir." Dad would be shaping.

The researchers who taught Jenny to cooperate with dental work used shaping (Allen, Loiben, Allen, & Stanley, 1992). The dentist started by giving her a rest break if she cooperated for 1 to 3 seconds. He differentially reinforced longer periods of cooperation until she was cooperating for 10 to 20 seconds.

Intermittent negative reinforcement. If only some instances of a behavior terminate or prevent an event, they are on an intermittent schedule of reinforcement. For example, if Jim has to say "Thanks" three times before Dad stops scowling, Dad is (negatively) reinforcing the response on a fixed-ratio schedule. If Jim has to say "Thanks" a differing number of times averaging three, then Dad is (negatively) reinforcing the response on a variable-ratio schedule. If Jim can eliminate the scowl only by the first response after ten seconds, then Dad is (negatively) reinforcing the response on a fixed-interval schedule. If Jim can eliminate the scowl with the first response after an average of ten seconds, then Dad is (negatively) reinforcing the response on a variable-interval schedule.

The pattern of responding for different schedules is the same for positive and negative reinforcement. For example, a fixed-ratio schedule of negative reinforcement will produce a pause after reinforcement followed by a rapid rate of responding. The longer scalloping effect of the fixed-interval schedule will be the same. The more uniform rates produced by variable-interval and variable-ratio schedules will also be produced by negative reinforcement, with the variable-ratio schedule producing the highest rate of responding.

Likewise, resistance to extinction will be greater with an intermittent schedule. Satiation will be less likely. Ratio strain may occur if the ratio is too high. Shaping will work more quickly if the teacher uses a continuous schedule of negative reinforcement.

Principle of contingent negative reinforcement. The termination or prevention of an event will be more effective if it occurs only when the behavior is emitted. For example, Dad's scowl will be most effective if it is terminated only when Jim says "Thank you, sir." If Dad sometimes stops scowling for a "Thank you," it will be less effective in reinforcing the desired behavior of "Thank you, sir."

Principle of immediate negative reinforcement. The more immediately the behavior terminates or prevents the event, the more effective it will be as a negative reinforcer. For example, if Dad stops scowling only several minutes after Jim says "Thank you, sir" the negative reinforcement will not be as effective.

Principle of size of a negative reinforcer. The larger the amount (or intensity) of a negative reinforcer, the more effective it will be. If Dad makes only a slight grimace when not thanked, it will not be as effective as if he makes a very obvious scowl. Scowling and yelling might be even more effective. Of course, a behavior analyst would not recommend doing that. In fact, most behavior analysts would question Dad's target behavior. They would probably advise father and son to adopt a more mutually reinforcing pattern of behavior.

Principle of deprivation of a negative reinforcer. The less recently an event has been terminated or prevented, the more effective it will be. Thus, if Dad scowls only very rarely, he will have more of an effect than if he scowls frequently.

How Not to Supervise Employees

Aubrey Daniels is a business consultant. He writes, "A manager using negative reinforcement says 'Do it or else!' The 'or else' is clearly something distinctly aversive or undesirable for the employee. The employee complies in order to avoid the negative consequence. As soon as the heat is off, the employee's pace slackens. The employee is motivated to do only enough work to reduce pressure from the boss. Typically, there are no consequences to doing more work than that. Thus, negative reinforcement teaches people to do just enough work to 'get by' " (Daniels, 1985). Daniels teaches managers to use positive reinforcement to improve productivity and quality. He claims that employees will work to get as much positive reinforcement as possible, thereby doing more than just enough to get by.

7. According to Daniels, managers will increase productivity and profit more if they use ______________ (negative, positive) reinforcement.

Discrimination training using negative reinforcement. If a behavior leads to the termination or prevention of an event in one situation but not in another, then the procedure being used is called *discrimination training*. Thus, saying "Thank you, sir" may terminate the scowl after borrowing money, but not after Dad has said, "Son, it is your turn to do the dishes."

Summary

Tactic #2 of the aversive control strategy is to increase desirable behavior through negative reinforcement as a last resort. Negative reinforcement is a form of reinforcement in which the desired behavior is followed by termination or prevention of an event. If this strengthens the behavior, the event is a negative reinforcer. The procedure of using a negative reinforcer is negative reinforcement. Negative reinforcement comes in the form of escape and avoidance, which behavior analysts have used to improve cooperation, social skills, and recovery from burns. Much coercive behavior is caused by negative reinforcement. Many people learn that others will do what they want in order to stop the coercive behavior. Behavior analysts have found that by giving in, you reinforce coercive behavior. They recommend reducing coercive behavior by reinforcing more desirable alternative behavior. No matter who uses it, negative reinforcement is analogous to positive reinforcement. It can be delivered according to the same schedules. Its effectiveness can be enhanced by the same principles of effectiveness. It can be used in shaping.

Behavior Analysis Example

Taking Pills on Time

Doctors regard the failure of patients to take their pills as a major problem that can undermine the medical treatment of a wide range of illnesses. Studies have estimated that as many as 35% of all patients fail to take their medication correctly. Doctors reviewed about 1400 medical research articles studying 34 different strategies for improving pill-taking. None of the strategies was based on behavior analysis, and none showed much effect.

Behavior analysts tried a behavioral approach. Researchers analyzed the pill-taking of 20 patients with a 100 mg dose of vitamin C four times a day (Epstein & Masek, 1978). They approached compliance as a behavioral problem. They devised a simple method for observing whether the patients took the pills as scheduled by adding a small amount of a "tracer" medicine to three of the 28 pills for one week. The tracer pills looked and tasted just like the regular vitamin C pills, but they caused the patient's urine to turn bright red within 12 hours of taking them. The researchers placed all 28 pills in a dispenser so that they would be taken in a fixed order. The tracer pills were placed in a random order known only to the doctors.

The patients reported any time they noticed red urine. Researchers found whether reports of red urine occurred within 12 hours of when they had scheduled a tracer pill. The patients did not know which pills contained the tracer medicine; they could not taste or see the difference. Thus, their report could be correct only if they took their pills on time and observed the red urine.

Figure 24-2 shows the results of observations

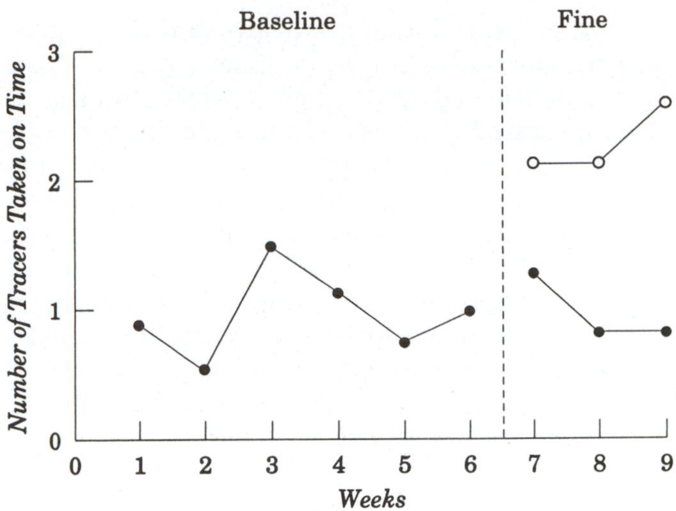

Figure 24-2. The number of pills taken at the prescribed time. The filled circles represent patients operating with no special consequences. The open circles represent patients who were fined $1 for failing to take at least two out of three tracer pills at the prescribed time. From "Behavioral Control of Medicine Compliance," by L. H. Epstein and B. J. Masek, *Journal of Applied Behavior Analysis,* 1978, *11,* 1–9. Copyright 1978 by the Society for the Experimental Analysis of Behavior, Inc. Used by permission.

during baseline. The patients took about 33% of their three tracer pills at the correct time. The doctors then required half of the patients to pay $1 if they did not take at least two of the three tracer pills. The patients who had to pay the fine started taking about 70% of their pills on time. This rose to 90%. The other patients, who did not have to pay the fine, continued at baseline level.

8. In this case, a correct report of red urine prevented the doctors from levying a fine of $1. The procedure increased the rate of correct reports from 33% to 90%. Therefore, you would label the event of a fine as a negative ______________________.

Note

Note #1

Some behavior analysts argue that the distinction between positive and negative reinforcement is often impossible to make objectively (Michael, 1975). For example, suppose a teacher lets kids play if they stay in their seats for 15 minutes

(Osborne, 1969). You might argue that this is positive reinforcement for staying seated. But it also might be viewed as negative reinforcement. If staying seated is aversive, then playing could be viewed as terminating an aversive situation (Iwata, 1987). Michael also provides an interesting description of the history of the distinction between positive and negative reinforcement and suggests that it be abandoned. Behavior analysis continues to make the distinction. But if you sometimes have a problem figuring out whether an event is a positive or a negative reinforcer, be assured you are not alone.

Helpful Hints

Helpful Hint #1

The key to discriminating between escape and avoidance is whether the negative reinforcer is present when the response is made. To escape from an event means to get away from it. You can get away from an event by terminating contact with it. You might do so by stopping the event or by moving away from it. You can terminate an event only if it is present. Therefore, if your behavior terminates a negative reinforcer that is present when you make the response, you are making an escape response. If your behavior prevents a negative reinforcer that is not present, then you are making an avoidance response. You can tell whether a behavior is escape by asking: "Was the negative reinforcer present at the moment of responding?" If it was present and the person's response terminated it, then the behavior is escape. If it was not present, and the person's response prevented it, then the behavior is an avoidance response.

9. If a negative reinforcer is present at the moment of responding, and the person's response terminates it, then the behavior is escape. If it is not present at the moment of responding, and the person's response prevents it, then the behavior is a(n) ______________ response.

For example, the $1 fine had not been levied when the patient took the tracer pill. It was not present. The patient prevented the fine from occurring. Therefore, you would label the behavior as avoidance.

10. Since the dental work was present when Jenny engaged in cooperative behavior, and her cooperative behavior terminated the dental work, you call the behavior a(n) ______________ response.
11. When the negative reinforcer is not present, and the person responds to prevent it from occurring, you call the behavior a(n) ______________ response. When the negative reinforcer is present, and the person responds to terminate it, you call the behavior a(n) ______________ response.

Helpful Hint #2

You do not have to name an event as a "negative" reinforcer. Behavior analysts refer to both positive and negative reinforcers with the single term *reinforcer.*

12. You do not have to name an event as a "negative" reinforcer. Behavior analysts refer to both positive and negative reinforcers with the single term ______________.

Helpful Hint #3

Sometimes you can view a procedure as either punishment or negative reinforcement. For example, if Mom spanks Ron for being dirty, you would normally label the spanking as punishment. That assumes that the spanking is for getting dirty. However, you might assume that the spanking is for Ron not washing. Ron can avoid such spankings by washing. On this assumption, you would label the spanking as negative reinforcement. This problem can arise whenever the person must make one of two responses. In such cases, be sure to answer the question as it is stated. Suppose the question is "What do you call spanking a child for getting dirty?" The correct answer is "punishment." Suppose the question is "What do you call spanking a child for failing to wash?" The correct answer is reinforcement (or negative reinforcement). Your answer will be considered incorrect if you do not answer the question as stated.

13. Suppose the question is "What do you call spanking a child for failing to wash?" The correct answer is ______________.
14. Even if you can't figure out anything else about the question, don't make the mistake

of calling a procedure that increases behavior *punishment* or a procedure that decreases behavior ________________.

Let's look at a situation involving punishment. For example, suppose Holly has a bad habit of nail-biting. Her mother decides to make her wear gloves for the rest of the day each time that she catches Holly biting her nails. After a few weeks of this treatment, Holly rarely bites her nails.

15. Because the rate of her nail-biting decreases, the procedure involved is ________________.

Now let's look at a situation that involves negative reinforcement. Stan does not like to clean up his room, but he loves to ask friends over to his house. Whenever his friends come over, they complain to Stan about how messy his room is. Consequently, Stan now cleans his room before inviting friends over to his house.

16. Because Stan's rate of cleaning his room has increased, the procedure involved is ________.

Helpful Hint #4

Be sure that all of the elements of negative reinforcement are described in any example. If one is missing, the procedure is "unknown."

17. For example, suppose that whenever your roommate leaves dirty dishes in the sink, you complain. If you are asked what procedure your complaining involves, you should answer ________________________.

Helpful Hint #5

To simplify this lesson, I will not ask you about escape or avoidance as a procedure. I will only ask about escape behavior or avoidance behavior. If I ask you to label a negative reinforcement procedure, you can be sure the answer will not be escape or avoidance.

18. For example, Baby Annie cries to get Mom's attention. Mom picks Baby Annie up, which terminates her crying. She picks up Baby Annie more and more often. What procedure is Annie using to increase Mom's rate of picking her up? ____________________________

Additional Readings

Ayllon, T., & Michael, J. (1959). The psychiatric nurse as a behavioral engineer. *Journal of the Experimental Analysis of Behavior, 2,* 323–334. Two psychiatric patients who refused to feed themselves, and thus required spoon feeding by a nurse, were exposed to avoidance. The researchers observed that both patients were extremely concerned about their appearance, so the nurse continued to feed both patients but now dropped a bit of food on the patients' clothing. The patients soon learned to feed themselves in order to avoid the spilled food.

Iwata, B.A. (1987). Negative reinforcement in applied behavior analysis: An emerging technology. *Journal of Applied Behavior Analysis, 20,* 361–378. This article discusses the current conceptualization of negative reinforcement. It discusses how undesirable behavior is learned through negative reinforcement and examines many methods for treating negatively reinforced behavior. Finally, it discusses using negative reinforcement as a treatment itself. Iwata suggests that behavior analysts examine any environment that they create to see whether it provides negative reinforcement for undesirable behavior.

Lovaas, O. I., Schaeffer, B., & Simmons, J. Q. (1965). Building social behavior in autistic children by use of electric shock. *Journal of Experimental Research in Personality, 1,* 99–109. This study deals with two children with autism. Psychiatric treatment had been totally ineffective in bringing them into contact with other individuals, so a program was started in which they were shocked for any self-stimulating behaviors. The shock was turned off if they approached the therapist (escape). This procedure rapidly increased the social behaviors of the children and provided a starting point for further behavioral therapy.

Reading Quiz

18. First, let's review the next tactic. Tactic #2 of the aversive control strategy is to increase desirable behavior through ________________ (negative, positive) reinforcement as a last resort.

84. When all else has failed to start someone emitting a behavior, you can use Tactic #2 of the aversive control strategy: increase desirable behavior through negative ________.

68. Review: Tactic #2 of the aversive control strategy is to increase desirable behavior through ________________ as a last resort.

78. The first goal of this section is to teach you about negative reinforcers. I will teach you about escape and avoidance a little later. Any event that is <u>terminated</u> or <u>prevented</u> by a behavior, and that causes the rate of that behavior to increase, is called a(n) ________ reinforcer. (Notice that I did not ask for the procedure.)

76. Suppose Mother picks up Liz when she is crying, and Liz's crying stops. Suppose Mother picks her up more often from then on. Notice that the termination of Liz's crying <u>follows</u> Mother's picking her up. Also, the rate at which Mother picks her up when she cries <u>increases</u>. Crying is an event called a(n) ________ for Mother's picking up Liz.

48. Review: Be careful to distinguish between <u>events</u> that function as negative reinforcers and the <u>procedure</u> of using those events. The procedure of using a negative reinforcer is called negative ________.

64. Review: Suppose Mother picks up Liz to <u>terminate</u> or <u>prevent</u> her crying. If Mother picks her up more often from then on, what procedure is Liz using without knowing it? ________ ________

65. Review: Suppose Mother picks up Liz to terminate or prevent her crying. If Mother picks her up more often from then on, what do you call the event of crying? ________

25. I will continue to follow the convention concerning events and procedures. Behavior analysts call an <u>event</u> that increases the rate of a behavior that <u>terminated</u> or <u>prevented</u> it a *negative* ________. They call the <u>procedure</u> that uses a negative reinforcer *negative* ________.

38. Key words in understanding the idea of negative reinforcer are <u>terminates</u> and <u>prevents</u>. A negative reinforcer is any event that increases the rate of a behavior that terminates or ________ that event.

1. <u>Terminates</u> and <u>prevents</u> are key words, because both of them help define a negative reinforcer. A negative reinforcer is any event that increases a behavior that ________ or prevents that event.

56. Review: If a behavior <u>terminates</u> or <u>prevents</u> an event, and the rate of that behavior does not change, you would label the event a(n) ________.

83. Three key words help define negative reinforcer. One of them is *increase*. Write the other two: ________ and ________.

49. Review: Both a positive reinforcer and a negative reinforcer have a similar effect. When either of them follows a behavior, it ________ the rate of that behavior.

4. A positive reinforcer is any event that follows a behavior and increases its rate. A negative reinforcer is any event that increases a behavior that ________ or ________ that event.

80. The next important goal is to teach you the relation between negative reinforcement and punishment. Should you ever label the procedure of negative reinforcement as the "punishment" for not making a response? ____

77. Suppose that when Joe does not turn off the TV during advertisements, he is exposed to loud advertisements he hates. Suppose his rate of not turning off the TV during advertisements decreases. Because his not turning off the TV during advertisements is followed by loud advertisements, and the rate of not turning it off decreases, you might incorrectly label the procedure as ________.

10. Behavior analysts describe Joe's situation differently. They describe it as a situation in which his behavior of turning off the TV can terminate an event—the loud ad. If the behavior increases in rate, they label the procedure as ________.

24. Here is the rule. Behavior analysts always define behavior as an act of doing something, never as the absence of doing something. This avoids the confusion of calling a procedure either punishment or negative reinforcement depending on your point of view. Thus, behavior analysts ______ (do, don't) consider not doing something as a behavior.

31. If Mom spanks Tommy when he fails to clean his room, and his rate of room cleaning doesn't change, what procedure has Mom used? ________

33. If Tommy's mother spanks him for forgetting to clean his room, and his rate of room clean-

ing increases, remember that "forgetting to clean" is the same as "not cleaning." Then you can rephrase the example as doing something. If Tommy cleans his room to prevent a spanking, you would call the procedure ______________.

32. If Tommy cleans his room to prevent a spanking, you would call the event of the spanking a negative ______________.
34. If Tommy's rate of swearing decreases because his mother spanks him when he does it, call the procedure ______________.
5. A punisher leads to a(n) ________ in the rate of a behavior; a negative reinforcer leads to a(n) ________ in the rate of a behavior.
39. Many psychologists equate the two terms *punisher* and ____________ *reinforcer;* behavior analysts do not.
81. The next major goal is to teach you about avoidance and escape. Behavior analysts distinguish between terminating the negative reinforcer and preventing it. They call the behavior in which the person terminates the negative reinforcer *escape*. They call the behavior in which the person prevents the negative reinforcer from occurring ____________.
11. Behavior analysts use *escape* and *avoid* consistently with everyday usage. We speak of avoiding something that has not yet happened. We avoid having to talk with Judith by crossing the street. Avoidance means ______________ (prevention, termination). We speak of escaping from something that is already present. We escape from a boring conversation. Escape means ____________ (prevention, termination).
88. You call the response to terminate a negative reinforcer an *escape* response. You call the response to prevent a negative reinforcer a(n) ______________ response.
26. If a behavior terminates a negative reinforcer, you call it a(n) ____________ response.
19. For escape behavior, a negative reinforcer is present in the environment until a response is made that ____________ (prevents, terminates) the negative reinforcer.
42. Mom yells at Nancy when she doesn't clean her room. Nancy can prevent being yelled at by just cleaning her room. Because it prevents being yelled at, cleaning her room is a(n) ______________ behavior.
41. Mom complains to Nancy until she washes the dishes. Nancy can terminate the complaints by washing the dishes. Because it terminates the complaining, washing the dishes is a(n) ____________ behavior.
12. Dad glares at Nancy when she wears her short shorts. Nancy can stop the glares by changing to regular shorts. Because it terminates the glaring, changing to regular shorts is a(n) ______________ behavior.
13. Dad grounds Nancy when she comes home late. Nancy can head off the grounding by coming home on time. Because it prevents the grounding, coming home on time is a(n) ______________ behavior.
15. Dad yells at Nancy when she grabs her food. Nancy doesn't get yelled at when she asks the person closest to the dish she wants to pass it. To figure out whether asking is avoidance or escape, you must decide whether it prevents or terminates the yelling. Because the yelling isn't going on when she asks, asking ______________ (prevents, terminates) the yelling. Therefore, asking is ______________ behavior.
14. Dad sulks when Nancy doesn't say hello to him when he comes home. Nancy can stop the sulking by saying hello. To figure out whether saying hello is avoidance or escape, you must decide whether it prevents or terminates the sulking. Because the sulking is going on when she says hello, saying hello ______________ (prevents, terminates) the sulking. Therefore, saying hello is ______________ behavior.
6. Allen and associates (1992) advised a dentist to tell uncooperative children that when they were acting calm, he would give them a brief break from the dental work. This resulted in an increase in cooperative behavior. If the children cooperated in order to terminate the dental treatment, their behavior would be called ______________ behavior.
47. Review: Azrin and Powell (1969) developed a pill dispenser that sounded a buzzer at the prescribed time for taking a pill. The buzzer could be turned off only by dispensing a pill. To decide whether this is avoidance or escape, figure out whether dispensing the pill terminates or avoids the buzzer. The behavior of dispensing the pill would be an example of a(n) ______________ behavior.
8. Avoidance is behavior in which a negative

reinforcer will be delivered in the future if a response is not made that ______________ (prevents, terminates) that stimulus from occurring.

23. Hegel and associates (1986) devised a treatment for severe burn victims. The patient could avoid being sent to a highly structured rehabilitation program by complying with a very flexible self-exercise program. Because stretching in the self-exercise program avoids the structured program, it is an example of ______________ behavior.
52. Review: Fichter and his colleagues (1976) nagged Joe anytime he failed to engage in acceptable social behavior. Because engaging in acceptable social behavior prevents being nagged, the acceptable social behavior would be a(n) ______________ behavior.
30. If Joe seeks to escape from a therapy unit that uses nagging to increase social skills, nagging as an event is a(n) ______________.
9. Azrin and his colleagues (1968) developed an apparatus that sounded a loud buzzer anytime a person slouched. Because maintaining good posture prevents the buzzer from sounding, it would be an example of a(n) ______________ behavior. If the person did slouch, he or she could turn the buzzer off only by adopting good posture. Because adopting good posture terminates the buzzer, it would be an example of a(n) ______________ behavior.
28. If clients and students attempt to prevent or terminate instruction, it is likely that the environment created by the teacher is providing ______________ reinforcement (Iwata, 1987).
62. Review: Remember, when a response prevents delivery of a negative reinforcer, you call the behavior ______________ behavior; when a response terminates delivery of a negative reinforcer, you call the behavior ______________ behavior.
37. Just a reminder. I will not ask you to tell the difference between escape and avoidance procedures—only escape and avoidance behaviors. Suppose Joe swats a mosquito to terminate its biting his arm. Suppose Joe's swatting increases. If I ask you what procedure nature is applying to Joe, which would be the letter of the correct answer: (a) escape or (b) negative reinforcement? ____
86. When faced with unpleasant and coercive behavior by others, we often inadvertently reinforce such behavior by giving in to it. If giving in to it terminates the coercive behavior, and our rate of giving in increases, then our giving in is what kind of behavior? ______________ behavior
35. If we allow Kim to control us by crying at bedtime until we comfort her, then our comforting behavior is ______________ behavior.
85. When attention by teachers reinforces disruptive behavior rather than punishing it, behavior analysts advise using attention to ______________ the rate of constructive behaviors.
40. Mental hospital staff could reduce patients' "crazy" behavior by using what behavioral procedure to increase desirable behavior? ______________
66. Review: Suppose Mr. Jones asks Sam, a person with retardation, to brush his teeth, and Sam then starts acting aggressive toward Mr. Jones. Mr. Jones might cancel the lesson on toothbrushing. Suppose Sam terminates acting aggressive, and the rate at which Mr. Jones lets Sam out of toothbrushing increases from then on. You would call Sam's aggressive action what kind of an event? A(n) ______________.
79. The most important rule in responding to coercive behavior is not to give in to it, because giving in will increase its rate through the behavioral procedure of ______________ ______________. Also important is to teach the person desirable ______________ that lets him or her obtain social reinforcement.
75. Suppose Mom withdraws her parenting attempt when Dave punishes it. If Dave's punishing behavior increases, we would say that Mom has unintentionally used the procedure of ______________.
45. Review: Any procedure or principle that applies to positive reinforcement also applies to ______________ reinforcement.
74. Review: When termination of a negative reinforcer no longer <u>follows</u> a behavior, and the rate of the behavior <u>decreases</u>, you label the procedure ______________.
58. Review: If one behavior terminates an event while other behaviors do not, and the relative rate of the first behavior increases, then what is the name of the total behavioral procedure? ______________

29. If each of a series of successive approximations to some target behavior terminates a negative reinforcer (while nonapproximations do not), the procedure is called ____________.
27. If an event is prevented by a varying number of responses, then the behavior is on what generic schedule of reinforcement? It is on a(n) ____________________ schedule.
73. Review: What intermittent schedule of negative reinforcement produces the highest rate of responding? ____________________
7. An intermittent schedule of negative reinforcement will reduce satiation and have greater resistance to ______________ (not satiation).
43. Review: "The termination or prevention of an event will be more effective if it occurs only when the behavior is emitted" is the principle of ______________.
82. The principle of immediacy states that in order to be most effective, a negative reinforcer should be terminated ____________________ after the behavior occurs.
2. "The larger the amount (or intensity) of a negative reinforcer, the more effective it will be" is the principle of ____________.
3. "The less often and less recently an event has been terminated or prevented, the more effective it will be" is the principle of ____________.
70. Review: The procedure being used when a behavior leads to the termination or prevention of an event in one situation, but the same behavior does not have that effect in another situation, is called ____________________.
53. Review: If a behavior is followed by the termination or prevention of an event, and the behavior is strengthened, the event is a(n) ____________________.
87. When the behavior terminates a negative reinforcer, call it a(n) _____________ response; when it prevents a negative reinforcer, call it a(n) _____________ response.
16. Epstein and Masek (1978) required that their patients pay a $1 fine if they failed to take their medication at the prescribed time. The patients' rate of taking their medication at the correct time increased to prevent the fine. The patients' behavior of taking the medication at the prescribed time would be called a(n) ____________________ response.
17. Epstein and Masek (1978) required their patients to pay a $1 fine if they did not take the medication at the prescribed time. The patients' rate of taking their medication at the prescribed time increased as a result. The $1 fine would be called a(n) ____________________.
20. From Helpful Hint #1: To decide whether a behavior is an escape behavior, ask, "Was the negative reinforcer present at the moment of responding?" If it was present, and the behavior terminated it, then the behavior is a(n) ____________________ behavior.
21. From Helpful Hint #1: When the negative reinforcer is not present, and the person responds to prevent it from occurring, you call the behavior a(n) ______________ response. When the negative reinforcer is present, and the person responds to terminate it, you call the behavior a(n) ______________ response.
36. If you decided that a procedure involves the termination or prevention of an event following a behavior, and the rate increases, you should label it as ____________________.
22. From Helpful Hint #3: If terminating or preventing an event that follows a behavior results in an <u>increase</u> in the behavior, the procedure involved is ____________________. When an event that follows a behavior results in a <u>decrease</u> in the behavior, the procedure involved is ______________.
71. Review: To use the aversive control strategy, (1) decrease undesirable behavior through punishment as a last resort, (2) increase desirable behavior through ____________________ as a last resort.
57. Review: If every fifth response is followed by the termination of a negative reinforcer, that behavior is on what schedule of intermittent reinforcement? ____________________
59. Review: If the rate of a behavior increases when it is followed by the termination of an event, the event is called a(n) ____________________.
50. Review: Do behavior analysts equate negative reinforcers and punishers? ______
61. Review: Positive reinforcers and negative reinforcers are both events that result in a(n) ______________ in the rate of a behavior.
54. Review: If a behavior terminates an event, and the rate of the behavior increases, the behavior is called a(n) ____________________ response.
72. Review: To use the aversive control strategy,

(1) decrease undesirable behavior through ______________ as a last resort; (2) increase desirable behavior through ______________ ______________ as a last resort.

55. Review: If a behavior prevents an event from occurring, and the rate of the behavior increases, the behavior is called a(n) __________ response.
60. Review: If you think that an example involves negative reinforcement, be sure to check to see whether the rate of the behavior increases. If the rate decreases, then the procedure _______ (can, can't) be negative reinforcement.
46. Review: Avoidance behavior is any behavior that ____________________ the occurrence of a negative reinforcer.
51. Review: Escape behavior is behavior that ____________________ a negative reinforcer.
67. Review: Suppose that every time a person emits a particular behavior, another person removes one of the first person's reinforcers. If the rate of that behavior decreases, what behavioral procedure is the second person using? ________________________
44. Review: A negative reinforcer is any event that is ____________ or ____________ by a behavior and that causes the rate of the behavior to increase.
69. Review: The second tactic of the aversive control strategy is to increase desirable behavior through ________________________ as a last resort.
63. Review: Sometimes students decide whether a procedure is punishment or negative reinforcement by looking only at the "unpleasant" event. If they think of it as a punisher, they label the procedure as punishment. For example, a fine can be used as a punisher. You fine someone for doing something. If doing so decreases the behavior, then the fine is a punisher. But a fine can also be used as a negative reinforcer. If you fine someone for not emitting a behavior, and the rate of the behavior increases, what procedure are you using? ______________________

Examples

1. When 4-year-old Mary got out of bed on a cold morning, she "froze" her feet. One morning she put on her slippers when her feet felt a cold floor. Putting on her slippers stopped her feet from feeling the cold floor. Because Mary did not put on her slippers before feeling the cold but only after feeling the cold, you would say that Mary ______________ (prevented, terminated) the cold feeling by putting on her slippers. From then on, she put on her slippers any morning that her feet felt a cold floor. Mary's behavior of putting on slippers when she felt a cold floor ____________ in rate after that first time. Because Mary terminated the cold feeling by putting on the slippers, and because Mary's rate of putting on the slippers increased in frequency, the event of feeling the cold floor would be classified as a(n) ________ ______________. Remember, you don't have to write both words.

2. One day Mary put on her slippers before she put her feet on the floor. On that day, the coldness never reached her feet. From that day on, Mary put on her slippers before getting out of bed. Because she put her slippers on before her feet ever felt cold, she ______________ (prevented, terminated) the cold feeling. The rate of Mary's putting on the slippers before getting out of bed __________. Therefore, the procedure she was reacting to is called ____________________.

3. The residents of Corbin Hall used to complain about the meals all the time. They then imposed a fine on anyone who complained about the food. Needless to say, you rarely hear any complaints about the food anymore. You might not be sure whether the fining procedure is negative reinforcement or punishment. Even if you think you know, check your guess by asking if the procedure increases or decreases the behavior. In this case, imposing a fine decreases complaining. Therefore, the fine is an example of what behavioral procedure? ________________

4. Hamm and Carey had been dating for quite a while. But Hamm had a bad habit. Somehow he would just lose track of time when talking with one of his friends and, as a result, would show up late for his date with Carey. When Hamm was late, Carey looked sad. When Hamm was on time, Carey looked happy. By showing up on time, Hamm could keep Carey from looking sad. Soon Hamm noticed the difference in Carey's look when he was on time and when he was late, so he started showing up on time. By showing up on time, Carey's looking sad was ________________ (prevented, terminated). The rate of Hamm's showing up on time

________________. Carey's sad look is an event called a(n) ____________________.

5. Sally never did her homework for Ms. Mann's social studies class, so Ms. Mann started keeping Sally after class every day she failed to do her homework. Of course, Sally could get out of having to stay after school by simply doing her homework. After two months, Sally still never did her homework. Sally could ________________ (terminate, prevent) being kept after school by doing her homework. The rate of Sally's doing her homework during the two months that Ms. Mann tried keeping her after school ________________ (decreased, increased, stayed the same). What procedure did Ms. Mann use with Sally? ____________________

6. Gene had a beautiful Siamese cat that would run around the apartment knocking over furniture and climbing up curtains. Gene started putting his cat in the basement to keep him out of trouble. After several weeks, the cat started to howl and cry when locked in the basement. Gene found that he could stop the cat's howling by letting him out of the basement. Gene now lets the cat out of the basement as soon as the cat howls. By letting the cat out of the basement as soon as he howls, Gene ____________ (prevents, terminates) the howling. The rate at which Gene let the cat out of the basement, after discovering that this would stop the howling, ____________. The event "stopping the howling" is an example of a(n) ________________. Gene's behavior of letting the cat out of the basement is called a(n) ____________ response. (Is the howling present when Gene lets the cat out of the basement?)

7. Ken wasn't doing well in sixth-grade math. When his mother and father had their regular conferences with the teacher, she told them that Ken handed in less than half of his homework assignments. Ken's parents started sending him to bed early as a "punishment" when he didn't do his homework. Ken handed in all of his homework assignments from then on. Ken could __________ (prevent, terminate) his parents from sending him to bed early by handing in his homework. Ken's behavior of doing his homework would be classified as ______________ behavior. What behavioral procedure produced Ken's increased rate of doing his homework? ________________

8. Eight-year-old Dan had trouble pronouncing "refrigerator." His parents always said "No, Dan, that wrong!" when he said it incorrectly. After a while, Dan got so he always pronounced "refrigerator" correctly. By pronouncing "refrigerator" correctly the first time, Dan could __________ (prevent, terminate) his parent's "No." Because telling him "No" increased the rate of correct pronunciation by Dan, his parents used what procedure? __________________. Dan's correct pronunciation of "refrigerator" is an example of what type of behavior? ____________

9. Jerry didn't do his homework often enough in his social studies class. His teacher, Mr. Johnson, decided to embarrass Jerry every day until he started to do his homework. The first day after this change in procedure, he called on Jerry first for every question on the assignment. Naturally, Jerry didn't know the answers to any of them. Mr. Johnson repeated the same pattern every day for a week. Jerry got called on an average of 10 to 15 times each day, and he never had the correct answer. Finally, Jerry did his homework, so the teacher didn't ask him any questions. From then on, Jerry usually did his homework. On the few days that he didn't, the teacher again asked him many questions in class. The increase in Jerry's homework behavior is due to the teacher's use of what behavioral procedure? ________________________

10. The students at a big Midwestern university were angry that their administration had put off hiring more female faculty members while a special committee was "studying the problem." They decided to sit in the president's office until he changed his mind. They sat there for three days, but the president still would not agree to hire any female faculty members right away. Finally, they gave up and went home. What behavioral procedure did the students use? ____________

11. Review: The children on the corner frequently got into arguments with Mr. Ryker, the candy store owner. Mr. Ryker yelled that they were killing his business by standing there and bothering people who walked by. The children replied that they were among his best customers, and they had a right to stay there. One day, Mr. Ryker got angrier than usual. In spite of his outburst, the children remained on the corner, so Mr. Ryker called the police. The children left before the police arrived, but they were angry. They threw a rock through one of his windows. Mr. Ryker never called the police again. What procedure did the children use to decrease Mr. Ryker's police-calling behavior? ____________

12. Review: The cooperative dorm had a problem getting its members to do the work needed to keep the house going. To solve the problem, the membership voted to fine any members who didn't do their share of the work during a given week. After this rule was instituted, everyone started doing a fair share of the work. Because working prevented a fine, and the rate of work increased, what procedure is fining members who don't do their share? ____________________

13. Review: When Dad says "Stop it" to Tommy for pestering him, Tommy stops immediately. Dad's "Stop it" follows the pestering and decreases it. It is a punisher. Dad is likely to say "Stop it" more often in the future because it terminates the pestering. Dad's saying "Stop it" is an example of ____________________ behavior.

14. Review: In some courses, if students don't score high enough on the daily quiz, they must take it over again. If this procedure gets the student to work hard to pass the quiz on the first try, the quiz repetition would be an example of what procedure? ____________________

15. Review: Mrs. Marlowe often reprimanded Ken for not doing his daily chores, but she usually waited many hours to give her reprimand. Ken's rate of doing his daily chores did not increase. The reprimand probably had little effect because it did not occur ____________ after his failure to respond.

16. Review: Dave didn't like waiting for Carol to come home at dinnertime when she had not called him. Finally, one day when she came home late without calling, he explained his feelings to her. From then on, Carol prevented Dave's complaint by calling when she was going to be late. Carol's calling behavior would be called ____________________ behavior.

17. Review: Jane hated it when Bob put his cigarette out on his dinner plate. Finally, she expressed her feelings to him. He usually did not put his cigarette out that way after that, and when he did, Jane again expressed her dislike for the practice. Eventually, Bob completely stopped doing it. Because Jane's expressions followed Bob's putting his cigarette out on his plate, and his rate decreased, what behavioral procedure did Jane use? ____________________

18. Review: People learn to use negative reinforcement and punishment procedures more rapidly and more easily than they learn to use reinforcement procedures. When a person uses either negative reinforcement or punishment, the change in another person's behavior is likely to occur immediately. When a person uses reinforcement techniques, he or she reinforces a behavior that has already happened and that may not be appropriate again for a long time. Thus, any change resulting from the reinforcement can't be seen until that later time. Which principle of reinforcer effectiveness suggests that such a long delay may radically reduce the reinforcing effectiveness of any resulting behavioral change? ____________________

19. Review: Kip had the bad habit of talking in the weekly dorm meetings without putting up his hand. Marianne, the chairperson of the meeting, finally started yelling at him each time he failed to raise his hand. Kip soon started to raise his hand. Kip's behavior of raising his hand would be called ____________ behavior.

20. Review: Todd was a very careful driver. He looked carefully at side streets, parked cars, and moving cars to prevent being hit; he stopped at traffic lights and stop signs to prevent accidents. He concluded that most of his driving should be classified as ____________ behavior.

LESSON

25 Review of Aversive Control

This unit introduced aversive control. Aversive control involves either withdrawing a reinforcer or delivering a punisher. Most people report "not liking" aversive control. Thus aversive control is sharply different from positive reinforcement control. Aversive control and reinforcement control occur within four types of contingencies.

Four Types of Contingencies

Figure 25-1 reviews the four types of contingencies you have learned in this book. Behavior analysts call the procedure in which an event follows and increases a behavior *reinforcement*. They call it *positive* reinforcement if it presents a stimulus, and *negative* reinforcement if it withdraws a stimulus. Both procedures are reinforcement, because the event follows and increases a behavior. Behavior analysts call the procedure in which an event follows and decreases a behavior *punishment*. It is punishment by contingent stimulation if it presents a stimulus, and punishment by contingent withdrawal if it withdraws a stimulus. Both procedures are punishment, because the event follows and decreases a behavior. Thus, the distinction between punishment and reinforcement is whether the behavior decreases or increases. Only positive reinforcement is not a form of aversive control.

Rate	*Presentation*	*Withdrawal*
Increase	Positive Reinforcement	Negative Reinforcement
Decrease	Punishment (contingent stimulation)	Punishment (contingent withdrawal)

Figure 25-1. Procedures for delivering contingent stimuli.

The Aversive Control Strategy

This unit described each of the aversive contingencies, which are built into our interactions with the physical world. People often use aversive contingencies in everyday life. Their use leads to immediate and obvious results and seems to be very reinforcing. Behavior analysts use them only as a last resort, when they can't get positive reinforcement to work. Each contingency defines a technique for using the aversive control strategy.

Tactic #1 in using the aversive control strategy is to decrease undesirable behavior through punishment as a last resort. One procedure is to use punishment by contingent stimulation. This involves delivering an event that reduces the rate of a behavior that it follows. Primary punishers include spanking, restraint, and shock. Behavior analysts use these events only as a last resort for dangerous behaviors that they can't control through positive reinforcement. Conditioned punishers include reprimands and feedback.

Another procedure is to use punishment by contingent withdrawal. This involves withdrawing an event so that the rate of the behavior it follows is reduced. Good examples include fines, suspension of privileges, and time out—mild forms of punishment that are widely acceptable.

Tactic #2 in using the aversive control strategy is to increase desirable behavior through negative reinforcement as a last resort. This involves a response that terminates or prevents an event and that increases the rate of the response. This procedure is often used to get someone to start behaving when we don't know how to get positive procedures to work. It may then be stopped and positive reinforcement applied to the behavior.

Behavior analysts usually view all these procedures as a last resort.

Reducing the Need for Aversive Control

Early behavior analysts saw the awesome power of positive reinforcement. Even before they applied it to human problems, they imagined its potential for helping people and predicted that its use would make it possible to abandon aversive control. They foresaw a world in which the science of human behavior could greatly reduce human suffering.

You realize by now that positive reinforcement is the most important discovery of behavior analysis. Many examples of positive reinforcement have given you a good idea of the enormous range of behaviors influenced by positive reinforcement. This range includes obvious behavior like football, subtle behavior like looking, internal behavior like muscle tension, and private behavior like pain. It includes both normal and abnormal behavior, both manual and cognitive behavior.

You have read about the effect of positive reinforcement on the behaviors of normal people in everyday situations. These behaviors include creating, relaxing, laboring, learning, talking, taking care of your health, and running a business. I have shown how these behaviors often start and continue because they lead to reinforcement. When they do not occur at an optimal rate, I have tried to show you how they can often be improved through positive reinforcement. We can help people by teaching them how to get more positive reinforcement, and by improving their environment.

You have read about the effect of the misuse of positive reinforcement that causes abnormal behaviors such as self-injury, acting crazy, aggression, complaining, crying, and even hallucinating. I have shown how these behaviors are often the result of misuses of reinforcement. The first step in eliminating them is to help the person learn more appropriate behaviors that produce reinforcement. But eliminating them entirely usually requires removing the misplaced reinforcement. Sometimes behavior analysts use aversive procedures to ensure elimination.

Applied behavior analysts often use positive reinforcement to change these behaviors, but they sometimes fail to find ways to change disruptive and dangerous behavior with positive reinforcement alone. This leads them to use primary punishment on such problems as self-injury and aggression. It leads them to use milder punishment on a wide range of behaviors—often temporarily, and often in conjunction with positive reinforcement. Many behavior analysts view such uses of aversive control as failures of the science (Sidman, 1989). Other behavior analysts view them as practical solutions to heartwrenching problems (Baer, 1970).

A new approach began to emerge in the 1980s (Iwata et al., 1982). In many ways it was a return to the vision of the early behavior analysts. Applied behavior analysts developed tools that have greatly reduced the failures that led to the use of aversive control. They call the key tool *functional analysis*.

Functional Analysis of Undesirable Behavior

Undesirable behavior often permits a person to avoid or escape from a situation. We saw that with Jenny's disruptive behavior: By pulling away and crying, she could stop the dentist from working on her teeth. Likewise, the burn victims, by not stretching, could avoid the pain of stretching the burned areas. Perhaps we saw it with the slouchers, who could avoid the effort of standing up straight by slouching. In all cases, the undesirable behavior avoided or escaped some aversive stimulus. Notice that these behaviors are not irrational or "crazy." They produce a reduction in immediate pain or discomfort.

Although these undesirable behaviors may make sense, they are not necessarily optimal behaviors. These people all stood to lose some important positive reinforcers by making their responses. Jenny would not get clean, pain-free teeth. The burn victims would not regain the ability to move freely. The slouchers would not have a smoothly functioning back free of pain. Helping all of these people learn more useful behaviors permitted them to gain additional reinforcers.

Some undesirable behaviors seem to make sense, but do all of them? Self-injury, refusing to eat, and aggression don't seem to make sense. One research team has analyzed the causes of self-injury (Iwata et al., 1994). The team found that misused positive social attention caused 26% of the cases. These cases stem from the misuse of positive reinforcement by parents and other caregivers. They may represent cases where the caregivers did not give attention except when the person engaged in SIB. Once we know that this is the source of a person's self-injury, we can use positive reinforcement to modify it. The new caregiver must withhold attention for self-injury and give it instead for more desirable behaviors. The person still gets the attention, but in the process learns new and more functional behaviors.

The team found that escape from task or other demands caused 38% of the cases. These cases stem from caregivers giving in to obnoxious behaviors, as in the case of Jenny, who was so disruptive that previous dentists had let her escape from dental treatment. In these cases, something about the caregiver's behavior is aversive to the person. Perhaps the caregiver treats him or her roughly. Perhaps the caregiver insists on teaching something that is too hard for the person. Other than self-injury, he or she has no way to stop the caregiver's behavior. Once we know that this is the source of self-injury, we can reduce the demands made by the caregivers. We can also teach the person more acceptable ways to stop the caregiver's behavior (Carr & Durand, 1985; Durand & Carr, 1992). People with moderate retardation may be able to learn a phrase such as "Please stop" or "I would like a rest." If they have severe retardation, they may learn to press a button that signals the caregiver to give them a rest. They get the same rest they got with their obnoxious behaviors, but they learn a more acceptable way to get it.

The team found that sensory stimulation caused 26% of the cases. These cases are perhaps the hardest to understand intuitively. They represent people who found the pain, sound, or other sensation involved in self-injury to be reinforcing. We don't know why this would be so. Perhaps they are so totally lacking in ways to produce reinforcers that this is the best they can do. However, once we know that this is the source of the self-injury, we can devise ways to eliminate the sensory reinforcement. You read about a case in which the person was required to wear mittens (Luiselli, 1991). This cushioned blows enough to make them no longer reinforcing. Such methods might be combined with teaching the person some simple skills with which to produce other reinforcers. The person still gets some reinforcement, but learns some useful skills to get it.

The kinds of analysis outlined above permit individualized treatment for each person. It modifies the specific aspect of the environment that caused the abnormal behavior in the first place. This approach produces many more successes. Iwata's team succeeded with about 85% of the cases. They resorted to punishment in the form of spraying a water mist in only seven cases, treating the rest by positive reinforcement, extinction or differential reinforcement. This marks a major change for applied behavior analysis. It is not only a shift away from having to use aversive control because nothing else works; it is also a movement toward finding ways to make positive reinforcement work. It is a step toward the dream of a world without coercion envisioned by the founders of behavior analysis.

Reducing the Use of Aversive Control

Does not behavior analysis "clearly stand out among other sciences by frequently claiming that wars can be prevented, prisoners can be rehabilitated, children can be taught... without resort to aversive contingencies? A few of these claims have been documented, but there is much to be learned, demonstrated, and applied. How will we acquire that learning? We will use every encounter with an aversive contingency... to learn more about the behavior in question, its controlling events, and ways in which reinforcement and extinction schedules may be used to bring about the behavioral displacement. Through these experiences, we may not only solve the immediate problem, but also acquire the skills necessary to deal with the really tough cases in our culture—the drug dealers, the murderers" (Iwata, 1988: p. 151).

1. Iwata claims that behavior analysis can use reinforcement and extinction instead of ______________ control.

Freedom

Skinner argues that the word *freedom* usually refers to the absence of aversive control. When we behave under the influence of positive rein-

Figure 25-2. Brian Iwata developed SIBIS, an effective method for reducing self-injury based on aversive control. At the same time, he pioneered functional analysis to increase the effectiveness of positive reinforcement to control self-injury. His work illustrates the way in which behavior analysis can pursue its founders' dream of a world whose people do not rely on aversive control.

forcement, we usually call ourselves free. We are not free from environmental influence, but simply from coercive influence. When our behavior leads to positive reinforcement, we act in our own interest. We behave because doing so helps us attain our own goals. The history of civilization has in many ways been the history of our struggle to throw off coercive control, whether it be from the king, the church, or the paternalistic family. "Movements for freedom... are in essence escape behaviors" (Richelle, 1993).

Behavior analysts see their science as providing the understanding and the tools by which civilization can increase the speed and sureness of its march toward a society based on positive reinforcement.

Glossary

The definitions of all terms introduced in this unit of the book are presented below. You can review the unit and prepare for your exam by testing yourself on the definitions and related facts presented for each term. You might use a piece of paper as a mask and leave only the term exposed; see if you can formulate a reasonable definition and remember other facts about that term. Then move the mask and check on yourself.

The **aversive control strategy** is to use aversive control if positive control fails. This strategy consists of two tactics:
1. Decrease undesirable behavior through punishment as a last resort.
2. Increase desirable behavior through negative reinforcement as a last resort.

Avoidance is any behavior that prevents a negative reinforcer from occurring.

A **conditioned punisher** is one that loses its effectiveness through unpaired presentations.

A **discriminative stimulus for punishment** (SP) is any stimulus that is associated with the punishment of a particular behavior.

Escape is any behavior that terminates a negative reinforcer.

A **generalized punisher** is any conditioned punisher that is associated with many other punishers.

A **negative reinforcer** is any event that, when terminated or prevented by a behavior, increases the rate of that behavior.
- A negative reinforcer is simply another form of reinforcer and thus can be used in shaping, discrimination training, and conditioned reinforcement.
- Both positive and negative reinforcers increase the rate of a behavior, but a positive reinforcer is an event that is delivered, whereas a negative reinforcer is an event that is terminated or prevented.

Negative reinforcement is the procedure of following a behavior with a negative reinforcer.

- Any procedure or principle that applies to positive reinforcement may also be applied to negative reinforcement.

A **primary punisher** is any punisher that loses its effectiveness only through satiation (adaptation). Primary punishers are usually basic physical events such as hitting, shock, and pinching.

A **punisher** is any event that follows a response and decreases the rate of that behavior. This definition of a punisher also applies to the withdrawal of an event following a behavior such that the rate of the behavior decreases—for instance, fining people or "timing them out" of a reinforcing activity.

Punishment is the procedure in which a punisher is administered contingent on an undesired behavior.

- Punishment by contingent stimulation involves delivery of a punisher, producing a decrease in the rate of the behavior.
- Punishment by contingent withdrawal involves withdrawal of a reinforcing event, producing a decrease in the rate of the behavior.
- When a person is removed from a reinforcing activity, that form of punishment by contingent withdrawal is called time out.

Practice Review

The following material has questions on every concept studied in Unit Four, as well as review questions from all prior units. By answering the questions and checking your answers, you can prepare yourself for the Review Exam, which will contain questions from all four units.

55. If a behavior analyst reinforces a particular behavior, the analyst becomes associated with reinforcement for that behavior. The behavior analyst then becomes a stimulus that influences that behavior. The name of that kind of stimulus is a(n) ________________ for that behavior.

162. The use of punishment and negative reinforcement to control behavior is known as ________________ control.

121. Review: If a response prevents a negative reinforcer, it is termed a(n) ________________ response.

6. A primary reinforcer is one that is weakened only temporarily by ________________.

126. Review: Tom frequently looks in his rearview mirror so that he won't have an accident. If having an accident is a negative reinforcer, then looking in his rearview mirror is an example of a(n) ________________ behavior.

64. If a teacher shows students how to do something, observes to see whether they do it the same way, and then reinforces them, we say that the teacher is using the method of ________________ training.

123. Review: If you stop delivering a reinforcer for an unrelated behavior whenever the person makes an undesirable response, and the rate of the undesirable behavior decreases, you are using what procedure? ________________. If you stop delivering a reinforcer following an undesirable response, and the rate decreases, you are using what procedure? ________________.

80. Instructional training involves explaining to someone how to do something. That explanation is called a(n) ________________ description.

139. The attention that one person pays to another is frequently associated with many other reinforcers. What kind of conditioned reinforcer is it? A(n) ________________ reinforcer

136. Tactic #1 in using the aversive control strategy is to decrease undesirable behavior through ________________ as a last resort.

61. If a reinforcer is produced by the first response that occurs after a fixed period of time, we say that it is being reinforced according to a(n) ________________ schedule.

13. A stimulus associated with reinforcement for a particular response is called a(n) ________________.

18. A stimulus/response chain is a sequence of responses in which the occurrence of one response serves as the ________________ for the next response. (Note carefully the order of events implied by this question.)

177. What principle of effective reinforcement is determined by asking, "Was the amount of the event used worthwhile?" The principle of ________________

1. A conditioned reinforcer is one that is weak-

ened permanently by ________ presentations.

100. People will continue to imitate the behavior of someone else only if they are ________ for doing so.

148. The method of observation based on dividing the observational period into many continuous intervals, and observing during each interval whether the behavior occurs, is called ________ recording.

133. Suppose Brad is praised for saying "9" when asked, "What is the sum of 5+4?" but ignored for saying anything else. Suppose he is praised for saying "12" when asked, "What is the sum of 8+4?" but ignored for saying anything else. Behavior analysts call this complex procedure ________ ________.

88. Mr. Cosgrove explained to his eighth-graders exactly how to find the square of a number. He then asked them to find the square of the number. He praised each student who got the right answer. What behavioral procedure was he using? ________ training

140. The baseline is a record of a behavior before the ________ condition.

87. Mr. Cosgrove displayed on the blackboard how to find the square of a number. He then erased his example and asked his students to find the square of that same number. He examined each student's work and praised him or her if it was correct. What behavioral procedure did he use? ________ training

151. The person who is consistently nice to other people may be reinforced by the smile of the other person. If the smile is usually associated with many other reinforcers from that other person, it would be an example of what type of reinforcer? ________ reinforcer

112. Review: A punisher is defined as any event that (1) ________ a response and (2) ________ the rate of that response.

62. If a response is reinforced after a fixed number of occurrences, this procedure is an example of a(n) ________ schedule.

26. Any conditioned reinforcer that is paired with many backup reinforcers is called a(n) ________ reinforcer.

119. Review: Barb used to throw tantrums often. Then Mom started making her go to her room for a half hour when she threw a tantrum. Her rate of throwing tantrums decreased. What procedure did Mom use to decrease Barb's rate of throwing tantrums? ________

57. If a behavior occurs more frequently in the presence of one stimulus and less frequently in the presence of another stimulus, we call it ________ behavior.

180. When civil rights groups measure the number of shoppers at a store prior to undertaking a boycott, the resulting data are called a(n) ________.

159. The supervisor checked on Jerry every 30 minutes. If Jerry was working at that time, the supervisor praised him. What schedule was Jerry on? A(n) ________ schedule

56. If a behavior analyst reinforces someone for chewing gum but not for smoking cigarettes, and if the person's rate of chewing gum increases, the behavior analyst would be using what procedure? ________

167. To decide whether the principle of immediacy was followed, ask, "Was the event delivered within a(n) ________ of the behavior (or while it was still occurring)?"

72. If Tommy has learned to call the funny little car a "beetle" but not the long sleek car, we say that the funny little car exerts ________ ________ over his behavior of calling it a "beetle."

120. Review: Husbands and wives often point out one another's thoughtless acts right after they occur. If pointing them out decreases the rate of thoughtless acts, it is an example of what behavioral procedure? ________

130. Shaping involves applying the procedure of ________ to a series of successive ________ to some target behavior.

70. If people have not received a particular reinforcer for a while, we say that they are ________ with respect to that reinforcer.

175. Two kinds of experimental designs that rule out both kinds of alternative explanations are the ________ design and the ________ design.

83. Larry wondered if Kevin's stuttering was decreasing, so he recorded each time Kevin

emitted a stuttered word in his presence. What method of direct observation was he using? ________________ recording

16. A stimulus event that occurs prior to a response and increases the frequency of that response is called a(n) ________________.
A stimulus event that occurs after a response and increases the frequency of that response is called a(n) ______________.

149. The more immediate the delivery of an event after the occurrence of the desired behavior, the more effective the reinforcer, according to the principle of ____________.

12. A snerkel is a card that can be exchanged for a wide range of privileges in the frat. A reinforcer of this type is effective because at least one of the backup reinforcers is likely to be an effective reinforcer at any given time due to what principle? __________

68. If one behavior is reinforced while another is extinguished in the presence of one stimulus, and if the first behavior is extinguished while the second is reinforced in the presence of a second stimulus, we have decided to label this complex procedure ____________ ________________.

158. The single-subject design in which a behavior is observed during baseline and then during treatment is called a(n) ______________ design.

71. If delivery of the reinforcer for a behavior is stopped, and the rate of that behavior decreases, this procedure is called ___________.

49. Fred and Charlie observed Murray's study behavior using the same definition but on different days. Is their agreement a measure of the reliability of their observations? _________

48. Frank argued long and loud against the idea that only coop members should be allowed to buy at reduced prices. If no one paid any attention to him, it is likely that this verbal behavior (arguing) would decrease. What procedure would be involved? ______________

7. A procedure for gradually changing a behavior is called ______________.

89. Mr. Jackson observed five students to determine whether they were studying. He first observed Diane for 12 seconds, then shifted to Ken and observed him for 12 seconds, and so on for the other three students. He started over again with Diane after having observed the others. What method of observation is he using to observe Diane? _________ ____________ recording

98. Paul praised Kim every time she acted assertively with others. Kim's rate of acting assertively did not change. What behavioral procedure did Paul use? _____________

45. Extinction involves stopping the delivery of a reinforcer for a behavior and observing a(n) ________________ in the rate of that behavior.

116. Review: Any response that terminates a negative reinforcer is called a(n) ____________ response.

182. When you arrange to deliver an event after each instance of a behavior, thereby increasing the rate of behavior, you refer to the procedure as ________________ and the event as a(n) ________________.

5. A positive reinforcer has to have two characteristics: It must be timed so that it ______________ a behavior, and it must __________ the frequency of the behavior.

105. Reinforcing a behavior in the presence of one stimulus and extinguishing that same behavior in the presence of another stimulus is called ________________.

173. Tom was always griping about the food at the frat. When he griped, people argued with him. The more they argued, the more he griped. What behavioral procedure did the other members use to increase his rate of griping? ___________

114. Review: An escape response is any response that __________ a negative reinforcer.

122. Review: If a stimulus signals the contingent withdrawal of a reinforcer, that stimulus is called a(n) ________________.

74. If Tommy is praised for calling the funny little car a "beetle" but not for calling other cars "beetles," what behavioral procedure is being used? ______________

20. An experimental design in which two behaviors are observed over different-length baselines prior to the introduction of the treatment is called a(n) ____________ design.

58. If a person is reinforced after varying numbers of responses, what schedule of reinforcement is being used? ____________

97. Outcome recording involves observing some relatively lasting ______________ of the response.

143. The differential reinforcement of a series of successive approximations to some target behavior is called ________________.

51. Generalization training consists of reinforcing a behavior in each of a series of situations until it ________________ to other members of that same stimulus class.

145. The funny-shaped little car is not a plane. Therefore, for the response "plane," it would be called a(n) ________.

137. Tactic #2 in using the aversive control strategy is to increase desirable behavior through ________________ reinforcement as a last resort.

25. Any behavior that prevents a negative reinforcer is called a(n) ____________ behavior.

38. Differential reinforcement is a procedure in which one response is ____________ and other responses are ________________.

86. May studied the child-rearing practices of college graduates by asking a random sample of 25 of them to answer such questions as "How many times last week did you tell your child to finish the rest of the food on his or her plate?" Since the parents did not record the observations when they occurred, the approach they used is an example of ________ ________ observation.

172. Tom's goal was to teach Mona how to play a particular chord on the guitar, step by step. He first praised her only when she held the guitar correctly, next only when she strummed it correctly, and finally only when she strummed a particular chord. Tom's goal of Mona playing a particular chord is called the ________ ______________ that he was trying to teach.

52. Henry helped Carol move by going to her old place with her, loading up his pickup truck, and taking the stuff to her new place. After each load, Carol gave him a beer. He loved beer but could never afford it himself. Even though it took three trips to move all her stuff, he didn't tire of drinking beer she offered. What principle of effective reinforcement, if any, did Carol neglect? ____________

14. A stimulus associated with extinction for a particular response is called a(n) ____________.

164. Time sample recording involves observing whether or not a behavior occurs during each of a series of ________________________ intervals.

40. Dr. Gold observed Maria's assertiveness prior to assertiveness training and then during the training. What experimental design was he using? ____________

63. If a response is reinforced every time it occurs, it is said to be on what generic schedule? A(n) ________________ schedule of reinforcement

95. Name four principles of effective reinforcement: ________________, ________________, ________________, and ________________.

132. Suppose Bob Behaviorist found that any time Ruby wasn't shocked for taking a cigarette, she smoked at her normal rate. This discovery would indicate that the effect of the shock on her rate of smoking did not ____________ to situations in which she wasn't shocked.

154. The principle of effective reinforcement that states, "The more deprived a person is with respect to the event, the more effective it will be," is called the principle of ____________.

44. Event recording involves recording each ________________ of a behavior.

73. If Tommy has learned to call the funny-shaped little car a "beetle" but not other cars, we would call his behavior of calling it a "beetle" ________________ behavior.

109. Reliability is a measure of the ____________ between two independent observers.

60. If a reinforcer is delivered to people for their first response after differing periods of time, they are said to be on what specific schedule? A(n) ________________________ schedule

152. The person who was to be the main observer for the experiment and Mary's teacher observed Mary's nearness to other children during the first day of observations. The following are their results for 10 observations (where F stands for further than two feet, and N stands for nearness).

Teacher:	F	F	N	F	F	F	F	N	F
Another:	F	F	F	F	F	F	N	N	F

Compute reliability: ____________ percent. Is the reliability of these observations acceptable? ____________

82. Jerry was a pretty good fisherman. He managed to hook the first fish that nibbled his bait, the fifth fish, and the third fish. What specific schedule of reinforcement is his fishing on? A(n) ________________ schedule

23. An S-delta is a stimulus that is associated

with the ______________ of a particular response.

50. Fred felt that it was important to determine whether the behaviors that he was observing and calling "studying" would be regarded by others as studying. He had a panel of individuals observe several students who were studying according to his definition and several who were not to see if the panel would agree with his definition. Fred was attempting to determine the ______________ of his definition of studying.

168. To decide whether the public areas of a building are clean enough, you might make up a checklist of things that should be clean (floors, ashtrays, trash baskets, and so on) and check once a day to see whether they are clean. You would be using what method of direct observing? __________ recording

22. An observation that is seen (or heard) by the observer and promptly recorded uses what approach to observation? ______________ observation

76. If you show someone how to do something, watch his or her behavior, and reinforce it when it is correct, your behavior is called the ____________ stimulus.

39. Differential reinforcement involves two basic behavioral procedures: ______________ and ______________.

163. The weakness of a simple comparison design is that it does not rule out ____________ causes of an observed change in the behavior.

102. Programming is the temporary use of a prompt to produce ______________ of behavior to a novel situation.

142. The design in which a behavior is observed during a baseline, during a treatment condition, and, finally, during a return to baseline, is called a(n) __________ design.

131. Students listening to a lecture are often regarded as being attentive if their eyes are open and their heads are pointed toward the speaker. If this were a statement of how to observe attentive behavior, it would be called a(n) ______________.

34. Brad was helping Carol change several of her behaviors. He started by doing baseline observations on her interrupting and arguing behaviors for one month. During the second month, he gave her a wrist counter and asked her to count interrupting but not arguing. During the third month, he gave her a second wrist counter and asked also to count arguing behaviors. They were happy to find that both behaviors decreased. What single-subject experimental design was he using? ______________ design

53. Henry was particularly interested in pictures of birds. When he looked through a book of photos, he skipped the pictures that were not of birds. What specific schedule of intermittent reinforcement was his picture-looking behavior on? ______________

96. Observation based on some physical <u>result</u> of a response rather than observation of the response itself is called ______________ recording.

66. If Jan's mother showed her a picture of a cow to help her learn to read the word *cow*, the picture of a cow would be called a(n) ______________.

90. Mr. James awarded Tom a token for every ten multiplication problems he got correct. What schedule of intermittent reinforcement was Mr. James using? ____________

36. Clearly stating what behavior to observe is called a(n) ______________.

46. Fading is a procedure used to help teach a specific ______________ that involves gradually withdrawing a stimulus called a prompt. (The answer is not behavior or response!)

59. If a person's behavior occurs in the presence of a novel stimulus, we call this the process of ______________.

81. Interval recording involves recording whether or not a behavior occurs during each of a series of ____________ intervals.

170. Tom the Peeper has to wait different lengths of time for Gloria to enter her room and begin disrobing, but it averages 45 minutes. What intermittent schedule of reinforcement is his peeping on? ______________

127. Sarah wanted to help Ken build his stone fireplace, so she volunteered to wheel the very heavy wet concrete from the mixer to the fireplace for Ken. Each time she brought a load, he said "Thanks" as soon as she arrived. He thanked her only for hauling the concrete. Sarah certainly did not get thanked too often for her work. However, she did not seem overwhelmed by just hearing "Thanks." What principle of effective reinforcement, if

any, did Ken neglect in his treatment of Sarah's help? ______

91. Mr. Janes taught Roberto to draw a map of Kansas by first praising any rectangle that was twice as long as it was high. He then praised the map only if the Missouri River was shown; finally he praised the map only if Wichita, Kansas City, and Topeka were shown. The behavioral procedure by which Mr. Janes taught Roberto to draw the map is called ______.

135. Suppose you hit Tom every time he tells you, "Your Momma's feet stink." Suppose he starts saying it even more often. You should conclude that hitting him is an event technically known as a(n) ______.

166. To decide whether the principle of deprivation was followed rather than violated, ask, "Has the reinforcer ______ been delivered?"

92. Mr. Warren, a high school teacher, was always negative in his class. Several of his students decided to observe him to find out how much of the time he was negative. They made their observations in consecutive 15-second blocks throughout the day and found that he was negative 75% of the time. What method of direct observation did they use? ______ recording

155. The procedure of having an event follow a behavior and increase its rate is called ______.

29. Anytime a response is not reinforced after every occurrence, we say that the response is on what generic schedule? A(n) ______ ______ schedule

161. The use of outside judges to determine whether a behavioral definition is acceptable to nonbehaviorists is called determining the ______ ______ of the definition.

32. Bev did a meticulous job on her math homework last Friday. Her teacher was so pleased that he showed her homework to everyone in class as the way homework should be done. Bev then did a meticulous job with her English homework. The occurrence of such a careful job in a second class without reinforcement is an example of what behavioral process? ______

9. A response will take longer to extinguish if it has been on what generic schedule? A(n) ______ schedule

110. Remember, if you tell people to do something and they do, this ______ (is, isn't) an example of reinforcement.

147. The longer the delay in providing reinforcement for a response, the ______ (more, less) effective the reinforcer will be.

150. The observation of a behavior prior to introducing a treatment is called the ______ condition.

47. Four basic methods of observation of behavior are ______ recording, ______ recording, ______ recording, and ______ recording.

169. To use the aversive control strategy, you (1) decrease undesirable behavior through ______ as a last resort, (2) increase desirable behavior through ______ reinforcement as a last resort.

107. Reinforcing one response while extinguishing a different response is called ______ ______.

2. A generalization may occur when a response has been reinforced in the presence of a stimulus so that the person emits the same response in the presence of a(n) ______ stimulus.

17. A stimulus that consistently signals the occurrence of punishment is called a(n) ______ ______.

37. Danny was trying to teach Marty to say "one." Every time Marty said something like "one," Danny said "Very good." At first Marty had a high rate of saying something close to "one." Then he slowed down, and finally he quit altogether. Marty probably quit because Danny was saying "Very good" too often. What principle of effective reinforcement did Danny violate? ______

171. Tom was teaching Mona to play the guitar. He first praised her only when she held it correctly, next only when she strummed properly, and finally only when she struck a particular chord. Holding the guitar properly is called a(n) ______ to playing it correctly.

146. The goal of shaping is to produce a specified behavior called a(n) ______.

118. Review: Avoidance behavior prevents an event called a(n) ______ from occurring.

65. If an event follows a behavior and increases its rate, it is called a(n) ______.

165. To decide whether the principle of contin-

gency was followed, ask, "Was the event given ________________ if the desired behavior occurred?"

103. Recording whether or not a behavior occurs during each of a series of discontinuous intervals is called ________________ recording.

33. Bob really liked Kay when she acted assertively, so he always made it a point to praise such behavior. After a while Kay always acted assertively around Bob, but for some reason her assertiveness did not spill over into her other relationships. However, after David also started reinforcing assertiveness, Kay began acting assertively with everyone she knew. What behavioral procedure did this series of friends use to change Kay's behavior in this way? ________________ training

104. Reinforcing a behavior in the presence of a series of situations until it generalizes to novel members of that same stimulus class is called ________________.

141. The collection of all works of art would be considered a(n) ________________.

138. The agreement between the observations of two independent observers is called the ________________ of those observations.

93. Mrs. Whalen observed Penny's study behavior prior to praising it, while she praised it, and after she had stopped praising it. What experimental design was she using? ________________ design

117. Review: As soon as Susie felt her feet get cold on the cold floor, she put her slippers on. Her rate of putting her slippers on increased over time. Putting her slippers on to stop the cold is called a(n) ________________ behavior.

124. Review: If you withdraw a reinforcer (unrelated to an undesirable behavior) every time that particular undesirable behavior occurs, and the undesirable behavior decreases, you are using what procedure? ________________

181. When Thurmond moved up north, no one paid any attention to his racially prejudiced statements. However, the statements did not decrease in rate. What behavioral procedure was being applied to his prejudiced behavior? ________________

30. Behavior analysis looks at ________________ events that ________________ behavior.

84. Lenny's mother was very interested in increasing his rate of comments reflecting a positive outlook on life. So she watched very carefully for such comments to occur and noted them to herself. She would then praise Lenny for each comment at a special meeting that they held every Sunday. She never praised comments that were not positive. Her praise was very important to Lenny, and he never seemed to get too much of it. What principle of effective reinforcement, if any, did his mother neglect? ________________

101. Pete designed the world's best token system for his third-grade pupils. They could trade tokens for snacks, TV lessons, meeting with the principal, having a story read, and lots of neat things. Pete never gave them so many tokens that they didn't want them any more, and he always gave the tokens immediately after the behavior that he desired. When he tried to reinforce them for pronouncing difficult words accurately, however, he had little success, because he was hard of hearing. Thus, he gave them tokens for both right and wrong pronunciation. What principle of effective reinforcement, if any, did he neglect? ________________

144. The effectiveness of an event will be maximized if it is delivered only when the desired behavior occurs, according to the principle of ________________.

160. The temporary use of a prompt to produce a generalization is called ________________.

41. Each of a series of behaviors that are similar to some target behavior is called a(n) ________________.

42. Eleanor learned to read the word *dog* from a special book. The book reinforced her when she called d-o-g "dog" but not when she called another word "dog." The book helped her start out by showing a picture of a dog when the word was first presented but gradually showed less and less of the dog—until Eleanor had to read the word without the help of the picture. What behavioral procedure did the book use? ________________

54. Here's a trick question: Is a generalized reinforcer defined as an event that can be used to reinforce a response as it generalizes to new situations? ________________

174. Tommy's mother wanted to teach him the idea of "boy," so she showed him a picture of Ken and asked "What kind of person is this—

you know, like Daddy?" and reinforced him when he said "boy." She then gave him less and less of the hint until Tommy always said "boy" when shown a picture of Ken. She then repeated the procedure with a picture of Joe until he learned to call Joe a boy. By this time, Tommy could label any picture of a young male as a boy. By adding the hint to the basic procedure, what procedure did his mother use? ______________

85. Mary was observed by the primary observer to talk with other children in her class 7 times. A reliability observer noted 10 instances of talking. Compute the reliability of these observations: __________ percent. Is it acceptable? __________
157. The reliability of a new behavioral definition should be at least ________ percent.
19. An added stimulus, used to help learn a discrimination or generalization, is called a(n) ______________.
11. A set of related stimuli is called a(n) ______________.
178. What two schedules of reinforcement produce lower rates of responding right after reinforcement and a higher rate as the time for the next reinforcement approaches? __________ and __________
183. Writing the date, the store's name, and the amount on a check usually precedes the signing of the check and the receiving of the store's merchandise. If signing the check is reinforced by receiving the merchandise, the sequence of writing behaviors is what is called a(n) ______________.
15. A stimulus class consists of a set of ________ stimuli.
129. Schedules of reinforcement that are based on time are called __________ schedules; schedules based on number of responses are called __________ schedules.
111. Review: A negative reinforcer is any event that is terminated or __________ by a behavior and that causes the rate of the behavior to __________.
128. Satiation, extinction, and punishment all have the effect of __________ the rate of a response.
108. Reinforcing one response and extinguishing a different response is called ______________ ______________. Reinforcing a response in one situation and extinguishing the same response in a different situation is called ______________.
8. A procedure used to help teach a specific discrimination that involves gradually withdrawing a prompt is called __________.
67. If observers check for 5 seconds every 14 minutes to see if a certain behavior is occurring, what method of direct observation are they using? __________ recording
21. An intermittent schedule of reinforcement will reduce satiation and also produce a greater resistance to ______________ than will a continuous schedule.
153. The principle of effective reinforcement that states "The more worthwhile the amount of an event that is delivered after the desired behavior, the more effective it will be" is called the principle of __________.
4. A method of direct observation based on counting instances of a behavior is called ________ recording.
43. Escape is a procedure in which a negative reinforcer is __________ following a response.
10. A sequence of responses in which the prior response serves as the discriminative stimulus for the succeeding response is called a(n) ______________.
134. Suppose two observers were recording the occurrence of nervous looks by witnesses at the Congressional hearings (where N stands for nervous and C stands for calm):

First observer:	N	N	N	N	N
Second observer:	N	N	C	N	N

Compute the reliability: ________ percent. If this is a new definition, is the reliability acceptable? __________

75. If you make a negative reinforcer most effective in increasing the rate of a response by removing it right after the response, you are using what principle of reinforcer effectiveness? The principle of __________
94. Ms. Whalen wanted to increase the amount of studying in her fourth-grade class so that the children would learn faster. She decided that she would walk through the room while the children were working on their math and would grade their work right then and there. Each child would then be allowed to play outside for ten minutes after he or she had completed ten problems correctly. She

found that the rate of work in the class went up dramatically as a result of this approach. The grade in this example was probably a(n) ______________ (conditioned, generalized, primary) reinforcer. Because a child could buy it with ten correct problems, the right to play would be a ______________ reinforcer for the grade.

115. Review: Any event that follows a response and reduces the probability of that response occurring is called a(n) ______________.
113. Review: A punisher that loses its effectiveness through unpaired presentations is called a(n) ______________ punisher.
99. People will continue to follow instructions only if they are ______________ for doing so.
179. Which two schedules of reinforcement produce uniform rates of responding? The ______________ schedule and the ______________ schedule
176. What is the best generic schedule of reinforcement to use when attempting to shape a new behavior? ______________ reinforcement
106. Reinforcing events that make conditioned reinforcers and generalized reinforcers effective as a result of being paired with them are called ______________ reinforcers.
78. In order for punishment to be most effective, it should follow the undesirable response ______________.
69. If people are reinforced only every 500 responses, their responding may become erratic and slower. This consequence is known as ______________.
184. Quite frequently, we can't reinforce someone immediately after the behavior we would like to encourage. The important thing about conditioned reinforcers, such as a smile or a thank-you, is that they can be delivered ______________, which enhances their effectiveness.
24. An SD is a stimulus that precedes a behavior and is present only if that behavior will be ______________. An S-delta is a stimulus that precedes a behavior and is present only if that behavior will be ______________.
35. Carol didn't like football, but she did like the interviews with the players. So she tuned in exactly at the start of halftime. The interviews always started 5 minutes after the start of halftime. What schedule of reinforcement was her TV viewing on? A(n) ______________ ______________ schedule
27. Any reinforcer that is weakened permanently by unpaired presentations is called a(n) ______________ reinforcer.
156. The procedure of reinforcing a desired behavior that has been verbally described to a person is called ______________.
3. A generalized reinforcer is any conditioned reinforcer that is paired with ______________ backup reinforcers.
125. Review: Mike's parents "punished" him by sending him to bed early on any day that he hadn't done his homework for school. Mike started doing his homework. What procedure increased Mike's rate of doing homework? ______________
77. If you withdraw an event contingent on a behavior, and the rate of that behavior decreases, the procedure is called ______________.
28. Any reinforcer that is weakened temporarily only by satiation is called a(n) ______________ reinforcer.
31. Behavior analysts don't consider negative reinforcement and ______________ to be the same.

References

ABRAMOWITZ, A. J., & O'LEARY, S. G. (1990). Effectiveness of delayed punishment in an applied setting. *Behavior Therapy, 21*(2), 231–239.

AHLES, T. A., COOMBS, D. W., JENSEN, L., STUKEL, T., MAURER, L. H., & KEEFE, F. J. (1990). Development of a behavioral observation technique for the assessment of pain behaviors in cancer patients. *Behavior Therapy, 21*, 449–460.

ALFORD, G. S., & TURNER, S. M. (1976). Stimulus interference and conditioned inhibition of auditory hallucinations. *Journal of Behavior Therapy and Experimental Psychiatry*, 7(2), 155–160.

ALLEN, G. J. (1973). Case study: Implementation of behavior modification techniques in summer camp settings. *Behavior Therapy*, 4(4), 570–575.

ALLEN, J. S., TARNOWSKI, K. J., SIMONIAN, S. J., ELLIOTT, D., & DRABMAN, R. S. (1991). The generalization map revisited: Assessment of generalized treatment effects in child and adolescent behavior therapy. *Behavior Therapy, 22*(3), 393–405.

ALLEN, K. D., LOIBEN, T., ALLEN, S. J., & STANLEY, R. T. (1992). Dentist-implemented contingent escape for management of disruptive child behavior. *Journal of Applied Behavior Analysis, 25*(3), 629–626.

ALLEN, K. D., & STOKES, T. F. (1987). Use of escape and reward in the management of young children during dental treatment. *Journal of Applied Behavior Analysis, 20*(4), 381–390.

ALLEN, K. E., HART, B. M., BUELL, J. S., HARRIS, F. R., & WOLF, M. M. (1964). Effects of social reinforcement on isolate behavior of a nursery school child. *Child Development, 35*, 511–518.

ALLEN, K. E., TURNER, K. D., & EVERETT, P. M. (1970). A behavior modification classroom for Head Start children with problem behaviors. *Exceptional Children*, 37, 119–127.

ALLPORT, G. W., & POSTMAN, L. F. (1945). The basic psychology of rumor. *Transactions of the New York Academy of Sciences, Series II*, 61–81.

APPLEBAUM, K. A., BLANCHARD, E. B., NICHOLSON, N. L., RADNITZ, C., KIRSCH, C., MIKULTKA, D., ATTANSIO, V., ANDRASIK, F., & DENTINGER, M. P. (1990). Controlled evaluation of the addition of cognitive strategies to a home-based relaxation protocol for tension headache. *Behavior Therapy, 21*(3), 293–304.

ARAUJO, J., & BORN, D. G. (1985). Calculating percentage agreement correctly but writing its formula incorrectly. *Behavior Analyst, 8*(2), 207–208.

AXELROD, S. (1991). Smoking cessation through functional analysis. *Journal of Applied Behavior Analysis, 24*(4), 717–718.

AYLLON, T. (1963). Intensive treatment of psychotic behavior by stimulus satiation and food reinforcement. *Behavior Research and Therapy, 1*, 53–61.

AYLLON, T., & AZRIN, N. H. (1964). Reinforcement and instructions with mental patients. *Journal of the Experimental Analysis of Behavior, 7*, 327–333.

AYLLON, T., & AZRIN, N. H. (1965). The measurement and reinforcement of behavior of psychotics. *Journal of the Experimental Analysis of Behavior, 8*(6), 357–383.

AYLLON, T., & AZRIN, N. H. (1968). *The token economy: A motivational system for therapy and rehabilitation*. Englewood Cliffs, NJ: Prentice Hall.

AYLLON, T., & MICHAEL, J. (1959). The psychiatric nurse as a behavioral engineer. *Journal of the Experimental Analysis of Behavior, 2*, 323–334.

AZRIN, N. H., & HOLZ, W. C. (1966). Punishment. In W. K. Honig (Ed.), *Operant behavior: Areas of research and application*. New York: Appleton-Century-Crofts.

AZRIN, N. H., & POWELL, J. (1968). Behavioral engineering: The reduction of smoking behavior by a conditioning apparatus and procedure. *Journal of Applied Behavior Analysis, 1*(3), 193–200.

AZRIN, N. H., & POWELL, J. (1969). Behavioral engineering: The use of response priming to improve prescribed self-medication. *Journal of Applied Behavior Analysis, 2*(1), 39–42.

AZRIN, N., RUBIN, H., O'BRIEN, F., AYLLON, T., & ROLL, D. (1968). Behavioral engineering: Posture control by a portable operant apparatus. *Journal of Applied Behavior Analysis, 1*(2), 99–108.

AZRIN, R. D., & HAYES, S. C. (1984). The discrimination of interest within a heterosexual interaction: Training, generalization, and effects on social skills. *Behavior Therapy, 15*(2), 173–184.

BACHRACH, A. J. (1962). *Psychological research: An introduction*. New York: Random House.

BACON, D. L., FULTON, B. J., & MALOTT, R. W. (1982). Improving staff performance through the use of task checklists. *Journal of Organizational Behavior Management, 4*(3–4), 17–25.

BAER, A. M., ROWBURY, T., & BAER, D. M. (1973). The development of instructional control over classroom activities of deviant preschool children. *Journal of Applied Behavior Analysis, 6*(2), 289–298.

BAER, D. M. (1962). Laboratory control of thumbsucking by withdrawal and representation of reinforcement. *Journal of the Experimental Analysis of Behavior, 5*, 525–528.

BAER, D. M. (1970). A case for the selective reinforcement of punishment. In C. Neuringer & J. L. Michael (Eds.), *Behavior modification in clinical psychology* (pp. 243–249). New York: Appleton-Century-Crofts.

BAER, D. M. (1976). The organism as host. *Human Development, 19*, 87–98.

BAER, D. M. (1977a). Perhaps it would be better not to know everything. *Journal of Applied Behavior Analysis, 10*(1), 167–172.

BAER, D. M. (1977b). Reviewer's comments: Just because it's reliable doesn't mean that you can use it. *Journal of Applied Behavior Analysis, 10*, 117–119.

BAER, D. M. (1987). Do we really want the unification of psychology? A response to Krantz. *New Ideas in Psychology, 5*(3), 355–359.

BAER, D. M., & DEGUCHI, H. (1985). Generalized imitation from a radical-behavioral viewpoint. In R. Bootzin & S. Reiss (Eds.), *Theoretical issues in behavior therapy* (pp. 179–217). Orlando, FL: Academic Press.

BAER, D. M., & GUESS, D. (1971). Receptive training of adjective inflections in mental retardates. *Journal of Applied Behavior Analysis, 4*(2), 129–140.

BAER, D. M., PETERSON, R. F., & SHERMAN, J. A. (1967). The development of imitation by reinforcing behavioral similarity to a model. *Journal of the Experimental Analysis of Behavior, 10*, 405–416.

BAER, D. M., WOLF, M. M., & RISLEY, T. R. (1968). Some current dimensions of applied behavior analysis. *Journal of Applied Behavior Analysis, 1*(1), 91–97.

BAER, D. M., WOLF, M. M., & RISLEY, T. R. (1987). Some still-current dimensions of applied behavior analysis. *Journal of Applied Behavior Analysis, 20*(4), 313–327.

BAER, R. A., & DETRICH, R. (1990). Tacting and manding in correspondence training: Effects of child selection of verbalization. *Journal of the Experimental Analysis of Behavior, 54*(1), 23–30.

BAILEY, S. L., POKRZYWINSKI, J., & BRYANT, L. E. (1983). Using water mist to reduce self-injurious and stereotypic behavior. *Applied Research in Mental Retardation, 4*(3), 229–241.

BANDURA, A. (1969). *Principles of behavior modification.* New York: Holt, Rinehart, & Winston.

BANDURA, A. (1971). *Psychological modeling: Conflicting theories.* Chicago: Aldine-Atherton.

BARLOW, D. H., HAYES, S. C., & NELSON, R. O. (1984). *The scientist practitioner: Research accountability in clinical and educational settings.* New York: Pergamon.

BARLOW, D. H., & HERSEN, M. (1984). *Single-case experimental design.* New York: Pergamon.

BARRETT, B. H., & LINDSLEY, O. R. (1962). Deficits in acquisition of operant discrimination and differentiation shown by institutionalized retarded children. *American Journal of Mental Deficiency, 67*, 424–436.

BASS, R. F. (1987). Computer-assisted observer training. *Journal of Applied Behavior Analysis, 20*(1), 83–88.

BASS, R. F., & ASERLIND, R. (1984). Interval and time-sample data collection procedures: Methodological issues. In K. V. Gadow (Ed.), *Advances in learning and behavioral disabilities* (vol. 3) (pp. 1–39). Greenwich, CT: JAI Press.

BECKMAN, P. J., & KOHL, F. L. (1987). Interactions of preschoolers with and without handicaps in integrated and segregated settings: A longitudinal study. *Mental Retardation, 25*(1), 5–11.

BEHRENS, B. C., SANDERS, M. R., & HALFORD, W. K. (1990). Behavioral marital therapy: An evaluation of treatment effects across high and low risk settings. *Behavior Therapy, 21*(4), 423–433.

BELLES, D., & BRADLYN, A. S. (1987). The use of the changing criterion design in achieving controlled smoking in a heavy smoker: A controlled case study. *Journal of Behavior Therapy and Experimental Psychiatry, 18*(1), 77–82.

BENTALL, R. P., & LOWE, C. F. (1987). The role of verbal behavior in human learning: III. Instructional effects in children. *Journal of the Experimental Analysis of Behavior, 47*(2), 177–190.

BEREITER, C., & MIDIAN, K. (1978). *Were some follow through models more effective than others?* Paper presented at American Educational Research Association, Toronto, March 30.

BERGIN, A. E., & STRUPP, H. H. (1972). *Changing frontiers in the science of psychotherapy.* New York: Wiley.

BERNARD, C. (1957). *An introduction to the study of experimental medicine.* New York: Dover.

BICKEL, W. K., DEGRANDPRE, R. J., HUGHES, J. R., & HIGGINS, S. T. (1991). Behavioral economics of drug self-administration: II. A unit-price analysis of cigarette smoking. *Journal of the Experimental Analysis of Behavior, 55*(2), 145–154.

BIJOU, S. W., PETERSON, R. F., & AULT, M. H. (1968). A method to integrate descriptive and experimental field studies at the level of data and empirical concepts. *Journal of Applied Behavior Analysis, 1*(2), 175–191.

BIRNBRAUER, J. S., BIJOU, S. W., WOLF, M. M., & KIDDER, J. D. (1965). Programmed instruction in the classroom. In L. P. Ullman & L. Krasner (Eds.), *Case studies in behavior modification.* New York: Holt, Rinehart & Winston.

BLAKE, P., & MOSS, T. (1967). The development of socialization skills in an electively mute child. *Behavior Research and Therapy, 5*, 349–356.

BLAMPIED, N. M., & KAHAN, E. (1992). Acceptability of alternative punishments: A community survey. *Behavior Modification, 16*(3), 400–413.

BLECHMAN, E. A., OLSON, D. H., & HELLMAN, I. D. (1976). Stimulus control over family problem-solving behavior: The Family Contract Game. *Behavior Therapy, 7*(5), 686–692.

BORKOVEC, T. D., WILKINSON, L., FOLENSBEE, R., & LERMAN, C. (1983). Stimulus control applications to the treatment of worry. *Behaviour Research and Therapy, 21*(3), 247–251.

BORNSTEIN, M. R., BELLACK, A. S., & HERSEN, M. (1977). Social-skills training for unassertive children: A multiple-baseline analysis. *Journal of Applied Behavior Analysis, 10*(2), 183–195.

BOURGEOIS, M. S. (1990). Enhancing conversation skills in patients with Alzheimer's disease using a prosthetic memory aid. Erratum. *Journal of Applied Behavior Analysis, 23*(3), 360.

BOURGEOIS, M. S. (1993). Effects of memory aids on the dyadic conversations of individuals with dementia. *Journal of Applied Behavior Analysis, 26*(1), 77–87.

BRANDT, R. M. (1972). *Studying behavior in natural settings.* New York: Holt, Rinehart & Winston.

BRAWLEY, E. R., HARRIS, F. R., ALLEN, K. E., FLEMING, R. S., & PETERSON, R. F. (1969). Behavior modification of an autistic child. *Behavioral Science, 14*, 87–97.

BRICKMAN, L. (1972). Environmental attitudes and actions. *Journal of Social Psychology, 87*, 223–224.

BRIGHAM, T. A., FINFROCK, S. R., BRUENIG, M. K., & BUSHELL, D. (1972). The use of programmed materials in the analysis of academic contingencies. *Journal of Applied Behavior Analysis, 5*(2), 177–182.

BRY, B. H. (1991). B. F. Skinner for behavior therapists. *Behavior Therapist, 14*(1), 9–10.

BUCHANAN, C. D. (1973). *Programmed reading.* New York: McGraw-Hill.

BUCKHOUT, R. (1980). Nearly 2,000 witnesses can be wrong. *Bulletin of the Psychonomic Society, 16*(4), 307–310.

BUDNEY, A. J., HIGGINS, S. T., DELANEY, D. D., KENT, L., & BICKEL, W. K. (1991). Contingent reinforcement of abstinence with individuals abusing cocaine and marijuana. *Journal of Applied Behavior Analysis, 24*(4), 657–665.

BUDZYNSKI, T. H., & STOYVA, J. M. (1969). An instrument for producing deep muscle relaxation by means of analog information feedback. *Journal of Applied Behavior Analysis, 2*(4), 231–237.

BURGESS, R. L., & BUSHELL, D. J. (1969). *Behavioral sociology.* New York: Columbia University Press.

BURGIO, L. D., BURGIO, K. L., ENGEL, B. T., & TICE, L. M. (1986). Increasing distance and independence of ambulation in elderly nursing home residents. *Journal of Applied Behavior Analysis, 19*(4), 357–366.

BURGIO, L. D., WHITMAN, T. L., & REID, D. H. (1983). A participative management approach for improving direct-care staff performance in an institutional setting. *Journal of Applied Behavior Analysis, 16*(1), 37–53.

BUSHELL, D. J. (1978). An engineering approach to the elementary classroom: The Behavior Analysis Follow Through Project. In A. C. Catania & T. A. Brigham (Eds.), *Handbook of applied behavior analysis: Social and instructional processes* (pp. 525–563). New York: Irvington Press/Halstead Press.

BUZAS, H. P., & AYLLON, T. (1981). Differential reinforcement in coaching tennis skills. *Behavior Modification, 5*(3), 372–385.

CAMPBELL, D. T., & STANLEY, J. C. (1963). *Experimental and quasi-experimental designs for research.* Chicago: Rand McNally.

CARPENTER, C. (1993, November). In the glass meadow. *Reader's Digest*, pp. 63–64.

CARR, E. G., & DURAND, V. M. (1985). Reducing behavior problems through functional communication training. *Journal of Applied Behavior Analysis, 18*(2), 111–126.

CARR, E. G., NEWSOM, C. D., & BINKOFF, J. A. (1980). Escape as a factor in the aggressive behavior of two retarded children. *Journal of Applied Behavior Analysis, 13*(1), 101–117.

CARROLL, L. J., & YATES, B. T. (1981). Further evidence for the role of stimulus control training in facilitating weight reduction after behavioral therapy. *Behavior Therapy, 12*(2), 287–291.

CARSTENS, C. (1982). Application of a work penalty threat in the treatment of a case of juvenile fire setting. *Journal of Behavior Therapy and Experimental Psychiatry, 13*(2), 159–161.

CARSTENSEN, L. L. (1988). The emerging field of behavioral gerontology. *Behavior Therapy, 19*(3), 259–281.

CARTWRIGHT, M., & D'ORSO, M. (1993). For the children. *Reader's Digest, 143*(856), 169–208.

CATANIA, A. C. (1984). *Learning*. Englewood Cliffs, NJ: Prentice-Hall.

CAUTELA, J. R. (1969). Behavior therapy and self-control: Techniques and implications. In C. M. Franks (Ed.), *Behavior therapy: Appraisal and status.* New York: McGraw-Hill.

CAVALLARO, C. C., & POULSON, C. L. (1985). Teaching language to handicapped children in natural settings. *Education & Treatment of Children, 8*(1), 1–24.

CHANDLER, L. K., LUBECK, R. C., & FOWLER, S. A. (1992). Generalization and maintenance of preschool children's social skills: A critical review and analysis. *Journal of Applied Behavior Analysis, 25*(2), 415–428.

CHAPLIN, J. P. (1985). *Dictionary of Psychology*. New York: Dell.

CINCIRIPINI, P. M., EPSTEIN, L. H., & MARTIN, J. E. (1979). The effects of feedback on blood pressure discrimination. *Journal of Applied Behavior Analysis, 12*(3), 345–353.

CLARK, H. B., ROWBURY, T., BAER, A. M., & BAER, D. M. (1973). Timeout as a punishing stimulus in continuous and intermittent schedules. *Journal of Applied Behavior Analysis, 6*(3), 443–455.

COMUNIDAD-LOS-HORCONES. (1986). News from now-here, 1986: A response to "News from Nowhere, 1984" *Behavior Analyst, 9*(1), 129–132.

COPE, J. G., ALLRED, L. J., & MORSELL, J. M. (1991). Signs as deterrents of illegal parking in spaces designated for individuals with physical disabilities. *Journal of Applied Behavior Analysis, 24*(1), 59–63.

COSE, E. (1995, August 21). Teaching kids to be smart. *Newsweek.*

CRITCHFIELD, T. S., & PERONE, M. (1990). Verbal self-reports of delayed matching to sample by humans. *Journal of the Experimental Analysis of Behavior, 53*(3), 321–344.

DAHLQUIST, L. M., & GIL, K. M. (1986). Using parents to maintain improved dental flossing skills in children. *Journal of Applied Behavior Analysis, 19*(3), 255–260.

DANIELS, A. C. (1985, Summer). Performance management: The behavioral approach to productivity improvement. *National Productivity Review*, pp. 225–236.

DANSKIN, D. G., & CROW, M. A. (1981). *Biofeedback: An introduction and guide.* Palo Alto, CA: Mayfield.

DAVIDSON, D. (1980). Psychology as philosophy. In D. Davidson (Ed.), *Essays on actions and events* (pp. 229–244). New York: Oxford.

DAVIS, J. R., RAWANA, E. P., & CAPPONI, D. R. (1989). Acceptability of behavioral staff management techniques. *Behavioral Residential Treatment, 4*(1), 23–44.

DAVIS, J. R., & RUSSELL, R. H. (1990). Behavioral staff management: An analogue study of acceptability and its behavioral correlates. *Behavioral Residential Treatment, 5*(4), 259–270.

DELPRATO, D. J. (1977). Observing covert behavior ("mind-reading") with Chevreul's pendulum. *Psychological Record, 27*(2), 473–478.

DELUCA, R. V., & HOLBORN, S. W. (1985). Effects of a fixed interval schedule of token reinforcement on exercise in obese and non-obese boys. *Psychological Record, 35*, 525–533.

DELUCA, R. V., & HOLBORN, S. W. (1990). Effects of fixed interval and fixed ratio schedules of token reinforcement on exercise in obese and non-obese boys. *Psychological Record, 40*, 67–82.

DELUCA, R. V., & HOLBORN, S. W. (1992). Effects of a variable-ratio reinforcement schedule with changing criteria on exercise in obese and non-obese boys. *Journal of Applied Behavior Analysis, 25*(3), 671–679.

DERRICKSON, J. G., NEEF, N. A., & CATALDO, M. F. (1993). Effects of signaling invasive procedures on a hospitalized infant's affective behaviors. *Journal of Applied Behavior Analysis, 26*(1), 133–134.

DICKERSON, M. G. (1979). FI schedules and persistence at gambling in the UK betting office. *Journal of Applied Behavior Analysis, 12*(3), 315–323.

DINSMOOR, J. A. (1995). Stimulus control: Part 1. *Behavior Analyst, 18*(1), 51–68.

DONAHOE, J. W., & PALMER, D. C. (1994). *Learning and complex behavior*. Boston: Allyn & Bacon.

DURAND, V. M., & CARR, E. G. (1992). An analysis of maintenance following functional communication training. *Journal of Applied Behavior Analysis, 25*(4), 777–794.

DURAND, V. M., & MINDELL, J. A. (1990). Behavioral treatment of multiple childhood sleep disorders. *Behavor Modification, 14*(1), 37–49.

DUSH, D. M., & SPOTH, R. L. (1988). Comprehensive behavioral medicine in community mental health: A needs assessment that needs assessment. *Evaluation and Program Planning, 11*(4), 297–306.

DYER, K., DUNLAP, G., & WINTERLING, V. (1990). Effects of choice making on the serious problem behaviors of students with severe handicaps. *Journal of Applied Behavior Analysis, 23*(4), 515–524.

ELDER, J., BODDY, P., BARRIGA, P., AGUILAR, A. L., & ESPINAL, H. (1991). Training Honduran health workers and mothers in infant acute respiratory infection control. *Boletin de la Officina Sanitaria Panamericana, 110*, 29–40.

ELDER, J. P., LOUIS, T., SUTISNAPUTRAS, O., SULAEIMAN, N. S., WARE, L., SHAW, W., MOOR, C., & GRAEFF, J. (1992). The use of diarrhoeal management counselling cards for community health volunteer training in Indonesia: The HealthCom Project. *Journal of Tropical Medicine and Hygiene, 95*, 301–308.

EPSTEIN, L. H., & MASEK, B. J. (1978). Behavioral control of medicine compliance. *Journal of Applied Behavior Analysis, 11*(1), 1–9.

ESPIE, C. A., LINDSAY, W. R., BROOKS, D. N., & HOOD, E. M. (1989). A controlled comparative investigation of psychological treatments for chronic sleep-onset insomnia. *Behaviour Research and Therapy, 27*(1), 79–88.

ESPOSITO, B. G., & KOORLAND, M. A. (1989). Play behavior of hearing impaired children: Integrated and segregated settings. *Exceptional Children, 55*(5), 412–419.

FAVELL, J. E., AZRIN, N., BAUMEISTER, A. A., CARR, E. G., DORSEY, M. F., FOREHAND, R., FOXX, R. M., LOVAAS, O. I., RINCOVER, A., RISLEY, T. R., ROMANCZYK, R. G., RUSSO, D. C., SCHROEDER, S. R., & SOLNICK, J. V. (1982). The treatment of self-injurious behavior. *Behavior Therapy, 13*(4), 529–554.

FICHTER, M. M., WALLACE, C. J., LIBERMAN, R. P., & DAVIS, J. R. (1976). Improving social interaction in a chronic psychotic using discriminated avoidance ("nagging"): Experimental analysis and generalization. *Journal of Applied Behavior Analysis, 9*(4), 377–386.

FISHER, E. B. (1979). Overjustification effects in token economies. *Journal of Applied Behavior Analysis, 12*(3), 407–415.

FIXSEN, D. L., PHILLIPS, E. L., PHILLIPS, E. A., & WOLF, M. M. (1976). The teaching-family model of group home treatment. In W. E. Craighead, A. E. Kazdin, & M. J. Mahoney (Eds.), *Behavior modification.* Boston: Houghton Mifflin.

FLANAGAN, B., GOLDIAMOND, I., & AZRIN, N. (1958). Operant stuttering: The control of stuttering behavior through response-contingent consequences. *Journal of the Experimental Analysis of Behavior, 1*(2), 173–177.

FORD, J. E. (1981). A simple punishment procedure for controlling employee absenteeism. *Journal of Organizational Behavior Management, 3*(2), 71–79.

FOXX, R. M., MCMORROW, M. J., BITTLE, R. G., & BECHTEL, D. R. (1986). The successful treatment of a dually-diagnosed deaf man's aggression with a program that included contingent electric shock. *Behavior Therapy, 17*(2), 170–186.

FRANCE, K. G., & HUDSON, S. M. (1990). Behavior management of infant sleep disturbance. *Journal of Applied Behavior Analysis, 23*(1), 91–98.

FUQUA, R. W., & SCHWADE, J. (1986). Social validation of applied behavioral research. In A. Poling & R. W. Fuqua (Eds.), *Research methods in applied behavior analysis: Issues and advances* (pp. 265–292). New York: Plenum.

GAINER, J. C. (1978). Temperature discrimination training in the biofeedback treatment of migraine headache. *Journal of Behavior Therapy and Experimental Psychiatry, 9*(2), 185–187.

GARCIA, E. (1974). The training and generalization of a conversational speech form in nonverbal retardates. *Journal of Applied Behavior Analysis, 7*(1), 137–149.

GARCIA, E., GUESS, D., & BYRNES, J. (1973). Development of syntax in a retarded girl using procedure of imitation, reinforcement, and modeling. *Journal of Applied Behavior Analysis, 6*(2), 299–310.

GETTINGER, M. (1993). Effects of invented spelling and direct instruction on spelling performance of second-grade boys. *Journal of Applied Behavior Analysis, 26*(3), 281–291.

GEWIRTZ, J. L., & BAER, D. M. (1958a). Deprivation and satiation of social reinforcers as drive conditions. *Journal of Abnormal and Social Psychology, 57*, 165–172.

GEWIRTZ, J. L., & BAER, D. M. (1958b). The effect of brief social deprivation on behaviors for a social reinforcer. *Journal of Abnormal and Social Psychology, 56*, 49–56.

GIBBS, J. W., & LUYBEN, P. D. (1985). Treatment of self-injurious behavior: Contingent versus noncontingent positive practice overcorrection. *Behavior Modification, 9*(1), 3–21.

GIEBENHAIN, J. E., & O'DELL, S. L. (1984). Evaluation of a parent-training manual for reducing children's fear of the dark. *Journal of Applied Behavior Analysis, 17*(1), 121–125.

GIL, K. M., KEEFE, F. J., SAMPSON, H. A., MCCASKILL, C. C., RODIN, J., & CRISSON, J. E. (1988). Direct observation of scratching behavior in children with atopic dermatitis. *Behavior Therapy, 19*(2), 213–227.

GLAISTER, B. (1985). A case of auditory hallucination treated by satiation. *Behaviour Research and Therapy, 23*(2), 213–215.

GLASSCOCK, S. G., FRIMAN, P. C., O'BRIEN, S., & CHRISTOPHERSEN, E. R. (1986). Varied citrus treatment of ruminant gagging in a teenager with Batten's disease. *Journal of Behavior Therapy and Experimental Psychiatry, 17*(2), 129–133.

GLENN, S. (1986). *Behavior: A gene for the social sciences* (pp. 1–6). Presented at poster session, American Psychological Association, Washington, DC.

GLOVER, J., & GARY, A. L. (1976). Procedures to increase some aspects of creativity. *Journal of Applied Behavior Analysis, 9*(1), 79–84.

GLYNN, S. M. (1990). Token economy approaches for psychiatric patients: Progress and pitfalls over 25 years. *Behavior Modification, 14*(4), 383–407.

GOETZ, E. M., & BAER, D. M. (1973). Social control of form diversity and the emergence of new forms in children's blockbuilding. *Journal of Applied Behavior Analysis, 6*(2), 209–217.

GOLDIAMOND, I. (1965). Self-control procedures in personal behavior problems. *Psychological Reports, 17*, 851–868.

GOLDSTEIN, H., & MOUSETIS, L. (1989). Generalized language learning by children with severe mental retardation: Effects of peers' expressive modeling. *Journal of Applied Behavior Analysis, 22*(3), 245–259.

GOLTZ, S. M. (1992). A sequential learning analysis of decisions in organizations to escalate investments despite continuing costs or losses. *Journal of Applied Behavior Analysis, 25*(3), 561–574.

GOODALL, K. (1972, November). Shapers at work. *Psychology Today*, pp. 53–63.

GRAHAM, S. R. (1990). Citation for outstanding lifetime contribution to psychology: Presented to B. F. Skinner, August 10, 1990. *American Psychologist, 45*(11), 1205.

GREEN, C. W., REID, D. H., CANIPE, V. S., & GARDNER, S. M. (1991). A comprehensive evaluation of reinforcer identification processes for persons with profound multiple handicaps. *Journal of Applied Behavior Analysis, 24*(3), 537–552.

GREEN, G. R., LINSK, N. L., & PINKSTON, E. M. (1986). Modification of verbal behavior of the mentally impaired elderly by their spouses. *Journal of Applied Behavior Analysis, 19*(4), 329–336.

GREEN, R. R., & HOATS, D. L. (1969). Reinforcing capabilities of television distortion. *Journal of Applied Behavior Analysis, 2*, 139–141.

GREER, R. D., DOROW, L., WILLIAMS, G., MCCORKLE, N., & ASNES, R. (1991). Peer-mediated procedures to induce swallowing and food acceptance in young children. *Journal of Applied Behavior Analysis, 24*(4), 783–790.

GRIFFITHS, H., & CRAIGHEAD, W. E. (1972). Generalization in operant speech therapy for misarticulation. *Journal of Speech and Hearing Disorders, 37*, 485–494.

GROSS, A. M., & DRABMAN, R. S. (Eds.). (1990). *Handbook of behavioral pediatrics*. New York: Plenum.

GROSS, A. M., WOJNILOWER, D. A., LEVIN, R. B., DALE, J., RICHARDSON, J. J., & DAVIDSON, P. C. (1983). Discrimination of blood glucose levels in insulin-dependent diabetics. *Behavior Modification, 7*(3), 369–382.

GUESS, D. (1969). A functional analysis of receptive language and productive speech: Acquisition of the plural phoneme. *Journal of Applied Behavior Analysis, 2*(1), 55–64.

GUESS, D., SAILOR, W., RUTHERFORD, G., & BAER, D. M. (1968). An experimental analysis of linguistic development: Productive use of the plural morpheme. *Journal of Applied Behavior Analysis, 1*, 297–306.

HALL, R. V. (1991). Behavior analysis and education: An unfulfilled dream. *Journal of Behavioral Education, 1*(3), 305–315.

HALL, R., AXELROD, S., TYLER, L., GRIEF, E., JONES, F., & ROBERTSON, R. (1972). Modification of behavior problems in the home with a parent as observer and experimenter. *Journal of Applied Behavior Analysis, 5*(1), 53–64.

HANDLIN, H. C. (1992). The company built upon the Golden Rule: Lincoln Electric. *Journal of Organizational Behavior Management, 12*(1), 151–163.

HARDYCKE, C. D., PETRINOVICH, L. F., & ELLSWORTH, D. W. (1966). Feedback of speech muscle activity during silent reading: Rapid extinction. *Science, 154*, 1467–1468.

HARRIS, M. (1979). *Cultural materialism: The struggle for a science of culture*. New York: Random House.

HARROP, A., FOULKES, C., & DANIELS, M. (1989). Observer agreement calculations: The role of primary data in reducing obfuscation. *British Journal of Psychology, 80*, 181–189.

HARTMANN, D. P., & HALL, R. V. (1976). The changing criterion design. *Journal of Applied Behavior Analysis, 9*(4), 527–532.

HARTMANN, D. P., & PETERSON, L. (1975). A neglected literature and an aphorism. *Journal of Applied Behavior Analysis, 8*, 231–232.

HATCH, J. P. (1990). Growth and development of biofeedback: A bibliographic update. *Biofeedback and Self-Regulation, 15*(1), 37–46.

HATCH, J. P., FISHER, J. G., & RUGH, J. D. (Eds.). (1987). *Biofeedback: Studies in clinical efficacy.* New York: Plenum.

HAUSERMAN, N., WALEN, S. R., & BEHLING, M. (1973). Reinforced racial integration in the first grade: A study in generalization. *Journal of Applied Behavior Analysis, 6*(2), 193–200.

HAYES, S. C. (1988). Contextualism and the next wave of behavioral psychology. *Behavior Analysis, 23*(1), 7–22.

HAYES, S. C., JOHNSON, V. S., & CONE, J. D. (1975). The marked item technique: A practical procedure for litter control. *Journal of Applied Behavior Analysis, 8*(4), 381–386.

HAYES, S. C., KOHLENBERG, B. S., & HAYES, L. J. (1991). The transfer of specific and general consequential functions through simple and conditional equivalence relations. *Journal of the Experimental Analysis of Behavior, 56*(1), 119–137.

HAYES, S. C., & WILSON, K. G. (1993). Some implications of a contemporary behavior-analytic account of verbal events. *Behavior Analyst, 16*(2), 283–301.

HEFFER, R. W., & KELLEY, M. L. (1987). Mothers' acceptance of behavioral interventions for children: The influence of parent race and income. *Behavior Therapy, 18*(2), 153–163.

HEGEL, M. T., AYLLON, T., VANDERPLATE, C., & SPIRO-HAWKINS, H. (1986). A behavioral procedure for increasing compliance with self-exercise regimens in severely burn-injured patients. *Behaviour Research and Therapy, 24*(5), 521–528.

HERSEN, M., EISLER, R., ALFORD, G., & AGRAS, W. S. (1973). Effects of token economy on neurotic depression: An experimental analysis. *Behavior Therapy, 4*, 392–397.

HINELINE, P. N. (1992). A self-interpretive behavior analysis. *American Psychologist, 47*(11), 1274–1286.

HINGTGEN, J. N., SANDERS, B. J., & DEMEYER, M. K. (1965). Shaping cooperative responses in childhood schizophrenics. In L. Ullman & L. Krasner, Eds., *Case studies in behavior modification* (pp. 130–183). New York: Holt, Rinehart & Winston.

HOELSCHER, T. J., LICHSTEIN, K. L., & ROSENTHAL, T. L. (1984). Objective vs subjective assessment of relaxation compliance among anxious individuals. *Behaviour Research and Therapy, 22*(2), 187–193.

HOGBEN, L. T. (1957). *Statistical theory: The relationship of probability, credibility, and error. An examination of the contemporary crisis in statistical theory from a behaviourist viewpoint.* New York: Norton.

HOLLAND, J. G. (1958). Human vigilance. *Science, 128*(3315), 61–67.

HOLLAND, J. G. (1960). Teaching machines: An application of principles from the laboratory. *Journal of the Experimental Analysis of Behavior, 3*, 275–287.

HOLLAND, J. G. (1965). Research on programming variables. In R. Glaser (Ed.), *Teaching machines and programming learning II: Data and directions.* Washington, DC: National Education Association.

HOLLANDSWORTH, J. G., GLAZESKI, R. C., & DRESSEL, M. E. (1978). Use of social-skills training in the treatment of extreme anxiety and deficient verbal skills in the job interview setting. *Journal of Applied Behavior Analysis, 11*(2), 259–269.

HOLZ, W. C., & AZRIN, N. H. (1966). Punishment. In W. K. Honig (Ed.), *Operant behavior: Areas of research and application.* New York: Appleton-Century-Crofts.

HOMME, L. E., DEBACA, P. C., DEVINE, J. V., STEINHORST, R., & RICKERT, E. J. (1963). Use of the Premack Principle in controlling the behavior of nursery school children. *Journal of the Experimental Analysis of Behavior, 6*(4), 544.

HOPKINS, B. L., & HERMANN, J. A. (1977). Evaluating interobserver reliability of interval data. *Journal of Applied Behavior Analysis, 10*(1), 121–126.

HORNER, R. D. (1971). Establishing use of crutches by a mentally retarded spina bifida child. *Journal of Applied Behavior Analysis, 4*(3), 183–189.

HORNER, R. H., MCDONNELL, J. J., & BELLAMY, G. T. (1986). Teaching generalized skills: General case instructions in simulation and community settings. In L. H. Meyers & H. D. Fredericks (Eds.), *Education of learners with severe handicaps: Exemplary service strategies* (pp. 289–314). Baltimore: Paul H. Brookes.

HORTON, G. O. (1975). Generalization of teacher behavior as a function of subject matter specific discrimination training. *Journal of Applied Behavior Analysis, 8*(3), 311–319.

HOULIHAN, D. D., SLOANE, H. N., JONES, R. N., & PATTEN, C. (1992). A review of behavioral conceptualizations and treatments of child noncompliance. *Education and Treatment of Children, 15*(1), 56–77.

HUME, K. M., & CROSSMAN, J. (1992). Musical reinforcement of practice behaviors among competitive swimmers. *Journal of Applied Behavior Analysis, 25*(3), 665–670.

HURSH, S. R. (1984). Behavioral economics. *Journal of the Experimental Analysis of Behavior, 42*(3), 435–452.

INGENMEY, R., & VAN HOUTEN, R. (1991). Using time delay to promote spontaneous speech in an autistic child. *Journal of Applied Behavior Analysis, 24*(3), 591–596.

INGHAM, P., & GREER, R. D. (1992). Changes in student and teacher responses in observed and generalized settings as a function of supervisor observations. *Journal of Applied Behavior Analysis, 25*(1), 153–164.

INOUE, M., & KOBAYASHI, S. (1992). Conversation skill training through videotape modeling in an autistic child. *Japanese Journal of Behavior Therapy, 18*(2), 22–29.

IRWIN, D. M., & BUSHNELL, M. M. (1980). *Observational strategies for child study.* New York: Holt, Rinehart & Winston.

ISAACS, W., THOMAS, J., & GOLDIAMOND, I. (1960). Application of operant conditioning to reinstate verbal behavior in psychotics. *Journal of Speech and Hearing Disorders, 25*, 8–12.

IWATA, B. A. (1987). Negative reinforcement in applied behavior analysis: An emerging technology. *Journal of Applied Behavior Analysis, 20*(4), 361–378.

IWATA, B. A. (1988). The development and adoption of controversial default technologies. *Behavior Analyst, 11*(2), 149–157.

IWATA, B. A., DORSEY, M. F., SLIFER, K. J., BAUMAN, K. E., & RICHMAN, G. S. (1982). Toward a functional analysis of self-injury. *Analysis and Intervention in Developmental Disabilities, 2*, 3–20.

IWATA, B. A., PACE, G. M., DORSEY, M. F., ZARCONE, J. R., VOLLMER, T. R., SMITH, R. G., RODGERS, T. A., LERMAN, D. C., SHORE, B. A., MAZELESKI, J. L., HAN-LEONG, G., COWDERY, G. E., KALSHER, M. J., MCCOSH, K. C., & WILLIS, K. D. (1994). The functions of self-injurious behavior: An experimental-epidemiological analysis. *Journal of Applied Behavior Analysis, 27*(2), 215–240.

JACKSON, D. A., & WALLACE, R. F. (1974). The modification and generalization of voice loudness in a fifteen-year-old retarded girl. *Journal of Applied Behavior Analysis, 7*(3), 461–471.

JAMES, J. E., RICCIARDELLI, L. A., HUNTER, C. E., & ROGERS, P. (1989). Relative efficacy of intensive and spaced behavioral treatment of stuttering. *Behavior Modification, 13*(3), 376–395.

JOHNSON, S. P., WELSH, T. M., MILLER, L. K., & ALTUS, D. E. (1991). Participatory management: Maintaining staff performance in a university housing cooperative. *Journal of Applied Behavior Analysis*, *24*(1), 119–127.

JOHNSTON, J. M., & PENNYPACKER, H. S. (1981). *Strategies and tactics of human behavioral research*. Hillsdale, NJ: Laurence Erlbaum.

JONES, F. H., FREMOUW, W., & CARPLES, S. (1977). Pyramid training of elementary school teachers to use a classroom management "skill package." *Journal of Applied Behavior Analysis*, *10*(2), 239–253.

JONES, R. R., WEINROTT, M. R., & VAUGHT, R. S. (1978). Effects of serial dependency on the agreement between visual and statistical inference. *Journal of Applied Behavior Analysis*, *11*(2), 277–283.

KAGEL, J. H., & WINKLER, R. C. (1972). Behavioral economics: Areas of cooperative research between economics and applied behavioral analysis. *Journal of Applied Behavior Analysis, 5*, 335–342.

KARLINS, M., & ANDREWS, L. H. (1972). *Biofeedback*. New York: Lippincott.

KAUFMAN, B. N. (1991). *Happiness is a choice*. New York: Fawcett Columbine.

KAZDIN, A. E. (1975). Characteristics and trends in applied behavior analysis. *Journal of Applied Behavior Analysis*, *8*(3), 332.

KAZDIN, A. E. (1977a). Assessing the clinical or implied importance of behavior change through social validation. *Behavior Modification*, *1*, 427–452.

KAZDIN, A. E. (1977b). Vicarious reinforcement and direction of behavior change in the classroom. *Behavior Therapy*, *8*(1), 57–63.

KAZDIN, A. E. (1980). Acceptability of time out from reinforcement procedures for disruptive child behavior. *Behavior Therapy*, *11*(3), 329–344.

KAZDIN, A. E., & POLSTER, R. (1973). Intermittent token reinforcement and response maintenance in extinction. *Behavior Therapy*, *4*(3), 386–391.

KEEFE, F. J., & BLUMENTHAL, J. A. (1980). The life fitness program: A behavioral approach to making exercise a habit. *Journal of Behavior Therapy and Experimental Psychiatry*, *11*(1), 31–34.

KELLEHER, R. T., & GOLLUB, L. R. (1962). A review of positive conditioned reinforcement. *Journal of the Experimental Analysis of Behavior*, *5*, 543–597.

KELLER, J. J. (1991). The recycling solution: How I increased recycling on Dilworth Road. *Journal of Applied Behavior Analysis*, *24*(4), 617–619.

KELLY, M. B. (1977). A review of the observational data-collecting and reliability procedures reported in The Journal of Applied Behavior Analysis. *Journal of Applied Behavior Analysis, 10*, 97–101.

KENNEDY, D. A., & THOMPSON, I. (1967). The use of reinforcement techniques with a first-grade boy. *Personality and Guidance Journal, 46*, 366–370.

KIRBY, K. C., & BICKEL, W. K. (1988). Toward an explicit analysis of generalization: A stimulus control interpretation. *Behavior Analyst*, *11*(2), 115–129.

KIRIGAN, K. A., BRAUKMANN, C. J., ATWATER, J. D., & WOLF, M. M. (1982). An evaluation of teaching-family (Achievement Place) group homes for juvenile offenders. *Journal of Applied Behavior Analysis*, *15*(1), 1–16.

KOEGEL, R. L., & FREA, W. D. (1993). Treatment of social behavior in autism through the modification of pivotal social skills. *Journal of Applied Behavior Analysis*, *26*(3), 369–377.

KOEGEL, R. L., & RINCOVER, A. (1977). Research on the difference between generalization and maintenance in extra-therapy responding. *Journal of Applied Behavior Analysis, 10*(1), 1–12.

KOEGEL, R. L., RUSSO, D. C., & RINCOVER, A. (1977). Assessing and training teachers in the generalized use of behavior modification with autistic children. *Journal of Applied Behavior Analysis*, *10*(2), 197–205.

KOHLER, F. W., & GREENWOOD, C. R. (1990). Effects of collateral peer supportive behaviors within the classwide peer tutoring program. *Journal of Applied Behavior Analysis*, *23*(3), 307–322.

KOMAKI, J., & BARNETT, F. T. (1977). A behavioral approach to coaching football: Improving the play execution of the offensive backfield on a youth football team. *Journal of Applied Behavior Analysis*, *10*(4), 657–664.

KRANTZ, P. J., & MCCLANNAHAN, L. E. (1993). Teaching children with autism to initiate to peers: Effects of a script-fading procedure. *Journal of Applied Behavior Analysis*, *26*(1), 121–132.

KRATOCHWILL, T. R., & BRODY, G. H. (1978). Single subject designs: A perspective on the controversy over employing statistical inference and implications for research and training in behavior modification. *Behavior Modification*, *2*(3), 291–307.

KULIK, J., KULIK, C., & COHEN, P. A. (1979). A meta-analysis of outcome studies of Keller's personalized system of instruction. *American Psychologist*, *34*, 307–318.

KUNKEL, J. H. (1975). *Behavior, social problems, and change: A social learning approach*. Englewood Cliffs, NJ: Prentice-Hall.

KUNKEL, J. H. (1985a). The Vicos Project: A cross-cultural test of psychological propositions. *Psychological Record*, *36*, 451–466.

KUNKEL, J. H. (1985b). Vivaldi in Venice: An historical test of psychological propositions. *Psychological Record*, *35*, 445–457.

KYMISSIS, E., & POULSON, C. L. (1990). The history of imitation in learning theory: The language acquisition process. *Journal of the Experimental Analysis of Behavior*, *54*(2), 113–127.

LA PIERRE, R. T. (1934). Attitudes vs actions. *Social Forces*, *13*, 230–237.

LARKIN, K. T., ZAYFERT, C., ABEL, J. L., & VELTUM, L. G. (1992). Reducing heart rate reactivity to stress with feedback: Generalization across task and time. *Behavior Modification*, *16*(1), 118–131.

LARSEN, J. A. (1991, January). A story for Valentine's Day. *Reader's Digest*, pp. 7–8.

LATHAM, G. P., & HUBER, V. L. (1992). Schedules of reinforcement: Lessons from the past and issues for the future. *Journal of Organizational Behavior Management*, *12*(1), 125–149.

LAVELLE, J. M., HOVEL, M. F., WEST, M. P., & WAHLGREN, D. R. (1992). Promoting law enforcement for child protection: A community analysis. *Journal of Applied Behavior Analysis*, *25*(4), 885–892.

LAWTON, C., FRANCE, K. G., & BLAMPIED, N. M. (1991). Treatment of infant sleep disturbance by graduated extinction. *Child and Family Behavior Therapy*, *13*(1), 39–56.

LEVINE, F. M., & FASNACHT, G. (1974). Token rewards may lead to token learning. *American Psychologist, 29*, 816–820.

LICHSTEIN, K. L., & JOHNSON, R. S. (1991). Older adults' objective self-recording of sleep in the home. *Behavior Therapy*, *22*(4), 531–548.

LINDSLEY, O. R. (1968). A reliable wrist counter for recording behavior rates. *Journal of Applied Behavior Analysis, 1*, 77.

LINSCHEID, T. R., IWATA, B. A., RICKETTS, R. W., WILLIAMS, D. E., & GRIFFIN, J. C. (1990). Clinical evaluation of the self-injurious behavior inhibiting system (SIBIS). *Journal of Applied Behavior Analysis*, *23*(1), 53–78.

LLOYD, K. E. (1980). Do as I say, not as I do. *New Zealand Psychologist*, *9*(1).

LLOYD, K. E. (1985). Behavioral anthropology: A review of Marvin Harris' Cultural Materialism. *Journal of the Experimental Analysis of Behavior*, *43*, 279–287.

LOMBARD, D., NEUBAUER, T. E., CANFIELD, D., & WINETT, R. A. (1991). Behavioral community intervention to reduce the

LINSCHEID, T. R., IWATA, B. A., RICKETTS, R. W., WILLIAMS, D. E., & GRIFFIN, J. C. (1990). Clinical evaluation of the self-injurious behavior inhibiting system (SIBIS). *Journal of Applied Behavior Analysis, 23*(1), 53–78.

LLOYD, K. E. (1980). Do as I say, not as I do. *New Zealand Psychologist, 9*(1).

LLOYD, K. E. (1985). Behavioral anthropology: A review of Marvin Harris' Cultural Materialism. *Journal of the Experimental Analysis of Behavior, 43*, 279–287.

LOMBARD, D., NEUBAUER, T. E., CANFIELD, D., & WINETT, R. A. (1991). Behavioral community intervention to reduce the risk of skin cancer. *Journal of Applied Behavior Analysis, 24*(4), 677–686.

LONG, G. M., & MCNAMARA, J. R. (1989). Paradoxical punishment as it relates to the battered woman syndrome. *Behavior Modification, 13*(2), 192–205.

LOOS, F. M., WILLIAMS, K. P., & BAILEY, J. S. (1977). A multi-element analysis of the effect of teacher aides in an "open style" classroom. *Journal of Applied Behavior Analysis, 10*(3), 437–448.

LOVAAS, O. I., SCHAEFFER, B., & SIMMONS, J. Q. (1965). Building social behavior in autistic children by use of electric shock. *Journal of Experimental Research in Personality, 1*, 99–109.

LOVAAS, O. I., & SIMMONS, J. (1969). Manipulation of self-destruction in three retarded children. *Journal of Applied Behavior Analysis, 2*, 143–157.

LOVE, S. R., MATSON, J. L., & WEST, D. (1990). Mothers as effective therapists for autistic children's phobias. *Journal of Applied Behavior Analysis, 23*(3), 379–385.

LOVITT, T. C., & ESVELDT, K. A. (1970). The relative effects on math performance of single versus multiple ratio schedules: A case study. *Journal of Applied Behavior Analysis, 3*, 261–270.

LUISELLI, J. K. (1991). Assessment-derived treatment of children's disruptive behavior disorders. *Behavior Modification, 15*(3), 294–309.

LUMSDAINE, A. A., & GLASER, R. (1960). *Teaching machines and programmed learning.* Washington, DC: National Education Association.

MACE, F. C. (1994). Basic research needed for stimulating the development of behavioral technologies. *Journal of the Experimental Analysis of Behavior, 61*(3), 529–550.

MACE, F. C., KRATOCHWILL, T. R., & FIELLO, R. A. (1983). Positive treatment of aggressive behavior in a mentally retarded adult: A case study. *Behavior Therapy, 14*(5), 689–696.

MACE, F. C., LALLI, J. S., SHEA, M. C., & NEVIN, J. A. (1992). Behavioral momentum in college basketball. *Journal of Applied Behavior Analysis, 25*(3), 657–663.

MADSEN, C. H., JR., BECKER, W. C., & THOMAS, D. R. (1968). Rules, praise, and ignoring: Elements of elementary classroom control. *Journal of Applied Behavior Analysis, 1*(2), 139–150.

MAGER, R. F. (1962). *Preparing instructional objectives.* Belmont, CA: Fearon.

MANN, J., TEN HAVE, T., PLUNKETT, J. W., & MEISELS, S. J. (1991). Time sampling: A methodological critique. *Child Development, 62*, 227–241.

MANN, R. A. (1972). The behavior-therapeutic use of contingency contracting to control an adult behavior problem: Weight control. *Journal of Applied Behavior Analysis, 5*(2), 99–109.

MANN, R. A., & BAER, D. M. (1971). The effects of receptive language training on articulation. *Journal of Applied Behavior Analysis, 4*(4), 291–298.

MARKLE, S. (1969). *Good frames and bad: A grammar of frame writing.* New York: Wiley.

MARKS, I. M., & GELDER, M. G. (1967). Transvestism and fetishism: Clinical and psychological changes during faradic aversion. *British Journal of Psychiatry, 113*, 711–729.

MARTENS, B. K., LOCHNER, D. G., & KELLY, S. Q. (1992). The effects of variable-interval reinforcement on academic engagement: A demonstration of matching theory. *Journal of Applied Behavior Analysis, 25*(1), 143–151.

MARTIN, G., & PEAR, J. (1988). *Behavior modification: What it is and how to do it* (3rd ed.). Englewood Cliffs, NJ: Prentice-Hall.

MASON, S. A., MCGEE, G. G., FARMER-DOUGAN, V., & RISLEY, T. R. (1989). A practical strategy for ongoing reinforcer assessment. *Journal of Applied Behavior Analysis, 22*(2), 171–179.

MATHEWS, J. R., HODSON, G. D., CRIST, W. B., & LAROCHE, G. R. (1992). Teaching young children to use contact lenses. *Journal of Applied Behavior Analysis, 25*, 229–235.

MATHEWS, R. M., & DIX, M. (1992). Behavior change in the funny papers: Feedback to cartoonists on safety belt use. *Journal of Applied Behavior Analysis, 25*(4), 769–776.

MAWHINNEY, V. T., BOSTOW, D. E., LAWS, D. R., BLUMENFELD, G. J., & HOPKINS, B. L. (1971). A comparison of students' studying behavior produced by daily, weekly, and three-week testing schedules. *Journal of Applied Behavior Analysis, 4*, 257–264.

MCEVOY, M. A., NORDQUIST, V. M., TWARDOSZ, S., HECKAMAN, K. A., WEHBY, J. H., & DENNY, R. K. (1988). Promoting autistic children's peer interaction in an integrated early childhood setting using affection activities. *Journal of Applied Behavior Analysis, 21*(2), 193–200.

MCFADDEN, A. C., MARSH, G. E., PRICE, B. J., & HWANG, Y. (1992). A study of race and gender bias in the punishment of school children. *Education and Treatment of Children, 15*(2), 140–146.

MCNEES, M. P., EGLI, D. S., MARSHALL, R. S., SCHNELLE, J. F., & RISLEY, T. R. (1976). Shoplifting prevention: Providing information through signs. *Journal of Applied Behavior Analysis, 9*(4), 399–405.

MCSWEENY, A. J. (1978). Effects of response cost on the behavior of a million persons: Charging for directory assistance in Cincinnati. *Journal of Applied Behavior Analysis, 11*(1), 47–51.

MELAMED, B. G., & BENNETT, C. G. (1985). Behavioral dentistry. In L. J. Siegel & C. Twentyman (Eds.), *Prevention and treatment in behavioral medicine*. New York: Springer.

MERTZ, W., TSUI, J. C., JUDD, J. T., REISER, J., HALLFRISCH, J., MORRIS, E. R., STEELE, P. D., & LASHLEY, E. (1991). What are people really eating? The relation between energy intake derived from estimated diet records and intake determined to maintain body weight. *American Journal of Clinical Nutrition, 54*, 291–295.

MICHAEL, J. (1974a). Statistical inference for individual organism research: Some reactions to a suggestion by Gentile, Riden, and Klein. *Journal of Applied Behavior Analysis, 7*(4), 627–628.

MICHAEL, J. (1974b). Statistical inference for single-subject research: Mixed blessing or curse? *Journal of Applied Behavior Analysis, 7*, 647–653.

MICHAEL, J. (1975). Positive and negative reinforcement, a distinction that is no longer necessary; or a better way to talk about bad things. *Behaviorism, 3*(1), 33–44.

MILLER, L. K. (1968a). Escape from an effortful situation. *Journal of the Experimental Analysis of Behavior, 11*, 619–627.

MILLER, L. K. (1968b). Determinancy vs. risk: A critique of contemporary statistical methodology in sociology. *Kansas Journal of Sociology, 4*, 71–78.

MILLER, L. K. (1970). Some punishing effects of response-force. *Journal of the Experimental Analysis of Behavior, 13*, 215–220.

MILLER, L. K., & FEALLOCK, R. A. (1975). A behavioral system for group living. In E. Ramp & G. Semb (Eds.), *Behavior analysis: Areas of research and application* (pp. 73–96). Englewood Cliffs, NJ: Prentice-Hall.

MILLER, L. K., & MILLER, O. L. (1970). Reinforcing self-help group activities of welfare recipients. *Journal of Applied Behavior Analysis, 3*, 57–64.

MILLER, L. K., & SCHNEIDER, R. L. (1970). The use of a token system in Project Head Start. *Journal of Applied Behavior Analysis, 3*, 213–220.

MILLER, L. K., & WEAVER, F. H. (1974). The use of "concept programming" to teach behavioral concepts to university students. In J. Johnston (Ed.), *Behavior research and technology in higher education*. Springfield, IL: Charles C. Thomas.

MILLER, W. C. (1976). Brainwaves and the creative state. *Behavioral Engineering, 3*(3), 73–75.

MINKIN, N. M., BRAUKMANN, C. J., MINKIN, B. L., TIMBERS, G. D., FIXSEN, D. L., PHILLIPS, E. L., & WOLF, M. M. (1976). The social validation and training of conversational skills. *Journal of Applied Behavior Analysis, 9*(2), 127–139.

MOERK, E. L. (1990). Three-term contingency patterns in mother-child verbal interactions during first-language acquisition. *Journal of the Experimental Analysis of Behavior, 54*(3), 293–305.

MONTESINOS, L., FRISCH, L. E., GREENE, B. F., & HAMILTON, M. (1990). An analysis of and intervention in the sexual transmission of disease. *Journal of Applied Behavior Analysis, 23*(3), 275–284.

MOORE, J. (1975). On the principle of operationism in a science of behavior. *Behaviorism, 3*(2), 120–138.

MOORE, J. (1980). On behaviorism and private events. *Psychological Record, 30*, 459–475.

MOORE, R., & GOLDIAMOND, I. (1964). Errorless establishment of visual discrimination using fading procedures. *Journal of the Experimental Analysis of Behavior, 7*, 269–272.

MORRIS, E. K. (1988). Contextualism: The world view of behavior analysis. *Journal of Experimental Child Psychology, 46*, 289–323.

MURPHY, J. K., & BRANTLEY, P. J. (1982). A case study reportedly involving possession. *Journal of Behavior Therapy and Experimental Psychiatry, 13*(4), 357–359.

NEALE, D. H. (1963). Behavior therapy and encopresis in children. *Behavior Research and Therapy, 1*, 139–149.

NEWSOM, C. D., & SIMON, K. M. (1977). A simultaneous discrimination procedure for the measurement of vision in nonverbal children. *Journal of Applied Behavior Analysis, 10*(4), 633–644.

NINNESS, H. C., FUERST, J., RUTHERFORD, R. D., & GLENN, S. S. (1991). Effects of self-management training and reinforcement on the transfer of improved conduct in the absence of supervision. *Journal of Applied Behavior Analysis, 24*(3), 499–508.

ODOM, S. L., CHANDLER, L. K., OSTROSKY, M., MCCONNELL, S. R., & REANEY, S. (1992). Fading teacher prompts from peer-initiation interventions for young children with disabilities. *Journal of Applied Behavior Analysis, 25*(2), 307–317.

O'LEARY, K. D. (Ed). (1979). Behavioral assessment [special issue]. *Journal of Applied Behavior Analysis, 12*(4), 489.

O'NEILL, G. W., BLANCK, L. S., & JOYNER, M. A. (1980). The use of stimulus control over littering in a natural setting. *Journal of Applied Behavior Analysis, 13*(2), 379–381.

OSBORNE, J. G. (1969). Free-time as a reinforcer in the management of classroom behavior. *Journal of Applied Behavior Analysis, 2*(2), 113–118.

OSBORNE, K., RUDRUD, E., & ZEZONEY, F. (1990). Improved curveball hitting through the enhancement of visual cues. *Journal of Applied Behavior Analysis, 23*(3), 371–377.

OSBORNE, M. L., & HIMADI, B. (1990). Evaluation of a shaping procedure with the changing-criterion design. *Behavioral Residential Treatment, 5*(2), 75–81.

PAINE, S. C., CARNINE, D. W., WHITE, W. A., & WALTERS, G. (1982). Effects of fading teacher presentation structure (covertization) on acquisition and maintenance of arithmetic problem-solving skills. *Education and Treatment of Children, 5*(2), 93–107.

PALMER, M. H., LLOYD, M. E., & LLOYD, K. E. (1977). An experimental analysis of electricity conservation procedures. *Journal of Applied Behavior Analysis, 10*(4), 665–671.

PARSONSON, B. S., & BAER, D. M. (1978a). The analysis and presentation of graphic data. In T. R. Kratochwill (Ed.), *Single-subject research: Strategies for evaluating change* (pp. 101–165). New York: Academic Press.

PARSONSON, B. S., & BAER, D. M. (1978b). Training generalized improvisation of tools by preschool children. *Journal of Applied Behavior Analysis, 11*(3), 363–380.

PATTERSON, G. R. (1977). A performance theory for coercive family interaction. In R. Cairns (Ed.), *Social interaction: Methods, analysis, and illustrations.* Society Research Child Development Monograph.

PATTERSON, G. R. (1993). Coercion as a basis for early age of onset for arrest. In J. McCord (Ed.), *Coercion and punishment in long-term perspective*. Cambridge, UK: Cambridge University Press.

PATTISHALL, E. G. J. (1989). The development of behavioral medicine: Historical models. *Annals of Behavioral Medicine, 11*(2), 43–48.

PAVLOV, I. P. (1927). *Conditioned reflexes: An investigation of the physiological activity of the cerebral cortex.* London: Oxford University Press.

PBERT, L. A., COLLINS, F. L., SMITH, S., & SHARP, B. (1988). Visual acuity improvement following Fading and Feedback training: II. Relationship to changes in refractive error. *Behaviour Research and Therapy, 26*(6), 467–473.

PFIFFNER, L. J., & O'LEARY, S. G. (1987). The efficacy of all-positive management as a function of the prior use of negative consequences. *Journal of Applied Behavior Analysis, 20*(3), 265–271.

PHILLIPS, E. L. (1968). Achievement Place: Token reinforcement procedures in home-style rehabilitation setting for "pre-delinquent" boys. *Journal of Applied Behavior Analysis, 1*(3), 213–223.

PHILLIPS, E. L., PHILLIPS, E. A., FIXSEN, D. L., & WOLF, M. M. (1971). Achievement Place: Modification of the behaviors of pre-delinquent boys within a token economy. *Journal of Applied Behavior Analysis, 4*(1), 45–59.

PIAZZA, C. C., & FISHER, W. W. (1991). Bedtime fading in the treatment of pediatric insomnia. *Journal of Behavior Therapy and Experimental Psychiatry, 22*(1), 53–56.

PIERCE, C. H., & RISLEY, T. R. (1974). Recreation as a reinforcer: Increasing membership and decreasing disruption in an urban recreation center. *Journal of Applied Behavior Analysis, 7*(3), 403–411.

PINKSTON, E. M., REESE, N. M., LEBLANC, J. M., & BAER, D. (1973). Independent control of a preschool child's aggression and peer interaction by contingent teacher attention. *Journal of Applied Behavior Analysis, 6*(1), 115–124.

PITTS, C. E. (1976). Behavior modification—1887. *Journal of Applied Behavior Analysis, 9*(2), 146.

PLACE, U. T. (1993). A radical behaviorist methodology for the empirical investigation of private events. *Behavior and Philosophy, 20*(2), 25–35.

PLUMMER, S., BAER, D. M., & LEBLANC, J. M. (1977). Functional considerations in the use of procedural timeout and an effective alternative. *Journal of Applied Behavior Analysis, 10*(4), 689–705.

POLIRSTOK, S. R., & GREER, R. D. (1977). Remediation of mutually aversive interactions between a problem student and four teachers by training the student in reinforcement techniques. *Journal of Applied Behavior Analysis, 10*(4), 707–716.

POPPEN, R. (1982). The fixed-interval scallop in human affairs. *Behavior Analyst, 5*(2), 127–136.

POULSON, C. L., & KYMISSIS, E. (1988). Generalized imitation in infants. *Journal of Experimental Child Psychology*, *46*, 324–336.

POULSON, C. L., KYMISSIS, E., REEVE, K., ANDREATOS, M., & RICHARDS, L. (1988). Generalized vocal imitation in infants. *Journal of Experimental Child Psychology*, *46*, 409–415.

POWELL, J., & AZRIN, N. (1968). The effects of shock as a punisher for cigarette smoking. *Journal of Applied Behavior Analysis*, *1*(1), 63–71.

PRUE, D. M., KRAPFL, J. E., & MARTIN, J. E. (1981). Brand fading: The effects of gradual changes to low tar and nicotine cigarettes on smoking rate, carbon monoxide, and thiocyanate levels. *Behavior Therapy*, *12*(3), 400–416.

PRYOR, K. (1984). *Don't shoot the dog*. New York: Bantam.

PRYOR, K. W., HAAG, R., & O'REILLY, J. (1969). The creative porpoise: Training for novel behavior. *Journal of the Experimental Analysis of Behavior*, *12*(4), 653–661.

QUINN, J. M., SHERMAN, J. A., SHELDON, J. B., QUINN, L. M., & HARCHIK, A. E. (1992). Social validation of component behaviors of following instructions, accepting criticism, and negotiating. *Journal of Applied Behavior Analysis*, *25*(2), 401–413.

QUINSEY, V. L., CHAPLIN, T. C., & CARRIGAN, W. F. (1980). Biofeedback and signaled punishment in the modification of inappropriate sexual age preferences. *Behavior Therapy*, *11*(4), 567–576.

RACHLIN, H. (1976). *Introduction to modern behaviorism*. San Francisco: Freeman.

RASING, E. J., & DUKER, P. C. (1992). Effects of a multifaceted training procedure on the acquisition and generalization of social behaviors in language-disabled deaf children. *Journal of Applied Behavior Analysis*, *25*(3), 723–734.

REDD, W. H., & BIRNBRAUER, J. S. (1969). Adults as discriminative stimuli for different reinforcement contingencies with retarded children. *Journal of Experimental Child Psychology*, *7*, 440–447.

REESE, E. P. (1978). *Human behavior: Analysis and application* (2nd ed.). Dubuque, IA: William C. Brown.

REICHLE, J., & WACKER, D. P. (1993). *Communicative alternatives to challenging behavior: Intergrating functional assessment and intervention strategies*. Baltimore: Paul H. Brookes.

RENNE, C. M., & CREER, T. L. (1976). Training children with asthma to use inhalation therapy equipment. *Journal of Applied Behavior Analysis*, *9*(1), 1–11.

REPP, A. C., ROBERTS, D. M., SLACK, D. J., REPP, C. F., & BERKLER, M. S. (1976). A comparison of frequency, interval, and time-sampling methods of data collection. *Journal of Applied Behavior Analysis*, *9*(4), 501–508.

RICHELLE, M. N. (1993). *B. F. Skinner: A reappraisal*. Hillsdale, NJ: Lawrence Erlbaum.

RIEGLER, H. C., & BAER, D. M. (1989). A developmental analysis of rule-following. In H. W. Reese (Ed.), *Advances in child development and behavior* (Vol. 21). New York: Academic Press.

RISLEY, T. R. (1968). The effects and side effects of punishing the autistic behaviors of a deviant child. *Journal of Applied Behavior Analysis*, *1*(1), 21–34.

RISLEY, T. R., & WOLF, M. M. (1972). Strategies for analyzing behavioral change over time. In J. Nesselroade & H. Reese (Eds.), *Life-span developmental psychology: Methodological issues*. New York: Academic Press.

ROBERTS, M. C., & SANTOGROSSI, D. A. (1976). Behavior analysis in the White House. *Journal of Applied Behavior Analysis*, *9*, 334.

ROBERTS, M. W., & POWERS, S. W. (1990). Adjusting chair timeout enforcement procedures for oppositional children. *Behavior Therapy*, *21*(3), 257–271.

RODGERS, M. A. (1993, September). How to handle a hostile driver. *Reader's Digest*, pp. 85–87.

RODGERS, T. A., & IWATA, B. A. (1991). An analysis of error-correction procedures during discrimination training. *Journal of Applied Behavior Analysis*, *24*(4), 775–781.

ROGERS, C. R., & SKINNER, B. F. (1956). Some issues concerning the control of human behavior. *Science*, *124*, 1057–1066.

ROLIDER, A., & VAN HOUTEN, R. (1985). Suppressing tantrum behavior in public places through the use of delayed punishment mediated by audio recordings. *Behavior Therapy*, *16*(2), 181–194.

ROSEN, R. C., SCHIFFMAN, H. R., & COHEN, A. S. (1984). Behavior modification and the treatment of myopia. *Behavior Modification*, *8*(2), 131–154.

ROSENTHAL, R., & ROSNOW, R. L. (1969). *Artifact in behavioral research*. New York: Academic Press.

ROSS, L. V., FRIMAN, P. C., & CHRISTOPHERSEN, E. R. (1993). An appointment-keeping improvement package for outpatient pediatrics: Systematic replication and component analysis. *Journal of Applied Behavior Analysis*, *26*(4), 461–467.

SACKETT, G. P., RUPENTHAL, G. C., & GLUCK, J. (1978). Introduction: An overview of methodological and statistical problems in observational research. In G. P. Sackett (Ed.), *Observing behavior: Data collection and analysis methods* (Vol. II, pp. 1–14). Baltimore: University Park Press.

SAGAN, C. (1989, September 10). Sagan on science. *Parade*, pp. 6–7.

SAIGH, P. A., & UMAR, A. M. (1983). The effects of a Good Behavior Game on the disruptive behavior of Sudanese elementary school students. *Journal of Applied Behavior Analysis*, *16*(3), 339–344.

SAMELSON, F. (1985). Organizing for the kingdom of behavior: Academic battles and organizational policies in the twenties. *Journal of the History of Behavioral Science*, *21*, 33–47.

SANDERS, M. R., & PARR, J. M. (1989). Training developmentally disabled adults in independent meal preparation: Acquisition, generalization, and maintenance. *Behavior Modification*, *13*(2), 168–191.

SAUNDERS, K. J., & SPRADLIN, J. E. (1990). Conditional discrimination in mentally retarded adults: The development of generalized skills. *Journal of the Experimental Analysis of Behavior*, *54*(3), 239–250.

SCHAEFER, H. H. (1963). A vocabulary program using language redundancy. *Journal of Programmed Instruction*, *2*, 9–16.

SCHOENFELD, W. N. (1978). "Reinforcement" in behavior theory. *Behavior Analyst*, *18*(1), 173–185.

SCHREIBMAN, L. (1975). Effects of within-stimulus and extra-stimulus prompting on discrimination learning in autistic children. *Journal of Applied Behavior Analysis*, *8*(1), 91–112.

SCHROEDER, S. R. (1972). Parametric effects of reinforcement frequency, amount of reinforcement, and required response force on sheltered workshop behavior. *Journal of Applied Behavior Analysis*, *5*, 431–441.

SCHUSSLER, N. G., & SPRADLIN, J. E. (1991). Assessment of stimuli controlling the requests of students with severe mental retardation during a snack routine. *Journal of Applied Behavior Analysis*, *24*(4), 791–798.

SCHWARTZ, B. (1977). Studies of operant and reflexive key pecks in the pigeon. *Journal of the Experimental Analysis of Behavior*, *27*(2), 301–313.

SCHWARTZ, G. J. (1977). College students as contingency managers for adolescents in a program to develop reading skills. *Journal of Applied Behavior Analysis*, *10*, 645–655.

SCHWARTZ, I. S., & BAER, D. M. (1991). Social-validity assessments: Is current practice state-of-the-art? *Journal of Applied Behavior Analysis*, *24*(2), 189–204.

SCHWARTZ, M. L., & HAWKINS, R. P. (1970). Applications of delayed reinforcement procedures to the behaviors of an elementary school child. *Journal of Applied Behavior Analysis*, *3*, 85–96.

SECAN, K. E., EGEL, A. L., & TILLEY, C. S. (1989). Acquisition, generalization, and maintenance of question-answering skills in autistic children. *Journal of Applied Behavior Analysis*, *22*(2), 181–196.

SEYMOUR, F. W., BAYFIELD, G., BROCK, P., & DURING, M. (1983). Management of night waking in young children. *Australian Journal of Family Therapy*, *4*, 217–223.

SHERMAN, J. A. (1963). Reinstatement of verbal behavior in a psychotic by reinforcement methods. *Journal of Speech and Hearing Disorders*, *28*(4), 398–401.

SHULL, R. L. (1995). Interpreting cognitive phenomena: A review of Donahoe and Palmer's *Learning and complex behavior*. *Journal of the Experimental Analysis of Behavior*, *63*, 347–358.

SIDMAN, M. (1960). *Tactics of scientific research*. New York: Basic Books.

SIDMAN, M. (1971). Reading and auditory-visual equivalences. *Journal of Speech and Hearing Research*, *14*, 5–13.

SIDMAN, M. (1978). Remarks. *Behaviorism*, *6*(2), 265–268.

SIDMAN, M. (1988). A behavior analyst's view of coercion. Paper presented at a meeting of the Eastern Psychological Association (Buffalo, NY).

SIDMAN, M. (1989). *Coercion and its fallout*. Boston: Authors Cooperative.

SIDMAN, M., & TAILBY, W. (1982). Conditional discriminations vs. matching-to-sample: An expansion of the testing paradigm. *Journal of the Experimental Analysis of Behavior*, *37*, 5–22.

SIMMONS, M. W., & LIPSITT, L. P. (1961). An operant discrimination apparatus for infants. *Journal of the Experimental Analysis of Behavior*, *4*, 233–235.

SINGH, N. N., & LEUNG, J. P. (1988). Smoking cessation through cigarette-fading, self-recording, and contracting: Treatment, maintenance and long-term follow up. *Addictive Behaviors*, *13*(1), 101–105.

SKINNER, B. F. (1945). The operational analysis of psychological terms. *Psychological Review*, *52*, 270–277.

SKINNER, B. F. (1948a). "Superstition" in the pigeon. *Journal of Experimental Psychology*, *38*, 168–172.

SKINNER, B. F. (1948b). *Walden two*. New York: Macmillan.

SKINNER, B. F. (1950). Are theories of learning necessary? *Psychological Review*, *57*, 193–216.

SKINNER, B. F. (1953a). *Science and human behavior*. New York: Macmillan.

SKINNER, B. F. (1953b). Personal control. In *Science and human behavior* (pp. 313–322). New York: Macmillan.

SKINNER, B. F. (1954). The science of learning and the art of teaching. *Harvard Educational Review*, *24*(2), 99–113.

SKINNER, B. F. (1958). *Cumulative record*. New York: Appleton-Century-Crofts.

SKINNER, B. F. (1972). *Beyond freedom and dignity*. New York: Knopf.

SKINNER, B. F. (1974). *About behaviorism*. New York: Vintage.

SKINNER, B. F. (1986). Is it behaviorism? *Behavioral and Brain Sciences*, *9*, 716.

SKINNER, B. F. (1989). The place of feelings in the analysis of behavior. In B. F. Skinner (Ed.), *Recent issues in the analysis of behavior* (pp. 3–11). Columbus, OH: Merrill.

SLIFER, K. J., CATALDO, M. F., LLORENTE, A. M., & GERSEN, A. C. (1993). Behavior analysis of motion control for pediatric neuroimaging. *Journal of Applied Behavior Analysis*, *26*(4), 469–470.

SNYDER, G. (1990). Burrhus Frederic Skinner—The man behind the science. *ABA Newsletter*, *13*(3), 3–5.

SOLNICK, J. V., RINCOVER, A., & PETERSON, C. R. (1977). Some determinants of the reinforcing and punishing effects of timeout. *Journal of Applied Behavior Analysis*, *10*(3), 415–424.

SPRUTE, K. A., WILLIAMS, R. L., & MCLAUGHLIN, T. F. (1990). Effects of a group response cost contingency procedure on the rate of classroom interruptions with emotionally disturbed secondary students. *Child and Family Behavior Therapy*, *12*(2), 1–12.

STAATS, A. W., & BUTTERFIELD, W. H. (1965). Treatment of nonreading in a culturally deprived juvenile delinquent: An application of reinforcement procedures. *Child Development*, *36*, 925–942.

STAATS, A. W., FINLEY, J. R., MINKE, K. A., & WOLF, M. (1964). Reinforcement variables in the control of unit reading responses. *Journal of the Experimental Analysis of Behavior*, *7*, 139–149.

STAATS, A. W., STAATS, C. K., SCHULTZ, R., & WOLF, M. M. (1962). The conditioning of textual responses using "extrinsic" reinforcers. *Journal of the Experimental Analysis of Behavior*, *5*, 33–40.

STARK, L. J., ALLEN, K. D., HURST, M., NASH, D. A., RIGNEY, B., & STOKES, T. F. (1989). Distraction: Its utilization and efficacy with children undergoing dental treatment. *Journal of Applied Behavior Analysis*, *22*(3), 297–307.

STARK, L. J., KNAPP, L. G., BOWEN, A. M., POWERS, S. W., JELALIAN, E., EVANS, S., PASSERO, M. A., MULVIHILL, M. M., & HOVELL, M. (1993). Increasing calorie consumption in children with cystic fibrosis: Replication with 2-year follow-up. *Journal of Applied Behavior Analysis*, *26*(4), 435–450.

STEIN, L., XUE, B. G., & BELLUZZI, J. D. (1994). In vitro reinforcement of hippocampal bursting: A search for Skinner's atoms of behavior. *Journal of the Experimental Analysis of Behavior*, *61*(2), 155–168.

STEPHENS, C. E., PEAR, J. L., WRAY, L. D., & JACKSON, G. C. (1975). Some effects of reinforcement schedules in teaching picture names to retarded children. *Journal of Applied Behavior Analysis*, *8*, 435–447.

STITZER, M. L., & BIGELOW, G. E. (1984). Contingent reinforcement for carbon monoxide reduction: Within-subject effects of pay amount. *Journal of Applied Behavior Analysis*, *17*(4), 477–483.

STOCK, L. Z., & MILAN, M. A. (1993). Improving dietary practices of elderly individuals: The power of prompting, feedback and social reinforcement. *Journal of Applied Behavior Analysis*, *26*(3), 379–387.

STOKES, T. (1992). Discrimination and generalization. *Journal of Applied Behavior Analysis*, *25*(2), 429–432.

STOKES, T. F., & BAER, D. M. (1976). Preschool peers as mutual generalization-facilitating agents. *Behavior Therapy*, *9*(4), 549–556.

STOKES, T. F., & BAER, D. M. (1977). An implicit technology of generalization. *Journal of Applied Behavior Analysis*, *10*(2), 349–367.

STOKES, T. F., BAER, D. M., & JACKSON, R. L. (1974). Programming the generalization of a greeting response in four retarded children. *Journal of Applied Behavior Analysis*, *7*(4), 599–610.

STOKES, T. F., & FAWCETT, S. B. (1977). Evaluating municipal policy: An analysis of a refuse-packaging program. *Journal of Applied Behavior Analysis*, *10*(3), 391–398.

STURGIS, E. T., TOLLISON, C. D., & ADAMS, H. E. (1978). Modification of combined migraine-muscle contraction headaches using BVP and EMG feedback. *Journal of Applied Behavior Analysis*, *11*(2), 215–223.

SULLIVAN, M. A., & O'LEARY, S. G. (1990). Maintenance following reward and cost token programs. *Behavior Therapy*, *21*(1), 139–149.

SULZER, B., & MAYER, G. R. (1972). *Behavior modification procedures for school personnel*. Hinsdale, IL: Dryden Press.

TALSMA, T. (1976). Thales on behavior modification. *Journal of Applied Behavior Analysis*, *9*, 178.

TATE, B. G., & BAROFF, G. S. (1966). Aversive control of self-injurious behavior in a psychotic boy. *Behavior Research and Therapy*, *4*, 281–287.

TAWNEY, J. W. (1972). Training letter discrimination in four-year-old children. *Journal of Applied Behavior Analysis, 5*(4), 455–465.

THOMAS, J. D., PRESLAND, I. E., GRANT, M. D., & GLYNN, T. L. (1978). Natural rates of teacher approval and disapproval in grade-7 classrooms. *Journal of Applied Behavior Analysis, 11*(1), 91–94.

THYER, B. A. (1988). Social work as a behaviorist views it: A reply to Nagel. *Social Work, 33*, 371–372.

TRUAX, C. B. (1966). Reinforcement and nonreinforcement in Rogerian psychotherapy. *Journal of Abnormal Psychology, 71*(1), 1–9.

TUDOR, R. M., & BOSTOW, D. E. (1991). Computer-programmed instruction: The relation of required interaction to practical application. *Journal of Applied Behavior Analysis, 24*(2), 361–368.

TURNER, S. M., BEIDEL, D. C., LONG, P. J., & GREENHOUSE, J. (1992). Reduction of fear in social phobics: An examination of extinction patterns. *Behavior Therapy, 23*(3), 389–403.

TWARDOSZ, S., & BAER, D. M. (1973). Training two severely retarded adolescents to ask questions. *Journal of Applied Behavior Analysis, 6*(4), 655–661.

ULLMAN, L. P., & KRASNER, L. (1965). *Case studies in behavior modification.* New York: Holt, Rinehart & Winston.

VAN HOUTEN, R. (1993). The use of wrist weights to reduce self-injury maintained by sensory reinforcement. *Journal of Applied Behavior Analysis, 26*(2), 197–203.

VAN HOUTEN, R., & NAU, P. A. (1980). A comparison of the effects of fixed and variable ratio schedules of reinforcement on the behavior of deaf children. *Journal of Applied Behavior Analysis, 13*(1), 13–21.

VARGAS, E. A., & VARGAS, J. S. (1991). Programmed instruction: What it is and how to do it. *Journal of Behavioral Education, 1*(2), 235–251.

VAUGHAN, W. J. (1984). Giving up the ghost. *Behavioral and Brain Sciences, 7*(4), 501.

VOLLMER, T. R., & IWATA, B. A. (1991). Establishing operations and reinforcement effects. *Journal of Applied Behavior Analysis, 24*(2), 279–291.

VOLLMER, T. R., IWATA, B. A., ZARCONE, J. R., SMITH, R. G., & MAZELESKI, J. L. (1993). The role of attention in the treatment of attention-maintained self-injurious behavior: Noncontingent reinforcement and differential reinforcement of other behavior. *Journal of Applied Behavior Analysis, 26*(1), 9–21.

VON BOZZAY, G. D. (1984). *Projects in biofeedback: A text/workbook.* Dubuque, IA: Kendall/Hunt.

WALKER, H. M., & BUCKLEY, N. K. (1968). The use of positive reinforcement in conditioning attending behavior. *Journal of Applied Behavior Analysis, 1*(3), 245–250.

WALKER, H. M., & BUCKLEY, N. K. (1972). Programming generalization and maintenance of treatment effects across time and across settings. *Journal of Applied Behavior Analysis, 5*(3), 209–224.

WALLACE, I., & PEAR, J. J. (1977). Self-control techniques of famous novelists. *Journal of Applied Behavior Analysis, 10*(3), 515–525.

WATSON, D. L., & THARP, R. G. (1972). *Self-directed behavior: Self-modification for personal adjustment.* Monterey, CA: Brooks/Cole.

WATSON, J. B. (1914). *Behavior.* New York: Holt.

WEAVER, F. H., & MILLER, L. K. (1975). Teaching students how to proctor in a PSI course by means of a role-playing procedure. In J. Johnston (Ed.), *Behavior research and technology in higher education.* Springfield, IL: Charles C. Thomas.

WEBSTER'S NEW COLLEGIATE DICTIONARY (1977). Springfield, MA: G & C Merriam.

WEINER, H. (1969). Controlling human fixed-interval performance. *Journal of the Experimental Analysis of Behavior, 12*(3), 349–373.

WEISBERG, P., & WALDROP, P. B. (1972). Fixed interval work habits of Congress. *Journal of Applied Behavior Analysis, 5*, 93–97.

WELSH, T. M., JOHNSON, S. P., MILLER, L. K., MERRILL, M. H., & ALTUS, D. E. (1989). A practical procedure for training meeting chairpersons. *Journal of Organizational Behavior Management, 10*(1), 151–165.

WELSH, T. M., MILLER, L. K., & ALTUS, D. E. (1994). Programming for survival: A meeting system that survives 8 years later. *Journal of Applied Behavior Analysis, 27*(3), 423–433.

WERLE, M. A., MURPHY, T. B., & BUDD, K. S. (1993). Treating chronic food refusal in young children: Home-based parent training. *Journal of Applied Behavior Analysis, 26*(4), 421–433.

WHEELER, H. (Ed.). (1973). *Beyond the punitive society.* San Francisco: W. H. Freeman.

WHITE, A. G., & BAILEY, J. S. (1990). Reducing disruptive behaviors of elementary physical education students with Sit and Watch. *Journal of Applied Behavior Analysis, 23*(3), 353–359.

WHITE, B., & SANDERS, S.H. (1986). The influence on patients' pain intensity rating of antecendent reinforcement of pain talk or well talk. *Journal of Behavior Therapy and Experimental Psychiatry, 17*, 155–159.

WHITE, M. A. (1975). Natural rate of teacher approval and disapproval in the classroom. *Journal of Applied Behavior Analysis, 8*(4), 367–372.

WHITEHEAD, W. E., RENAULT, P. F., & GOLDIAMOND, I. (1975). Modification of human gastric acid secretion with operant-conditioning procedures. *Journal of Applied Behavior Analysis, 8*(2), 147–156.

WHITMAN, T. L., & DUSSAULT, P. (1976). Self control through the use of a token economy. *Journal of Behavior Therapy and Experimental Psychiatry, 7*(2), 161–166.

WICKER, A. W. (1969). Attitudes versus actions: The relationship of verbal and overt behavioural responses to attitude objects. *Journal of Social Issues, 25*, 41–78.

WILLIAMS, B. A. (1994). Conditioned reinforcement: Experimental and theoretical issues. *Behavior Analyst, 17*(2), 261–285.

WILLIAMS, C. D. (1959). The elimination of tantrum behavior by extinction procedures. *Journal of Abnormal and Social Psychology, 59*(269), 142–145.

WILLIAMS, J. A., HURST, M. K., & STOKES, T. F. (1983). Peer observation in decreasing uncooperative behavior in young dental patients. *Behavior Modification, 7*(2), 225–242.

WILLIS, J., & GILES, D. (1976). *Great experiments in behavior modification.* Indianapolis, IN: Hackett.

WILSON, G. T., LEAF, R. C., & NATHAN, P. E. (1975). The aversive control of excessive alcohol consumption by chronic alcoholics in the laboratory setting. *Journal of Applied Behavior Analysis, 8*(1), 13–26.

WINETT, R. A., KRAMER, K. D., WALKER, W. B., MALONE, S. W., & LANE, M. K. (1988). Modifying food purchases in supermarkets with modeling, feedback, and goal-setting procedures. *Journal of Applied Behavior Analysis, 21*(1), 73–80.

WINKLER, R. C. (1970). Management of chronic psychiatric patients by a token reinforcement system. *Journal of Applied Behavior Analysis, 3*(1), 47–55.

WOLF, M. M. (1978). Social validity: The case for subjective measurement or how applied behavior analysis is finding its heart. *Journal of Applied Behavior Analysis, 11*, 203–214.

WOLF, M. M., BIRNBRAUER, J., LAWLER, J., & WILLIAMS, T. (1970). The operant extinction, reinstatement, and re-extinction of vomiting behavior in a retarded child. In R. Ulrich, T. Stachnik, & J. Mabry (Eds.), *Control of human behavior* (Vol. 2). Glenview, IL: Scott, Foresman.

WOLF, M. M., RISLEY, T. R., & MEES, H. L. (1964). Application of operant conditioning procedures to the behavior problems of an autistic child. *Behavior Research and Therapy, 1*, 305–312.

WRIGHT, H. (1960). Observational child study. In P. Mussen (Ed.),

Handbook of research methods in child development. New York: Wiley.

WULBERT, M., NYMAN, B. A., SNOW, D., & OWEN, Y. (1973). The efficacy of stimulus fading and contingency management in the treatment of elective mutism: A case study. *Journal of Applied Behavior Analysis, 6*(3), 435–441.

WYATT, W. J., HAWKINS, R. P., & DAVIS, P. (1986). Behaviorism: Are reports of its death exaggerated? *Behavior Analyst, 9*(1), 101–105.

ZEILBERGER, J., SAMPEN, S. E., & SLOANE, H. N. J. (1968). Modification of a child's problem behavior in the home with the mother as therapist. *Journal of Applied Behavior Analysis, 1*, 47–54.

Answer Key

Introduction

Text

1. analysis 2. learn 3. problems 4. example 5. respond 6. sections 7. Reading 8. Quiz 9. check 10. Examples 11. hints 12. check 13. Quiz 14. Reading; Quiz; Examples; Quiz 15. review 16. Exam 17. Class; Review 18. read; write; check 19. read 20. write 21. check 22. boldface; underlined 23. Reading 24. References 25. examples 26. checking 27. different 28. every

Reading Quiz

1. check 2. check 3. Exam 4. problems 5. learn 6. underlined 7. Reading 8. Examples 9. check 10. different 11. every 12. calculator 13. Review 14. boldface [or bold] 15. read 16. different 17. read [or reread or review] 18. write 19. check 20. read; write; check 21. Reading; examples 22. Examples 23. Quiz 24. Class 25. behavior 26. check 27. Reading 28. review 29. behavior 30. respond 31. sections 32. Hints 33. analysis 34. example 35. hints

Lesson 1

Text

1. behaviorism 2. facts 3. applied 4. everyday 5. 1970 6. change 7. explain 8. feelings 9. yes 10. behavioral 11. methods 12. private 13. Skinner 14. different 15. same 16. environmental; change

Reading Quiz

1. environmental 2. moderate 3. severe 4. explain 5. private 6. change [or modify or cause] 7. behavioral [or social] 8. applied 9. everyday 10. analysis 11. facts 12. Skinner 13. different 14. multiple-choice 15. analysis 16. behavior 17. private 18. greatest [or leading or best] 19. resisted 20. behavioral 21. private 22. behavior 23. Skinner 24. environmental [or external or public or observable]; change [or modify or cause] 25. Skinner 26. change [or modify or cause] 27. 1970 28. no 29. explain 30. behavioral 31. public 32. behavioral 33. 1970 34. voluntary 35. explain 36. voluntary 37. environmental 38. behavioral 39. behavior analysis 40. environmental [or external or public] 41. explain 42. everyday 43. behavior analysis [or applied behavior analysis] 44. behavior analysis 45. feelings 46. events 47. analysis 48. recognition 49. private 50. behavioral 51. four 52. environmental [or external or public] 53. strategy 54. behavior 55. private 56. environmental [or external or public] 57. major 58. response 59. behavior analysis 60. public 61. public 62. everyday

Lesson 2

Text

1. does 2. behavior 3. behavior 4. observe 5. inaccurate 6. inaccurate [or wrong] 7. see; record 8. observed 9. definition 10. behavior 11. definition 12. behavior 13. isn't 14. whole 15. direct observation 16. behavioral definition 17. direct observation 18. records 19. approach

Reading Quiz

1. doesn't 2. exclude 3. behavioral definition 4. behavior 5. doesn't 6. record 7. observations 8. communication 9. consistent 10. behavioral 11. clearer [or clear] 12. environmental [or external or public]; change [or modify or cause] 13. direct 14. definition 15. observation 16. observation 17. behavior 18. behavior 19. self-reports [or self reports] 20. behavioral definition 21. behavioral 22. behavioral definition 23. behavioral 24. behavioral 25. behavioral 26. direct 27. records 28. approach 29. whole [or entire] 30. communication; observation 31. observed 32. 1 [or 1%] 33. definition 34. do 35. behavior 36. direct 37. behavioral definition 38. observe 39. observe 40. behavioral definition 41. don't 42. behavior 43. behavioral definition; direct observations 44. direct observation 45. behavior 46. does 47. communication; observations 48. behavioral definition 49. don't 50. do 51. behavioral definition; direct observation 52. direct [or direct observation] 53. sees [or hears]; records 54. behavioral definition 55. behavioral definition 56. behavioral; behavior 57. direct observation 58. behavior; behavioral 59. see; record 60. see [or hear]; record 61. inaccurate [or false or wrong] 62. inaccurate [or false or wrong] 63. behavior analysis 64. result 65. direct 66. direct 67. direct; self-report [or self report] 68. self-report [or self report] 69. self-report [or self report] 70. direct observation 71. direct; self-report [or self report]

72. direct observation 73. communicate; consistent 74. result 75. inaccurate 76. self-report [or self report]; direct 77. self 78. reports 79. observation 80. isn't 81. result 82. behavioral 83. self-reports [or self reports] 84. behavior 85. behavior 86. behavior 87. record 88. see 89. do 90. inaccurate [or false or wrong] 91. behavior analysis 92. do 93. self-report [or self report] 94. behavior 95. direct 96. inaccurate

Examples

1. behavioral; direct 2. result; behavioral definition 3. direct; self-report [or self report] 4. behavioral definition 5. direct; behavior analysis 6. direct observation; behavior analysis 7. no 8. yes 9. direct 10. direct observation

Lesson 3

Text

1. result 2. outcome 3. instance 4. event 5. event 6. continuous 7. Y [or yes]; Y [or yes] 8. discontinuous 9. aren't 10. discontinuous 11. doesn't 12. interval 13. 16 [or 16th] 14. event 15. outcome 16. replace 17. time sample 18. response 19. event; 90 [or 90%] 20. event 21. event 22. results; continuous 23. time sample 24. interval 25. method 26. interval

Reading Quiz

1. after 2. event; outcome 3. interval 4. outcome 5. outcome 6. outcome 7. time sample 8. intervals 9. event; interval; outcome 10. result 11. continuous 12. event 13. instance 14. is 15. discontinuous 16. event 17. instance 18. outcome 19. couldn't 20. continuous 21. no 22. event [or event recording]; direct observation 23. event 24. 90 25. event 26. during 27. interval 28. outcome 29. 150 30. yes 31. interval 32. time sample 33. event 34. outcome 35. result 36. results 37. nonuniform 38. time 39. method 40. behavioral; behavior 41. intervals 42. instances 43. instances 44. continuous 45. result 46. response 47. time sample; interval 48. outcome 49. time sample 50. interval 51. time sample 52. interval 53. outcome 54. event 55. interval; outcome; time sample; event 56. continuous 57. response; behavior 58. time sample 59. outcome 60. discontinuous 61. time sample [or time-sample] 62. event; outcome 63. continuous 64. outcome 65. event; interval; time sample 66. behavioral definition 67. direct observation 68. discontinuous 69. intervals; continuous; results 70. no 71. event 72. behavior; response 73. discontinuous 74. e 75. direct observation 76. behavioral definition; direct observation 77. interval 78. interval 79. results 80. behavior 81. uniform 82. wrong 83. instance 84. discontinuous 85. time sample 86. interval 87. aren't 88. outcome 89. time 90. different 91. observation 92. direct 93. event 94. continuous; results 95. intervals; continuous; results 96. continuous 97. direct observation 98. time 99. interval 100. no 101. discontinuous 102. discontinuous 103. continuous 104. time sample 105. outcome 106. interval [or time sample] 107. can't 108. time sample 109. sample [or time sample or time-sample] 110. instance 111. event 112. result 113. continuous

Examples

1. yes; yes; interval 2. no; yes; outcome 3. yes; no; time sample 4. no; no; event 5. no; yes; outcome 6. yes; no; time sample 7. yes; yes; interval 8. yes; yes; interval 9. outcome 10. behavioral definition 11. time sample 12. interval 13. event 14. direct observation 15. event 16. outcome 17. interval 18. behavioral definition 19. event 20. self report [or self-report]

Lesson 4

Text

1. validity 2. agreement 3. reliability 4. behavioral definition; responses 5. each 6. agreements 7. 5 8. 3; 5 9. 3; 6 10. count 11. 90 [or ninety] 12. outside 13. validity 14. validity 15. social 16. reliability 17. social validity 18. reliability 19. reliability 20. social validity 21. social validity 22. 29 [or 29%] 23. old; new 24. social validity; reliability 25. 100%xA/(A+D) 26. didn't

Reading Quiz

1. reliability; social validity 2. can't 3. true 4. reliability 5. stable 6. reliability 7. time sample 8. validity 9. 3; 1; 4 10. new 11. social validity 12. smaller 13. 3; 2; 5; 3; 5; .6 [or .60 or 0.6 or 0.60]; 60 14. .80 [or 0.80 or 0.8 or .8]; 80 15. yes; 3; 5; .6 [or 0.6 or 0.60 or .60]; 60 16. responses; 3; 6; .5 [or 0.5 or 0.50 or .50]; 50 17. 40; 10; 50 18. new 19. reliability 20. old; 90% 21. old 22. can't 23. no 24. same; same 25. outside judges 26. social validity 27. outcome; event 28. 90 29. agreement; outside judges 30. many 31. behavioral definition; responses 32. reliability 33. reliability 34. agreements [or A] 35. trial 36. outcome; event 37. 100%xA/(A+D) 38. social validity 39. time sample; interval 40. behavioral definition; responses 41. behavioral definition; responses 42. agreement 43. outcome; event 44. outside judges 45. outside judges 46. social validity 47. 100%xA/(A+D) 48. 100%xA/(A+D) 49. behavior analysis 50. social validity 51. direct observation 52. discontinuous 53. reliability; social validity 54. reliability; social validity 55. direct observation; reliability; social validity 56. trial; frequency 57. frequency 58. 80; 90 59. trial; frequency 60. reliability; social validity 61. 90; 80 62. 90; 80 63. judges 64. trial 65. social validity 66. no 67. new; 80 68. behavioral definitions 69. responses 70. yes 71. can't 72. can't 73. 80 74. social validity 75. outside 76. behavioral definition 77. (A+D) 78. agree 79. (A+D) 80. A/(A+D) 81. same 82. social 83. responses 84. social 85. 8; 10; .8 [or 0.8 or 0.80 or .80]; 80 86. social validity 87. reliability 88. no 89. can't 90. frequency 91. trial 92. reliability 93. can 94. validity 95. trial 96. 100% 97. social validity 98. 100%xA/(A+D)

Examples

1. yes; 8; 2; 10; .8 [or 0.8 or .80 or 0.80]; 80 2. yes; 9; 1; 10; .90 [or 0.90 or .9 or 0.9]; 90 3. no 4. yes; 60; 80; no; c 5. yes; 90; yes 6. no; no 7. social validity 8. yes; 90; yes 9. 80; no 10. social validity 11. 80; no 12. event 13. time sample 14. a 15. behavioral definition 16. no 17. 90; yes 18. yes 19. 80; no 20. 80; yes

Lesson 5

Text

1. experiment 2. modify 3. treatment 4. baseline 5. cause 6. alternative 7. one [or 1] 8. treatment 9. comparison 10. reversal 11. reversal 12. alternative 13. two [or 2] 14. baseline 15. multiple-baseline 16. 18 17. 26 18. reversal 19. comparison 20. notes 21. experiment 22. group 23. alternating 24. treatment 25. different

Reading Quiz

1. didn't 2. comparison 3. baseline 4. multiple 5. time 6. subject 7. treatment 8. different 9. outcome 10. treatment 11. multiple-baseline 12. reversal 13. cause 14. doesn't 15. 2 [or two] 16. 1 17. cause 18. multiple-baseline 19. reversal 20. treatment 21. different 22. reversal 23. individual 24. treatment 25. single-subject 26. comparison 27. comparison 28. multiple-baseline; reversal 29. treatment 30. comparison 31. reversal; multiple-baseline 32. comparison; reversal; multiple-baseline 33. multiple-baseline 34. comparison 35. multiple-baseline 36. treatment 37. 100%xA/(A+D) 38. alternative 39. baseline; treatment 40. baseline; treatment 41. baseline 42. reliability; social validity 43. modify [or change] 44. single-subject 45. single-subject 46. social validity; single-subject 47. time; individual 48. individual; time 49. treatment 50. discontinuous 51. treatment 52. alternative 53. multiple-baseline 54. treatment 55. comparison; reversal 56. alternative 57. time 58. reversal 59. time 60. can't 61. time; individual 62. treatment 63. yes; multiple-baseline 64. alternative 65. can't 66. alternative 67. yes; multiple-baseline 68. no; reversal 69. can't 70. 2 [or two] 71. treatment 72. reversal 73. treatment 74. different 75. modify 76. comparison 77. reversal 78. multiple-baseline 79. treatment 80. single-subject 81. individual 82. modify [or change] 83. yes 84. can't 85. backward 86. backward 87. treatment 88. treatment 89. different 90. treatments 91. alternative 92. reversal 93. comparison 94. treatment

Examples

1. baseline; treatment; no; no; yes; comparison 2. baseline; treatment; baseline; no; yes; no; reversal 3. yes; multiple-baseline 4. no; no; yes; comparison 5. multiple-baseline 6. treatment; comparison 7. reversal 8. reliability 9. multiple-baseline 10. comparison 11. 87; no 12. baseline 13. alternative 14. event 15. treatment 16. behavioral definition 17. reversal 18. alternative 19. 80; no 20. social validity

Lesson 6

Text

1. didn't 2. convincing 3. overlap; trend 4. 2; 5 5. 0 [or zero] 6. 4 7. 4; 2 8. 100 9. would 10. isn't 11. is 12. do 13. do 14. 1 15. 5 16. 4; 3 17. yes 18. no 19. visual 20. 30 21. no; yes 22. 0; no 23. 20; no 24. analysis 25. yes; yes 26. experiments 27. no 28. difference; cause 29. the same

Reading Quiz

1. does 2. first 3. higher 4. treatment 5. trend 6. 60; 4; 80; 3; 70; no 7. shouldn't 8. visual; alternative 9. no; no; yes; yes 10. 10 [or ten] 11. lowest; 2 12. 30; 30; no; yes; no 13. less 14. no; yes 15. causes [or caused] 16. overlap; 5; 50 17. trends; 3; baseline 18. reversal; reversal 19. overlap; trends; alternative 20. has 21. yes 22. end 23. 20; no; no; yes 24. no; no; yes; yes 25. visual 26. behavior 27. 0; no; no; yes 28. can 29. is 30. shouldn't 31. yes; no; yes 32. visual 33. 3 34. higher 35. 50 36. 100%xA/(A+D) 37. single-subject 38. behavior analysis; behavioral definition 39. convincing 40. overlap; trend 41. alternative 42. visual 43. visual 44. single-subject; visual 45. 30; no; yes 46. convincing 47. 5 [or five] 48. overlap; trend 49. no 50. 30 51. 0; no 52. 2; 2; 40; no 53. 3; 3; 60; yes 54. 5; 5; 100; yes 55. 5 56. no 57. yes 58. yes 59. no; no; are 60. lower 61. no; yes 62. yes; no 63. yes; no 64. lower 65. 0; yes 66. 10 67. largest 68. convincing 69. highest; 1 70. less 71. less 72. less 73. smaller 74. overlap 75. can't 76. overlap; trends 77. visual 78. alternative 79. yes; time; no 80. 0; no 81. 0; 0; 0 82. no; no; no 83. convincing 84. convincing 85. convincing 86. largest 87. smallest 88. largest 89. 2 90. 50 91. no; yes 92. yes; more 93. doesn't 94. caused [or causes] 95. convincing 96. overlap; trends 97. alternative

Examples

1. no; no; no; yes; no; no 2. no; no; no; no; yes; yes; yes 3. no; no; no; no; yes; yes; yes 4. yes; no; no; no 5. no; yes; no; no 6. no; yes; no; no 7. no; no; yes; yes 8. baseline; treatment; reversal; reversal; alternative 9. time sample 10. multiple-baseline 11. no; yes; no; no 12. baseline 13. no; no; yes; yes 14. alternative; comparison 15. no; yes; no; no 16. interval 17. no; no; yes; yes 18. behavioral definition 19. yes; yes; no; no 20. 80; yes

Lesson 7

Text

1. time sample 2. unexpected 3. Practice

Practice Review

1. behavior 2. yes 3. multiple-baseline 4. comparison 5. expected 6. interval 7. reversal 8. interval 9. comparison 10. time sample 11. event

12. behavioral definition 13. alternative 14. multiple-baseline 15. multiple-baseline 16. alternative 17. reversal 18. environmental [or external or public]; change [or modify or cause] 19. behaviors [or private events] 20. Skinner 21. yes; yes 22. behavioral 23. behavior analysis [or applied behavior analysis] 24. interval 25. reversal 26. treatment 27. treatment 28. interval 29. 85; yes 30. no 31. reversal [or multiple-baseline] 32. direct observation 33. 80 34. comparison 35. social validity 36. 100%xA/(A+D) 37. behavioral [or behavior] 38. 75; no 39. event 40. time sample 41. outcome 42. reliability 43. baseline 44. environmental [or external or public] 45. convincing 46. one [or 1] 47. see [or hear]; record 48. explain 49. discontinuous 50. behavioral definition 51. visual 52. social validity 53. 1970 54. 80; no 55. behavioral definition; single-subject 56. baseline 57. comparison 58. time sample 59. behavior analysis 60. event 61. overlap; trend 62. time sample 63. multiple-baseline 64. 80; yes 65. 80; no 66. time; behavioral definition [or definition] 67. event 68. single-subject

Lesson 8

Text

1. reinforcement 2. follows; increases 3. increase 4. event; procedure 5. reinforcers 6. reinforcers 7. reinforcement 8. reinforcer 9. reinforcement 10. reinforcer 11. baseline; treatment 12. reinforcement 13. multiple-baseline; reversal 14. reinforcer 15. behavior 16. reinforcement 17. increase 18. can't; unknown 19. reinforcer 20. reinforcer 21. unknown 22. reinforcer; reinforcement

Reading Quiz

1. no 2. reinforcers 3. increases 4. follows 5. reinforcer 6. follows; increase 7. reinforcer; reinforcement 8. unknown 9. reinforcers 10. unknown 11. can't 12. unknown 13. behavior 14. reinforcement 15. unknown 16. reinforcers 17. reinforcers 18. precede 19. reinforcer 20. reinforcer 21. reinforcer 22. reinforcer 23. behavior 24. reinforcement 25. history 26. history; reinforcement 27. increase 28. behavioral definition 29. social validity 30. unknown 31. unknown 32. no 33. correct 34. no 35. reinforcement 36. unknown 37. unknown 38. reinforcer 39. reinforcer 40. reinforcement 41. unknown 42. unknown 43. reinforcement 44. isn't 45. follows; increases 46. follows; increases 47. reversal; multiple-baseline 48. reinforcement 49. reinforcer 50. reinforcement 51. reinforcer 52. reinforcer 53. reinforcer 54. unknown 55. reinforcer 56. unknown 57. unknown 58. reinforcer; reinforcement 59. unknown 60. behavior 61. unknown 62. reinforcer 63. unknown 64. unknown 65. reinforcement 66. reinforcement 67. reinforcement; reinforcer 68. increase 69. behavior 70. reinforcer 71. unknown 72. unknown 73. unknown 74. unknown 75. unknown 76. reinforcer 77. unknown 78. unknown 79. reinforcement 80. reinforcement 81. reinforcement 82. increase 83. reinforcer 84. reinforcer 85. unknown 86. preceding 87. reinforcer 88. reinforcer

Examples

1. followed; increased; reinforcer 2. followed; steadied; unknown 3. followed; increased; reinforcer 4. preceded; increased; unknown; can't 5. followed; increased; reinforcer 6. follow; increased; reinforcer 7. follow; increased; reinforcer 8. unknown 9. reinforcer; reinforcement 10. reinforcement; reinforcer 11. reinforcer 12. reinforcement 13. unknown 14. reinforcement 15. reinforcer 16. unknown 17. reinforcer 18. reinforcement 19. unknown 20. reinforcement

Lesson 9

Text

1. extinction 2. stopping; decrease 3. extinction 4. extinction 5. extinction 6. is 7. extinction 8. wouldn't 9. unknown 10. wouldn't 11. unknown 12. extinguishing

Reading Quiz

1. extinction 2. extinction burst 3. increase 4. decreased 5. reinforcers 6. stopped; decrease 7. reinforce [or reinforced] 8. extinction 9. extinction 10. decrease [or be reduced] 11. behavior 12. decrease [or reduction] 13. stopping 14. reinforcer 15. wouldn't 16. unknown 17. wouldn't 18. unknown 19. unknown 20. extinguishing 21. is 22. extinction 23. didn't 24. history 25. unknown 26. desirable 27. extinction 28. extinction 29. behavioral definition 30. extinction 31. unknown 32. unknown 33. unknown 34. extinction 35. extinction 36. decreases [or decreased] 37. extinction burst 38. extinction 39. stopping; decrease 40. unknown 41. unknown 42. unknown 43. extinction 44. extinction 45. extinction 46. unknown; unknown 47. unknown 48. unknown 49. extinction 50. reinforcement; extinction 51. extinction 52. stopping [or stop]; decrease 53. extinction 55. unknown 56. extinguishing 57. unknown 58. extinction 59. extinguishing 60. extinction 61. reinforcement 62. reinforcement 63. extinction 64. increases; extinction 65. extinction 66. stop; decrease 67. unknown

Examples

1. yes; yes; extinction 2. yes; no; unknown 3. no; yes; unknown 4. yes; yes; extinction 5. extinction 6. unknown 7. extinction 8. unknown 9. unknown 10. extinction 11. reinforcement 12. unknown 13. reinforcement 14. extinction 15. reinforcement 16. unknown 17. extinction 18. unknown 19. reinforcer 20. extinction

Lesson 10

Text

1. reinforcement 2. different; reinforced; extinguished 3. reinforcement 4. reinforced [or reinforces]

5. reinforcement 6. differential reinforcement 7. history 8. incompatible 9. unknown 10. muscles 11. aren't 12. no 13. yes 14. aren't 15. no 16. yes 17. isn't 18. no 19. isn't 20. one 21. differential reinforcement 22. extinction 23. reinforcement

Reading Quiz

1. reinforcement 2. no 3. differential reinforcement 4. reinforcement 5. differential reinforcement 6. different 7. unknown 8. differential reinforcement 9. increases; decreases [or reduces] 10. alternative 11. two [or 2] 12. unknown 13. muscles 14. differential reinforcement 15. unknown 16. yes 17. history 18. differential reinforcement 19. differential reinforcement 20. differential reinforcement 21. aren't 22. reinforcement 23. differential reinforcement 24. aren't 25. no 26. yes 27. yes 28. yes 29. no 30. no 31. no 32. no 33. yes 34. incompatible 35. unknown 36. differential reinforcement 37. differential reinforcement 38. differential reinforcement 39. aren't 40. different 41. unknown 42. are 43. are 44. reinforcement 45. extinction 46. differential reinforcement 47. differential reinforcement 48. unknown 49. unknown 50. differential reinforcement 51. different; reinforcement; extinction 52. unknown 53. differential reinforcement 54. extinction 55. reinforcement 56. differential reinforcement 57. yes 58. differential reinforcement 59. differential reinforcement 60. differential reinforcement 61. different; reinforcement; extinction 62. differential reinforcement 63. reinforcement; extinction 64. differential reinforcement 65. unknown 66. isn't 67. aren't 68. reinforcement; extinction 69. are 70. differential reinforcement 71. reinforcer 72. social validity 73. differential reinforcement 74. can 75. differential reinforcement 76. unknown 77. differential reinforcement 78. one [or 1] 79. extinction 80. reinforcement 81. differential reinforcement 82. isn't 83. reinforcement 84. reinforcement 85. extinction 86. differential 87. differential; differentially

Examples

1. yes; yes; yes; differential reinforcement 2. no; unknown 3. no; unknown 4. yes; yes; yes; differential reinforcement 5. yes; yes; yes; differential reinforcement 6. differential reinforcement 7. unknown 8. unknown 9. reinforcement 10. reinforcement 11. unknown 12. differential reinforcement 13. reinforcement 14. unknown 15. extinction 16. unknown 17. differential reinforcement 18. reinforcement 19. unknown 20. differential reinforcement

Lesson 11

Text

1. shaping 2. approximations 3. target 4. target 5. successive approximations 6. shaping 7. approximations 8. successive approximations 9. shaping 10. reinforcer 11. shaping 12. differential reinforcement 13. reinforcement 14. target behavior 15. approximation 16. shaping 17. new

Reading Quiz

1. approximations [or successive approximations] 2. can 3. shaping 4. new 5. shaping 6. new 7. yes 8. shaping 9. extinction 10. differential reinforcement 11. target behavior 12. approximation 13. shaping 14. shaping 15. differential reinforcement 16. target behavior 17. target behavior 18. approximation [or successive approximation] 19. differential reinforcement 20. shaping 21. differential reinforcement 22. approximation [or successive approximation] 23. shaping 24. increase 25. differential reinforcement 26. approximation [or successive approximation] 27. approximations 28. can't 29. target behavior 30. successive approximations [or approximations] 31. differential reinforcement 32. approximation [or successive approximation] 33. target behavior 34. shaping 35. differential reinforcement 36. shaping 37. target behavior 38. approximation [or successive approximation] 39. target behavior 40. target behavior; approximations [or successive approximations] 41. target behavior; approximations [or successive approximations] 42. shaping 43. shaping 44. shaping 45. shaping 46. target behavior 47. approximation [or successive approximation] 48. target behavior 49. differential reinforcement 50. approximation [or successive approximation] 51. differential reinforcement; shaping 52. target behavior; successive approximations [or approximations] 53. shaping 54. differential reinforcement 55. target behavior 56. can't 57. shaping 58. shaping 59. shaping 60. approximations [or successive approximations] 61. shaping 62. old 63. approximation [or successive approximation] 64. behavior 65. behavior; approximations 66. approximations 67. behavior 68. social validity 69. target 70. shaping 71. extinction 72. shaping 73. approximations

Examples

1. approximation [or successive approximation]; differential reinforcement; target behavior; shaping 2. successive approximations [or approximations]; target behavior; differential reinforcement; shaping 3. differential reinforcement 4. target behavior; differential reinforcement; approximation [or successive approximation]; shaping 5. target behavior; approximation [or successive approximation]; shaping 6. successive approximation [or approximation]; shaping 7. differential reinforcement 8. unknown 9. reinforcement 10. unknown 11. shaping 12. differential reinforcement 13. shaping 14. unknown 15. unknown 16. target behavior 17. reinforcement 18. approximation [or successive approximation] 19. unknown 20. shaping

Lesson 12

Text

1. reinforcer 2. only 3. only 4. immediately 5. minute 6. amount 7. worthwhile 8. recently; long 9. deprived 10. rarely 11. contingency 12. immediacy 13. deprivation 14. deprivation 15. contingency; deprivation; size; immediacy 16. reinforcement; extinction; differential reinforcement; shaping 17. worthwhile 18. unknown; none

Reading Quiz

1. quickly 2. behavior 3. decreases 4. increase 5. reinforcer 6. contingency 7. contingent 8. deprivation 9. yes 10. deprivation 11. incompatible 12. daily 13. size 14. worthwhile 15. contingency 16. is 17. deprived of 18. size 19. worthwhile 20. deprivation 21. worthwhile 22. immediacy 23. reinforcement [or reinforcer] 24. rarely 25. deprivation 26. only 27. worthwhile 28. contingency; immediacy; size; deprivation 29. immediacy 30. deprivation 31. size 32. contingency 33. deprivation 34. deprivation 35. immediacy 36. immediacy 37. satiated 38. contingency 39. no; yes 40. contingency 41. reinforcer effectiveness 42. contingency; immediacy; size; deprivation 43. reinforcer effectiveness 44. contingency; immediacy; size; deprivation 45. deprived 46. immediacy 47. only 48. deprivation 49. deprived 50. worthwhile 51. size 52. only 53. minute 54. rarely 55. rarely 56. shaping; reinforcer effectiveness 57. reinforcer effectiveness 58. deprived 59. deprivation 60. contingency 61. effectiveness 62. contingency 63. increases 64. effectiveness 65. reinforcer 66. only 67. satiated with 68. no 69. desired [or desirable] 70. only 71. rarely 72. minute 73. immediate 74. amount 75. reinforcer 76. liked 77. reinforcer effectiveness 78. contingency 79. satiated

Examples

1. only; minute; worthwhile; rarely; deprivation 2. yes; yes; yes; yes; none 3. yes; yes; yes; yes; none 4. yes; yes; yes; no; deprivation 5. size 6. unknown 7. size 8. immediacy 9. reinforcer 10. immediacy 11. deprivation 12. contingency 13. unknown 14. deprivation 15. none 16. size 17. unknown 18. immediacy 19. shaping 20. contingency

Lesson 13

Text

1. continuous; intermittent 2. ratio 3. fixed 4. pause 5. fixed-ratio 6. fixed-ratio 7. variable 8. extinction 9. satiation 10. shaping 11. strain 12. continuous 13. variable-ratio [or VR-5] 14. fixed-ratio [or FR-30] 15. FR-5; VR-53 16. varying 17. continuous 18. no 19. continuous; intermittent; extinction

Reading Quiz

1. continuous 2. big 3. higher 4. pause 5. variable 6. intermittent 7. yes 8. increase 9. no 10. fixed-ratio [or FR-30] 11. FR-5; VR-10 12. varying 13. continuous [or FR-1] 14. no 15. behavioral definition 16. new 17. variable; fixed 18. continuous; extinction; intermittent 19. intermittent 20. extinction 21. continuous 22. fixed-ratio 23. variable-ratio; VR-5 24. fixed; variable 25. fixed 26. ratio strain 27. lower 28. no 29. extinction 30. fixed-ratio 31. variable-ratio; fixed-ratio; continuous 32. extinction; satiation 33. variable-ratio; fixed-ratio; continuous 34. shaping; ratio strain 35. continuous [or FR-1] 36. satiation 37. variable-ratio [or VR-4] 38. variable-ratio 39. variable-ratio 40. extinction; satiation 41. extinction 42. fixed-ratio [or FR-13] 43. intermittent 44. variable-ratio [or VR-50] 45. ratio strain 46. extinction; satiation 47. fixed-ratio; variable-ratio 48. continuous [or FR-1] 49. variable-ratio 50. extinction; satiation 51. shaping; ratio strain 52. continuous [or FR-1] 53. fixed-ratio 54. ratio 55. fixed 56. variable-ratio 57. fixed-ratio 58. variable-ratio 59. ratio 60. variable-ratio 61. variable-ratio; fixed-ratio 62. ratio 63. effectiveness; ratio 64. continuous [or FR-1] 65. ratio strain 66. continuous; intermittent; extinction 67. ratio 68. variable-ratio 69. variable-ratio [or VR-5] 70. b 71. variable-ratio [or VR-5] 72. intermittent 73. faster 74. intermittent 75. intermittent 76. fixed-ratio [or FR-10] 77. variable-ratio [or VR-10] 78. intermittent 79. variable-ratio [or VR-15] 80. quickly 81. slowly 82. slowly 83. intermittent 84. extinction 85. intermittent [or variable-ratio or fixed-ratio] 86. fixed-ratio 87. extinction 88. variable-ratio 89. high 90. ratio 91. shaping; ratio strain 92. continuous 93. strain 94. variable-ratio [or VR-8] 95. paused 96. intermittent; fixed-ratio; variable-ratio 97. variable-ratio 98. every time

Examples

1. variable-ratio; a; c 2. fixed-ratio [or FR-5]; b; d; pause; yes 3. fixed-ratio [or FR-2] 4. variable-ratio [or VR-3]; ratio strain 5. target behavior; shaping; continuous [or FR-1] 6. variable-ratio [or VR-4] 7. extinction 8. contingency 9. continuous [or FR-1]; variable-ratio 10. variable-ratio [or VR-4] 11. fixed-ratio [or FR-6] 12. shaping 13. variable-ratio [or VR-4] 14. reinforcement 15. variable-ratio [or VR-4] 16. shaping 17. satiation 18. fixed-ratio [or FR-5] 19. intermittent [or variable-ratio or fixed-ratio] 20. immediacy

Lesson 14

Text

1. interval 2. fixed-interval 3. scallop 4. fixed 5. variable; response 6. uniform 7. variable 8. interval 9. fixed 10. no 11. ratio 12. sooner 13. one [or 1] 14. interval 15. fixed-interval; FI-3 16. variable 17. time sample

Reading Quiz

1. intermittent 2. b 3. fixed 4. fixed-interval 5. counting 6. responses; time 7. ratio 8. one [or 1] 9. sooner 10. ratio; interval 11. variable-interval [or interval] 12. ratio 13. interval 14. FI; VI 15. VI-2 16. variable 17. superstitious reinforcement 18. law 19. intermittent 20. ratio 21. variable-interval; VI-5 22. fixed-interval; FI-5 23. ratio; interval 24. shaping; reinforcers 25. lower 26. variable-ratio 27. one [or 1] 28. interval 29. scallop; uniform 30. uniform 31. fixed-interval [or FI-3] 32. fixed-ratio; fixed-interval 33. faster 34. time sample 35. won't 36. fixed 37. fixed; response 38. variable 39. variable; response 40. variable-ratio [or VR-10] 41. scallop 42. scallop 43. variable-interval [or VI-6] 44. ratio strain 45. ratio; interval 46. satiation; extinction 47. fixed-interval [or FI-10] 48. a 49. b 50. variable-ratio [or VR-20] 51. fixed-interval 52. fixed-ratio; fixed-interval 53. variable-interval 54. variable-

interval 55. interval 56. interval 57. variable-interval 58. fixed-interval 59. variable-interval 60. one [or 1] 61. interval 62. ratio; interval 63. uniform 64. sooner 65. variable-ratio 66. continuous; extinction; intermittent 67. scallop 68. timing 69. fixed-ratio 70. response 71. ratio 72. scallop 73. variable-ratio 74. variable 75. interval 76. response 77. one [or 1] 78. one [or 1]; sooner 79. scallop 80. increases 81. fixed-interval [or FI-10] 82. increase 83. intermittent 84. no 85. no 86. fixed-ratio 87. interval

Examples

1. no; yes; variable-interval 2. no; yes; variable-interval [or VI-15] 3. yes; no; fixed-ratio [or FR-13] 4. no; yes; fixed-interval [or FI-30] 5. no; yes; variable-ratio [or VR-20] 6. interval; variable-interval [or VI-93] 7. variable-ratio [or VR-5] 8. fixed-interval [or FI-10] 9. variable-ratio [or VR-4] 10. variable-interval [or VI-4] 11. immediacy 12. fixed-interval [or FI-15] 13. extinction 14. differential reinforcement 15. fixed-ratio [or FR-3] 16. variable-ratio [or VR-10] 17. reinforcer 18. variable-interval 19. fixed-interval [or FI-2] 20. variable-ratio

Lesson 15

Text

1. reinforcement 2. reinforcer 3. reinforcers 4. variable-interval 5. c [or (c)]

Practice Review

1. unknown 2. unknown 3. outcome 4. reinforcement; extinction; differential reinforcement; shaping; reinforcer effectiveness; ratio; interval 5. reversal 6. 90; yes 7. reliability 8. interval 9. reinforcer 10. unknown 11. unknown 12. discontinuous 13. continuous 14. event 15. multiple-baseline 16. unknown 17. 90 [or ninety] 18. fixed-ratio [or FR-7] 19. multiple-baseline 20. comparison 21. unknown 22. follows; increases 23. unknown 24. unknown 25. shaping 26. approximation [or successive approximation] 27. target behavior 28. reinforcement 29. variable-ratio 30. reinforcement; extinction 31. different 32. immediacy 33. continuous [or continuous reinforcement] 34. ratio strain 35. fixed-ratio [or FR-2] 36. variable-ratio 37. satiated 38. differential reinforcement 39. intermittent 40. contingency 41. extinction 42. variable-interval 43. fixed-interval 44. unknown 45. behavioral; reinforcement 46. extinction 47. unknown 48. immediacy 49. deprivation 50. reinforcers 51. variable-interval 52. successive approximations [or approximations] 53. target behavior 54. stopped; decreases [or decreased] 55. amount 56. fixed-interval [or FI-1] 57. interval 58. contingency 59. fixed-ratio 60. variable-ratio 61. variable-ratio 62. differential reinforcement 63. none 64. behavioral definition 65. unknown 66. shaping 67. treatment 68. baseline 69. environmental [or external or public]; change [or modify or cause] 70. reinforcement; reinforcer 71. reliability; social validity 72. social validity 73. discontinuous 74. shaping 75. ratio 76. reinforcement 77. differential reinforcement 78. interval 79. extinction 80. effectiveness 81. fixed-interval; fixed-ratio 82. 75; no 83. continuous 84. variable-ratio; variable-interval 85. rarely

Lesson 16

Text

1. stimulus 2. behavior 3. discrimination 4. reinforcing; extinguishing 5. discriminative stimulus [or SD] 6. S-delta 7. discriminated 8. stimulus [or SD] 9. stimulus 10. SD 11. stimulus 12. training 13. stimulus 14. equivalent to 15. before 16. discrimination training

Reading Quiz

1. discriminative 2. stimulus control 3. discrimination 4. discriminated 5. discrimination training 6. discrimination 7. extinction 8. stimulus 9. discriminative 10. discriminative 11. extinction 12. S-delta 13. discrimination training 14. precedes 15. reinforcing 16. SD [or discriminative stimulus] 17. hadn't 18. discrimination training 19. discrimination training 20. extinguishing 21. SD [or discriminative stimulus]; reinforcer 22. discrimination training 23. reinforcing 24. increased 25. response 26. shaping 27. ed 28. reinforced 29. SD [or discriminative stimulus] 30. stimulus 31. SD; reinforcer 32. is 33. discrimination training 34. differential reinforcement; discrimination training 35. discrimination training 36. discrimination training 37. differential reinforcement 38. differential reinforcement 39. stimulus 40. stimulus control 41. reinforcer; SD [or discriminative stimulus] 42. differential reinforcement 43. more 44. discriminative stimulus 45. SD [or discriminative stimulus or prompt]; reinforcer 46. response 47. S-delta 48. complex 49. 1 [or one]; 2 [or two] 50. ion; ive; ed 51. ive 52. discrimination training 53. differential reinforcement 54. discriminated 55. discrimination training 56. SD [or discriminative stimulus or prompt] 57. discrimination; discriminative; SD; S-delta 58. discriminated 59. discrimination training 60. follows 61. stimulus 62. stimulus control 63. SD [or discriminative stimulus or prompt] 64. discriminated behavior 65. SD [or discriminative stimulus or prompt]; reinforcer 66. S-delta 67. reinforcement 68. S-delta 69. SD [or discriminative stimulus]; reinforcer 70. discrimination training 71. S-delta 72. stimulus control 73. stimulus control 74. discrimination training 75. discrimination training 76. differential reinforcement 77. discrimination training 78. discrimination training 79. SD 80. discrimination training 81. discrimination training 82. discrimination training 83. stimulus control 84. stimulus control 85. stimulus control 86. discrimination training 87. discrimination training; differential reinforcement 88. discriminated 89. stimulus control 90. stimulus 91. discriminated 92. discrimination training; differential reinforcement 93. SD [or discriminative stimulus or prompt] 94. SD [or discriminative stimulus or prompt]; S-delta 95. stimulus 96. discriminated 97. discrimination training 98. differential reinforcement 99. discrimination training 100. differential reinforcement 101. yes 102. discrimination training 103. discrimination training 104. differential reinforcement 105. discrimination training

106. discrimination training 107. discriminated; response; stimulus 108. differential reinforcement 109. stimulus control 110. discrimination 111. discriminative stimulus; SD; S-delta 112. stimulus 113. discriminated behavior; discriminated response 114. discrimination training 115. differential reinforcement 116. discrimination 117. stimuli 118. discrimination 119. SD 120. SD 121. extinction 122. discrimination training 123. is 124. discriminated 125. SD [or discriminative stimulus]; S-delta 126. discrimination training 127. discrimination training 128. training 129. discrimination 130. reinforcer 131. discrimination training 132. SD [or discriminative stimulus or prompt] 133. control; discriminated 134. stimulus 135. less 136. discriminated 137. discriminated 138. reinforcer; SD [or discriminative stimulus] 139. discriminative 140. stimulus 141. control 142. stimulus control

Examples

1. 1 [or one]; 2 [or two]; discrimination training
2. 1 [or one]; 3 [or three]; differential reinforcement
3. 2 [or two]; 1 [or one]; discrimination training
4. 1 [or one]; 2 [or two]; differential reinforcement
5. 2 [or two]; 2 [or two]; discrimination training
6. 1 [or one]; 2 [or two]; differential reinforcement
7. yes; no; discrimination training 8. discrimination training
9. discrimination training 10. stimulus control
11. discrimination training 12. stimulus control
13. SD [or discriminative stimulus or prompt]
14. discrimination training 15. differential reinforcement
16. SD [or discriminative stimulus]; S-delta
17. discrimination training 18. stimulus control
19. SD [or discriminative stimulus or prompt]; S-delta
20. discriminated

Lesson 17

Text

1. generalization 2. stimulus class 3. generalization 4. generalization 5. stimuli 6. generalization 7. generalization 8. behavior [or response] 9. generalization 10. generalization 11. generalization 12. generalization 13. generalization 14. generalization; generalization training 15. generalization; discrimination 16. 2; 1

Reading Quiz

1. concept 2. generalization 3. behavior [or response] 4. generalization training 5. class 6. related; novel 7. similar 8. related 9. more than one 10. generalization 11. stimulus class 12. generalization training 13. eliminates 14. generalization; generalization training 15. generalization training; discrimination training 16. 2; 1 17. generalization 18. generalization 19. generalization 20. novel; stimulus class 21. generalization training 22. behavioral definition 23. generalization training 24. draws 25. generalization 26. similar 27. generalization 28. generalization training 29. procedure; process 30. generalized [or generalizes] 31. generalize 32. doesn't 33. generalization training 34. stimulus class; generalization 35. stimulus class 36. novel 37. novel 38. generalization training 39. novel 40. novel stimulus 41. generalizes 42. generalization 43. class 44. generalization 45. discrimination training 46. generalization 47. stimulus class 48. stimulus control 49. generalization 50. discrimination training 51. novel 52. generalization training 53. generalization training 54. series; generalizes; stimulus class 55. series; generalizes; stimulus class 56. generalization training 57. discrimination training; generalization training 58. generalization training 59. generalization training 60. reinforcement 61. generalization training 62. novel 63. discrimination training 64. generalization training 65. hope 66. hasn't 67. related 68. generalization 69. generalization training 70. training 71. generalization 72. stimulus class 73. generalizes; stimulus class 74. series; generalizes; stimulus class 75. generalization 76. series 77. generalizes 78. series of 79. generalizes 80. stimulus 81. generalized [or generalizes] 82. social validity 83. eliminates 84. discrimination training 85. generalization training; discrimination training 86. novel 87. extinguishing

Examples

1. generalization; stimulus class; generalization training
2. generalization; discrimination training; generalization training 3. SD [or discriminative stimulus or prompt]; S-delta; discrimination training; generalization training
4. discrimination training; generalization training
5. generalize; generalization training 6. generalization [or overgeneralization]; discrimination training 7. generalization; generalization training 8. discrimination training
9. S-delta; SD [or discriminative stimulus or prompt]; stimulus control 10. generalization 11. discrimination training
12. stimulus class 13. discriminated 14. generalization
15. discrimination training 16. generalization training
17. discriminated 18. stimulus control 19. differential reinforcement 20. generalization training

Lesson 18

Text

1. prompts 2. stimulus 3. fading 4. prompt 5. discriminated [or prompted] 6. generalization 7. discrimination 8. response; feedback; steps 9. prompt 10. programming 11. programming 12. programming; fading 13. behavior; stimulus 14. differential reinforcement

Reading Quiz

1. new 2. prompt; SD [or discriminative stimulus] 3. discrimination 4. discrimination 5. discrimination; generalization 6. behavior 7. stimulus 8. behavior; stimulus 9. programming 10. fading 11. prompt 12. prompt 13. fading; programming 14. prompt 15. prompt 16. programming 17. small 18. step 19. feedback 20. response 21. generalization 22. generalization 23. generalization; discrimination 24. generalization; discrimination 25. fading 26. fading; programming 27. prompt 28. prompt 29. fading 30. fading 31. prompt 32. fading 33. prompt 34. prompt 35. control 36. fading 37. response; feedback; steps 38. steps 39. generalization 40. generalization 41. programming

42. programming 43. prompt 44. fading 45. discrimination 46. programmed 47. fading 48. prompts 49. generalization training; prompts 50. instruction 51. programming 52. few 53. programming 54. prompt 55. generalization [or generalizing] 56. fading 57. novel 58. programming 59. generalization 60. prompt 61. generalization 62. prompts 63. prompts 64. prompts 65. programming; fading 66. fading 67. programming; fading 68. prompt

Examples

1. prompt; fading 2. generalization; programming 3. programmed instruction [or programming] 4. generalization; prompt; programming 5. fading 6. generalization training; programming 7. programming [or programmed instruction] 8. shaping 9. fading; discrimination training 10. shaping 11. SD [or discriminative stimulus or prompt]; S-delta 12. generalization 13. discrimination training; fading 14. differential reinforcement 15. fading 16. programming 17. fading 18. generalization training 19. discrimination training 20. fading

Lesson 19

Text

1. imitation 2. imitative; imitative; reinforces 3. instructional 4. imitation 5. discrimination training 6. fading 7. imitation 8. demonstrate 9. imitation; imitative; imitative 10. instructional; instructed 11. differential reinforcement 12. imitation 13. fading

Reading Quiz

1. generalization training 2. reinforce 3. instructed behavior 4. reinforce 5. instructed 6. reinforcer 7. behavior 8. extinction 9. programming 10. fading 11. reinforcement 12. verbal description 13. imitative stimulus 14. describe 15. discrimination training 16. instructional 17. imitative stimulus; imitative behavior; reinforces 18. extinction 19. imitation training 20. imitation 21. discrimination; generalization 22. imitative stimulus 23. stimulus; behavior 24. instructional 25. training 26. behavior 27. ion 28. imitation 29. instructional; imitation 30. verbal description 31. imitation training 32. instructional training 33. instructed 34. imitative 35. imitative stimulus 36. reinforced 37. SD [or discriminative stimulus or prompt] 38. verbal description; instructed behavior; reinforce 39. SD [or discriminative stimulus or prompt] 40. verbal description; imitative stimulus 41. SD [or discriminative stimulus or prompt] 42. imitation; instructional 43. imitation; instructional 44. training 45. imitative stimulus; imitative behavior 46. verbal description; instructed behavior 47. imitation training 48. imitative stimulus 49. instructional training 50. imitation; instructional 51. prompts; instructional 52. generalization 53. discrimination 54. verbal; instructed 55. description 56. instructional 57. imitation; instructional 58. imitation; instructional 59. imitative 60. behavior 61. reinforce 62. reinforces 63. imitative 64. imitation training 65. instructed behavior 66. verbal description 67. imitative behavior 68. imitative behavior 69. instructional 70. imitation 71. imitative stimulus 72. stimulus 73. imitative 74. verbal 75. imitation training; instructional training 76. instructional 77. instructional training 78. imitation 79. stimulus; behavior 80. imitation 81. imitative stimulus 82. imitative behavior 83. reinforces 84. verbal description 85. instructed behavior 86. imitative

Examples

1. description; behavior; reinforcer [or reinforcement]; described 2. imitative; imitative; reinforcer [or reinforcement]; demonstrated 3. imitative stimulus; imitative behavior; reinforcer; imitation training 4. verbal description; instructed behavior; reinforcer; instructional training 5. imitation training; imitative behavior 6. programming 7. imitation training 8. instructional training; reinforcer [or reinforcement]; verbal description 9. extinction; continuous [or FR-1 or reinforcement]; differential reinforcement 10. imitative stimuli [or imitative stimulus]; imitation training 11. imitation training 12. differential reinforcement 13. instructional training 14. discrimination training 15. generalization training 16. SD [or discriminative stimulus or prompt]; S-delta 17. discrimination training 18. fading 19. generalization 20. imitation training

Lesson 20

Text

1. conditioned 2. primary 3. unpaired 4. backup 5. many 6. conditioned 7. generalized 8. chain 9. generalized 10. generalized 11. no 12. no; generalized 13. conditioned; generalized 14. conditioned; backup

Reading Quiz

1. conditioned 2. backup 3. many 4. all 5. backup 6. after 7. generalized 8. unpaired 9. response 10. stimulus 11. immediacy 12. money 13. primary 14. token [or point or token economy] 15. generalized [or generalized reinforcer] 16. backup 17. conditioned 18. immediately 19. B 20. conditioned 21. generalized; generalization 22. many 23. conditioned 24. backup 25. backup 26. 1 [or one] 27. sequence; discriminative stimulus [or SD]; reinforcement; sequence; discriminative stimulus [or SD]; reinforcement; chain 28. unpaired 29. satiated 30. stimulus; response 31. SD [or discriminative stimulus or prompt] 32. primary 33. SD [or discriminative stimulus or prompt] 34. conditioned; generalized; backup 35. unpaired 36. primary 37. many 38. satiation 39. primary 40. backup 41. conditioned 42. generalized 43. chain [or stimulus/response chain] 44. chain [or stimulus/response chain] 45. SD [or discriminative stimulus]; reinforcement 46. backup 47. conditioned 48. satiation; unpaired; generalized reinforcers [or generalized] 49. conditioned [or generalized] 50. immediacy 51. SD [or discriminative stimulus or prompt] 52. satiated 53. conditioned 54. deprived 55. generalized 56. chain [or stimulus/response chain] 57. backup reinforcers [or backups] 58. conditioned 59. instructional; conditioned 60. conditioned 61. no 62. generalized 63. backup 64. generalized

65. stimulus/response chain 66. generalized 67. conditioned 68. conditioned 69. sequence 70. SD [or discriminative stimulus] 71. primary 72. chain 73. conditioned 74. conditioned 75. SD [or discriminative stimulus] 76. does 77. sequence 78. reinforcement 79. primary 80. can't 81. backup 82. backup 83. chain 84. immediacy 85. chain 86. discriminative stimulus 87. sequence; discriminative stimulus [or SD]; reinforcement 88. chain 89. reinforcement

Examples

1. conditioned; backup; satiated 2. generalized; backup; deprived; immediacy 3. primary 4. yes; SD [or discriminative stimulus or prompt]; reinforcer; chain [or stimulus/response chain] 5. generalized; backup; deprivation; paired 6. satiated; primary 7. satiated; conditioned; generalized 8. generalized; backup 9. backup; conditioned 10. conditioned; backup; immediacy 11. backup; unpaired; conditioned 12. discrimination training 13. conditioned; backup 14. SD [or discriminative stimulus or prompt] 15. generalization 16. fading 17. chain [or stimulus/response chain] 18. conditioned 19. generalization 20. generalized

Lesson 21

Text

1. extinguishing 2. discriminated 3. S-delta 4. stimulus control

Practice Review

1. fading 2. fixed-ratio [or FR-100] 3. variable-ratio 4. deprivation 5. discrimination training 6. programming 7. stimulus [or prompt or SD]; behavior [or response] 8. 80; yes 9. ratio strain 10. comparison 11. increases 12. intermittent 13. imitation 14. many 15. satiation 16. backup 17. after; before 18. stimulus class 19. S-delta 20. SD [or discriminative stimulus or prompt] 21. prompt 22. generalization 23. backup 24. discriminated 25. generalization 26. stimulus control 27. discriminated 28. SD [or discriminative stimulus or prompt] 29. generalization 30. chain [or stimulus/response chain] 31. discrimination training 32. instructional training 33. programming 34. deprived 35. imitative 36. generalized 37. instructional; imitation 38. stimulus control 39. imitative 40. chain [or stimulus/response chain] 41. generalization training 42. discrimination training; differential reinforcement 43. conditioned 44. discrimination training 45. discrimination; generalization; prompts; instructional; conditioned 46. generalization training 47. prompts 48. imitation; instructional 49. conditioned 50. shaping 51. imitation; instructional 52. variable-ratio; variable-interval 53. differential reinforcement 54. prompt

Lesson 22

Text

1. reinforcement 2. punishment 3. follows; decreases 4. punishment 5. conditioned [or generalized] 6. punisher 7. primary 8. unpaired 9. generalized 10. SP 11. punisher 12. punishment 13. punishment; SP 14. differential reinforcement 15. punishment 16. punisher 17. punishment; punisher 18. unknown 19. reinforcer

Reading Quiz

1. stimulus 2. punisher 3. aversive 4. conditioned [or generalized] 5. immediacy 6. undesirable 7. punisher 8. reinforcers 9. punishers 10. discriminative 11. punishment 12. punishment 13. punishers 14. a 15. punishment 16. punishment; punisher 17. differential reinforcement 18. discrimination training 19. punishment 20. instructional 21. punishment 22. unknown 23. reinforcement 24. punishment 25. least 26. punishment 27. discriminative stimulus [or SP] 28. punishment 29. punishment 30. punishment 31. extinction 32. punishment 33. unpaired 34. many 35. satiation [or adaptation] 36. follows; decreases [or reduces] 37. discriminative; SP 38. SP [or discriminative stimulus for punishment]; punisher 39. discriminative stimulus for punishment [or SP] 40. punisher 41. punisher 42. punisher 43. conditioned 44. discriminative; SP 45. punisher 46. generalized 47. conditioned 48. unknown 49. follow 50. decrease [or reduction] 51. contingency; immediacy; deprivation; size 52. punisher 53. primary 54. punishment 55. punishment 56. aversive 57. aversive 58. primary; conditioned; generalized 59. primary; conditioned; generalized 60. punishment 61. generalization 62. aversive 63. no 64. no 65. reinforcement 66. punishment [or aversive control] 67. most 68. can't 69. punishment 70. punisher 71. decreases 72. decreases 73. unknown 74. extinction 75. punishment 76. extinction 77. punishment 78. unknown 79. unknown 80. unknown 81. unknown 82. punishment 83. punisher 84. decreases 85. aversive 86. aversive 87. punisher 88. decreases 89. decreases 90. aversive 91. aversive 92. immediately [or right] 93. punishment; extinction 94. SIB 95. extinction 96. punishment 97. no 98. punishment 99. instructional 100. punisher 101. extinction

Examples

1. no; no; punishment 2. no; no; punisher 3. no; no; punishment 4. yes; no; punisher; SP [or discriminative stimulus] 5. punisher; conditioned 6. extinction 7. punishment 8. conditioned 9. punisher; punishment 10. punishment; reinforcement [or positive reinforcement] 11. punisher; SP 12. punishment 13. extinction 14. discrimination training 15. immediacy 16. differential reinforcement 17. reinforcement 18. conditioned 19. punishing 20. extinction

Lesson 23

Text

1. withdrawing; decrease 2. not making 3. punisher 4. punisher 5. punishment 6. extinction 7. punishment 8. unknown

Reading Quiz

1. permanent 2. punishment 3. time out 4. punishment 5. rarely 6. punishment 7. time out 8. rarely 9. punishment; time out 10. punishment 11. no 12. punishment 13. don't 14. extinction 15. punisher 16. time out 17. unknown 18. punishment 19. reinforcement 20. unknown 21. unknown 22. unknown 23. unknown 24. extinction 25. extinction 26. temporary 27. punishment 28. punishment 29. withdrawal 30. decrease 31. withdrawal 32. unknown 33. follows; decreases [or reduces] 34. time out 35. time out 36. time out 37. punisher; SP 38. punishment 39. unknown 40. punishment 41. extinction 42. punishment 43. unknown 44. unknown 45. punishment 46. conditioned 47. punishment 48. punishment 49. punishment 50. extinction 51. reinforcer 52. primary; conditioned 53. punishment 54. punishment 55. punishment 56. extinction 57. punisher; punishment 58. unknown 59. punishment 60. punishment 61. unknown 62. punisher 63. time out 64. unknown 65. punishment 66. unknown 67. is 68. time out 69. punishment 70. punishment 71. punisher; decreases [or reduces] 72. unknown 73. punishment 74. punishment 75. didn't 76. do 77. out 78. aren't 79. punishment 80. reinforcement 81. withdrawal

Examples

1. no; punishment 2. no; punishment 3. yes; extinction 4. unknown 5. extinction 6. unknown 7. punishment 8. punishment 9. extinction 10. punishment 11. punishment 12. punishment 13. extinction 14. punishment 15. generalization training 16. unknown 17. punishment 18. extinction 19. punishment [or time out] 20. extinction

Lesson 24

Text

1. negative 2. prevented; increase 3. prevents 4. negative 5. negative 6. reinforcement 7. positive 8. reinforcer 9. avoidance 10. escape 11. avoidance; escape 12. reinforcer 13. reinforcement [or negative reinforcement] 14. reinforcement [or negative reinforcement] 15. punishment 16. reinforcement [or negative reinforcement] 17. unknown 18. reinforcement [or negative reinforcement]

Reading Quiz

1. terminates 2. size 3. deprivation 4. terminates; prevents 5. decrease [or reduction]; increase 6. escape 7. extinction 8. prevents 9. avoidance; escape 10. negative reinforcement [or reinforcement] 11. prevention; termination 12. escape 13. avoidance 14. terminates; escape 15. prevents; avoidance 16. avoidance 17. reinforcer [or negative reinforcer] 18. negative 19. terminates 20. escape 21. avoidance; escape 22. reinforcement [or negative reinforcement]; punishment 23. avoidance 24. don't 25. reinforcer; reinforcement 26. escape 27. intermittent [or variable-ratio] 28. negative 29. shaping 30. reinforcer [or negative reinforcer] 31. unknown 32. reinforcer 33. negative reinforcement [or reinforcement] 34. punishment 35. escape 36. reinforcement [or negative reinforcement] 37. b 38. prevents 39. negative 40. reinforcement [or positive reinforcement] 41. escape 42. avoidance 43. contingency 44. terminated [or terminate]; prevented [or prevent] 45. negative 46. prevents 47. escape 48. reinforcement 49. increases 50. no 51. terminates 52. avoidance 53. negative reinforcer [or reinforcer] 54. escape 55. avoidance 56. unknown 57. fixed-ratio [or FR-5] 58. differential reinforcement [or negative reinforcement] 59. negative reinforcer [or reinforcer] 60. can't 61. increase 62. avoidance; escape 63. negative reinforcement 64. reinforcement [or negative reinforcement] 65. negative reinforcer [or reinforcer] 66. negative reinforcer [or reinforcer] 67. punishment 68. negative reinforcement 69. negative reinforcement 70. discrimination training 71. negative reinforcement 72. punishment; negative reinforcement 73. variable-ratio 74. extinction 75. reinforcement [or negative reinforcement] 76. negative reinforcer [or reinforcer] 77. punishment 78. negative 79. reinforcement [or negative reinforcement]; behavior 80. no 81. avoidance 82. immediately 83. terminates; prevents 84. reinforcement 85. increase 86. escape 87. escape; avoidance 88. avoidance

Examples

1. terminated; increased; reinforcer [or negative reinforcer] 2. prevented; increased; reinforcement [or negative reinforcement] 3. punishment 4. prevented; increased; negative reinforcer [or reinforcer] 5. prevent; stayed the same; unknown 6. terminate; increased [or increase]; negative reinforcer [or reinforcer]; escape 7. prevent; avoidance; negative reinforcement [or reinforcement] 8. prevent; negative reinforcement [or reinforcement]; avoidance 9. negative reinforcement [or reinforcement] 10. unknown 11. punishment 12. negative reinforcement [or reinforcement] 13. escape 14. negative reinforcement [or reinforcement] 15. immediately 16. avoidance 17. punishment 18. immediacy 19. avoidance 20. avoidance

Lesson 25

Text

1. aversive

Practice Review

1. unpaired 2. novel 3. many 4. event 5. follows; increase 6. satiation 7. shaping 8. fading 9. intermittent 10. chain [or stimulus/response chain] 11. stimulus class 12. deprivation 13. SD [or discriminative stimulus or prompt] 14. S-delta 15. related 16. SD [or discriminative stimulus or prompt]; reinforcer 17. discriminative stimulus for punishment [or SP] 18. SD [or discriminative stimulus or prompt] 19. prompt 20. multiple-baseline 21. extinction 22. direct 23. extinction 24. reinforced; extinguished 25. avoidance 26. generalized 27. conditioned 28. primary 29. intermittent 30. environmental [or external or public];

change [or modify] 31. punishment 32. generalization 33. generalization 34. multiple-baseline 35. fixed-interval [or FI-5] 36. behavioral definition 37. deprivation 38. reinforced; extinguished 39. reinforcement; extinction 40. comparison 1. successive approximation [or approximation] 42. fading 43. terminated [or terminate] 44. instance 45. decrease [or reduction] 46. discrimination 47. outcome; event; interval; time sample 48. extinction 49. no 50. social validity 51. generalizes 52. none 53. variable-ratio 54. no 55. SD [or discriminative stimulus or prompt] 56. differential reinforcement 57. discriminated 58. variable-ratio 59. generalization 60. variable-interval 61. fixed-interval 62. fixed-ratio 63. continuous 64. imitation 65. reinforcer 66. prompt [or SD or discriminative stimulus] 67. time sample 68. discrimination training 69. ratio strain 70. deprived 71. extinction 72. stimulus control 73. discriminated 74. discrimination training 75. immediacy 76. imitative 77. punishment 78. immediately 80. verbal 81. continuous 82. variable-ratio [or VR-3] 83. event 84. immediacy 85. 70; no 86. self report [or self-report] 87. imitation 88. instructional 89. time sample 90. fixed-ratio [or FR-10] 91. shaping 92. interval 93. reversal 94. conditioned; backup 95. contingency; immediacy; size; deprivation 96. outcome 97. result 98. unknown 99. reinforced 100. reinforced 101. contingency 102. generalization 103. time sample 104. generalization training 105. discrimination training 106. backup 107. differential reinforcement 108. differential reinforcement; discrimination training 109. agreement

110. isn't 111. prevented; increase 112. follows; decreases [or reduces] 113. conditioned 114. terminates [or terminated] 115. punisher 116. escape 117. escape 118. negative reinforcer 119. punishment 120. punishment 121. avoidance 122. discriminative stimulus for punishment [or SP] 123. punishment; extinction 124. punishment 125. negative reinforcement [or avoidance or reinforcement] 126. avoidance 127. size 128. decreasing [or reducing or decrease] 129. interval; ratio 130. differential reinforcement; approximations 131. behavioral definition 132. generalize 133. discrimination training 134. 80; yes 135. reinforcer 136. punishment 137. negative 138. reliability 139. generalized 140. treatment 141. stimulus class 142. reversal 143. shaping 144. contingency 145. S-delta 146. target behavior 147. less 148. interval 149. immediacy 150. baseline 151. generalized 152. 80; no 153. size 154. deprivation 155. reinforcement 156. instructional training 157. 80 158. comparison 159. fixed-interval [or FI-30] 160. programming 161. social validity 162. aversive 163. alternative 164. discontinuous 165. only 166. rarely 167. minute 168. outcome 169. punishment; negative 170. variable-interval [or VI-45] 171. approximation [or successive approximation] 172. target behavior 173. reinforcement 174. programming 175. reversal; multiple-baseline 176. continuous 177. size 178. fixed-ratio; fixed-interval 179. variable-interval; variable-ratio 180. baseline 181. unknown 182. reinforcement; reinforcer 183. chain [or stimulus/response chain] 184. immediately

Class Quizzes

Introduction **Form A**

Name ____________________

Grade ____________________

Date ____________________

1. This book introduces you to the science of behavior __________.

2. The book differs from other introductory textbooks by inviting you to actively __________ to it.

3. If you can answer 90% or more of the questions in a Class Quiz, you should have little trouble scoring well on the __________ Exam.

4. Words referring to basic concepts initially appear in __________ type.

5. The Class Quizzes and Review Exams test you on the Helpful __________.

6. Which is the correct name for the science: *behavioral analysis* or *behavior analysis?* ____________________.

7. If you have trouble scoring 90% on the Class Quizzes, consider three practices. First, __________ every section of the lessons. Second, __________ your answers to every question. Third, __________ all of your answers.

8. Some of the questions on your Class Quiz will come from the __________ Quiz already completed; others will be shortened forms of __________.

9. I have changed some of the Class Quiz questions that are based on the Reading Quiz and the examples enough to make a(n) __________ answer correct.

10. Behavior analysis studies how people __________ the rich variety of behaviors that mark their lives.

11. Short answer question A: Explain what you should do if you have trouble scoring 90% on the Class Quizzes.

____

____

____

____

Lesson 1 Form A **Grade** ______________________

Name ______________________ **Date** ______________________

---

1. Behavior analysis is the science that studies __________ events that __________ behavior.

2. Who do behavior analysts view as the founder of their field? __________

3. Behavior analysis is the modern form of the philosophy of __________.

4. Behavior analysts call the practical application of laws of behavior __________ *behavior analysis*.

5. The problem with explaining behavior using private events is that we still must __________ __________ the private events.

6. The first strategy taught in this book is to define your problem as a behavioral problem and to gather information about it. I call this the __________ strategy.

7. B. F. Skinner argued that operant behavior is __________ behavior.

8. The principle of public events is to look for the causes of behavior in __________ events.

9. Which of the following is a private event? __________ (hitting, thinking, walking)

10. Many articles about applied behavior analysis began to appear in about the year __________.

11. Short answer question A: Define behavior analysis.

____
____
____
____
____
____
____

Lesson 1 **Form B**

Name ____________________

Grade ____________________

Date ____________________

1. Behavior analysts view both mental and physical actions as forms of ____________.

2. Applied behavior analysis burst on the American scientific scene about ____________.

3. Behavior analysis is the science that studies ____________ events that ____________ behavior.

4. The first strategy for changing behavior is to define problems in behavioral terms. I call this the ____________ strategy.

5. Behavior analysts call events like thoughts, feelings, and attitudes ____________ events.

6. Seeking the causes of behavior in environmental events conforms to the principle of ________ events.

7. B. F. Skinner argued that operant behavior is ________ behavior.

8. Skinner founded the modern form of behaviorism called the science of ____________ ____________________.

9. The problem with private events is that we still must ______________ them.

10. Did Skinner deny the existence of such private events as thinking and feeling? ________

11. Short answer question B: What is the problem with using private events to explain behavior?

____

____

____

____

Lesson 2 **Form A** Grade ______________________

Name ______________________ **Date** ______________________

1. The observers in the Goetz and Baer study did not watch children building novel block structures. Because they recorded any resulting block structure as soon as they saw it, this was an example of the approach to observation called ______________ *observation.*

2. Behavior analysts view everything that people do as ______________.

3. John defined "understanding" a word as meaning that the person correctly defined the word on the English test. John asked Ming if she correctly defined the term *reify* on last Friday's test. Ming said "yes." Because John did not personally see Ming's answer but relied on her description, he used what approach to observing her behavior? ______________

4. Behavior analysts create a successful behavioral definition by describing exactly what behavior they will ______________.

5. One of the problems with self-reports is that when you ask people to report on their own behavior from memory, the results are usually ______________.

6. The science that studies external events that modify what people do is called ______________ ______________.

7. The principle of direct observation requires a trained observer who ______________ the behavior and ______________ his or her observation at the time.

8. Dr. Quail tried to explain poor learning by students in terms of a poor attitude. Because the poor attitude must itself be explained, Dr. Quail's explanation shows the problem with ______________ events.

9. The cooperative dorm developed a list to help the inspector determine when the living room is clean. The list includes a clean floor, emptied ashtrays, and a vacuumed rug. This specification of what is meant by "cleanness" is called a(n) ______________.

10. The principle of public events is to seek the causes of behavior in ______________ events.

11. Short answer question A: Give two benefits for creating specific behavioral definitions.
____
____
____

Lesson 2 Form B **Grade** ______________________

Name ______________________ **Date** ______________________

---

1. Ahles et al. (1990) defined pain behavior as patients "guarding, bracing, rubbing, expressing and grimacing." Behavior analysts call the statement in quotes listing observable behaviors associated with pain a(n) ______________ ______________.

2. Direct observation usually applies only to situations in which the observer personally sees the behavior occurring. The one exception is when the observer sees the physical ______________ of some behavior.

3. Bry claims that "Instead of taking awareness as a given, Skinner views the act of becoming aware . . . as another learned behavior." Skinner views awareness as a form of learned ______ ______________.

4. A statement that pinpoints what behavior to observe is called a(n) ______________.

5. The problem with using private events to explain other behavior is that they must still be ______________.

6. An observer who immediately records any observation that he or she personally <u>sees</u> (or hears) is using the principle of ______________ ______________.

7. John asked Mrs. Muniz how much trash her family had generated last week. John's approach will probably be quite inaccurate because of the problem with ______________.

8. Dr. Casey found that sixth-graders studied more if they signed a contract with their teacher. The contract said that they could go to an early recess as soon as they learned their spelling words for the day. Because the contract is part of the students' environment, Dr. Casey was using the principle of ______________ events.

9. A friend studied whether Leila initiated conversations with men. By "initiated conversations," he meant whether she "approached a man and was the first to speak." The phrase in quotes is called a *behavioral definition* because it describes what to ______________.

10. As long as an action is something that people do and it is physical and produces a result, behavior analysts call the action ______________.

11. Short answer question B: Give one reason why behavior analysts usually rely on direct observation rather than observations that involve memory, such as those evoked by questionnaires or interviews.

____

____

____

Lesson 2 **Form C** **Grade** ____________________

Name ____________________ **Date** ____________________

1. Behavior is everything that a person ________.

2. Behavior analysts view everything that people do as ____________.

3. Carmen defined "studying" the social code as being able to answer the ten questions listed at the end of it. She asked Ann if she could answer those questions. Ann said "yes." Using her answer of "yes" to observe studying the social codes is called ______________ observation.

4. To develop a sound behavioral definition, the behavior analyst must clearly describe what behavior he or she will ______________.

5. The problem with using private events to explain other behavior is that they must still be ______________.

6. The science that studies environmental events that alter what people do is called __________ analysis; a statement that specifies exactly what to observe is called a(n) ______________ definition.

7. When an observer writes down an observation as soon as he or she sees it, we call it ____________________ observation. When it is written down from memory, we call it ____________________ observation.

8. B. F. Skinner's statement that "a student giving correct answers to more and more difficult questions" defines learning is called a(n) ______________.

9. The cooperative dorm developed a list to help the inspector determine when the living room is clean. The list includes a clean floor, emptied ashtrays, and a vacuumed rug. The list is a behavioral definition because it describes what behavior to ____________.

10. As long as an action is something that people do and it is physical and produces a result, behavior analysts call it ____________.

11. Short answer question C: Explain how behavior analysts view thinking. How might thinking be similar to silent reading?

____

____

____

____

____

Lesson 3 **Form A**

Name ______________________ **Grade** ______________________ **Date** ______________________

1. Heddy watched family A for 15 seconds to see if they dropped litter; she then turned to family B and watched them for 15 seconds; she also watched families C and D, each for 15 seconds. Every minute, she would return to family A and start the routine over again. To observe family A, she was using what method of observation? ____________ recording

2. Event recording is based on counting ________ of the behavior.

3. When the Bakers checked their son's room each day to see whether it had been cleaned, they were using what method of direct observation? ________________ recording

4. Behavior analysis studies ________________ events that ____________ behavior.

5. The observation of whether or not a behavior occurs during a series of continuous intervals is called ____________________ recording.

6. If you immediately note the number of times that you say something positive to another person during the day, you are using what method of observation? ________________ recording

7. The observation of behavior during a series of discontinuous intervals is called ________ ________________ recording.

8. If a mother wanted to find out how much of the class period her child spent studying in math class, she might go to the school and observe whether her child was studying during each 20-second period during the class. She would be using what method of observation? ______________ recording

9. Walker and Buckley (1968) analyzed the study behavior of a fourth-grader by writing down each time he was "looking at the assigned page, working problems, and recording responses." This statement would be called a behavioral definition, because it describes what to ____________.

10. One of the behavior analysts observed Juan's study behavior in spelling. He noted when Juan was studying during a 15-second interval every five minutes. The behavior analyst had other chores during the rest of the five minutes when he was not observing Juan. What method of observation was the behavior analyst using? ____________ recording

11. Short answer question A: Define time sample. Explain how it differs from interval recording.

____

____

____

____

____

____

Lesson 3 **Form B** **Grade** ______________________

Name ______________________ **Date** ______________________

1. The method that involves observation of behavior during continuous periods of time is called ______________ recording.

2. When a teacher gives a written test, he or she is using the method of observation that is called ____________________ recording.

3. The problem with using private events to explain behavior is that the events must still be __________________.

4. Outcome recording, event recording, and interval recording all involve trained observers writing down their observations as they make them. Therefore, they follow the principle of ________________________________.

5. When Dee observed the number of times any child struck another child at the alternative school, she was using what method of observation? ______________ recording

6. Outcome recording is based on observing a(n) ________________ of behavior, rather than the behavior itself.

7. Lindsley (1968) recommended the use of a simple wrist counter so that people could count the number of cigarettes they smoked, the number of smiles, and so on. These would be examples of ______________ recording.

8. Willie observed his political science professor during 30-second intervals over a whole 50-minute period. He noted each 30-second interval during which his professor talked to the pretty blonde. He was using what technique of direct observation? ________________ recording

9. Time sample recording involves the observation of behavior during a series of brief intervals that are ____________________ from one another.

10. Being a bit of a gossip, you want to know what percent of the time Ali has his girlfriend in his room. To find out, you briefly check once every hour to see whether she is there. You study the rest of the time. You are using what method of observation? ______________ recording

11. Short answer question B: Both outcome recording and event recording observe uniform behavior. Explain the major difference between them.

____
____
____
____
____
____
____

Lesson 3 Form C **Grade** ______________________________

Name ______________________________ **Date** ______________________________

---

1. The principle of public events is to look for the causes of behavior in ________________ events.

2. Counting the occurrence of instances of a behavior is called ________________ recording; observing a behavior for a brief time several times a day is called ________________ recording.

3. When John counted the number of times during the lecture that his English professor split his infinitives, he was using what method of direct observation? ______________ recording

4. What two methods involve dividing the period of observation into smaller units of time? ______________ and ______________ recording

5. The checklist covering the results of cleaning behavior used by Feallock and Miller (1976) is an example of what method of observation? ______________ recording

6. A racing heart, racing feet, racing thoughts, and racing words are all activities that people do. Therefore, they are all called ______________ by behavior analysts.

7. The method of observation that involves the results of behavior rather than the behavior itself is called ______________ recording.

8. To discover the level of violence of a TV show, you might note how many 15-second intervals contain some form of violence. You would be using what method of observation? ________________ recording

9. David Lombard observed whether swimmers wore a shirt; got in the shade; and wore a hat, sunglasses, zinc oxide, and sunscreen lotion. What method of observation did he use? ________________ recording

10. Maria checked on her son ten times an evening, at randomly selected times, to see whether he was studying. What method of observation was she using? ______________ recording

11. Short answer question C: What questions can you ask to decide the method of observation that is being used?

____

____

____

____

Lesson 4 Form A **Grade** ______________________

Name ______________________ **Date** ______________________

1. Dan counted the number of consecutive 15-second intervals during which his baby sister was smiling. He was using ______________ recording.

2. The formula for reliability is: ______________.

3. Tom and Pam observed the chairperson of the ecology committee during ten-second intervals to see if he was dominating the meetings. The first ten observations were (with "T" indicating talking and "O" indicating others talking):

Tom:	O	T	T	T	T	O	T	O	T	O
Pam:	O	T	T	T	T	O	T	O	T	T

What is their reliability? ______________ percent. Does the evidence indicate that the observations are reliable? ______________

4. Reliability is a measure of the extent to which there is ______________ between two independent observers.

5. Kim and Jose counted shooting stars one night. Kim saw 17, and Jose saw 20. Compute their reliability: ______________ percent. Is it acceptable? ______________

6. You and your friend both measure the accuracy of your observations about Johnny's behavior by observing the same responses and then comparing the results. This is called a test of ______________.

7. Alice and Janet watched ten commercials shown on late-night TV to determine how many of them were advertising products that were ecologically harmful. They developed their own behavioral definition. Their results were (where "H" stands for harmful commercials):

Alice:	H	N	H	N	H	H	H	N	N	H
Janet:	H	N	H	N	H	H	H	H	H	H

Compute their reliability: ______________ percent. Would this be acceptable? ______________

8. Minkin et al. (1976) investigated whether adult ratings of conversations and the level of three "good conversation behaviors" correlated. They were testing the ______________ of their behavioral definition.

9. Eileen checked to see whether her lazy roommate was studying during a short observation made at 19 random times during the day. What method of observation was she using? ______________ recording

10. Behavior analysts consider everything that people do to be ______________.

11. Short answer question A: Explain in words the formula to compute the reliability of two observers using interval recording.

____

____

____

____

Lesson 4 Form B **Grade** ____________________

Name ____________________ **Date** ____________________

---

1. When we ask people what TV programs they watch, they name educational programs more often than they actually watch them. This is an example of the problem with what approach to observing behavior? ____________

2. Dave and Pat were assigned to check on the bookkeeper in the food co-op. They used an established checklist of ten job tasks. They found:

Dan:	X	X	O	X	O	O	O	O	X	X
Pat:	X	X	X	X	O	X	O	O	X	X

   What is their reliability? ____________ percent. Is their agreement acceptable? ______

3. Kim wanted to observe how well the typists for large companies typed. She counted the number of errors appearing in a letter from Exxon; she found 6. She is using what method to observe that typist's typing? ____________ recording

4. Barb and Gary wanted to find out how much time the children at Yellow Brick Road Free School were spending learning to read, write, and do arithmetic. They developed their own behavioral definition and observed in 30-second blocks of time. Their first ten intervals were (S=studying; N= not studying. :

Barb:	N	S	S	N	S	N	N	N	N	N
Gary:	S	S	S	N	N	N	N	N	N	N

   What is their reliability? ____________ percent. Is their reliability acceptable? _____

5. Reliability can be measured only when two people use the same behavioral definition to observe the same ____________.

6. Joan counted the number of times Professor Brainbuster said "uh" during Monday's lecture and found that he said it 50 times. If Nel counts 50 "uh's" during Wednesday's lecture, can we conclude that their observations are reliable? ____________

7. Larry observed how often Professor Green encouraged students to make comments in his discussion class. Larry decided to record whenever the professor agreed with a comment. He also recorded praise of the comment. Larry's decision about what to record would be called a(n) ____________.

8. With a new behavioral definition, researchers will accept a reliability figure of ________ percent.

9. The extent of agreement between two sets of observations is called their ____________.

10. Quinn et al. (1992) showed that adults rated accepting criticism as high when roommates kept calm and repeated the criticism. They showed that using those behaviors to define accepting criticism has ____________.

11. Short answer question B: Suppose that one observer using event recording counts 25 responses, and a second observer counts 20. What observations do you assume they agree on and what observations do you assume they disagree on? Compute the reliability for this case.

____

____

____

____

Lesson 4 Form C **Grade** ____________________

Name ____________________ **Date** ____________________

---

1. Dolores and Richard noted how many times, at five selected inspection intervals, the ping-pong table was being used. They came up with the following data:

   Dolores: O O O X O
   Richard: O O O X X

   What is their reliability? ____________ percent. Is it acceptable? ____________

2. When the doctor weighs Morgan as a measure of eating behavior, he uses what method of observation? ____________ recording

3. If two observers agree on their observations, you cannot conclude that their observations are reliable unless they were made on the same ____________.

4. Most of us tend to look for the causes of behavior in people's thoughts. The problem with such private events is that we must still ____________ them.

5. Dom observed the stories on the evening news one day. He found that nine of the news items were biased. Jan also watched the evening news on the same day and found that ten were biased. She decided that Dom's observations were reliable. Do you agree with her conclusion? ____________

6. Marge felt that good teaching involved a great deal of personal contact. She observed the number of personal contacts that Tom made with his students by means of an event-recording approach and found it to be very low. She then explained her observation to Tom and suggested that he engage in more personal contact with his pupils, which he was observed to do. Marge then had ten parents view a videotape of Tom's teaching. In quality of teaching, they rated Tom low before and high after the discussion. These results indicated to Marge that her behavioral definition of good teaching had ____________.

7. The principle of public events is that we look for the causes of behavior in ____________ events.

8. Barb inspected the cleaning jobs according to a 50-item checklist at 8:00 Thursday night. She found that 46 items had been done. Vince inspected the same cleaning jobs according to the same checklist at 9:00 Thursday night and found only 30 of them done. Is this evidence that their observations are not reliable?

   ____

9. The general formula for calculating reliability is ____________.

10. Williams et al. (1983) had two observers record noncooperation occurrences. They found an 83% agreement rate. They were measuring the ____________ of the observations.

11. Short answer question C: Suppose you define pain behavior as holding the pained area, moaning, and complaining of pain. Suppose observers using this behavioral definition find Mark not engaging in those behaviors during videotape A. Suppose they find him engaging in those behaviors during videotape B. How would you use a nurse to test the social validity of your behavioral definition?

    ____
    ____
    ____
    ____
    ____

Lesson 5 **Form A** **Grade** ______________________

Name ______________________ **Date** ______________________

1. If two students measure the amount of time that another student, Nate, dominates the discussion before trying to get him to change, their agreement is a measure of the __________ of these data.

2. Comparing a baseline condition with the treatment condition is called a __________ design.

3. Dave observed the cleaning behavior of his children. If he started giving cookies for a clean room to one of them after one week, to the second one after two weeks, and to the third one after three weeks, he would be using what single-subject design? __________ __________ design

4. Professor Brainbuster based his lectures on the text *Moldy History* for five weeks and found most students sleeping. He then based his lectures on the new text called *Hip History* and found that most students stayed awake. He used what experimental design? __________ design

5. Steve and Cleo, who were performing in a play, agreed to determine whether their friend was reciting his lines loud enough to be heard in the last row. Since they were also reading their own scripts, they agreed to listen to his loudness at random times throughout his recitation. They were using what method of observation? __________ recording

6. The Cornucopia Food Co-op assigned a clerk to count the number of customers prior to their advertising campaign. They are gathering data during the __________ period.

7. The strength of a reversal design is that it can rule out __________ explanations of an observed behavior change.

8. The process of exposing the same person to both the baseline and the treatment is the principle of __________ experiments.

9. If you observed the vocabulary of ten 2-year-olds before and after instituting a half-hour reading time each day, you would be using a __________ design.

10. The purpose of an experiment is to find out whether a treatment changes the rate of a behavior. To do this, the researcher observes the behavior during a period of time prior to introducing the treatment. This initial period of time is called the __________ condition.

11. Short answer question A: Define baseline and treatment conditions.

____

____

____

____

____

____

Lesson 5 **Form B** **Grade** ______________________

Name ______________________ **Date** ______________________

1. If parents transfer their two children from a public school to a free school in order to see whether the children will be more willing to go to school, the parents would be using a(n) ______________ design.

2. Observing whether math tutoring improves Abdul's test scores tells you his behavior rate during the ______________ condition.

3. The name of the design in which you measure the behavior for three periods of time—one before, one during, and one after the treatment—is what single-subject design? A(n) ______________ design

4. Komaki and Barnett (1977) provided feedback for football play performance after ten sessions for the option play, after 14 sessions for the power sweep, and after 18 sessions for the counter. What experimental design did they use? ______________ design

5. Observing how well a student does in math before he or she starts receiving help from a tutor would be called determining the student's rate of behavior during what condition? ______________

6. During consecutive 15-second intervals, Steve recorded whether his friend was reciting his lines loud enough during play practice to be heard in the last row. What method of observation did Steve use? ______________ recording

7. If a teacher made class attendance optional for one student and then a week later made it optional for a second student (to see whether it affected their participation), the teacher would be using a(n) ______________ design.

8. The antipollution committee observed that Greg, and other members like him, came to their weekly meeting about 15% of the time. They then started scheduling short Greenpeace films at each meeting and found that Greg came about 65% of the time. They later stopped the films, and attendance fell back to under 20% for Greg. What single-subject design did they use to study the effects of the films? A(n) ______________ design

9. Steve and Clare were both supposed to record during 15-second intervals whether their friend was talking loud enough during his play practice to be heard in the last row. The first ten observations were (where L stands for loud enough, and S for too soft):

Steve:	L	L	L	L	S	L	L	S	L	S
Clare:	L	L	S	L	S	L	L	S	L	L

What is the reliability of their observations? ________ percent. Is it acceptable? ________

10. To use the behavioral strategy: (1) create a behavioral definition, (2) use a method of direct observation, (3) check the reliability and social validity of your observations, and (4) design a(n) ______________ experiment.

11. Short answer question B: Explain why the reversal design and the multiple-baseline design are strong designs.

____

____

____

Lesson 5 Form C **Grade** ______________________

Name ______________________ **Date** ______________________

---

1. If the teacher introduced Old West material to Bernie in his history and literature classes at the same time and compared his performance using Old West material with his performance using the regular material, the teacher would be using which single-subject design? A(n) __________ design

2. Observing Juanita's grades on math homework before, during, and after she has had a tutor is a strong research design because it can rule out __________ explanations of any improvement in her grades during the time she had the tutor.

3. The multiple-baseline design gets its name from the fact that the researcher finds baselines for __________ or more behaviors.

4. The record of a behavior prior to some attempt to change it is called a(n) __________.

5. Suppose three people have been annoying you. If this week you ask the first one to stop annoying you, next week the second one, and a week later the third one, you are using a(n) ______________________ design.

6. Palmer and associates (1977) measured people's electricity usage for a time period when not giving them cost information, for a period of time while giving it, and for a period of time after no longer giving them the information. They used what single-subject experimental design? ______________________ design

7. Frank had a behavioral definition for acting sexy. He observed that Bud didn't come close. He asked five of his girlfriends to rate Bud's sexiness, and they rated him low. When Bud complained that he couldn't get any dates, Frank told him how to act. Frank observed that Bud was doing what he suggested. Frank again asked five of his girlfriends to rate the sexiness of the new Bud, and they rated him high. Frank was trying to establish the __________ __________ of his behavioral definition for acting sexy.

8. Marie's roommates observed the amount of cleaning that she did for a period of time. They then assigned a specific job to her for another period of time. Finally, they relieved her of that job for a time. They used what single-subject design to study the effect of giving her a specific job? A(n) __________ design

9. In a simple comparison design, we compare the rate of a behavior during two periods of time called the ______________ and the __________ conditions.

10. The problem with asking people to tell us about their own behavior is that their reports are often ______________ or of unknown accuracy.

11. Short answer question C: Name the conditions in a reversal design.

____

____

____

Lesson 6 **Form A** **Grade** ____________________

Name ____________________ **Date** ____________________

---

1. Last week with George, Bonnie used a new counseling technique called empathy self-actualization. This week, she asked George to compare how depressed he was before and after the new counseling technique. He said he was a lot less depressed after the counseling. Behavior analysts would call the approach to observation that George used for his earlier depression ____________ observation, because he did not record it immediately.

2. You cannot conclude that a treatment caused a difference when using a comparison design, because it rules out ____________ differences but not ____________ coincidences.

3. Baseline: 5, 1, 4, 3, 4, 3, 5, 2
   Treatment: 4, 5, 5, 5, 7, 10, 15, 14

   Should you conclude that the conditions have high overlap? ____________

4. Ken drank too much beer, so he tried "just saying no" whenever he got the urge. Later he forget to just say no. He drank the following number of beers a day:

   Before saying no: 22, 21, 22, 15, 24, 18, 20, 22
   During saying no: 15, 17, 16, 17, 11, 13, 9, 12
   After saying no: 13, 15, 18, 14, 18, 22, 19, 18

   Can you conclude that just saying no caused a reduction in drinking beer? ____________

5. Here's a multiple-baseline experiment involving two persons:

   Marty's baseline: 4, 6, 2, 3, 3
   Marty's treatment: 3, 5, 4, 6, 8, 7, 9, 8, 9, 8
   Terry's baseline: 3, 6, 5, 3, 5, 6, 4, 3, 5, 3
   Terry's treatment: 5, 7, 9, 7, 8

   High overlap? ____. Converging trend? ____. Convincing differences? ______. Treatment caused differences? ______

6. Two single-subject experimental designs that rule out alternatives are the ____________ and ____________ designs.

7. The formula for reliability is 100% x ____/ (________).

8. Tommy studied 30% during baseline and 90% when praised. Marie studied 40% during baseline and 70% when praised. To decide if these are real differences, you should ask: Do the data for conditions have high ____________? Do the data for conditions show a converging ____________?

9. The method introduced during an experiment to modify the rate of a behavior is the ____________. The period of an experiment without the treatment is called the ____________.

10. To decide whether the difference between conditions is convincing, look for high ________ and look for converging ____________.

11. Short answer question A: Explain how to visually analyze data.

____
____
____
____
____
____
____
____

Lesson 6 **Form B** **Grade** ____________________

Name ____________________ **Date** ____________________

1. Data are not convincing if there is overlap of more than _______ percent.

2. The reversal design looks at behavior during __________, __________, and __________.

3. Behavior analysis is the science that studies ______________ events that ______________ behavior.

4. Baseline: 6, 5, 4, 7, 8
   Treatment: 8, 9, 10, 12, 19

   Should you conclude that baseline is trending toward treatment? ____________

5. Lavelle encouraged police to give safety tickets. After baseline, the police gave out coupons permitting violators to go to class to escape the ticket. Later, the coupons were withdrawn. Number of tickets issued:

No coupons:	5,	5,	0,	10
Coupons:	20,	40,	30,	50
No coupons:	25,	15,	20,	15

   High overlap? ____. Converging trend? ____. Convincing differences? ____. Treatment caused differences? ____

6. List three single-subject designs that can rule out individual differences. ______________ design, ______________ design, and ______________ design

7. If people's observations are based on memory and do not use a consistent definition, they are often inaccurate. This is the problem of ______________. Looking inside the person for the causes of behavior requires relying on events that must themselves be explained. This is the problem of ______________.

8. Sally wanted Terry to spend more time reading to their daughter Jill. After a baseline period, she asked Terry to read more to Jill. Terry spent the following amounts of time with her:

   Before request: 10, 6, 11, 7, 15, 25, 28
   After request: 20, 30, 23, 27, 25, 23, 28

   Can you conclude that Sally's request caused a change in Terry's reading? ____________

9. The extent to which outside judges agree with your behavioral definition is called ______________.

10. When you do an experiment, you compare behavior during treatment and baseline. To conclude that the treatment made a difference, you must find a convincing difference (not high overlap, not converging trend) and you must rule out ______________ explanations.

11. Short answer question B: Explain the principle of single-subject experiments.

____

____

____

____

Lesson 6 **Form C**

Name ______________________ **Grade** ______________________

Date ______________________

1. To decide whether differences between conditions are convincing, you must ask if the conditions have high ______________ and if they show a converging ______________.

2. A single-subject design in which two behaviors are subjected to the same treatment at different times is called a(n) ______________ ______________________ design.

3. The principle of visual analysis is to look for differences that are ______________.

4. Baseline is 3, 5, 4, 7, and 2. Treatment is 6, 7, 10, 13, and 9. Do these conditions have high overlap? _____

5. Bourgeois found that elderly patients made relevant comments with a memory booklet. She withdrew it and then used it again in a backward reversal design. The elderly patients made the following number of relevant comments per day:

Booklet:	5,	3,	3
No booklet:	1,	1,	2
Booklet:	7,	4,	4

High overlap? ____. Converging trend? ____. Convincing differences? ____. Treatment caused differences? ____

6. Rob and Jan observed Professor Brainbuster to find out whether he was looking at students when he lectured. They did this in 15-second intervals. The first ten observations were:

Rob:	O	O	O	O	X	O	O	X	O	O
Jan:	O	X	O	O	O	O	O	X	O	O

Compute the reliability. ______________ percent. Is this an acceptable level? ____________

7. Ted counts the number of compliments you make to Seth and Jean each day. He starts praising you first for Seth and later for Jean. You make the following number of compliments:

Seth/no praise:	1, 2, 1, 2, 0
Seth/praise:	5, 7, 9, 8, 8, 7, 9, 8, 7, 8
Jean/no praise:	2, 0, 3, 4, 3, 3, 4, 3, 5, 2
Jean/praise:	4, 6, 7, 8, 7

High overlap? ____. Converging trend? ____. Convincing differences? ____. Treatment caused differences? ____

8. A trend must involve a minimum of ____________ points that progressively change toward the values in the other condition.

9. The problem with using private events to explain behavior is that we must still ____________ the private events.

10. When determining whether there is overlap, usually look at only the last ______________ data points in each condition.

11. Short answer question C: Name and describe two ways to break a trend.

____

____

____

Lesson 7 **Form A** **Grade** ______________________

Name ______________________ **Date** ______________________

1. Dad noticed that Tim didn't hug his sister very often, so he started nagging Tim to hug more. Tim hugged his sister the following number of times per week:

   Before nagging: 0, 1, 1, 0, 0
   During nagging: 17, 10, 5, 3, 2

   Can you conclude that there is a convincing difference? ______

2. An experimental design that studies a behavior before the treatment, during the treatment, and after the treatment is called a(n) ________________ design.

3. Behavor analysts view thinking and feeling as ______________.

4. Experimenting with one person at a time is called the principle of ____________ designs.

5. Using the behavioral strategy: first, creating a behavioral definition; second, using the approach of ____________; third, checking reliability and social validity; fourth, using single-subject experimental design; and fifth, doing a(n) ____________ analysis of the data.

6. Lou took time out from his work to check on his children every little while. He checked to see if Jim was playing nicely outside. Then he went back to work. Then he checked to see if May was playing nicely near the TV. Then he worked. Then he checked again on Jim. He continued this pattern. He was using ________ ________ recording.

7. A measure of the amount of agreement between two observers is called ____________.

8. Behavior analysis is a behavioral science that examines ____________ events that ______ behavior.

9. Minkin and his colleagues (1976) investigated the correlation between two measures. First, they applied their own behavioral definition of good conversation skills to teenagers talking to each other. Second, they obtained ratings of the conversational skills of the same teenagers made by a cross section of adults. The researchers were evaluating the ________ ________ of their behavioral definition.

10. Name an experimental design that rules out both time coincidence and individual differences as alternative explanations of any observed change in behavior. ____________

11. Short answer question A: Explain why behavior analysts do not use private events to explain behavior.

____

____

____

____

Lesson 7 Form B **Grade** ______________________

Name ______________________ **Date** ______________________

---

1. Mary's teacher and another observer made the following 25 observations of Mary's nearness to other children (where N stands for near and F stands for far):

   Teacher: F N F N F F F N F F
   Another: F N F F F F F N N F

   What is their reliability? __________ percent.
   Is this an acceptable level of reliability? ______

2. The principle of public events is to seek the causes of behavior in _____________ events.

3. Dave observed the cleaning behavior of his children. He started giving cookies for a clean room to one of them after one week, to the second after two weeks, and to the third one after three weeks. He was using what kind of design? _____________ design

4. Name a single-subject experimental design that doesn't rule out both alternative explanations of any observed change in behavior. _____________ design

5. The problem with using private events to explain behavior is that you still must ________ them.

6. The method of observing that counts occurrences of behavior is called ______________ recording.

7. The problem with self-reports is that they are usually ____________ or can't be checked.

8. You observe John's study behavior during a series of intervals 15 seconds long. You used what method of observation? ______________ recording

9. Harry was a poor reader. He read 25, 15, 30, 20, and 10 percent of the time during the first week of observation. During the second week, he was told that he could stay at recess for an extra ten minutes on any day that he read more than 70% of the time. That week he read 60, 85, 80, 95, and 85 percent of the time. What experimental design was being used to determine the effectiveness of the extra recess time? _____________

10. The principle of visual analysis is to look for differences between baseline and treatment that are convincing. To decide if differences are convincing, look for high ______________ between conditions or a converging __________ toward each other.

11. Short answer question B: Explain why a comparison design is a weak design.

    ____
    ____
    ____
    ____

Lesson 7 **Form C** **Grade** ____________________

Name ____________________ **Date** ____________________

1. The statement "Giving support means to make a positive comment" is an example of a(n) ______________.

2. Ben didn't get many letters. He tried writing some letters so he would get more, but then he got busy and forgot to write letters. He got the following number of letters per month:

Didn't write:	0,	1,	0,	0,	2
Did write:	4,	5,	7,	9,	8
Didn't write:	5,	3,	0,	2,	1

Are you convinced that there are differences? ______. Can you conclude that the treatment caused the difference? ______

3. Suppose a teacher observes the amount of studying that two students do for a month. Then, for the second month, the teacher gives daily quizzes to one student but not the other. Finally, for the third month, the teacher gives daily quizzes to both students. The teacher is using what single-subject design? A(n) ______________ design

4. If you see a behavior and immediately record it, you are using the principle of ______________ ______________.

5. Janet applies for a driver's license. The Department of Motor Vehicles gives her a driving manual to bring home and read. Janet returns to the department, where they test her on the manual. They are observing her reading of that manual with the method of direct observation called ______________ recording.

6. Frank counted the number of times the president referred to a human rights violation in another country and the number of times he referred to the mistreatment of Native Americans in the United States. He found 123 mentions of other countries and no mention of Native Americans. He concluded that these data constituted a classic example of hypocrisy. What method of observation was he using? ______________ recording

7. About one student per week joined the new compact disc buying co-op. Then the co-op decided to try a newspaper advertisement. As a result, about 20 students per week joined. The members concluded that advertising pays, since the ad had succeeded in getting new members. This is not a good experimental design because it doesn't ______________.

8. The basic formula for computing reliability is ______________.

9. Hineline (1992) discusses when a behavior analysis explanation of behavior by environmental events sounds right or wrong in our culture. The behavioral approach may sound right to you when it uses an external cause to explain an expected behavior. However, it is likely to sound wrong to you when it uses an external cause to explain a(n) ______________ (expected, unexpected) behavior.

10. Dr. Smith developed a way to observe depressed behavior and a treatment to reduce it. She asked a group of psychiatrists to rate Jake's depression before and after the treatment. If these ratings correlated with her behavioral observations, she would have evidence that her behavioral definition of nondepressed behavior had ______________.

11. Short answer question C: Give one reason why behavior analysts usually rely on direct observation, rather than observations that involve memory such as questionnaires or interviews.

____

____

____

Lesson 8 Form A Grade ______________________

Name ______________________ Date ______________________

1. Kay was the only person in the group who supported the war. She always said things in favor of the war, and the other group members would always argue with her. She gradually said more and more things supporting the war. Another member of the group saying, "I think that war is immoral" would be an example of a(n) ____________ for Kay to make statements favoring the war.

2. Increasing the rate of a behavior by delivering a reinforcer after it occurs is called ____________________.

3. Glover and Gary (1976) gave points to students following each word they used in describing functions of an object. Since this procedure increased the number of words they used, you would term the procedure of delivering points ____________.

4. Tactic #1 in using the reinforcement strategy to solve human problems is to increase desired behavior through ____________.

5. Frank was given $10 by his father for cleaning the garage. During the next year, Frank's father asked him to clean the garage again, but he never did. The $10 is an example of what? ____________________

6. When Priscilla complained about life, Linda tried to cheer her up by talking with her. But the more often she talked with Priscilla about her complaints, the more often Priscilla complained about life. By talking with Priscilla after she complained, Linda was using what behavioral procedure? ________________

7. If an event follows a behavior, and the frequency of that behavior becomes greater, the event is called a(n) ____________.

8. Linda paused after giving a customer his coin change and before giving him the bills. He left without the bills. From then on, Linda did not pause after giving the coin part of someone's change. Having the customer leave without his bills is an example of ____________.

9. If an instruction precedes a behavior and increases the rate of the behavior, it is called a(n) ____________.

10. Jerome didn't do his share of cleaning, so every time the apartment became dirty, Bob asked Jerome to help clean it. After he was asked, Jerome would do his share. As a result, Jerome's rate of cleaning increased. Bob's request for help is a(n) ____________.

11. Short answer question A: Define a reinforcer.
____
____
____
____

Lesson 8 **Form B** **Grade** ______________

Name ______________ **Date** ______________

1. Jose tried tapping his TV set when the picture went out. His tapping restored the picture, but Jose still forgets to tap his TV set when the picture goes out. The restored picture is an example of a(n) ____________.

2. The teacher firmly told Francie to start doing her homework. Immediately thereafter, Francie started doing her homework. The teacher's demand is an example of what? ____________

3. Any event that occurs after the beginning of a behavior and leads to an increase in the rate of the behavior is called a(n) ____________.

4. Four-year-old Tony almost never greeted his father when he came home from work at night. The father then started giving Tony a big kiss every time he greeted his father at the door. Within a week, Tony was greeting his father every night. What behavioral procedure was the father using? ____________

5. Suppose that every time Jed fails to do what you want him to do, you tell him to do it. If this increases the rate at which Jed does what you want him to do, the arrangement would be called a(n) ____________.

6. Janice carefully typed her term paper for the first time. She received an A grade for the paper, and thereafter she frequently typed her term papers. The A is an example of what? ____________

7. Glover and Gary (1976) gave students one point for each different verb form that they used in describing possible functions of an object. The delivery of points increased the students' rate of using different verb forms. The points would be a good example of a(n) ____________.

8. Marty complained of a headache, so his teacher let him lay his head on the desk. Marty doesn't complain about headaches anymore. The teacher's permission to put his head down is an example of a(n) ____________.

9. Dana didn't kiss his girlfriend very often. One day she bit him just after a kiss. He kisses her quite often now, and she always bites him just after the kiss. Her bite is an example of a(n) ____________.

10. If you arrange to deliver an event following every instance of a behavior, and the rate of the behavior increases, you would refer to this procedure as ____________.

11. Short answer question B: Explain how a behavioral scientist would prove that an event is a reinforcer and disprove that an alternative event is the cause of the increase in behavior.

____

____

____

____

Lesson 8 Form C **Grade** ____________

Name ____________ **Date** ____________

1. An event that seems unpleasant but increases the rate of a behavior that it follows would be called a(n) ____________.

2. When Sue was a tiny infant, her father had a bright idea. Maybe it would increase her rate of smiling if he followed each adorable smile with a lullaby. It did. Sue's father was using what behavioral procedure? ____________

3. Suppose a person is late to class, and the teacher asks him to be on time in the future. If the person starts coming to class on time more often, the teacher's request would be an example of ____________.

4. An event is called a reinforcer if it ____________ a behavior and ____________ the probability of that behavior.

5. May came home from school and told her parents that she had finally beaten up the little boy who had been tormenting her every day. May's father took her out for a special ice cream treat for beating up the little boy. May has not beaten up the horrible little boy since then. The ice cream treat is an example of a(n) ____________.

6. Glover and Gary (1976) delivered points to students after each different function that students listed for an object. If the rate of listing different functions increased, the procedure of delivering the points would be called ____________.

7. When Larry commented that he liked long hair, his friends always agreed. They then frequently discussed how stupid other people's reactions to long hair were. Larry commented on the virtues of long hair more and more frequently. The event consisting of one of his friends saying, "Yeah, man, that's right" would be an example of a(n) ____________.

8. Verna spanked Tom every time he interrupted her. Tom seemed to interrupt even more than usual after she started spanking him. The event of spanking Tom would be called a(n) ____________.

9. To prove that an event is a reinforcer, you would have to use a(n) ____________ design.

10. Kim complained of problems every once in awhile. One day when Kim complained, his teacher, concerned that the problems might be interfering with school, had a long talk with him. After that, Kim complained more often about his problems and thus had more talks with the teacher. By talking with Kim after a complaint, the teacher was using what behavioral procedure? ____________

11. Short answer question C: Explain the difference between terms *reinforcer* and *reinforcement*.

____

____

____

____

Lesson 9 **Form A**

Name ____________________

Grade ____________________

Date ____________________

---

1. Dave always started pestering his mother for a snack just about the time she started cooking dinner. Although this irritated her, she tried to be a good mother and explain why he couldn't have a snack at that time. She finally decided that this wasn't working and that she would be better off ignoring his requests. What procedure would she be using if she ignored his requests, and he stopped making them? ____________

2. When Sam was young, he often started talking with his father about his day at school. His father usually listened and asked questions. Sam started talking with his father more often as a result. What behavioral procedure was Sam's father using? ____________

3. For five weeks, Professor Johnson told his students to type their weekly take-home exam, and they did. He then forgot to tell them during the rest of the semester, and all of them stopped typing their exams. By forgetting to tell them, Professor Johnson inadvertently used what procedure? ____________

4. One day Harry stroked Tabby softly, and the cat started to purr. Thereafter, he frequently stroked Tabby softly. Tabby's purr is an example of a(n) ____________.

5. Karen told John to stop using cocaine immediately, and John never used cocaine again. John's change in behavior is an example of what behavioral concept? ____________

6. Ann thought it would be cute to teach her son to swear. So every time he swore, she laughed and paid a lot of attention. Her son did not swear any more as a result. What behavioral procedure was Ann using? ____________

7. If you tell someone to stop a behavior, and the behavior decreases, you are using what behavioral procedure? ____________

8. Pinkston and her colleagues (1973) instructed the preschool teacher to stop paying attention to Cain's aggressive behavior, which she did. Cain's aggressive behavior decreased. What behavioral procedure was the teacher using?
____

9. Professor Adams disrupted faculty meetings with insane ideas, and his colleagues argued vehemently with him. However, the chairman finally convinced them simply to ignore Adams. Soon, Adams wasn't disrupting meetings anymore. The faculty ignoring Adams's insane ideas is an example of ____________.

10. When Jaime complained about how bad life was, Dad asked many questions. Later Dad stopped asking questions, but Jaime complained as much as before. What behavioral procedure was Dad using when he stopped asking questions? ____________

11. Short answer question A: Define the term *extinction*.
____
____
____
____

Lesson 9 Form B **Grade** ____________________

Name ____________________ **Date** ____________________

1. Extinction is defined as ____________ the delivery of a reinforcer following a behavior, thereby producing a(n) ____________ in the rate of that behavior.

2. Angela spent little of her time with her classmates, so her fourth-grade teacher started complimenting her whenever she did spend time with them. Soon, Angela spent a lot of time working on class projects with other children. One of the teacher's compliments would be an example of a(n) ____________.

3. Mimi asked Gary to help her remember to count calories. For a month, he reminded her. Then he stopped reminding her, and Mimi's rate of counting calories decreased. What behavioral procedure did Gary inadvertently use to produce the decrease? ____________

4. Fay used to ask Harry to go to the store. However, since he took up jogging, Harry won't go to the store when Fay asks. After ten weeks of asking with no results, Fay finally gave up asking Harry to go to the store. What behavioral procedure did Harry use to eliminate Fay's requests? ____________

5. If Pinkston and her colleagues (1973) had told the preschool teacher to tell Cain to stop being aggressive, and he had stopped, what behavioral procedure would the teacher have been using? ____________

6. Martha's son pinched her all the time, and she invariably asked him not to do it or told him it wasn't nice. Eventually, Martha stopped paying any attention to the pinching, and it stopped. What behavioral procedure did she eventually use? ____________

7. Dollie wanted Jim to light her cigarettes for her, so she started kissing him whenever he did so. Pretty soon he was lighting her cigarettes all the time. What behavioral procedure was she using? ____________

8. Within six months after they all moved into Happiness House, each member had stopped praising other members for cleaning the house. So, the amount of cleaning behavior drastically decreased for each member. This is an example of what behavioral procedure? ____________

9. Ben teased Jan about her weight a lot, and she usually protested. Then Jan decided that she would simply ignore his teasing. She noticed that Ben's rate of teasing did not change. What behavioral procedure was Jan using? ____________

10. Dan wanted Karen to smile more, so he worked up his nerve and said to her, "Karen, you have a beautiful smile; I sure would like it if you smiled more." To his delight, Karen smiled more. What behavioral procedure did he use to increase her rate of smiling? ____________

11. Short answer question B: Sometimes, when you stop delivering a reinforcer, the person's rate of behavior may briefly increase. Explain why stopping the reinforcer can still be an example of extinction.

____

____

____

____

Lesson 9 **Form C** **Grade** ____________________

Name ____________________ **Date** ____________________

1. Joyce started fixing her husband a fancy breakfast whenever he hung up his clothes. She noticed that he started hanging up his clothes most of the time after that. What behavioral procedure did Joyce use? ____________

2. During the reversal condition, Pinkston and her colleagues (1973) instructed the preschool teachers to pay attention to Cain's aggressive behavior, as they had done during baseline. Cain's aggressive behavior once again increased. An instance of the teacher's attention is an example of a(n) ____________.

3. Ben did a good job of vacuuming, as long as the president asked him first. Ben's rate of vacuuming decreased dramatically when the president no longer asked him. The president's procedure is called ____________.

4. The temporary increase in a behavior after it has been put on extinction is called a(n) ____________.

5. Laura asked silly questions that caused the professor to get mad. He tried ignoring the questions and found that Laura kept asking silly questions. Ignoring her questions is an example of what behavioral procedure? ____________

6. Mary often interrupted Sally while she was with her friends, and her friends paid attention to her interruptions rather than Sally's conversation. Sally finally talked them into ignoring Mary, and Mary's rate of interruptions decreased. What behavioral concept does the group's ignoring of Mary's interruptions illustrate? ____________

7. John could be a star swimmer if he would only practice more. The coach had talked with him and praised him when he did swim many laps, but still John did not practice enough. Finally, the coach told him in no uncertain terms to practice. John's rate of practice increased dramatically. The coach's talk is a good example of what behavioral procedure? ____________

8. Suppose you have been in the habit of telling people to perform behavior A, and they do it. If you now stop telling them to do it, and they stop doing it, what behavioral procedure are you using? ____________

9. If you stop delivering event A following a behavior, and the rate of the behavior decreases, what behavioral procedure are you using? ____________

10. Bull, a regular at the restaurant, was always calling for Ronald's service by yelling, "Hey boy, come here." This annoyed Ronald greatly, so he finally decided not to serve Bull when he called him a boy. Pretty soon, Bull stopped calling him "boy." What behavioral procedure did Ronald use? ____________

11. Short answer question C: Explain why telling someone to stop doing something is not an example of extinction even if the person stops doing it.

____

____

____

____

____

____

Lesson 10 Form A **Grade** ____________________

Name ____________________ **Date** ____________________

1. By asking the sanitation workers to rate how well the trash was packaged before and after the new rules were enforced, Stokes and Fawcett (1977) were determining the ____________ ____________ of the behavioral definition implicit in the new rules.

2. Gary's parents were a problem. They frequently ranted and raved about all the "yuppies" running around the university. Gary decided to change this by ignoring all unfavorable comments about young people and by praising his parents for being so in touch with young people when they made favorable comments. His parents gradually started talking more nicely about young people. What behavioral procedure did Gary use to change his parents' comments? ____________________

3. If one behavior is increased through reinforcement and all others are decreased through extinction, the procedure is called ____________ ____________________.

4. Parents who find their son reading a serious novel will probably ask him questions about his reading. Parents who find their son reading a western will often ignore him altogether. If the son starts reading serious novels more often and westerns less often, what behavioral procedure would account for the change? ____________________

5. Janice Johnson was a new social-welfare caseworker. Mrs. Brooks, one of her clients, became annoyed at Janice's habit of discussing her own children but never trying to find what help Mrs. Brooks needed. So Mrs. Brooks started ignoring all discussions about Janice's children and paid attention only when her own welfare problems came up. If Janice started talking more about Mrs. Brooks's problems, this would be an example of ____________ ____________________.

6. Mel was new to the ecology club. At first, he talked about how hard it is to sort your garbage into plastics, wet vegetation, cans, and so on. But everyone ignored him. When he talked about how everyone should do their share for the environment, everyone enthusiastically agreed. Pretty soon he was talking about everyone doing their share and not complaining about how hard sorting your garbage is. The members of the ecology club were using what behavioral procedure to change Mel's behavior? ____________________

7. Gale's teacher watched her while she practiced writing the letter "l." The teacher praised her when the loops were smooth and said nothing when they were rough or irregular. Gradually, Gale learned to write a smooth and beautiful "l." What procedure did her teacher use? ____________________

8. Good discussion leaders are remarkably successful in getting everyone into a discussion. They generally praise anyone who speaks. Even shy people, if praised, will contribute their ideas more often. This increase in the rate of everyone's talking is the result of what behavioral procedure? ____________________

9. When they were alone, Juan politely pulled out Maria's chair for her. She thanked him, and he did it more often over time. When they were with friends, Juan used to politely pull out Mary's chair for her. She did not thank him, because she was embarassed by this old-fashioned politeness. He did it less often with friends around. What behavioral procedure did Maria use to increase his politeness when alone and decrease it when with friends? ____________________

10. One characteristic of differential reinforcement is that one behavior should be increased through the use of ____________.

11. Short answer question A: Explain how you determine whether two behaviors are the same.
____
____
____
____

Lesson 10 Form B **Grade** ______________________

Name ______________________ **Date** ______________________

1. Mr. Howard taught ninth-grade geography class. One boy, Ben, said very little. Mr. Howard decided that rather than continue to put Ben on the spot by constantly asking him questions, he would compliment him when he said anything. If Ben's rate of talking increased, Mr. Howard would be using what behavioral procedure? ______________

2. Stokes and Fawcett (1977) found that correct trash-packaging behaviors increased and incorrect ones decreased when only correctly packaged trash was collected. What behavioral procedure did they use? ______________

3. If David always moved his eyes forward even when he had forgotten a previous word, he found that he read much faster. When David frequently stopped to move his eyes backward to look at a previous word, he found that he read much slower. Gradually he learned to always move his eyes forward and to stop moving them back. Suppose that reading faster is reinforcing and reading slower is extinguishing. What behavioral procedure caused him to change his reading behavior? ______________

4. Gary found that if he smiled when he was with Jane, she would pay a lot of attention to him. However, if he smiled when he was with Gloria, she would ignore him. Naturally, Gary started smiling a lot when he was around Jane but hardly at all when he was around Gloria. What behavioral procedure is at work changing his pattern of smiling? ______________

5. Rolando found that he could not pound in a nail if he struck with a pushing movement. But he could pound it in if he struck with a swinging movement. He quickly learned to strike with a swinging movement. What behavioral procedure is this an example of? ______________

6. Differential reinforcement involves the behavioral procedures of ______________ and ______________.

7. Manuel smiled broadly and said "Bueno" every time that Sara properly trilled her r's in "perro," the Spanish word for dog. He let improper trills just pass by without comment. Gradually Sara learned to make the correct trill. What behavioral procedure did Manuel use? ______________

8. A baby may say "Dada" to many adult males other than his father. The parents will probably ignore every misdirected "Dada" and pay attention to every "Dada" addressed to the father. If the baby comes to call his father "Dada" more often than other males, what behavioral procedure is this an example of? ______________

9. Bernie decided that it would be good for his girlfriend to jog more often, so he told her that she had to do it. She did. What behavioral procedure did Bernie use to increase her rate of jogging? ______________

10. Mr. Green, the football coach, made a point of praising Ann when she blocked her opponent away from the runner. He ignored her when she missed her block or blocked her opponent toward the ball. As a result, her blocking away from the ball increased relative to poor blocks. What behavioral procedure was the coach using? ______________

11. Short answer question B: What is the difference between reinforcement and differential reinforcement?

____
____
____
____
____
____

Lesson 10 **Form C**

Name ______________________ **Grade** ______________________

Date ______________________

1. John and Darrin always welcomed Lee when he sat with them during lunch. One day John and Darrin ignored Lee when he sat down, because they were having an important conversation. From then on, John and Darrin ignored Lee when he sat with them. Eventually, Lee stopped sitting with them. What behavioral procedure accounts for Lee's changed behavior? ______________

2. Stokes and Fawcett (1977) studied the effect of collecting properly packaged trash and not collecting improperly packaged trash. Does the example involve two (or more) different behaviors? ______________

3. When Frank was 5 years old, he used jerky movements of his fingers to tune his radio, and he could rarely get his favorite station. Sometimes his movements were less jerky by accident, and he could get the station. Gradually he developed a smooth movement that let him tune his favorite station quite easily. What behavioral procedure, built into the way radio tuners work, leads to smooth tuning movements? ______________

4. One characteristic of differential reinforcement is that all but one behavior should be decreased through the use of ______________.

5. Ben was an excellent ski instructor. He made a nice comment when you made your turn smoothly but said nothing when you goofed it up. He didn't even laugh when you fell down. His students learned smooth turns quickly. What behavioral procedure did he use to teach smooth turning? ______________

6. Roger's parents get on his case when he watches TV cartoons but ignore him when he watches educational programs. His rate of watching TV cartoons increases. What behavioral procedure have his parents inadvertently used to increase his watching cartoons but not educational programs? ______________

7. Grannies often spoil a child even when the parents are careful not to. If a child learns to beg for candy from Granny but does not beg from her parents, what procedure is unwittingly being used by the adults? ______________ ______________

8. When people are learning to drive a car with a manual transmission, they often have trouble learning how to shift. One problem is that, if they take their foot off the accelerator too slowly when they start to shift, the engine races. On the other hand, if they take their foot off the accelerator too rapidly, the car will suddenly slow down. They must learn to let the accelerator off at just the right speed. The process of decreasing responses that are too slow or too fast while increasing responses that are the right speed is the result of what behavioral procedure? ______________

9. If a single behavior is reinforced in one situation and extinguished in another situation, the behavioral procedure that is being used is called ______________.

10. John's coach, Ms. Davidson, permitted him to leave practice early on any day that he correctly performed a high dive. John's rate of correct high dives increased as a result. The event "time-off from practice" is an example of a(n) ______________.

11. Short answer question C: Why is being reinforced for reading about physics while being extinguished for reading about poverty problems not an example of differential reinforcement?

____

____

____

Lesson 11 **Form A**

Grade ______________________

Name ______________________ Date ______________________

1. Mrs. Baker began the process of overcoming the tone-deafness of Toneless Tony by asking him to sing A flat, which she then played on the piano. She praised him when he came within a half tone of it and simply asked him to try again if he did not. It took two lessons to teach him to sing within a half tone of A flat. Mrs. Baker was using what behavioral procedure to teach Tony to sing within a half tone of A flat? ______________

2. John's teacher helped him overcome acting like a loner. At first the teacher paid attention to him only when he looked at other children, then only when he was near them, and finally only when he was playing with them. What procedure did the teacher use to modify John's loner behavior? ______________

3. Frank never opened a door for Marsha. She decided to kiss him every time that he did so. Pretty soon Frank was opening the door for Marsha all the time. What behavioral procedure did Marsha employ to get him to open doors? ______________

4. Sammy's mother praised him every time he took out the garbage, and he did so regularly. When he was 12, she stopped praising him, feeling that he was old enough to accept responsibility. Sammy's rate of taking out the trash rapidly decreased after that. What behavioral procedure did Sammy's mother inadvertently use to reduce his rate of taking out the garbage? ______________

5. The term *shaping* is used to describe a particular use of what behavioral procedure that involves reinforcement? ______________

6. Dean taught Jason to hit badminton shots at least three steps away from Dean. Here's how he did it. First, Dean praised Jason only when he hit a shot at least one step away from him. Next he praised Jason only when he hit a shot two steps from him. Finally, he praised Jason only when he hit a shot three steps away from him. Hitting a shot one step away from Dean is called a(n) ______________ to hitting a shot three steps away from Dean.

7. By giving tickets to David only when he looked at the dial 4 out of 15 times, and then only when he looked at the dial 5 out of 15, and changing that criterion until completely correct use developed, Renne and Creer (1976) were using what behavioral procedure? ______________

8. Yancey noticed that when he said to Fran, "You look nice today," she smiled and thanked him for his compliment. However, when he said to Dan "You look nice today," Dan looked slightly embarrassed and ignored the compliment. Soon Yancey was frequently saying, "You look nice today" to Fran but almost never to Dan. What behavioral process is involved in changing Yancey's rate of saying this compliment to his two friends? ______________

9. Tom smoked only 15 cigarettes yesterday, and Vera praised his willpower mightily. Vera was sure that such praise would help Tom learn to stop smoking altogether. Stopping smoking would be called Vera's ______________.

10. Reinforcing one behavior and extinguishing all others, then changing to another behavior that more closely approximates the target behavior and repeating the process, is called ______________.

11. Short answer question A: Explain what an approximation is.

____

____

____

____

Lesson 11 **Form B** **Grade** ______________________

Name ______________________ **Date** ______________________

---

1. Tactic #4 in using the reinforcement strategy to solve human problems is to create new behavior through ____________.

2. A behavior that is similar to a target behavior would be called a(n) ________________.

3. Tad wanted to run a mile in under 6 minutes. So during the first week, he bought himself a Super Sundae every time he ran a mile under 12 minutes. During the next week, he bought himself a Super Sundae when he ran the mile in under 11 minutes. He continued this process until he ran a mile under 6 minutes. What behavioral procedure did he use on himself to attain this goal? ____________

4. Jawan wanted to teach his best friend to recognize what music was appropriate for dancing the Twirling Chicken. He let her initiate the dancing each time, praising her when she did the Twirling Chicken to the right music and saying nothing when she did the Twirling Chicken to the wrong music. Her ability to do the Twirling Chicken with the right music increased rapidly. What behavioral procedure did Jawan use to help her learn what was the correct music? (Note: Almost every student gets this wrong, so be sure to check the elements required for your answer.) ______________________

5. Ralph Radical wanted Bob to be against clearcutting the redwoods. At first Ralph agreed with Bob whenever he said anything mildly against clearcutting. Then Ralph agreed only when Bob made strong statements against clearcutting; pretty soon Bob was often making strong statements against clearcutting. Ralph used what procedure to change Bob's statements about clearcutting? ____________

6. Shaping begins with the selection of an ultimate goal called a(n) ________________.

7. Clarence's father told him to undertake more projects that involved the use of a hammer, so he did. What behavioral procedure was his father using to increase the rate of using a hammer? ______________________

8. Renne and Creer (1976) attempted to teach the correct use of inhalation equipment to asthmatic children. The correct use of the equipment would be called the ____________ of their experiment.

9. Charlie Brown smiled at the little redheaded girl only when she sat within five feet of him at lunch, then only when she sat within two feet, and finally only when she sat next to him. Charlie Brown's goal of getting her to sit next to him is called the ______________.

10. John often smelled gamey, because he usually forgot to put on his underarm deodorant. Barb decided to do something about it. For the next two months she praised John every time he remembered to put on his deodorant. John eventually remembered to put on his deodorant more often. What behavioral procedure was Barb using? ____________

11. Short answer question B: Define shaping.
____
____
____
____

Lesson 11 **Form C** **Grade** ______________________

Name ______________________ **Date** ______________________

---

1. Renne and Creer (1976) gave David a ticket at first for looking at the dial 4 times out of 15 breaths; that would be called a(n) ________ ________ to their ultimate goal of looking at it for all 15 breaths.

2. Kerr's teachers showed interest in his reading during the first month of school. As soon as Kerr finished a reading, they asked him to report on what he had learned. During later months, they lost their enthusiasm and stopped asking him for reports. Kerr gradually stopped reading. What behavioral procedure were they using when they stopped asking him about his reading? ______________________

3. Dr. Franklin used a portable railing for Roberto to lean on and learn to walk again. She moved this farther and farther away from him until he stood on his own and actually walked. She first reinforced Roberto just for standing with his weight on the railing, then reinforced him only when he leaned just a little, and finally reinforced him only when he stood on his own. She was using what behavioral procedure to change Roberto's behavior? ______________

4. For a situation to involve shaping, two conditions must be met: a(n) ______________ must be specified, and differential reinforcement must be applied to a series of ______________.

5. Marie told Fred to stop swearing whenever a minor annoyance occurred, and Fred's rate of swearing decreased as a result. What behavioral procedure did Marie use? ______________

6. Bobby was trying to pronounce the word correctly, but the best he could say was "refrigelator." June, his Mom, praised him for saying it so well. "Refrigelator" would be called a(n) ______________ to June's target behavior of "refrigerator."

7. Last week Mary started kissing Dave every time he lit her cigarette, in hopes that he would light her cigarette more often. Dave didn't get the message, however, and still doesn't light her cigarette very often. What behavioral procedure did Mary use? ________ ______________________

8. At first, Mary necked with John only after they had been discussing their problems. Later, Mary necked with John only after a fight. Finally, she necked with him only after a terrible, screaming fight. What behavioral process accounts for the increasing severity of John and Mary's fights? ______________

9. Dave's coach praised him only when he swam the 100-yard freestyle in under 50 seconds but ignored him when he swam it in over 50 seconds. Dave soon got so he could do it. What behavioral procedure was his coach using? ______________________

10. Bobby didn't start playing very much chess until after he started winning. Now he plays a lot. The event of winning is an example of what behavioral concept? ______________

11. Short answer question C: Explain how you use differential reinforcement within shaping.

____

____

____

Lesson 12 **Form A** **Grade** ______________________

Name ______________________ **Date** ______________________

1. Geraldo's mother agreed to teach him how to sew. She paid attention to him by pointing out only the good aspects of his sewing skill. She did this while he was sewing. This attention was very important to Geraldo. She kept her lessons brief so that Geraldo received attention rarely. What principle of effective reinforcement, if any, did Geraldo's mother neglect? ______________

2. If a person has recently had a lot of a certain reinforcer, the person is ______________ with respect to that reinforcer.

3. Bob usually didn't pay his share of the rent on time. Alicia praised him only when he paid his rent on time. She praised him as soon as she learned that he had paid—usually within a week. Alicia praised him rarely. Alicia's praise was a big deal for Bob. What principle did Alici fail to use, if any, to maximize the effectiveness of her praise? ______________ (Many students get this wrong. Ask questions!)

4. Janella's brother wasn't a very warm person. She felt that he would be friendlier if he would just hug people a little bit. She decided to praise him—first, only if he stood close. Next she praised him only if he touched her hand or shoulder briefly. Finally, she praised him only if he hugged her. Getting him to hug her would be termed a(n) ______________.

5. Reinforcers should be delivered only when the desired behavior occurs. This is called the principle of ______________.

6. John reinforced Marty with an M&M for reading sentences out loud. He gave Marty an M&M as soon as Marty finished reading the sentence. Marty worked eagerly for the M&M's at first, but after about 50 sentences, Marty didn't want to read anymore. Had John continued at that point, he would have violated what principle of effective reinforcement? ______________

7. Reinforcers should be delivered as soon after the behavior has occurred as possible. This is called the principle of ______________.

8. Kay decided to go out for basketball. She went to practice six days a week, usually putting in three hours of practice. The coach praised her play only when she played well, and immediately after good plays. Even with that, she didn't feel that she got praised too often. The coach restricted her praise to "good play," but never gave any other feedback, pointers for improvement, indication of appreciation for efforts, or even a friendly comment. Kay quit after concluding that such mechanical praise just didn't make all that work worth doing. What principle of effective reinforcement did the coach neglect? ______________

9. Brigham and his colleagues (1972) delivered tokens to children to get them to work more on their handwriting. The researchers gave tokens immediately after the children first sat down, whether or not they had done any handwriting. The tokens could be traded for activities that they enjoyed but did not get to participate in too often. Delivering tokens immediately after sitting down, in order to reinforce the accuracy of writing, violates what principle of effective reinforcement, if any? ______________

10. Mrs. Upton allowed Betty to stay home from school whenever she complained of being sick. Mrs. Upton did not let Betty stay home for talking about any other problems. Now Betty complains often about her illnesses, but not about other problems. What behavioral procedure accounts for Betty's becoming a hypochondriac? ______________

11. Short answer question A: Name the four principles that govern the effectiveness of a reinforcer.

____

____

Lesson 12 **Form B** **Grade** ______________________

Name ______________________ **Date** ______________________

1. Mr. Mack wanted to teach his infant son to sit up before any other children his age could do so. When his son was 4 months old, Mr. Mack designated the half hour after dinner as time to reward his son for sitting up by giving him a spoon of applesauce. His son didn't seem interested in the applesauce. A behavior analyst would guess that the applesauce did not work very well because the baby was already ____________ on food. (Use the technical term.)

2. The principle of contingency states that the reinforcer should be delivered ____________ when the behavior occurs.

3. The Spanish Club met for lunch each day. You were passed the ice cream if you asked for it in Spanish, but not if you asked for it in English. Members soon used the Spanish word for ice cream and stopped using the English word. What procedure was the club using to increase asking for ice cream in Spanish rather than English? ____________

4. Judy encouraged Tom to read by patting his head. She patted while he was reading. She patted only when he was reading. Attention was important to Tom, because Judy gave him few pats or other attention. However, because each pat lasted about a second, he didn't even seem to notice. Tom soon stopped reading. What principle of effective reinforcement, if any, does Judy's procedure omit? ____________________

5. Hall and his colleagues (1972) gave Jerry 25 cents at the end of the month for each time that he was observed wearing his braces (and only for wearing his braces). The money permitted him to buy things that he wanted, and he never seemed to have too much money. What principle of effective reinforcement, if any, did they violate? ____________

6. Marcella and Ken played tic-tac-toe in class. Marcella was apparently reinforced by the challenge of Ken's responses. He made his mark immediately after she made her mark. He made a mark only when she made a mark. By the 20th game, they were tired of tic-tac-toe. What principle of effective reinforcement accounts for their getting tired of the game? ____________

7. Members of the Utopian Village agreed to rely on expressions of love to maintain work behaviors in their community. The members provided each other with these expressions immediately after work behaviors. They also provided these expressions after goofing-off behaviors. These expressions of love were extremely important to every member of the group, and no one ever got too many of them. What principle of effective reinforcement, if any, did they neglect? ____________

8. Carey tutored Dave, the star football tackle, in poetry by having him compose short poems on a blackboard while she watched. She reserved her praise for the good aspects of his compositions and gave the praise as soon as he wrote a line. She kept the sessions short so that he wouldn't tire of the tutoring. To her surprise, her praise was very important to him. What principles, if any, did she omit in her procedure? ____________

9. The principle of size states that you must be sure to give the person enough of the reinforcer to be ____________.

10. Janella's brother wasn't a very warm person. She decided to praise him only when he stood close to people. Then she praised him only when he stood close and touched them briefly on the arm. Finally, she praised him only when he also hugged them. Because her goal was to have him stand close and hug people, standing close to someone would be called a(n) ____________ to that goal.

11. Short answer question B: State the principle of size.

____

____

____

Lesson 12 Form C **Grade** ____________________

Name ____________________ **Date** ____________________

1. Señor Jimenez taught 4-year-old Janice to say his name right by saying a syllable, "hee" and hugging her only when she said it right. Next he said "hee-mayn" and hugged her only when she said both syllables right. Finally, he said "hee-mayn-ays" and hugged her only when she said his whole name right. What procedure did he use to teach her how to say his name? ____________

2. Reinforcers should be selected according to whether the person has not had a lot of that reinforcer recently. This is known as the principle of ____________.

3. Janella's brother wasn't a very warm person. So every time he acted cold and distant, she would tell him to stand close and touch people. His rate of standing close and touching people increased after she started the procedure. What is the name of her procedure? ____________

4. Hal did not invite Dana to parties very often. Dana decided to change this by quickly offering free tutoring only when Hal invited him to a party. Dana made these offers immediately after an invitation. These offers were terribly important to Hal, because Dana was the only person who could explain the material well enough to enable Hal to pass the exams. Hal rarely received these offers from Dana. What principle of effective reinforcement, if any, did Dana neglect? ____________

5. Enough of the reinforcer must be delivered to be worthwhile. This is known as the principle of ____________.

6. He was every employee's dream. He praised your work no matter how poorly you did it. He gave it right after you finished a job. He didn't give you too much praise. You felt important afterwards. Still, it wasn't effective—no one improved the quality of his or her work. What principle of effective reinforcement, if any, did he neglect? ____________

7. Kevin lent his truck and his muscles to help Bob move. At first he carried boxes to the front door, where Bob took them and carried them inside and put them in the right room. Bob always thanked Kevin as soon as he brought a box to the door, and at no other time. Bob did not give praise so much or so often that Kevin tired of it. But when Kevin saw Bob drinking a beer without offering him any, he decided that getting thanks didn't justify all the hard work. What principle of effective reinforcement, if any, did Bob neglect? ____________

8. Sarah tried to help Juan overcome his shyness by praising him for being assertive. She conveyed her praise about his assertive behaviors after they returned home from social gatherings. During these conversations, she praised him only for the assertive acts that he had made during the event. Juan never got too much praise from Sarah during these conversations. Every instance of her praise was very important to him. What principle of effective reinforcement, if any, did Sarah neglect in providing help to Juan in this way? ____________

9. Ayllon (1963) gave Doris towels only when she was in her room; she had hoarded them for nine years, so each one was important to her. By the time she had been given 600 towels, she started removing them from her room. Ayllon used what principle of reinforcer effectiveness to reduce the reinforcing properties of towels for Doris? ____________

10. Tactic #5 in using the reinforcement strategy is to use the principles of ____________ ____________.

11. Short answer question C: State the principle of immediacy.

____

____

____

Lesson 13 **Form A** **Grade** ______________________

Name ______________________ **Date** ______________________

1. Maria earned a portion of her allowance doing chores. The money was given to her right after she told them that she had done the chore. The pay was pretty good—for example, 10 cents for taking out the garbage, 25 cents for doing the dishes. Maria was always broke, so the money was welcome. But her parents hardly every bothered to check the job after Maria told them it had been completed. As a result, it often wasn't done right, and sometimes it wasn't done at all. They were weakening the effectiveness of their reinforcer by ignoring the principle of ____________.

2. When someone is reinforced for every response, he or she is said to be on the generic schedule called the ____________ schedule of reinforcement.

3. Don's father used to have an endless interest in hearing about the latest chapter in Don's science fiction books. Later his father listened only after Don had read an entire book. If you consider a response to be the reading of one chapter, and three books had 6, 19, and 11 chapters each, what schedule of reinforcement was his father using later to reinforce reading of chapters? ____________

4. If a person is reinforced for different numbers of responses each time, he or she is on the specific schedule called a(n) ____________ ____________ schedule.

5. Jake is complimented for just saying "No" every 13 times. What schedule of reinforcement are Jake's "no's" on? ____________

6. Staats and associates (1964) studied the rate of reading-acquisition responses of children when they were given a reinforcer after every response and when they were given a reinforcer after varying numbers of responses that averaged five. Name the schedule that produced the highest rate of responding. ____________

7. When Donnell came home late at night, the door was always locked. So he would dig out his keys, insert the key in the lock, and turn it. The door never opened, so he would turn it again. Then it would open. What schedule of reinforcement was his key-turning behavior on? ____________

8. Francisco wanted to increase the rate at which his infant daughter Alicia imitated his behavior when he said, "Can you do this?" So he gave her a bite of ice cream each time she imitated. She usually lost interest after about 15 imitations. If Francisco asked you how he could increase the number of times she imitated him while still using ice cream, you should suggest that he switch to what generic schedule? A(n) ____________ schedule

9. The ratio schedule that produces alternating periods of responding and pausing is called a(n) ____________.

10. Tactic #6 in using the reinforcement strategy for solving human problems is to increase response rate with a(n) ____________ schedule of reinforcement.

11. Short answer question A: Describe one advantage and one disadvantage of the ratio schedules.

____

____

____

____

Lesson 13 Form B

Name ______________________

Grade ______________________

Date ______________________

1. Professor Irving often talks with students about what field to major in; she tries to interest them in psychology. She finds that about one in ten, on the average, end up by becoming psychology majors. If getting majors is a reinforcer for her, what schedule is her talking with students on? ____________

2. Maria's parents put her on a well-administered chore system. She earned one chocolate-covered peanut right after completing such chores as washing dishes and mowing the lawn. They gave her the peanut only after verifying that she had done a good job on the chore. Maria never got peanuts too often. Maria didn't do too many of her chores. Her parents weakened the effectiveness of the peanuts by ignoring the principle of ____________.

3. Staats and associates (1964) delivered a reinforcer after varying numbers of reading-acquisition responses that averaged 5. What is the name of the schedule that they were using? ____________

4. A person who is reinforced for some responses but not for every response is said to be on what generic schedule? A(n) ____________ schedule

5. Koegel and Rincover (1977) found that children with retardation would imitate without reinforcement for much longer when they had been trained on what schedule—continuous or fixed-ratio? ____________

6. In Professor Lopez's course, students could start on the next lesson only after they had correctly answered ten questions about the current lesson. If starting on the next lesson is a reinforcer, then having to make ten correct responses would define a(n) ____________ schedule of reinforcement.

7. David was very obnoxious in class. His teacher used to tell him to stop, explain why what he was doing was inappropriate, and generally spend a lot of attention on him. She finally decided to totally ignore his obnoxious behavior. David kept right on doing it, however. What procedure did his teacher use to try to decrease his obnoxious behavior? ____________

8. What schedule of reinforcement is usually used with shaping? ____________

9. Ann worked in a special room on her algebra homework problems. Dr. Otterman could observe through a one-way mirror and tell when she had completed seven problems. He then went in and complimented her on her progress. What schedule is she on for working problems? ____________

10. The schedule that produces the highest and most uniform rate of responding is called a(n) ____________.

11. Short answer question B: Name and define two specific types of schedules that involve counting the number of responses.

____

____

____

Lesson 13 **Form C** **Grade** ____________________

Name ____________________ **Date** ____________________

1. What schedule of reinforcement would you use in order to maximize the length of time it takes for a response to extinguish after reinforcement is stopped? ____________

2. If every 100th response is reinforced, the person may stop responding or start responding irregularly. The effect of such a large ratio is known as ____________________.

3. Maria's parents put her on a well-designed chore system. She was paid right after correctly doing a chore and only for doing it correctly. She felt that the amount of money was plenty for the work, but Maria already earned more money babysitting than she could spend. The parents were weakening the money reinforcer by ignoring the principle of ____________.

4. Staats and associates (1964) found that reading-acquisition responses could be increased by delivering a marble after every response. What is the label for the generic schedule of reinforcement they were using? ____________

5. Sarah sold Tupperware to Barbara, but Barbara would usually not buy the newest item on the first try. Usually Sarah had to try 2, 3, 4, or 5 times, but Barbara always bought the new item eventually. What schedule is Sarah's selling behavior on? ____________

6. Rich agreed to paint the house as part of his chores if he could have a rest break after every 100 brush strokes. After he counted 100 strokes, he got a drink of water and took a brief break. What schedule of reinforcement is his painting on? ____________

7. Maria's parents had her on a well-designed chore system. They checked carefully to see if she did the chore and kept a careful record of her chore behavior. They paid her at the end of the week, and Maria seemed to like the amount of money they paid her. They weakened the effectiveness of the money by ignoring the principle of ____________.

8. Angie seemed to have a hearing problem. She never answered a question the first time it was asked of her. She always said "What?" and then answered the second time it was asked. What is the name of the schedule that the questioner is on? ____________

9. Bob lived near the common phone in the dorm, so he had to answer it much of the time. Most of the dorm members didn't bother to thank him for answering it. He found that, on the average, he got thanked only once in four times. His phone answering was reinforced according to what schedule? ____________

10. A schedule of reinforcement in which the response is never reinforced is called ____________.

11. Short answer question C: Describe the rate of responding with a fixed-ratio schedule and a variable-ratio schedule.

____

____

____

Lesson 14 **Form A** **Grade** ______

Name ______ **Date** ______

1. Ken gets credit for one unit of work every time he tightens 18 nuts on the frame of a washing machine. What schedule is he on for getting credit? ______

2. In most books, there are passages or scenes that are boring. However, most people just keep reading, in the hope that a really exciting scene or passage will soon come along. Such a scene may occur on the average of only once in 33 pages, yet most people continue reading. Their reading behavior is on a(n) ______ schedule.

3. Of the four intermittent schedules that you have studied, which one produces the highest rate of responding? ______

4. Chester works in a factory in which his supervisor comes by to check on him every ten minutes. If it is reinforcing for Chester to be found working, what schedule is he working on? ______

5. Gladys loved rock music. While driving, she listened intently when music was being played but stopped listening when the announcer started talking, doing a commercial, or reading the news. Music as an event would be called a(n) ______ for Gladys's listening behavior.

6. Mawhinney and associates (1971) might have given tests in either of two ways: (a) after every three weeks or (b) after differing periods of time averaging three weeks. Which schedule would produce the more uniform rate of studying? ______

7. Do people maintain a uniform rate of responding on (a) a fixed-interval or (b) variable-interval schedule? ______

8. Ron and Betty are only interested in the few scenes of the movie that show dancing. These come after 5, 25, 15, and 15 minutes. What schedule of reinforcement is their movie viewing on? ______

9. If you think that an example involves an interval schedule, you should ask, "If the person makes no response at all, will there eventually arrive a time at which ______ response will produce the reinforcer?"

10. Richard is a radar scanner whose job is to look for unidentified planes on his radar screen. He usually sees one on an average of every four hours. What schedule is his looking behavior on? ______

11. Short answer question A: Name and define the two interval schedules.

______

______

______

Lesson 14 **Form B** **Grade** ______________________

Name ______________________ **Date** ______________________

---

1. In which interval schedule do people work at a gradually increasing rate as the time for the reinforcement approaches? ____________

2. Teachers frequently check on their students' work by walking around the room and looking to see whether or not they are working. The students are being reinforced for working on what schedule? ____________

3. Marty's teacher complimented him after he completed 6, 8, 6, and 4 problems. What type of schedule was he on? ____________

4. If you think that an example involves an interval schedule ask, "If the person does not emit the behavior for a time, will there eventually arrive a time when emitting ____________ response will produce the reinforcer?"

5. A schedule in which the person is reinforced for the first response that occurs after a constant period of time is called a(n) ____________ schedule.

6. Sarah wanted her son Dan to become a bookworm, so she encouraged him to read books. Every time he showed her an interesting fact in a book, she gave him some money right then and there. She gave him the money only if he showed her a fact. Dan seemed delighted with the amount. He never seemed to get the money too often. What principle of effective reinforcement, if any, did Sarah fail to employ? ____________

7. Mawhinney and associates (1971) studied student study patterns. They used two schedules: (a) they tested the students daily, and (b) they tested them every three weeks. If the professor stopped giving tests without telling the students, which of the two schedules that he used would lead to more enduring studying behavior? ____________

8. John stays "properly" dressed in his room, expecting visitors. (He is a bit pompous.) He has a visitor on the average of once every 65 minutes. If he is reinforced by his visitors for being properly dressed, what schedule is he on? ____________

9. John's father gives him an extra dessert when he has brought his own plate into the kitchen for four meals. What schedule is John on for bringing his plate into the kitchen? ____________ ____________

10. Darrel didn't like football, but he sure liked the cheerleaders. So he tuned in at the beginning of halftime. Exactly five minutes later, the cheerleaders came on and did a routine. What schedule was Darrel's watching behavior on? ____________

11. Short answer question B: Describe the pattern of responding produced by each of the four schedules.

____

____

____

Lesson 14 Form C **Grade** ____________________

Name ____________________ **Date** ____________________

1. In most joke books, an average of only one in ten jokes is hilarious, and the rest are terrible. But most people will plow through all the jokes, looking for the good ones. What schedule of reinforcement is a joke reader on? ____________

2. If you think that an example involves a ratio schedule, ask, "If the person makes the response very rapidly, will the next reinforcer arrive ____________?"

3. The author of a behavior analysis textbook sits in his office hour after hour, typing new examples. His writing is reinforced by finally finishing the 20th example for a lesson. If typing out one example is the response, what schedule of reinforcement is his writing on?

   ____

4. What two types of intermittent schedules produce a tendency for people to stop responding after reinforcement? ____________ and ____________

5. Bernie's mother used to remind him to start his homework as soon as he got home from school. But she stopped doing it last month, and Bernie almost never starts his homework right after school like he used to do. What behavioral procedure did his mother use to produce this disastrous change in behavior?

   ____

6. When Danny gets in the car to go on a trip (no matter how long), he immediately begins asking, "Are we there yet?" Sometimes the trips last just three minutes to the corner market; at other times, they last 30 minutes to a nearby lake. Assuming that having one of his parents say, "Yes, we are there" is a reinforcer, Danny is on what schedule of reinforcement for his questions? ____________

7. A schedule in which the person is reinforced for the first response that he or she makes after differing periods of time is called a(n) ____________________ schedule.

8. If the author of a book were to put his or her climactic scenes too far apart in the book, readers might quit reading even though they were still being reinforced occasionally. This would be an example of ____________.

9. Mawhinney and associates (1971) tested students at three-week intervals. Their study behavior would be on what schedule of reinforcement? ____________

10. Tactic #7 in using the reinforcement strategy for solving human problems is to reduce reinforcer frequency with a(n) ____________ schedule.

11. Short answer question C: Explain why being reinforced every ten minutes isn't necessarily a fixed-interval schedule.

    ____

    ____

    ____

    ____

Lesson 15 **Form A** **Grade** ____________________

Name ____________________ **Date** ____________________

1. If a response produces reinforcement after differing periods of time, we say that response is being reinforced according to a(n) __________ __________ schedule (two words).

2. Katherine got fed up with Gladys's lack of enthusiasm, so she had a long talk with Gladys one day and told her to act more enthusiastic. Gladys became a changed person, acting much more enthusiastic as a result. What behavioral procedure did Katherine use to increase Gladys's enthusiasm? __________

3. Two observers counted the number of times Fearsome Freddy hit another child. Observer 1 counted 15 hits, and Observer 2 counted 20 hits. Compute the reliability? ______ percent. Is it adequate? __________

4. Karen liked target shooting with a .38 magnum. She found that from 50 feet, she could hit a bullseye about once in ten tries—sometimes more, sometimes less. If hitting the bullseye was the reinforcer for shooting, what schedule was her shooting on? __________

5. If a person is required to make a high number of responses for each reinforcement, his or her responding may decrease because of what is called __________.

6. Professor King gave Margo, the star basketball player, the assignment of composing a poem to hand in every day of the semester. The next class period, he read the poem and returned it with praise of its good aspects. The professor praised only the good features of the poems and was careful not to provide too much praise. His praise seemed to be very important to Margo. In spite of his careful procedure, Margo's poetry writing did not improve. What principle of effective reinforcement, if any, did he neglect? __________

7. The Barker Street babysitting club awards ten points to any mother who takes care of another club member's child for an hour and charges ten points to a mother whose child is cared for. Marge's rate of babysitting for other club members increased after she joined the club and was awarded points. The points would be called a(n) __________.

8. Shaping involves the differential reinforcement of a series of responses that are successive approximations to a(n) __________ __________.

9. If a person's behavior is no longer reinforced, and its rate decreases, what schedule of reinforcement is it said to be on? __________

10. Sally tried to teach Harry how to throw a frisbee. She praised him right after every correct throw, and only when he threw it well. Harry was turned on by Sally, so her praise was really important to him. He never seemed to get too much of it. What principle of effective reinforcement, if any, did Sally fail to employ? __________

11. Short answer question A: Name the four principles that govern the effectiveness of a reinforcer.

____

____

____

____

Lesson 15 Form B Grade ____________________

Name ____________________ Date ____________________

1. Name the four principle s that govern the effectiveness of a reinforcer: __________, __________, __________, and __________.

2. When Flora studied in history class, the teacher praised her efforts. When she studied in English class, the teacher ignored her. Flora soon came to study more in history than in English. What behavioral procedure were these two teachers accidently using to increase studying in one class compared to the other? ____________________

3. Backward Ben hated the idea that behavioral methods might improve the ease of learning. As he worked through this very book, he rejoiced every time he missed an answer, saying to himself, "See, behavior analysis isn't so hot after all!" But he found that, try as he might, he could miss only an average of one question in 89. What schedule of reinforcement is his question answering on? ____________________

4. If you were concerned about the problem of satiating people by reinforcing them for every instance of behavior they emit, name the generic schedule that you would use to reduce the problem. ____________________

5. Juan's teacher helped him overcome being a loner. At first she paid attention to him only when he looked at other children, then only when he was near them, and finally only when he was playing with them. What procedure did the teacher use to modify Juan's loner behavior? ____________________

6. Experimental designs are used to discover exactly why a behavior changed. They are used to rule out __________ explanations based on coincidence.

7. If you reinforce the first response that occurs after a fixed amount of time has passed, you are following a(n) __________ schedule.

8. Clarence had to write a five-page essay for his art history class every week. If a page is one response, what schedule of reinforcement was his essay-writing behavior on? ____________________

9. When shaping a new behavior, both reinforcement and extinction are used in the procedure of differential reinforcement. What is the best generic schedule to use for the reinforcement part of differential reinforcement? ____________________

10. Johnny used to be very brave, but one day when he fell down and skinned his knee, he cried. His mother immediately rushed over to him and held him. She brought him inside for an ice cream treat to help him forget his pain. Johnny now cries a lot when he hurts himself. His mother always comforts him and gives him an ice cream treat. What behavioral procedure did his mother unintentionally use to increase Johnny's crying? ____________________

11. Short answer question B: Explain the relationship between shaping and differential reinforcement.

____

____

____

____

____

Lesson 15 **Form C**

Name ______________________

Grade ______________________

Date ______________________

1. Roy always looked for an insert in the newspaper announcing food sales. He found that inserts occurred sometimes after a week and sometimes after five weeks, but he found one on the average of every two weeks. If finding an insert reinforced his looking for one, what schedule of reinforcement was his looking on?
   ____

2. Interval recording is a method of observation in which a response is recorded if some part of a behavioral episode is observed within one of a series of ____________ intervals. Time sample recording differs only in that the intervals are ____________.

3. Jason Johnson aspired to become a great poet, but he couldn't sit still long enough to write very much poetry. He set himself the goal of writing a 25-stanza poem each day. He started by writing a one-stanza poem, then a two-stanza poem, and so on until he had worked up to 25 stanzas. Writing a one-stanza poem would be called a(n) ____________ to the 25-stanza poem.

4. What level of reliability is considered acceptable for a new behavioral definition? ________ percent

5. Differential reinforcement involves two basic behavioral processes. They are ____________ and ____________.

6. There are two questions you should ask to decide whether data show a convincing difference. You should ask if the data for different conditions ____________ or if they show a converging ____________.

7. Dan was concerned about his son's small vocabulary, so he decided to promote crossword puzzles as a way to build vocabulary. He bought a book of crossword puzzles and paid his son $5 for finishing a complete puzzle. He paid for the puzzle as soon as it was completed. His son always seemed to need money to fix his old dragster, and he apparently felt that $5 was good pay for completing a puzzle. When Dan's son didn't seem to have an improved vocabulary after 25 puzzles, Dan got suspicious and checked the puzzle book. He found that the answers were listed in the back. What principle of effective reinforcement did the presence of the answers negate? ____________

8. The elementary school teacher who grades students' tests as soon as they finish them is enhancing the effectiveness of her grade as a reinforcer by what principle? ____________

9. Reliability is computed by the formula ________ ____________.

10. Harvey earned money picking pears. He was paid 25 cents for every ten that he picked. What schedule of reinforcement was his pear-picking behavior on? ____________

11. Short answer question C: Explain why being reinforced every ten minutes isn't necessarily a fixed-interval schedule.
    ____
    ____
    ____
    ____
    ____
    ____
    ____

Lesson 16 **Form A** **Grade** ____________________

Name ____________________ **Date** ____________________

1. Johnny made many baby noises. However, when he said "Dada," his parents paid a lot of attention to him. When he made other sounds, they ignored him. He came to say "Dada" a lot. What procedure accounts for Johnny saying "Dada" a lot? ____________________

2. If a behavior occurs with increased probability in the presence of an SD, we say that the stimulus exerts ____________________ over the behavior.

3. A discriminative stimulus (SD) is a stimulus that precedes a behavior and is present only if what procedure will be applied to the behavior? ____________

4. Jeff swears a lot around the dorm but doesn't swear much at home. His dorm friends encourage swearing; his parents don't. What procedure accounts for the fact that Jeff swears more in the dorm than at home? ____________ ____________________.

5. The first tactic in using the stimulus control strategy for solving human problems is to narrow stimulus control through ____________ ____________________.

6. If the question "What is 2+2?" always gets Ward to say "4," we say that the question exerts ____________ over his behavior.

7. Redd and Birnbrauer (1969) had Bill give a child with retardation edibles for playing cooperatively with other children and had Bob not reward the child for cooperative play. Bill would be called a(n) ____________ for playing cooperatively, while Bob would be called a(n) ____________.

8. Staats and Butterfield (1965) showed Carlos 700 cards, each with one word on it. They gave him a token if he said the word on that card but nothing if he said the word on another card. What procedure did they use to teach Carlos to read 700 words? ____________ ____________________

9. Burris's classmates helped him learn the meaning of *reinforcer* by asking him two questions. First, "If Rose asked for some candy and got it but didn't ask for any more in the future, what is the candy called?" Second, "If Rose asked for some candy and got it, and if she asked for more in the future, what is the candy called?" His classmates praised him if he said "reinforcer" in response to the second but not the first question. He soon came to answer the questions correctly. His behavior of answering "reinforcer" is called ____________ behavior.

10. The cooperative dorm uses a green tag as a "welcome signal" for anyone who is welcoming visitors. Assume that welcoming a visitor reinforces visiting behavior. If the occupant welcomes visitors only if the green tag is out, the green tag is a(n) ____________ for visiting behavior.

11. Short answer question A: Explain the difference between discrimination training and differential reinforcement.

____
____
____
____
____
____
____

Lesson 16 **Form B** **Grade** ____________________

Name ____________________ **Date** ____________________

1. Adolf asked Gert to help him learn German pronunciation. Gert showed him a card with the German word "der" on it. Gert praised him when he pronounced "der" like "dayrr." Gert ignored him when he pronounced "der" like "dur." After 30 trials, Adolf was always saying "dayrr." What procedure improved Adolph's pronunciation of "der"? ____________________

2. When a person is more likely to emit a particular behavior in the presence of the SD than in the presence of the S-delta, we call the behavior ____________.

3. Sheila was trying to become more assertive around men. When she was assertive with Bill, he responded favorably. When she was assertive with Ken, he ignored her. As a result, Sheila became more assertive around Bill but not around Ken. The increased probability of assertive behavior in the presence of Bill means that Bill came to exert __________ __________ over her assertive behavior.

4. When Charlie Brown smiled at the little redheaded girl, she ignored him. When he smiled at Lucy, she was very nice to him. If Charlie Brown's smiles were reinforced by "niceness," what type of stimulus is Lucy? ____________

5. Reinforcing one behavior and extinguishing a different behavior in the presence of the same stimulus is called ____________________.

6. The third strategy in solving human problems is the ____________________ strategy.

7. Reinforcing one behavior while extinguishing a second behavior in the presence of stimulus A and extinguishing the first behavior while reinforcing the second behavior in the presence of stimulus B is considered to be an example of what procedure? ____________________

8. Redd and Birnbrauer (1969) studied the results of having one behavior analyst give a child with retardation edibles when he played cooperatively with other children, while a second behavior analyst did not. The child learned to play cooperatively when the first adult was present but not when the second adult was present. What procedure accounts for this result? ____________________

9. Jeff's dorm friends paid attention when he said "X@#!" but not when he said "gosh" or "darn." Jeff gradually said only "X@#!" What procedure is at work? ____________

10. Dickie's mother taught him to recognize the picture of her favorite candidate, Aaron Burr, by sometimes showing him a picture of Burr and sometimes of Jefferson and asking, "Who is this?" She praised him when he answered correctly. Soon he answered "Burr" to the first picture but not the second. His behavior of calling only the first picture "Burr" is called ____________________.

11. Short answer question B: Explain the difference between a reinforcer and a discriminative stimulus.

____

____

____

____

Lesson 16 Form C **Grade** ______________________

Name ______________________ **Date** ______________________

1. Kenny had trouble learning how to pronounce 1776, so his teacher praised "seventeen seventy six" and ignored "seventy seventy six." In a few days, Kenny was saying it right. What procedure did the teacher use to teach Kenny the correct pronunciation? ______________________

2. Adolf had 100 flash cards with German words like *und*, *der*, and *kopf* written on their fronts and the translations written on their backs. Adolf looked at the front of each card and said the English translation. Then he turned the card over to see if he was right. After about a month, he was always right. If saying the English word on the back of the card was a reinforcer and saying a different word was extinction, what procedure was at work here? ______________________

3. Professor Tod always made positive comments about statements Gene made. Professor Rose rarely had a reaction. Gene talked a lot to Professor Tod and only a little to Professor Rose. Professor Rose was what kind of stimulus for talking to him? ______________

4. Donna used to be confused about what constituted a straight in poker. Her husband often asked her two questions. First, "What is 4,5,6,7, and 8 called?" Second, "What is five hearts called?" He praised her when she said "straight" to the first question but not when she said "straight" to the second question. Gradually, she came to say "straight" only when asked the first question. Her <u>behavior</u> of saying "straight" is called ______________.

5. Ted ignored Dick when he pronounced Aaron Burr's name as "Boor" and praised him when he said "Bur." Pretty soon Dick always pronounced it as "Bur." What procedure was Ted using? ______________________

6. After much practice, Xavier had learned the square root of many numbers. If his teacher asked him, "What is the square root of 81?" he promptly said "9." But he did not give 9 as the square root of any other number. The increased probability of saying "9" when asked the square root of 81 means that the question had come to exert ______________ over that behavior.

7. Jonah had three goldfish. He played a game with his friend Robert to see if Robert could name his goldfish. If he called the big goldfish "Whale," Jonah praised him. He ignored him if he called the big goldfish "Tiny." If he called the small goldfish "Tiny," Jonah praised him, but not if he called the small goldfish "Whale." What procedure was Jonah using? ______________________

8. A stimulus that occurs before a behavior and increases the rate of the behavior is called a(n) ______________. A stimulus that occurs after a behavior and increases the rate of the behavior is called a(n) ______________.

9. If a stimulus that precedes a behavior is associated with extinction, it is called a(n) ______________________.

10. Doug got a lot of attention if he was reading a mechanics book, but his father ignored him if he was reading anything else. Doug became an avid reader of mechanics books. What procedure increased Doug's reading of mechanics books? ______________

11. Short answer question C: Define stimulus control.

____

____

____

____

Lesson 17 **Form A** **Grade** ______________________

Name ______________________ **Date** ______________________

1. Mr. Wyler worked long and hard to teach Fran to study most of the time when she was in history class. However, this did not change her habit of goofing off all the time in other classes. Mr. Wyler suggested to Ms. Green that she also reinforce Fran for studying in math. Pretty soon, Fran was the champion studier in all of her classes. What procedure had her teachers used to bring about this remarkable change? ______________

2. Reinforcing a behavior in each of a series of situations, until the behavior generalizes to other members of that same stimulus class, is what procedure? ______________

3. Professor Smart always got a big smile from the pretty brunette whenever he referred to her as "Kay" in class, but he didn't seem to recognize her outside of class. However, walking across campus one day, he looked up, saw the pretty brunette, and said, "Hi, Kay." He was rewarded by a giant smile. The occurrence of the naming behavior outside of class would be an example of what process? ______________

4. If a behavior is more likely to occur in the presence of the SD than the S-delta, the behavior is called a(n) ______________ behavior.

5. The grouping of all situations in which Professor Smart might encounter Kay at the University—class, hallway, campus, student union, and so on—would be called a(n) ______________.

6. Bornstein and associates (1977) taught Jane to be assertive in response to being interrupted by another person. They then taught her to be assertive in several other types of situations. When they tested her assertiveness in three situations, they found her to be quite assertive. What behavioral procedure did they use? ______________

7. Reinforcing a behavior in the presence of a particular stimulus and extinguishing it in the presence of other stimuli is called ______________.

8. James usually acted very businesslike around Mr. Smith, because he seemed to appreciate it. James usually did not act businesslike around Mr. Clevis, because he ignored such behavior and acted in a slower and more relaxed manner. In this situation, we would say that Mr. Smith exerted ______________ over James's businesslike behavior.

9. A set of related stimuli is called a(n) ______________.

10. Dr. Rutherford taught Karen a number of "nonshy" behaviors, using role playing in his clinic. However, she could never get up the nerve to employ them anywhere else, so Dr. Rutherford arranged to have another psychologist reinforce Karen for nonshy behavior in another role-playing situation. Karen then acted in a nonshy way with her archaeology instructor. The occurrence of nonshy behavior outside the role-playing situation would be an example of ______________.

11. Short answer question A: Define *generalization* (not *generalization training*).

____

____

____

Lesson 17 **Form B** **Grade** ______________________

Name ______________________ **Date** ______________________

1. Sally was a health-food nut. Whenever Ralph ate healthy food at home, she praised his diet. Then he started eating healthy food when they ate at their favorite restaurant, and she praised him. Pretty soon he was eating only healthy foods no matter where he ate. What behavioral procedure did Sally use? ______________________

2. Miller and Weaver (1974) showed students a series of examples of extinction. If you regard each example as a stimulus, then the collection of all examples of extinction would be termed a(n) ______________________.

3. Generalization is defined as the occurrence of a behavior in the presence of a(n) ______________________.

4. Professor Brainbuster usually got a smile when he called the student in the front row Ted but not if he called him Dan. Likewise, he usually got a smile when he called the burly athlete in the back row Dan but not if he called him Ted. What behavioral procedure are these guys unknowingly applying to the prof's behavior? ______________________

5. If Danny is reinforced for calling the giant old tree in front of his house a tree, he might see the giant oak down the street and call it a tree also. If he does, the occurrence of his labeling behavior for the second tree is called ______________________.

6. The second tactic in using the stimulus control strategy to help people is to broaden stimulus control through ______________________.

7. Peggy never volunteered to answer a question in class. In one of her classes, however, a question arose concerning her greatest love, classical art, and she got so excited that she volunteered. The teacher praised her for having the right answer. She volunteered often in that class from then on. Somewhat later, the same thing happened in another class, and again she volunteered and had the right answer. After that, she started to volunteer in all of her classes. Even though no one was intentionally arranging it, Peggy's behavior changed as a result of what procedure? ______________________

8. The Klines praised little Sarah when she called their dog "doggy." One day she called the neighbor's dog "doggy" also. What behavioral process occurred? ______________________

9. The increased probability of a discriminated behavior that is produced by a stimulus is called ______________________.

10. Any stimulus in whose presence a behavior has not previously been reinforced is called a(n) ______________________ stimulus.

11. Short answer question B: Define *generalization training.*

____
____
____
____
____
____
____
____

Lesson 17 Form C **Grade** ____________________

Name ____________________ **Date** ____________________

1. The occurrence of a behavior in the presence of a novel stimulus is called ____________.

2. Generalization training is a procedure in which a behavior is reinforced in each of a series of situations until it ____________ to other members of that same stimulus class.

3. Davey looked at the big old elm and said, "That's a tree, Mom" to his surprised mother. She praised him for knowing it, and he often told her that the elm was a tree. One day he said, "Hey mom, that is a tree too, isn't it?" and pointed to a giant oak. Again she made a big fuss over his knowledge. After several more trees, Davey started referring to all big woody plants as trees. What behavioral procedure did his mother use? ____________

4. A stimulus that precedes the behavior and is present only if the behavior will be reinforced is called a(n) ____________. A stimulus that precedes the behavior and is present only if the behavior will be extinguished is called a(n) ____________.

5. Dr. Rutherford taught Karen a number of "nonshy" behaviors, using role playing in his clinic. However, she never could get up enough nerve to apply them anywhere else. So Dr. Rutherford arranged to have another psychologist reinforce Karen for nonshy behavior, also in a role-playing situation. Karen then started to act in nonshy ways at school, on her job, and even among strangers. What behavioral procedure did Dr. Rutherford employ to help Karen? ____________

6. Professor Smart always got a big smile from the pretty brunette whenever he referred to her as "Kay" in class, but he didn't seem to recognize the brunette outside of class. While crossing campus one day, he looked up, saw the brunette, and said, "Hi, Kay." He was rewarded with a giant smile. From then on, he recognized Kay no matter where he saw her. What behavioral procedure did Kay use to teach Professor Smart to recognize her in all places outside of class? ____________

7. The collection of all people you encounter during a day would be called a(n) ____________.

8. Miller and Weaver (1974) reinforced students for correctly labeling the examples contained in this textbook. They then observed that the students could correctly label examples that they had not seen before. The occurrence of the students' labeling behavior in the presence of the new examples would be called ____________.

9. Rex praised his daughter for saying "15" when asked "What does 8 + 7 equal?" but not when asked "What does 9 + 4 equal?" What procedure was Rex using? ____________

10. Damien helped his little sister learn addition by showing her simple problems, printed on flash cards. Damien gave her a chocolate-covered peanut after showing her the card "3 + 9 = ?" if she said "12," but not if she said "12" when he showed her the card "8 + 7 = ?" Damien used the same approach to answers to other cards. What procedure did he use? ____________

11. Short answer question C: Define *stimulus class.*
____
____
____

Lesson 18 **Form A** **Grade** ______________________

Name ______________________ **Date** ______________________

1. Terry was taught to add by a teacher who showed him two piles of blocks, with two and three blocks in each, and asked the question, "How much is 2 + 3?" As the training went on, the blocks were moved farther and farther from Terry. The blocks would be called a(n) ______________________.

2. The book showed Roger a picture of a red ant. It used many repetitions of "This is a --- ant." It reinforced him for the correct answer. Later the book showed Roger a red mat. The first time he saw the mat he answered "red" when the book showed "This is a --- mat." The occurrence of his response to the new example of a red object is an example of what behavioral process? ______________

3. Melba taught Hilda to read the word *dog* by making cards with the word *dog* printed across the head of a picture of a dog. She then made a series of cards, with less and less of the dog sketched in. She praised Hilda for reading "dog" when that was the word but ignored her when it was another word. Hilda used what procedure to teach Hilda to read the word *dog*? ______________

4. Tom got a ride home from school every day from Carol. He praised Carol every time she made the correct turn. The first day she didn't know the way, so he told her which way to turn at Five Corners; the next day, he only said "here" at the turn and didn't tell her which way to turn; on subsequent days, he gave no instructions at all. Carol learned the way perfectly in three days. What behavioral procedure did Tom use? ______________

5. An added stimulus that increases the probability that a person will make the correct response is called a(n) ______________.

6. Mr. Kline taught Roberta to label the kitchen floor as a rectangle by asking her, "What shape is that? A rect-----?"; then asking, "What shape is that? A rrrr----------------?"; and finally, giving no prompt. He praised her when she said "rectangle." Mr. Kline taught Roberta to label the shape of a piece of paper in the same way. Roberta came to label as a rectangle any novel object with parallel sides, right angles, and length greater than width. What procedure did Mr. Kline use? ______________________

7. Schaefer (1963) used the German word *ich* to replace the English *I* in several short stories by Poe. The context of redundant sentences was enough to serve as an effective prompt for proper translation. By placing the German word in many different sentences, students learned to recognize that word. What behavioral procedure did Schaefer use to teach the meaning of *ich*? ______________

8. Programmed instruction requires a written response, provides immediate ______________ on the correctness of the response, and uses small steps.

9. Programming is the temporary use of a prompt during generalization training to establish a(n) ______________.

10. Professor Brainbuster shunned Samantha when she wore jeans, but another student, David, didn't mind. Samantha learned to wear jeans around David but not around the prof. What procedure influenced her when she wore jeans? ______________________________

11. Short answer question A: Define the procedure of fading.
____
____
____
____
____

Lesson 18 Form B **Grade** ____________________

Name ____________________ **Date** ____________________

---

1. In the book *Programmed Reading,* the child is shown a picture of a girl in a bag and then is required to fill in the blank: "That is Ann in the ba-." Showing one or more letters contained in the correct answer is called a(n) ____________________.

2. To use the stimulus control strategy to help solve human problems, (3) create new stimulus control by using ____________.

3. Fran taught Jimmy to write "P" when shown a "P" but not when shown a "B." Fran drew some light dashed lines that Jimmy drew over. She made the dashed lines fainter until they were no longer needed. What behavioral procedure did Fran use? ____________

4. The teacher praised Juanita if she said "car" when he showed her the word *car,* but not when he showed her the word *cat*. To help her learn *car,* he put a picture of a car next to the word. He gradually made the picture smaller until Juanita could no longer see it. What behavioral procedure was the teacher using? ____________

5. The temporary use of a prompt to establish a generalization is called ____________.

6. The gradual elimination of a prompt when teaching a discrimination is called __________.

7. Ann pointed to the table, asked Shigura, "What is this?", and then said "table" so he could hear it. She praised him when he also said "table." Gradually, she said the word more and more softly. What behavioral procedure did Ann use to teach Shigura to label this table correctly? ____________

8. A prompt is an added ____________ that increases the probability of a person's making the correct response in the presence of a novel stimulus.

9. Darlene praised her daughter for saying "crow" when shown a picture of the large black bird and ignored her for saying "crow" when shown the picture of the small black bird. What better behavioral procedure was Darlene using? ____________________________

10. Bob showed Tom a big red ball and asked, "What is this?" When Tom answered "ball," Bob gave him a tiny candy. After many trials, Tom would always say "ball." Next, Tom held a little green ball up many times, asked what it was, and gave Tom a candy when he said "ball." When Bob held up any kind of ball after that, Tom always called it a ball. What behavioral procedure did Bob use to teach Tom the idea of a ball? ____________

11. Short answer question B: Define the procedure of programming.

____

____

____

____

Lesson 18 Form C

Name ______________________ Grade ______________________

Date ______________________

1. Moore and Goldiamond (1964) had the correct answer light up while the incorrect answers remained dark. They always used the same problem with the same correct answer. They reinforced pushing the correct answer but ignored pushing the incorrect answer. They then gradually increased the brightness of the incorrect answers until they were as bright as the correct answer. What behavioral procedure were they using when they gradually made the correct and incorrect answers equally bright? ____________

2. Fading is the use of a prompt to establish a specific ____________.

3. A method for gradually changing a behavior is called ______________________; a method for gradually changing one stimulus is called ____________.

4. Darlene praised her daughter for saying "crow" when shown a picture of the large black bird and ignored her for saying "crow" when shown the picture of the small black bird. Darlene then gave the child hints for "bigness" when showing the picture of the crow. She gradually withdrew these hints. What behavioral procedure was Darlene using? ____________

5. Roger was shown a picture of a red ant and the words, "This is a r-d ant." (He had been taught to fill in such a blank.) Next he got a picture of a red ant and the words, "This is a r-- ant." After each problem, Roger was given an M&M if he filled in the blank correctly and was ignored if he got it wrong. As the sequence developed, fewer of the letters in "red" were given to him. Those letters would be called a(n) ____________.

6. Marvin ignored Sheila when he was using the headphones to listen to his new stereo. Marvin gave her a lot of attention when he was listening to the stereo without headphones. Sheila started sitting next to Marvin only when he did not have the headphones on. What behavioral procedure influenced when Sheila sat next to Marvin? ______________________

7. Carol's workbook showed her pictures of many red objects: ants, balls, houses, fire engines. It asked her, "What color is this? ---." The book reinforced Carol for writing "red" in response to this series of objects. At first, the question had one or more of the letters in "red" attached to the blank as a clue, but the book gradually eliminated these letters. Eventually Carol could label an object as red even when she had not seen it before and had no prompt. What behavioral procedure did the book use to teach Carol to label red objects as red? ______________________

8. Mr. Hearthstone taught Greg to sing middle C by first playing the note loudly on the piano and asking Greg to copy it, which he could do easily. Mr. Hearthstone then played the note more and more softly until Greg was singing the note without any reminder from the piano. What procedure did Mr. Hearthstone use? ____________

9. Suppose Bev called the baseball a ball but she didn't call the bat a ball. Because the behavior of saying "ball" is higher in the presence of the ball than in the presence of the bat, we call the behavior ____________ behavior.

10. The temporary use of a prompt to establish a generalization is called ____________.

11. Short answer question C: Define a prompt.
____
____
____

Lesson 19 **Form A** **Grade** ____________________

Name ____________________ **Date** ____________________

---

1. Buzz explained to Carol how to grip the ball in order to throw a curve. She tried it and threw a perfect curve! What behavioral procedure did Buzz use? ____________

2. If a teacher provides a behavioral demonstration of what another person is supposed to do, the teacher's behavior is called the ________ ____________.

3. When a teacher describes a behavior that he or she would like a learner to produce, this description would be called a(n) ____________ (not an *instruction*).

4. If a learner produces a behavior that someone else describes orally, the learner's behavior would be an example of ____________ behavior.

5. Henri found that when he typed out the full word in the rough copy of his book, his typist did too. However, if he used abbreviations in the rough copy of his book, his typist did not type the full word out but simply copied the abbreviations. Since Henri wanted the full word typed out, he gradually stopped using abbreviations and started typing full words. The change in Henri 's typing behavior is the result of what behavioral procedure? ________ ____________

6. Shawn showed Sherril several shimmering seashells and asked, "What are these? Are they several shimmering seashells?" Shawn praised Sherril for saying, "They are several shimmering seashells." The next time Shawn asked, he gave as a hint only the phrase, "several shimmering sea..." Each successive time, he dropped a word from the hint. Finally, Sherril could say the whole thing without any part of the hint. What behavioral procedure did Shawn use? ____________

7. Carol told Buzz how to sew a buttonhole, in detail. He tried it and sewed a perfect hole the first time. What behavioral procedure did Carol use? ____________

8. Ada demonstrated the essential elements of fielding: getting her body in front of the ball, kneeling to one knee, keeping her eye on the ball, and so on. Then she hit some balls to the children and had them try to field them. When they fielded the ball correctly, she praised them. What procedure increasing correct fielding was Ada using? ____________

9. Professor Brainbuster showed his students what a multiple-baseline graph looked like. When his students drew their own graphs in the same way, he praised them and gave them a good grade. What procedure did he use to teach his students to make good multiple-baseline graphs? ____________

10. Ada had Gordie stand at the plate and call "strike" for only the good pitches. She praised him when he called a good pitch a strike but ignored him when he called a bad pitch a strike. What procedure was she using to teach Gordie to call "strike" for the good pitches and not for the bad pitches? ____________

11. Short answer question A: Explain what question to ask to differentiate between instructional and imitation training.

____

____

____

Lesson 19 Form B **Grade** ________________

Name ________________ **Date** ________________

1. Frank explained in detail how Felicia should sight the rifle on the target. His explanation would be referred to as a(n) ____________ in the behavioral procedure of instructional training.

2. Because the imitative stimulus is associated with reinforcement for the imitative behavior, it is technically known as a(n) ____________ for the imitative behavior.

3. Ada hit several ground balls to Billy. If he kneeled with one knee on the ground when fielding a ball, she praised him. If he bent down with his knees straight when fielding the ball, she ignored him. Ada used what procedure to teach Billy to put one knee down when fielding? ____________

4. Marcia's roommate explained what clothing to buy and how to put on makeup in order to be in style. Marcia did these things and found that she got asked out for a lot more dates. Marcia's behavior changed as a result of what behavioral procedure? ____________

5. Sometimes a nontalker in a discussion class may learn to use an effective argument simply by listening to another person use it. The nontalker may, in the future, use that same line of argument and be reinforced. Changing the person's behavior in this way would be an example of ____________.

6. Imitation training and instructional training will continue to work only if the person's imitative or instructed behavior is ____________.

7. If a learner copies the behavior of another person, the learner's behavior is called ____________ ____________.

8. Hollandsworth and colleagues (1978) demonstrated for Herbert how to ask questions designed to clarify interview questions. They then watched his ability to ask such questions in a simulated interview and reinforced correct performance. What behavioral procedure did they use to teach Herbert how to ask questions of the interviewer? ____________

9. Sam can learn from a lecture in two ways. He can do things that the lecturer tells him to do; in that case, the lecturer would be using what procedure? ____________. Or Sam can copy arguments contained in the lecture; in that case, the lecturer would be using what procedure? ____________

10. Dr. Feelgood taught Marcia to act assertively toward Howard. He praised her when she acted assertively toward him. He then brought in Felix and praised her when she acted assertively toward him. The good doctor used a series of males until Marcia started acting assertively to new males without reinforcement. What behavioral procedure did Dr. Feelgood and his assistant use to create this result? ____________

11. Short answer question B: Define imitation training, referring to its three parts.

____

____

____

Lesson 19 **Form C** **Grade** ____________________

Name ____________________ **Date** ____________________

1. The fourth tactic in the stimulus control strategy is to create complex stimulus control through ____________ training or ____________ training.

2. The use of verbal descriptions of behavior and reinforcement to teach a new behavior is called ____________.

3. John's father sawed the first board to show John how to use the power saw. He then watched John cut a board and praised him when he followed the father's example. This is an example of what behavioral procedure? ____________

4. Ada patiently explained to Sam exactly where to look when he was pitching. She then had him throw several pitches while she was watching and praised him only when he did it right. What procedure for changing Sam's behavior did Ada use? ____________

5. Tom explained in detail how Frank should operate the chain saw, watched him try, and praised his performance. What behavioral procedure did Tom use? ____________

6. Cursive writing is often taught in school by showing children examples of the properly formed letters and words. The children are required to copy these letters over and over. The teacher praises good copies. This is an example of what behavioral procedure? ____________

7. Mary showed Tommy two blocks and asked, "How many are there? Two?" She praised him when he said "two." She then repeated the question at various times during the day, each time saying "two" softer and softer until Tommy answered "two" without any help. Mary then showed Tommy two toys and repeated the procedure. When she showed him two spoons and asked him how many, he said "two" without any hint. By reinforcing Tommy's response of "two" in the presence of a series of stimuli until he could apply it to a novel stimulus, Mary used what behavioral procedure? ____________

8. Because the teacher's verbal description concerning what behavior the learner should produce is associated with reinforcement for the instructed behavior, the verbal description would technically be called a(n) ____________ for the instructed behavior.

9. Hollandsworth and his colleagues (1978) gave Herbert a verbal description of how he should make clear responses to interview questions. They then observed his performance in a simulated interview session and reinforced correct responses. The behavior analysts were using what behavioral procedure to teach Herbert to make clear answers? ____________

10. Barb showed Kenny a picture of a tree and asked, "What is this? Say 'tree.'" Kenny said "tree." Several other times during the week, she showed him the same picture and asked him, "What is this, a tree?" But she said "tree" more and more softly until he called it a tree without her hint. Barb was using what behavioral procedure? ____________

11. Short answer question C: Define instructional training, referring to its three parts.
____
____
____
____

Lesson 20 Form A Grade ______________________

Name ______________________ Date ______________________

1. Carey earned a point for every page of the SRA Reading Program that she finished. She could trade each point for one cookie. Carey's parents noted that she usually earned a few points early in the morning and then quit working for that day. The points probably lost their effectiveness as a conditioned reinforcer because Carey soon became ______________ with cookies.

2. The fifth tactic in using the stimulus control strategy to solve human problems is to make reinforcement more practical by creating ______________ reinforcers.

3. Larry often forgot to wear safety goggles when using the chain saw. Dad reminded him by putting on his own goggles. Dad later reminded Larry by simply putting his own goggles on his forehead but not slipping them over his eyes. Still later, Dad reminded Larry by simply picking up his goggles without putting them on. Finally, Dad was able to stop giving any hint; Larry always put on his safety goggles when operating the chain saw. What behavioral procedure did Larry's father use to teach him to wear safety goggles? ______________

4. One day, Mary wore her hair loose, and Kevin stopped and talked with her for the first time ever. Don also stopped to talk with her, and he complimented her on her hair. When she went home for Thanksgiving break, she again decided to wear her hair loose. If home was a situation where she had not been reinforced for wearing her hair loose, then occurrence of wearing her hair loose at home would be an example of what behavioral process? ______________________________

5. Any reinforcer that loses its effectiveness permanently through unpaired presentation is called a(n) ______________ reinforcer.

6. When the towels were no longer backed up with social attention by Ayllon and Michael (1959), the towels lost their effectiveness as reinforcers. Thus, towels would be considered a(n) ______________________ reinforcer.

7. A reinforcer associated with <u>many</u> other reinforcers is called a(n) ______________ reinforcer.

8. Ms. Whalen walked through the room while the children were working on their math. She marked all correct work with a big, red C. Each child was allowed to play outside for ten minutes after he or she had gotten ten C's. Ms. Whalen found that the rate of work in the class went up dramatically as a result of this approach. We call playing outside a(n) ______________ reinforcer for Ms. Whalen's C's.

9. Marlon's teachers gave him a button every time he picked up his toys after he finished playing. Marlon could use the button to get a snack, a story, or a long walk. If these three events were reinforcers, you would call the button a(n) ______________ reinforcer.

10. Bev learned to cube the number 5 by the sequence of multiplying 5 x 5 to get 25. This 25 was then an SD for multiplying by another 5 to get the answer, 125. Her teacher always praised her final answer. Bev's behavior in this example constituted a(n) ______________ ______________.

11. Short answer question A: Define stimulus/response chain.

____

____

____

____

____

____

____

Lesson 20 **Form B** **Grade** ______________________

Name ______________________ **Date** ______________________

1. A stimulus/response chain consists of several related responses; the results of one response serve as a(n) ____________ for the next response.

2. Whitman and Dussault (1976) helped James set up a system in which he earned points by studying and attending class. He spent them on such activities as visiting his girlfriend and watching TV. Visiting his girlfriend and watching TV would be considered __________ reinforcers for the points.

3. Willie's mother reinforced him for doing something thoughtful with an immediate "Thank you" and later an M&M. Then she decided to reinforce his thoughtful behavior only with a "Thank you." He started doing fewer thoughtful things, and he eventually stopped altogether. This pattern indicates that "Thank you" was what type of reinforcer? ____________

4. Suppose the teacher gave Juan two math problems, such as "2+2=?" and "4+3=?" Juan's responses would not constitute a stimulus/response chain, because the response to one problem does not serve as a(n) ____________ for the response to the second problem.

5. Any event that loses its effectiveness only temporarily through satiation is called a(n) __________ reinforcer.

6. One major advantage that conditioned reinforcers have over their backups, with respect to their effectiveness as reinforcers, is that conditioned reinforcers can easily be delivered according to the principle of __________.

7. One day Fat Frank was once again teasing Slim Simpson. Simpson gave Frank a look that he had never used before. The look said, "I'm going to hurt you very much if you do that again!" Frank immediately started being very nice. Simpson used that same look many times with Frank in the following days. One day, Heavy Harry started teasing Simpson. Simpson gave Harry the same look he had used with Frank. He had never used the look before with Harry. What is the name of the behavioral process that accounts for Simpson looking at Harry that way? ____________

8. A generalized reinforcer is an event that is associated with ____________ other reinforcers.

9. Carol's teacher showed her a picture of a maple tree and asked, "What is this? Is it a tree?" She gave Carol a token whenever she said "tree," but ignored her when she said the flower was a tree. On subsequent occasions, the teacher asked, "Is it a tree?" more and more softly until Carol could identify it as a tree without the hint. When she had succeeded, Carol could identify the maple as a tree. What behavioral procedure had the teacher used? ____________

10. In Sociology 71, students had to pay credits if they wanted to come to class. In class they could see movies, listen to guest speakers, and participate in discussions. The credits would be classified as what kind of reinforcer? ____________ reinforcer

11. Short answer question B: Define conditioned reinforcer

____

____

____

____

Lesson 20 **Form C** **Grade** ______________________

Name ______________________ **Date** ______________________

1. What type of reinforcer is most likely always to be an effective reinforcer, even if you have just had a lot of it? ____________ reinforcer.

2. When reciting "Mary had a little lamb," you would first say "Mary," and this response would serve as a discriminative stimulus for the second response, "had," and so on. The entire sequence would be called a(n) ____________ (if there were some "final" reinforcement).

3. Everyone at Sunflower House had to earn 100 points a week to be eligible to continue living there. In January, Sunflower House changed that rule. Members were now on their honor to earn 100 points a week to help keep the house running. Soon the members earned fewer and fewer points each week. These results suggest that points should be classified as what kind of reinforcer? ____________

4. A reinforcer that makes a conditioned reinforcer effective is called a(n) ____________ reinforcer.

5. Members of the behavioral dorm gave a ticket worth one point to anyone they saw complimenting another person. These points could be traded for tickets to the theatre or sports events, a special dessert at dinner, or the use of a computer or other house property. You call the points a(n) ____________ reinforcer; you call the desserts and other privileges a(n) ____________ reinforcer for the points.

6. Getting the correct answer on a self-quiz may be a minor reinforcer for a student. However, if getting the correct answer on the self-quiz is associated with doing well on a class quiz, it may be a fairly strong reinforcer. What type of reinforcer is getting correct answers on the self-quiz if it is associated with a good grade on the class quiz? ____________ reinforcer

7. Claire started using the word *ephemeral* when she was around Dale, because he complimented her for having such a good vocabulary. One day Kevin also complimented her for using the word *ephemeral*. After that, she used the word in her conversations with many people. What behavioral procedure did Dale and Kevin combine to employ to have her use the word with new people who had never reinforced her? ____________

8. Every time Jean made an approving statement to her teachers, Polirstok and Greer (1977) gave her a token. The tokens could be exchanged for music tapes, extra gym time, lunch with a favorite teacher, or extra English credit. These tokens could be considered to be a(n) ____________ reinforcer.

9. Melody's father praised her for using the word *gregarious* for the first time one day. After that, Melody used the word in a conversation with her mother. What is the name for the process of using the word with her mother without ever having been reinforced by her mother? ____________

10. A sequence of responses in which the results of one response serve as an SD for the next response and in which the last response leads to a reinforcer is called a(n) ____________.

11. Short answer question C: Define generalized reinforcer.

____

____

____

____

Lesson 21 **Form A** **Grade** ______________________

Name ______________________ **Date** ______________________

1. A person will continue to follow instructions only if frequently ____________ for doing so.

2. If a behavior occurs more frequently in the presence of the SD than the S-delta, we say that the stimulus exerts ______________ over that behavior.

3. We often think of people who bubble over with "fun" as having that trait ingrained in their personality. Yet a group could accidentally eliminate this behavior by ignoring it. They would be unintentionally applying the procedure called ____________.

4. Flora taught her daughter Melody to read the word *cat* by printing the word on a card and asking her, "What is this word?" She made a delighted fuss when Melody said "cat" in the presence of that word but ignored her when she said "cat" in the presence of any other word. To help Melody, Flora showed her a picture of a cat with the word *cat*. Each time, she showed the picture of the cat for a briefer time, until she stopped showing it at all. What behavioral procedure was Flora using? ______________

5. The name for reinforcers that are paired with other events to make them effective conditioned reinforcers is ____________ reinforcers.

6. Crazy Harry made a card showing a photo of an Amanita Muscaria mushroom with the word *Amanita* written underneath. He also made cards showing pictures of other mushrooms. When he showed the Amanita to Jeff, he uncovered a bit of the label until Jeff could name the mushroom. When Jeff said Amanita, Harry praised him. Crazy Harry showed less of the label until Jeff could name it without looking at the label at all. Crazy Harry then repeated the process for a series of photos of different Amanita mushrooms until Jeff could name them without looking at the label. Crazy Harry found that Jeff could name any picture of a new Amanita. What behavioral procedure did Harry use when he showed less of the label for each of a series of photos of different mushrooms until Jeff could always identify the new photo? ______________

7. In the process of teaching Marty to say "elephant," Danny would show Marty how to say "elephant" by saying it himself. Danny would then praise Marty if he said it correctly. The method that Danny used to teach Marty to say "elephant" is called ____________ training.

8. Primary reinforcers lose their effectiveness only temporarily through the process called ______________; conditioned reinforcers lose their effectiveness permanently through being ______________ with their backups.

9. Anytime Karen used a new word longer than three syllables, her father immediately gave her a quarter and praised her improving vocabulary. Her father never did this unless Karen had used a new word. Karen always needed the money and seemed to think of it as a reasonable payoff for learning a new word. What principle of effective reinforcement, if any, did Karen's father fail to employ? ______________

10. Everyone was given a "snerkel" each time he or she said something positive about the food. People could cash in the snerkels for a small amount of money or for privileges in the house (such as the use of games). What kind of reinforcer is the snerkel? ____________

11. Short answer question A: Explain the difference between discrimination training and differential reinforcement.

____

____

____

Lesson 21 **Form B** **Grade** ____________________

Name ____________________ **Date** ____________________

1. Fred will neck with Gloria only in a drive-in theatre. Assuming that Gloria finds it reinforcing to neck with Fred, the drive-in would be called a(n) __________ for necking.

2. Olivia explained to Juan in detail how to do a particular dance, even drawing out little diagrams showing where he should move his feet. Juan tried it, and Olivia provided feedback to him until he could do it perfectly. What behavioral procedure was Olivia using to teach Juan the dance? __________

3. Gladys's parents never listened to her during dinner, preferring to discuss the day's news instead. However, one day Gladys criticized the Republicans, and her father had a long argument with her about politics. As a result, Gladys became an ardent critic of Republicans at home. Later, she criticized Republicans around a series of her parents' friends and similarly got an argument and lots of attention. Gladys now criticizes Republicans whenever she is in the presence of conservative, business-oriented people. What behavioral procedure produced this change in Gladys? __________

4. Mr. Howard pointed to a VW going by and asked little Alicia, "What is that? Vroom, vroom." She said "car." Mr. Howard pointed to another Beetle later and said the "vroom, vroom" much more softly. He repeated this until Alicia could identify a VW as a car without the addition of the "vroom, vroom." Mr. Howard then used the same approach on a Mustang. From then on, Alicia could identify any passenger vehicle as a car. What behavioral procedure did Mr. Howard use? __________

5. You define generalization as the occurrence of a behavior in the presence of a(n) __________ stimulus.

6. Generalization training involves reinforcing a behavior in the presence of each of a series of situations until generalization occurs to other members of that same __________.

7. Replacing a baby's diaper consists of placing the child on her back, removing the old diaper, and putting on and securing a new diaper. This sequence of behaviors would be called a(n) __________.

8. Sue frequently told Ken that she couldn't jog with him because she didn't know how to run. To help her learn how, Ken took her out on their lawn and jogged for her, showing her where on the foot to land, how to extend the legs, and how to coordinate swinging the arms with the leg movements. Sue then tried, and Ken provided feedback. In a few minutes, Sue was able to run almost as smoothly as Ken. What behavioral procedure did Ken employ to teach Sue how to jog? __________

9. If the probability of a behavior decreases because an event that used to follow it has been stopped, what behavioral procedure is being used? __________

10. Discrimination training is a procedure in which a behavior is __________ in the presence of one stimulus and __________ in the presence of a second stimulus.

11. Short answer question B: Explain how to differentiate between instructional training and imitation training.

____
____
____
____
____
____
____

Lesson 21 **Form C** **Grade** ____________________

Name ____________________ **Date** ____________________

---

1. Katie showed her son the word *house*. She praised him if he said "house" when shown that word, but not when shown other words. To help him, she showed him a picture of a house along with the word. She showed the picture for successively briefer times. Because it helped establish the response of reading the word, the picture would be called a(n) ____________.

2. Mary's mother checked every 15 minutes to see if she was cleaning her room. If it was reinforcing for Mary to be found cleaning, what schedule was she on? ____________ schedule

3. Fran praised Melanie when she said that she had been studying. Unfortunately, Melanie lied. When Melanie said she had been studying, Fran immediately gave Melanie a special snack. Melanie loved the snacks—in fact, she would do anything to get one. She never got too much of the snack. What principle of effective reinforcement, if any, was Fran failing to employ? ____________

4. If a reinforcer is paired with one backup reinforcer, it is called a(n) ____________ reinforcer; if it is paired with many backup reinforcers, it is called a(n) ____________ reinforcer.

5. During World War II, Colonel Peterson frequently showed a photo of a British Spitfire fighter plane to his Civilian Defense recruits and asked them what it was. To help them, he made a spitting sound. Every time he showed the picture, he made a slightly softer spitting sound until everyone could identify the Spitfire with no clue. Later he showed them a different picture of the Spitfire and repeated the process. He had to teach them four different pictures before they could identify new photos. What behavioral procedure had Col. Peterson used? ____________

6. If Gloria peeps only when the light is on in Todd's room, then we would call her peeping a(n) ____________ behavior.

7. Eli wanted to teach his friend to say "Hi" when Eli said "Yassou," the Greek word for "Hi." So at first he said "Yassou" and waved at his friend. Gradually he delayed the wave until his friend was responding "Hi" even before the wave. The wave used in addition to the greeting is called a(n) ____________.

8. Davey's friends explained to him how to highlight important points, how to review them, and how to work in an area without distractions. They praised him when he followed their suggestions. Davey tried their suggestions and got all A's that semester, while his friends got C's. What behavioral procedure did his friends use to teach him how to study effectively? ____________

9. Barb and Carey loved to go window shopping. Barb had undertaken to teach Carey how to dress in the latest fashions. When Carey expressed the opinion that some garment looked really cool, Barb would praise her taste. She did it immediately, but only if Carey was correct. Carey was always delighted when Barb told her she had good taste and never seemed to get too much praise of this sort. What principle of effective reinforcement, if any, did Barb overlook? ____________

10. Cutting a tree down with the chain saw required Tom to do the following: get the chain saw, check its fuel if necessary, open the choke, start it, and cut a wedge from the front of the tree and a straight cut in the back. Then the tree fell on his cabin and wrecked it. What is the name for this sequence of behaviors that Tom so carefully carried out? ____________

11. Short answer question C: Define the term *generalized reinforcer*.

____

____

____

Lesson 22 **Form A** **Grade** ______________________

Name ______________________ **Date** ______________________

1. Three types of punishers are ______________, ______________, and ______________.

2. Tom told his mother several times that disco dancing Saturday night was far more important to him than saving his soul Sunday morning. She simply ignored him each time that he said that. Pretty soon he stopped saying that. The reduction in his frequency of making that statement was the result of what behavioral procedure? ______________

3. Here are the principles of effective punishment. A punishing stimulus should be ________ only on the behavior that you want to decrease in frequency. It should follow the behavior ______________. The person should be relatively ______________ of the punisher. The ______________ (or intensity) of the stimulus should be sufficiently large.

4. To use the aversive control strategy, (1) decrease undesirable behavior through ________ as a last resort.

5. Every time Bob broke the rule about dinner complaints, Paul reminded him that he had broken the rule. Bob's rate of breaking the rule increased. The reminder was an event called a(n) ______________ for Bob.

6. A punisher is defined as an event that (1) ______________ a behavior and (2) ______________ the frequency of that behavior.

7. On the few occasions that Marty swore, his mother told him, "Stop that, I'm going to tell your father," and his father spanked him. Recently, however, she took pity on him. While still telling Marty, "Stop that, I'm going to tell your father," she did not tell his father. Pretty soon Marty was swearing all the time. His mother's statement is a(n) ______________ punisher.

8. Professor Ann Klein ridiculed Ronnie Republican because he made what she considered to be trivial comments. As a result, Ronnie made even more comments. The increase in Ronnie's comments is a result of what behavioral procedure? ______________

9. Bob broke the written rule about dinner complaints. Another member of the group reminded him that he had broken the rule, and he never complained at dinner again. If you view the written rule about dinner complaints as a stimulus, what is its technical name? ________

10. Kevin repeatedly said racist things in the presence of members of his frat. One day he made a racist comment, and another member said, "Kevin, please don't say that anymore. It was disrespectful." Kevin never repeated that comment again. Kevin's racist comment was eliminated by what procedure? ______________

11. Short answer question A: Define the term *punisher*.

____

____

____

Lesson 22 **Form B** **Grade** ______________________

Name ______________________ **Date** ______________________

1. When Ben insulted his friends, they used to argue with him about the insults. Now they no longer argue with him but just pretend that he didn't say anything. Ben's rate of insults has decreased dramatically. What behavioral procedure is at work here? __________

2. Mary tried to teach her child to count by saying, "No, that's wrong" whenever the child made a mistake. The child never repeated those mistakes. Mary's statement is an example of an event called a(n) ____________.

3. Abdul ran a red light one day when he was in a hurry to get to class. A police officer caught him and gave him a ticket, and Abdul didn't go through a red light again after that. The red light would be called a(n) ____________ for going through it.

4. The fourth strategy for changing human behavior is the ____________ control strategy.

5. The terms *punisher* and *reinforcer* both refer to events that are timed to ____________ a behavior.

6. Gloria hit Lenny every time he attempted a soul kiss. His rate of attempting a soul kiss increased. What behavioral procedure did Gloria use to bring about this increased rate? ____________

7. A stimulus that occurs before the behavior and is associated with the punishment of that behavior would be called a(n) ____________.

8. Bob broke the rule about dinner complaints, but a reminder didn't work to stop his complaining. The group members decided to fine him 25 cents in addition to the reminder. This worked. The reminder now works all by itself for Bob. The reminder is a(n) ____________ punisher.

9. Tito was spanked every time he teased his little sister Janet. His rate of teasing increased as a result. Spanking would be called a(n) ____________.

10. If a person's behavior is decreased through punishment in one situation, any decrease in other situations without punishment would be called ____________, which will not necessarily occur.

11. Short answer question B: Name four principles that determine the effectiveness of punishment.

____
____
____
____
____
____

Lesson 22 **Form C** **Grade** ______________________

Name ______________________ **Date** ______________________

1. One day, Mr. King spanked Marcie in front of the class right after he caught her teasing a friend. Marcie never teased a friend in class again. Her teasing decreased due to what behavioral procedure? ____________

2. Punishment and extinction both result in a(n) __________ in the frequency of a behavior.

3. The procedure in which a punisher is administered for the occurrence of a particular behavior, and reduces the rate of that behavior, is called ____________.

4. Mary nagged her mother for snacks while dinner was being cooked. Mary's mother repeatedly said "No," but Mary nagged even more. Mary's mother finally screamed "No!" at Mary, and Mary stopped nagging. One of mother's screams would be an example of what behavioral event? ____________

5. Punisher A reduced the rate of the behavior as long as it was paired with punisher B. But when it was no longer paired, its effectiveness gradually diminished. Behavior analysts call punisher A a(n) ____________ punisher.

6. Every time Tom threw a ball in the house, Paula, his mother, spanked him. For some unknown reason, Tom threw the ball around inside the house even more after that. What behavioral procedure did Paula use to produce this change in Tom's ball-throwing? ________________

7. Yvonne told everyone in her class that she didn't think that President Nixon should have taken the troops out of Vietnam until the United States had won. Her classmates ignored her, knowing that she liked to get attention by taking controversial positions. They ignored this same statement every time she made it; pretty soon she stopped saying it. What behavioral procedure had her class members used to reduce her rate of making that statement? ________________

8. Steve used to pester Carla for a date. However, Carla completely ignored his requests. Steve no longer pesters Carla for a date. What behavioral procedure did she use to decrease the rate of requests? ____________

9. An event that follows a behavior and reduces the future probability of that behavior is called a(n) ____________.

10. McNees and his associates (1976) posted stars identifying clothing that was most often stolen. Customers stole much less after the posting than before. If the customers stole less because they had in the past been punished in similar situations for stealing, then the star would technically be called a(n) __________.

11. Short answer question C: Explain in behavioral terms why people use punishment so often.

____

____

____

Lesson 23 **Form A** **Grade** ______________________

Name ______________________ **Date** ______________________

1. Pierce and Risley (1974) posted the number of minutes early that a recreation center would have to close each time a rule violation was observed. This reduced rule violations dramatically. If these numbers were no longer paired with the actual closing of the center, they would probably lose their effect. If they did, what type of punisher would they be? A(n) ____________ punisher

2. Frank's parents took away his new erector set each time he played too roughly with it. If Frank's rate of rough play decreased, this would be an example of what behavioral procedure? ____________

3. Previously when Beth burped at the dinner table, her parents argued with her about it. Now they no longer argue with her, and her rate of burping has decreased. What behavioral procedure did her parents use to decrease her burping? ____________

4. Tommy hit his little brother frequently and was always spanked for it. After a while, his mother decided to stop spanking Tommy. She was surprised to see that Tommy rarely hit his little brother after she stopped spanking him. What behavioral procedure accounts for the decrease in Tommy's hitting his brother? ____________

5. Tommy hit his little brother frequently. One day Tommy's mother just happened to see Tommy hitting him and immediately ran and spanked Tommy. Tommy hit his brother again, and again his mother spanked him. Tommy rarely hit his brother after that, but when he did, he got a spanking. Spanking in this case is an example of what behavioral procedure? ____________

6. Tommy hit his little brother frequently. One day Tommy's mother just happened to see Tommy hitting him and immediately ran and spanked Tommy. Tommy hit his brother again, and again his mother spanked him. Tommy hit his brother even more often after that and always got a spanking. The event of spanking in this case is an example of a(n) ____________.

7. When Larry pouted, Carol used to sympathize with him. Since she has stopped sympathizing with his pouting, his rate of pouting has decreased sharply. What procedure did Carol use to decrease Larry's pouting behavior? ____________

8. There are two types of punishment. In one, a behavior produces an event, and the rate of the behavior decreases. In the second, a behavior is followed by withdrawal of an event, and the rate ____________.

9. A <u>punisher</u> is any event (produced or withdrawn) timed such that it ____________ a behavior and ____________ the rate of the behavior.

10. If an event that is normally in a person's environment is withdrawn following a behavior, and the rate of the behavior decreases, then the procedure is called ____________.

11. Short answer question A: Define time out, and explain how it conforms to the definition of punishment.

____

____

____

____

____

____

Lesson 23 **Form B** **Grade** ______________________

Name ______________________ **Date** ______________________

1. The procedure of stopping the delivery of a reinforcer that follows a behavior and finding a decrease in the rate of the behavior is called ______________.

2. If a stimulus precedes the withdrawal of a reinforcer when a particular behavior occurs, that stimulus is called a(n) ______________.

3. Tactic #1 in using the aversive control strategy for solving human problems is to decrease undesirable behavior through ______________ as a last resort.

4. If Pierce and Risley (1974) had ignored all rule-violating behavior, and the rate of such behavior had decreased, what procedure would they have been using? ______________

5. Lora's parents made her stay indoors each time she pinched her little brother. If she stopped pinching him, this would be an example of what behavioral procedure? ______________

6. Dave frequently made gross comments about the food, and his friends always acted outraged. His friends then decided to no longer act outraged when he complained. Dave stopped complaining. The decrease in Dave's complaining is the result of what behavioral procedure? ______________

7. Alice griped about the dorm food a lot. Every time she made such a comment, she was fined 25 cents. She quickly stopped making such comments. The decrease in Alice's griping was the result of what behavioral procedure? ______________

8. Tommy hit his little brother frequently. His mother decided that she would send Tommy to his room whenever he hit his little brother. Tommy stopped hitting his little brother after this change in his mother's behavior. Sending Tommy to his room for hitting is a good example of what behavioral procedure? ______________

9. Frank frequently explained his theory of politics. Melody defeated Frank's theory with her criticism. Soon Frank stopped explaining his theory. The event "Melody defeated Frank's theory" would be called a(n) ______________.

10. When Tommy first suggested vigilante action to oppose the liberal government, other conservatives supported his ideas. However, now that they have stopped agreeing with his positions, he is making fewer and fewer vigilante proposals. The group used what procedure to reduce Tommy's violent proposals? ______________

11. Short answer question B: State the two elements that define punishment by contingent withdrawal.

____

____

____

____

Lesson 23 **Form C** **Grade** ______________________

Name ______________________ **Date** ______________________

---

1. The procedure in which the failure to make a response is followed by the delivery of an aversive event ____________ (should, shouldn't) be labeled *punishment*.

2. If an event is normally in a person's environment but is taken away whenever the person emits a particular behavior, and if the rate of that behavior decreases, the procedure is an example of ____________.

3. The temporary loss of a privilege contingent on the occurrence of a particular behavior is a form of punishment by withdrawal called ____________.

4. Every time Paco pouted, his parents took away some of his play time by sending him to his room. Afterward, they discussed with him why they had sent him to his room. He pouted more often. What procedure did his parents use? ____________

5. Pierce and Risley (1974) withdrew the privilege of playing in the recreation center when a rule was violated. The rule-violating behavior decreased dramatically. What behavioral procedure did they use? ____________

6. Hedley started all sorts of stories about members of the group. They decided to suspend him for 24 hours whenever he told such a story, and Hedley stopped doing so. The decrease in his storytelling is the result of what behavioral procedure? ____________

7. The frat members no longer argued with Larry when he griped about the food. Soon he stopped making such comments. This is an example of what behavioral procedure? ____________

8. Marge used to cook meals for John. Ever since he started following each meal with "Thank you," her rate of cooking meals has decreased. "Thank you" is an event called a(n) ____________ for Marge's meal-cooking behavior.

9. When Professor Odd made absurd statements to his friends, they would argue with him. Recently, they have stopped arguing with him when he makes absurd statements, and his rate of making absurd statements has decreased. What behavioral procedure did they use? ____________

10. One day Ken said something about engineering students that Bob didn't like, and Bob said, "Why don't you shut up, you damned fool? You don't know anything about engineering!" Ken never said anything about engineering students around Bob. The decrease in Ken's comments about engineering students is the result of what behavioral procedure? ____________

11. Short answer question C: Explain how to tell whether a procedure that decreases behavior is extinction.

____

____

____

Lesson 24 **Form A** **Grade** ______________________

Name ______________________ **Date** ______________________

1. Larry used to argue a lot, but he finally realized that every time he got into a really intense argument, he lost a good friend. So Larry decided to stop arguing, and in fact he never argued again. What behavioral procedure did his social environment use to reduce his rate of arguing? ____________

2. Azrin and Powell (1969) developed a pill dispenser that sounded a buzzer at the prescribed time for taking a pill. The buzzer could be turned off only by dispensing a pill. The behavior of dispensing the pill is an example of ____________ behavior.

3. If every third response is followed by the termination of a negative reinforcer, that behavior is on what schedule of intermittent reinforcement? ____________

4. The moment Brad guessed that he might get a cold, he started taking a lot of vitamin C. He never got a cold. Taking vitamin C would be an example of a(n) ____________ behavior.

5. Terry used to come home late from school. Then his mother started scolding him every day that he was not home on time. He started coming home on time. Coming home on time would be an example of ____________ behavior for Terry.

6. If the termination of an event increases the rate of a behavior that the termination follows, the event is called a(n) ____________.

7. Andy frequently forgot to bring any money along on his dates with Leslie, so she usually paid for the movie or drinks. Finally, Leslie explained that she couldn't afford to pay for all their dates. From then on, Andy brought along money. What behavioral procedure did Leslie use to increase Andy's rate of bringing along money for their dates? ____________

8. Tactic #2 of the aversive control strategy is to increase desirable behavior through ____________ ____________ as a last resort.

9. Penny just hated it when Kenny got fresh with her. So she would always haul off and slap the hell out of him when he did. Kenny is no longer fresh with Penny. What behavioral procedure did Penny use to stop Kenny from acting fresh? ____________

10. Anytime Reginald played with any of his toys in any part of the house outside of his own room, his parents picked them up and kept them for a week before returning them. Reginald stopped playing with his toys in the rest of the house. What behavioral procedure did his parents use to eliminate the behavior of playing with the toys in the rest of the house? ____________

11. Short answer question A: Define escape and avoidance behavior.

____

____

____

Lesson 24 **Form B** **Grade** ____________________

Name ____________________ **Date** ____________________

1. When Lester showed up for a date with Felicia in his grubby clothes, she wouldn't let him put his arm around her in the movie—in fact, she wouldn't let him touch her at all. Lester stopped showing up for dates with Felicia in his grubbies. Felicia used what procedure to reduce his rate of showing up in his grubby clothes? ____________

2. Bev didn't like doing any kind of dirty work at the sorority. On "work Saturdays," she would start working but after a little while she would remember a doctor's appointment and have to leave immediately. Leaving for a doctor's appointment would be an example of ________ behavior.

3. Everyone at the police station was pretty sure that Paul knew more about the crime than he was admitting. Captain Thomas kept questioning him until he finally "broke" and admitted what he knew. Captain Thomas immediately stopped the questioning. Later, under similar questioning, Paul admitted knowing about a number of other crimes. Paul's confessions would be an example of ____________ behavior.

4. Epstein and Masek (1978) required their patients to pay a $1 fine if they failed to take their medication at the prescribed time. The patients' rate of taking their medication at the correct time increased as a result of being fined. The patients' behavior would be called a(n) ______________________ response.

5. Positive reinforcers and negative reinforcers are both events that can be used to ________ the rate of a behavior.

6. Larry was a conservationist. When he and Fran went for a hike, he would always remind her when she littered by saying something like, "Hey, you dropped something." Pretty soon Fran stopped littering when on a hike with Larry. What behavioral procedure did Larry use to eliminate littering? ____________

7. If a behavior <u>terminates</u> a negative reinforcer, the behavior is called a(n) ____________ behavior.

8. Frank and Jerry used to whisper and giggle a lot in the movie theater. One day, the manager kicked them out of the theater for being noisy. They never made noise again in the theater. What behavioral procedure did the manager use to decrease their whispering and giggling? ____________

9. If a behavior <u>prevents</u> a negative reinforcer from occurring, it is called a(n) ____________ behavior.

10. Professor Brainbuster had an uncanny knack for guessing when Meredith had not read the assignment. On those days, he would inevitably call on her to answer a question about the material. After having this happen a few times, Meredith always read the assignment. What behavioral procedure did the professor use to increase her frequency of reading the assignment? ____________

11. Short answer question B: Define a negative reinforcer, and distinguish it from a positive reinforcer. (Hint: it has nothing to do with whether the event is pleasant or unpleasant.)

____

____

____

____

____

____

Lesson 24 **Form C**

Name ______________________

Grade ______________________

Date ______________________

1. Mrs. Norris had become annoyed by Carol's frequent failure to do her homework for her American history course. So she started making Carol do her homework during the outside recess period. Carol soon started doing her homework the night before so that she wouldn't have to miss recess. Mrs. Norris used what behavioral procedure to increase Carol's frequency of doing her homework the night before? ______________________

2. Avoidance behavior could be any behavior that ______________ the occurrence of a negative reinforcer.

3. Escape behavior is behavior that ____________ a negative reinforcer.

4. A negative reinforcer could be any event that is ______________ or ____________ by a behavior and that causes the rate of the behavior to increase.

5. Epstein and Masek (1978) required their patients to pay a $1 fine if they failed to take their medication at the prescribed time. The patients' rate of taking their medication at the correct time increased as a result. The $1 fine would be an event called a(n) ____________ ______________.

6. Frank and Jerry used to whisper and giggle a lot in the movie theater. One day, the theatre manager came in and asked them to follow him. He made them miss five minutes of the movie because they were bothering other customers. They never whispered and giggled again after that. What behavioral procedure did the manager use to reduce their noise-making? ______________________

7. Karen hated to have work pile up on her to the extent that she had to rush to get her assignments done. When a term paper was assigned early in the semester, she immediately started to work on it a little each day, to keep from being overburdened. Karen's working a little each day would be an example of ____________ behavior.

8. Melody didn't really start working hard on her studies until the work piled up. Since she didn't like having work piled up, she would start to work practically day and night to get out from under the burden. Melody's rate of work when work had piled up would be an example of ______________ behavior.

9. Billy got up about every 15 minutes to sharpen a pencil. Mrs. Feingold started glaring at Billy. As a result, Billy's rate of pencil sharpening decreased. What procedure did Mrs. Feingold use to reduce Billy's frequency of pencil sharpening? ____________

10. Barb was on a point system at home. She lost points for teasing her little brother and soon stopped teasing him. What behavioral procedure was used to reduce her rate of teasing her brother? ____________

11. Short answer question C: Explain what "punishing someone for not making the desired response" would be called by a behavior analyst and why.

____

____

____

____

____

____

Lesson 25 **Form A** **Grade** ____________________

Name ____________________ **Date** ____________________

---

1. Wendy agreed to encourage Carol to speak more loudly, as a step toward helping her become more assertive. At first Wendy praised Carol only if she could hear her; later only if she could hear her five feet away; and still later only if she could hear her from ten feet away. Carol speaking loud enough to be heard from five feet away is called a(n) ____________ to the ultimate goal.

2. Because the answer to the question "What is the sum of 8 and 2?" is "10," with regard to the response of "4," the question is called a(n) ____________________.

3. Mr. Levin observed five groundskeepers to determine whether they were working. He first observed Ken for 30 seconds, then shifted to Diane for 30 seconds, and so on for the other three workers. He started over again every two and a half minutes. What method of direct observation was he using? ____________________

4. If a behavior is reduced in frequency by removing an event that is usually in the person's environment anytime the behavior occurs, the name of the procedure is ____________. If a behavior is reduced in frequency by stopping the delivery of an event that had followed the behavior in the past, the name of the procedure is ____________.

5. Judy was curious to find out how much of the time the president was smiling, so she watched several of his news conferences. She divided the conferences into a series of intervals 15 seconds long and recorded whether he was smiling or not during each interval. (He smiled 79% of the time.) What method of direct observation was she using? ____________________ recording

6. Jim broke the rule about dinner complaints, and a reminder didn't stop him from complaining. The group decided to fine him $1 in addition to the reminder, and that worked. What procedure decreased Jim's complaining? ____________________

7. Gail liked to go dancing, but Harvey almost never took her. She finally started nagging him relentlessly until he would say, "All right, we'll go dancing tonight." Harvey takes her dancing more often now. What procedure did Gail use to increase Harvey's rate of taking her dancing? ____________

8. To use the aversive control strategy, you should (1) decrease undesirable behavior through ____________________, or (2) increase desirable behavior through ____________________, reinforcement as a last resort.

9. Bob observed Ruby's rate of smoking during three different periods: before the cigarette case shocked her, while the case shocked her, and after the case stopped shocking her. Bob used what type of design to study the effect of the shocks on Ruby's smoking? ____________ design.

10. Sally hates to carry out the garbage after dinner, so her father does it for her if she has studied for at least an hour after dinner. Since he has started doing that, Sally has done a lot more studying. Because studying prevents her having to take out the garbage, her study behavior is an example of ____________________ behavior.

11. Short answer question A: Explain in behavioral terms why people use punishment so often.

____

____

____

____

Lesson 25 Form B

Grade ____________________

Name ____________________

Date ____________________

1. Suppose Dr. Brown developed a behavioral definition of generosity. He might then ask a number of nonbehaviorists to rate the generosity of several individuals appearing on videotape. If he compared their ratings of generosity with the level of generosity according to his behavioral definition, he would determine the ________________ of his definition.

2. Customers in grocery stores used to be given trading stamps as incentive to continue buying at a particular store. The trading stamps could later be exchanged for anything from a toaster to a vacation. What kind of reinforcers were the trading stamps? ____________ reinforcers.

3. Jane kept track of her reading speed for two weeks for each homework assignment. She read about 150 words per minute and usually didn't finish her homework. Then she took a speed reading course. After finishing the course, she observed her reading speed again for two weeks and found that it had increased to 700 words a minute. Her homework was much easier to finish as a result. What kind of design was she using to determine the effect of the course on her reading rate? ____________ __________ design

4. If Tommy learns to say "49" when asked "What is the square of seven?" but not when asked for the square of other numbers, we would say that the question "What is the square of seven?" has come to exert ______________ over his behavior of saying "49."

5. Peter used to drink beer after beer immediately upon arriving home from work. His wife begged him for months to stop doing it, but to no avail. Finally, she decided to leave the house anytime he drank beer and stay gone until the next day. Peter has stopped drinking beer. What behavioral procedure did his wife use to decrease beer drinking? ____________

6. A behavior will take longer to extinguish if it has been on what generic schedule? A(n) ____________________ schedule

7. Responding to terminate a negative reinforcer is called a(n) ____________ response. Responding to prevent a negative reinforcer is called a(n) ____________ response.

8. Wendy agreed to encourage Carol to speak more loudly, as a step toward helping her to become more assertive. Wendy's goal was to get Carol to speak loudly enough that she could be heard ten feet away. At first Wendy praised Carol only if she could hear her from two feet; later only if she could hear her from five feet; finally only if she could hear her from ten feet away. Hearing her from ten feet away is an example of a(n) ____________.

9. Mrs. Franklin taught Jimmy to label a large circular line as a circle. When he labeled a circle as circle, she would praise him. When he labeled any other figure a circle, she ignored him. She helped him learn by adding onto her question "You know, a circle" and praising him when he said "circle." Next she gave as a hint only "You know, a cirk," leaving the "le" sound off. Finally, she gave no hint at all, and Jimmy could label the circle correctly. What behavioral procedure did Mrs. Franklin use? ____________

10. Sue repeatedly said racist things in the presence of members of her group. One day she made a racist comment, and another member said "Sue, that's ugly talk." She never repeated that comment again. Sue's racist comment was eliminated by what procedure? ____________

11. Short answer question B: Explain how to distinguish between punishment by contingent withdrawal and extinction.

____

____

____

____

Lesson 25 **Form C** **Grade** ______________________

Name ______________________ **Date** ______________________

---

1. The statement, "Shyness is the behavior of avoiding eye contact, speaking so softly that the words cannot be heard, and failing to make one's wishes known" would be an example of a(n) ______________________.

2. Howard's swearing bothered his friend Barbara. Every time he swore, she gave him a look designed to singe his eyebrows, but Howard's rate of swearing remained unchanged. What behavioral procedure did Barbara use with respect to Howard's swearing? __________

3. Ken was only interested in those parts of the movie that showed scenes of Hawaii, where he had lived as a boy. These scenes came after 13 minutes, then another 18, then another 2, and finally another 7 minutes of the movie. What specific schedule of reinforcement was his movie watching on? __________ __________ schedule

4. Two observers, who worked in the same office as Ruby, observed to see whether she was smoking during each 15-minute period of the day.

First:	S	N	S	N	S	N	N	S	N	N
Second:	S	N	S	N	S	N	N	N	S	N

   What is the reliability of their observations? _____ percent. If this is not a new definition, is it acceptable? __________

5. For punishment or reinforcement to be effective, it is necessary to deliver them (or a promise) very soon after the behavior has occurred. This is known as the principle of __________.

6. If a book asks a child to read a word like *cat* and shows the child a picture of a cat as a hint, but then shows less and less of the cat on subsequent pages where the child must read the word, the picture of the cat would be called a(n) __________.

7. Martin wore a wrist counter to count the number of times that he said something positive to someone. On any day that he counted at least 15 positive statements, he permitted himself to watch TV that night. What kind of reinforcer is the counter? A(n) __________ reinforcer. Watching TV would serve as a(n) __________ reinforcer for the counts.

8. Flora wanted to teach her daughter to be an opera singer. When the daughter was two years old, Flora started devoting the half hour after dinner to singing lessons. She used ice cream to reinforce singing. Because it was right after dinner, her daughter didn't seem very interested in the ice cream. What principle of effective reinforcement, if any, had Flora neglected in choosing a time right after dinner? __________

9. Claire likes to ride her snowmobile without a hat. If the cold becomes too intense after driving for a while, she puts on a hat. Putting on a hat after feeling intense cold is an example of __________ behavior.

10. Ruby was using a special cigarette case that counted the number of times she opened the case to take out a cigarette. Bob Behaviorist recorded the number of such openings for three weeks prior to helping Ruby stop smoking. This three-week period of measurement is called a(n) __________.

11. Short answer question C: Define a negative reinforcer, and distinguish it from a positive reinforcer.

____

____

____

____

____

____

Subject Index

Name Index

Photo Credits

Chapter 1: 4, (left), Archives of the History of American Psychology; **4, (right),** The Bettmann Archive; **5,** Courtesy of Montrose Wolfe. **Chapter 2: 16,** Bob Clay/Clay Images; **19,** Elizabeth Crews/Stock, Boston; **22,** Ray Ellis/Photo Researchers; **23,** Courtesy of The Iris and B. Gerald Cantor Foundation; **25,** Greg Mancuso/Stock, Boston. **Chapter 3: 36,** Petit/Photo Researchers, Inc.; **38,** Eric Gregg/Allsport. **Chapter 4: 61 (left),** Addison Geary/Stock, Boston; **61 (right),** Bob Daemmrich/Stock, Boston; **64;** Jean Claude LeJeune/Stock, Boston. **Chapter 8: 132,** Kathleen Olson; **135 (left),** Fred Palmer/Stock, Boston; **135 (right),** PhotoEdit/D. Young-Wolff; **137,** Gary Conner/PhotoEdit. **Chapter 9: 150,** Myrleen Ferguson/ PhotoEdit. **Chapter 10: 164 (left and right),** Bob Daemmrich/Stock, Boston. **Chapter 11: 177,** San Francisco Ballet/Photo: Marty Sohl. **Chapter 12: 196,** Richard Hutchings/Photo Researchers. **Chapter 17: 200,** Courtesy of Trevor Stokes; **201,** Courtesy of Don Baer. **Chapter 20: 327,** Courtesy of Ted Ayllon; **330,** Jerry Brendt/Stock, Boston. **Chapter 22: 356,** Courtesy of Nathan Azrin. **Chapter 23: 404,** Courtesy of Brian Iwata.